SAFETY SYMBOLS

SAFETY SYMBOLS	HAZARD	PRECAUTION	REMEDY
Disposal	Special disposal required	Dispose of wastes as directed by your teacher.	Ask your teacher how to dispose of laboratory materials.
Biological	Organisms that can harm humans	Avoid breathing in or skin contact with organisms. Wear dust mask or gloves. Wash hands thoroughly.	Notify your teacher if you suspect contact.
Extreme Temperature	Objects that can burn skin by being too cold or too hot	Use proper protection when handling.	Go to your teacher for first aid.
Sharp Object	Use of tools or glassware that can easily puncture or slice skin	Practice common sense behavior and follow guidelines for use of the tool.	Go to your teacher for first aid.
Fumes	Potential danger from smelling fumes	Must have good ventilation and never smell fumes directly.	Leave foul area and notify your teacher immediately.
Electrical	Possible danger from electrical shock or burn	Double-check setup with instructor. Check condition of wires and apparatus.	Do not attempt to fix electrical problems. Notify your teacher immediately.
Irritant	Substances that can irritate your skin or mucous membranes	Wear dust mask or gloves. Practice extra care when handling these materials.	Go to your teacher for first aid.
Chemical	Substances (acids and bases) that can react with and destroy tissue and other materials	Wear goggles and an apron.	Immediately flush with water and notify your teacher.
Toxic	Poisonous substance	Follow your teacher's instructions. Always wash hands thoroughly after use.	Go to your teacher for first aid.
Fire	Flammable and combustible materials may burn if exposed to an open flame or spark	Avoid flames and heat sources. Be aware of locations of fire safety equipment.	Notify your teacher immediately. Use fire safety equipment if necessary.

Eye Safety
This symbol appears when a danger to eyes exists.

Clothing Protection
This symbol appears when substances could stain or burn clothing.

Animal Safety
This symbol appears whenever live animals are studied and the safety of the animals and students must be ensured.

New York, New York Columbus, Ohio Woodland Hills, California Peoria, Illinois

A Glencoe Program

California Edition

Glencoe Science Voyages

California Student Edition
California Teacher Wraparound Edition
Assessment
- Chapter Review
- California Science Content Standards Practice Questions
- Performance Assessment
- Assessment—Chapter and Unit Tests
- ExamView Test Bank Software
- Performance Assessment in the Science Classroom
- Alternate Assessment in the Science Classroom

Study Guide for Content Mastery, SE and TE
Chapter Overview Study Guide, SE and TE
Reinforcement
Enrichment
Critical Thinking/Problem Solving
Multicultural Connections
Activity Worksheets
Laboratory Manual, SE and TE
Science Inquiry Activities, SE and TE
California Home Involvement
Teaching Transparencies
Section Focus Transparencies
Science Integration Transparencies
Spanish Resources
California Lesson Plans
Lab and Safety Skills in the Science Classroom
Cooperative Learning in the Science Classroom
Exploring Environmental Issues
MindJogger Videoquizzes and Teacher Guide
English/Spanish Audiocassettes
Interactive Lesson Planner CD-ROM
Interactive CD-ROM
Internet Site
Using the Internet in the Science Classroom

The "Test-Taking Tip" and "Test Practice" features in this book were written by The Princeton Review, the nation's leader in test preparation. Through its association with McGraw-Hill, The Princeton Review offers the best way to help students excel on standardized assessments.

The Princeton Review is not affiliated with Princeton University or Educational Testing Service.

Glencoe/McGraw-Hill

A Division of The ***McGraw-Hill*** *Companies*

Send all inquiries to:
Glencoe/McGraw-Hill
8787 Orion Place
Columbus, OH 43240

ISBN 0-07-823976-1
Printed in the United States of America.
4 5 6 7 8 9 10 071/043 10 09 08 07 06

Series Authors

Alton Biggs
Biology Instructor
Allen High School
Allen, Texas

John Eric Burns
Science Teacher
Ramona Jr. High School
Chino, California

Lucy Daniel, Ph.D.
Teacher, Consultant
Rutherford County Schools
Rutherfordton, North Carolina

Cathy Ezrailson
Science Department Head
Oak Ridge High School
Conroe, Texas

Ralph Feather, Jr., Ph.D.
Science Department Chair
Derry Area School District
Derry, Pennsylvania

Patricia Horton
Math and Science Teacher
Summit Intermediate School
Etiwanda, California

Thomas McCarthy, Ph.D.
Science Department Chair
St. Edwards School
Vero Beach, Florida

Ed Ortleb
Science Consultant
St. Louis Public Schools
St. Louis, Missouri

Susan Leach Snyder
Science Department Chair
Jones Middle School
Upper Arlington, Ohio

Eric Werwa, Ph.D.
Department of Physics and Astronomy
Otterbein College
Westerville, Ohio

National Geographic Society
Educational Division
Washington D.C.

Contributing Authors

Al Janulaw
Science Teacher
Creekside Middle School
Rohnert Park, California

Penny Parsekian
Science Writer for
The National Geographic Society
New London, Connecticut

Gerry Madrazo, Ph.D.
Mathematics and Science Education Network
University of North Carolina, Chapel Hill
Chapel Hill, North Carolina

Series Consultants

Chemistry

Douglas Martin, Ph.D.
Chemistry Department
Sonoma State University
Rohnert Park, California

Cheryl Wistrom, Ph.D.
Associate Professor of Chemistry
Saint Joseph's College
Rensselaer, Indiana

Earth Science

Maureen Allen
Science Resource Specialist
Irvine Unified School District
Laguna Hills, California

Tomasz K. Baumiller, Ph.D.
Museum of Paleontology
University of Michigan
Ann Arbor, Michigan

Connie Sutton, Ph.D.
Department of Geoscience
Indiana University
Indiana, Pennsylvania

Physics

Thomas Barrett, Ph.D.
Department of Physics
The Ohio State University
Columbus, Ohio

David Haase, Ph.D.
Professor of Physics
North Carolina State University
Raleigh, North Carolina

Life Science

William Ausich, Ph.D.
Department of Geological Sciences
The Ohio State University
Columbus, Ohio

Dennis Stockdale
Asheville High School
Asheville, North Carolina

Daniel Zeigler, Ph.D.
Director
Bacillus Genetic Stock Center
The Ohio State University
Columbus, Ohio

Reading

Nancy Farnan, Ph.D.
School of Teacher Education
San Diego State University
San Diego, California

Gary Kroesch
Mount Carmel High School
San Diego, California

Safety

Mark Vinciguerra
Lab Safety Instructor
Department of Physics
The Ohio State University
Columbus, Ohio

Curriculum

Tom Custer, Ph.D.
Maryland State Department of Education
Challenge/Reconstructed Schools
Baltimore, Maryland

Series Reviewers

Jhina Alvarado
Potrero Hill Middle School for the Arts
San Francisco, California

Richard Cheeseman
Bert Lynn Middle School
Torrance, California

Linda Cook
Rider High School
Wichita Falls, Texas

John B. Davis
Niagara-Wheatfield Central School
Sanborn, New York

Shirley Ann DeFilippo
Timothy Edwards Middle School
South Windsor, Connecticut

Janet Doughty
H J McDonald Middle School
New Bern, North Carolina

Jason Druten
Jefferson Middle School
Torrance, California

Lin Harp
Magellan Middle School
Raleigh, North Carolina

Doris Holland
West Cary Middle School
Raleigh, North Carolina

Deborah Huffine
Noblesville Intermediate School
Noblesville, Indiana

Paul Osborne
DeValls Bluff High School
DeValls Bluff, Arkansas

Erik Resnick
Robert E. Peary Middle School
Gardena, California

Robert Sirbu
Lowell Junior High School
Oakland, California

Michael Tally
Wake County Public Schools
Raleigh, North Carolina

Cindy Williamson
Whiteville City Schools
Whiteville, North Carolina

Maurice Yaggi
Middlebrook School
Wilton, Connecticut

Donna York
Anchorage School District
Anchorage, Alaska

Activity Testers

Clayton Millage
Science Teacher
Lynden Middle School
Lynden, Washington

Science Kit and Boreal Laboratories
Tonawanda, New York

Contents in Brief

GRADE EIGHT: FOCUS ON PHYSICAL SCIENCE

What are science content standards and why does California have them? Standards are guidelines for schools, students, and parents that describe the essential science concepts and skills for understanding the world in which we live. In 1999, The California State Board of Education established science content standards, and these standards will be the basis for state assessments that measure student achievement in science.

ADDITIONAL CONTENT STANDARDS FOR GRADE 8

- California Science Standards and Case Studies, found at the back of the book
- California Science Content Standards Assessment Practice booklets
- Chapter Assessments at the end of each chapter
- Science Voyages Website at www.glencoe.com/sec/science/ca

Motion

1. The velocity of an object is the rate of change of its position. As a basis for understanding this concept, students know:

a. position is defined relative to some choice of standard reference point and a set of reference directions.
Sections 11-1, 17-2, 20-4, page 478

b. average speed is the total distance traveled divided by the total time elapsed. The speed of an object along the path traveled can vary.
Sections 11-1, 17-1, 19-1, 19-2, page 478

c. how to solve problems involving distance, time, and average speed.
Sections 11-1, 19-1, 19-2, page 479

d. to describe the velocity of an object, one must specify both direction and speed.
Section 11-1, page 479

e. changes in velocity can be changes in speed, direction, or both.
Sections 11-1, 11-2, page 480

f. how to interpret graphs of position versus time and speed versus time for motion in a single direction.
Section 11-1, page 480

Forces

2. Unbalanced forces cause changes in velocity. As a basis for understanding this concept, students know:

a. a force has both direction and magnitude.
Sections 5-1, 12-1, 12-2, 12-3, 12-4, 17-2, page 482

b. when an object is subject to two or more forces at once, the effect is the cumulative effect of all the forces.
Sections 5-2, 12-1, 12-2, 24-4, 25-3, page 482

c. when the forces on an object are balanced, the motion of the object does not change.
Sections 12-1, 12-4, 24-4, pages 482–483

d. how to identify separately two or more forces acting on a single static object, including gravity, elastic forces due to tension or compression in matter, and friction.
Sections 12-1, 25-3, page 483

e. when the forces on an object are unbalanced, the object will change its motion (that is, it will speed up, slow down, or change direction).
Sections 7-1, 12-1, 12-2, 12-3, 12-4, 17-2, 24-3, 25-3, page 483

f. the greater the mass of an object, the more force is needed to achieve the same change in motion.
Sections 11-2, 12-2, 12-3, 19-2, page 484

g. the role of gravity in forming and maintaining planets, stars, and the solar system.
Sections 17-2, 17-3, 18-2, 19-1, 19-2, 19-3, 19-4, 20-3, 20-4, page 484

Structure of Matter

3. Elements have distinct properties and atomic structure. All matter is comprised of one or more of over 100 elements. As a basis for understanding this concept, students know:

a. the structure of the atom and how it is composed of protons, neutrons, and electrons.
Sections 5-1, 5-2, 7-1, 7-2, 9-2, 10-1, page 487

b. compounds are formed by combining two or more different elements. Compounds have properties that are different from the constituent elements.
Sections 4-1, 4-2, 5-1, 7-2, 8-1, 9-1, 9-2, 10-1, 10-2, 10-3, page 487

c. atoms and molecules form solids by building up repeating patterns such as the crystal structure of NaCl or long chain polymers.
Sections 4-1, 7-2, 10-3, pages 487–488

d. the states (solid, liquid, gas) of matter depend on molecular motion.
Sections 4-1, 4-2, 4-3, pages 262–263

e. in solids the atoms are closely locked in position and can only vibrate, in liquids the atoms and molecules are more loosely connected and can collide with and move past one another, while in gases the atoms or molecules are free to move independently, colliding frequently.
Sections 4-1, 4-2, 4-3, 9-1, pages 262–263

f. how to use the Periodic Table to identify elements in simple compounds.
Sections 6-1, 6-2, 6-3, 7-1, 7-1, pages 488–489

Earth in the Solar System (Earth Science)

4. The structure and composition of the universe can be learned from the study of stars and galaxies, and their evolution. As a basis for understanding this concept, students know:

a. galaxies are clusters of billions of stars, and may have different shapes.
Section 20-4, page 490

b. the sun is one of many stars in our own Milky Way galaxy. Stars may differ in size, temperature, and color.
Sections 19-1, 19-3, 20-1, 20-2, 20-3, 20-4, page 490

c. how to use astronomical units and light years as measures of distance between the sun, stars, and Earth. Sections 19-2, 19-3, 20-1, 20-4, page 490

d. stars are the source of light for all bright objects in outer space. The moon and planets shine by reflected sunlight, not by their own light. Sections 17-1, 18-2, 18-3, 19-1, 19-2, 20-3, pages 490–491

e. the appearance, general composition, relative position and size, and motion of objects in the solar system, including planets, planetary satellites, comets, and asteroids. Sections 17-2, 17-3, 18-1, 18-2, 18-3, 19-1, 19-2, 19-3, 19-4, page 491

Reactions

5. Chemical reactions are processes in which atoms are rearranged into different combinations of molecules. As a basis for understanding this concept, students know:

a. reactant atoms and molecules interact to form products with different chemical properties. Sections 8-1, 8-2, 9-3, 10-1, 10-2, 10-3, 22-2, 23-1, page 494

b. the idea of atoms explains the conservation of matter: in chemical reactions the number of atoms stays the same no matter how they are arranged, so their total mass stays the same. Section 8-1, page 494

c. chemical reactions usually liberate heat or absorb heat. Sections 8-1, 9-2, 26-2, page 494

d. physical processes include freezing and boiling, in which a material changes form with no chemical reaction. Sections 4-1, 4-2, 8-1, 9-1, 9-2, page 495

e. how to determine whether a solution is acidic, basic or neutral. Sections 9-3, 22-2, 27-1, page 496

Chemistry of Living Systems (Life Science)

6. Principles of chemistry underlie the functioning of biological systems. As a basis for understanding this concept, students know:

a. carbon, because of its ability to combine in many ways with itself and other elements, has a central role in the chemistry of living organisms. Sections 6-2, 10-1, 10-2, 10-3, 21-1, 21-2, 22-2, 23-1, 26-2, page 498

b. living organisms are made of molecules largely consisting of carbon, hydrogen,nitrogen, oxygen, phosphorus and sulfur. Sections 10-1, 10-2, 10-3, 21-2, 23-1, pages 498–499

c. living organisms have many different kinds of molecules including small ones such as water and salt, and very large ones such as carbohydrates, fats, proteins and DNA. Sections 9-3, 10-1, 10-3, 23-1, 23-3, 24-4, pages 498–499

Periodic Table

7. The organization of the Periodic Table is based on the properties of the elements and reflects the structure of atoms. As a basis for understanding this concept, students know:

a. how to identify regions corresponding to metals, nonmetals and inert gases. Sections 6-1, 6-2, 6-3, 7-2, page 501

b. elements are defined by the number of protons in the nucleus, which is called the atomic number. Different isotopes of an element have a different number of neutrons in the nucleus. Sections 5-2, 6-1, page 501

c. substances can be classified by their properties, including melting temperature, density, hardness, heat, and electrical conductivity. Sections 6-1, 6-2, 6-3, 7-1, page 502

Density and Buoyancy

8. All objects experience a buoyant force when immersed in a fluid. As a basis for understanding this concept, students know:

a. density is mass per unit volume. Sections 1-2, 4-3, 18-1, pages 504–505

b. how to calculate the density of substances (regular and irregular solids, and liquids) from measurements of mass and volume. Sections 1-2, 4-3, pages 504–506

c. the buoyant force on an object in a fluid is an upward force equal to the weight of the fluid it has displaced. Sections 4-3, 25-1, pages 504–505

d. how to predict whether an object will float or sink. Sections 1-2, 4-3, pages 504–505

Investigation and Experimentation

9. Scientific progress is made by asking meaningful questions and conducting careful investigations. As a basis for understanding this concept, and to address the content of the other three strands, students should develop their own questions and perform investigations. Students will:

a. plan and conduct a scientific investigation to test a hypothesis. Sections 1-1, 1-2, 4-2, 4-3, 5-1, 5-2, 6-2, 6-3, 7-1, 7-2, 8-1, 8-2, 9-2, 10-3, 11-1, 20-4, 21-1, 24-3, 25-4, 27-1, pages 127, 482, 483, 484, 486, 487, 489, 494, 495, 496, 507

b. evaluate the accuracy and reproducibility of data. Sections 1-1, 5-1, 5-2, 6-3, 7-1, 8-1, 17-2, 21-1, 24-3, 25-4, pages 481, 483, 493, 495, 503

c. distinguish between variable and controlled parameters in a test. Sections 1-1, 1-2, 6-3, 8-1, 8-2, 9-2, 11-2, 12-2, 18-1, 21-1, 21-2, 24-3, 25-4, 27-1, pages 481, 482, 483, 488, 494, 495, 497, 500, 503, 555

d. recognize the slope of the linear graph as the constant in the relationship $y=kx$ and apply this to interpret graphs constructed from data. Sections 11-1, 26-1, pages 479, 480, 498, 953–954, 978

e. construct appropriate graphs from data and develop quantitative statements about the relationships between variables. Sections 1-1, 1-2, 4-1, 4-2, 5-2, 6-1, 9-2, 10-1, 25-1, 25-4, 26-1, pages 121, 149, 233, 479, 480, 498, 502, 978

f. apply simple mathematical relationships to determine one quantity given the other two (including speed = distance/time, density = mass/volume, force = pressure x area, volume = area x height). Sections 1-1, 1-2, 4-1, 4-2, 4-3, 5-2, 7-1, 8-2, 9-2, 10-1, 10-3, 11-1, 11-2, 11-3, 12-4, 17-1, 17-2, 19-2, 21-2, 23-3, 26-1, 27-1, pages 324, 357, 479, 499, 505

g. distinguish between linear and nonlinear relationships on a graph of data. Sections 1-1, 4-1, 4-2, 5-2, 10-1, 11-1, pages 325, 480, 491, 502, 953–954, 978

Contents

Contents

Contents

UNIT 6 Life's Diversity 734

Contents

Science Connections

Reading & Writing in Science

Science & Society

History of Science

How it Works

Activities

Explore Activities

Problem Solving

MiniLab

Try at Home MiniLab

Skill Activities

Skill Builders

UNIT 5

Astronomy

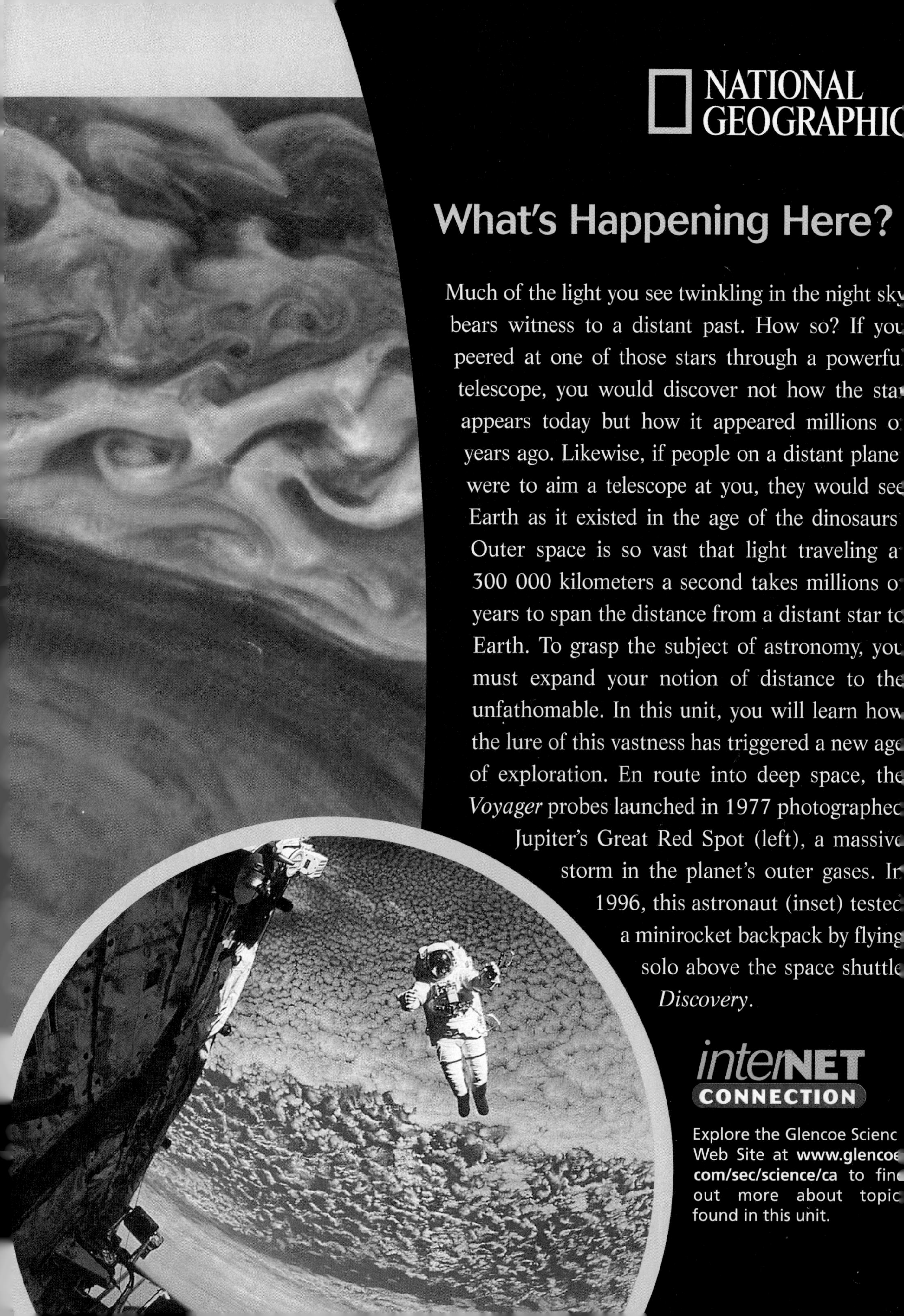

NATIONAL GEOGRAPHIC

What's Happening Here?

Much of the light you see twinkling in the night sky bears witness to a distant past. How so? If you peered at one of those stars through a powerfu telescope, you would discover not how the sta appears today but how it appeared millions o years ago. Likewise, if people on a distant plane were to aim a telescope at you, they would see Earth as it existed in the age of the dinosaurs Outer space is so vast that light traveling a 300 000 kilometers a second takes millions o years to span the distance from a distant star to Earth. To grasp the subject of astronomy, you must expand your notion of distance to the unfathomable. In this unit, you will learn how the lure of this vastness has triggered a new age of exploration. En route into deep space, the *Voyager* probes launched in 1977 photographed Jupiter's Great Red Spot (left), a massive storm in the planet's outer gases. In 1996, this astronaut (inset) tested a minirocket backpack by flying solo above the space shuttle *Discovery*.

interNET CONNECTION

Explore the Glencoe Scienc Web Site at **www.glencoe com/sec/science/ca** to find out more about topic found in this unit.

CHAPTER 17

Exploring Space

Chapter Preview

Skills Preview

Skill Builders
- Sequence
- Map Concepts

MiniLabs
- Analyze Data
- Infer

Activities
- Draw Conclusions

Reading Check

As you read this chapter about space, write four or five questions that are answered in each section.

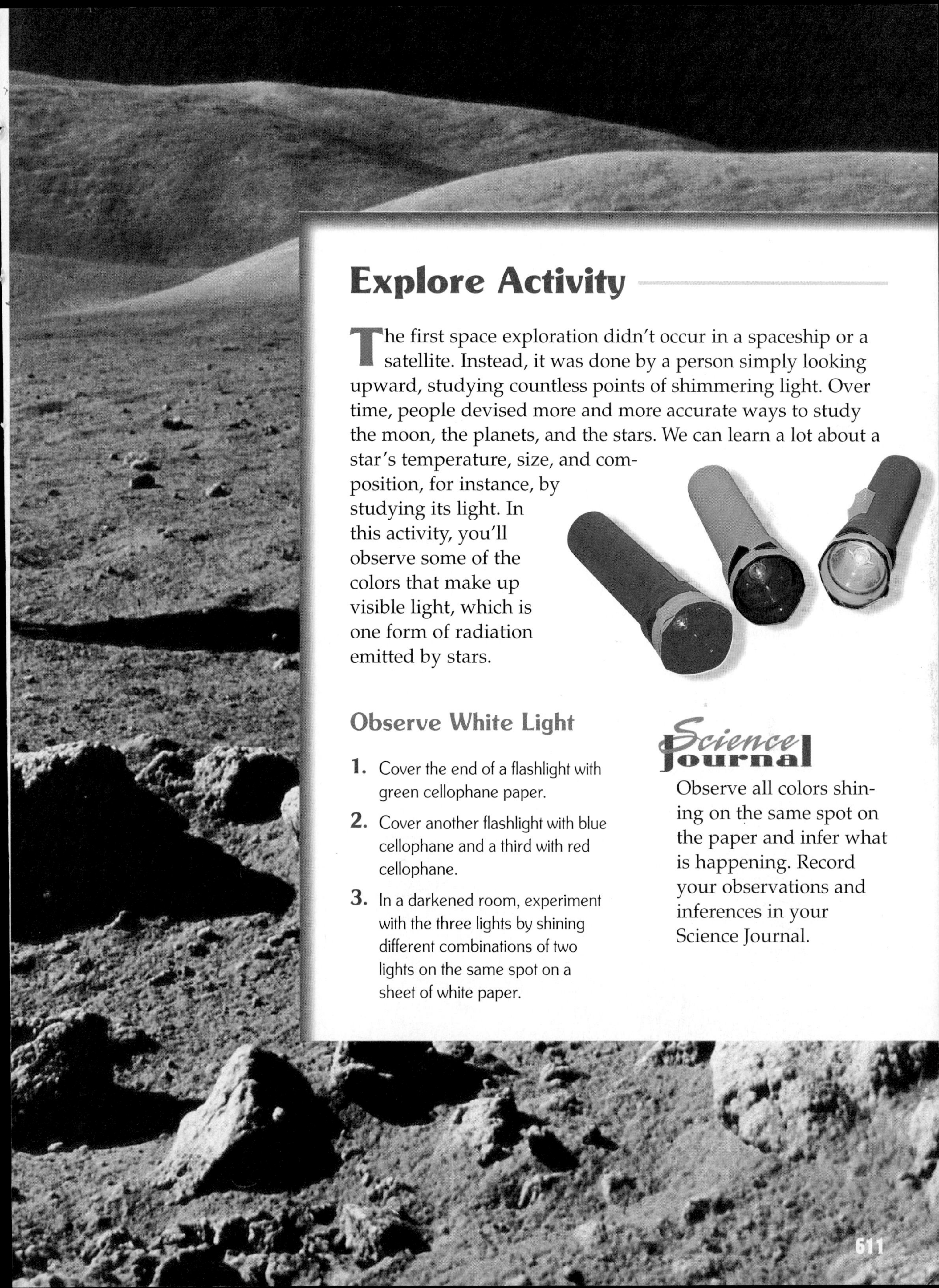

Explore Activity

The first space exploration didn't occur in a spaceship or a satellite. Instead, it was done by a person simply looking upward, studying countless points of shimmering light. Over time, people devised more and more accurate ways to study the moon, the planets, and the stars. We can learn a lot about a star's temperature, size, and composition, for instance, by studying its light. In this activity, you'll observe some of the colors that make up visible light, which is one form of radiation emitted by stars.

Observe White Light

1. Cover the end of a flashlight with green cellophane paper.
2. Cover another flashlight with blue cellophane and a third with red cellophane.
3. In a darkened room, experiment with the three lights by shining different combinations of two lights on the same spot on a sheet of white paper.

Science Journal

Observe all colors shining on the same spot on the paper and infer what is happening. Record your observations and inferences in your Science Journal.

17•1 Radiation from Space

What You'll Learn

- The electromagnetic spectrum
- The differences between refracting and reflecting telescopes
- The differences between optical and radio telescopes

Vocabulary

electromagnetic spectrum
refracting telescope
reflecting telescope
observatory
radio telescope

Why It's Important

- You'll learn about the tools and methods used to study space.

Electromagnetic Waves

On a crisp, autumn evening, you take a break from your homework to gaze out the window at the many stars that fill the night sky. Looking up at the stars, it's easy to imagine future spaceships venturing through space and large space stations circling above Earth, where people work and live. But, when you look into the night sky, what you're really seeing is the distant past, not the future.

Light from the Past

When you look at a star, you see light that left the star many years ago. The light that you see travels fast. Still, the distances across space are so great that it takes years for the light to reach Earth—sometimes millions of years.

The light and other energy leaving a star are forms of radiation. Recall that radiation is energy that's transmitted from one place to another by electromagnetic waves. Because of the electric and magnetic properties of this radiation, it's called electromagnetic radiation. Electromagnetic waves carry energy through empty space as well as through matter.

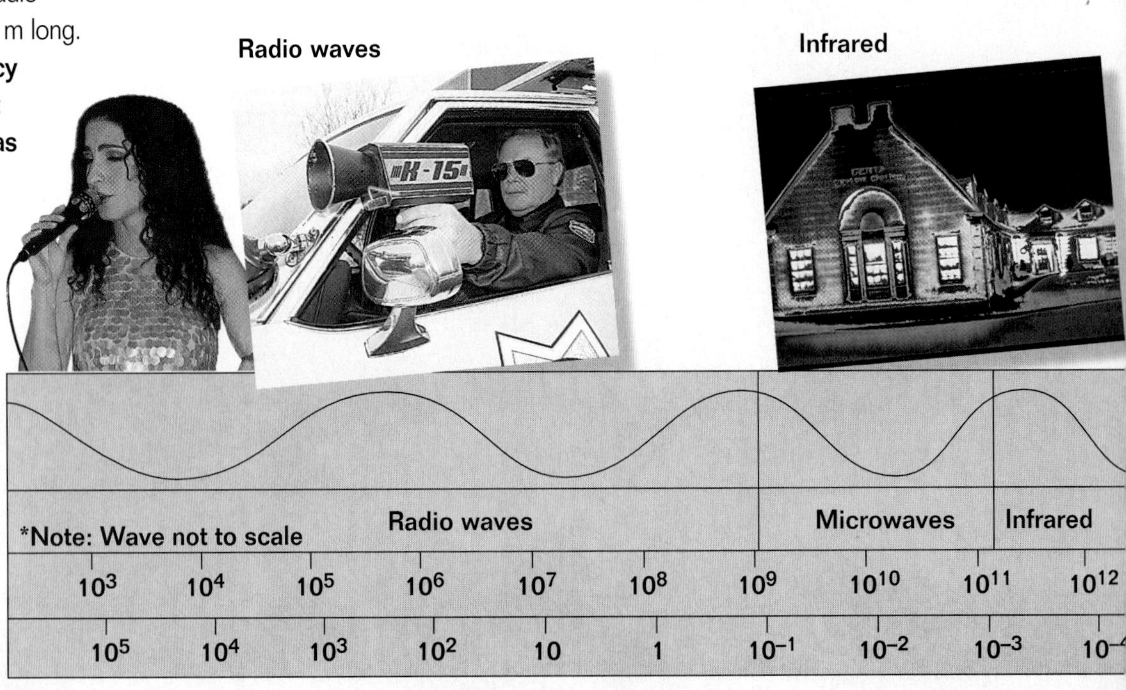

Figure 17-1 The electromagnetic spectrum ranges from gamma rays with wavelengths of less than 0.000 000 000 01 m to radio waves more than 100 000 m long. **What happens to frequency (the number of waves that pass a point per second) as wavelength shortens?**

Electromagnetic Radiation

Sound waves, a type of mechanical wave, can't travel through empty space. How do we hear the voices of the astronauts while they're in space? When they speak into a microphone, the sound is converted into electromagnetic waves called radio waves. The radio waves travel through space and through our atmosphere. They are then converted back into sound by electronic equipment and audio speakers.

Radio waves and visible light from the sun are just two types of electromagnetic radiation. The other types include gamma rays, X rays, ultraviolet waves, infrared waves, and microwaves. **Figure 17-1** shows these forms of electromagnetic radiation arranged according to their wavelengths. This arrangement of electromagnetic radiation is called the **electromagnetic spectrum.**

Although the various electromagnetic waves differ in their wavelengths, they all travel at the speed of 300 000 km/s in a vacuum. You're probably more familiar with this speed as the "speed of light." Visible light and other forms of electromagnetic radiation travel at this incredible speed, but the universe is so large that it takes millions of years for the light from some stars to reach Earth.

Once electromagnetic radiation from stars and other objects reaches Earth, we can use it to learn about the source of the electromagnetic radiation. What tools and methods do scientists use to discover what lies beyond our planet? One tool for observing electromagnetic radiation from distant sources is a telescope.

Bending Light
Pass a beam of white light through a prism. Note that different colors of light are bent, forming a spectrum. Infer how the white light and prism form a spectrum with violet on one end and red on the other.

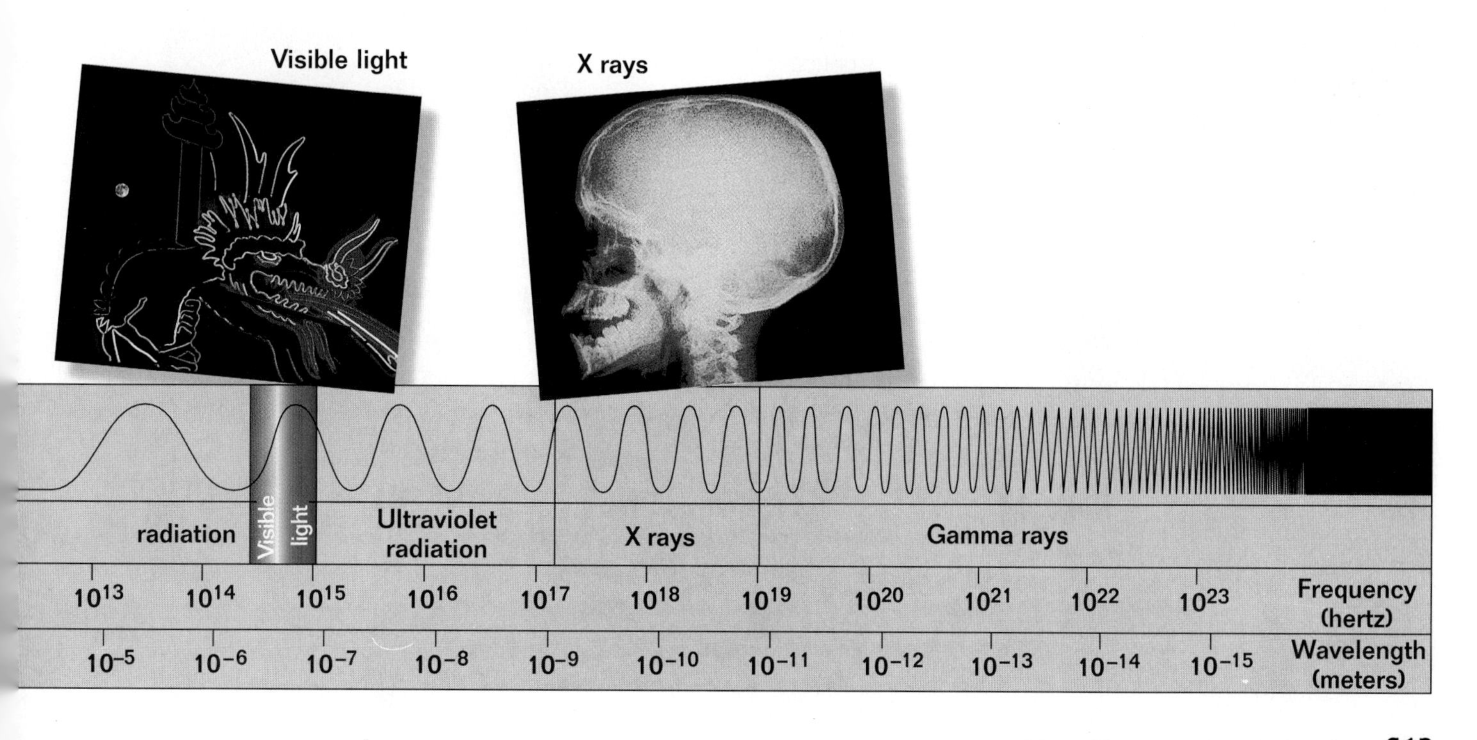

Optical Telescopes

Optical telescopes produce magnified images of objects. Light is collected by an objective lens or mirror, which then forms an image at the focal point of the telescope. The eyepiece lens then magnifies the image. The two types of optical telescopes are shown in **Figure 17-2.**

In a **refracting telescope,** the light from an object passes through a double convex objective lens and is bent to form an image on the focal point. The image is then magnified by the eyepiece.

A **reflecting telescope** uses a mirror as an objective to focus light from the object being viewed. Light passes through the open end of a reflecting telescope and strikes a concave mirror at its base. The light is then reflected to the focal point to form an image. A smaller mirror is often used to reflect the light into the eyepiece lens so the magnified image can be viewed.

Figure 17-2 These diagrams show how each type of optical telescope collects light and forms an image.

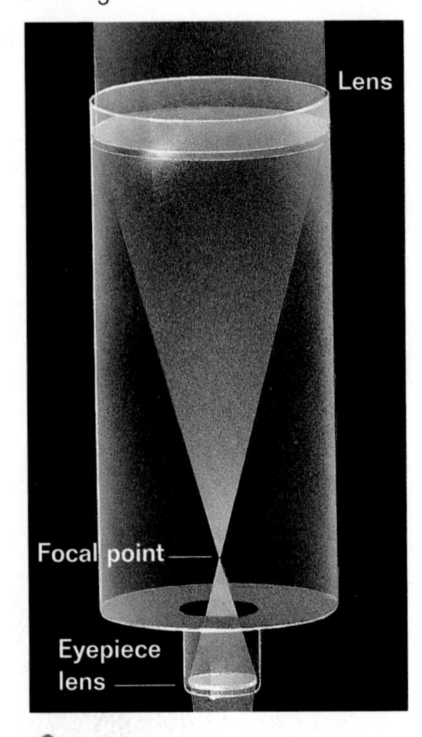

A In a refracting telescope, a double convex lens focuses light to form an image at the focal point.

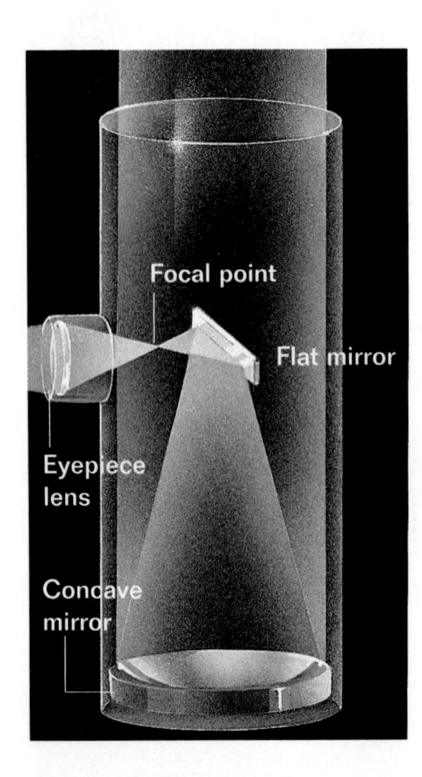

B In a reflecting telescope, a concave mirror focuses light to form an image at the focal point.

Using Optical Telescopes

Most optical telescopes used by professional astronomers are housed in buildings called **observatories.** Observatories often have a dome-shaped roof that opens up to let in light. However, not all telescopes are in observatories.

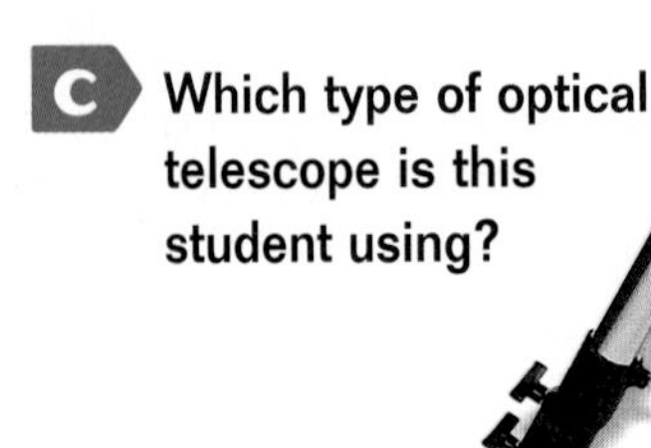

C **Which type of optical telescope is this student using?**

The *Hubble Space Telescope,* shown in **Figure 17-3,** was launched in 1990 by the space shuttle *Discovery.* Earth's atmosphere absorbs and distorts some of the energy received from space. Because *Hubble* didn't have to view space through our atmosphere, it should have produced clear images. However, when the largest mirror of this reflecting telescope was shaped, there was a mistake. Images obtained by the telescope were not as clear as expected. In December 1993, a team of astronauts repaired *Hubble's* telescope mirror and other equipment. Now, the clear images obtained by *Hubble Space Telescope* are changing scientists' ideas about space.

Figure 17-3 The *Hubble Space Telescope* was released from the cargo bay of the space shuttle *Discovery* on April 25, 1990. It's now orbiting Earth, sending back images and data about distant space objects.

Problem Solving

Interpreting Telescope Data

The magnifying power *(Mp)* of a telescope is determined by the focal lengths of the telescope's objective lens and eyepiece. Once built, you cannot easily change the objective lens, but you can easily change the eyepiece. That's why telescopes are often sold with three or four eyepieces—each with a different focal length. The magnifying power of a telescope is equal to the focal length of its objective lens divided by the focal length of its eyepiece.

Telescopes also have light-gathering power (LGP). Generally, the larger the diameter (aperture) of a telescope's objective, the more light the telescope can gather. Therefore, a telescope with an objective aperture of 125 mm will gather more light than a telescope with an objective aperture of 75 mm.

The following table lists the characteristics of two telescopes. Study the data about each telescope and interpret which has the greater magnifying power and which has the greater light-gathering power.

Telescope Data

Telescope	Aperture	Objective Focal Length	Eyepiece Focal Length
1	75 mm	1200 mm	9 mm, 12 mm
2	125 mm	900 mm	9 mm, 12 mm

Think Critically: Which telescope would you want to use to observe stars? Which telescope would you want to use to observe craters on the moon? Explain your selections.

Active Optics

Since the early 1600s, when the Italian scientist Galileo Galilei first turned a telescope toward the stars, people have been searching for better ways to study what lies beyond our atmosphere, such as the twin Keck telescopes shown in **Figure 17-4.** Today, the largest reflector has a segmented mirror 10 m wide. The most recent innovations in optical telescopes involve active and adaptive optics. With active optics, a computer is used to compensate for changes in temperature, mirror distortions, and bad viewing conditions. Even more ambitious is adaptive optics, which uses a laser to probe the atmosphere and relay information to a computer about air turbulence. The computer then adjusts the telescope's mirror thousands of times per second, thus reducing the effects of atmospheric turbulence.

Figure 17-4 The twin Keck telescopes on Mauna Kea in Hawaii can be used together, more than doubling the resolving power. Each individual telescope has an objective mirror 10 m in diameter. To cope with the difficulty of building such a large mirror, this telescope design used several smaller mirrors positioned to work as one. **Although the Keck telescopes are much larger than the *Hubble Space Telescope*, the *Hubble* is able to achieve better resolution. Why?**

Radio Telescopes

As you know, stars and other objects radiate energy throughout the electromagnetic spectrum. A **radio telescope,** such as the one shown in **Figure 17-5,** is used to study radio waves traveling through space. Unlike visible light, radio waves pass freely through Earth's atmosphere. Because of this, radio telescopes are useful 24 hours a day under most weather conditions.

Radio waves reaching Earth's surface strike the large, curved dish of a radio telescope. This dish reflects the waves to a focal point where a receiver is located. The information allows scientists to detect objects in space, to map the universe, and to search for intelligent life on other planets.

Figure 17-5 This radio telescope is used to study radio waves traveling through space.

In the remainder of this chapter, you'll learn about the instruments that travel into space and send back information that telescopes on Earth's surface cannot obtain.

Section Assessment

1. What is the difference between radio telescopes and optical telescopes?
2. The frequency of electromagnetic radiation is the number of waves that pass a point in a specific amount of time. If red light has a longer wavelength than blue light, which would have a greater frequency?
3. **Think Critically:** It takes light from the closest star to Earth (other than the sun) about four years to reach us. If there were intelligent life on a planet circling that star, how long would it take for us to send them a radio transmission and for us to receive their reply?
4. **Skill Builder**
   Sequencing Sequence these electromagnetic waves from longest wavelength to shortest wavelength: *gamma rays, visible light, X rays, radio waves, infrared waves, ultraviolet waves,* and *microwaves.* If you need help, refer to Sequencing in the **Skill Handbook** on page 950.

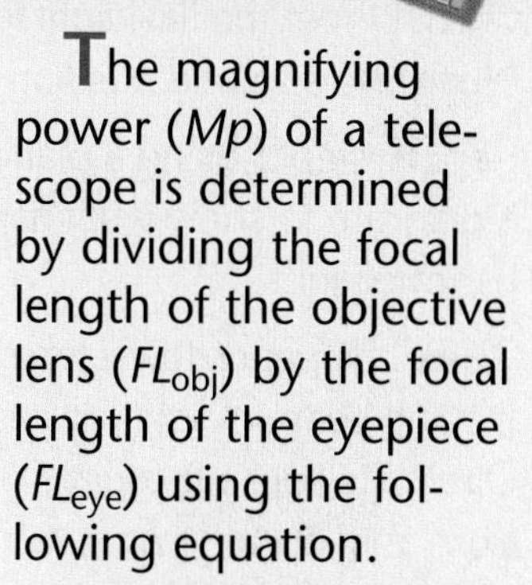

Using Math

The magnifying power (Mp) of a telescope is determined by dividing the focal length of the objective lens (FL_{obj}) by the focal length of the eyepiece (FL_{eye}) using the following equation.

$$Mp = \frac{FL_{obj}}{FL_{eye}}$$

If $FL_{obj} = 1200$ mm and $FL_{eye} = 6$ mm, what is the telescope's magnifying power?

Activity 17•1

Using Scientific Methods

Telescopes

Materials

- Candle
- White cardboard (50 cm × 60 cm)
- Flashlight
- Hand lens
- Large glass of water
- Concave mirror
- Plane mirror
- Masking tape
- Convex mirror
- Empty paper-towel tube

You have learned that optical telescopes use lenses and mirrors as objectives to collect light from an object. They use eyepiece lenses to magnify images of that object. Try this activity to see how the paths of light differ in reflecting and refracting telescopes.

What You'll Investigate

In what way are paths of light affected by the lenses and mirrors in refracting and reflecting telescopes?

Goals

- **Observe** how different mirrors and lenses affect light and the appearance of objects.

Procedure

1. **Observe** your reflection in plane, convex, and concave mirrors.
2. Hold an object in front of each of the mirrors. **Compare** the size and position of the images.
3. **Darken** the room and hold the convex mirror in front of you at a 45° angle, slanting downward. Direct the flashlight toward the mirror. **Note** the size and position of the reflected light.
4. Repeat step 3 using a plane mirror. **Draw** a diagram to show what happens to the beam of light.
5. **Tape** the paper-towel tube to the flashlight so that the beam of light will pass through the tube. Direct the light into a glass of water, first directly from above, then from an angle 45° to the water's surface. **Observe** the direction of the light rays when viewed from the side of the glass.
6. **Light** a candle and set it some distance from the vertically held cardboard screen. **CAUTION:** *Keep hair and clothing away from the flame.* Using the hand lens as a convex lens, move it between the candle and the screen until you have the best possible image.
7. **Move** the lens closer to the candle. Note what happens to the size of the image. Move the cardboard until the image is in focus.

Conclude and Apply

1. How did you **determine** the position of the focal point of the hand lens in step 6? What does this tell you about the position of the light rays?
2. **Compare and contrast** the effect the three types of mirrors had on your reflection.
3. **Compare and contrast** the path of light in refracting and reflecting telescopes.
4. What is the purpose of the concave mirror in a reflecting telescope?

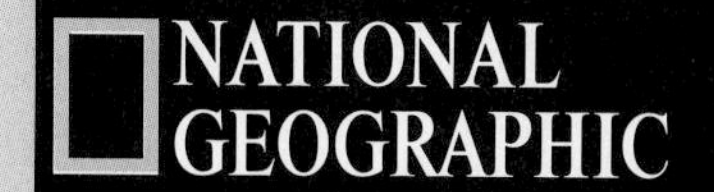

Seeing in 3-D

Why do humans have two eyes? One reason is that the second eye lets us see more of the world. It increases our field of view. Many animals have eyes set on opposite sides of their heads, so each eye sees a separate half of the world. But, human eyes are set closer together. They see almost the same scene but from a slightly different angle. Look at the student in front of you, first through only your right eye then only your left eye. You'll notice that each eye sees a slightly different view. But, your brain puts the two different views together, giving you the ability to figure out which object is closer to you and which is farther away. You see in three dimensions (3-D).

In the figure on the left, notice how the green block appears to the left of the yellow cylinder when seen by the left eye but to the right when seen by the right eye. Your brain interprets these two images, and you know that the yellow cylinder is in front of the green block.

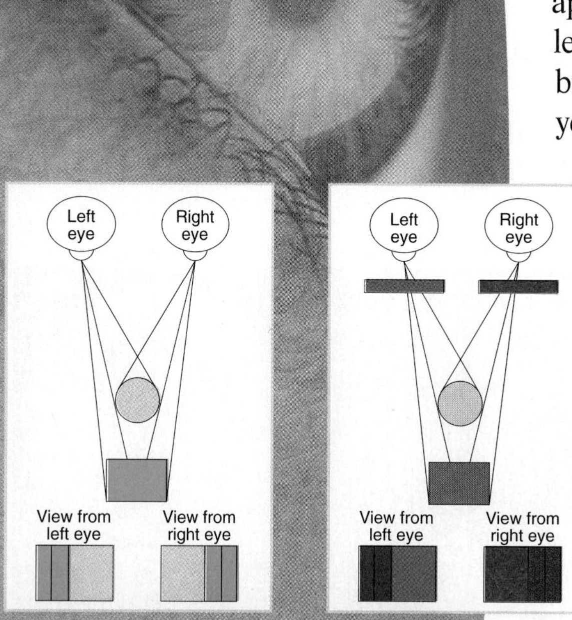

Movies and Television

How can you have a 3-D experience at the movies or on a TV? A camera with two lenses a few inches apart records the images on film or videotape. But, one lens has a red filter in front of it and the other a blue, as shown in the figure on the right. So, the image recorded by one lens is in shades of red, while the one recorded by the other lens is in shades of blue. The viewer watches the film through 3-D glasses that have the same color filters. Because the red filter allows only red light through it, only the image meant for that eye passes through that filter. The filters send the images meant for the right eye only to the right eye and the images meant for the left only to the left. The brain does the rest of the work. It combines the two colors, giving different shades of gray and interprets the slightly different images so that you can tell which object is in front and which is behind.

Career CONNECTION

Research how 3-D technology is being used in the latest computer animation software. Find out how the 3-D images used in computer animations are made.

17•2 Early Space Missions

What You'll Learn

- How to compare and contrast natural and artificial satellites
- The differences between artificial satellites and space probes
- The history of the race to the moon

Vocabulary
satellite
orbit
space probe
Project Mercury
Project Gemini
Project Apollo

Why It's Important

- Learning about space exploration will help you better understand the vastness of space.

The First Steps into Space

If you had your choice of watching your favorite sports team on television or from the stadium, which would you prefer? You would probably want to be as close as possible to the game so you wouldn't miss any of the action. Scientists feel the same way about space. Even though telescopes have taught them a great deal about the moon and planets, they want to learn more by actually going to those places or by sending spacecraft where they can't go.

Satellites

Space exploration began in 1957 when the former Soviet Union used a rocket to send *Sputnik I* into space. It was the first artificial satellite. A **satellite** is any object that revolves around another object. When an object enters space, it travels in a straight line unless a force such as gravity deflects it. When Earth's gravity pulls on a satellite, it falls toward Earth. The result of the satellite traveling forward while at the same time falling toward Earth is a curved path, called an **orbit,** around Earth. This is shown in **Figure 17-6.**

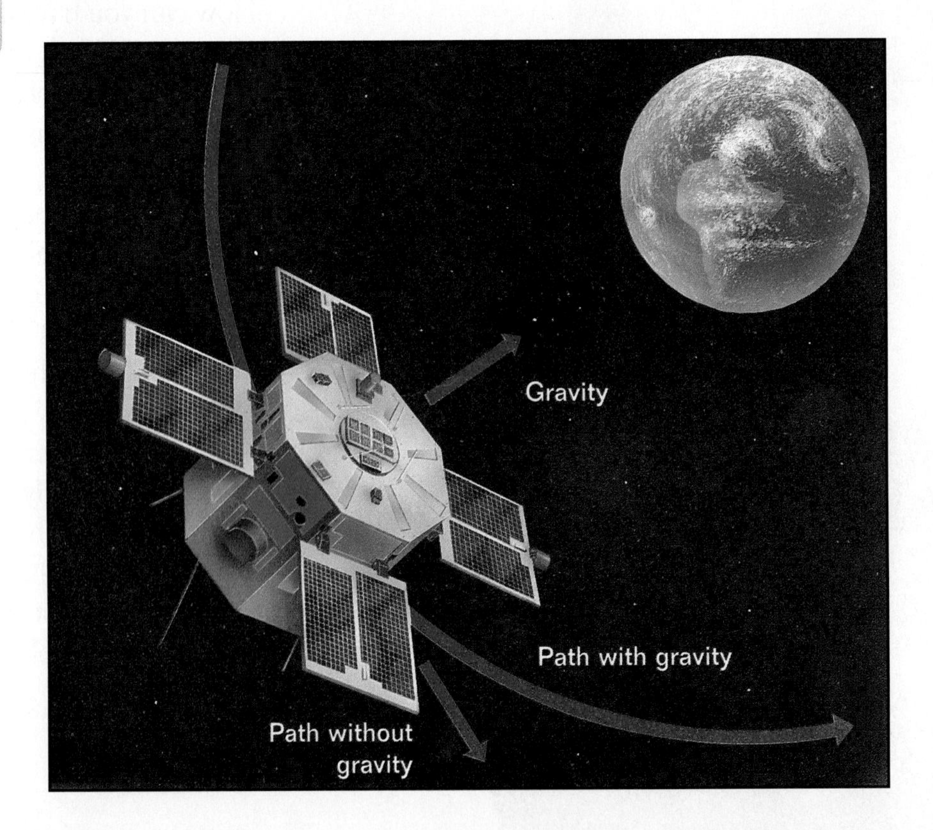

Figure 17-6 The combination of the satellite's forward movement and the gravitational attraction of Earth causes the satellite to travel in a curved path, called an orbit. **What would happen if the forward speed of the satellite decreased?**

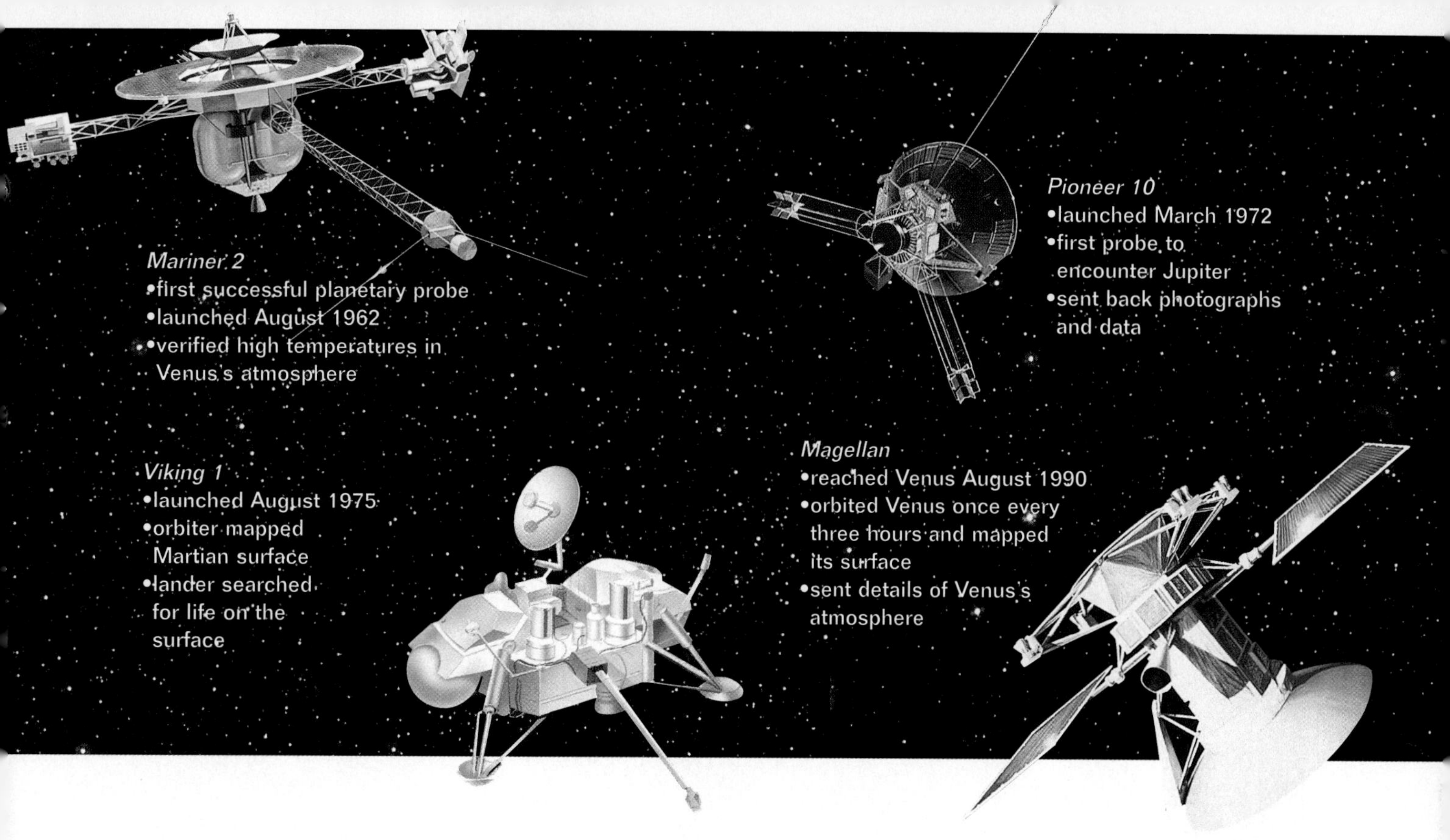

Figure 17-7 Some early U.S. space probes and their missions provided much useful data.

Satellite Uses

The moon is a natural satellite of Earth. It completes one orbit every month. *Sputnik I* orbited Earth for 57 days before gravity pulled it back into the atmosphere, where it burned up. *Sputnik I* was an experiment to show that artificial satellites could be made. Today, thousands of artificial satellites orbit Earth.

Present-day communication satellites transmit radio and television programs to locations around the world. Other satellites gather scientific data that can't be obtained from Earth, and weather satellites constantly monitor Earth's global weather patterns.

Using Math

Suppose a spacecraft is launched at a speed of 40 200 km per hour. Express this speed in kilometers per second.

Space Probes

Not all objects carried into space by rockets become satellites. Rockets also can be used to send instruments into space. A **space probe** is an instrument that gathers information and sends it back to Earth. Unlike satellites that orbit Earth, space probes travel far into the solar system. Some have even traveled out of the solar system. Space probes, like many satellites, carry cameras and other data-gathering equipment, as well as radio transmitters and receivers that allow them to communicate with scientists on Earth. **Figure 17-7** shows some of the early space probes launched by NASA (National Aeronautics and Space Administration).

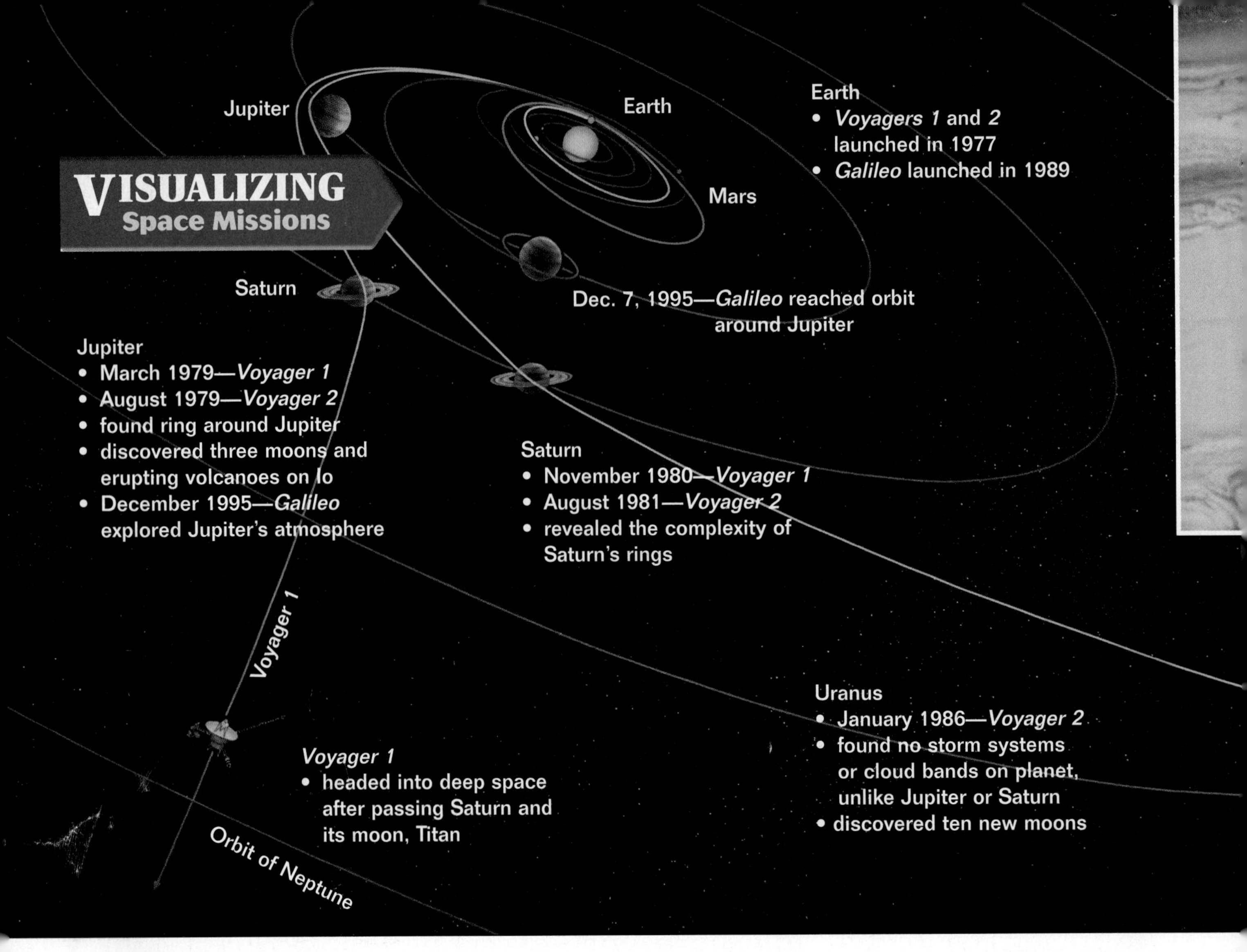

Figure 17-8 The *Voyager* and *Galileo* spacecraft helped make many major discoveries.

You've probably heard of the space probes *Voyager 1* and *Voyager 2*. These two probes were launched in 1977 and are now heading toward deep space. *Voyager 1* flew past Jupiter and Saturn. *Voyager 2* flew past Jupiter, Saturn, Uranus, and Neptune. **Figure 17-8** describes some of what we've learned from the *Voyager* probes. Now, these probes are exploring beyond our solar system as part of the Voyager Interstellar Mission. Scientists expect these probes to continue to transmit data to Earth for at least 20 more years.

The fate of a probe is never certain, and not all probes are successful. In 1993, *Mars Observer* was only days away from entering orbit around Mars when it was lost. The problem was most likely a critical failure in the propulsion system.

Galileo, launched in 1989, reached Jupiter in 1995. In July 1995, *Galileo* released a smaller probe that began a five-month approach to Jupiter. The small probe took a parachute ride through Jupiter's violent atmosphere in December 1995.

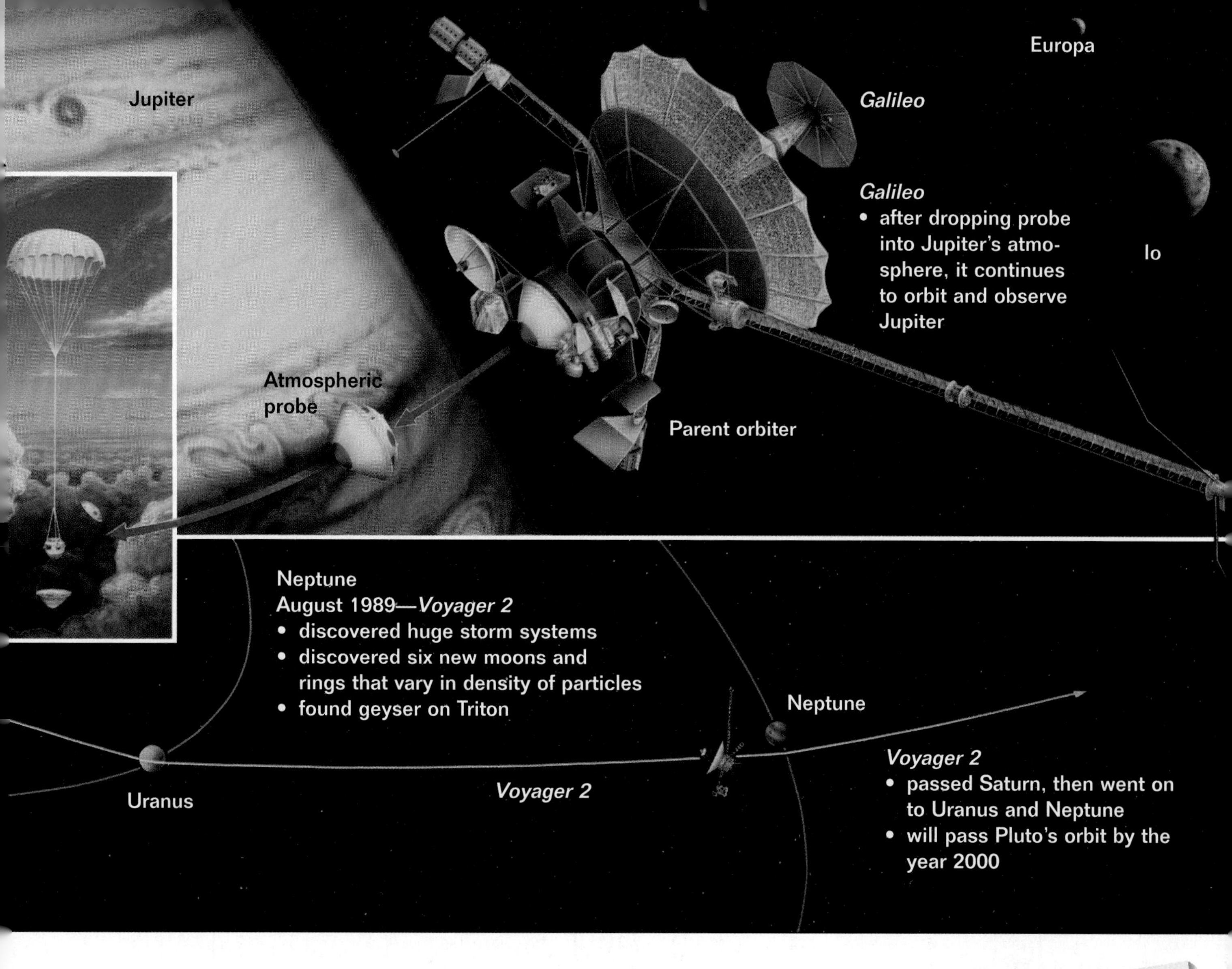

Before being crushed by the atmospheric pressure, it transmitted information about Jupiter's composition, temperature, and pressure to the ship orbiting above. *Galileo* studied Jupiter's moons, rings, and magnetic fields and then relayed this information back to scientists who were eagerly waiting for it on Earth. ☑

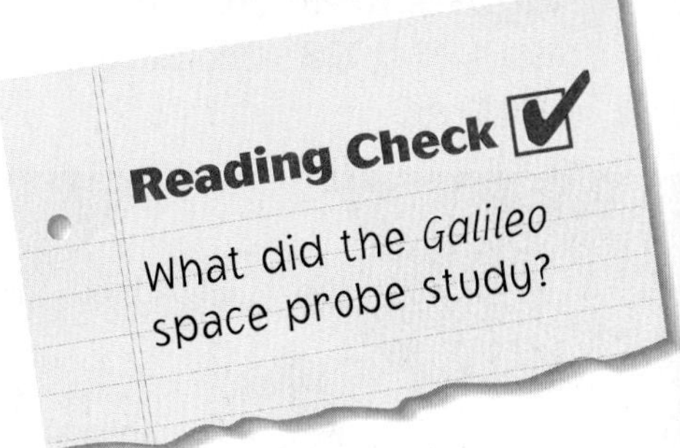

Galileo

Recent studies of Jupiter's moon Europa by *Galileo* indicate that an ocean of water or ice may exist under the outer layer of ice that covers Europa's cracked surface. The cracks in the surface may be caused by geologic activity that heats the ocean underneath the surface. Sunlight penetrates these cracks, further heating the ocean and setting the stage for the possible existence of life on Europa. *Galileo* studied Europa through 1999. More advanced probes will be needed to determine whether molecular life actually does exist on this icy moon.

Comparing the Effects of Light Pollution

Procedure

1. Obtain a cardboard tube from an empty roll of paper towels.
2. Select a night when clear skies are predicted. Go outside about two hours after sunset and look through the cardboard tube at a specific constellation decided upon ahead of time.
3. Count the number of stars you are able to see without moving the observing tube. Repeat this three times.
4. Determine the average number of observable stars at your location.

Analysis

1. Compare and contrast the number of stars visible from other students' homes.
2. Explain the cause and effect of differences in your observations.

The Race to the Moon

Throughout the world, people were shocked when they turned on their radios and television sets in 1957 and heard the radio transmissions from *Sputnik I* as it orbited over their heads. All that *Sputnik I* transmitted was a sort of beeping sound, but people quickly realized that putting a human into space wasn't far off.

In 1961, the Soviet cosmonaut Yuri A. Gagarin became the first human in space. He orbited Earth and then returned safely. Soon, President John F. Kennedy called for the United States to place people on the moon and return them to Earth by the end of that decade. The "race for space" had begun.

The U.S. program to reach the moon began with **Project Mercury.** The goals of Project Mercury were to orbit a piloted spacecraft around Earth and to bring it safely back. The program provided data and experience in the basics of space flight. On May 5, 1961, Alan B. Shepard became the first U.S. citizen in space. In 1962, *Mercury* astronaut John Glenn became the first U.S. citizen to orbit Earth. **Figure 17-9** shows Glenn preparing for liftoff. In 1998, Glenn returned to space aboard the space shuttle *Discovery.* You'll learn more about space shuttles in the next section.

Figure 17-9 John Glenn was the first U.S. astronaut to orbit Earth.

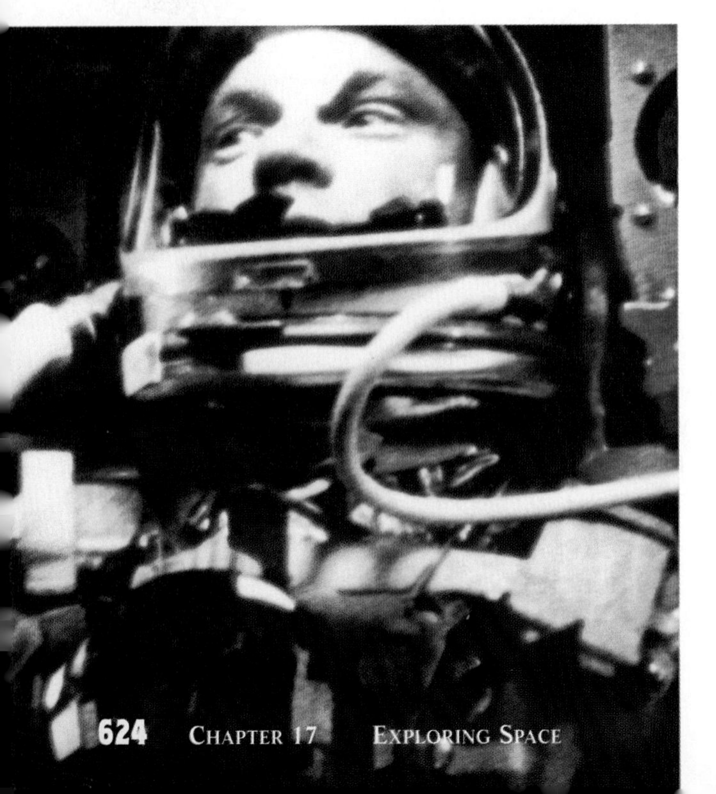

Project Gemini

Project Gemini was the next step in reaching the moon. Teams of two astronauts in the same *Gemini* spacecraft orbited Earth. One *Gemini* team met and connected with another spacecraft in orbit—a skill that would be needed on a voyage to the moon.

Along with the *Mercury* and *Gemini* programs, a series of robotic probes was sent to the moon. *Ranger* proved we could get spacecraft to the moon. *Surveyor* landed gently on the moon's surface, indicating that the moon's surface could support spacecraft and humans. The mission of *Lunar Orbiter* was to take pictures of the moon's surface to help determine the best landing sites on the moon.

Project Apollo

The final stage of the U.S. program to reach the moon was **Project Apollo.** On July 20, 1969, *Apollo* 11 landed on the lunar surface. Neil Armstrong was the first human to set foot on the moon. His first words as he stepped onto its surface were, "That's one small step for man, one giant leap for mankind." Edwin Aldrin, the second of the three *Apollo* 11 astronauts, joined Armstrong on the moon, and they explored its surface for two hours. Michael Collins remained in the Command Module orbiting the moon, where Armstrong and Aldrin returned before beginning the journey home. A total of six lunar landings brought back more than 2000 samples of moon rock and soil for study before the program ended in 1972. **Figure 17-10** shows astronauts on the moon.

Figure 17-10 The Lunar Rover Vehicle was first used during the *Apollo 15* mission. Riding in the moon buggy, *Apollo 15, 16,* and *17* astronauts explored large areas of the lunar surface.

During the past three decades, most missions in space have been carried out by individual countries, often competing to be the first or the best. Today, there is much more cooperation among countries of the world to work together and share what each has learned. Projects are now being planned for cooperative missions to Mars and elsewhere. As you read the next section, you'll see how the U.S. program has progressed since the days of Project Apollo, and where it may be going in the future.

Section Assessment

1. Currently, no human-made objects are orbiting Neptune, yet Neptune has eight satellites. Explain.
2. *Galileo* was considered a space probe as it traveled to Jupiter. Once there, however, it became an artificial satellite. Explain.
3. **Think Critically:** Is Earth a satellite of any other body in space? Explain your answer.
4. **Skill Builder**
   Concept Mapping Make an events-chain concept map that lists the events in the U.S. space program to place people on the moon. If you need help, refer to Concept Mapping in the **Skill Handbook** on page 950.

Using Computers

Spreadsheet Use the spreadsheet feature on your computer to generate a table of recent successful satellites and space probes launched by the United States. Include a description of the craft, the date launched, and the mission. If you need help, refer to page 974.

On The Internet

Activity 17•2

Star Sightings

For thousands of years, humans have used the stars to learn about the planet we live on. From star sightings, you can map the change of seasons, navigate the oceans, and even determine the size of Earth.

Polaris, or the North Star, has occupied an important place in human history. The location of Polaris is not affected by Earth's rotation. At any given observation point, it always appears at the same angle above the horizon. At Earth's north pole, Polaris appears directly overhead. At the equator, it is just above the northern horizon. Polaris provides a standard from which other locations can be measured. Such star sightings can be made using the astrolabe, an instrument used to measure the height of a star above the horizon.

Recognize the Problem

How can you determine the size of Earth?

Form a Hypothesis

Think about what you have learned about sightings of Polaris. How does this tell you that Earth is round? Knowing that Earth is round, **form a hypothesis** about whether you can estimate the circumference of Earth based on star sightings.

Goals

- **Record** your sightings of Polaris.
- **Share** the data with other students to **calculate** the circumference of Earth.

Safety Precautions

Do not use the astrolabe during the daytime to observe the sun.

Data Sources

Go to the Glencoe Science Web Site at **www.glencoe.com/sec/science/ca** to obtain instructions on how to make an astrolabe, for more information about the location of Polaris, and for data from other students.

Test Your Hypothesis

Plan

1. Obtain an astrolabe or **construct** one using the instructions posted on the Glencoe Science Web Site.
2. **Design** a data table in your Science Journal similar to the one below.
3. Decide as a group how you will make your observations. Does it take more than one person to make each observation? When will it be easiest to see Polaris?

Do

1. Make sure your teacher approves your plan before you proceed.
2. Carry out your observations.
3. **Record** your observations in your data table.
4. **Average** your readings and post them in the table provided on the Glencoe Science Web Site.

Analyze Your Data

1. **Research** the names of cities that are at approximately the same longitude as your hometown. **Gather** astrolabe readings at the Glencoe Science Web Site from students in one of those cities.
2. **Compare** your astrolabe readings. **Subtract** the smaller reading from the larger one.
3. Determine the distance between your star sighting location and the other city.
4. To calculate the circumference of Earth, use the following relationship.

$$\text{Circumference} = \frac{(360°)(\text{distance between locations})}{\text{difference between readings}}$$

Draw Conclusions

1. How does the circumference of Earth that you calculated compare with the accepted value of 40 079 km?
2. What are some possible sources of error in this method of determining the size of Earth? What improvements would you suggest?

Polaris Observations

Your location:		
Date	Time	Astrolabe Reading
Average astrolabe reading:		

17•3 Recent and Future Space Missions

What You'll Learn

- The benefits of the space shuttle
- The usefulness of orbital space stations
- Future space missions

Vocabulary
space shuttle
space station

Why It's Important

- Many exciting things are planned for the future of space exploration.

The Space Shuttle

Imagine spending millions of dollars to build a machine, sending it off into space, and watching its 3000 metric tons of metal and other materials burn up after only a few minutes of work. That's exactly what NASA did for many years. The early rockets lifted a small capsule holding the astronauts into orbit. Sections of the rocket separated from the rest of the rocket body and burned as they reentered the atmosphere.

A Reusable Spacecraft

NASA administrators, like many others, realized that it would be less expensive and less wasteful to reuse resources. The reusable spacecraft that transports astronauts, satellites, and other materials to and from space is the **space shuttle.** The space shuttle is shown in **Figure 17-11.**

At launch, the space shuttle stands on end and is connected to an external liquid-fuel tank and two solid-fuel booster rockets. When the shuttle reaches an altitude of about 45 km, the emptied solid-fuel booster rockets drop off and parachute back to Earth. They are recovered and used again. The larger, external liquid-fuel tank eventually separates and falls back to Earth, but it isn't recovered.

Once the space shuttle reaches space, it begins to orbit Earth. There, astronauts perform many different tasks. The cargo bay can carry a self-contained laboratory, where astronauts conduct scientific experiments and determine the effects of space flight on the human body. On missions in which the cargo bay isn't used as a laboratory, the shuttle can launch, repair, and retrieve satellites.

To retrieve a satellite, a large mechanical arm in the cargo bay is extended. An astronaut inside the shuttle moves the arm by remote control. The arm grabs the satellite and pulls it back into the cargo bay. The doors are closed, and it is then returned to Earth.

Figure 17-11 The space shuttle is designed to make many trips into space.

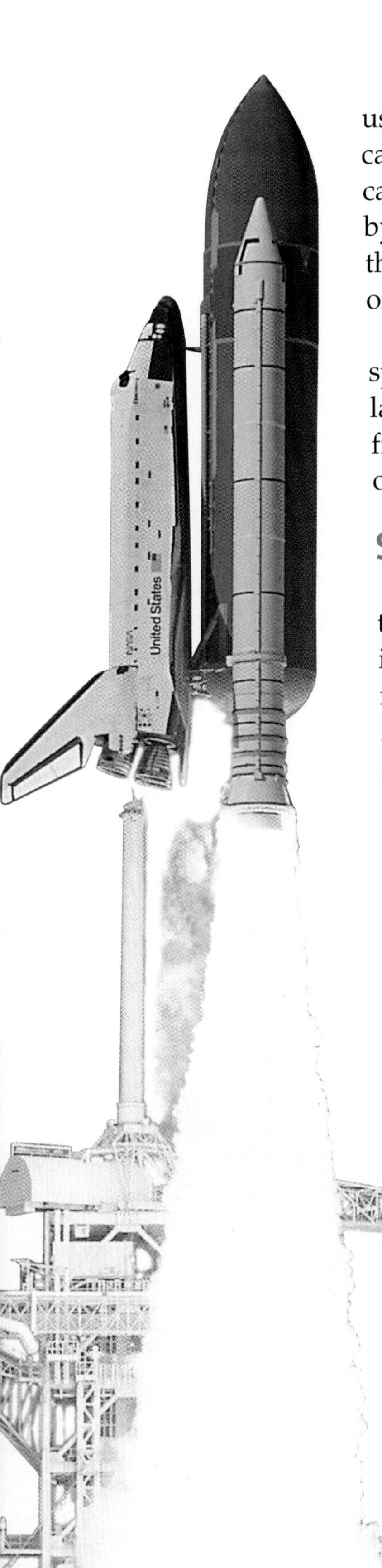

Similarly, the mechanical arm can be used to lift a satellite or probe out of the cargo bay and place it into space. In some cases, a defective satellite can be pulled in by the mechanical arm, repaired while in the cargo bay, and then placed into space once more.

After each mission is completed, the space shuttle glides back to Earth and lands like an airplane. A large landing field is needed because the gliding speed of the shuttle is 335 km/hr.

Space Stations

Astronauts can spend only a short time in space in the space shuttle. Its living area is small, and the crew needs more room to live, exercise, and work. A **space station** has living quarters, work and exercise areas, and all the equipment and support systems needed for humans to live and work in space.

The United States had such a station in the past. The space station *Skylab* was launched in 1973. Crews of astronauts spent up to 84 days in it performing experiments and collecting data on the effects that living in space had on humans. In 1979, the abandoned *Skylab* fell out of orbit and burned up as it entered Earth's atmosphere.

interNET CONNECTION

In 1962, John Glenn became the first U.S. citizen to orbit Earth. In 1998, Glenn returned to space aboard the space shuttle *Discovery*. Visit the Glencoe Science Web Site at **www.glencoe.com/sec/science/ca** for more information about the historical significance of Glenn's *Discovery* flight.

Modeling Gravity

Procedure

1. Locate a stereo record album and turntable you can use for this activity.
2. Fold 8-cm-wide strips of construction paper in half, then unfold them.
3. Wrap the strips along the fold around the circumference of the record so there is a 4-cm wall around the outside edge of the disc.
4. Securely tape the rest underneath the record.
5. Place the record on a turntable and place three marbles at its center.
6. Switch on the turntable.

Analysis

1. What did you observe about the movements of the marbles?
2. Hypothesize how what you've observed could be useful for simulating the effects of gravity on a space station.

Crews from the former Soviet Union have spent the most time in space aboard the space station *Mir.* Cosmonaut Dr. Valery Polyakov returned to Earth after 438 days in space studying the long-term effects of weightlessness.

Cooperation in Space

In 1995, the United States and Russia began an era of cooperation and trust in exploring space. Early in the year, Dr. Norman Thagard was launched into orbit aboard the Russian *Soyuz* spacecraft, along with two Russian cosmonaut crewmates. Dr. Thagard was the first U.S. astronaut launched into space by a Russian booster and the first American resident of the Russian space station *Mir*.

In June 1995, Russian cosmonauts rode into orbit aboard the space shuttle *Atlantis,* America's 100th crewed launch. The mission of *Atlantis* involved, among other studies, a rendezvous and docking with space station *Mir*. The cooperation that existed on this mission continued through

Figure 17-12 The proposed International Space Station is scheduled for completion in 2003.

eight more space shuttle-*Mir* docking missions. Each was an important step toward building and operating the International Space Station.

The International Space Station

The International Space Station (ISS) will be a permanent laboratory designed to use in long-term research. Diverse topics will be studied, such as researching the growth of protein crystals. This project will help scientists determine protein structure and function. This could enhance work on drug design and the treatment of diseases.

The space station will draw on the resources of more than 16 nations. Various nations will build units for the space station, which will then be transported into space aboard the space shuttle and Russian launch rockets. The station will be constructed in space. **Figure 17-12** shows what the completed station will look like.

NASA is planning the space station program in three phases. Phase One, now concluded, involved the space shuttle-*Mir* docking missions. Phase Two began in 1998 with the launch of the Russian-built Functional Cargo Block, and will end with the delivery of a U.S. laboratory aboard the space shuttle. During Phase Two, a crew of three people will be delivered to the space station. This is expected to occur by January 2000.

Figure 17-13 Using the space shuttle, scientists have already performed extensive experiments in the weightlessness of space.

Living in Space

The project will continue with Phase Three when the Japanese Experiment Module, the European Columbus Orbiting Facility, and another Russian lab will be delivered.

The U.S. hopes to deliver its Habitation module in 2003, although this date may be delayed. This will end Phase Three and make the International Space Station fully operational and ready for its permanent six- or seven-person crew. A total of 45 separate launches are required to take all components of ISS into space. NASA plans for crews of astronauts to stay on board the station for several months at a time. As shown in **Figure 17-13,** NASA has already conducted numerous tests to prepare astronauts for extended space missions. One day, the station could be a construction site for ships that will go to the moon and Mars.

Exploring Mars

Two of the most successful missions in recent years were the 1996 launchings of the Mars *Global Surveyor* and Mars *Pathfinder*. *Surveyor* orbited Mars, taking high-quality photos of the planet's surface. *Pathfinder* descended to the Martian surface, using rockets and a parachute system to slow its descent. Large balloons were used to absorb the shock of landing. *Pathfinder* carried technology to study the surface of the planet, including a remote-controlled robot rover called *Sojourner.* Using information gathered by the rover and photographs taken by *Surveyor*, scientists determined that areas of the planet's surface were once covered with water during Mars's distant past.

Exploring the Moon

Does water exist in the craters of the moon's poles? This is one question NASA intends to explore with data gathered from the *Lunar Prospector* spacecraft. Launched in 1998, the *Lunar Prospector's* one-year mission was to orbit the moon, taking photographs of the moon's surface for mapping purposes. Early data obtained from the spacecraft indicate that hydrogen is present in the rocks of the moon's poles. Hydrogen is one of the elements found in water. Scientists now theorize that ice on the floors of the moon's polar craters may be the source of this hydrogen.

Figure 17-14 *Cassini* will reach Saturn in 2004.

Cassini

In October 1997, NASA launched the space probe *Cassini.* Destination: Saturn. *Cassini* will not reach its goal until 2004. At that time, the space probe will explore Saturn and surrounding areas for four years. One part of its mission is to deliver the European Space Agency's *Huygens* probe to Saturn's largest moon, Titan, as shown in **Figure 17-14.** Some scientists theorize that Titan's atmosphere may be similar to the atmosphere of early Earth.

Section Assessment

1. What is the main advantage of the space shuttle?
2. Why were the space shuttle-*Mir* docking missions so important?
3. Describe Phase Three of the International Space Station program.
4. Recent space missions have been characterized by a spirit of cooperation. How does this compare and contrast with early space missions?
5. **Think Critically:** Why is the space shuttle more versatile than earlier spacecraft?
6. **Skill Builder**
   Using Numbers *Lunar Prospector* was placed in lunar orbit to photograph the moon's surface. Do the **Chapter 17 Skill Activity** on page 978 to learn more about satellites placed in orbit around Earth.

Suppose you're in charge of assembling a crew for a new space station. Select 50 people you want for the station. Remember, you will need people to do a variety of jobs, such as farming, maintenance, scientific experimentation, and so on. In your Science Journal, explain whom you would select and why.

Chapter 17 Reviewing Main Ideas

For a **preview** of this chapter, study this Reviewing Main Ideas before you read the chapter. After you have studied this chapter, you can use the Reviewing Main Ideas to **review** the chapter.

The Glencoe MindJogger, Audiocassettes, and CD-ROM provide additional opportunities for review.

Section

17-1 RADIATION FROM SPACE

Electromagnetic waves are arranged in the electromagnetic spectrum according to their wavelengths. Optical telescopes produce magnified images of objects. A **refracting telescope** bends light to form an image. A **reflecting telescope** uses mirrors to focus light to produce an image. **Radio telescopes** collect and record radio waves given off by some space objects. ***Why can radio telescopes be used during the day or night and in all types of weather?***

Section

17-2 EARLY SPACE MISSIONS

A **satellite** is an object that revolves around another object. The moons of planets are natural satellites. Artificial satellites are those made by people. An artificial satellite collects data as it **orbits** a planet. A **space probe** travels into the solar system, gathers data, and sends the information back to Earth. Some space probes become artificial satellites of the planet or other object they are sent to study. ***Why can the* Galileo *spacecraft be referred to both as a probe and as an artificial satellite of Jupiter?***

Reading Check

Review the space missions discussed in the chapter. Then, create a timeline that shows these discoveries in chronological order.

Section

17-3 RECENT AND FUTURE SPACE MISSIONS

The **space shuttle** is a reusable spacecraft that carries astronauts, satellites, and other equipment to and from space. **Space stations,** such as *Mir* and *Skylab,* provide the opportunity to conduct research not possible on Earth. The International Space Station will be constructed in Earth orbit with the cooperation of 16 different nations. Completion of the ISS should occur in the year 2003, if all goes as planned. ***What advantage does the space shuttle have over other launch vehicles?***

Chapter 17 Assessment

Using Vocabulary

a. electromagnetic spectrum
b. observatory
c. orbit
d. Project Apollo
e. Project Gemini
f. Project Mercury
g. radio telescope
h. reflecting telescope
i. refracting telescope
j. satellite
k. space probe
l. space shuttle
m. space station

The sentences below include italicized terms that have been used incorrectly. Change the incorrect terms so that the sentences read correctly. Underline your change.

1. A *reflecting telescope* uses lenses to bend light toward a focal point.
2. A *space probe* is an object that revolves around another object.
3. *Project Apollo* was the first piloted U.S. space program.
4. A *space station* carries people and tools to and from space.
5. In an *observatory,* electromagnetic waves are arranged according to their wavelengths.

Checking Concepts

Choose the word or phrase that best answers the question.

6. Which spacecraft has sent back images of Venus?
   A) *Voyager* C) *Apollo 11*
   B) *Viking* D) *Magellan*
7. Which telescope uses mirrors to collect light?
   A) radio C) refracting
   B) electromagnetic D) reflecting
8. *Sputnik I* was the first what?
   A) telescope C) observatory
   B) artificial satellite D) U.S. space probe
9. Which telescope can be used during day or night and during bad weather?
   A) radio C) refracting
   B) electromagnetic D) reflecting
10. When fully operational, the International Space Station will be crewed by up to how many people?
    A) 3 C) 15
    B) 7 D) 50
11. Which space mission had the goal to put a spacecraft in orbit and bring it back safely?
    A) Project Mercury C) Project Gemini
    B) Project Apollo D) *Viking I*
12. The space shuttle reuses which of the following?
    A) liquid-fuel tanks C) booster engines
    B) *Gemini* rockets D) *Saturn* rockets
13. What does the space shuttle use to place a satellite into space?
    A) liquid-fuel tank C) mechanical arm
    B) booster rocket D) cargo bay
14. What was *Skylab?*
    A) space probe C) space shuttle
    B) space station D) optical telescope
15. Which of the following is a natural satellite of Earth?
    A) *Skylab* C) the sun
    B) the space shuttle D) the moon

Thinking Critically

16. How would a moon-based telescope have advantages over the Earth-based telescopes being used today?
17. Would a space probe to the sun's surface be useful? Explain.
18. Which would you choose—space missions with people aboard or robotic space probes? Why?

19. Suppose two astronauts were outside the space shuttle, orbiting Earth. The audio speaker in the helmet of one astronaut quits working. The other astronaut is 1 m away, so she shouts a message to him. Can he hear her? Explain.

20. No space probes have visited the planet Pluto. Nevertheless, probes have crossed Pluto's orbit. How?

Developing Skills

If you need help, refer to the Skill Handbook.

21. **Measuring in SI:** Explain whether or not the following pieces of equipment could be used aboard the space shuttle as it orbits Earth: a balance, a meterstick, and a thermometer.

22. **Making and Using Tables:** Copy the table below. Use information in the chapter as well as news articles and other resources to complete your table.

U.S. Space Probes

Probe	Launch Date	Destinations	Planets or Objects Visited
Vikings 1 & 2			
Galileo			
Lunar Prospector			
Mars Pathfinder & Sojourner			

23. **Classifying:** Classify the following as a satellite or a space probe: *Cassini, Sputnik I, Hubble Space Telescope, space shuttle,* and *Voyager 2.*

Test-Taking Tip

Best Times If your test is going to be timed, then practice under timed conditions. Try timing yourself on specific sections to see if you can improve your overall speed while maintaining accuracy.

Test Practice

Use these questions to test your Science Proficiency.

1. Large telescopes are usually reflectors. Which of the following statements **BEST** explains why this is true?
   A) Reflecting telescopes are easier to use and carry around.
   B) Reflecting telescopes have greater magnifying power.
   C) Reflecting telescopes are less expensive to build and maintain.
   D) In reflecting telescopes, the objective mirror can be supported from beneath and, therefore, can be made larger.

2. The *Lunar Prospector* was classified as a space probe when launched but is now classified as a satellite. What does this illustrate about this spacecraft's flight?
   A) The *Lunar Prospector* is in orbit around Earth.
   B) The *Lunar Prospector* was a space probe on its flight to the moon and became a satellite when it went into orbit around the moon.
   C) The *Lunar Prospector* is moving out of our solar system.
   D) The *Lunar Prospector* was launched from Earth, went into orbit around the moon, and landed on the moon.

CHAPTER

18 The Sun-Earth-Moon System

Chapter Preview

Skills Preview

Skill Builders
- Sequence

Activities
- Make a Model
- Interpret Data

MiniLabs
- Compare and Contrast
- Use Numbers

Reading Check

As you read about the phases of the moon and other topics in this chapter, write down the signal words that indicate a sequence, such as *shortly after* and *just before.*

Explore Activity

Earth, the moon, and the sun are constantly moving through space. That's why one night you may see a shining full moon and weeks later see no moon at all. Is the appearance of the moon the only thing that changes because of these movements? No, seasons change, too, because of Earth's tilted axis as it moves around the sun. Let's explore how this happens.

Model Seasons 

1. Use a lamp without a shade to represent the sun.
2. Turn on the lamp and hold a globe of Earth about 2 m from the lamp.
3. Tilt the globe slightly so the northern half points toward the sun.
4. Keeping the globe tilted in the same direction, walk halfway around the sun. Be careful not to turn or twist the globe as you walk.

Science Journal

In which direction is the northern hemisphere pointing relative to the sun in step 3? In step 4? In your Science Journal, describe which seasons these positions represent for the northern hemisphere.

18•1 Planet Earth

What You'll Learn

- Physical data about Earth
- The difference between the rotation and revolution of Earth
- How Earth's revolution and tilt cause seasons to change on Earth

Vocabulary

sphere, ellipse, axis, equinox, rotation, solstice, revolution

Why It's Important

- The movements of Earth cause night and day.

Planet Earth Data

You rise early in the morning, while it's still dark outside. You sit by the window and watch the sun come up. Finally, day breaks, and the sun begins its journey across the sky. But, is the sun moving, or are you?

Today, we know that the sun appears to move across the sky because Earth is spinning as it travels around the sun. But, it wasn't long ago that people believed Earth was the center of the universe. They believed Earth stood still and the sun traveled around it.

As recently as the days of Christopher Columbus, some people also believed Earth was flat. They thought that if you sailed far out to sea, you eventually would fall off the edge of the world. How do you know this isn't true? How have scientists determined Earth's shape?

Earth's Shape

Space probes and artificial satellites have sent back images that show Earth is sphere-shaped. A **sphere** (SFIHR) is a round, three-dimensional object. Its surface at all points is the same distance from its center. Tennis balls and basketballs are examples of spheres. But, people had evidence of Earth's true shape long before cameras were sent into space.

Around 350 B.C., the Greek astronomer and philosopher Aristotle reasoned that Earth was spherical because it always casts a round shadow on the moon during an eclipse, as shown in **Figure 18-1.** Only a spherical object always produces a round shadow. If Earth were flat, it would cast a straight shadow.

Other evidence of Earth's shape was observed by early sailors. They watched as ships approached from across the ocean and saw that the top of the ship would come into view first. As they continued to watch the ship, more and more of it

Figure 18-1 If Earth were flat, its shadow during an eclipse would be straight on the moon, not curved, as shown.

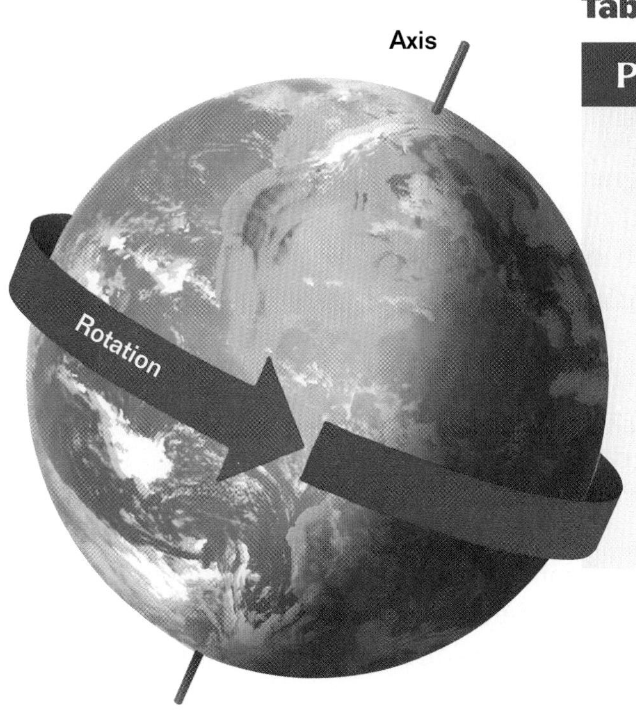

Table 18-1

Physical Properties of Earth	
Diameter (pole to pole)	12 714 km
Diameter (equator)	12 756 km
Circumference (poles)	40 008 km
Circumference (equator)	40 075 km
Mass	5.98×10^{27} g
Density	5.52 g/cm^3
Average distance to the sun	149 600 000 km
Period of rotation (1 day)	23 hr, 56 min
Period of revolution (1 year)	365 days, 6 hr, 9 min

would appear until they could see all of it. This was possible only if Earth was a sphere.

Today, we know that Earth is sphere-shaped, but it is not a perfect sphere. It bulges slightly at the equator and is somewhat flattened at the poles. The poles are located at the north and south ends of Earth's axis. Earth's **axis** is the imaginary line around which Earth spins. The spinning of Earth on its axis, called **rotation,** causes day and night to occur.

Earth's Rotation

As Earth rotates, the sun comes into view at daybreak. Earth continues to spin, making it seem as if the sun moves across the sky until it sets at night. During night, your area of Earth has spun away from the sun. Because of this, the sun is no longer visible. Earth continues to rotate steadily, and the sun eventually comes into view the next morning. One complete rotation takes about 24 hours, or one day. How many rotations does Earth complete during one year? As you can see in **Table 18-1,** it completes about 365 rotations during its journey around the sun.

Comparing Spheres

Procedure 

1. Use a long piece of string to measure the circumference of a basketball or volleyball.
2. Measure the circumference of the ball at a right angle to your first measurement.
3. Determine the roundness ratio by dividing the larger measurement by the smaller one.
4. Compare these data with the roundness ratio data about Earth's circumference provided in **Table 18-1.**

Analysis

1. How round is Earth compared with the ball?
2. Is Earth larger through the equator or through the poles?
3. Explain how your observations support your answer.

Earth's Magnetic Field

Convection currents inside Earth's mantle power the movement of tectonic plates. Scientists hypothesize that movement of material inside Earth along with Earth's rotation generates a magnetic field, as shown in **Figure 18-2.**

The magnetic field of Earth is much like that of a bar magnet. Earth has a north and a south magnetic pole, just as a bar magnet has opposite magnetic poles at its ends. **Figure 18-3** illustrates the effects of sprinkling iron shavings over a bar magnet. The shavings align with the magnetic field of the magnet. Earth's magnetic field is similar, almost as if Earth had a giant bar magnet in its core.

Magnetic North

When you observe a compass needle pointing toward the north, you are seeing evidence of Earth's magnetic field. Earth's magnetic axis, the line joining its north and south magnetic poles, does not align with its rotational axis. The magnetic axis is inclined at an angle of 11.5° to the rotational axis. If you followed a compass needle pointing north, you would end up at the magnetic north pole rather than the geographic (rotational) north pole.

Earth's magnetic field and other physical properties affect us every day. What occurrences can you explain in terms of Earth's physical properties and movement in space?

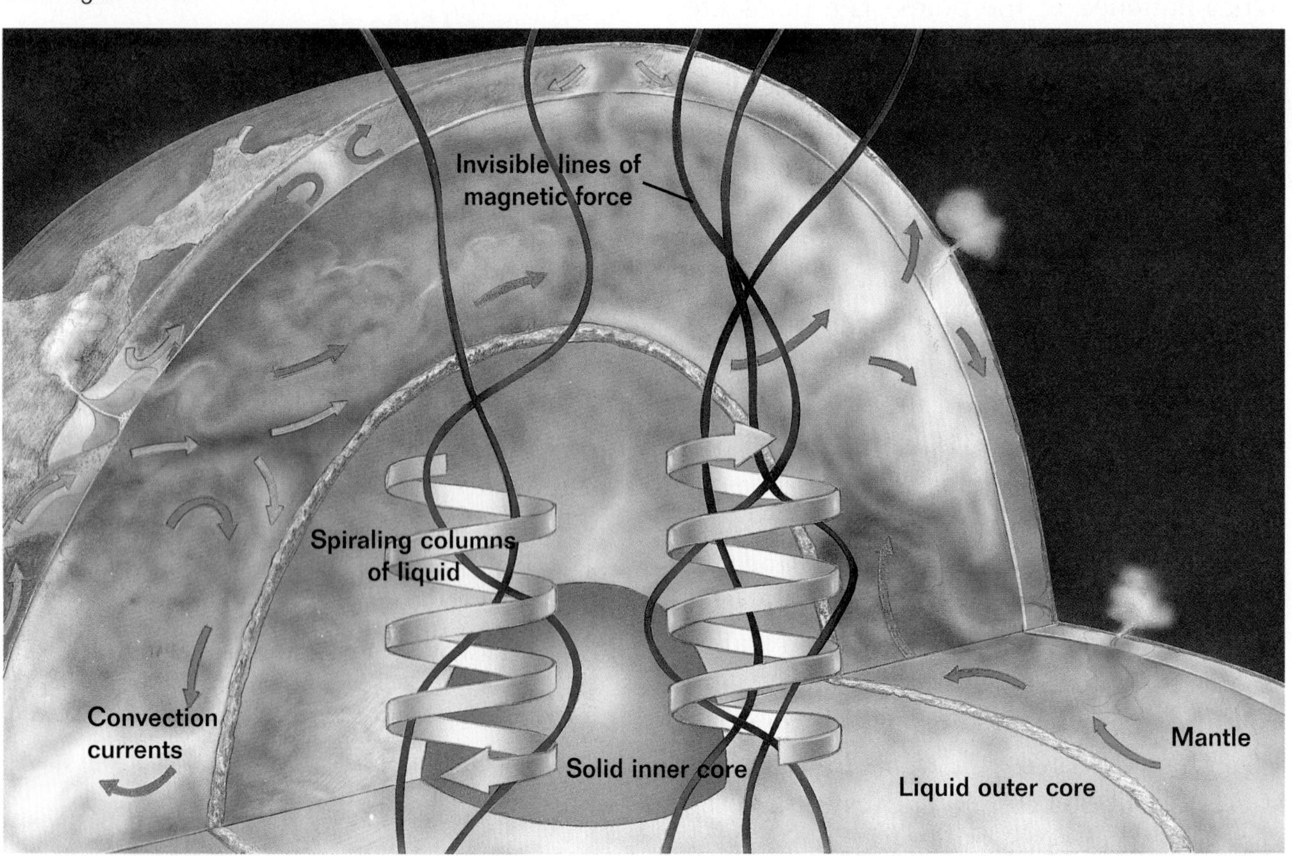

Figure 18-2 Heat and pressure within Earth cause the liquid outer core to move continuously. Driven by Earth's rotation and convection currents deep within Earth, the molten liquid forms spiraling columns. These spirals generate mechanical energy, which in turn generates electricity that creates the magnetic field.

Figure 18-3 Particles in the solar wind streaming through space from the sun distort Earth's magnetic field. As a result, Earth's magnetic field isn't symmetrical. It doesn't have the same shape as a magnetic field surrounding a bar magnet, which is symmetrical.

Seasons

Autumn is coming, and each day it gets colder outside. Dawn comes later each morning, and the sun appears lower in the sky. A month ago, it was light enough to ride your bike at 8:00 P.M. Now, it's dark at 8:00 P.M. What is causing this change?

Earth's Revolution

You learned earlier that Earth's rotation causes day and night. Another important motion of Earth is its **revolution,** or yearly orbit around the sun. Just as the moon is a satellite of Earth, Earth is a satellite of the sun. If Earth's orbit were a circle and the sun were at the center of the circle, Earth would maintain a constant distance from the sun. However, this is not the case. Earth's orbit is an **ellipse** (ee LIHPS), which is an elongated, closed curve. As **Figure 18-4** shows, the sun is offset from the center of the ellipse. Because of this, the distance between Earth and the sun changes during Earth's yearlong orbit. Earth gets closest to the sun—about 147 million km away—around January 3. The farthest point in Earth's orbit is about 152 million km away from the sun and is reached around July 4.

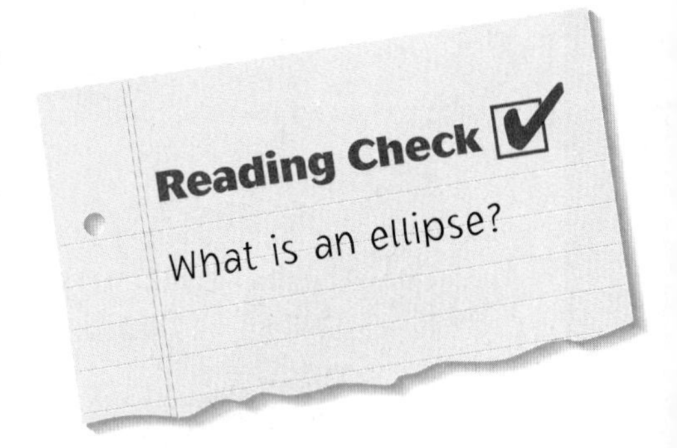

Does this elliptical orbit cause seasonal temperatures on Earth? If it did, you would expect the warmest days in January. You know this isn't the case in the northern hemisphere. Something else causes the change.

Even though Earth is closest to the sun in January, the overall amount of energy Earth receives from the sun changes little throughout the year. However, the amount of energy any one place on Earth receives can vary greatly.

Figure 18-4 The northern hemisphere experiences summer when Earth is farthest from the sun. It experiences winter when Earth is closest to the sun. **Is the change of seasons caused by Earth's elliptical orbit? Explain your answer.**

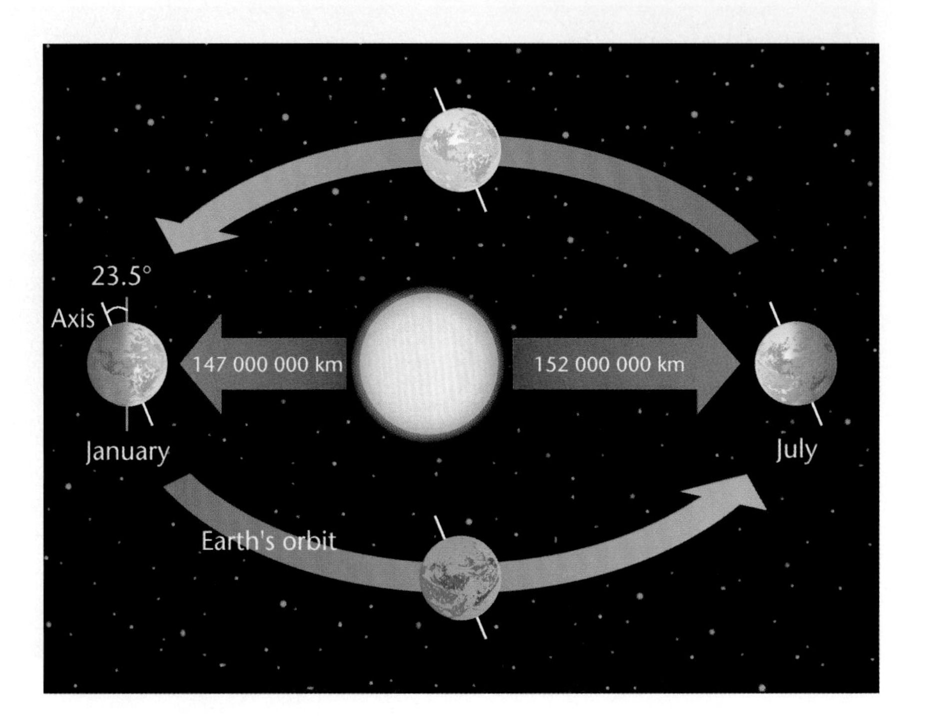

Earth's Tilted Axis

Earth's axis is tilted 23.5° from a line perpendicular to its orbit. This tilt causes the seasons. Daylight hours are longer for the hemisphere tilted toward the sun. Think of how early it gets dark in the winter compared to the summer. As shown in **Figure 18-4,** the hemisphere tilted toward the sun receives more hours of sunlight than the hemisphere tilted away from the sun.

Earth's tilt also causes the sun's radiation to strike the hemisphere tilted toward it at a higher angle than it does the other hemisphere. Because of this, the hemisphere tilted toward the sun receives more electromagnetic radiation per unit area than the hemisphere tilted away. In other words, if you measured the amount of radiation received in a 1-km^2 area in the northern hemisphere and, at the same time, measured it for 1 km^2 in the southern hemisphere, you would find a difference. The hemisphere tilted toward the sun would be receiving more energy.

A summer season results when the sun's electromagnetic radiation strikes Earth at a higher angle. Just the opposite occurs during winter. **Figure 18-5** shows scenes from winter and summer.

Figure 18-5 Temperatures during summer are warmer than those during winter. **Why?**

Equinoxes and Solstices

Because of the tilt of Earth's axis, the sun's position relative to Earth's equator constantly changes. Most of the time, the sun is north or south of the equator. Two times during the year, however, the sun is directly over the equator.

Visit the Glencoe Science Web Site at **www.glencoe.com/sec/science/ca** for more information about seasons.

Equinox

Look at **Figure 18-6.** When the sun reaches an **equinox** (EE kwuh nahks), it is directly above Earth's equator, and the number of daylight hours equals the number of nighttime hours all over the world. At that time, neither the northern nor the southern hemisphere is tilted toward the sun. In the northern hemisphere, the sun reaches the spring equinox on March 20 or 21 and the fall equinox on September 22 or 23. In the southern hemisphere, the equinoxes are reversed. Spring occurs in September and fall occurs in March.

Solstice

The **solstice** is the point at which the sun reaches its greatest distance north or south of the equator. In the northern hemisphere, the sun reaches the summer solstice on June 21 or 22, and the winter solstice occurs on December 21 or 22. Just the opposite is true for the southern hemisphere. When the sun is at the summer solstice, there are more daylight

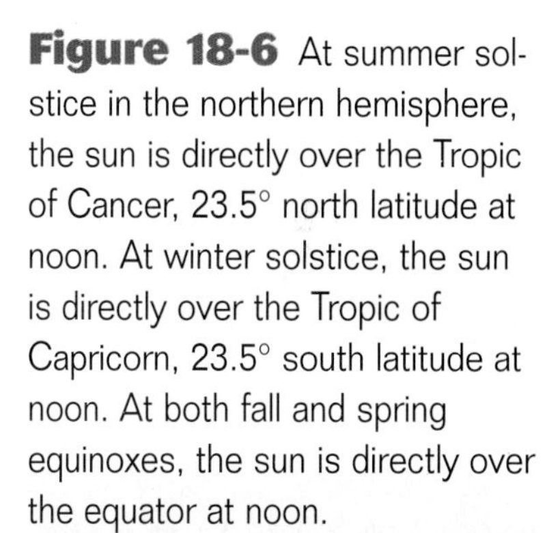

Figure 18-6 At summer solstice in the northern hemisphere, the sun is directly over the Tropic of Cancer, 23.5° north latitude at noon. At winter solstice, the sun is directly over the Tropic of Capricorn, 23.5° south latitude at noon. At both fall and spring equinoxes, the sun is directly over the equator at noon.

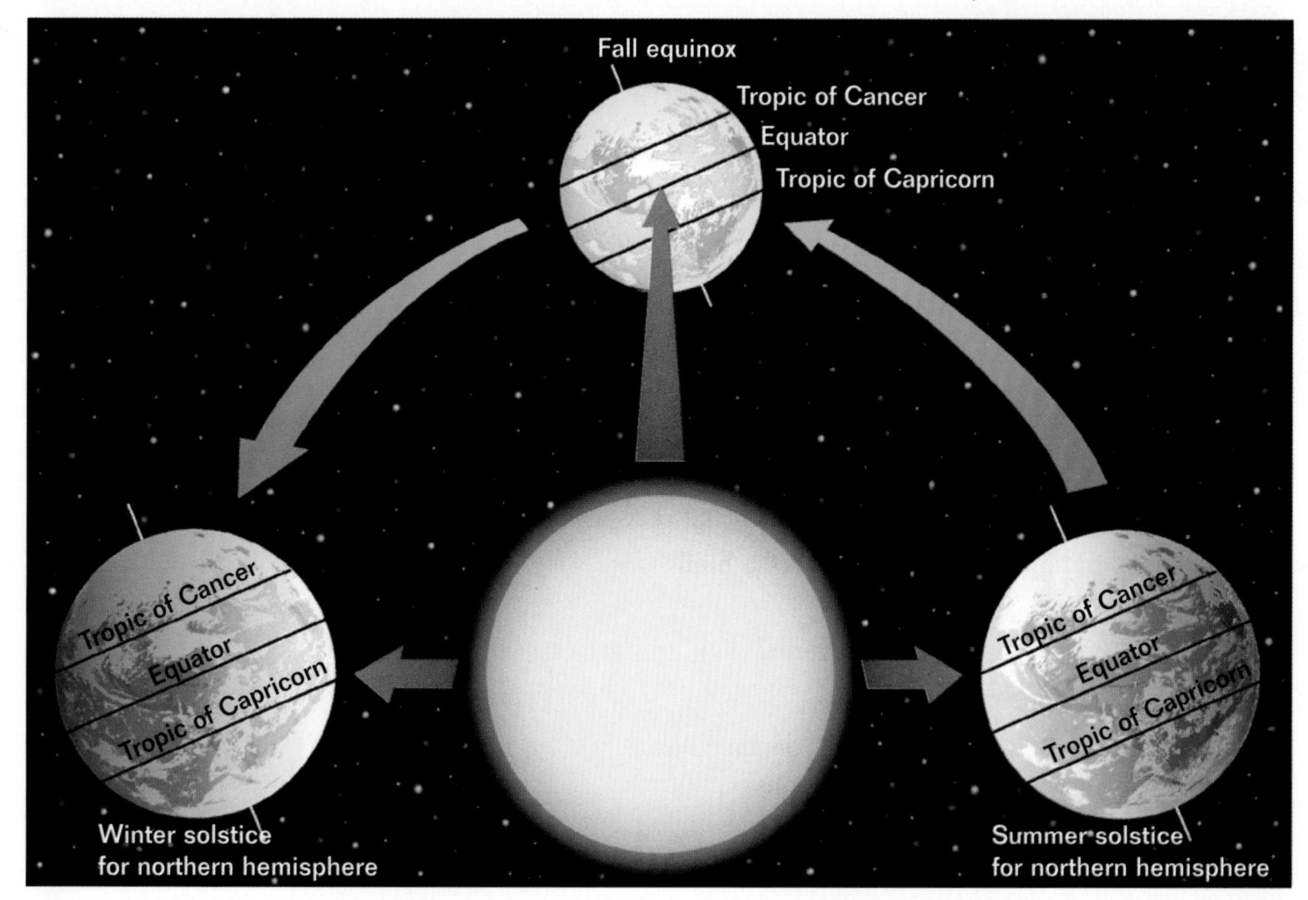

hours than during any other day of the year. When it's at the winter solstice, on the shortest day of the year, the most nighttime hours occur.

Earth Data Review

Earth, shown in **Figure 18-7,** is an imperfect sphere that bulges very slightly at the equator and is somewhat flattened at the poles. The rotation of Earth causes day and night. Earth's tilted axis is responsible for the seasons you experience, and our revolution around the sun marks the passing of a year. In the next section, you will read how Earth's nearest neighbor, the moon, is also in constant motion and how you observe this motion each day.

Figure 18-7 In this photo, Earth appears to be nearly a perfect sphere. In reality, its diameter is 42 km larger at the equator than at the poles.

Section Assessment

1. Which Earth motion causes night and day?
2. Why does summer occur in Earth's northern hemisphere when Earth's north pole is tilted toward the sun?
3. **Think Critically:** **Table 18-1** lists Earth's distance from the sun as an average. Why isn't there one exact measurement of this distance?
4. **Skill Builder**
   Recognizing Cause and Effect
   Answer these questions about the sun-Earth-moon relationship. If you need help, refer to Recognizing Cause and Effect in the **Skill Handbook** on page 957.
   a. What causes seasons on Earth?
   b. What causes winter?
   c. Earth is closest to the sun in January. What effect does this have on seasons?

Using Computers

Spreadsheet Using the table or spreadsheet capabilities of a computer program, generate a table of Earth's physical data showing its diameter, mass, period of rotation, and other data. Then, write a description of the planet based on the table you have created. If you need help, refer to page 974.

A Brave and Startling Truth
by Maya Angelou

In this chapter, you have learned some of the physical characteristics of our planet. Now, find out how one poet, Maya Angelou, uses Earth-science imagery to describe the human race and the quest for world peace. Below are several excerpts, or parts, from her poem "A Brave and Startling Truth."

We, this people, on a small and lonely planet
Traveling through casual space
Past aloof stars, across the way of indifferent suns
To a destination where all signs tell us
It is possible and imperative that we learn
A brave and startling truth...

When we come to it
Then we will confess that not the Pyramids
With their stones set in mysterious perfection
Nor the Gardens of Babylon
Hanging as eternal beauty
In our collective memory
Not the Grand Canyon
Kindled into delicious color
By Western sunsets
These are not the only wonders of the world...

When we come to it
We, this people, on this wayward, floating body
Created on this earth, of this earth
Have the power to fashion for this earth
A climate where every man and every woman
Can live freely without sanctimonious piety
And without crippling fear

When we come to it
We must confess that we are the possible
We are the miraculous, the true wonder of this world
That is when, and only when
We come to it.

interNET CONNECTION

Visit the Glencoe Science Web Site at **www.glencoe.com/sec/science/ca** to learn more about Maya Angelou and her works. Do her other books and poems also contain Earth-science imagery? Using your knowledge of Earth science, write a short poem that uses Earth-science imagery to describe a social issue important to you.

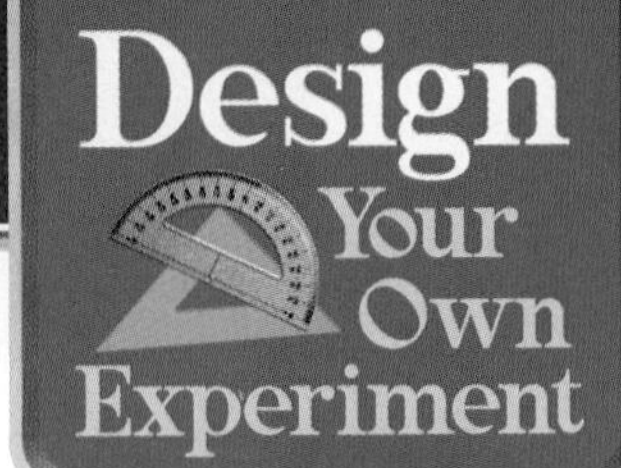

Activity 18 • 1

Tilt and Temperature

Possible Materials

- Tape
- Black construction paper (one sheet)
- Gooseneck lamp with 75-watt bulb
- Celsius thermometer
- Watch
- Protractor

Have you ever noticed how hot the surface of a blacktop driveway can get during the day? The sun's rays hit Earth more directly as the day progresses. Now, consider the fact that Earth is tilted on its axis. How does this affect the amount of heat an area on Earth receives from the sun?

Recognize the Problem

How is the angle at which light strikes an area on Earth related to the changing of the seasons?

Form a Hypothesis

State a hypothesis about how the angle at which light strikes an area affects the amount of heat energy received by that area.

Goals

- **Measure** the amount of heat generated by a light as it strikes a surface at different angles.
- **Describe** how light striking a surface at different angles is related to the changing of the seasons on Earth.

Safety Precautions

Do not touch the lamp without safety gloves. The lightbulb and shade can be hot even when the lamp has been turned off. Handle the thermometer carefully. If it breaks, do not touch anything. Inform your teacher immediately.

Test Your Hypothesis

Plan

1. As a group, agree upon and write out your hypothesis statement.
2. As a group, **list the steps** you need to take to test your hypothesis. Be specific, describing exactly what you will do at each step. List your materials.
3. **Make a list** of any special properties you expect to observe or test.
4. Read over your entire experiment to make sure that all steps are in a logical order.
5. **Identify** any constants, variables, and controls in the experiment.
6. Will you **summarize** data in a graph, table, or some other format?
7. How will you **determine** whether the length of time the light is turned on affects heat energy?
8. How will you **determine** whether the angle at which light strikes an area causes changes in heat and energy?

Do

1. Make sure your teacher approves your plan before you proceed.
2. **Carry out** the experiment as planned.
3. **Complete** the data table in your Science Journal.

Analyze Your Data

1. **Describe** your experiment, including how you used independent variables to test your hypothesis.
2. What happened to the temperature of the area being measured as you modified your variables?
3. **Identify** the dependent variable in your experiment.

Draw Conclusions

1. Did your experiment support your hypothesis? **Explain.**
2. If not, **determine** how you might change the experiment in order to retest your hypothesis. How might you change your hypothesis?

18•2 Earth's Moon

What You'll Learn

- How the moon's phases depend on the relative positions of the sun, the moon, and Earth
- Why eclipses occur and how solar and lunar eclipses compare
- What the surface features of the moon may tell us about its history

Vocabulary

moon phase, new moon, waxing, first quarter, full moon, waning, third quarter, solar eclipse, lunar eclipse, maria

Why It's Important

- The moon is our closest neighbor in space.

Motions of the Moon

You have probably noticed how the moon's apparent shape changes from day to day. Sometimes, just after sunset, you can see a full, round moon low in the sky. Other times, only half of the moon is visible, and it's high in the sky at sunset. Sometimes, the moon is visible during the day. Why does the moon look the way it does? What causes it to change its appearance and position in the sky?

The Moon's Rotation and Revolution

Just as Earth rotates on its axis and revolves around the sun, the moon rotates on its axis and revolves around Earth. The moon's revolution causes changes in its appearance. If the moon rotates on its axis, why don't we see it spin around in space? The moon rotates on its axis once every 27.3 days. It takes the same amount of time to revolve once around Earth. As **Figure 18-8** shows, because these two motions take the same amount of time, the same side of the moon always faces Earth.

Figure 18-8 In about one month, the moon orbits Earth. It also completes one rotation on its axis during the same period. **Does this affect which side of the moon faces Earth? Explain.**

Figure 18-9 The phases of the moon are: (A) new moon, (B) waxing crescent, (C) first quarter, (D) waxing gibbous, (E) full moon, (F) waning gibbous, (G) third quarter, and (H) waning crescent.

You can show this by having a friend hold a ball in front of you. Instruct your friend to move the ball around you while keeping the same side of it facing you. Everyone else in the room will see all sides of the ball. You will see only one side.

Why the Moon Shines

The moon shines because it reflects sunlight from its surface. Just as half of Earth experiences day as the other half experiences night, half of the moon is lighted while the other half is dark. As the moon revolves around Earth, you see different portions of its lighted side, causing the moon's appearance to change. **Moon phases,** as shown in **Figure 18-9,** are the changing appearances of the moon as seen from Earth. The phase you see depends on the relative positions of the moon, Earth, and the sun.

Phases of the Moon

A new moon occurs when the moon is between Earth and the sun. During a **new moon,** the lighted half of the moon is facing the sun and the dark side faces Earth. The moon is in the sky, but it cannot be seen.

Waxing Phases

Shortly after a new moon, more and more of the moon's lighted side becomes visible—the phases are **waxing.** About 24 hours after a new moon, you can see a thin slice of the side of the moon that is lighted by the sun. This phase is called the waxing crescent. About a week after a new moon, you can see half of the lighted side, or one-quarter of the moon's surface. This phase is **first quarter.**

The phases continue to wax. When more than one-quarter is visible, it is called waxing gibbous. A **full moon** occurs when all of the moon's surface that faces Earth is lit up.

Using Math

Earth rotates through an angle of 360° in one day. How many degrees does Earth rotate in one hour?

MiniLab

Comparing the Sun and Moon

Procedure

1. Find an area where you can make a chalk mark on pavement or another surface.
2. Tie a piece of chalk to one end of a string that's 400 cm long.
3. Hold the other end of the string to the pavement.
4. Have a friend pull the string tight and walk around you, leaving a mark on the pavement as he or she circles you.
5. Draw a circle with a 1-cm diameter in the middle of the large circle.

Analysis

1. The small circle represents the moon, and the larger circle represents the sun. How big is the sun compared to the moon?
2. The diameter of the sun is 1.39 million km. The diameter of the Earth is 12 756 km. Draw two new circles modeling the sizes of the sun and Earth.
3. What are the diameters of your two new circles?

Figure 18-10 The orbit of the moon is not in the same plane as Earth's orbit around the sun. If it were, we would experience a solar eclipse each month during the new moon. The plane of the moon's orbit is tilted about 5° to the plane of Earth's orbit.

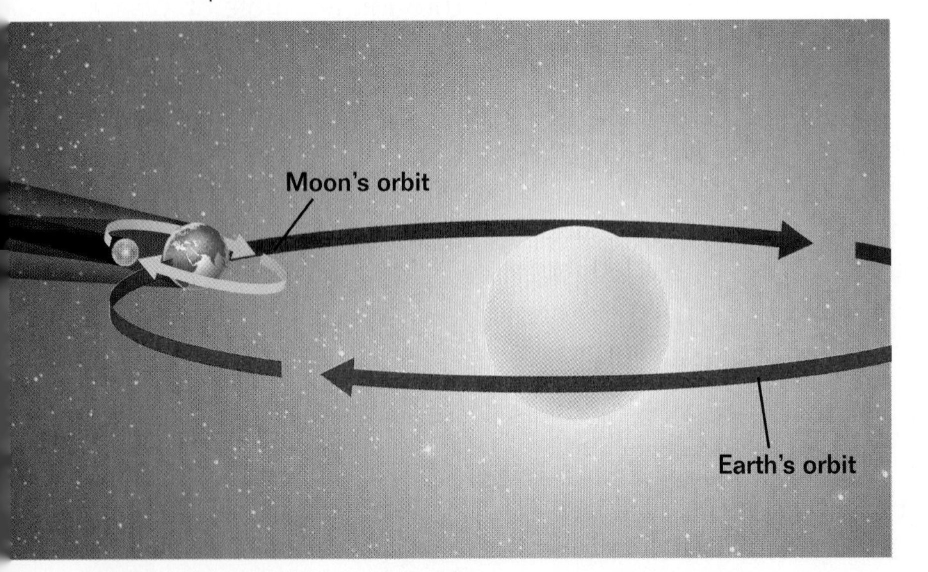

Waning Phases

After a full moon, the amount of the moon's lighted side that can be seen becomes smaller. The phases are said to be **waning.** Waning gibbous begins just after a full moon. When you can see only half of the lighted side, the **third-quarter** phase occurs. The amount of the moon that can be seen continues to become smaller. Waning crescent occurs just before another new moon. Once again, you can see a small slice of the lighted side of the moon.

The complete cycle of the moon's phases takes about 29.5 days. Recall that it takes about 27.3 days for the moon to revolve around Earth. The discrepancy between these two numbers is due to Earth's revolution. It takes the moon about two days to "catch up" with Earth's advancement around the sun.

Eclipses

Imagine yourself as one of your ancient ancestors, living 10 000 years ago. You are out foraging for nuts and other fruit in the bright afternoon sun. Gradually, the sun disappears from the sky, as if being swallowed by a giant creature. The darkness lasts only a short time, and the sun soon returns to full brightness. You realize something unusual has happened, but you don't know what caused it. It will be almost 8000 years before anyone can explain the event that you just experienced.

The event just described was a total solar eclipse (ih KLIPS). Today, we know what causes such eclipses, but for our early ancestors, they must have been terrifying events. Many animals act as if night has come. Cows return to their barns, and chickens go to sleep. What causes the day to suddenly change into night and then back into day?

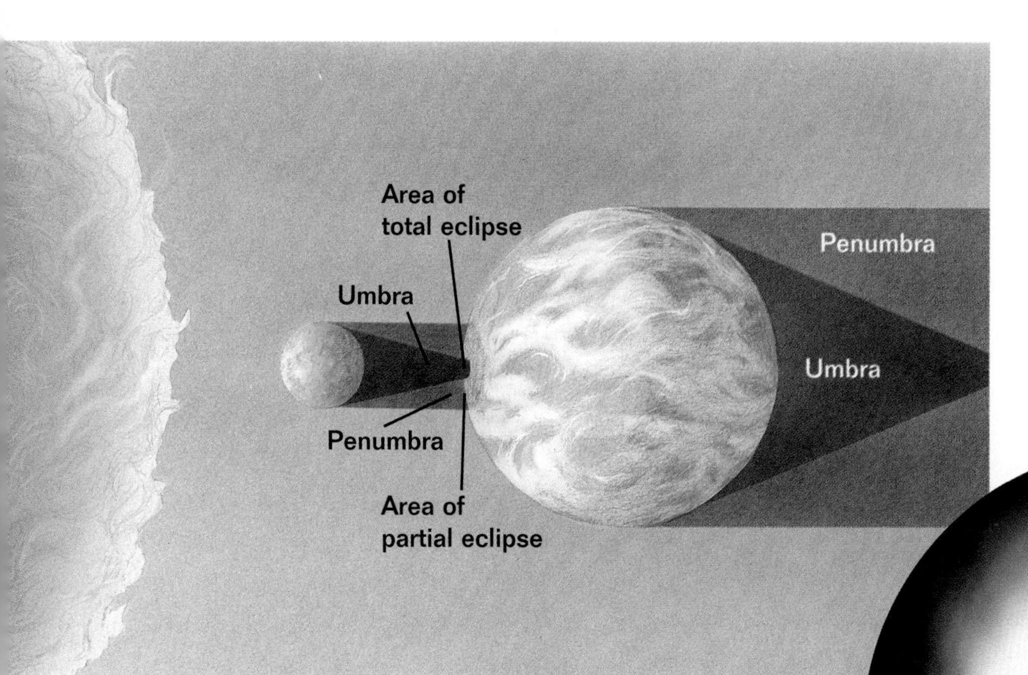

Figure 18-11 Only a small area of Earth experiences a total solar eclipse during the eclipse event. Only the outer portion of the sun's atmosphere is visible during a total solar eclipse. Distances are not drawn to scale.

The Cause of Eclipses

Revolution of the moon causes eclipses. Eclipses occur when Earth or the moon temporarily blocks the sunlight reaching the other. Sometimes, during a new moon, a shadow cast by the moon falls on Earth and causes a solar eclipse. During a full moon, a shadow of Earth can be cast on the moon, resulting in a lunar eclipse.

Eclipses can occur only when the sun, the moon, and Earth are lined up perfectly. Look at **Figure 18-10.** Because the moon's orbit is not in the same plane as Earth's orbit around the sun, eclipses happen only a few times each year.

Solar Eclipses

A **solar eclipse,** such as the one in **Figure 18-11,** occurs when the moon moves directly between the sun and Earth and casts a shadow on part of Earth. The darkest portion of the moon's shadow is called the umbra (UM bruh). A person standing within the umbra experiences a total solar eclipse. The only portion of the sun that is visible is part of its atmosphere, which appears as a pearly white glow around the edge of the eclipsing moon.

Surrounding the umbra is a lighter shadow on Earth's surface called the penumbra (puh NUM bruh). Persons standing in the penumbra experience a partial solar eclipse. **CAUTION:** *Regardless of where you are standing, never look directly at a solar eclipse. The light can permanently damage your eyes.*

Changing Seasons

Suppose that Earth's rotation took twice the time that it presently does. Write a report on how conditions such as global temperatures, work schedules, plant growth, and other factors might be different.

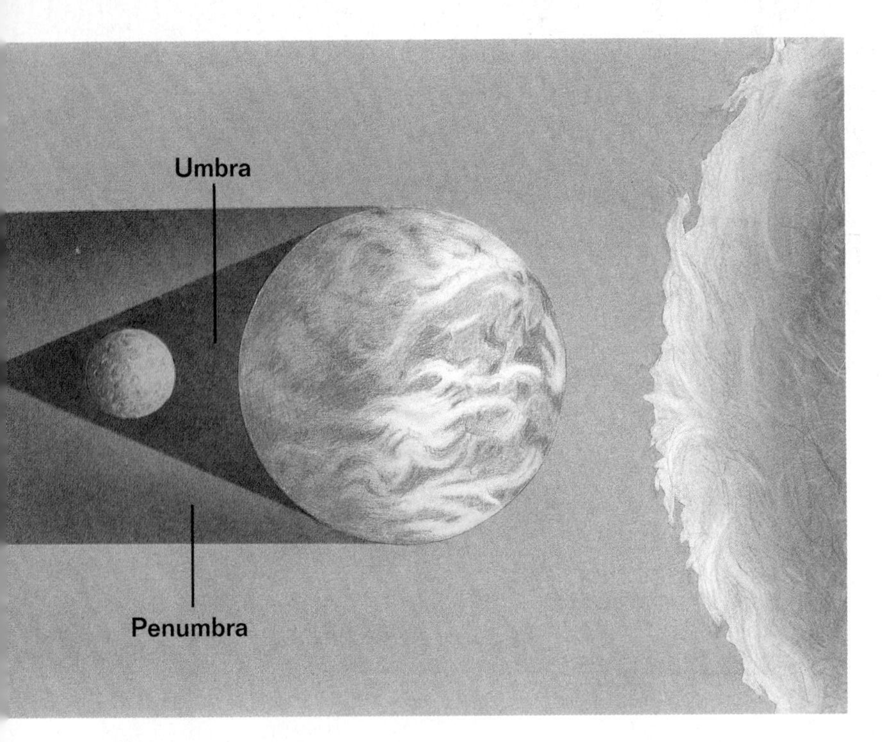

Figure 18-12 During a total lunar eclipse, Earth's shadow blocks light coming from the sun.

Lunar Eclipses

When Earth's shadow falls on the moon, a **lunar eclipse** like the one shown in **Figures 18-12** and **18-13** occurs. A lunar eclipse begins when the moon moves into Earth's penumbra. As the moon continues to move, it enters Earth's umbra and you see a curved shadow on the moon's surface. It was from this shadow that Aristotle concluded that Earth's shape was spherical. When the moon moves completely into Earth's umbra, the moon becomes dark red because light from the sun is refracted by Earth's atmosphere onto the moon. A total lunar eclipse has occurred.

A partial lunar eclipse occurs when only a portion of the moon moves into Earth's umbra. The remainder of the moon is in Earth's penumbra and, therefore, receives some direct sunlight.

A total solar eclipse occurs up to two times every year, yet most people live their entire lives without witnessing one. You may not be lucky enough to see a total solar eclipse, but it is almost certain you will have a chance to see a total lunar eclipse in your lifetime. The reason it is so difficult to view a total solar eclipse is that only those people in the small region where the moon's umbra strikes Earth can witness one. In contrast, anyone on the nighttime side of Earth can see a total lunar eclipse.

Figure 18-13 These photographs show the moon moving from right to left into Earth's umbra, then out again.

Structure of the Moon

When you look at the moon, you can see many of its larger surface features. The dark-colored, relatively flat regions are called **maria.** Maria formed when ancient lava flows from the moon's interior filled large basins on the moon's surface. The basins formed early in the moon's history.

Craters

Many depressions on the moon were formed by meteorites, asteroids, and comets, which strike the surfaces of planets and their satellites. These depressions are called craters. During impact, cracks may have formed in the moon's crust, allowing lava to reach the surface and fill in the large craters, forming maria. The igneous rocks of the maria are 3 to 4 billion years old. They are the youngest rocks found on the moon thus far.

The Moon's Interior

Seismographs left on the moon by *Apollo* astronauts have enabled scientists to study moonquakes. The study of earthquakes allows scientists to map Earth's interior. Likewise, the study of moonquakes has led to a model of the moon's interior. One model of the moon shows that its crust is about 60 km thick on the side facing Earth and about 150 km thick on the far side. Below the crust, a solid mantle may extend to a depth of 1000 km. A partly molten zone of the mantle extends farther down. Below this may be an iron-rich, solid core.

interNET CONNECTION

Visit the Glencoe Science Web Site at **www.glencoe.com/sec/science/ca** to learn more about the *Apollo* space missions.

Problem Solving

Survival on the Moon

You and your crew have crash-landed on the moon, far from your intended landing site at the moon colony. It will take one day to reach the colony on foot. The side of the moon that you are on will be facing away from the sun during your entire trip back. You manage to salvage the following items from your wrecked ship: food, rope, solar-powered heating unit, battery-operated heating unit, three 70-kg oxygen tanks, map of the constellations, magnetic compass, oxygen-burning signal flares, matches, 8 L of water, solar-powered radio receiver and transmitter, three flashlights and extra batteries, signal mirror, and binoculars. Keep in mind that the moon's gravity is about one-sixth that of Earth's, and it lacks a magnetic field. Determine which items will be of no use to you. Determine which items to take with you on your journey to the colony.

Think Critically: Based on what you have learned about the moon, describe why each of the salvaged items is useful or not useful.

1. How did the moon's physical properties affect your decisions?
2. How did the lack of sunlight affect your decisions?

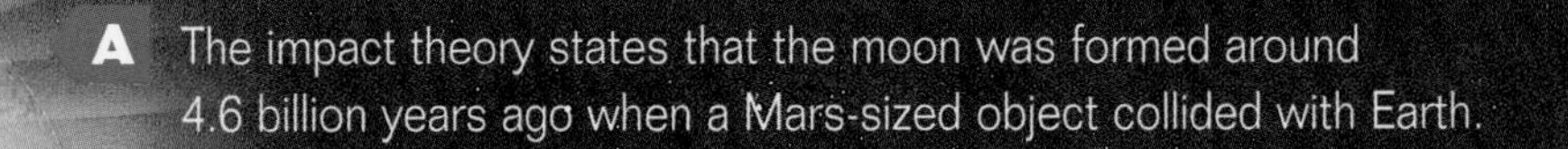

VISUALIZING Moon Formation

Figure 18-14 Evidence suggests that the impact theory may be the best explanation of the moon's origin.

Origin of the Moon

Prior to the data obtained from the *Apollo* space missions, there were three theories about the moon's origin. The first was that the moon was captured by Earth's gravity. It had formed elsewhere and wandered into Earth's vicinity. The second theory was that the moon condensed from loose material surrounding Earth during the early formation of the solar system. The last theory was that a blob of molten material was ejected from Earth while Earth was still in its early molten stage.

Impact Theory

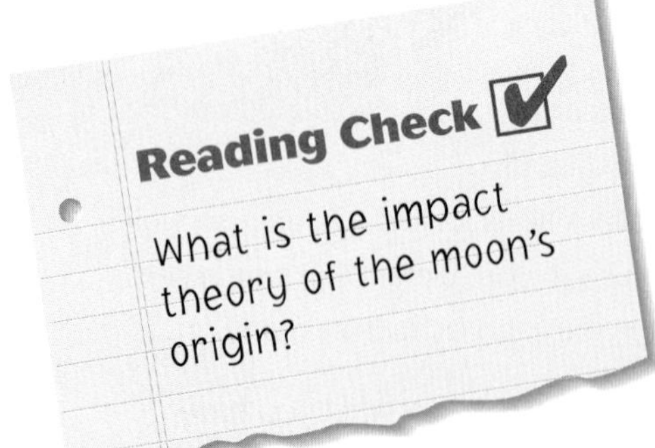

The data gathered by the *Apollo* missions have led many scientists to support a new impact theory. According to the impact theory, the moon was formed about 4.6 billion years ago when a Mars-sized object collided with Earth, throwing gas and debris into orbit. The gas and debris then condensed into one large mass, forming the moon. **Figure 18-14** illustrates the impact theory.

Regardless of the moon's true origin, it has played an important role in our history. It was a source of curiosity for many early astronomers. Studying the phases of the moon and eclipses led people to conclude that Earth and the moon were in motion around the sun. Earth's shadow on the moon proved that Earth's shape was spherical. When Galileo first turned his telescope to the moon, he found a surface scarred by craters

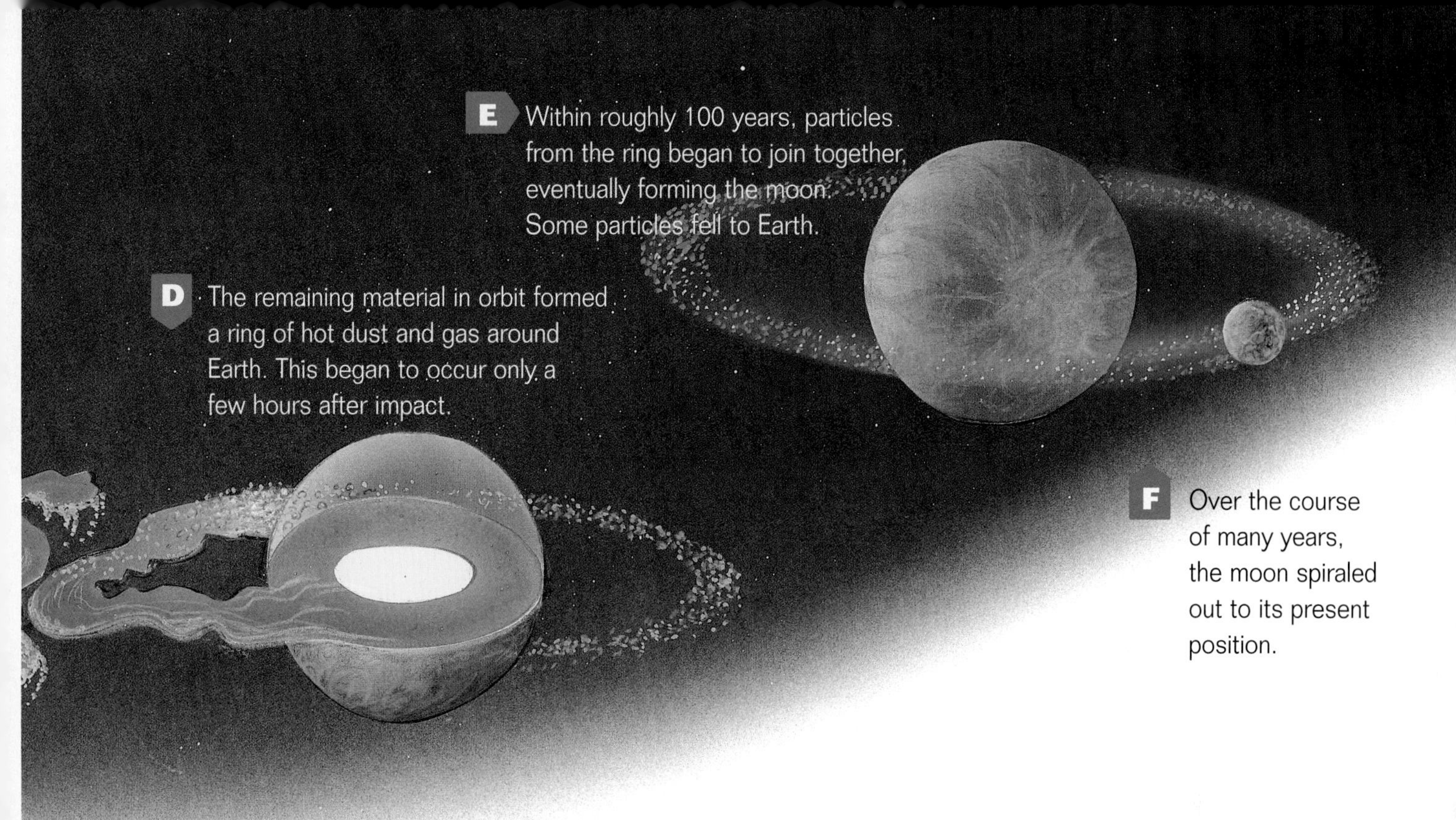

and maria. Before that time, many people believed that all planetary bodies were perfect, without surface features.

By studying the moon, we can learn about ourselves and the planet we live on. As you will read in the next section, not only is the moon important as an object from our past, but it is important to our future, as well.

Section Assessment

1. What are the relative positions of the sun, the moon, and Earth during a full moon?
2. Why does a lunar eclipse occur only during a full moon?
3. Compare and contrast umbra and penumbra.
4. **Think Critically:** What provides the force necessary to form craters on the moon?
5. **Skill Builder**
   Interpreting Scientific Illustrations By tracking the changing positions of the sun, Earth, and the moon, scientists can predict solar eclipses. Do the **Chapter 18 Skill Activity** on page 979 to see when and where future solar eclipses will occur.

Science Journal

Research the moon's origin in astronomy books and magazines. In your Science Journal, write a report about the various theories, including the theory about a Mars-sized object colliding with Earth. Make a drawing of each theory.

18-3 Exploration of the Moon

What You'll Learn

- Recent information about the moon discovered by spacecraft
- Facts about the moon's poles that may be important to future space travel

Vocabulary

mascon

Why It's Important

- Future missions to the moon may lead to important discoveries about Earth's origin.

Early Moon Missions

For centuries, astronomers have studied the moon for clues to its makeup and origin. In 1958, the former Soviet Union took studies of the moon into space with the launching of the *Luna* spacecraft. Three years later, the United States launched the first *Ranger* spacecraft, beginning its own lunar space exploration program.

Early U.S. moon missions, such as those involving the uncrewed *Ranger* and later the *Lunar Orbiter* spacecraft, focused on taking detailed photographs of the moon's surface. The *Lunar Orbiter* missions were followed by the *Surveyor* missions, wherein seven *Surveyor* spacecraft landed on the moon in preparation for the ultimate goal: to land astronauts on the moon. In 1969, this goal was realized with the launching of *Apollo 11*. By 1972 when the *Apollo* missions ended, 12 U.S. astronauts had walked on the moon.

Return to the Moon

More than 20 years passed before the United States resumed its studies of the moon from space. In 1994, the *Clementine* spacecraft was placed into lunar orbit to conduct a two-month survey of the moon's surface. *Clementine's* mission was to test new sensors for tracking cold objects, such as satellites, in space.

Figure 18-15 This false-color photograph, taken by cameras on the *Clementine* spacecraft, shows the moon, the sun, and the planet Venus.

In addition, *Clementine* was placed in lunar orbit to take high-resolution photographs in order to compile a detailed map of the moon's surface. **Figure 18-15** shows a photograph taken by *Clementine. Clementine's* four cameras were able to resolve features as small as 200 m across, enhancing our knowledge of the moon's surface.

Reading Check Why was *Clementine* placed in lunar orbit?

The Moon's South Pole

The South Pole-Aitken Basin is the oldest identifiable impact feature on the moon's surface. It is also the largest and deepest impact basin or depression found thus far anywhere in the solar system, measuring 12 km in depth and 2500 km in diameter. Data returned by *Clementine* gave scientists the first set of high-resolution photographs of this area of the moon. Much of this depression stays in shadow throughout the moon's rotation, forming a cold area where ice deposits from impacting comets may have collected. Radio signals reflected from *Clementine* to Earth indicated the presence of ice at the moon's south pole. Also, a large plateau that is always in sunlight was discovered in this area. If there truly is ice near the plateau, this would be an ideal location for a moon colony powered by solar energy.

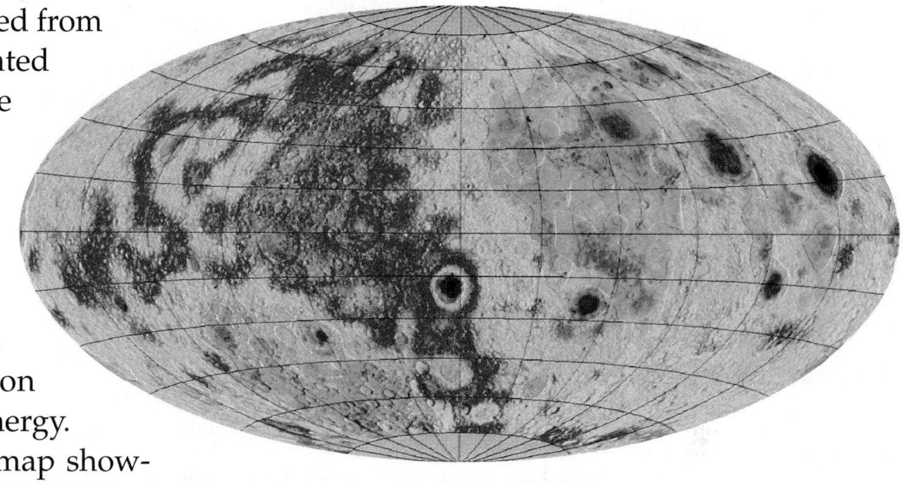

Figure 18-16 is a global map showing the moon's crustal thickness based on *Clementine* data. According to the data, the moon's crust thins under impact basins. Also, the moon's crust on the side facing Earth is much thinner than on the far side. Such maps show the location of **mascons,** which are concentrations of mass. Mascons are located under impact basins. Data collected by *Clementine* also provided information on the mineral content of moon rocks. In fact, this part of its mission was instrumental in naming the spacecraft. Clementine was the daughter of a miner in the ballad "My Darlin' Clementine."

Figure 18-16 This computer-enhanced map based on *Clementine* data indicates the thickness of the moon's crust. The crust of the side of the moon facing Earth, shown mostly in red, is thinner than the crust on the far side of the moon.

The Lunar Prospector

The success of *Clementine* at a relatively low cost opened the door for further moon missions. In 1998, NASA launched the *Lunar Prospector* spacecraft. Its mission was to orbit the moon, taking photographs of the lunar surface for mapping purposes. These maps confirmed the *Clementine* data. The

Lunar Prospector also was scheduled to conduct a detailed study of the moon's surface, searching for clues as to the origin and makeup of the moon.

Icy Poles

Early data obtained from the *Lunar Prospector* indicate that hydrogen is present in the rocks found in the craters at the moon's poles, as shown in **Figure 18-17.** Hydrogen is one of the elements that make up water. These data, combined with data from *Clementine,* have led scientists to theorize that ice may exist in the floors of the craters at both of the moon's poles. These craters are deep and cold. Sunlight never reaches their floors, where temperatures are as low as –233°C—definitely cold enough to have preserved any ice that may have collected in the craters from colliding comets or meteorites.

Based on the *Lunar Prospector* data, scientists estimate that 6 billion tons of ice lie under the surface of the moon's poles. The ice may be buried under about 40 cm of crushed rock. Data from *Lunar Prospector* also have enabled scientists to conclude that the moon has a small, iron-rich core about 600 km across.

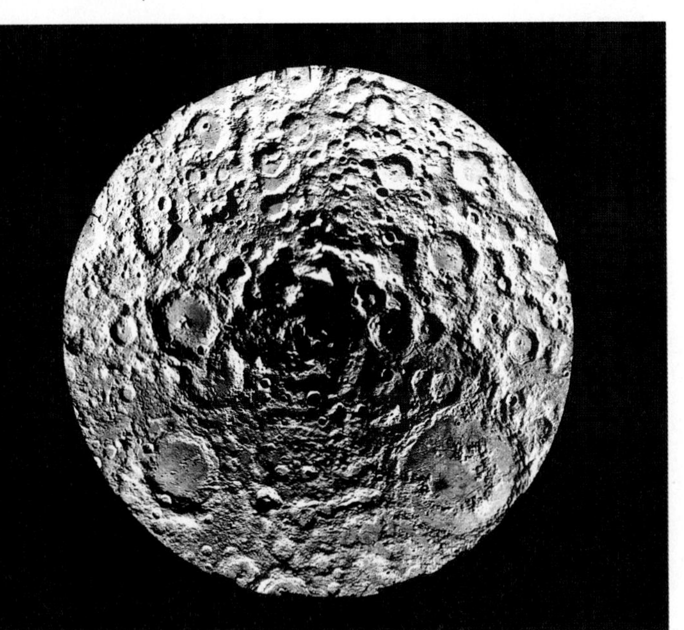

Figure 18-17 Data from *Lunar Prospector* indicate the presence of twice as much ice at the moon's north pole as at its south pole.

Section Assessment

1. List two discoveries about the moon made by the *Clementine* spacecraft.
2. What was the main mission of the *Lunar Prospector?*
3. How did studies of the moon change after the 1950s?
4. **Think Critically:** Why would the discovery of ice at the moon's poles be important to future space flights?
5. **Skill Builder**
   Sequencing Sequence the following moon missions in the order in which they occurred: *Surveyor, Lunar Prospector, Apollo, Lunar Orbiter, Ranger,* and *Clementine.* If you need help, refer to Sequencing in the **Skill Handbook** on page 950.

Using Math

The moon's orbit is tilted at an angle of about 5° to Earth's orbit around the sun. Using a protractor, draw an angle of 5°. Draw a model of the moon's orbit around Earth.

Activity 18•2

Moon Phases and Eclipses

Materials

- Light source (unshaded)
- Polystyrene ball on pencil
- Globe

You know that moon phases and eclipses result from the relative positions of the sun, the moon, and Earth. In this activity, you will demonstrate the positions of these bodies during certain phases and eclipses. You also will see why only people on a small portion of Earth's surface see a total solar eclipse.

What You'll Investigate

Can a model be devised to show the positions of the sun, the moon, and Earth during various phases and eclipses?

Goals

- **Model** moon phases.
- **Model** solar and lunar eclipses.

Procedure

1. Review the illustrations of moon phases and eclipses shown in Section 18-2.
2. **Use** the light source as a model sun and a polystyrene ball on a pencil as a model moon. **Move** the model moon around the globe to duplicate the exact position that would have to occur for a lunar eclipse to take place.
3. **Move** the model moon to the position that would cause a solar eclipse.
4. **Place** the model moon at each of the following phases: first quarter, full moon, third quarter, and new moon. **Identify** which, if any, type of eclipse could occur during each phase. Record your data.
5. **Place** the model moon at the location where a lunar eclipse could occur. **Move** it slightly toward Earth, then away from Earth. Note the amount of change in the size of the shadow causing the eclipse. Record this information.
6. **Repeat** step 5 with the model moon in a position where a solar eclipse could occur.

Conclude and Apply

1. During which phase(s) of the moon is it possible for an eclipse to occur?
2. **Describe** the effect that a small change in the distance between Earth and the moon has on the size of the shadow causing the eclipse.
3. As seen from Earth, how does the apparent size of the moon **compare** with the apparent size of the sun? How can an eclipse be used to confirm this?
4. **Infer** why a lunar and solar eclipse do not occur every month.
5. Suppose you wanted to more accurately model the movement of the moon around Earth. **Explain** how your model moon moves around the globe. Would it always be in the same plane as the light source and the globe?
6. Why have only a few people seen a total solar eclipse?

Moon Phase Observations

Moon Phase	Observations
first quarter	
full	
third quarter	
new	

Chapter 18 Reviewing Main Ideas

For a **preview** of this chapter, study this Reviewing Main Ideas before you read the chapter. After you have studied this chapter, you can use the Reviewing Main Ideas to **review** the chapter.

The Glencoe MindJogger, Audiocassettes, and CD-ROM provide additional opportunities for review.

Section
18-1 PLANET EARTH

Earth is a **sphere** that is slightly flattened at its poles. Earth **rotates** once each day and **revolves** around the sun in a little more than 365 days. Seasons on Earth are due to the amount of solar radiation received by a hemisphere at a given time. The tilt of Earth on its **axis** causes the amount of solar energy to vary. ***How does Earth's interior act like an electromagnet?***

Section
18-2 EARTH'S MOON

Earth's moon goes through **phases** that depend on the relative positions of the sun, the moon, and Earth. Eclipses occur when Earth or the moon temporarily blocks sunlight from the other. A **solar eclipse** occurs when the moon moves directly between the sun and Earth. A **lunar eclipse** occurs when Earth's shadow falls on the moon. The moon's **maria** are the result of ancient volcanism. Craters on the moon's surface formed from impacts with meteorites, asteroids, and comets. ***If the moon is between Earth and the sun for each new moon, why are there only one or two solar eclipses each year?***

Reading Check

Use these words in sentences that do not relate to the sun, Earth, or moon: *sphere, axis, rotation, revolution, ellipse, waxing,* and *waning.*

Section

18-3 EXPLORATION OF THE MOON

The *Clementine* spacecraft took detailed, high-resolution photographs of the moon's surface. Data from *Clementine* indicate that the moon's South Pole-Aitken Basin may contain ice deposits that could supply water for a moon colony. The *Clementine* spacecraft also noted that **mascons** occur beneath impact basins on the moon. NASA has returned to exploring the moon with its latest spacecraft, the *Lunar Prospector.* Data from *Lunar Prospector* seem to support the ice theory and also indicate that the moon's north pole may contain twice as much ice as the south pole. ***How did the* Clementine *spacecraft get its name?***

Career CONNECTION

Gibor Barsi, Astronomer

Gibor Barsi is an astronomer who works with the Keck Telescopes on Mauna Kea, Hawaii. The summit of Mauna Kea is considered the world's premier site for astronomical observation. Gibor is interested in answering the questions, "How many planets are there around other stars, what are they like, and how do they form?" He feels that the next generation of astronomers and technology will answer these questions. ***Why do you suppose astronomers are interested in finding new planets?***

Chapter 18 Assessment

Using Vocabulary

a. axis	j. new moon
b. ellipse	k. revolution
c. equinox	l. rotation
d. first quarter	m. solar eclipse
e. full moon	n. solstice
f. lunar eclipse	o. sphere
g. maria	p. third quarter
h. mascon	q. waning
i. moon phase	r. waxing

Each phrase below describes a science term from the list. Write the term that matches the phrase describing it.

1. causes day and night to occur on Earth
2. occurs when the sun's position is directly above the equator
3. moon phase in which all of the lighted side of the moon is seen
4. eclipse that occurs when the moon is between Earth and the sun
5. concentration of mass on the moon located under an impact basin

Checking Concepts

Choose the word or phrase that completes the sentence.

6. How long does it take for the moon to rotate?
   A) 24 hours C) 27.3 hours
   B) 365 days D) 27.3 days
7. Where is Earth's circumference greatest?
   A) equator C) poles
   B) mantle D) axis
8. During an equinox, the sun is directly over what part of Earth?
   A) southern hemisphere
   B) northern hemisphere
   C) equator
   D) pole
9. Why does the sun appear to rise and set?
   A) Earth revolves.
   B) The sun moves around Earth.
   C) Earth rotates.
   D) Earth orbits the sun.
10. How long does it take for the moon to revolve?
    A) 24 hours C) 27.3 hours
    B) 365 days D) 27.3 days
11. As the lighted portion of the moon appears to get larger, what is it said to be?
    A) waning C) rotating
    B) waxing D) crescent shaped
12. During what kind of eclipse is the moon directly between the sun and Earth?
    A) solar C) full
    B) new D) lunar
13. What is the darkest part of the shadow during an eclipse?
    A) waxing gibbous C) waning gibbous
    B) umbra D) penumbra
14. What are depressions on the moon called?
    A) eclipses C) phases
    B) moonquakes D) craters
15. What fact do data gathered from the *Clementine* spacecraft support?
    A) The moon rotates once in 29.5 days.
    B) The moon has a thinner crust on the side facing Earth.
    C) The moon revolves once in 29.5 days.
    D) The moon has a thicker crust on the side facing Earth.

Thinking Critically

16. How would the moon appear to an observer in space during its revolution? Would phases be observable? Explain.
17. Would you weigh more at Earth's equator or at the north pole? Explain.

18. Tides occur due to the gravitational attraction among the sun, the moon, and Earth. During which phases of the moon are tides the highest? Explain.
19. If you were lost on the moon's surface, why would it be more beneficial to have a star chart rather than a compass?
20. Which of the moon's motions are real? Which are apparent? Explain.

Developing Skills

If you need help, refer to the **Skill Handbook.**

21. **Hypothesizing:** Why do locations near Earth's equator travel faster during one rotation than places near the poles?
22. **Using Variables, Constants, and Controls:** Describe a simple activity to show how the moon's rotation and revolution work to keep one side facing Earth at all times.
23. **Comparing and Contrasting:** Compare and contrast a waning moon with a waxing moon.
24. **Concept Mapping:** Copy and complete the cycle map shown on this page. Show the sequences of the moon's phases.

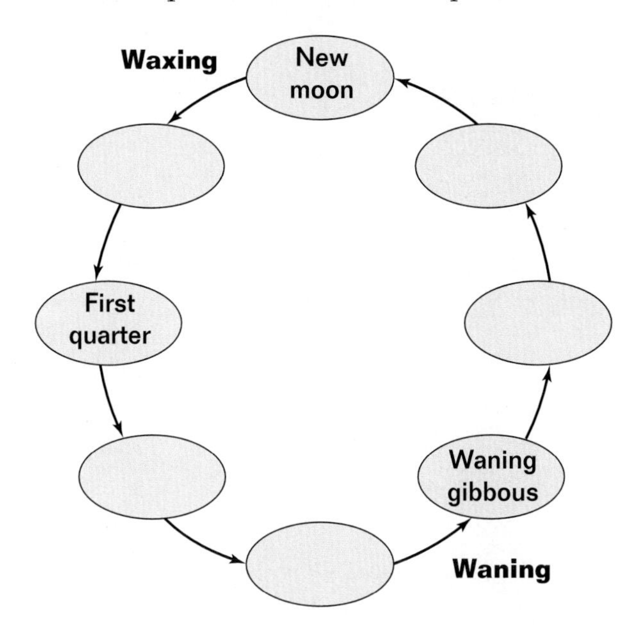

Test-Taking Tip

Practice, Practice, Practice Practice to improve *your* performance. Don't compare yourself with anyone else.

Test Practice

Use these questions to test your Science Proficiency.

1. As the moon revolves around Earth, it keeps the same side facing Earth. Which of the following statements **BEST** explains why this is so?
   A) The moon rotates once on its axis as it makes one complete revolution around Earth.
   B) The moon does not rotate as it revolves.
   C) The speed of rotation for the moon exactly equals its speed of revolution.
   D) The speed of revolution for the moon is constant and therefore keeps one side facing Earth at all times.
2. More craters are on the far side of the moon than on the side facing Earth. Which of the following statements would **BEST** explain this fact?
   A) A greater number of volcanoes occur on the far side of the moon.
   B) Earth's gravity attracts more of the objects that would produce craters on the side of the moon facing Earth.
   C) Earth blocks the paths of any objects that would collide with the side of the moon facing Earth.
   D) The far side of the moon is always facing away from the sun.

CHAPTER

19 The Solar System

Chapter Preview

Skills Preview

Skill Builders
- Map Concepts

Activities
- Make a Model

MiniLabs
- Observe and Infer

Reading Check

As you read this chapter, identify and describe the cause-effect relationships that control the structure of the solar system.

Explore Activity

The planets of our solar system are our neighbors in space. But to us on Earth, they look like tiny points of light among the thousands of others visible on a clear night. With the help of telescopes and space probes, the points of light become giant colorful spheres, some with rings, others pitted with countless craters. This false-color image of Mars shows the space rover *Sojourner* exploring the planet's surface. Mars has two heavily cratered moons. In this activity, you'll explore how craters are made on the surfaces of planets and moons.

Model Comet Collisions

1. Place fine white flour into a cake pan to a depth of 3 cm, completely covering the bottom of the pan.
2. Cover the flour with 1 cm of fine, gray, dry cement mix, or try different colors of gelatin powder.
3. From different heights ranging from 10 cm to 25 cm, drop various-sized objects into the pan. Use marbles, lead weights, bolts, and nuts.

In your Science Journal, draw what happened to the surface of the powder in the pan when each object was dropped from different heights.

19•1 The Solar System

What You'll Learn

- The sun-centered and Earth-centered models of the solar system
- Current models of the formation of the solar system

Vocabulary
solar system
inner planet
outer planet

Why It's Important

- You'll learn how views of the solar system have changed over time.

Early Ideas About the Solar System

Imagine yourself on a warm, clear summer night lying in the grass and gazing at the stars and the moon. The stars and the moon seem so still and beautiful. You may even see other planets in the solar system, thinking they are stars. Although the planets are different from the stars, they blend in with the stars and are usually hard to pick out.

Earth-Centered Model

It is generally known today that the sun and the stars appear to move through the sky because Earth is moving. This wasn't always an accepted fact. Many early Greek scientists thought the planets, the sun, and the moon were embedded in separate spheres that rotated around Earth. The stars were thought to be embedded in another sphere that also rotated around Earth. Early observers described moving objects in the night sky using the term *planasthai,* which means "to wander." The word *planet* comes from this term.

This model is called the Earth-centered model of the solar system. It included Earth, the moon, the sun, five planets—Mercury, Venus, Mars, Jupiter, and Saturn—and the sphere of stars.

Figure 19-1 Each of the nine planets in the solar system is unique. The sizes of the planets and sun are drawn to scale but the distances between the planets and sun are not to scale.

Sun-Centered Model

The idea of an Earth-centered solar system was held for centuries until the Polish astronomer Nicholas Copernicus published a different view in 1543. Using an idea proposed by an early Greek scholar, Copernicus stated that the moon revolved around Earth, which was a planet. Earth, along with the other planets, revolved around the sun. He also stated that the daily movement of the planets and the stars was due to Earth's rotation. This is the sun-centered model of the solar system.

Using his telescope, the Italian astronomer Galileo Galilei found evidence that supported the ideas of Copernicus. He discovered that Venus went through phases like the moon's. These phases could be explained only if Venus were orbiting the sun. From this, he concluded that Venus revolves around the sun and that the sun is the center of the solar system.

Modern View of the Solar System

We now know that the **solar system** is made up of the nine planets, including Earth, and many smaller objects that orbit the sun. The sizes of the nine planets and the sun are shown to scale in **Figure 19-1.** However, the distances between the planets are not to scale. The dark areas on the sun are sunspots, which you will learn about later. Notice how small Earth is compared with some of the other planets and the sun, which is much larger than any of the planets.

The solar system includes a vast territory extending billions of kilometers in all directions from the sun. The sun contains 99.86 percent of the mass of the whole solar system. Because of its gravitational pull, the sun is the central object around which other objects of the solar system revolve.

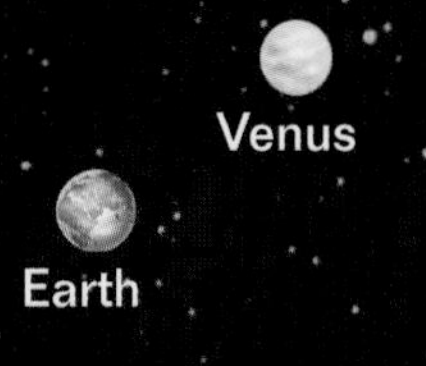

VISUALIZING The Early Solar System

Figure 19-2 Through careful observations, astronomers have found clues that help explain how our solar system may have formed.

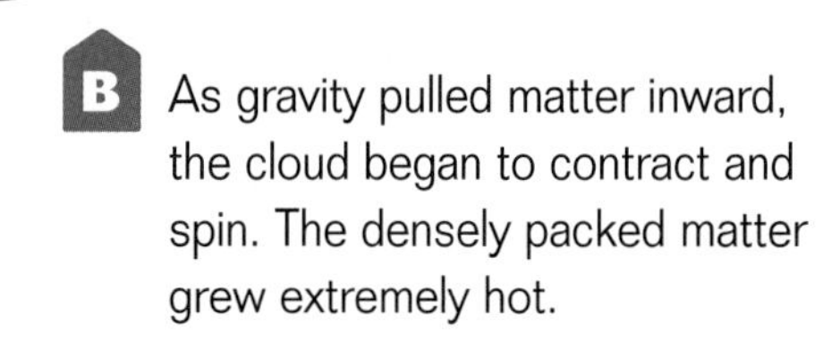

As gravity pulled matter inward, the cloud began to contract and spin. The densely packed matter grew extremely hot.

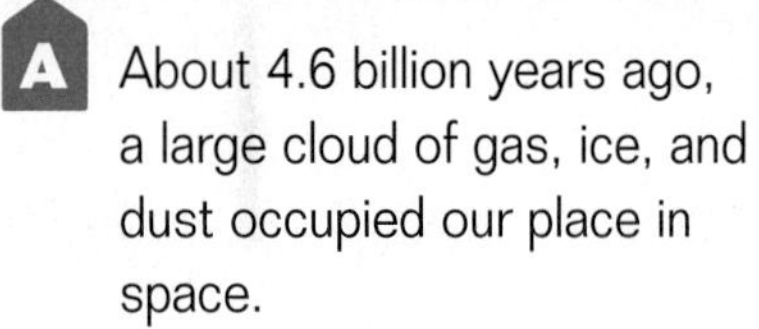

About 4.6 billion years ago, a large cloud of gas, ice, and dust occupied our place in space.

How the Solar System Formed

Scientists hypothesize that the sun and the solar system formed from a cloud of gas, ice, and dust about 4.6 billion years ago. **Figure 19-2** illustrates how this may have happened. This cloud was slowly rotating in space. A nearby star may have exploded, and the shock waves from this event may have caused the cloud to start contracting. At first, the cloud was rotating slowly. As it contracted, the matter in the cloud was squeezed into less space. The cloud's density became greater and the increased attraction of gravity pulled more gas and dust toward the cloud center. This caused the cloud to rotate faster, which in turn caused it to flatten into a disk with a dense center.

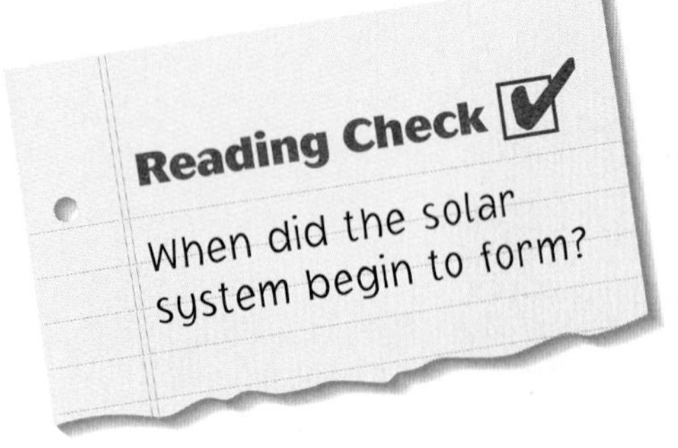

As the cloud contracted, the temperature began to increase. Eventually, the temperature in the core of the cloud reached about 10 million °C and nuclear fusion began. A star was born—this was the beginning of our sun. Nuclear fusion occurs when atoms with low mass, such as hydrogen, combine to form heavier elements, such as helium. The new, heavy element contains slightly less mass than the sum of the light atoms that formed it. The lost mass is converted into energy.

Not all of the nearby gas, ice, and dust were drawn into the core of the cloud. Remaining gas, ice, and dust particles

C The center of the rotating disk continued to heat. Meanwhile, gas and dust particles in the outer rim clumped together, forming larger objects.

D The larger clumps continued to grow as more objects collided.

collided and stuck together, forming larger objects that in turn attracted more particles because of the stronger pull of gravity. Close to the sun, the temperature was hot, and the easily vaporized elements could not condense into solids. This is why light elements are more scarce in the planets closer to the sun than in planets farther out in the solar system. Instead, the inner solar system is dominated by small, rocky planets with iron cores.

The **inner planets**—Mercury, Venus, Earth, and Mars—are the solid, rocky planets closest to the sun. The **outer planets**—Jupiter, Saturn, Uranus, Neptune, and Pluto—are those farthest from the sun. Except for Pluto, which is made of rock and ice, the outer planets are made mostly of lighter elements such as hydrogen, helium, methane, and ammonia.

E Eventually, the larger clumps gathered enough matter to become planets. The core of the disk grew even denser and hotter.

F Nuclear fusion began in the core, and the sun became a star. Some of the smaller objects became moons and rings around the planets.

Motions of the Planets

PHYSICS INTEGRATION

When Nicholas Copernicus developed his sun-centered model of the solar system, he thought that the planets orbited the sun in circles. In the early 1600s, the German mathematician Johannes Kepler began studying the orbits of the planets. He discovered that the shapes of the orbits are not circular, but elliptical. He also calculated that the sun is not at the center of the ellipse but is offset from the center.

Kepler also discovered that the planets travel at different speeds in their orbits around the sun. By studying these speeds, you can see that the planets closer to the sun travel faster than planets farther away from the sun. As a result, the outer planets take much longer to orbit the sun than the inner planets do.

Copernicus's ideas, considered radical at the time, led to the birth of modern astronomy. Early scientists didn't have technology such as space probes to learn about the planets. They used instruments such as the one shown in **Figure 19-3.** Nevertheless, they developed theories about the solar system that we still use today. In the next section, you'll learn about the inner planets—our nearest neighbors in space.

Figure 19-3 This instrument, called an astrolabe, was used for a variety of astronomical calculations.

Section Assessment

1. What is the difference between the sun-centered and the Earth-centered models of the solar system?
2. How do scientists hypothesize the solar system formed?
3. The outer planets are rich in water, methane, and ammonia—the materials needed for life. Yet life is unlikely on these planets. Explain.
4. **Think Critically:** Would a year on the planet Uranus be longer or shorter than an Earth year? Explain.
5. **Skill Builder**
   Concept Mapping Make a concept map that compares and contrasts the Earth-centered model with the sun-centered model of the solar system. If you need help, refer to Concept Mapping in the **Skill Handbook** on page 950.

Using Math

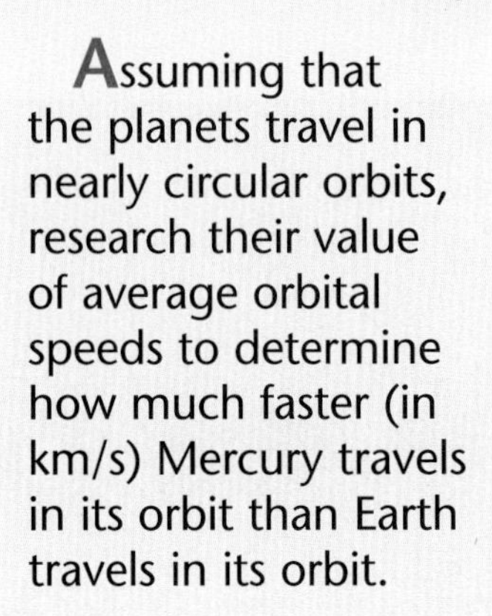

Assuming that the planets travel in nearly circular orbits, research their value of average orbital speeds to determine how much faster (in km/s) Mercury travels in its orbit than Earth travels in its orbit.

Activity 19•1

Planetary Orbits

Planets travel around the sun along fixed paths called orbits. Early theories about the solar system stated that planetary orbits were perfect circles. As you construct a model of a planetary orbit, you will observe that the shape of planetary orbits is an ellipse, not a circle.

Materials

- Thumbtacks or pins
- Metric ruler
- String (25 cm)
- Pencil
- Cardboard (23 cm × 30 cm)
- Paper (21.5 cm × 28 cm)

What You'll Investigate

How can a model be constructed that will show planetary orbits to be elliptical?

Goals

- **Model** planetary orbits.
- **Calculate** changes in ellipses.

Procedure

1. **Place** a blank sheet of paper on top of the cardboard and insert two thumbtacks or pins about 3 cm apart.
2. **Tie** the string into a circle with a circumference of 15 to 20 cm. **Loop** the string around the thumbtacks. With someone holding the tacks or pins, **place** your pencil inside the loop and **pull** it tight.

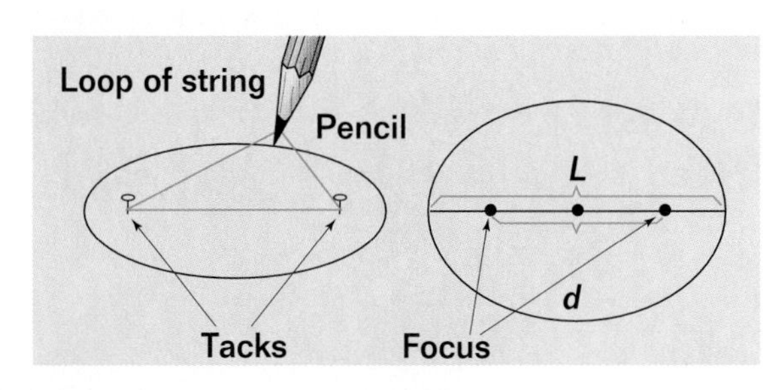

3. **Move** the pencil around the tacks, keeping the string tight, until you have completed a smooth, closed curve, called an ellipse.
4. **Repeat** steps 1 through 3 several times. First, **vary** the distance between the tacks, then **vary** the length of the string. However, change only one of these each time. Make a data table to record the changes in the sizes and shapes of the ellipses.
5. Orbits usually are described in terms of eccentricity (*e*). The eccentricity of any ellipse is determined by dividing the distance (*d*) between the foci (fixed points—here, the tacks) by the length of the major axis (*L*). See the diagram at left.
6. **Calculate** and **record** the eccentricity of the ellipses that you constructed.
7. **Research** the eccentricities of planetary orbits.
8. **Construct** an ellipse with the same eccentricity as Earth's orbit. **Repeat** this step with the orbit of either Pluto or Mercury.

Conclude and Apply

1. **Analyze** the effect a change in the length of the string or the distance between the tacks has on the shape of the ellipse.
2. **Hypothesize** what must be done to the string or placement of tacks to decrease the eccentricity of a constructed ellipse.
3. **Describe** the shape of Earth's orbit. Where is the sun located within the orbit?
4. **Identify** the planets that have the most eccentric orbits.
5. **Describe** the path of an orbit with an eccentricity of zero.

19•2 The Inner Planets

What You'll Learn

- The inner planets in their relative order from the sun
- Important characteristics of each inner planet
- How Venus and Earth compare and contrast

Vocabulary

Mercury
Venus
Earth
astronomical unit
Mars

Why It's Important

- Other planets have characteristics that are different from those of Earth.

Inner Planets

We have learned much about the solar system since the days of Copernicus and Galileo. Advancements in telescopes allow astronomers to observe the planets from Earth. The planets shine by sunlight reflected from their surfaces. In addition, space probes have explored much of our solar system, adding greatly to the knowledge we have about the planets. Let's take a tour of the solar system through the "eyes" of the space probes.

Mercury

The closest planet to the sun is **Mercury.** It is also the second-smallest planet. The first and only American spacecraft mission to Mercury was in 1974-1975 by *Mariner 10,* which flew by the planet and sent pictures back to Earth. *Mariner 10* photographed only 45 percent of Mercury's surface—we do not know what the other 55 percent looks like. What we do know is that the surface of Mercury has many craters and looks much like our moon. It also has cliffs as high as 3 km on its surface, as seen in **Figure 19-4.** These cliffs may have formed when Mercury apparently shrank about 2 km in diameter.

Why did Mercury apparently shrink? Scientists think the answer may lie inside the planet. *Mariner 10* detected a weak magnetic field around Mercury, indicating that the planet has a large iron core. Some scientists hypothesize that the crust of Mercury solidified while the iron core was still hot and

Figure 19-4 Giant cliffs on Mercury, like the one marked by the arrow, suggest that the planet might have shrunk.

Mercury

molten. Then, as the core cooled and solidified, it contracted, causing the planet to shrink. The large cliffs may have resulted from breaks in the crust caused by this contraction, similar to what happens when an apple dries out and shrivels up.

Because of Mercury's small size and low gravitational pull, most gases that could form an atmosphere escape into space. Mercury's thin atmosphere is composed of hydrogen, helium, sodium, and potassium. The sodium and potassium may diffuse upward through the crust. The thin atmosphere and the nearness of Mercury to the sun cause this planet to have large extremes in temperature. Mercury's surface temperature can reach 450°C during the day and drop to –170°C at night.

Using Math

The average distance from the sun to Earth is 150 million km. How many minutes does it take light traveling at 300 000 km/s to reach Earth? Use the equation

$$\text{Time} = \frac{\text{distance}}{\text{speed}}$$

Venus

The second planet outward from the sun is **Venus.** Venus is sometimes called Earth's twin because its size and mass are similar to Earth's. One major difference is that the entire surface of Venus is blanketed by a dense atmosphere. The atmosphere of Venus, which has 96 times the surface pressure of Earth's at sea level, is mostly carbon dioxide. The clouds in the atmosphere contain droplets of sulfuric acid, which gives them a slightly yellow color.

Clouds on Venus are so dense that only two percent of the sunlight that strikes the top of the clouds reaches the planet's surface. The solar energy that reaches the surface is trapped by the carbon dioxide gas and causes a greenhouse effect similar to but more intense than Earth's greenhouse effect. Due to this intense greenhouse effect, the temperature on the surface of Venus is 470°C.

The former Soviet Union led the exploration of Venus. Beginning in 1970 with the first *Venera* probe, the Russians have photographed and mapped the surface of Venus using radar and surface probes. Between 1990 and 1994, the *U.S. Magellan* probe used its radar to make the most detailed maps yet of Venus's surface. *Magellan* revealed huge craters, faultlike cracks, and volcanoes with visible lava flows, as seen in **Figure 19-5.**

Figure 19-5 Although Venus is similar to Earth, there are important differences. **How could studying Venus help us learn more about Earth?**

Earth

Earth, shown in **Figure 19-6,** is the third planet from the sun. The average distance from Earth to the sun is 150 million km, or one astronomical unit (AU). **Astronomical units** are used to measure distances to objects in the solar system.

Unlike other planets, surface temperatures on Earth allow water to exist as a solid, liquid, and gas. Earth's atmosphere causes most meteors to burn up before they reach the surface. The atmosphere also protects life from the sun's intense radiation.

Mars

Mars, the fourth planet from the sun, is called the red planet because iron oxide in the weathered rocks on its surface gives it a reddish color, as seen in **Figure 19-7.** Other features of Mars visible from Earth are its polar ice caps, which get larger during the Martian winter and shrink during the summer. The ice caps are made mostly of frozen carbon dioxide and frozen water.

Figure 19-6 More than 70 percent of Earth's surface is covered by liquid water. **What is unique about surface temperatures on Earth?**

Most of the information we have about Mars came from the *Mariner 9*, *Viking* probes, *Mars Global Surveyor*, and *Mars Pathfinder*. *Mariner 9* orbited Mars in 1971–1972. It revealed long channels on the planet that may have been carved by

Problem Solving

Interpret Planetary Data

Your teacher asks you to determine which planet's surface is hotter, Mercury or Venus. You must also explain the temperature difference. You decide that this assignment is going to be easy. Of course, Mercury has to be hotter than Venus because it is much closer to the sun. Venus is almost twice as far away as Mercury. You write your answer and turn in your paper. Later, when you receive your paper back, you find out that your assumptions were evidently wrong. Your teacher suggests that you research the question further, using the table on this page as a guide. As a further hint, your teacher tells you to consider how a greenhouse works to keep it warmer inside than outside and to relate this to what might happen to a planet with a thick atmosphere.

Data for Mercury and Venus

	Mercury 0.39 AU from sun	**Venus 0.72 AU from sun**
Surface Temperature (High)		
Atmosphere Density		
Atmosphere Compostion		

Think Critically: What causes Venus to have a higher surface temperature than Mercury? Explain.

flowing water. *Mariner 9* also discovered the largest volcano in the solar system, Olympus Mons. Like all Mars's volcanoes, Olympus Mons is extinct. Large rift zones that formed in the Martian crust were also discovered. One such rift, Valles Marineris, is shown in **Figure 19-7.**

The Viking probes

In 1976, the *Viking 1* and *2* probes arrived at Mars. Each spacecraft consisted of an orbiter and a lander. The *Viking 1* and *2* orbiters photographed the entire surface of Mars from orbit, while the *Viking 1* and *2* landers touched down on the planet's surface to conduct meteorological, chemical, and biological experiments. The biological experiments found no evidence of life in the soil. The *Viking* landers also sent back pictures of a reddish-colored, barren, rocky, and windswept surface.

Inferring Effects of Gravity

Procedure

1. Suppose you are a crane operator who is sent to Mars to help build a Mars colony.
2. You know that your crane can lift 44 500 N on Earth, but the gravity on Mars is only 40 percent of Earth's gravity.
3. Using Appendix B, determine how much mass your crane could lift on Mars.

Analysis

1. How can what you have discovered be an advantage over construction on Earth?
2. In what ways might construction advantages change the overall design of the Mars colony?

Figure 19-7 Valles Marineris is more than 4000 km long, up to 240 km wide, and more than 6 km deep.

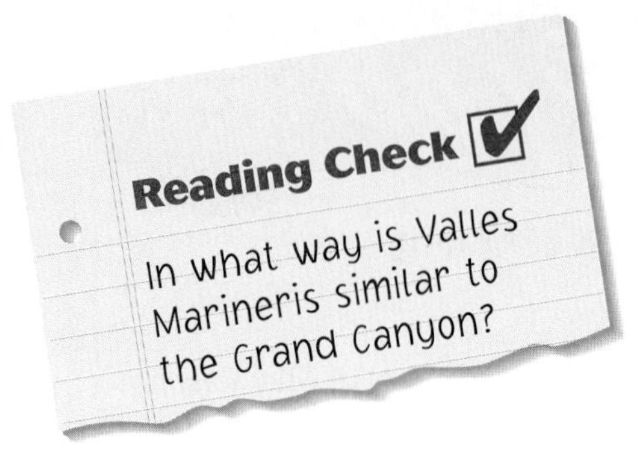

Global Surveyor and Pathfinder

The *Mars Pathfinder,* shown in **Figure 19-8,** gathered data that indicated that iron in Mars's crust may have been leached out by groundwater. In addition, high-quality cameras on board *Global Surveyor* showed that the walls of Valles Marineris have distinct layers similar to the Grand Canyon on Earth. *Global Surveyor* also noticed that a vast flat region, similar to a dried-up seabed or mudflat, covers a large area of Mars's northern hemisphere. This evidence, combined with evidence gathered from *Mariner 9,* indicates that large amounts of water were once present on the planet. Where has all the water gone? Many believe it is frozen into Mars's crust at the poles, shown in **Figure 19-9,** or has soaked into the ground. 

CHEMISTRY INTEGRATION

Mars has always been known as the red planet. Research the composition of surface rocks on Mars. Describe the chemical reaction in the Martian soil responsible for the planet's red color.

The Martian atmosphere is much thinner than Earth's and is composed mostly of carbon dioxide, with some nitrogen and argon. The thin atmosphere does not filter out harmful rays from the sun as Earth's atmosphere does. Surface temperatures range from 35°C to –170°C. The temperature difference between day and night sets up strong winds on the planet, which can cause global dust storms during certain seasons.

A

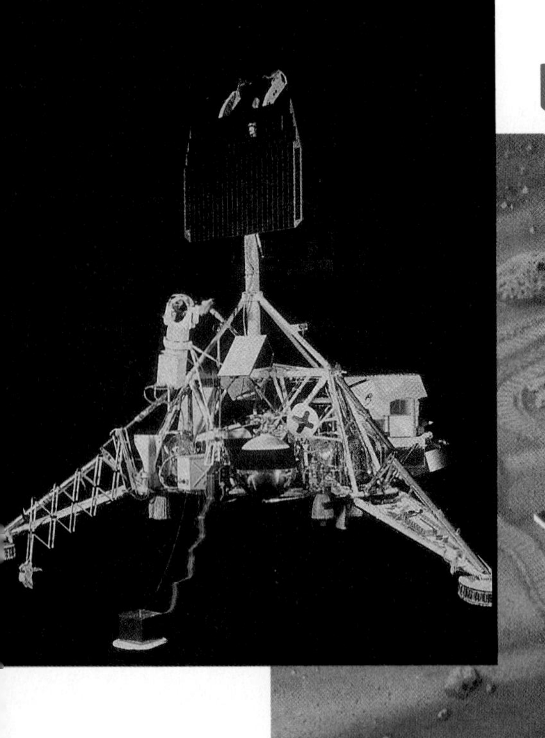

B

Figure 19-8 *Mars Pathfinder* (A) arrived at Mars in 1997. Upon landing, the craft opened its three petal-shaped doors, and the robot rover *Sojourner* began exploring the planet's surface (B).

Figure 19-9 These photos show two features of Mars.

A Olympus Mons is the largest volcano in the solar system.

B Water that flowed on Mars long ago may now be frozen in polar ice caps.

Martian Moons

Mars has two small, heavily cratered moons. Phobos is 25 km in diameter, and Deimos is 13 km in diameter. Phobos's orbit is slowly spiraling inward toward Mars. Phobos is expected to impact the Martian surface in about 50 million years.

As you toured the inner planets using the "eyes" of the space probes, you saw how each planet is unique. Mercury, Venus, Earth, and Mars are different from the outer planets, which you'll explore in the next section.

Section Assessment

1. How are Mercury and Earth's moon similar?
2. List one important characteristic of each inner planet.
3. Although Venus is often called Earth's twin, why would life as we know it be unlikely on Venus?
4. Name the inner planets in order from the sun.
5. **Think Critically:** Do the closest planets to the sun always have the hottest surface temperatures? Explain your answer.
6. **Skill Builder**
   Interpreting Data Using the information in this section, explain how Mars is like Earth. How are they different? If you need help, refer to Interpreting Data in the **Skill Handbook** on page 960.

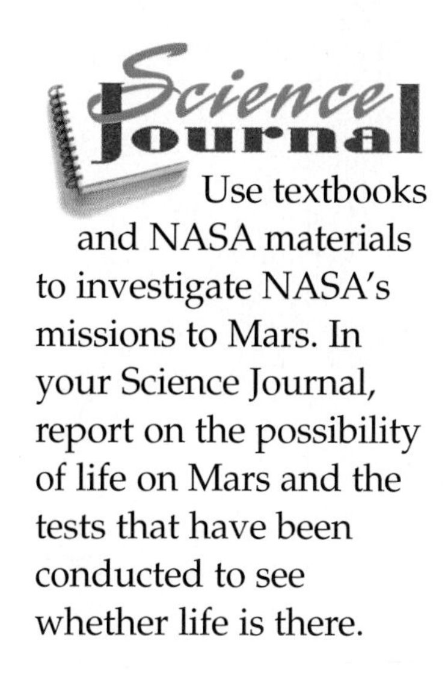

Science Journal

Use textbooks and NASA materials to investigate NASA's missions to Mars. In your Science Journal, report on the possibility of life on Mars and the tests that have been conducted to see whether life is there.

19•3 The Outer Planets

What You'll Learn

- The major characteristics of Jupiter, Saturn, Uranus, and Neptune
- How Pluto differs from the other outer planets

Vocabulary
Jupiter
Great Red Spot
Saturn
Uranus
Neptune
Pluto

Why It's Important

- You'll learn about the planets in our solar system that differ most from Earth.

Outer Planets

You have learned that the inner planets are small, solid, rocky bodies in space. By contrast, the outer planets, except for Pluto, are large, gaseous objects.

You may have heard or read about the *Voyager* and *Galileo* spacecraft. Although they were not the first probes to the outer planets, they have uncovered a wealth of new information about Jupiter, Saturn, Uranus, and Neptune. Let's follow the spacecraft on their journeys to the outer planets of the solar system.

Jupiter

In 1979, *Voyager 1* and *Voyager 2* flew past **Jupiter,** the largest planet and the fifth planet from the sun. *Galileo* reached Jupiter in 1995. The major discoveries of the probes include new information about the composition and motion of Jupiter's atmosphere and the discovery of three new moons. *Voyager* probes also discovered that Jupiter has faint dust rings around it and that one of its moons has volcanoes on it.

Jupiter is composed mostly of hydrogen and helium, with some ammonia, methane, and water vapor as well. Scientists theorize that the atmosphere of hydrogen and helium gradually changes to a planetwide ocean of liquid hydrogen and helium toward the middle of the planet. Below this liquid layer may be a solid rocky core. The extreme pressure and temperature, however, make the core different from any rock on Earth.

You've probably seen pictures from the probes of Jupiter's colorful clouds. Its atmosphere has bands of white, red, tan, and brown clouds, as shown in **Figure 19-10.** Continuous storms of swirling, high-pressure gas have been observed on Jupiter. The **Great Red Spot** is the most spectacular of these storms. Lightning also has been observed within Jupiter's clouds.

Figure 19-10 Jupiter (A) is the largest planet in our solar system, containing more mass than all of the other planets combined. The Great Red Spot (B) is a giant storm about 12 000 km from top to bottom.

Moons of Jupiter

Sixteen moons orbit Jupiter. The four largest, shown in **Table 19-1,** were discovered by Galileo in 1610. Io is the closest large moon to Jupiter. Jupiter's tremendous gravitational force and the gravity of Europa pull on Io. This force heats up Io, causing it to be the most volcanically active object in the solar system. The next large moon is Europa. It is composed mostly of rock with a thick, smooth crust of ice, which may indicate the presence of an ocean under the ice. Next is Ganymede, which is the largest moon in the solar system. It's larger than the planet Mercury. Callisto, the last of the large moons, is composed of ice and rock. Studying these moons and events such as the comet collision shown in **Figure 19-11** further our knowledge of the solar system.

Saturn

The next planet surveyed by the *Voyager* probes was Saturn, in 1980 and 1981. **Saturn** is the sixth planet from the sun and is also known as the ringed planet. Saturn is the second-largest planet in the solar system but has the lowest density. Its density is so low that the planet would float on water.

Table 19-1

Large Moons of Jupiter

Io The most volcanically active object in the solar system; sulfur lava gives it its distinctive red and orange color; has a thin oxygen, sulfur, and sulfur dioxide atmosphere.

Europa Rocky interior is covered by a 100-km-thick ice crust, which has a network of cracks, indicating tectonic activity; has a thin oxygen atmosphere.

Ganymede Has an ice crust about 100 km thick, covered with grooves; crust may surround a mantle of water or slushy ice; has a rocky core and a thin hydrogen atmosphere.

Callisto Has a heavily cratered, ice-rock crust several hundred kilometers thick; crust may surround a salty ocean around a rock core; has a thin atmosphere of hydrogen, oxygen, and carbon dioxide.

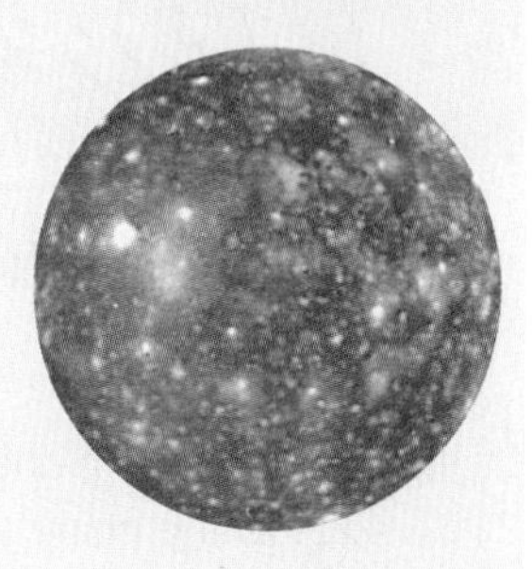

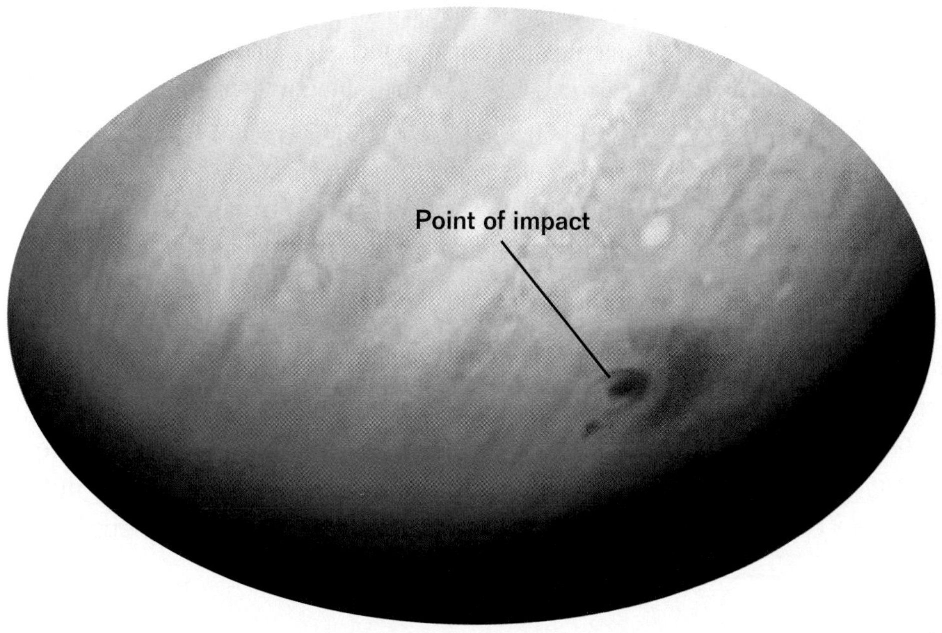

Figure 19-11 In 1994, comet Shoemaker-Levy 9 collided into Jupiter causing a series of spectacular explosions. Information from this impact gives us clues about what might happen if such an impact occurred on Earth.

Figure 19-12 Saturn's rings are composed of pieces of rock and ice.

Modeling Planets

Procedure

1. Research the planets to determine how the sizes of the planets in the solar system compare with each other.
2. Select a scale for the diameter of Earth based on the size of your paper.
3. Make a model by drawing a circle with this diameter on paper.
4. Using Earth's diameter as 1.0, draw each of the other planets to scale.

Analysis

1. At this scale, how far would your model Earth need to be located from the sun?
2. What would 1 AU be equal to in this model?
3. Using a scale of 1 AU = 2 m, how large would the sun and Earth models have to be to remain in scale?

Similar to Jupiter, Saturn is a large, gaseous planet with a thick outer atmosphere composed mostly of hydrogen and helium. Saturn's atmosphere also contains ammonia, methane, and water vapor. As you go deeper into Saturn's atmosphere, the gases gradually change to liquid hydrogen and helium. Below its atmosphere and liquid ocean, Saturn may have a small rocky core.

The *Voyager* probes gathered new information about Saturn's ring system and its moons. The *Voyager* probes showed that Saturn has several broad rings, each of which is composed of thousands of thin ringlets. Each ring is composed of countless ice and rock particles ranging in size from a speck of dust to tens of meters across, as shown in **Figure 19-12.** This makes Saturn's ring system the most complex of all the outer gaseous planets.

At least 20 moons orbit Saturn. That's more than any other planet in our solar system. The largest of these, Titan, is larger than Mercury. It has an atmosphere of nitrogen, argon, and methane. Thick clouds prevent us from seeing the surface of Titan.

Uranus

After touring Saturn, *Voyager 2* flew by Uranus in 1986. **Uranus,** shown in **Figure 19-13,** is the seventh planet from the sun and wasn't discovered until 1781. It is a large, gaseous planet with 17 satellites and a system of thin, dark rings.

Voyager revealed numerous thin rings and ten moons that had not been seen earlier. *Voyager* also detected that the planet's magnetic field is tilted 55 degrees from its rotational poles.

The atmosphere of Uranus is composed of hydrogen, helium, and some methane. The methane gives the planet its blue-green color. Methane absorbs the red and yellow light, and the clouds reflect the green and blue. No cloud bands and few storm systems are seen on Uranus. Evidence suggests that under its atmosphere, Uranus has a mantle of liquid water, methane, and ammonia surrounding a rocky core.

Figure 19-13 The atmosphere of Uranus gives the planet its distinct blue-green color.

One of the most unique features of Uranus is that its axis of rotation is tilted on its side compared with the other planets. The axes of rotation of the other planets, except Pluto, are nearly perpendicular to the planes of their orbits. Uranus, however, has a rotational axis nearly parallel to the plane of its orbit, as shown in **Figure 19-14.** Some scientists believe a collision with another object turned Uranus on its side.

interNET CONNECTION

Visit the Glencoe Science Web Site at **www.glencoe.com/sec/science/ca** for more information about the *Voyager* space probes.

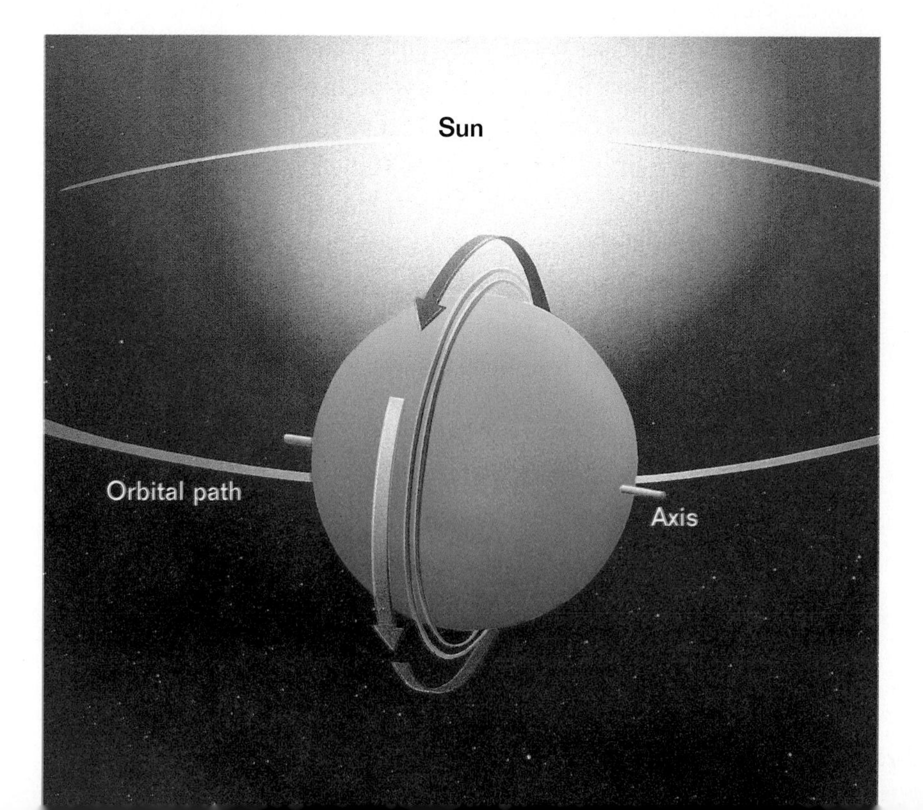

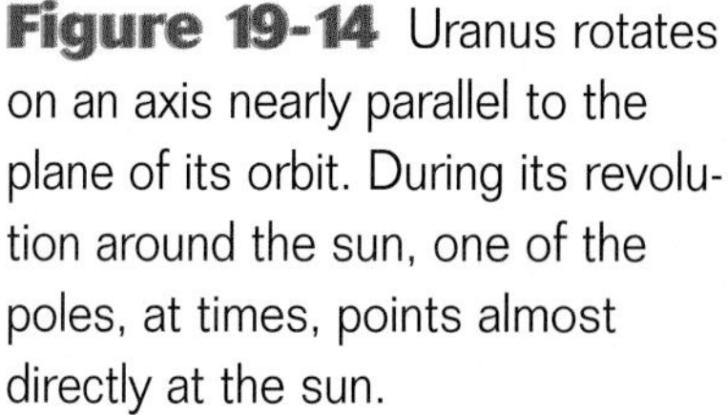

Figure 19-14 Uranus rotates on an axis nearly parallel to the plane of its orbit. During its revolution around the sun, one of the poles, at times, points almost directly at the sun.

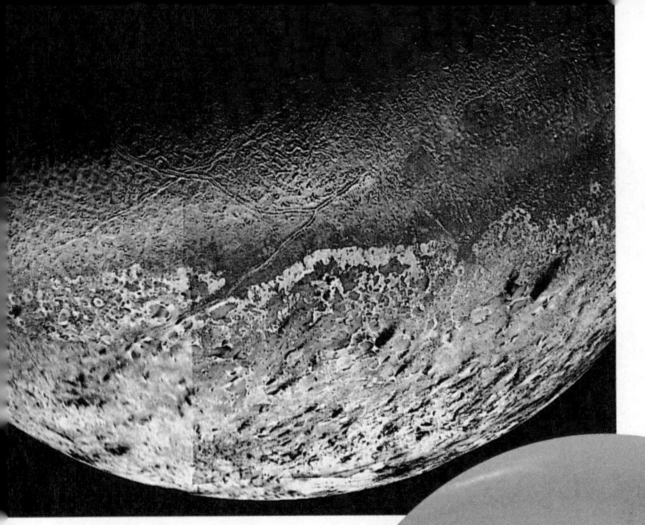

Figure 19-15
Triton, above, is Neptune's largest moon.

Neptune

From Uranus, *Voyager 2* traveled on to Neptune, a large, gaseous planet. Discovered in 1846, **Neptune** is usually the eighth planet from the sun. However, Pluto's orbit crosses inside Neptune's during part of its voyage around the sun. Between 1979 and 1998, Pluto was closer to the sun than Neptune. In 1999, Pluto once again became the farthest planet from the sun.

Neptune's atmosphere is similar to that of Uranus. The methane content gives Neptune, shown in **Figure 19-15,** its distinctive blue-green color, just as it does for Uranus.

Neptune has dark-colored, stormlike features in its atmosphere that are similar to the Great Red Spot on Jupiter. One discovered by *Voyager* is called the Great Dark Spot.

Under its atmosphere, Neptune is thought to have liquid water, methane, and ammonia. Neptune probably has a rocky core.

Neptune

Voyager 2 detected six new moons, so the total number of Neptune's known moons is now eight. Of these, Triton is the largest. Triton, shown in **Figure 19-15,** has a diameter of 2700 km and a thin atmosphere composed mostly of nitrogen. *Voyager* detected methane geysers erupting on Triton. *Voyager* also detected that Neptune has rings that are thin in some places and thick in other places. Neptune's magnetic field is tilted 47 degrees from its rotational axis. In comparison, Earth's magnetic field is tilted only 11.5 degrees from its rotational axis.

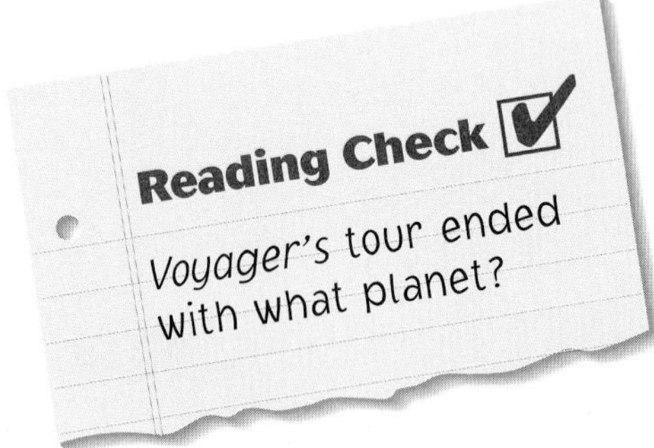

Voyager ended its tour of the solar system with Neptune. Both *Voyager* probes are now beyond the orbits of Pluto and Neptune. They will continue into space, studying how far the sun's power reaches into the outer limits of our solar system.

Pluto

The smallest planet in our solar system, and the one we know the least about, is Pluto. Because **Pluto** is farther from the sun than Neptune during most of its orbit around the sun, it is considered the ninth planet from the sun. Pluto is not like the other outer planets. It's surrounded by only a thin atmosphere, and it's the only outer planet with a solid, icy-rock surface.

Pluto's only moon, Charon, has a diameter about half the size of Pluto's. Charon orbits close to Pluto. Pluto and Charon are shown in **Figure 19-16.** Because of their close size and orbit, they are sometimes considered to be a double planet.

Recent data from the *Hubble Space Telescope* indicate the presence of a vast disk of icy comets near Neptune's orbit, called the Kuiper belt. Some of the ice comets are hundreds of kilometers in diameter. Are Pluto and Charon members of this belt? Are they escaped moons of one of the larger gaseous giants, or did they simply form at the distance they are? Maybe planets at that distance from the sun should be small and composed of icy rock. We may not find out until we send a probe to Pluto.

With the *Voyager* probes, we entered a new age of knowledge about the solar system. The space probe *Galileo*, which arrived at Jupiter in 1995, and the *Cassini* probe, which will arrive at Saturn in 2004, will continue to extend our understanding of the solar system.

Figure 19-16 The *Hubble Space Telescope* gave astronomers their first clear view of Pluto and Charon as distinct objects.

Section Assessment

1. What are the differences between the outer planets and the inner planets?
2. Are any moons in the solar system larger than planets? If so, which ones?
3. How does Pluto differ from the other outer planets?
4. **Think Critically:** Why is Neptune sometimes the farthest planet from the sun?
5. **Skill Builder**
   Recognizing Cause and Effect
   Answer the following questions about Jupiter. If you need help, refer to Recognizing Cause and Effect in the **Skill Handbook** on page 957.
   a. What causes Jupiter's surface color?
   b. How is the Great Red Spot affected by Jupiter's atmosphere?
   c. How does Jupiter's mass affect its gravitational force?

Using Computers

Spreadsheet Design a table using spreadsheet software of the nine planets. Compare their characteristics, such as size, distance from the sun, orbital speed, and number of satellites. If you need help, refer to page 974.

Design Your Own Experiment

Activity 19.2

Solar System Distance Model

Possible Materials

- Meterstick
- Scissors
- Pencil
- String (several meters)
- Paper (several sheets of notebook paper)

Distances between the planets of the solar system are large. Can you design a model that will demonstrate the large distances between and among the sun and planets in the solar system?

Recognize the Problem

How can a model be designed that will show the relative distances between and among the sun and planets of the solar system?

Form a Hypothesis

State a hypothesis about how a model with scale dimensions of the solar system can be constructed.

Goals

- **Make a table** of scale distances that will represent planetary distances to be used in a model of the solar system.
- **Research** planetary distances.
- **Make a model** of the distances between the sun and planets of the solar system.

Safety Precautions

Take care when handling scissors.

Planetary Distances

Planet	Distance to Sun (km)	Distance to Sun (AU)	Scale Distance (1 AU = 10 cm)	Scale Distance (1 AU = 2 m)
Mercury	5.8×10^7			
Venus	1.08×10^8			
Earth	1.50×10^8			
Mars	2.28×10^8			
Jupiter	7.80×10^8			
Saturn	1.43×10^9			
Uranus	2.88×10^9			
Neptune	4.51×10^9			
Pluto	5.92×10^9			

Test Your Hypothesis

Plan

1. As a group, **agree** upon and write out your hypothesis statement.
2. **List** the steps that you need to take in making your model to **test** your hypothesis. Be specific, describing exactly what you will do at each step.
3. **Make** a list of the materials that you will need to complete your model.
4. **Make a table** of scale distances you will use in your model.
5. **Write** a description of how you will **build** your model, **explaining** how it will demonstrate relative distances between and among the sun and planets of the solar system.

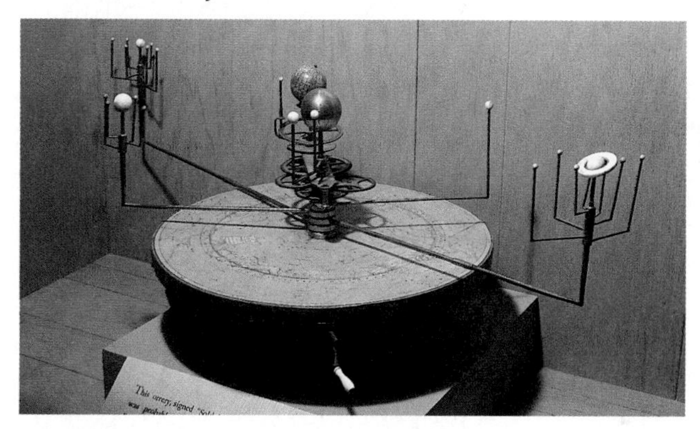

Do

1. Make sure your teacher approves your plan before you proceed.
2. **Construct the model** as planned using your scale distances.
3. While constructing the model, **write** down any observations that you or other members of your group make and complete the data table in your Science Journal.
4. **Calculate** the scale distance that would be used in your model if 1 AU = 2 m.

Analyze Your Data

1. **Explain** how a scale distance is determined.
2. How much string would be required to construct a model with a scale distance 1 AU = 2 m?

Draw Conclusions

1. Was it possible to work with your scale? **Explain** why or why not.
2. Proxima Centauri, the closest star to our sun, is about 270 000 AU from the sun. Based on your scale, how much string would you need to place this star on your model?

19•4 Other Objects in the Solar System

What You'll Learn

- Where a comet comes from and how a comet develops as it approaches the sun
- Comets, meteoroids, and asteroids

Vocabulary
comet
Oort Cloud
meteor
meteorite
asteroid

Why It's Important

- Comets, meteoroids, and asteroids may be composed of material that formed early in the history of the solar system.

Comets

Although the planets and their moons are the most noticeable members of the sun's family, many other objects orbit the sun. Comets, meteoroids, and asteroids are other objects in the solar system.

You've probably heard of Halley's comet. A **comet** is composed of dust and rock particles mixed in with frozen water, methane, and ammonia. Halley's comet was last seen from Earth in 1986. English astronomer Edmund Halley realized that comet sightings that had taken place about every 76 years were really sightings of the same comet. This comet, which takes about 76 years to orbit the sun, was named after him. Halley's comet is just one example of the many other objects in the solar system besides the planets. The Dutch astronomer Jan Oort proposed the idea that a large collection of comets lies in a cloud that completely surrounds the solar

Figure 19-17 Comet Hale-Bopp was visible in March and April 1997.

Figure 19-18 A comet consists of a nucleus, a coma, and a tail.

system. This cloud is located beyond the orbit of Pluto and is called the **Oort Cloud.** Evidence suggests that the gravity of the sun and nearby stars interacts with comets in the Oort Cloud. Comets either escape from the solar system or get captured into much smaller orbits. As mentioned earlier, another belt of comets, called the Kuiper belt, may exist near the orbit of Neptune.

On July 23, 1995, two backyard astronomers made an exciting discovery—a new comet was headed toward the sun. This comet, Comet Hale-Bopp, is larger than most that approach the sun and was the brightest comet visible from Earth in 20 years. Shown in **Figure 19-17,** it was at its brightest in March and April 1997.

Visit the Glencoe Science Web Site at **www.glencoe.com/sec/science/ca** for more information about comets.

Structure of Comets

The structure of a comet, shown in **Figure 19-18,** is like a large, dirty snowball or a mass of frozen ice and rock. But as the comet approaches the sun, it develops a distinctive structure. Ices of water, methane, and ammonia begin to vaporize because of the heat from the sun. Dust and bits of rock are released. The vaporized gases and released dust form a bright cloud called a coma around the nucleus, or solid part, of the comet. The solar wind pushes on the gases and released dust in the coma. These particles form a tail that always points away from the sun.

After many trips around the sun, most of the frozen ice in a comet has vaporized. All that is left are small particles that spread throughout the orbit of the original comet.

VISUALIZING Meteorites

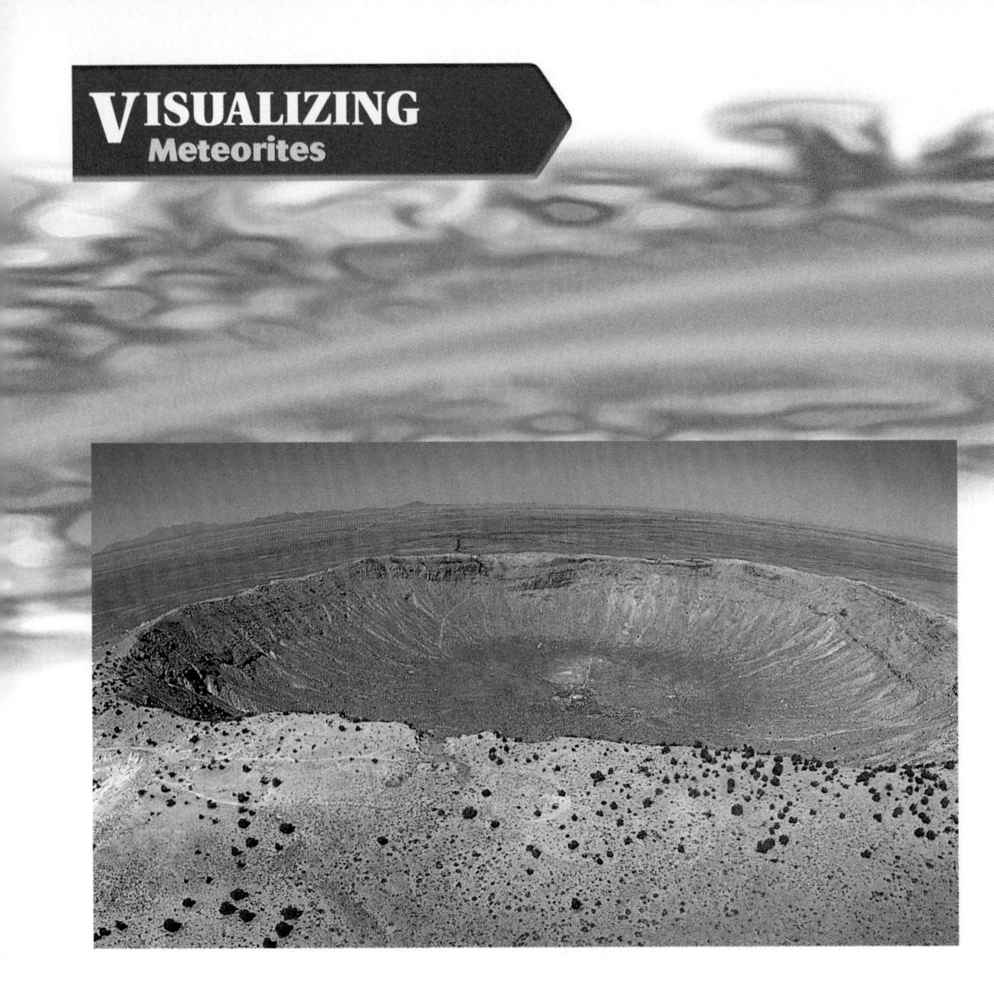

Figure 19-19 Meteorites strike the surface of a moon or planet.

A A large meteorite struck Arizona 50 000 years ago.

Visit the Glencoe Science Web Site at **www.glencoe.com/sec/science/ca** for more information about meteor craters.

Meteoroids, Meteors, and Meteorites

You learned that comets tend to break up after they have passed close to the sun several times. The small pieces of the comet nucleus spread out into a loose group within the original orbit of the broken comet. These small pieces of rock moving through space are then called meteoroids.

When the path of a meteoroid crosses the position of Earth, it enters our atmosphere at between 15 and 70 km/s. Most meteoroids are so small that they are completely vaporized in Earth's atmosphere. A meteoroid that burns up in Earth's atmosphere is called a **meteor.** People often see these and call them shooting stars.

Each time Earth passes through the loose group of particles within the old orbit of a comet, many small particles of rock and dust enter the atmosphere. Because more meteors than usual are seen, this is called a meteor shower.

If the meteoroid is large enough, it may not completely burn up in Earth's atmosphere. When it strikes Earth, it is called a **meteorite.** Meteor Crater in Arizona, shown in **Figure 19-19A,** was formed when a large meteorite struck Earth about 50 000 years ago. Most meteorites are probably debris from asteroid collisions or broken-up comets, but some are from the moon and Mars.

B This crater made by a meteorite is on the moon.

C A meteoroid that burns up in Earth's atmosphere is called a meteor.

Asteroids

An **asteroid** is a piece of rock similar to the material that formed into the planets. Most asteroids are located in an area between the orbits of Mars and Jupiter called the asteroid belt, shown in **Figure 19-20.** Why are they located there? The gravity of Jupiter may have kept a planet from forming in the area where the asteroid belt is now located.

Other asteroids are scattered throughout the solar system—they may have been thrown out of the belt by gravity. Some may have since been captured as moons around other planets.

Figure 19-20 The asteroid belt lies between the orbits of Mars and Jupiter.

Asteroid Size

The sizes of the asteroids in the asteroid belt range from tiny particles to 940 km. Ceres is the largest and the first one discovered. The next three in size are Pallas (523 km), Vesta (501 km), and Juno (244 km). Two asteroids, Gaspra and Ida, were photographed by *Galileo* on its way to Jupiter, as shown in **Figure 19-21.**

Comets, meteoroids, and asteroids are probably composed of material that formed early in the history of the solar system. Scientists study the structure and composition of these space objects in order to better understand what the solar system may have been like long ago. Understanding what the early solar system was like could help scientists to better understand the formation of Earth and its relationship to other objects in the solar system.

Figure 19-21 The asteroid Ida (A) is about 56 km long. Gaspra (B) is about 20 km long.

Section Assessment

1. How does a comet's tail form as it approaches the sun?
2. What type of feature might be formed on Earth if a large meteorite reached its surface?
3. Describe differences among comets, meteoroids, and asteroids.
4. **Think Critically:** What is the chemical composition of comets? Are comets more similar to the inner or the outer planets?
5. **Skill Builder**
   Inferring Scientists can learn a lot about a planet's history by studying its impact craters. Do the **Chapter 19 Skill Activity** on page 980 to infer how scientific illustrations can be used to determine the ages of impact craters.

The asteroid belt contains many objects—from tiny particles to objects 940 km in diameter. In your Science Journal, describe how mining the asteroids for valuable minerals might be accomplished.

Science & Society

Mission to Mars

Scientists are currently developing plans for further exploration of Mars. But even at its closest, Mars is 55 million km away from Earth, a distance that would take astronauts three years to travel round-trip. Given the long flight, not to mention conditions astronauts would face living on Mars, a journey to the Red Planet would be full of risks. This raises a question: Should humans or robots be sent to explore Mars?

Risks to Humans

Getting to and from Mars would take a toll on the human body. In the near-zero gravity of outer space, bones lose calcium and gradually become weaker. Muscles lose their strength as well, because they don't have to work against gravity to support and move body parts. Furthermore, in a weightless environment, body fluids don't flow downward as they do on Earth. Unusual circulation of body fluids can interfere with kidney function and lead to dehydration.

Assuming humans survived the long flight to Mars in good health, they would face other challenges upon arrival. To explore Mars properly, a team of astronauts would probably have to live on the planet for months, even years. The NASA painting, left, shows a module that could house explorers. Such a structure would have to withstand the Martian environment and protect astronauts from high levels of solar radiation.

The Case for Robots

Because of the many risks a Mars mission would pose for humans, some scientists suggest sending specialized robots that could operate equipment and carry out scientific experiments. These robots would be equipped with artificial senses that would allow researchers on Earth to experience the planet's surface in a way second only to being there in person. However, radio signals sent back and forth between robots on Mars and operators on Earth would take up to 20 minutes to travel each way. Scientists are working to solve this problem in the hope that extensive exploration of Mars will soon be a reality—by people or by machines.

Science JOURNAL

How do you think Mars should be further explored? Write a proposal to your class explaining how you would explore Mars.

Chapter 19 Reviewing Main Ideas

For a **preview** of this chapter, study this Reviewing Main Ideas before you read the chapter. After you have studied this chapter, you can use the Reviewing Main Ideas to **review** the chapter.

The Glencoe MindJogger, Audiocassettes, and CD-ROM provide additional opportunities for review.

Section

19-1 THE SOLAR SYSTEM

Early astronomers thought that the planets, the moon, the sun, and the stars were embedded in separate spheres that rotated around Earth. The sun-centered model of the **solar system** states that the sun is the center of the solar system. Using a telescope, Galileo discovered evidence that supported the sun-centered model. Later, Kepler discovered that the planets orbit the sun in elliptical orbits, not circles. ***What type of evidence did Galileo discover that indicated the sun-centered model was correct?***

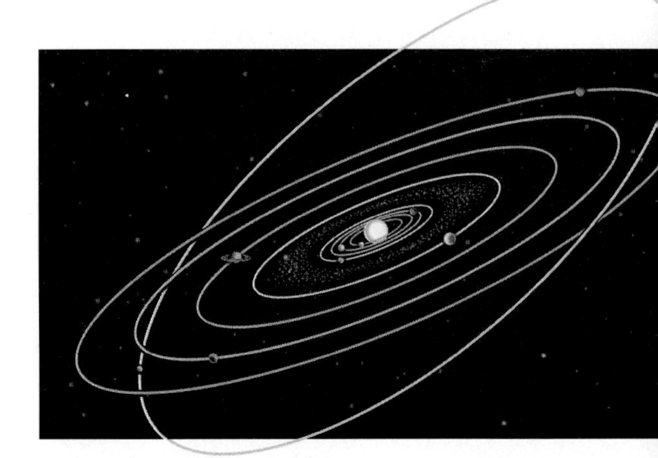

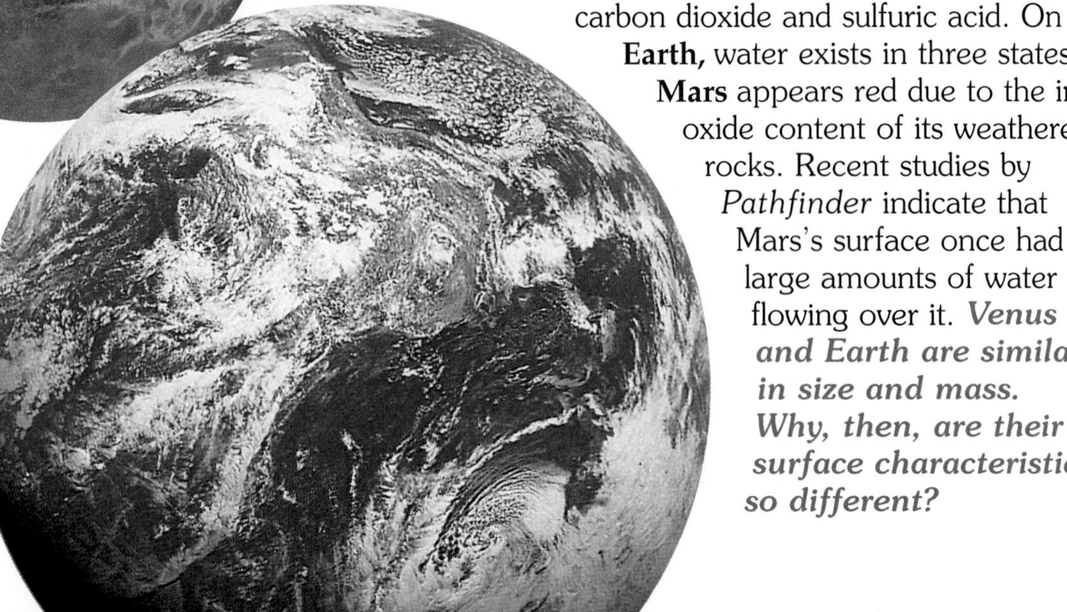

Section

19-2 THE INNER PLANETS

The **inner planets,** in increasing distance from the sun are Mercury, Venus, Earth, and Mars. The moonlike **Mercury** has craters and cliffs on its surface. **Venus** has a dense atmosphere of carbon dioxide and sulfuric acid. On **Earth,** water exists in three states. **Mars** appears red due to the iron oxide content of its weathered rocks. Recent studies by *Pathfinder* indicate that Mars's surface once had large amounts of water flowing over it. ***Venus and Earth are similar in size and mass. Why, then, are their surface characteristics so different?***

Reading Check ✔

Locate a legend, myth, or folktale from another culture that explains the origin of all or part of the solar system. Share it with the class.

Section

19-3 THE OUTER PLANETS

Faint rings and 16 moons orbit the gaseous **Jupiter.** Jupiter's Great Red Spot is a high-pressure storm generated by huge thunderstorms in Jupiter's atmosphere. **Saturn** is made mostly of gas and has pronounced rings. **Uranus** is a large, gaseous planet with many moons and several rings. **Neptune** is similar to Uranus in size, composition, and stormlike features. **Pluto** has a thin, changing atmosphere, and its surface is icy rock. ***Why would the average densities of the four large, outer planets be so low when compared with the average densities of the inner planets?***

Section

19-4 OTHER OBJECTS IN THE SOLAR SYSTEM

As a **comet** approaches the sun, vaporized gases form a bright coma around the comet's nucleus and solar wind forms a tail that points away from the sun. Meteoroids form when asteroids collide, when comets break up, or when **meteorites** collide with the moon or other planets. An **asteroid** is a piece of rock usually found in the asteroid belt. ***Why does the tail of a comet always point away from the sun?***

Chapter 19 Assessment

Using Vocabulary

a. asteroid
b. astronomical unit
c. comet
d. Earth
e. Great Red Spot
f. inner planet
g. Jupiter
h. Mars
i. Mercury
j. meteor
k. meteorite
l. Neptune
m. Oort Cloud
n. outer planet
o. Pluto
p. Saturn
q. solar system
r. Uranus
s. Venus

Distinguish between the terms in each of the following pairs.

1. asteroid, comet
2. inner planet, outer planet
3. meteor, meteorite
4. Great Red Spot, Oort Cloud
5. Neptune, Uranus

Checking Concepts

Choose the word or phrase that best answers the question.

6. Who proposed a sun-centered solar system?
   A) Ptolemy
   B) Copernicus
   C) Galileo
   D) Oort
7. How does the sun produce energy?
   A) magnetism
   B) nuclear fission
   C) nuclear fusion
   D) the greenhouse effect
8. What is the shape of planetary orbits?
   A) circles
   B) ellipses
   C) squares
   D) rectangles
9. Which planet has extreme temperatures because it has essentially no atmosphere?
   A) Earth
   B) Jupiter
   C) Mars
   D) Mercury
10. Water is a solid, liquid, and gas on which planet?
    A) Pluto
    B) Uranus
    C) Saturn
    D) Earth
11. Where is the largest known volcano in the solar system?
    A) Earth
    B) Jupiter
    C) Mars
    D) Uranus
12. What do scientists call a rock that strikes Earth's surface?
    A) asteroid
    B) comet
    C) meteorite
    D) meteoroid
13. Which planet has a complex ring system made of hundreds of ringlets?
    A) Pluto
    B) Saturn
    C) Uranus
    D) Mars
14. Which planet has a magnetic pole tilted 60 degrees?
    A) Uranus
    B) Earth
    C) Jupiter
    D) Pluto
15. How does the tail of a comet always point?
    A) toward the sun
    B) away from the sun
    C) toward Earth
    D) away from the Oort Cloud

Thinking Critically

16. Why is the surface temperature on Venus so much higher than that on Earth?
17. Describe the relationship between the mass of a planet and the number of satellites it has.
18. Why are probe landings on Jupiter or Saturn unlikely events?
19. What evidence suggests that water is or once was present on Mars?
20. An observer on Earth can watch Venus go through phases much like Earth's moon does. Explain why this is so.

Developing Skills

If you need help, refer to the Skill Handbook.

21. **Concept Mapping:** Complete the concept map on this page to show how a comet changes as it travels through space.

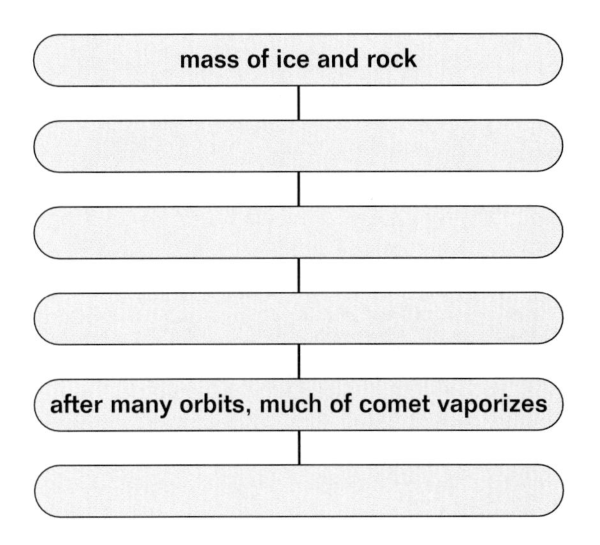

22. **Hypothesizing:** Mercury is the closest planet to the sun, yet it does not reflect much of the sun's light. What can you say about Mercury's color?
23. **Sequencing:** Arrange the following planets in order from the planet with the most natural satellites to the one with the fewest: Earth, Jupiter, Saturn, Neptune, Uranus, and Mars.
24. **Making and Using Tables:** Make a table that summarizes the main characteristics of each planet in the solar system.
25. **Measuring in SI:** The Great Red Spot of Jupiter is about 40 000 km long and about 12 000 km wide. What is its approximate area in km^2?

Test-Taking Tip

Get to the Root of Things If you don't know a word's meaning, you can still get an idea of its meaning if you focus on its roots, prefixes, and suffixes. For instance, words that start with *non-*, *un-*, *a-*, *dis-*, and *in-* generally reverse what the rest of the word means.

Test Practice

Use these questions to test your Science Proficiency.

1. Earth is probably the only planet in our solar system on which life exists. Which of the following statements **BEST** explains why this is true?
   A) Earth is the only planet on which water exists in all three states.
   B) Earth has frozen ice caps at its poles.
   C) Earth has carbon dioxide in its atmosphere.
   D) Earth has an atmosphere.
2. Both Copernicus and Kepler proposed a model of the solar system. What was the major difference between the two models?
   A) Copernicus's model had the sun in the center. Kepler's model had Earth in the center.
   B) Copernicus's model included Saturn. Kepler's model did not.
   C) Copernicus's model included circular orbits for the planets. Kepler's model included elliptical orbits for the planets.
   D) Copernicus's model showed the moon as a planet. Kepler's model showed the moon as a satellite of Earth.

CHAPTER

20 Stars and Galaxies

Chapter Preview

Skills Preview

Skill Builders
- Predict

Activities
- Measure in SI

MiniLabs
- Make a Model

Reading Check

Summarize the main ideas in Section 20-1. Then, compare your summary with the Reviewing Main Ideas at the end of the chapter.

Explore Activity

This photo may look like science fiction, but it shows a real event. It is a photo of two galaxies colliding. Other galaxies are moving away from each other. The universe is full of billions of galaxies, each containing billions of stars. By studying deep space, astronomers have observed that the universe is expanding in all directions. In the following activity, you can model how the universe might be expanding.

Model the Universe 

1. Partially inflate a balloon. Clip the neck shut with a clothespin.
2. Draw six evenly spaced dots on the balloon with a felt-tip marker. Label the dots A through F.
3. Use a string and ruler to measure the distance, in millimeters, from dot A to each of the other dots.
4. Remove the clothespin and inflate the balloon some more.
5. Measure the distance of each dot from A again.
6. Inflate the balloon again, tie the neck shut, and take new measurements.

Science Journal

If each dot represents a galaxy and the balloon represents the universe, describe the motion of the galaxies relative to one another. Is the universe expanding? Explain.

20•1 Stars

What You'll Learn

- Why the positions of the constellations change throughout the year
- Absolute magnitude and apparent magnitude
- How parallax is used to determine distance

Vocabulary
constellation
absolute magnitude
apparent magnitude
parallax
light-year

Why It's Important

- You'll learn to recognize groups of stars found in the night sky.

Constellations

Have you ever watched clouds drift by on a summer day? It's fun to look at the clouds and imagine they have shapes familiar to you. One may look like a face. Another might resemble a rabbit or a bear. People long ago did much the same thing with patterns of stars in the sky. They named certain groups of stars, called **constellations,** after animals, characters in mythology, or familiar objects.

From Earth, a constellation looks like a group of stars that are relatively close to one another. In most cases, the stars in a constellation have no relationship to each other in space.

The position of a star in the sky can be given as a specific location within a constellation. For example, you can say that the star Betelgeuse (BEE tul jooz) is in the shoulder of the mighty hunter Orion. Orion's faithful companion is his dog, Canis Major. The brightest star in the sky, Sirius, is in the constellation Canis Major. Orion and Canis Major are shown in **Figure 20-1.**

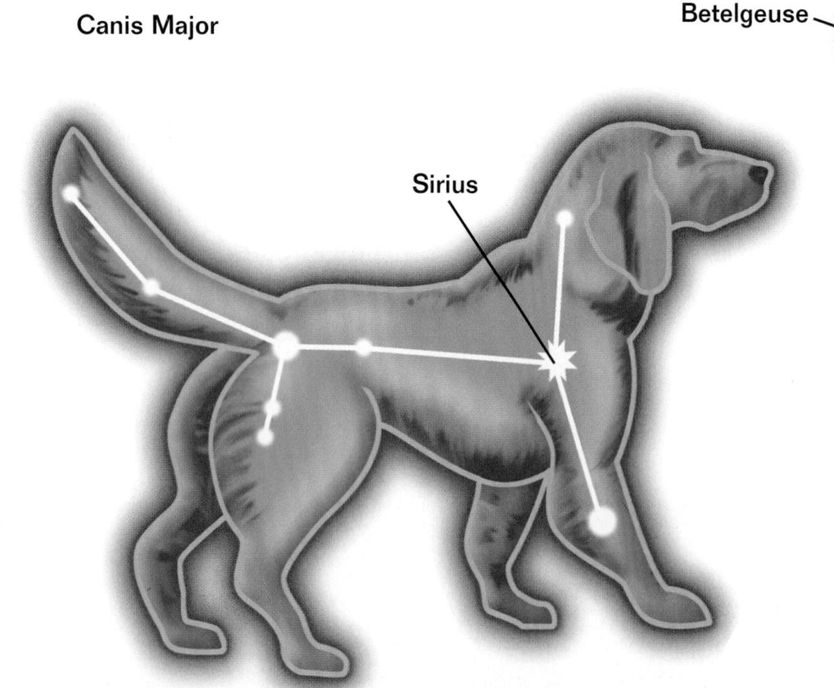

Figure 20-1 Groups of stars can form patterns that look like familiar objects or characters.

Summer

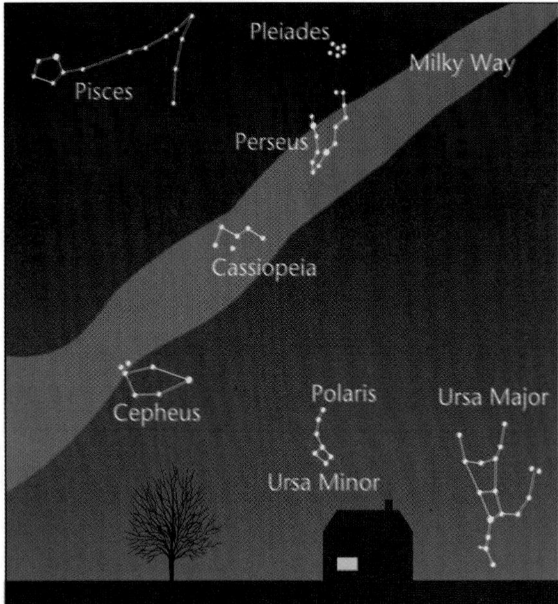

Winter

Figure 20-2 Some constellations are visible only during certain seasons of the year. Others, such as those close to Polaris, are visible year-round.

Early Greek astronomers named many constellations. Modern astronomers used many of these names to divide the sky into 88 constellations. You may already know some of them. Have you ever tried to find the Big Dipper? It's part of the constellation Ursa Major, shown in **Figure 20-2.** Notice how the front two stars of the Big Dipper point directly at the star Polaris. Polaris, also known as the North Star, is located at the end of the Little Dipper in the constellation Ursa Minor. Polaris is almost directly over Earth's north pole. You'll learn how to locate Polaris and constellations in the **Field Guide to Backyard Astronomy** at the end of this chapter.

Circumpolar Constellations

As Earth rotates, you can watch Ursa Major, Ursa Minor, and other constellations in the northern sky circle around Polaris. Because these constellations circle Polaris, they are called circumpolar constellations.

All of the constellations appear to move because Earth is moving. Look at **Figure 20-3.** The stars appear to complete one full circle in the sky in just under 24 hours as Earth rotates on its axis. The stars also appear to change positions in the sky throughout the year as Earth revolves around the sun.

Figure 20-3 This photograph shows the path of circumpolar stars over several hours. Polaris is almost directly over the north pole. **Does Polaris appear to move as Earth rotates? Explain.**

Circumpolar constellations are visible all year long, but other constellations are not. As Earth orbits the sun, different constellations come into view while others disappear. Orion, which is visible in the winter in the northern hemisphere, can't be seen in the summer because the daytime side of Earth is facing it.

Absolute and Apparent Magnitudes

When you look at constellations, you'll notice that some stars are brighter than others. Sirius looks much brighter than Rigel. But is Sirius actually a brighter star, or is it just closer to Earth, which makes it appear to be brighter? As it turns out, Sirius is 100 times closer to Earth than Rigel. If Sirius and Rigel were the same distance from Earth, Rigel would appear much brighter in the night sky than would Sirius.

When you refer to the brightness of a star, you can refer to either its absolute magnitude or its apparent magnitude. The **absolute magnitude** of a star is a measure of the amount of light it actually gives off. A measure of the amount of light received on Earth is called the **apparent magnitude.** A star that's actually rather dim can appear bright in the sky if it's close to Earth. A star that's actually bright can appear dim if it's far away. If two stars are the same distance away, what factors might cause one of them to be brighter than the other?

You can experience the effect of distance on apparent magnitude when driving in a car at night. Observe the other cars' headlights as they approach. Which cars' headlights are brighter—those that are closer to you or those that are farther away?

Problem Solving

Star Light, Star Bright

Mary conducted an experiment to determine the relationship between distance and the brightness of stars. She used a meterstick, a light meter, and a lightbulb. The bulb was mounted at the zero end of the meterstick. Mary placed the light meter at the 20-cm mark on the meterstick and recorded the distance and the light-meter reading in the data table below. Readings are in luxes, which are units for measuring light intensity. Mary doubled and tripled the distance and took more readings.

Think Critically: What happened to the amount of light recorded when the distance was increased from 20 cm to 40 cm? From 20 cm to 60 cm? What does this indicate about the relationship between light intensity and distance? What would the light intensity be at 100 cm?

Effect of Distance on Light

Distance (cm)	Meter Reading (luxes)
20	4150.0
40	1037.5
60	461.1
80	259.4

How far are stars?

How do we know when a star is close to our solar system? One way is to measure its parallax. **Parallax** is the apparent shift in the position of an object when viewed from two different positions. You are already familiar with parallax. Hold your hand at arm's length and look at one finger first with your left eye closed and then with your right eye closed. Your finger appears to change position with respect to the background. Now, try the same experiment with your finger closer to your face. What do you observe? The nearer an object is to the observer, the greater its parallax.

We can measure the parallax of relatively close stars to determine their distances from Earth, as shown in **Figure 20-4.** When astronomers first realized how far away stars actually are, it became apparent that a new unit of measure would be needed to record their distances. Measuring star distances in kilometers would be like measuring the distance between cities in millimeters.

Distances in space are measured in light-years. A **light-year** is the distance that light travels in one year. Light travels at 300 000 km/s, or about 9.5 trillion km in one year. The nearest star to Earth, other than the sun, is Proxima Centauri. Proxima Centauri is 4.2 light-years away, or about 40 trillion km.

Observing Star Patterns

Procedure

1. On a clear night, go outside after dark and study the stars. Take an adult with you and see if you can help each other find constellations.
2. Let your imagination go to work and try to see any patterns of stars in the sky that look like something with which you are familiar.
3. Draw the stars you see, where they are in the sky, and include a drawing of what you think the star pattern resembles.

Analysis

1. How do your constellations compare with those observed by your classmates?
2. How do you think recognizing star patterns could be useful?

Figure 20-4 Parallax can be seen if you observe the same star while Earth is at two different points during its orbit around the sun (A). The star's position relative to more-distant background stars will appear to change (B and C).

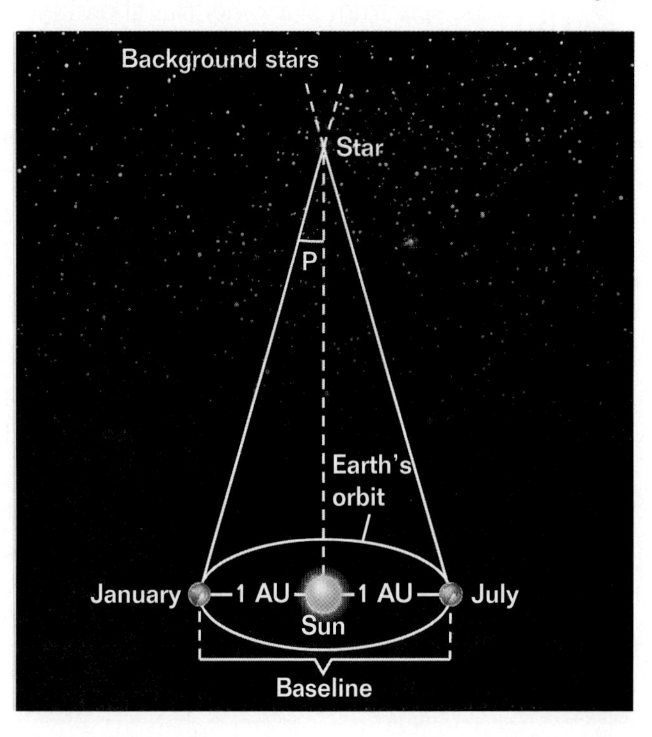

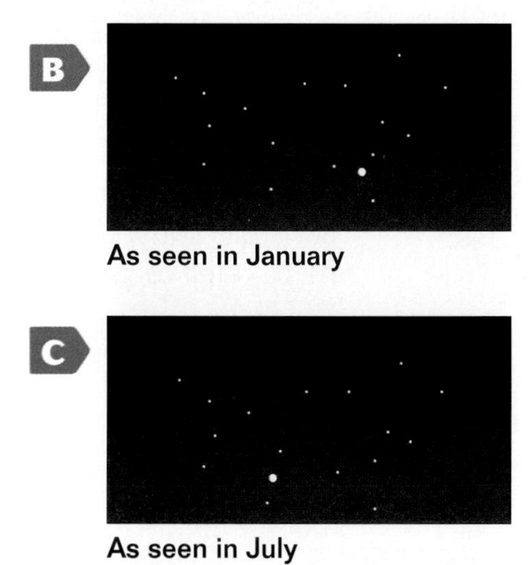

How hot are stars?

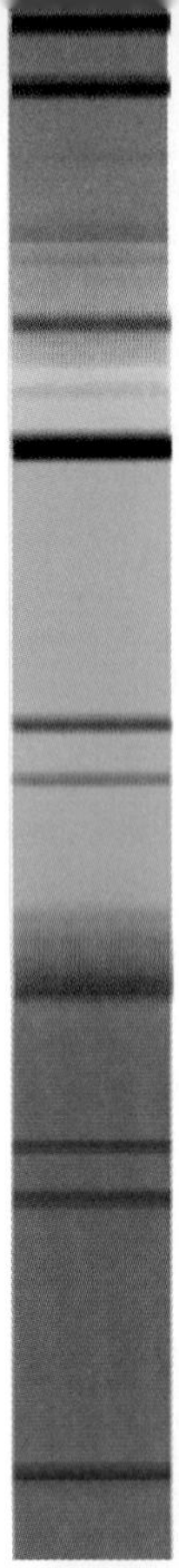

The color of a star indicates its temperature. For example, hot stars are a blue-white color. A relatively cool star looks orange or red. Stars the temperature of our sun have a yellow color.

Figure 20-5
These star spectra were made by placing a prism over a telescope's objective lens. **What causes the lines in spectra?**

Astronomers learn about other properties of stars by studying their spectra. They use spectrographs to break visible light from a star into its component colors. If you look closely at the spectrum of a star, such as the ones shown in **Figure 20-5,** you will see dark lines in it. The lines are caused by elements in the star's atmosphere.

As light radiated from a star passes through the star's atmosphere, some of it is absorbed by elements in the atmosphere. The wavelengths of visible light that are absorbed appear as dark lines in the spectrum. Each element absorbs certain wavelengths, producing a certain pattern of dark lines. The patterns of lines can be used to identify which elements are in a star's atmosphere.

Section Assessment

1. Explain how Earth's revolution affects constellations that are visible throughout the year.
2. If two stars give off the same amount of light, what might cause one to look brighter than the other?
3. If the spectrum of another star shows the same absorption lines as the sun, what can be said about its composition?
4. **Think Critically:** Only about 700 stars can be studied using parallax. Most stars are invisible to the naked eye. What does this indicate about their apparent magnitudes?
5. **Skill Builder**
Recognizing Cause and Effect
Suppose you viewed Proxima Centauri through a telescope. How old were you when the light that you see left Proxima Centauri? Why might Proxima Centauri look dimmer than the star Betelgeuse, a large star 310 light-years away? If you need help, refer to Recognizing Cause and Effect in the **Skill Handbook** on page 957.

Using Computers

Graphics Use drawing software on a computer to make a star chart of major constellations visible from your home during the current season. Include reference points to help others find the charted constellations. If you need help, refer to page 970.

The Sun

20•2

Layers of the Sun

More than 99 percent of all of the matter in our solar system is in the sun. The sun is the center of our solar system, and it makes life possible on Earth. But in the grand scheme of the universe, our sun is just another star in the sky.

The sun is an average, middle-aged star. Its absolute magnitude is about average and it shines with a yellow light. Like other stars, the sun is an enormous ball of gas, producing energy by fusing hydrogen into helium in its core. **Figure 20-6** is a model of the sun's interior and atmosphere.

What You'll Learn

- How energy is produced in the sun
- That sunspots, prominences, and solar flares are related
- Why our sun is considered an average star and how it differs from stars in binary systems

Vocabulary
photosphere
chromosphere
corona
sunspot
binary system

Why It's Important

- The sun is the source of most energy on Earth.

The Sun's Atmosphere

The lowest layer of the sun's atmosphere and the layer from which light is given off is the **photosphere.** The photosphere is often called the surface of the sun. Temperatures there are around 6000 K. Above the photosphere is the **chromosphere.** This layer extends upward about 2000 km above the photosphere. A transition zone occurs between 2000 and 10 000 km above the photosphere. Above the transition zone is the **corona.** This is the largest layer of the sun's atmosphere and extends millions of kilometers into space. Temperatures in the corona are as high as 2 millionK. Charged particles continually escape from the corona and move through space as solar wind.

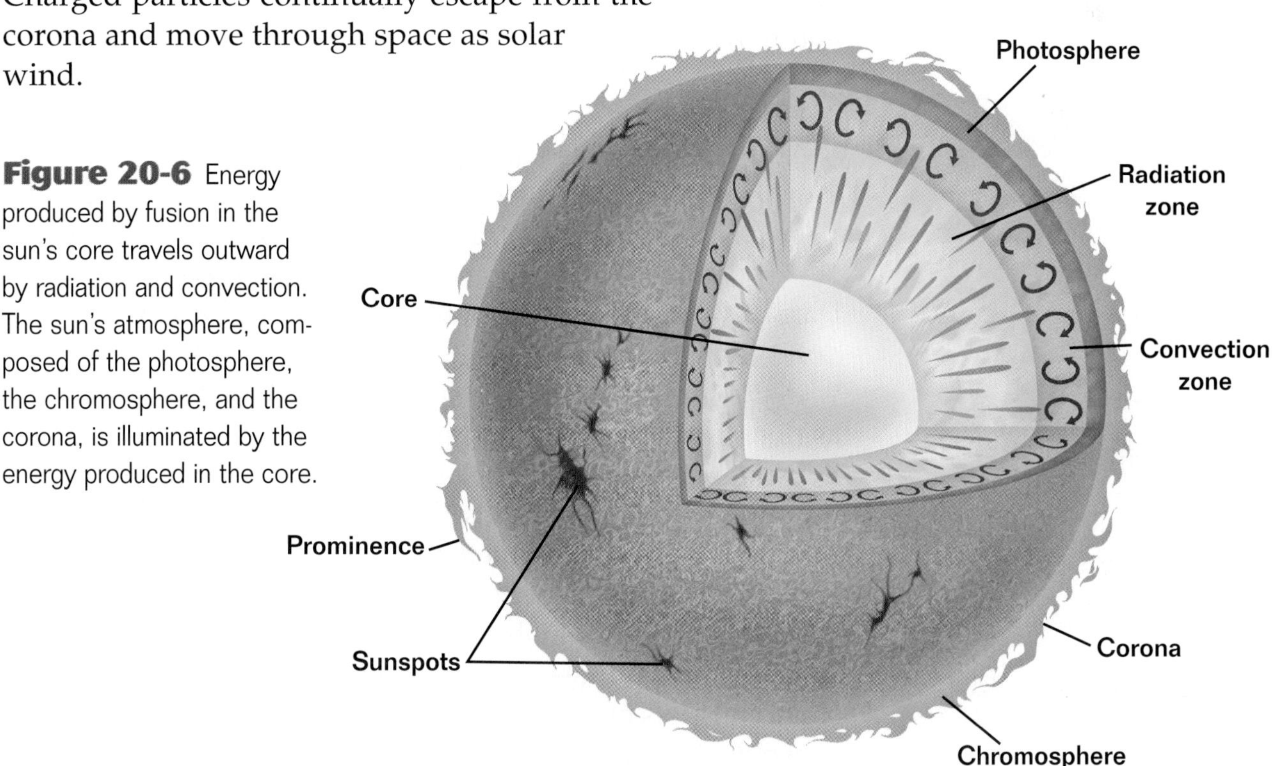

Figure 20-6 Energy produced by fusion in the sun's core travels outward by radiation and convection. The sun's atmosphere, composed of the photosphere, the chromosphere, and the corona, is illuminated by the energy produced in the core.

Figure 20-7 Sunspots are bright, but when viewed against the rest of the photosphere, they appear dark. The small photo is a close-up of a sunspot.

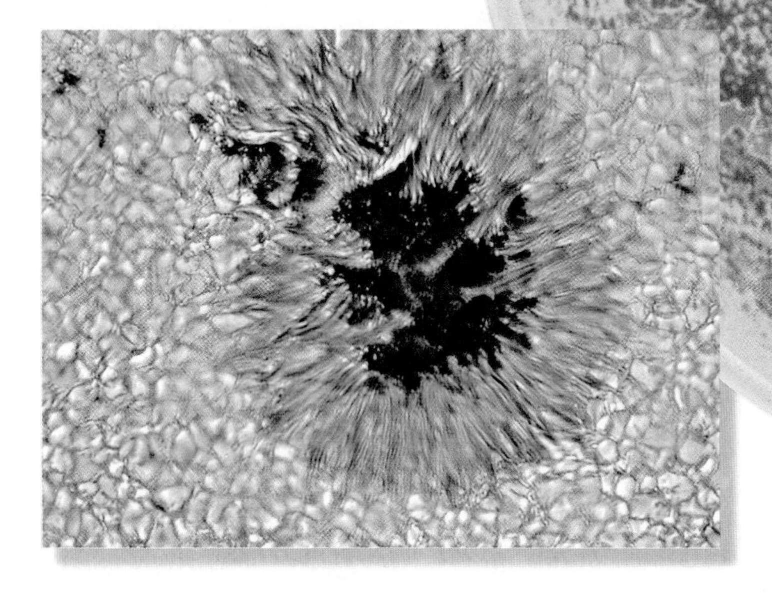

Surface Features of the Sun

Because the sun is a ball of hot gas, it's hard to imagine its surface as anything but a smooth layer. In reality, the sun's surface has many features, including sunspots, prominences, and flares.

Sunspots

Areas of the sun's surface that appear to be dark because they are cooler than surrounding areas are called **sunspots.** Ever since Galileo identified sunspots like those in **Figure 20-7,** scientists have been studying them. One thing we've learned by studying sunspots is that the sun rotates. We can observe the movement of individual sunspots as they move with the sun's rotation. The sun doesn't rotate as a solid body, as does Earth. It rotates faster at its equator than at its poles. Sunspots near the equator take about 27 days to go around the sun. At higher latitudes, they take 31 days.

Sunspots aren't permanent features on the sun. They appear and disappear over a period of several days, weeks, or months. Also, there are times when there are many large sunspots—a sunspot maximum—and times when there are only a few small sunspots or none at all—a sunspot minimum. Periods of sunspot maximum occur about every 11 years.

Prominences and Flares

Sunspots are related to several features on the sun's surface. The intense magnetic field associated with sunspots may cause prominences, which are huge arching columns of gas. Some prominences blast material from the sun into space at speeds ranging from 600 km/s to more than 1000 km/s.

Gases near a sunspot sometimes brighten up suddenly, shooting gas outward at high speed. These violent eruptions from the sun, shown in **Figure 20-8,** are called solar flares.

Ultraviolet light and X rays from solar flares can reach Earth and cause disruption of radio signals. Solar flares make communication by radio and telephone difficult at times. High-energy particles emitted by solar flares are captured by Earth's magnetic field, disrupting communication equipment. These particles also interact with Earth's atmosphere near the polar regions and create light. This light is called the aurora borealis, or northern lights, when it occurs in the northern hemisphere. In the southern hemisphere, it is called the aurora australis.

interNET CONNECTION

Visit the Glencoe Science Web Site at **www.glencoe.com/sec/science/ca** for more information about sunspots, solar flares, and prominences.

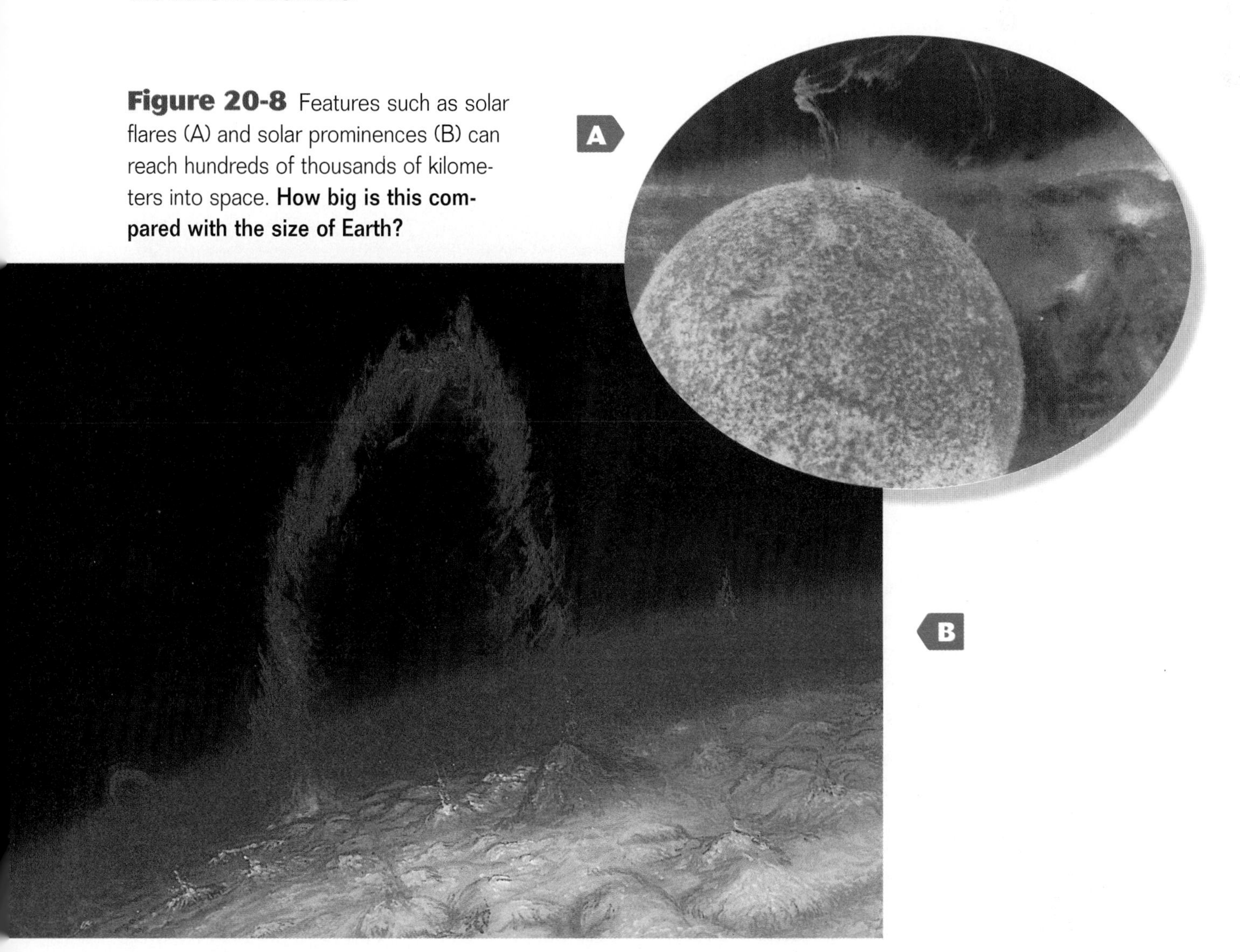

Figure 20-8 Features such as solar flares (A) and solar prominences (B) can reach hundreds of thousands of kilometers into space. **How big is this compared with the size of Earth?**

Our Sun—A Typical Star?

Figure 20-9 Pleiades is a cluster of stars that are gravitationally bound to each other.

Although our sun is an average star, it is somewhat unusual in one way. Most stars are in systems in which two or more stars orbit each other. When two stars orbit each other, they make up a **binary system.**

In some cases, astronomers can detect binary systems because one star occasionally eclipses the other. The total amount of light from the star system becomes dim and then bright again on a regular cycle. Algol in Perseus is an example of this.

In many cases, stars move through space together as a cluster. In a star cluster, many stars are relatively close to one another and are gravitationally attracted to each other. The Pleiades star cluster, shown in **Figure 20-9,** can be seen in the constellation of Taurus in the winter sky. On a clear, dark night, you may be able to see seven of the stars of this cluster. Most star clusters are far from our solar system and appear as a fuzzy patch in the night sky.

Section Assessment

1. How are sunspots, prominences, and solar flares related?
2. What properties does the sun have in common with other stars? What property makes it different from most other stars?
3. **Think Critically:** Because most stars are found in multiple-star systems, what might explain why the sun is a single star?
4. **Skill Builder**
   Interpreting Scientific Illustrations Use **Figure 20-6** to answer the questions below. If you need help, refer to Interpreting Scientific Illustrations in the **Skill Handbook** on page 962.
   a. Which layers make up the sun's atmosphere?
   b. What process occurs in the sun's convection zone that enables energy produced in the core to reach the surface?

Write a brief description in your Science Journal that explains how the sun generates energy. Hypothesize what might happen to the sun when it exhausts the supply of hydrogen in its core.

Activity 20•1

Sunspots

Sunspots are dark, relatively cool areas on the surface of the sun. They can be observed moving across the face of the sun as it rotates. Do this activity to measure the movement of sunspots, and use your data to determine the sun's period of rotation.

Materials

- Several books
- Cardboard (about 8 cm × 12 cm)
- Clipboard
- Drawing paper (5 sheets)
- Small refracting telescope
- Small tripod
- Scissors

What You'll Investigate

Can sunspot motion be used to determine the sun's period of rotation?

Goals

- **Observe** sunspots.
- **Estimate** sunspot size and rate of apparent motion.

Procedure

1. **Find** a location where the sun may be viewed at the same time of day for a minimum of five days. **CAUTION:** *Do not look directly at the sun. Do not look through the telescope at the sun. You could damage your eyes.*
2. **Set up** the telescope with the eyepiece facing away from the sun, as shown below. Align the telescope so that the shadow it casts on the ground is the smallest size possible. **Cut** and **attach** the cardboard as shown in the photo.
3. **Use** books to prop the clipboard upright. Point the eyepiece at the drawing paper.
4. If the telescope has a small finder scope attached, **remove** the finder scope or keep it covered.
5. **Move** the clipboard back and forth until you have the largest possible image of the sun on the paper. Adjust the telescope to form a clear image. **Trace** the outline of the sun on the paper.
6. **Trace** any sunspots that appear as dark areas on the sun's image. Repeat this step at the same time each day for a week.
7. Using the sun's diameter (approximately 1 390 000 km), **estimate** the size of the largest sunspots that you observed.
8. **Calculate** how many kilometers any observed sunspots appear to move each day.
9. At the rate determined in step 8, **predict** how many days it will take for the same group of sunspots to return to about the same position in which you first observed them.

Conclude and Apply

1. What was the average number of sunspots observed each day?
2. What was the estimated size and rate of apparent motion of the largest sunspots?
3. **Infer** how sunspots can be used to determine that the sun's surface is not solid like Earth's.

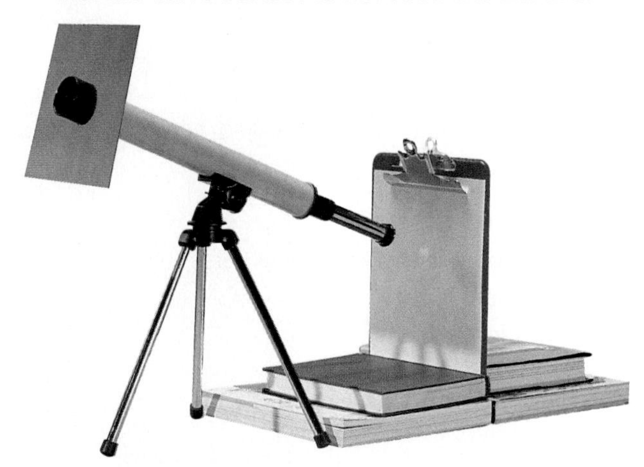

20•3 Evolution of Stars

What You'll Learn

- How stars are classified
- How the temperature of a star relates to its color
- How a star evolves

Vocabulary

main sequence, **nebula**, **giant**, **white dwarf**, **supergiant**, **neutron star**, **black hole**

Why It's Important

- The evolution of stars helps explain the theory for the evolution of the universe.

The H-R Diagram

In the early 1900s, Ejnar Hertzsprung and Henry Russell noticed that for most stars, the higher their temperatures, the brighter their absolute magnitudes. They developed a graph to show this relationship.

Hertzsprung and Russell placed the temperatures of stars across the bottom of the graph and the absolute magnitudes of stars up one side. A graph that shows the relationship of a star's temperature to its absolute magnitude is called a Hertzsprung-Russell (H-R) diagram. **Figure 20-10** shows a variation of an H-R diagram.

The Main Sequence

As you can see, stars seem to fit into specific areas of the chart. Most stars fit into a diagonal band that runs from the upper left to the lower right of the chart. This band, called the **main sequence,** contains hot, blue, bright stars in the upper left and cool, red, dim stars in the lower right. Yellow, medium-temperature, medium-brightness stars fall in between. The sun is a yellow main sequence star.

About 90 percent of all stars are main sequence stars, most of which are small, red stars found in the lower right of the H-R diagram. Among main sequence stars, the hottest stars generate the most light and the coolest generate the least. But,

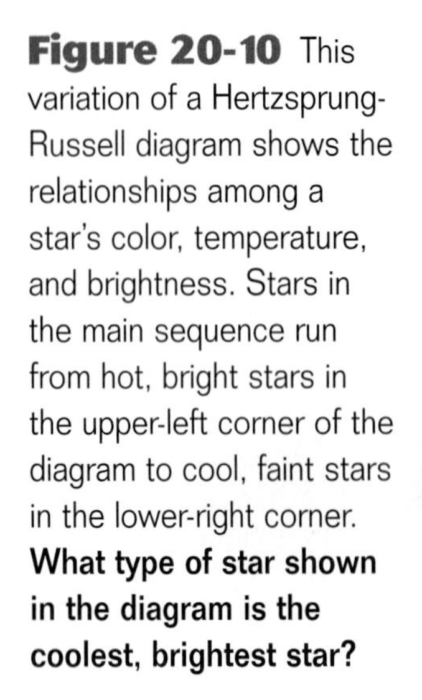

Figure 20-10 This variation of a Hertzsprung-Russell diagram shows the relationships among a star's color, temperature, and brightness. Stars in the main sequence run from hot, bright stars in the upper-left corner of the diagram to cool, faint stars in the lower-right corner. **What type of star shown in the diagram is the coolest, brightest star?**

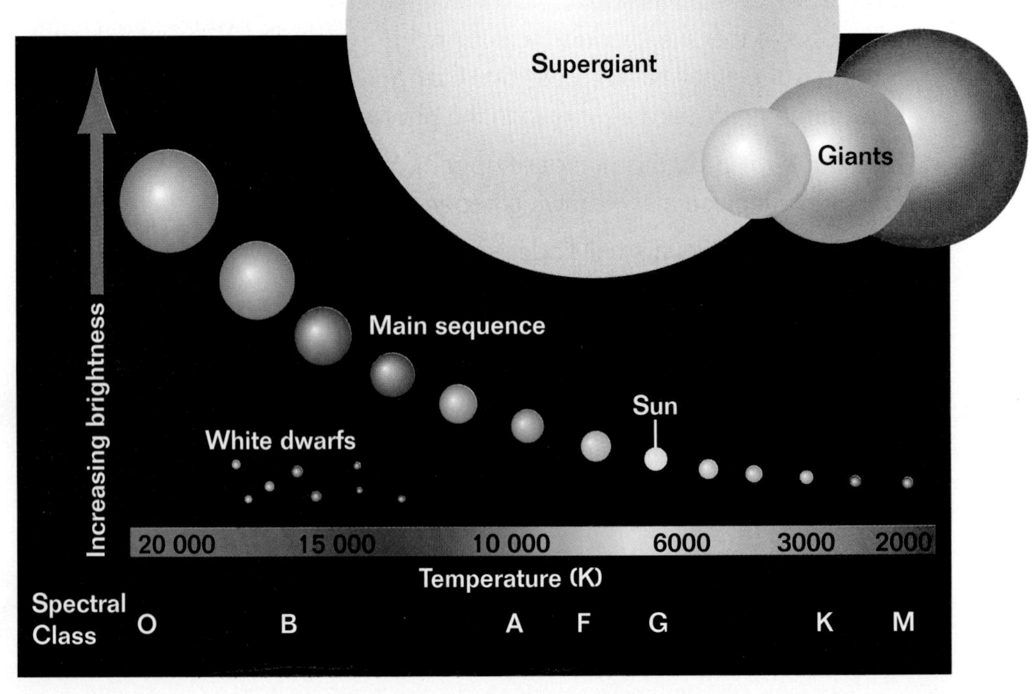

what about the remaining ten percent? Some of these stars are hot but not bright. These small stars are located on the lower left of the H-R diagram and are called white dwarfs. Other stars are extremely bright but not hot. These large stars on the upper right of the H-R diagram are called giants, or red giants because they are usually red in color. The largest giants are called supergiants. The relative sizes of stars are shown in **Figure 20-11.**

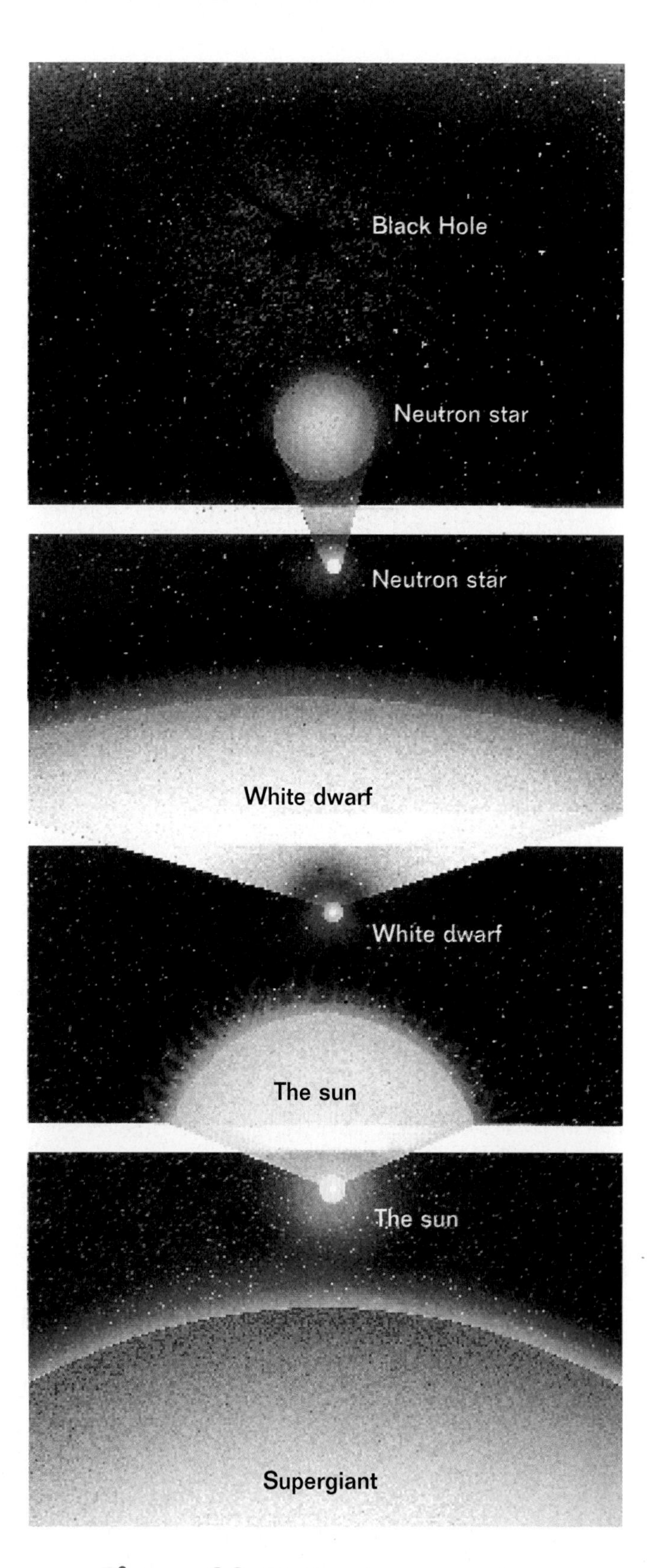

Figure 20-11 The relative sizes of stars range from supergiants as much as 800 times larger than the sun to neutron stars and black holes possibly 30 km or less across. The relative sizes of a supergiant, the sun, a white dwarf, a neutron star, and a black hole are shown.

Fusion

When the H-R diagram was developed, scientists didn't know what caused stars to shine. Hertzsprung and Russell developed their diagram without knowing what produced the light and heat of stars.

For centuries, people had been puzzled by the question of what stars were and what made them shine. It wasn't until the early part of the twentieth century that scientists began to understand how a star could shine for billions of years. Until that time, many had estimated that Earth was only a few thousand years old. The sun could have been made of coal and shined for that long. But what material could possibly burn for billions of years?

Generating Energy

In 1920, one scientist hypothesized that temperatures in the center of the sun must be high. Another scientist then suggested that with these high temperatures, hydrogen could fuse to make helium in a reaction that would release tremendous amounts of energy. **Figure 20-12** on the next page illustrates how four hydrogen nuclei could combine to create one helium nucleus. The mass of one helium nucleus is less than the mass of four hydrogen nuclei, so some mass is lost in the reaction. In the 1930s, scientists hypothesized that carbon could be used as a catalyst in fusion reactions. This explained the energy production in hotter stars.

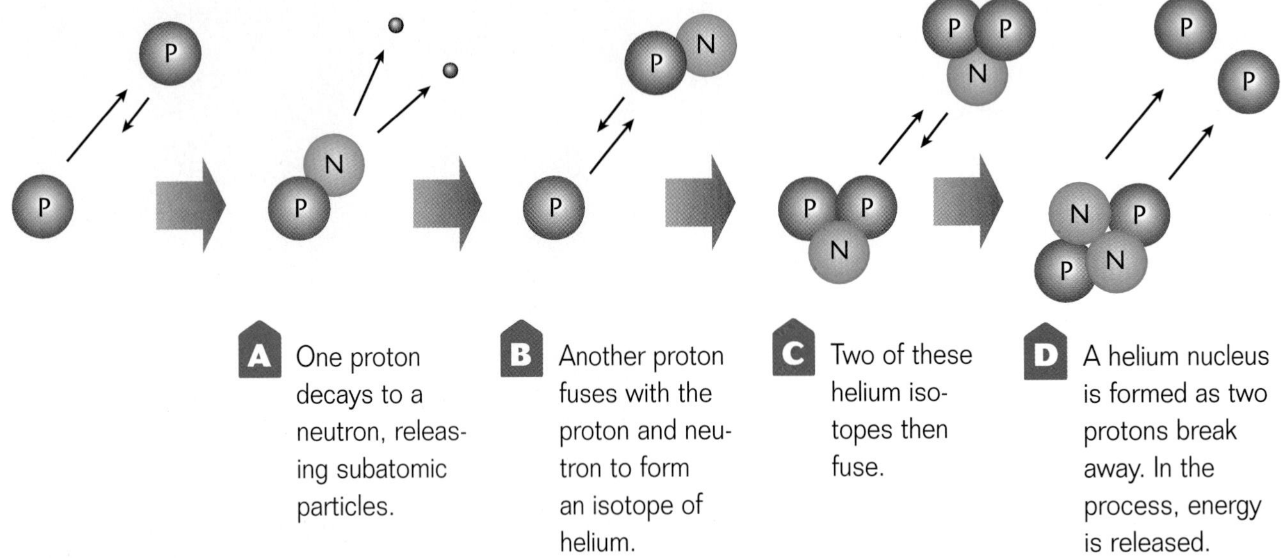

Figure 20-12 In a star's core, fusion begins as two hydrogen nuclei (protons) are forced together. **What happens to the "lost" mass during this process?**

Years earlier, in 1905, Albert Einstein had proposed a theory stating that mass can be converted into energy. This was stated as the famous equation $E = mc^2$, where E is the energy produced, m is the mass, and c is the speed of light. The small amount of mass "lost" when hydrogen atoms fuse to form a helium atom is converted to a large amount of energy.

Fusion occurs in the cores of stars. Only in the core are temperatures and pressures high enough to cause atoms to fuse. Normally, they would repel each other, but in the core of a star, atoms are forced close enough together that their nuclei fuse together.

The Evolution of Stars

The H-R diagram and other theories explained a lot about stars. But they also led to more questions. Many wondered why some stars didn't fit in the main sequence group and what happened when a star exhausted its supply of hydrogen fuel. Today, we have a theory of how stars evolve, what makes them different from one another, and what happens when they die. **Figure 20-13** illustrates the lives of different types of stars.

Nebula

Stars begin as a large cloud of gas and dust called a **nebula.** The particles of gas and dust exert a gravitational force on each other, and the nebula begins to contract. Gravitational forces cause instability within the nebula. The nebula can fragment into smaller pieces. Each will eventually collapse to form a star.

As the particles in the smaller clouds move closer together, the temperatures in each nebula increase. When temperatures inside each nebula reach 10 millionK, fusion begins. The energy released radiates outward through the condensing ball of gas. As the energy radiates into space, stars are born.

Star Spectrum
The spectrum of a star shows absorption lines of helium and hydrogen and is bright in the blue end. Describe as much as you can about the star's composition and surface temperature.

Main Sequence to Giant Stars

In the newly formed star, the heat from fusion causes pressure that balances the attraction due to gravity, and the star becomes a main sequence star. It continues to use up its hydrogen fuel.

When hydrogen in the core of the star is exhausted, there is no longer a balance between pressure and gravity. The core contracts, and temperatures inside the star increase. This causes the outer layers of the star to expand. In this late stage of its life cycle, a star is called a **giant.**

Once the core temperature reaches 100 millionK, helium nuclei fuse to form carbon in the giant's core. By this time, the star has expanded to an enormous size, and its outer layers are much cooler than they were when it was a main sequence star. In about 5 billion years, our sun will become a giant.

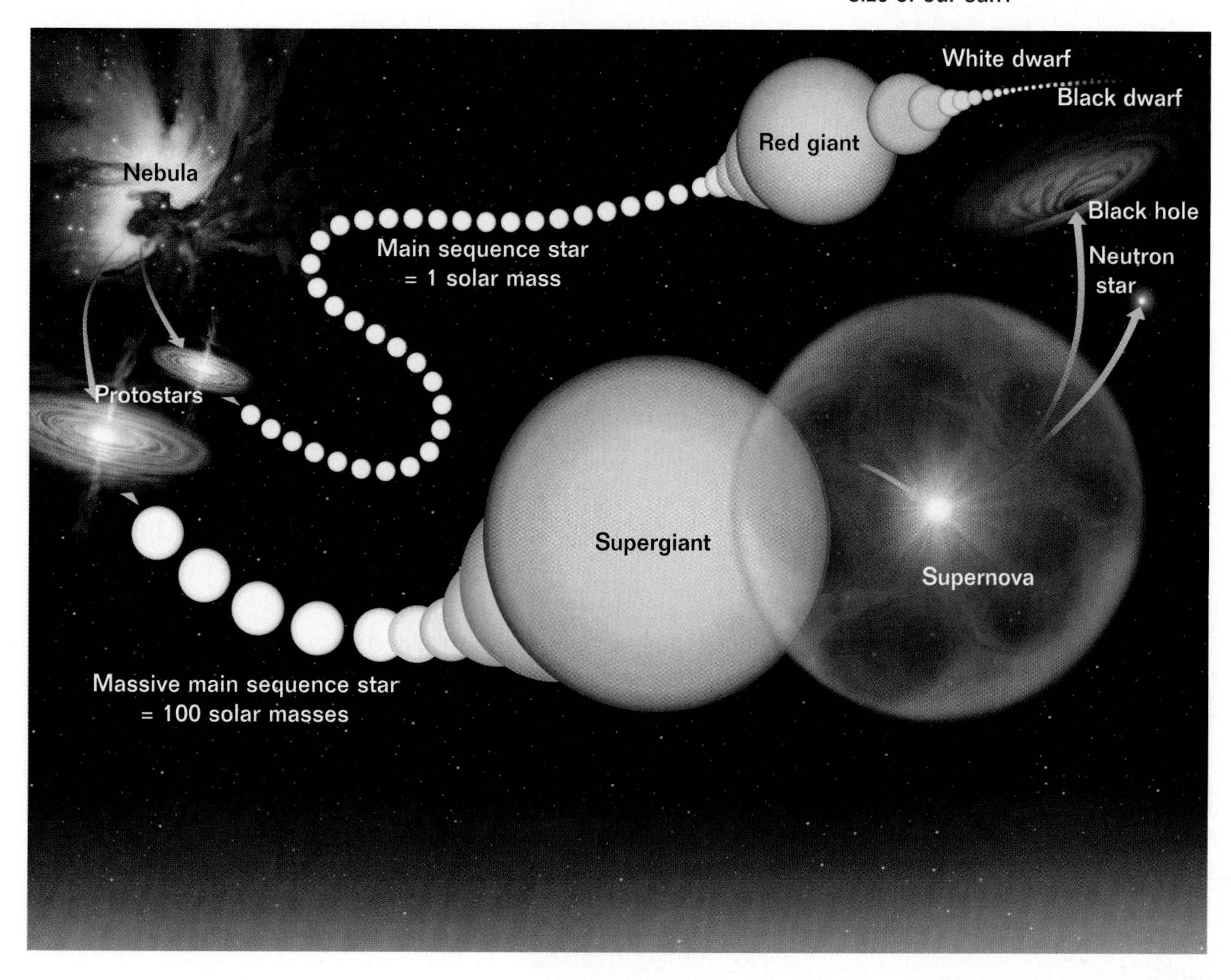

Figure 20-13 The life of a star depends greatly on its mass. Massive stars eventually become neutron stars, or possibly black holes. **What happens to stars the size of our sun?**

White Dwarfs

After the star's core uses up its supply of helium, it contracts even more. As the core of a star like the sun runs out of fuel, its outer layers escape into space. This leaves behind the hot, dense core. The core contracts under the force of gravity. At this stage in a star's evolution, it is a **white dwarf.** A white dwarf is about the size of Earth.

Supergiants and Supernovas

In stars that are over ten times more massive than our sun, the stages of evolution occur more quickly and more violently. The core heats up to much higher temperatures. Heavier and heavier elements form by fusion. The star expands into a **supergiant.** Eventually, iron forms in the core. Fusion can no longer occur once iron forms. The core collapses violently, sending a shock wave outward through the star. The outer portion of the star explodes, producing a supernova like the one shown in **Figure 20-14.** A supernova can be billions of times brighter than the original star.

Figure 20-14 This photo shows a supernova, the explosion of a star. **Explain why a supernova occurs.**

Neutron Stars

The collapsed core of a supernova shrinks to about 10 km to 15 km in diameter. Only neutrons can exist in the dense core, and the supernova becomes a **neutron star.**

If the remaining dense core is more than two times more massive than the sun, probably nothing can stop the core's collapse. It quickly evolves into a **black hole**—an object so dense that nothing can escape its gravity field.

Black Holes

If you could shine a flashlight on a black hole, the light wouldn't illuminate the black hole. The light would simply disappear into it. So, how do scientists locate black holes? Matter being pulled into a black hole can collide with other material, generating X rays. Astronomers have located X-ray sources around possible black holes. Extremely massive black holes probably exist in the centers of galaxies.

What are nebulas?

A star begins its life as a nebula, shown in **Figure 20-15.** But where does the matter in a nebula come from? Nebulas form partly from the matter that was once in other stars. A star ejects enormous amounts of matter during its lifetime. This matter can be incorporated into other nebulas, which can evolve into new stars. The matter in stars is recycled many times.

What about the matter created in the cores of stars? Are elements such as carbon and iron recycled also? Some of these elements do become parts of new stars. In fact, spectrographs have shown that our sun contains some carbon, iron, and other such elements. Because the sun is a main sequence star, it is too young to have created these elements itself. Our sun condensed from material that was created in stars that died many billions of years ago.

Figure 20-15 Stars are forming in the Crescent Nebula.

Some elements condense to form planets and other bodies rather than stars. In fact, your body contains many atoms that were fused in the cores of ancient stars. Evidence suggests that the first stars formed from hydrogen and helium and that all the other elements have formed in the cores of stars.

Section Assessment

1. Explain why giants are not in the main sequence on the H-R diagram. How do their temperatures and absolute magnitudes compare with those of main sequence stars?
2. What can be said about the absolute magnitudes of two equal-sized stars whose colors are blue and yellow?
3. Outline the history and probable future of our sun.
4. **Think Critically:** Why doesn't the helium currently in the sun's core undergo fusion?
5. **Skill Builder**
   Sequencing Sequence the following in order of most evolved to least evolved: *main sequence star, supergiant, neutron star,* and *nebula.* If you need help, refer to Sequencing in the **Skill Handbook** on page 950.

Using Math

Assume that a star's core has shrunk to a diameter of 12 km. What would be the circumference of the shrunken stellar core? Use the equation $C = \pi d$. How does this compare with the circumference of Earth with a diameter of 12 756 km?

Reading & Writing in Science

Dreamtime Down Under

The Aborigines of Australia believe that the world began long ago—before anyone can remember—when Dreamtime began. At first, Earth was cold and dark, and the spirit Ancestors slept underground.

When the Ancestors awoke, they moved to Earth's surface and created the sun for warmth and light. Some Ancestors became people. Others became plants, animals, clouds, or stars. As the Ancestors moved over Earth, they sang, and their singing created hills, rivers, and other features.

Leaving a Path

The movement of the Ancestors left Dreaming Tracks that the Aborigines still treasure. When the Ancestors tired, they returned underground. The bodies of some Ancestors remain on Earth's surface as rock outcroppings, trees, islands, and other natural features, such as the formation in the inset, below right.

Ancient Aborigines drew maps to show where the Ancestors came out, walked, and returned underground. Drawings with traditional dot patterns (see bark painting, far right) form the basis of Aboriginal art.

Dreaming the Big Bang

Some compare the Dreamtime forces that shaped Earth to the big bang theory—huge fields of energy interacting and forming planets. Later, more energy—more Dreaming—created today's continents, including Australia.

Today, Aborigines are struggling to maintain ancient traditions while living in modern Australia. They believe that the Ancestors still live in the land and that Dreamtime continues with no foreseeable end.

Science JOURNAL

In your Science Journal, write a poem that expresses your own view of our relationship to nature and to the land.

Galaxies and the Universe

20•4

Galaxies

One reason to study astronomy is to learn about your place in the universe. Long ago, people thought they were at the center of the universe and everything revolved around Earth. Today, you know this isn't the case. But, do you know where you are in the universe?

You are on Earth, and Earth orbits the sun. But does the sun orbit anything? How does it interact with other objects in the universe? The sun is one star among many in a galaxy. A **galaxy** is a large group of stars, gas, and dust held together by gravity. Our galaxy, called the Milky Way, is shown in **Figure 20-16.** It contains about 200 billion stars, including the sun. Galaxies are separated by huge distances—often millions of light-years.

Just as stars are grouped together within galaxies, galaxies are grouped into clusters. The cluster the Milky Way belongs to is called the Local Group. It contains about 30 galaxies of various types and sizes.

What You'll Learn

- The three main types of galaxies
- Several characteristics of the Milky Way Galaxy
- How the big bang theory explains the observed Doppler shifts of galaxies

Vocabulary
galaxy
big bang theory

Why It's Important

- You'll explore theories about how the universe may have formed.

Figure 20-16 The Milky Way Galaxy is usually classified as a normal spiral galaxy. Its spiral arms, composed of stars and gas, radiate out from an area of densely packed stars called the nucleus.

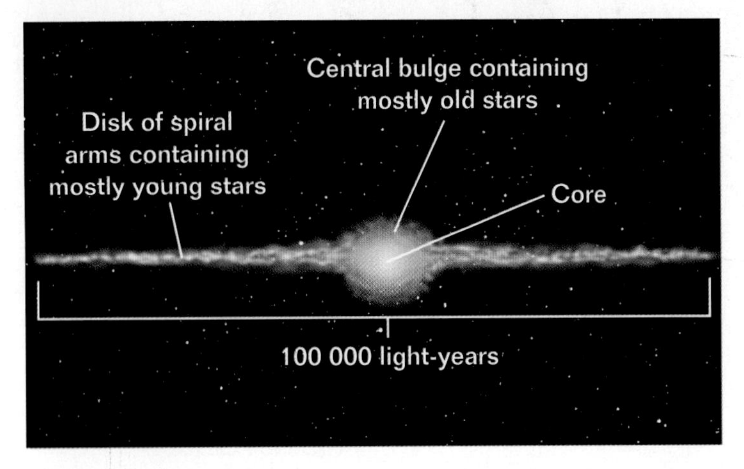

Figure 20-17 These illustrations show a side view and an overhead view of the Milky Way. **The Milky Way is part of what group of galaxies?**

Spiral Galaxies

The three major types of galaxies are elliptical, spiral, and irregular. Spiral galaxies have spiral arms that wind outward from inner regions. The Milky Way is a spiral galaxy, as shown in **Figure 20-17.** Its spiral arms are made up of bright stars and dust. The fuzzy patch you can see in the constellation of Andromeda is actually a spiral galaxy. It's so far away that you can't see its individual stars. Instead, it appears as a hazy spot in our sky. The Andromeda Galaxy is a member of the Local Group. It is about 2.2 million light-years away.

Arms in a normal spiral start close to the center of the galaxy. Barred spirals have spiral arms extending from a large bar of stars and gas that passes through the center of the galaxy.

Elliptical Galaxies

Probably the most common type of galaxy is the elliptical galaxy, shown in **Figure 20-18.** These galaxies are shaped like large, three-dimensional ellipses. Many are football-shaped, but others are round. Some elliptical galaxies are small, while some are so large that the entire Local Group of galaxies would fit inside one of them. **Figure 20-19** shows the Local Group and its relation to the solar system, the Milky Way, and large galaxy clusters.

Figure 20-18 This photo shows an example of an elliptical galaxy. **What are the two other types of galaxies?**

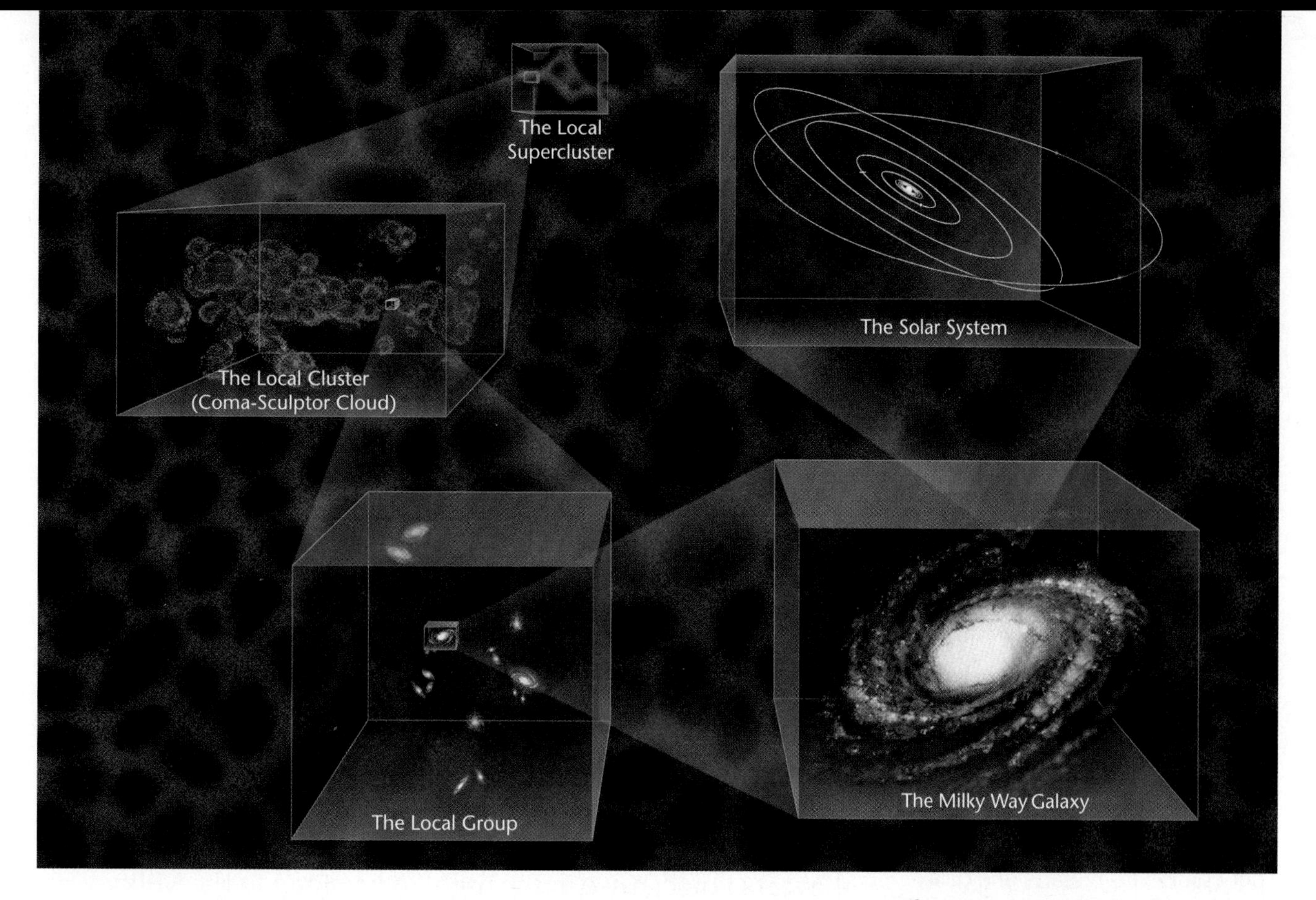

Figure 20-19 There may be more than 100 billion galaxies in the universe, and nearly all of them seem to be organized into clusters.

Irregular Galaxies

The third type of galaxy, irregular, includes most of those galaxies that don't fit into the other classifications. Irregular galaxies have many different shapes and are smaller and less common than the other types. Two irregular galaxies called the Clouds of Magellan orbit the Milky Way. The Large Magellanic Cloud is shown in **Figure 20-20.**

Figure 20-20 The Large Magellanic Cloud is an irregular galaxy. It's a member of the Local Group, and it orbits our own galaxy.

The Milky Way Galaxy

The Milky Way contains more than 200 billion stars. The visible disk of stars is about 100 000 light-years across, and the sun is located about 30 000 light-years out from its center. In our galaxy, all stars orbit around a central region. Based on a distance of 30 000 light-years and a speed of 235 km/s, the sun orbits around the center of the Milky Way once every 240 million years.

The Milky Way is usually classified as a normal spiral galaxy. However, recent evidence suggests that it might be a barred spiral. It is difficult to know for sure because we can never see our galaxy from the outside.

You can't see the normal spiral or barred shape of the Milky Way because you are

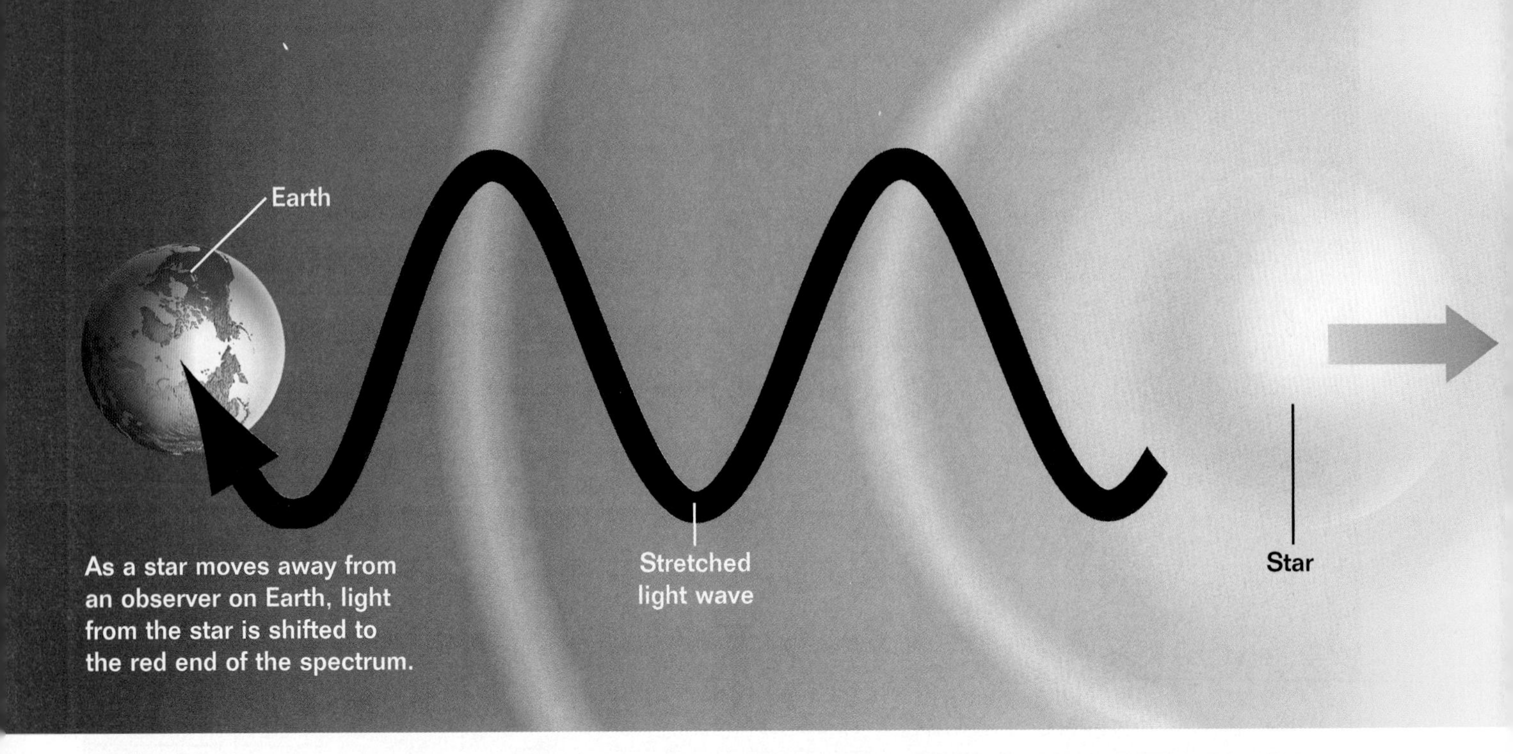

Figure 20-21 The Doppler shift causes the wavelengths of light coming from starts and galaxies to be compressed or stretched.

located within one of its spiral arms. You can see the Milky Way stretching across the sky as a faint band of light. All of the stars you can see in the night sky belong to the Milky Way Galaxy.

Measuring Distance in Space

Procedure

1. On a large sheet of paper, draw an overhead view of the Milky Way Galaxy. If necessary, refer to **Figure 20-17.** Choose a scale to show distance in light-years.
2. Mark the approximate location of our solar system, about two-thirds of the way out on one of the spiral arms.
3. Draw a circle around the sun indicating the 4.2 light-year distance of the next closest star to the sun, Proxima Centauri.

Analysis

1. What scale did you use to represent distance on your model?
2. At this scale, interpret how far away the next closest spiral galaxy—the Andromeda Galaxy—would be located.

Expansion of the Universe

What does it sound like when a car is blowing its horn while it drives past you? The horn has a high pitch as the car approaches you, then the horn seems to drop in pitch as the car drives away. This effect is called the Doppler shift. The Doppler shift occurs with light as well as with sound. **Figure 20-21** shows how the Doppler shift causes changes in the light coming from distant stars and galaxies. If a star is moving toward us, its wavelengths of light are pushed together. If a star is moving away from us, its wavelengths of light are stretched.

The Doppler Shift

Look at the spectrum of a star in **Figure 20-22A.** Note the position of the dark lines. How do they compare with the lines in **Figures 20-22B** and **C?** They have shifted in position. What caused this shift? As you just learned, when a star is moving toward Earth, its wavelengths of light are

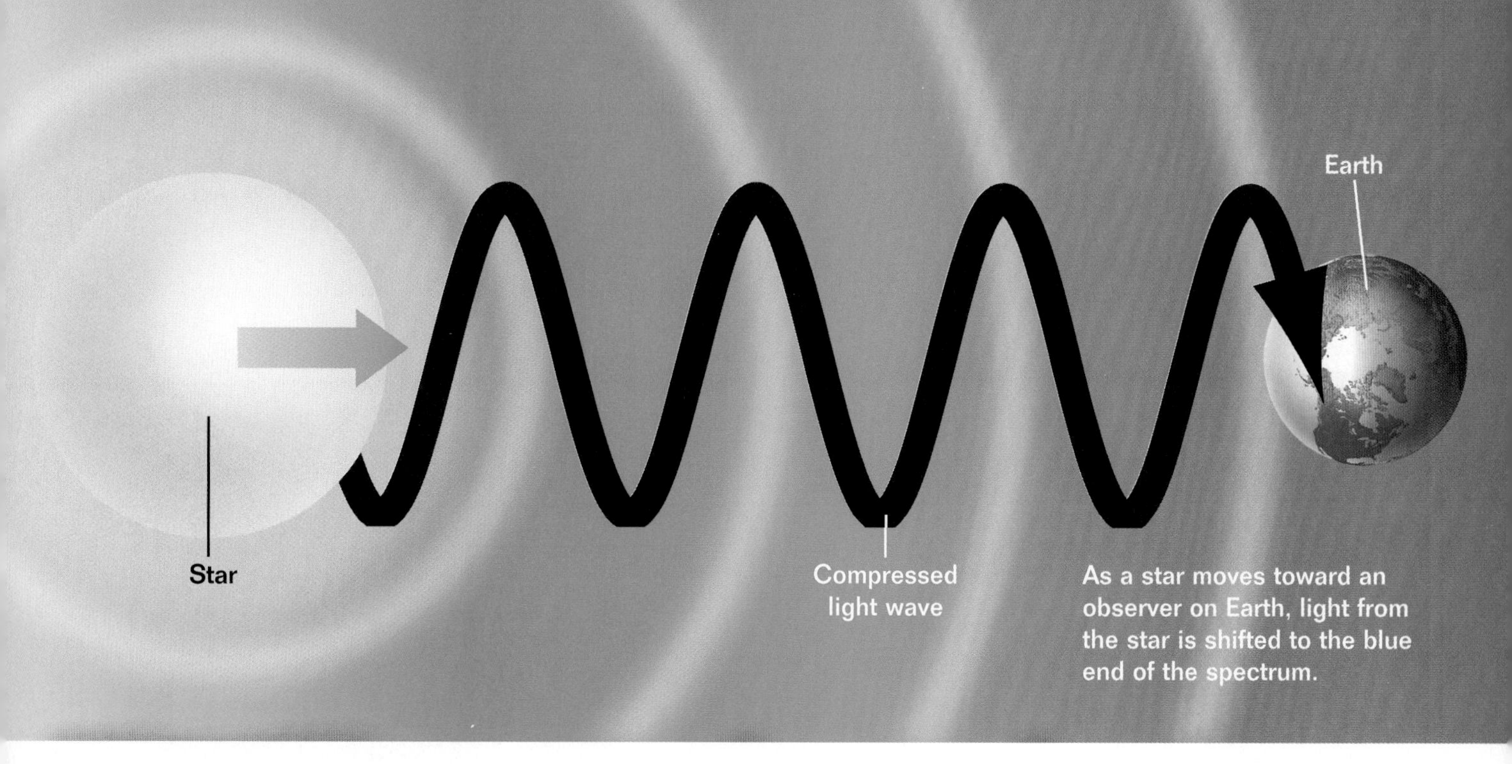

pushed together, just as the sound waves from the car's horn are. This causes the dark lines in the spectrum to shift toward the blue-violet end of the spectrum. A red shift in the spectrum occurs when a star is moving away from Earth. In a red shift, the dark lines shift toward the red end of the spectrum.

In the early twentieth century, scientists noticed an interesting fact about the light coming from most galaxies. When a spectrograph is used to study light from galaxies beyond the Local Group, there is a red shift in the light. What does this red shift tell you about the universe?

Because all galaxies beyond the Local Group show a red shift in their spectra, they must be moving away from Earth. If all galaxies outside the Local Group are moving away from Earth, this indicates that the entire universe must be expanding. Think of the Explore Activity at the beginning of the chapter. The dots on the balloon moved apart as the model universe expanded. Regardless of which dot you picked, all the other dots moved away from it. Galaxies beyond the Local Group move away from us just as the dots moved apart on the balloon.

Visit the Glencoe Science Web Site at **www.glencoe.com/sec/science/ca** for more information about the Doppler shift.

Figure 20-22 The dark lines in the spectra (A) are shifted toward the blue-violet end when a star is moving toward Earth (B). A red shift (C) indicates that a star is moving away from Earth.

VISUALIZING The Big Bang Theory

Figure 20-23 The universe probably began billions of years ago with a fiery explosion.

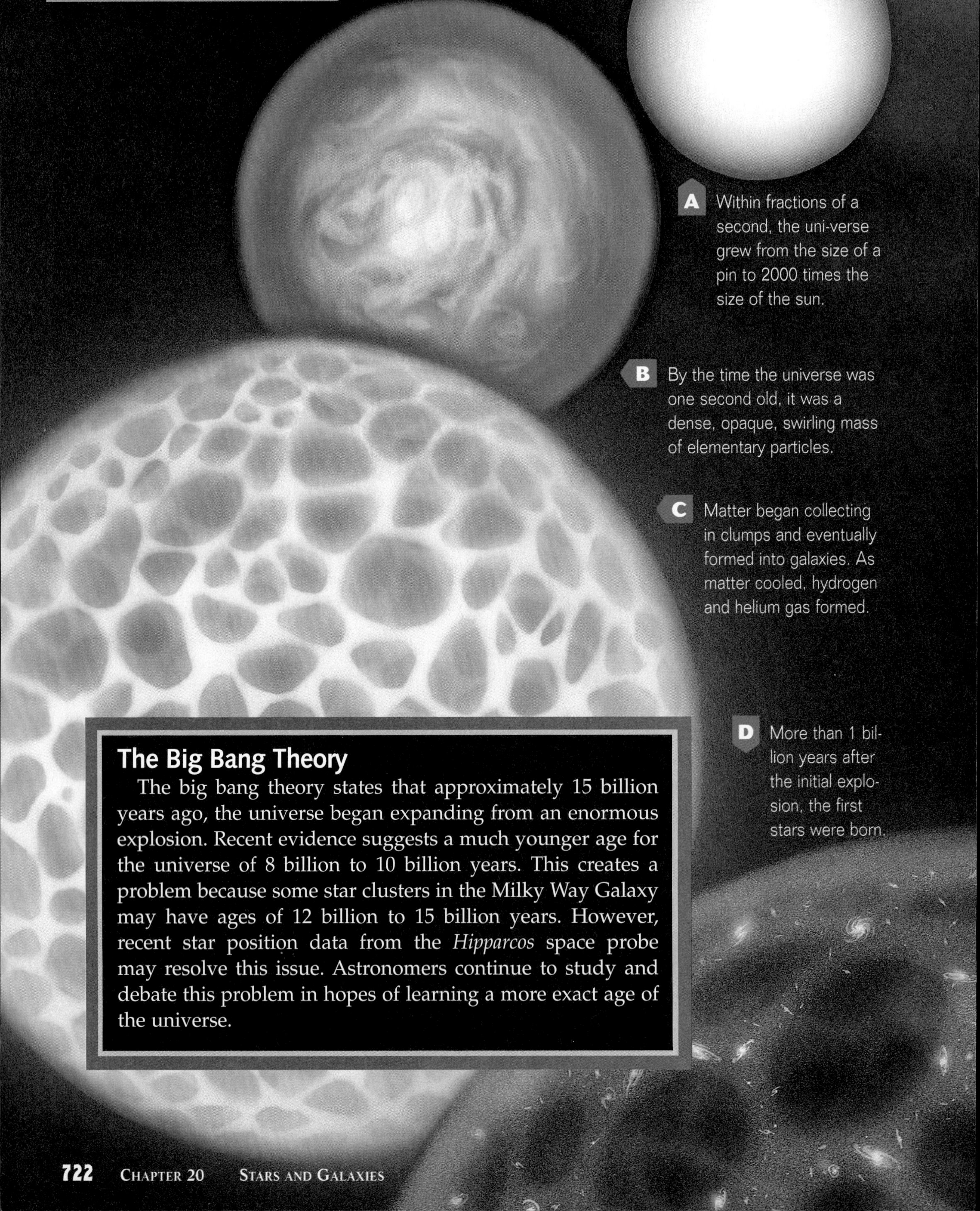

A Within fractions of a second, the uni-verse grew from the size of a pin to 2000 times the size of the sun.

B By the time the universe was one second old, it was a dense, opaque, swirling mass of elementary particles.

C Matter began collecting in clumps and eventually formed into galaxies. As matter cooled, hydrogen and helium gas formed.

D More than 1 billion years after the initial explosion, the first stars were born.

The Big Bang Theory

The big bang theory states that approximately 15 billion years ago, the universe began expanding from an enormous explosion. Recent evidence suggests a much younger age for the universe of 8 billion to 10 billion years. This creates a problem because some star clusters in the Milky Way Galaxy may have ages of 12 billion to 15 billion years. However, recent star position data from the *Hipparcos* space probe may resolve this issue. Astronomers continue to study and debate this problem in hopes of learning a more exact age of the universe.

The Big Bang Theory

When scientists determined that the universe was expanding, they realized that galaxy clusters must have been closer together in the past. The leading theory about the formation of the universe, called the big bang theory, is based on this explanation. **Figure 20-23** illustrates the **big bang theory,** which states that approximately 15 billion years ago, the universe began with an enormous explosion.

The time-lapse photograph shown in **Figure 20-24** was taken in December 1995 by the *Hubble Space Telescope*. It shows more than 1500 galaxies at a distance of more than 10 billion light-years. These galaxies may date back to when the universe was no more than 1 billion years old. The galaxies are in various stages of development. One astronomer indicates that we may be looking back to a time when our own galaxy was forming. Studies of this nature will eventually enable astronomers to determine the approximate age of the universe.

Whether the universe expands forever or stops depends on how much matter is in the universe. All matter exerts a gravitational force. If there's enough matter, gravity will halt the expansion, and the universe will contract until everything comes to one point.

Figure 20-24 The light from these galaxies in this photo mosaic took billions of years to reach Earth.

Section Assessment

1. List the three major classifications of galaxies. What do they have in common?
2. What is the name of the galaxy that you live in? What motion do the stars in this galaxy exhibit?
3. **Think Critically:** All galaxies outside the Local Group show a red shift in their spectra. Within the Local Group, some galaxies show a red shift and some show a blue shift. What does this tell you about the galaxies in the Local Group and outside the Local Group?
4. **Skill Builder**
   Predicting Astronomical distances are measured in light-years, the distance light travels in one year. It takes light from the star Betelgeuse 310 light-years to reach Earth. Do the **Chapter 20 Skill Activity** on page 981 to predict what was happening on Earth when light from distant stars began traveling toward our solar system.

Research and write a report in your Science Journal about the most recent evidence supporting or disputing the big bang theory. Describe how the big bang theory explains observations of galaxies made with spectrometers.

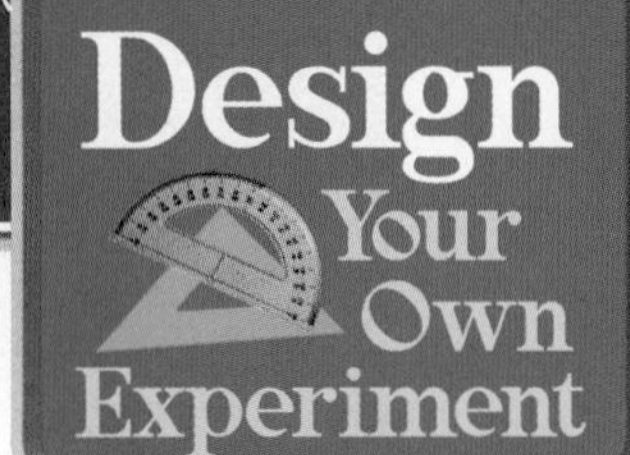

Activity 20•2

Measuring Parallax

Possible Materials

- Meterstick
- Metric ruler
- Masking tape
- Pencil

Parallax is the apparent shift in the position of an object when viewed from two locations. The nearer an object is to the observer, the greater its parallax. Do this activity to design a model and use it in an experiment that will show how distance affects the amount of observed parallax.

Recognize the Problem

How can you build a model to show the relationship between distance and parallax?

Form a Hypothesis

State a hypothesis about how a model must be built in order for it to be used in an experiment to show how distance affects the amount of observed parallax.

Goals

- **Design a model** to show how the distance from an observer to an object affects the object's parallax shift.
- **Design an experiment** that shows how distance affects the amount of observed parallax.

Safety Precautions

CAUTION: *Be sure to wear goggles to protect your eyes.*

Test Your Hypothesis

Plan

1. As a group, agree upon and write out your hypothesis statement.
2. List the steps that you need to take to build your model. Be specific, describing exactly what you will do at each step.
3. Devise a method to test how distance from an observer to an object, such as a pencil, affects the relative position of the object.
4. List the steps you will take to test your hypothesis. Be specific, describing exactly what you will do at each step.
5. Read over your plan for the model to be used in this experiment.
6. How will you determine changes in observed parallax? Remember, these changes should occur when the distance from the observer to the object is changed.
7. You should measure shifts in parallax from several different positions. How will these positions differ?
8. How will you measure distances accurately and compare relative position shift?

Do

1. Make sure your teacher approves your plan before you proceed.
2. Construct the model your team has planned.
3. Carry out the experiment as planned.
4. While conducting the experiment, write down any observations that you or other members of your group make in your Science Journal.

Analyze Your Data

1. **Compare** what happened to the object when it was viewed with one eye closed, then the other.
2. At what distance from the observer did the object appear to shift the most?

Draw Conclusions

1. **Infer** what happened to the apparent shift of the object's location as the distance from the observer was increased or decreased.
2. How might astronomers use parallax to study stars?

FIELD GUIDE to Backyard Astronomy

FIELD ACTIVITY

Study the star maps included in this field guide. Each night for a week, about one hour after sundown, observe the stars and identify at least three constellations. Draw and label the constellations in your Science Journal. Then, using the key of constellations visible in the northern hemisphere, make drawings of the objects, animals, or characters your constellations represent.

To help them study the night sky, early astronomers developed ways to organize stars into recognizable patterns. We call these patterns constellations. Think of constellations as drawings in the sky. They represent objects, animals, or characters in stories—things that were familiar to ancient stargazers. Using this field guide, you can observe the stars year-round.

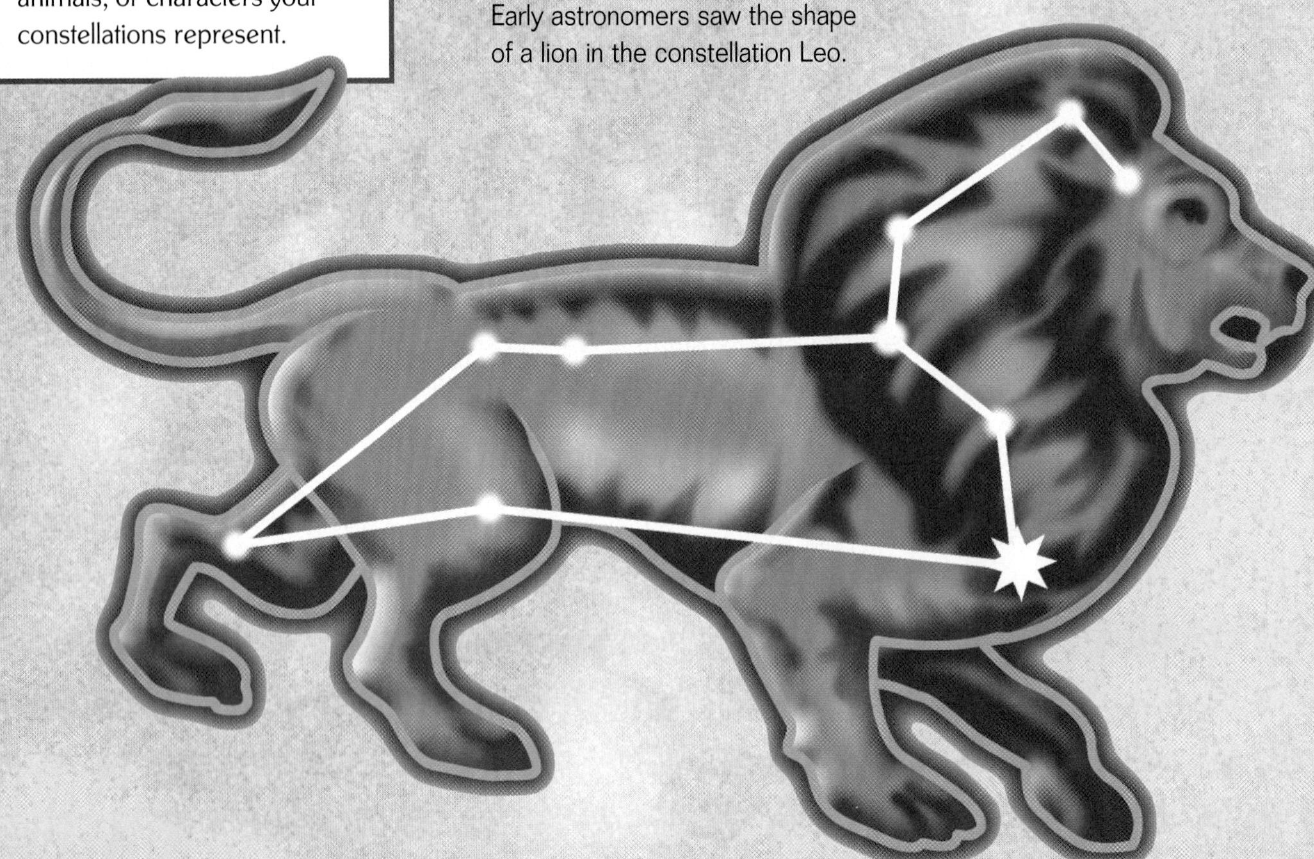

Early astronomers saw the shape of a lion in the constellation Leo.

Major Constellations Visible in the Northern Hemisphere

Name	Represents	Name	Represents
Andromeda	Princess	Lyra	Harp
Aquila	Eagle	Orion	Hunter
Bootes	Herdsman	Pegasus	Winged Horse
Canis Major	Big Dog	Sagittarius	Archer
Canis Minor	Little Dog	Scorpius	Scorpion
Cygnus	Swan (Northern Cross)	Taurus	Bull
Gemini	Twins	Ursa Major	Great Bear (Big Dipper)
Hercules	Hercules	Ursa Minor	Little Bear (Little Dipper)
Leo	Lion	Virgo	Virgin (Maiden)

This map shows the constellations that appear to circle the North Star, also known as Polaris. Because these constellations appear to circle Polaris, which is located almost directly over the north pole, they are called circumpolar constellations. Look toward the north to locate these constellations. To orient yourself, first locate Polaris, which is found by looking directly north, then up at an angle of roughly 35° to 45°.

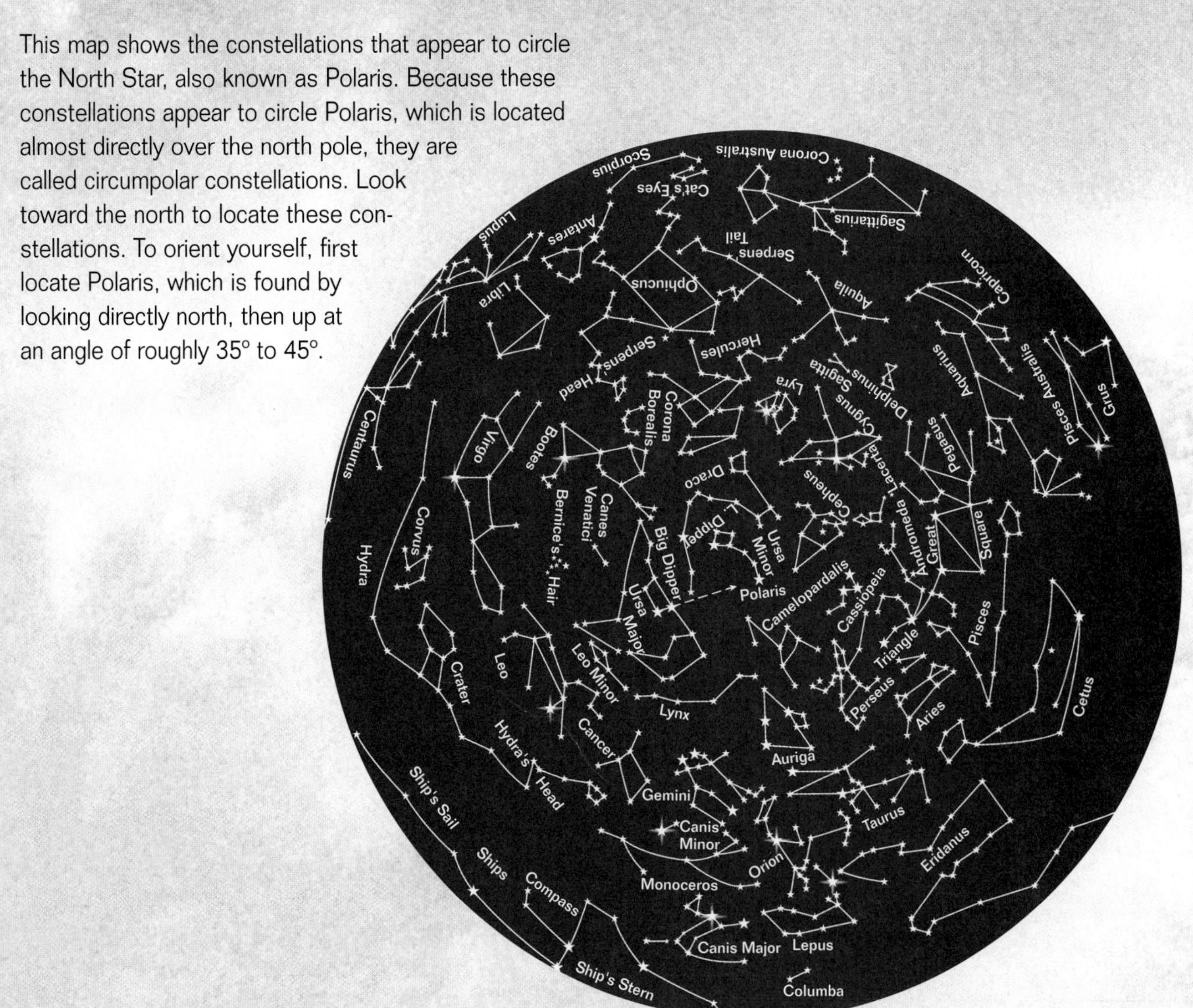

Different constellations are visible during different seasons, so this guide includes four star maps—one for each season. Choose the correct seasonal map, and face south. Hold the sky map above you, with the north part of the map pointing north (behind you). Look toward the southern sky between your zenith (the highest point above you) and the horizon to locate these constellations.

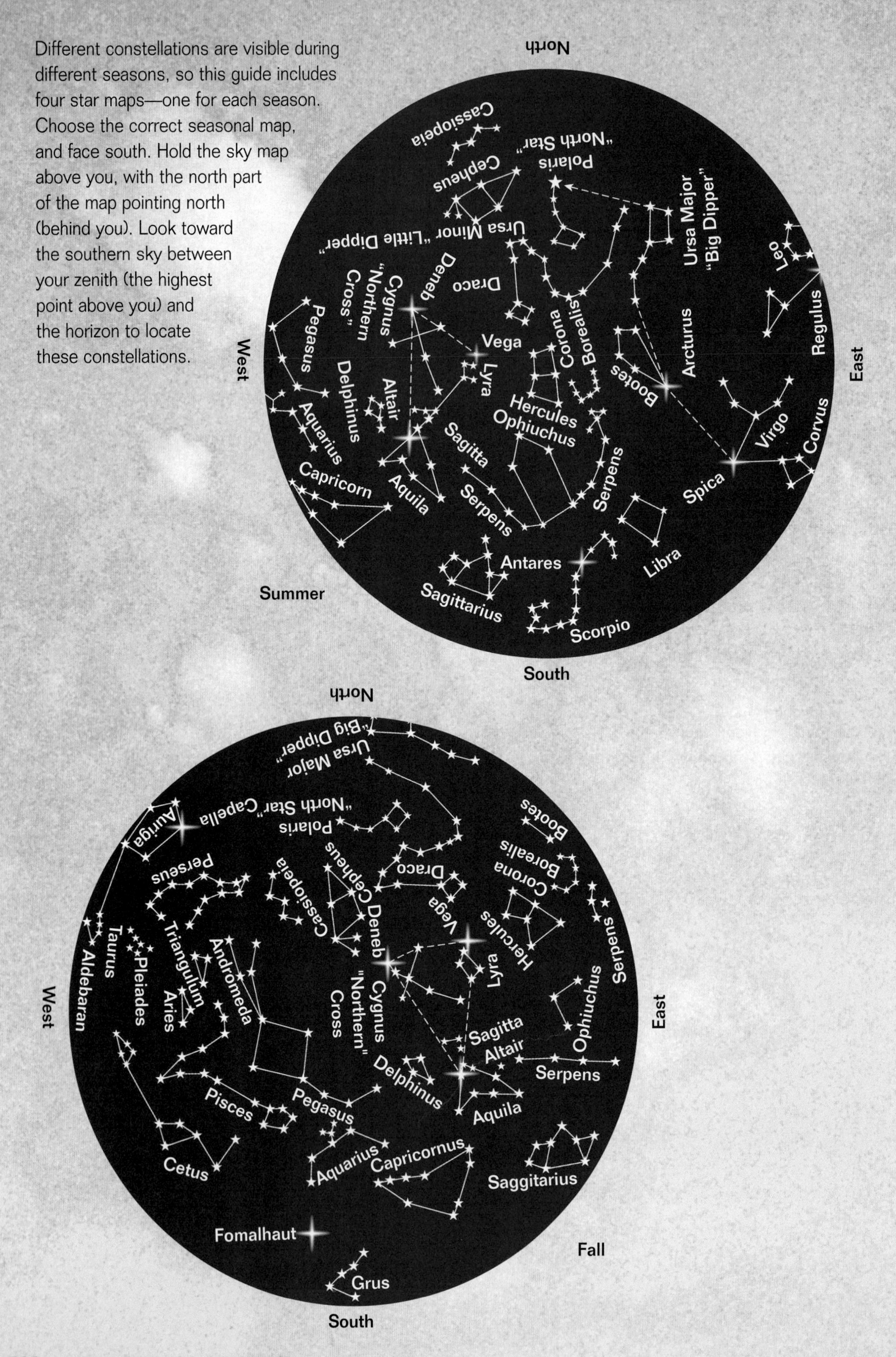

FIELD•GUIDE•FIELD•GUIDE•FIELD•GUIDE•FIELD•GUIDE•FIELD

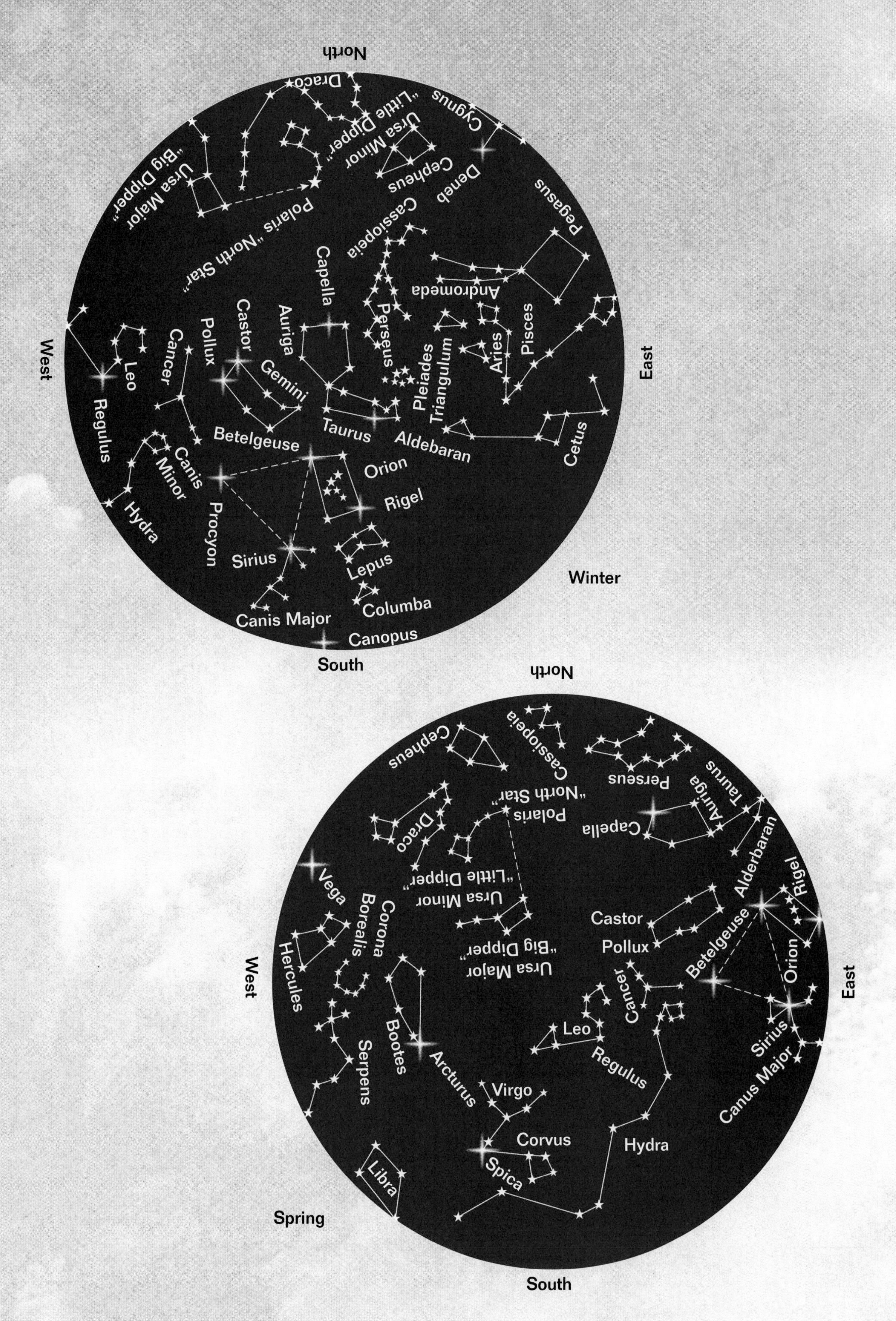
North
West
East
South
Winter
Draco
Cygnus
"Little Dipper"
Ursa Minor
Ursa Major
"Big Dipper"
Cepheus
Deneb
Pegasus
Polaris "North Star"
Cassiopeia
Capella
Andromeda
Castor
Auriga
Perseus
Pollux
Cancer
Leo
Gemini
Pleiades
Triangulum
Aries
Pisces
Regulus
Betelgeuse
Taurus
Aldebaran
Cetus
Canis Minor
Orion
Rigel
Hydra
Procyon
Sirius
Lepus
Columba
Canis Major
Canopus
North
West
East
South
Spring
Cepheus
Cassiopeia
Perseus
Polaris "North Star"
Taurus
Auriga
Capella
Draco
Vega
"Little Dipper"
Ursa Minor
Alderbaran
Rigel
Corona Borealis
Castor
Hercules
"Big Dipper"
Ursa Major
Pollux
Betelgeuse
Orion
Cancer
Leo
Bootes
Serpens
Arcturus
Regulus
Sirius
Canus Major
Virgo
Corvus
Hydra
Spica
Libra

FIELD•GUIDE•FIELD•GUIDE•FIELD•GUIDE•FIELD•GUIDE•FIELD•GUIDE•FIE

Chapter 20 Reviewing Main Ideas

For a **preview** of this chapter, study this Reviewing Main Ideas before you read the chapter. After you have studied this chapter, you can use the Reviewing Main Ideas to **review** the chapter.

The Glencoe MindJogger, Audiocassettes, and CD-ROM provide additional opportunities for review.

Section 20-1 STARS

The magnitude of a star is a measure of the star's brightness. **Absolute magnitude** is a measure of the light emitted. **Apparent magnitude** is a measure of the amount of light received on Earth. **Parallax** is the apparent shift in the position of an object when viewed from two different positions. The closer to Earth a star is, the greater its shift in parallax. A star's temperature and composition can be determined from the star's spectrum. ***What term describes how bright a star looks from Earth?***

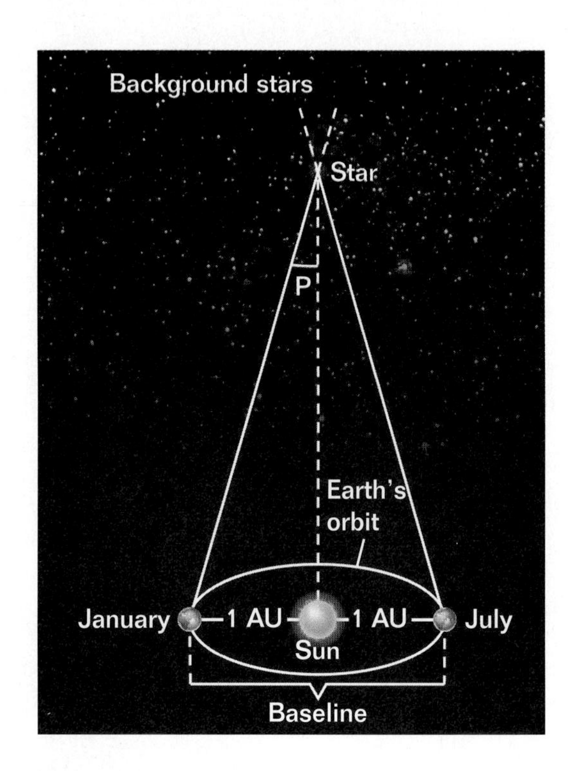

Section 20-2 THE SUN

The sun produces energy by fusing hydrogen into helium in its core. Light is given off from the photosphere, which is the lowest layer of the sun's atmosphere. **Sunspots** are areas of the sun that are cooler and less bright than surrounding areas. Sunspots, prominences, and flares are caused by the intense magnetic field of the sun, which is a main sequence star. ***Why is the sun considered an average star?***

Reading Check

The big bang theory is still controversial. What part of this theory is supported by evidence? What part is opinion?

Section 20-3 EVOLUTION OF STARS

When hydrogen is used up in a **main sequence** star, the star's core collapses and its temperature increases. The star becomes a **giant** or a **supergiant,** which uses helium as fuel. As the star evolves, its outer layers escape into space and the star becomes a **white dwarf.** Stars containing high amounts of mass can explode. During a supernova explosion, the outer layers of a star are blown away and the remaining core evolves into a **neutron star** or **black hole.** ***At what temperature does fusion begin inside a nebula?***

Section 20-4 GALAXIES AND THE UNIVERSE

A **galaxy** is a large group of stars, gas, and dust held together by gravity. Galaxies can be elliptical, spiral, or irregular in shape. The galaxy that our sun belongs to, the Milky Way, contains about 200 billion stars. There may be more than 100 billion galaxies in the universe. The most accepted theory about the origin of the universe is the **big bang theory.** ***What is the Local Group of galaxies?***

Chapter 20 Assessment

Using Vocabulary

a. absolute magnitude
b. apparent magnitude
c. big bang theory
d. binary system
e. black hole
f. chromosphere
g. constellation
h. corona
i. galaxy
j. giant
k. light-year
l. main sequence
m. nebula
n. neutron star
o. parallax
p. photosphere
q. sunspot
r. supergiant
s. white dwarf

Explain the differences in the terms given below. Then explain how the terms are related.

1. absolute magnitude, apparent magnitude
2. black hole, neutron star
3. chromosphere, photosphere
4. binary system, constellation
5. light-year, parallax

Checking Concepts

Choose the word or phrase that best answers the question.

6. What do constellations form?
   A) clusters
   B) giants
   C) black holes
   D) patterns
7. What is a measure of the amount of a star's light received on Earth?
   A) absolute magnitude
   B) apparent magnitude
   C) fusion
   D) parallax
8. What increases as an object comes closer to an observer?
   A) absolute magnitude
   B) red shift
   C) parallax
   D) size
9. What begins once a nebula contracts and temperatures increase to 10 millionK?
   A) main sequencing
   B) a supernova
   C) fusion
   D) a white dwarf
10. What is about 10 km in size?
    A) giant
    B) white dwarf
    C) black hole
    D) neutron star
11. Our sun fuses hydrogen into what?
    A) carbon
    B) oxygen
    C) iron
    D) helium
12. What are loops of matter flowing from the sun?
    A) sunspots
    B) auroras
    C) coronas
    D) prominences
13. What are groups of galaxies called?
    A) clusters
    B) supergiants
    C) giants
    D) binary systems
14. Which galaxies are sometimes shaped like footballs?
    A) spiral
    B) elliptical
    C) barred
    D) irregular
15. What do scientists study to determine shifts in wavelengths of light?
    A) spectrum
    B) surface
    C) corona
    D) chromosphere

Thinking Critically

16. What is significant about the 1995 discovery by the *Hubble Space Telescope* of more than 1500 galaxies at a distance of more than 10 billion light-years?
17. How do scientists know that black holes exist if these objects don't emit any visible light?
18. Use the autumn star chart in Appendix K to determine which constellation is directly overhead at 8 P.M. on November 23 for an observer in North America.
19. How are radio waves used to detect objects in space?
20. What kinds of reactions produce the energy emitted by stars?

Developing Skills

If you need help, refer to the Skill Handbook.

21. **Concept Mapping:** Complete the concept map on this page that shows the evolution of a main sequence star with a mass similar to that of the sun.

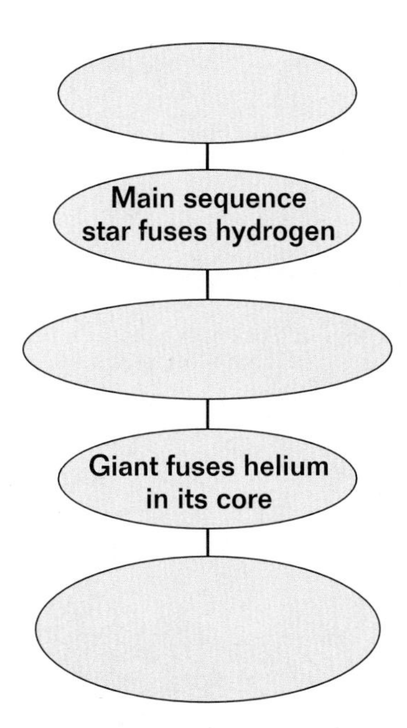

22. **Comparing and Contrasting:** Compare and contrast the sun with other stars on the H-R diagram.
23. **Measuring in SI:** The Milky Way Galaxy is 100 000 light-years in diameter. What scale would you use if you were to construct a model of the Milky Way with a diameter of 20 cm?
24. **Designing an Experiment:** Design and carry out an experiment that uses sunspot locations to compare rotational periods of different latitudes of the sun.
25. **Making a Model:** Design and construct scale models of a spiral and a barred spiral Milky Way Galaxy. Show the approximate position of the sun in each.

Test-Taking Tip

Read the Label No matter how many times you've taken a particular test or practiced for an exam, it's always a good idea to skim through the instructions provided at the beginning of each section.

Test Practice

Use these questions to test your Science Proficiency.

1. A white dwarf star is located in the lower-left-hand corner of an H-R diagram. Which of the following statements **BEST** explains why it is positioned there?
   A) White dwarf stars have low absolute magnitudes and high surface temperatures.
   B) White dwarf stars have low absolute magnitudes and low surface temperatures.
   C) White dwarf stars have high absolute magnitudes and high surface temperatures.
   D) White dwarf stars have high absolute magnitudes and low surface temperatures.
2. Sunspots are dark areas of the sun's surface. Which of the following statements **BEST** explains why this is true?
   A) Sunspots are areas of the sun's surface that do not give off light.
   B) Sunspots appear dark because they give off more energy than surrounding areas of the sun's surface.
   C) Sunspots are hotter than surrounding areas of the sun's surface.
   D) Sunspots are cooler than surrounding areas of the sun's surface.

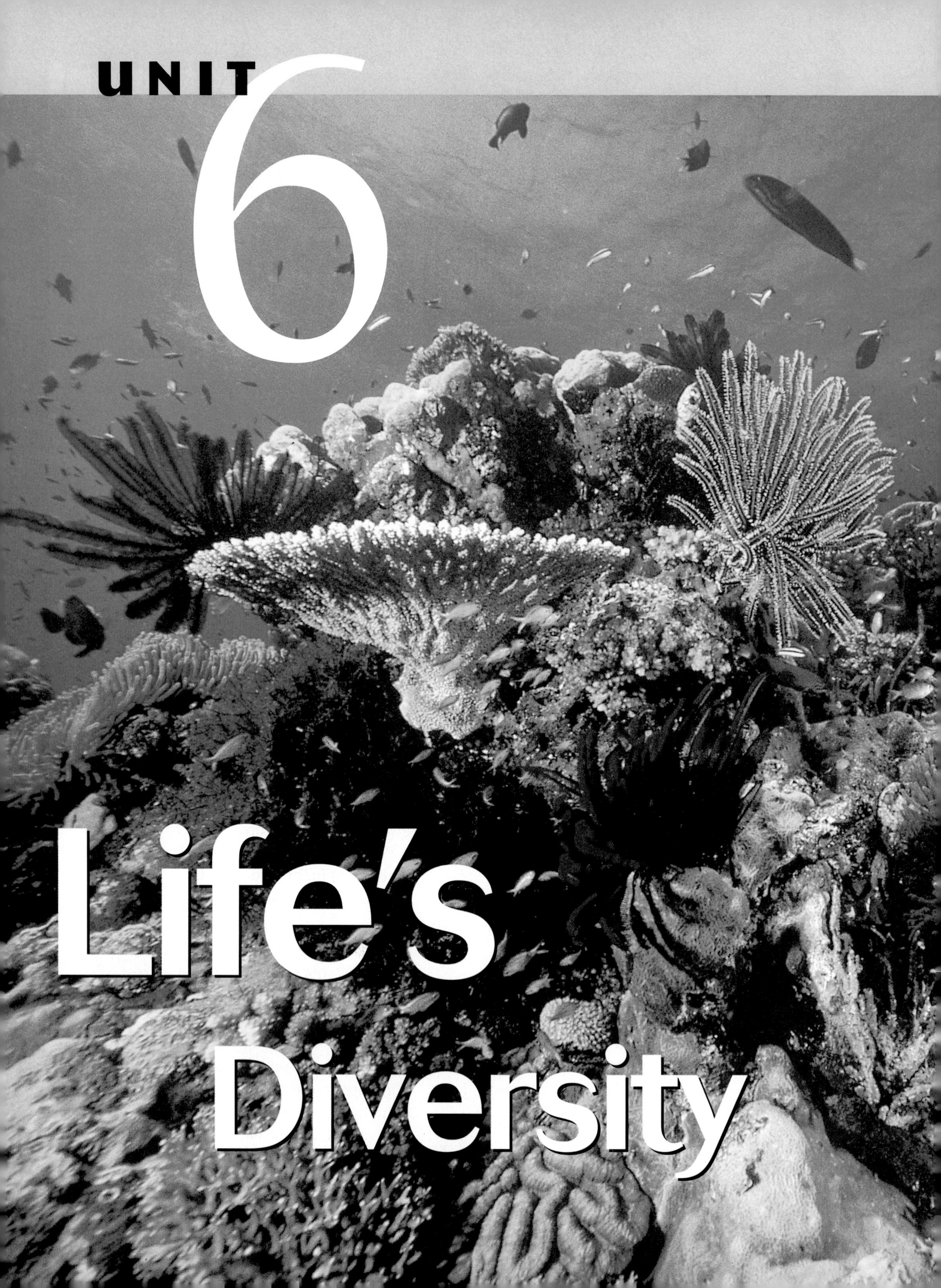

UNIT 6

Life's Diversity

NATIONAL GEOGRAPHIC

What's Happening Here?

In the shallow, sunlit waters between 30 degrees north and south of the equator are the rain forests of the ocean—coral reefs. Hundreds of species of organisms live in marine communities like this one (left) in the Bismarck Sea off New Britain Island, Papua New Guinea. Coral itself is an animal, although it stays put all its life. It belongs to the same phylum as jellyfish, which float freely in the current. Why is coral considered an animal and not a plant? How is it similar to jellyfish? These are some of the questions you will answer as you learn about life's diverse forms. You will also learn about forms of life that are difficult to pigeonhole. Some thrive in the world's most hostile places, such as this Morning Glory Pool (below) in Yellowstone's Upper Geyser Basin. Here, boiling springs bring to the surface minerals that nourish algae and bacteria and tint the formations in pastel colors.

interNET CONNECTION

Explore the Glencoe Science Web Site at **www.glencoe.com/sec/science/ca** to find out more about topics found in this unit.

CHAPTER 21 Bacteria

Chapter Preview

Section 21-1
Two Kingdoms of Bacteria

Section 21-2
Bacteria in Your Life

Skills Preview

Skill Builders

- Hypothesize
- Map Concepts

Activities

- Design an Experiment
- Organize Data

MiniLabs

- Recognize Cause and Effect
- Infer

Reading Check

As you read this chapter, find out the differences among the meanings of the prefixes *a-*, *anti-*, and *ana-*. List and define two words that begin with each prefix.

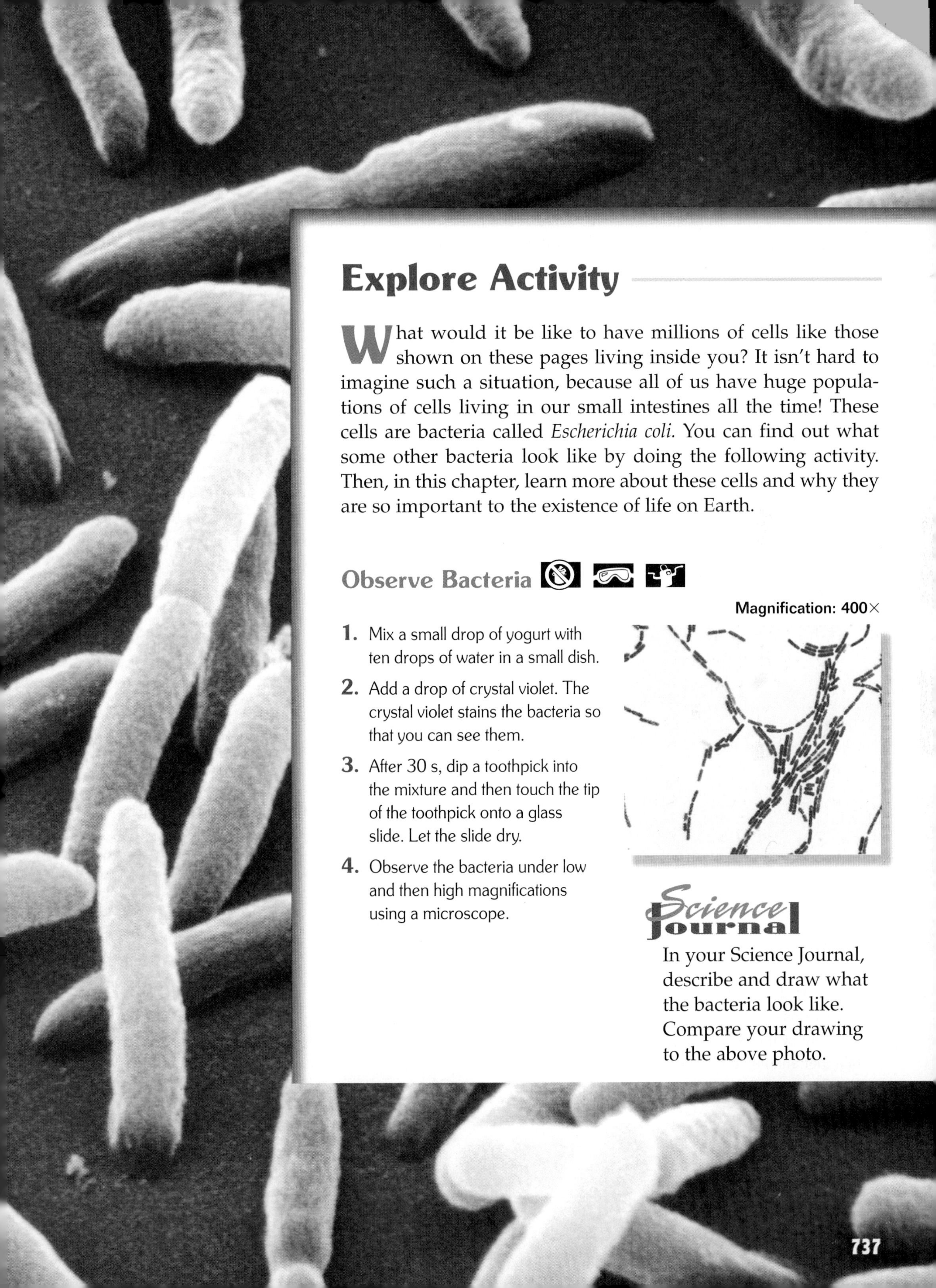

Explore Activity

What would it be like to have millions of cells like those shown on these pages living inside you? It isn't hard to imagine such a situation, because all of us have huge populations of cells living in our small intestines all the time! These cells are bacteria called *Escherichia coli*. You can find out what some other bacteria look like by doing the following activity. Then, in this chapter, learn more about these cells and why they are so important to the existence of life on Earth.

Observe Bacteria

1. Mix a small drop of yogurt with ten drops of water in a small dish.
2. Add a drop of crystal violet. The crystal violet stains the bacteria so that you can see them.
3. After 30 s, dip a toothpick into the mixture and then touch the tip of the toothpick onto a glass slide. Let the slide dry.
4. Observe the bacteria under low and then high magnifications using a microscope.

Magnification: 400×

Science Journal

In your Science Journal, describe and draw what the bacteria look like. Compare your drawing to the above photo.

21•1 Two Kingdoms of Bacteria

What You'll Learn

- The characteristics of bacterial cells
- The differences between aerobic and anaerobic organisms

Vocabulary

flagella	aerobe
fission	anaerobe

Why It's Important

- Bacteria are found in all environments. They affect all living things.

What are bacteria?

When most people hear the word *bacteria,* they probably associate it with sore throats or other illnesses. However, very few bacteria cause illness. Most are important for other reasons. Bacteria are almost everywhere—in the air you breathe, the food you eat, the water you drink, and even at great ocean depths. A shovelful of soil contains billions of them. Millions of bacteria live on and in your body. Many are beneficial to you.

There are two types of cells—prokaryotic and eukaryotic. Bacteria are prokaryotes because they have no true nucleus. The nuclear material of a bacterial cell is made up of one or more circular chromosomes. Bacteria have cell walls and cell membranes and also contain ribosomes. Structures inside bacterial cells are not surrounded by membranes.

Types of Bacteria

Bacteria are grouped into two kingdoms—eubacteria (yoo bak TIHR ee uh) and archaebacteria (ar kee bak TIHR ee uh). Some eubacteria, such as the cyanobacteria in **Figure 21-1,** contain chlorophyll, which enables them to make their own food. They obtain their energy from the sun by photosynthesis. Most eubacteria do not make their own food. Some break down dead organisms to obtain energy. Others live as parasites and absorb nutrients from living organisms. Archaebacteria live in habitats where few organisms can live and obtain energy in other ways.

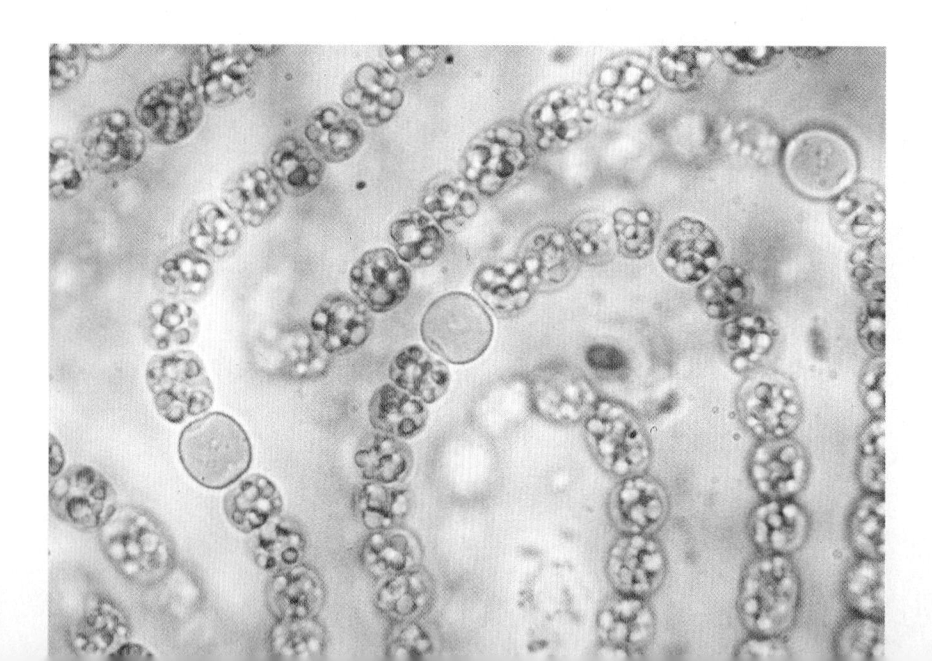

Figure 21-1 These cyanobacteria make their own food. **What do cyanobacteria contain that enables them to make food?**

Magnification: 1250×

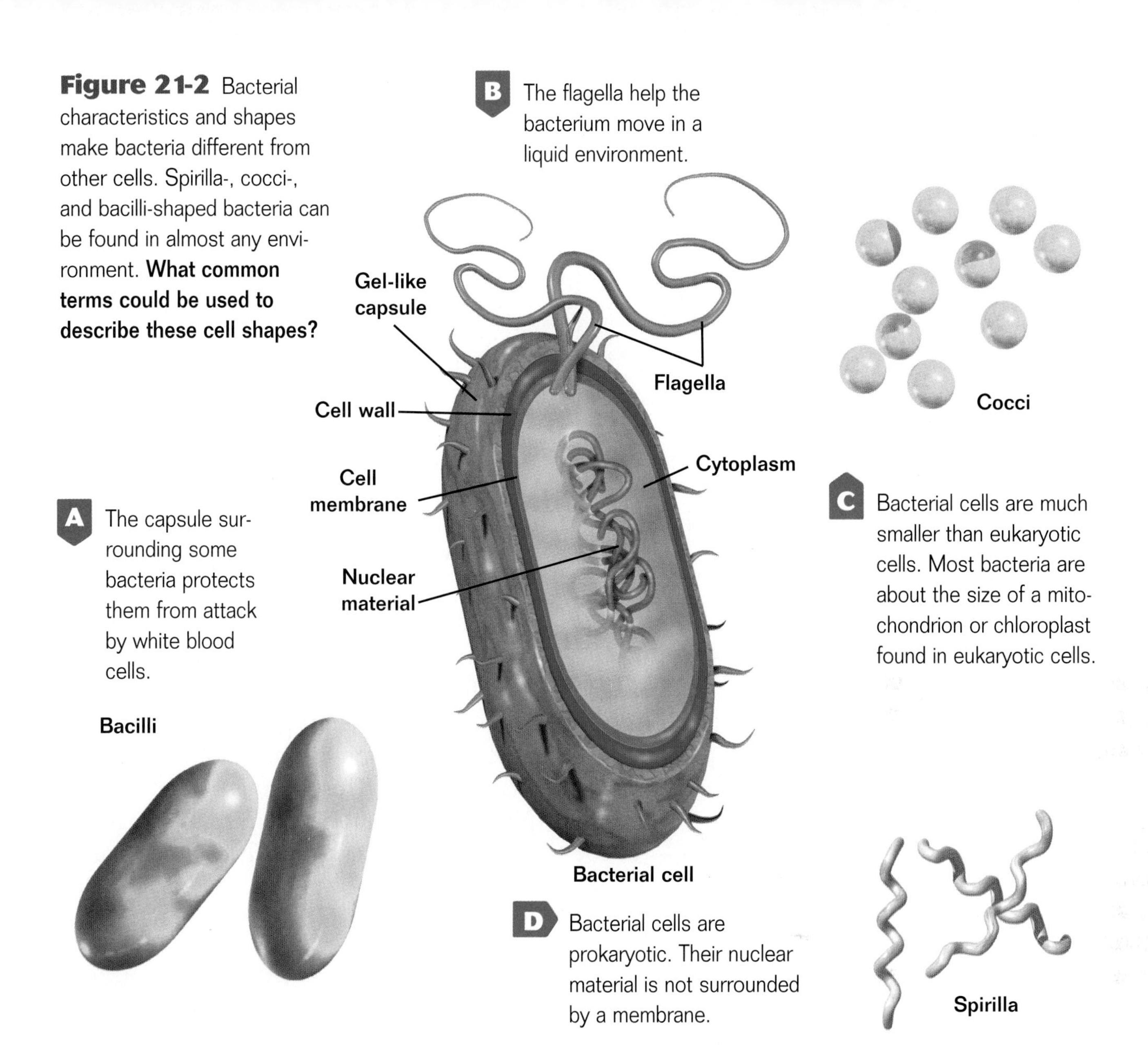

Figure 21-2 Bacterial characteristics and shapes make bacteria different from other cells. Spirilla-, cocci-, and bacilli-shaped bacteria can be found in almost any environment. **What common terms could be used to describe these cell shapes?**

A The capsule surrounding some bacteria protects them from attack by white blood cells.

B The flagella help the bacterium move in a liquid environment.

C Bacterial cells are much smaller than eukaryotic cells. Most bacteria are about the size of a mitochondrion or chloroplast found in eukaryotic cells.

D Bacterial cells are prokaryotic. Their nuclear material is not surrounded by a membrane.

Bacterial Shapes

The bacteria that normally inhabit your home and body have three basic shapes—spheres, rods, and spirals. Sphere-shaped bacteria are called *cocci* (sing. *coccus*), rod-shaped bacteria are called *bacilli* (sing. *bacillus*), and spiral-shaped bacteria are called *spirilla* (sing. *spirillum*). The general characteristics of bacteria can be seen in the bacillus shown in **Figure 21-2.** It contains cytoplasm surrounded by a cell membrane and wall. Bacterial chromosomes are not located in a membrane-bound nucleus but are found in the cytoplasm. Some bacteria have a thick, gel-like capsule around the cell wall. The capsule helps the bacterium stick to surfaces. How does a capsule help a bacterium to survive?

Many bacteria float freely in the environment on air and water currents, your hands, your shoes, and even the family dog or cat. Many that live in moist conditions have whiplike tails called **flagella** to help them move.

Observing Bacterial Growth

Procedure   

1. Obtain two or three dried beans.
2. Break them into halves and place the halves into 10 mL of distilled water in a glass beaker.
3. Observe how many days it takes for the water to become cloudy and develop an unpleasant odor.
4. Use methylene blue to dye a drop of water from the beaker and observe it under the microscope.

Analysis

1. How long did it take for the water to become cloudy?
2. What did you observe on the slide that would make the water cloudy?
3. What do you think the bacteria were feeding on?

Eubacteria

Eubacteria is the larger of the two bacterial kingdoms. It contains so many organisms that it is hard to classify. All bacteria except archaebacteria, which you will learn about later in this chapter, are considered to be eubacteria, or "true bacteria." These organisms live in much less harsh environments than archaebacteria. As illustrated in **Figure 21-3,** eubacteria include many diverse groups, from species that live off other organisms to those that can make their own food.

Cyanobacteria

One type of eubacteria is known as cyanobacteria. Cyanobacteria are eubacteria that are producers. They make their own food using carbon dioxide, water, and energy from sunlight. Cyanobacteria contain chlorophyll and another pigment that is blue. This pigment combination gives cyanobacteria their common name, blue-green bacteria. However, some cyanobacteria are yellow, black, or red. The Red Sea gets its name from red cyanobacteria.

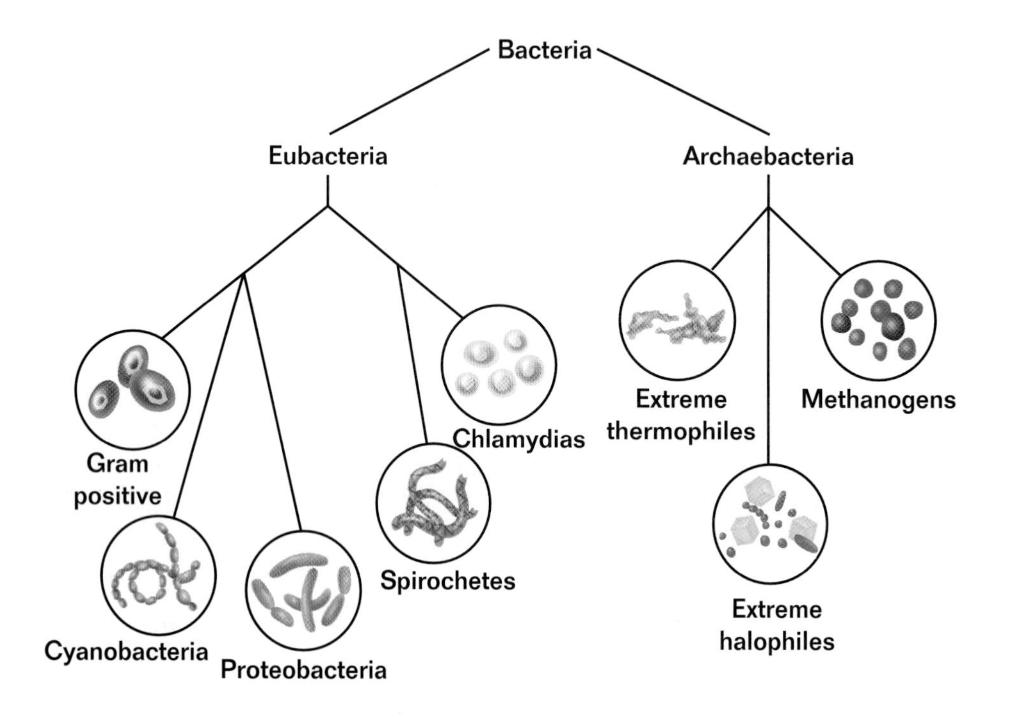

Figure 21-3 Bacteria are divided into two main groups—archaebacteria and eubacteria. **Which group contains the largest variety of organisms?**

All species of cyanobacteria are one-celled organisms. However, some of these organisms live together in long chains or filaments. Look again at **Figure 21-1.** Many are covered with a gel-like substance. This adaptation enables cyanobacteria to live in globular groups called colonies. Cyanobacteria are important for food production in lakes and ponds. Since cyanobacteria make food from carbon dioxide, water, and the energy from sunlight, fish in a healthy pond can eat them and use the energy released from that food.

Have you ever seen a pond covered with smelly, green, bubbly slime? When large amounts of nutrients enter a pond, cyanobacteria and various algae increase in number and produce a matlike growth called a bloom. Available resources are quickly consumed and the cyanobacteria and various algae die. Bacteria feed on them and use up all the oxygen in the water. As a result, fish and other organisms die.

Using Math

Figure 21-4 shows a bacterium that is dividing into two cells. Measure the length of one of the new cells in millimeters. Determine the actual size of the cell by dividing the measured length by the magnification.

Problem Solving

Controlling Bacterial Growth

Bacteria may be controlled by slowing their growth, preventing their growth, or killing them. When trying to control bacteria that affect humans, it is often desirable to slow just their growth because substances that prevent bacteria from growing or that kill bacteria may harm humans. For example, bleach often is used to kill bacteria in bathrooms or on kitchen surfaces, but it is poisonous if swallowed. Antiseptic is the word used to describe substances that slow the growth of bacteria. Advertisers often claim that a substance kills bacteria, when in fact, the substance only slows the bacteria's growth. Many mouthwash advertisements, however, make this claim. How could you test several mouthwashes to see which one is the best antiseptic?

Solve the Problem

1. Choose three mouthwashes and describe an experiment that you could do to find the best antiseptic mouthwash of the three.
2. What controls would you use in your experiment?

Think Critically: Read the ingredients label on one of the bottles of mouthwash. List the ingredients in the mouthwash. What ingredient do you think is the antiseptic? Explain you answer.

Figure 21-4 In this color-enhanced electron micrograph, a bacterium is shown undergoing fission.

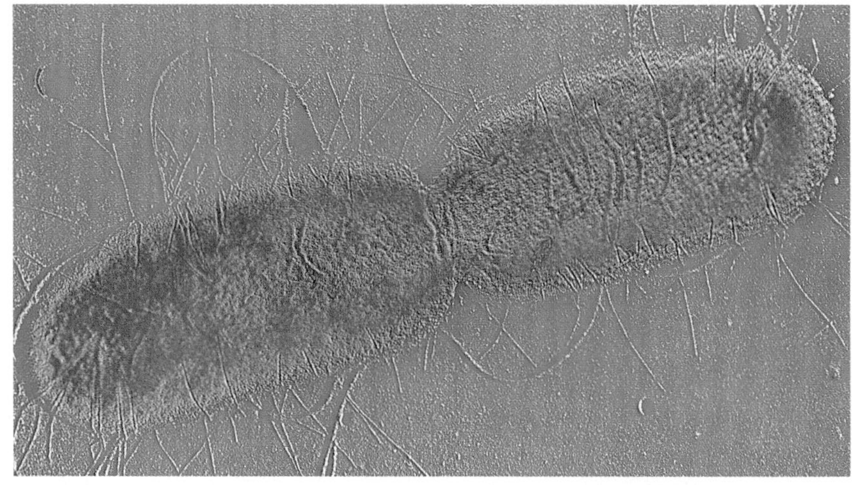

Magnification: 14 400×

Reproduction

Bacteria reproduce by fission, as shown in **Figure 21-4.** **Fission** produces two cells with genetic material identical to that of the parent cell. It is the simplest form of asexual cell reproduction. Some bacteria exchange genetic material through a process similar to sexual reproduction. Two bacteria line up beside each other and exchange DNA through a fine tube. This results in cells with different genetic material than their parents. As a result, the bacteria may have variations that give them an advantage for surviving in changing environments.

Most bacteria live in places where there is a supply of oxygen. An organism that uses oxygen for respiration is called an **aerobe** (AY rohb). You are an aerobic organism. In contrast, some organisms, called **anaerobes** (AN uh rohbz), have variations that allow them to live without oxygen.

Figure 21-5 Bacteria that live in mineral hot springs like Morning Glory Pool, shown below, are anaerobes. **What problems would bacteria have to overcome to live in conditions such as these?**

Archaebacteria

Kingdom Archaebacteria contains certain kinds of anaerobic bacteria, which, like eubacteria, are thought to have existed for billions of years. They are found in extreme conditions, such as the hot springs shown in **Figure 21-5,** salty lakes, muddy swamps, the intestines of cattle, and near deep ocean vents where life exists without sunlight. The conditions in which archaebacteria live today may resemble conditions found on early Earth.

Archaebacteria are divided into three groups, based on how they get energy. There are methanogens, halophiles, and thermophiles. The methanogens use carbon dioxide for energy and produce the methane gas that bubbles up out of swamps and marshes. The extreme halophiles live in salty environments such as the Great Salt Lake in Utah and the Dead Sea. Some of them require a habitat ten times saltier than seawater to grow. The last group of archaebacteria is the extreme thermophiles that survive in hot areas like the one shown in **Figure 21-6.**

Figure 21-6 Thermophiles get energy by breaking down sulfur compounds such as those escaping from the deep-sea vent found near these tube worms.

Section Assessment

1. What are the characteristics of bacteria?
2. How do aerobic and anaerobic organisms differ?
3. How do bacteria reproduce?
4. **Think Critically:** A mat of cyanobacteria is found growing on a lake with dead fish floating along the edge. What has caused these events to occur?
5. **Skill Builder**
   Interpreting Data Do the **Chapter 21 Skill Activity** on page 982 to interpret the data to determine which substance best prevents bacterial growth.

Using Math

Some bacteria may reproduce every 20 minutes. Suppose that one bacterium is present at the beginning of a timed period. How long would it take for the number of bacteria to increase to more than 1 million?

Activity 21•1

Using Scientific Methods

Observing Cyanobacteria

Materials

- Micrograph photos (see below)
  **prepared slides of* Gloeocapsa *and* Anabaena
  **microscope*

**Alternate Materials*

You can obtain many species of cyanobacteria from ponds. When you look at these organisms under a microscope, you will find that they have many similarities but that they are also different from each other in important ways. In this activity, you will compare and contrast species of cyanobacteria.

What You'll Investigate

What do cyanobacteria look like?

Goals

- **Observe** several species of cyanobacteria.
- **Describe** the structure and function of cyanobacteria.

Safety Precautions  

Procedure

1. **Make a data table** in your Science Journal. Indicate whether each cyanobacterium sample is in colony form or filament form. Write a *yes* or *no* for the presence or absence of each characteristic in each type of cyanobacterium.

Oscillatoria

Anabaena

Nostoc

Gloeocapsa

2. **Observe** photos or prepared slides, if available, of *Gloeocapsa* and *Anabaena.* If using slides, observe under the low and high power of the microscope. Notice the difference in the arrangement of the cells. In your Science Journal, draw and label a few cells of each species of cyanobacterium.
3. **Observe** photos of *Nostoc* and *Oscillatoria.* In your Science Journal, draw and label a few cells of each.

Conclude and Apply

1. How does the color of cyanobacteria compare with the color of leaves on trees? What can you infer from this?
2. How can you tell by **observing** them that cyanobacteria belong to Kingdom Eubacteria?
3. **Describe** the general appearance of cyanobacteria.

Cyanobacteria Observations

Structure	Anabaena	Gloeocapsa	Nostoc	Oscillatoria
Filament or colony				
Nucleus				
Chlorophyll				
Gel-like layer				

Bacteria in Your Life

Beneficial Bacteria

Have you had any bacteria for lunch lately? Any time you eat cheese or yogurt, you eat some bacteria. Bacteria break down substances in milk to make many everyday products. Cheese-making is illustrated in **Figure 21-7.** If you have eaten sauerkraut, you ate a product made with cabbage and a bacterial culture. Vinegar is also produced by a bacterium.

What You'll Learn

- Some ways bacteria are helpful
- The importance of nitrogen-fixing bacteria
- How some bacteria cause disease

Vocabulary

saprophyte
nitrogen-fixing bacteria
pathogen
antibiotic
vaccine
toxin
endospore

Why It's Important

- Discovering the ways bacteria affect your life can help you understand biological processes.

Figure 21-7 Bacteria that break down proteins in milk are used in production of various kinds of cheese.

A Bacteria such as *Streptococcus lactis* added to milk cause the milk to curdle, or separate into curds (solids) and whey (liquids).

B Other bacteria are added to the curds. Curds are then allowed to ripen into cheese. Which type of cheese is made depends on the bacterial species added to the curds.

Uses of Bacteria

Bacteria called saprophytes (SAP ruh fitz) help maintain nature's balance. A **saprophyte** is any organism that uses dead material as a food and energy source. Saprophytes digest dead organisms and recycle nutrients so that they are available for use by other organisms. Without saprophytic bacteria, there would be layers of dead material deeper than you are tall spread over all of Earth.

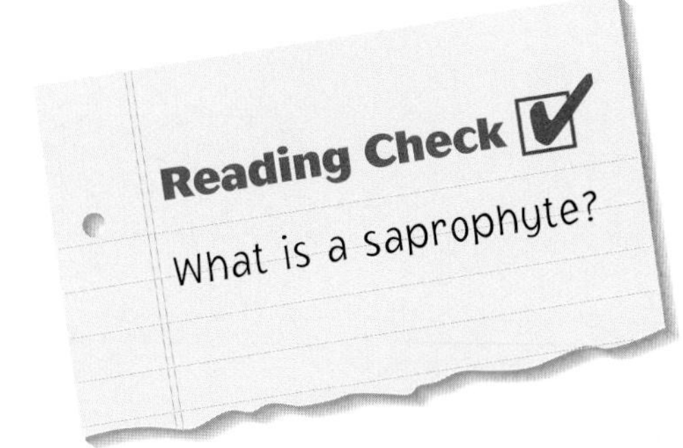

VISUALIZING Nitrogen Fixation

Figure 21-8 Root nodules, which form on the roots of peanuts, peas, and other legumes, contain nitrogen-fixing bacteria.

A Root hairs curl before infection by the bacteria.

B Bacteria enter the roots through an infection thread, which carries the bacteria into the root.

Bacteria

Root hair

Infection thread

The roots of some plants develop nodules when nitrogen-fixing bacteria enter them, as illustrated in **Figure 21-8.** This is especially true of legumes, a plant group that includes peas, peanuts, and clover. These **nitrogen-fixing bacteria** change nitrogen from the air into forms useful for plants and animals. Both plants and animals need nitrogen for making needed proteins and nucleic acids.

Many industries rely on bacteria. Biotechnology is putting bacteria to use in making medicines, enzymes, cleansers, adhesives, and other products. The ability of bacteria to digest oil has been extremely important in helping to clean up the extensive oil spills in Alaska, California, and Texas.

Visit the Glencoe Science Web Site at **www.glencoe.com/sec/science/ca** for more information about toxin-producing bacteria.

Harmful Bacteria

Some bacteria are pathogens. A **pathogen** is any organism that produces disease. If you have ever had strep throat, you have had firsthand experience with a bacterial pathogen. Other pathogenic bacteria cause anthrax in cattle, and diphtheria, tetanus, and whooping cough in humans. Bacterial diseases in humans and animals are usually treated effectively with antibiotics. An **antibiotic** is a substance produced by one organism that inhibits or kills another organism. Penicillin, a well-known antibiotic, works by preventing bacteria from making cell walls. Without cell walls, bacteria cannot survive.

Some bacterial diseases can be prevented by vaccines. A **vaccine** is made from damaged particles taken from bacterial

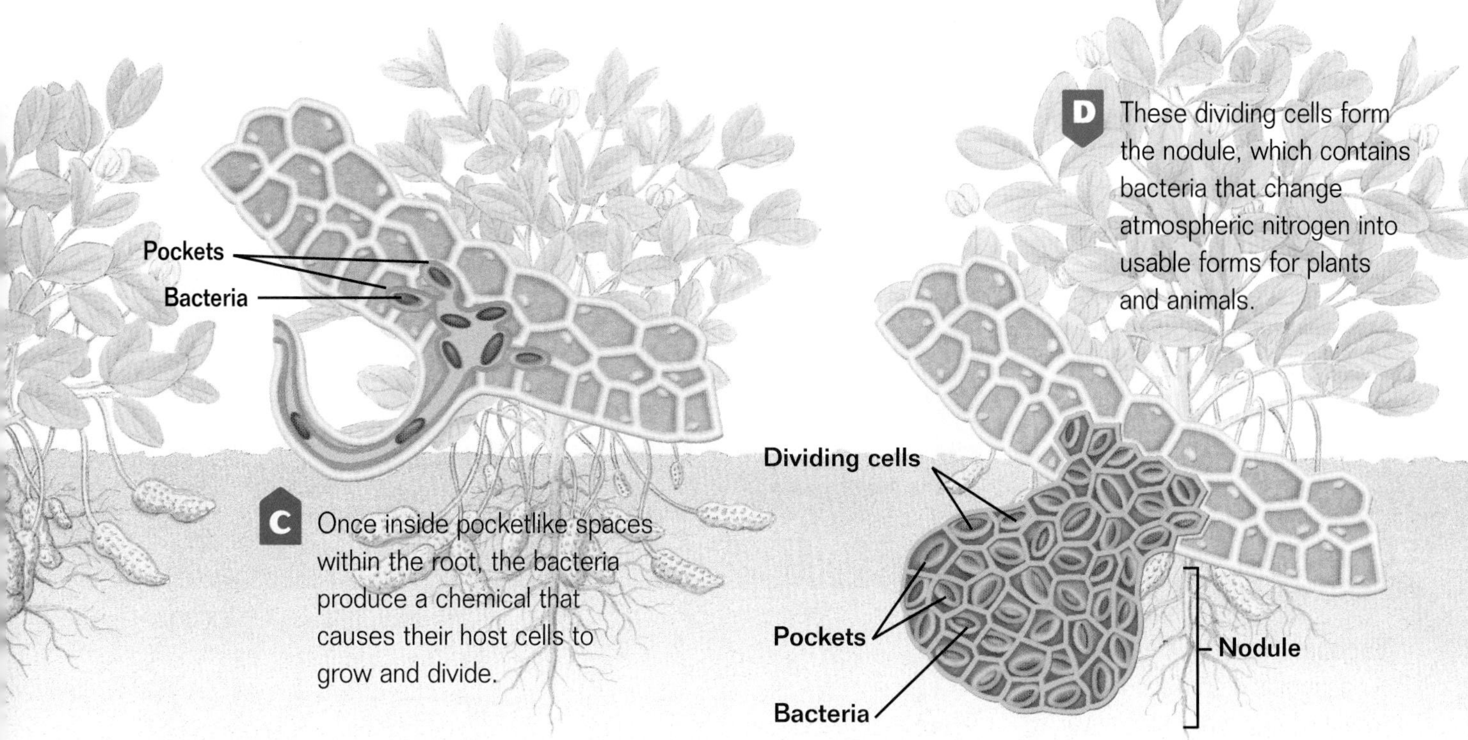

cell walls or from killed bacteria. Once injected, the white blood cells in the body learn to recognize the bacteria. If the particular bacteria then enter the body at a later time, the white blood cells immediately attack and overwhelm them. Vaccines have been produced that are effective against many bacterial diseases.

Some pathogens produce poisons. The poison produced by a bacterial pathogen is called a **toxin.** Botulism, a type of food poisoning, is caused by a toxin that can cause paralysis and death. The bacterium that causes botulism is *Clostridium botulinum.* Many bacteria that produce toxins are able to produce thick walls around themselves when conditions are unfavorable. This thick-walled structure is called an **endospore,** illustrated in **Figure 21-9.** Endospores can exist for hundreds of years before they begin to grow again. Botulism endospores must be exposed to heat for a long time to be destroyed. Once the endospores are in canned food, the bacteria can change back to regular cells and start producing toxins. Botulism bacteria are able to grow inside cans because they are anaerobes and do not need oxygen to live.

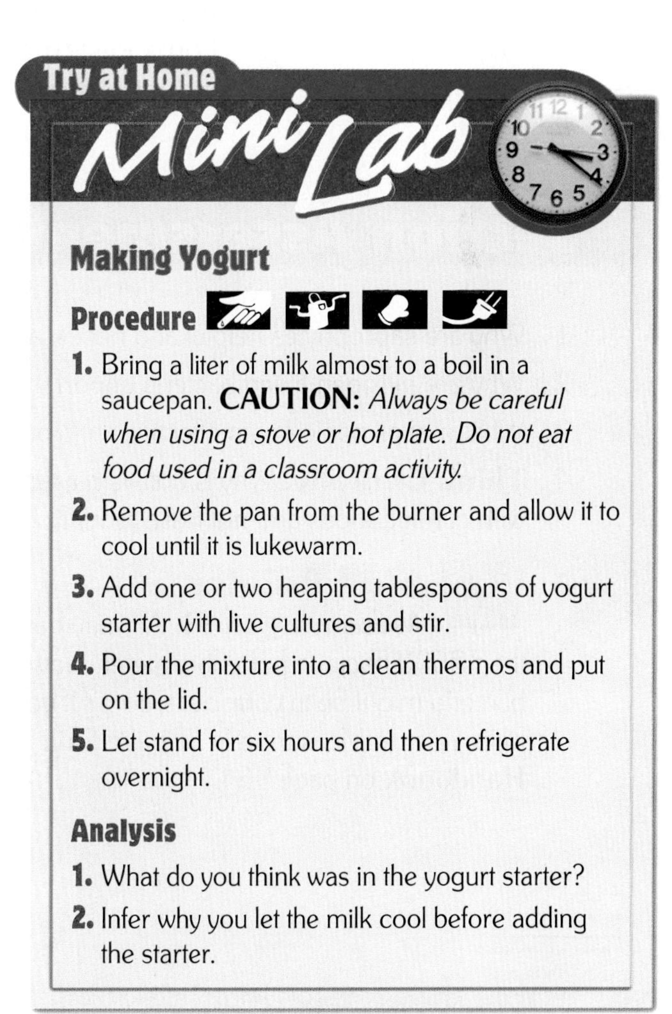

Try at Home

MiniLab

Making Yogurt

Procedure

1. Bring a liter of milk almost to a boil in a saucepan. **CAUTION:** *Always be careful when using a stove or hot plate. Do not eat food used in a classroom activity.*
2. Remove the pan from the burner and allow it to cool until it is lukewarm.
3. Add one or two heaping tablespoons of yogurt starter with live cultures and stir.
4. Pour the mixture into a clean thermos and put on the lid.
5. Let stand for six hours and then refrigerate overnight.

Analysis

1. What do you think was in the yogurt starter?
2. Infer why you let the milk cool before adding the starter.

Figure 21-9 Bacteria sometimes form endospores when conditions become unfavorable. These structures can survive harsh winters, dry conditions, and heat. In this photo, the blue in the center of each structure is the endospore. The golden part is the cellular material. **How can botulism endospores be destroyed?**

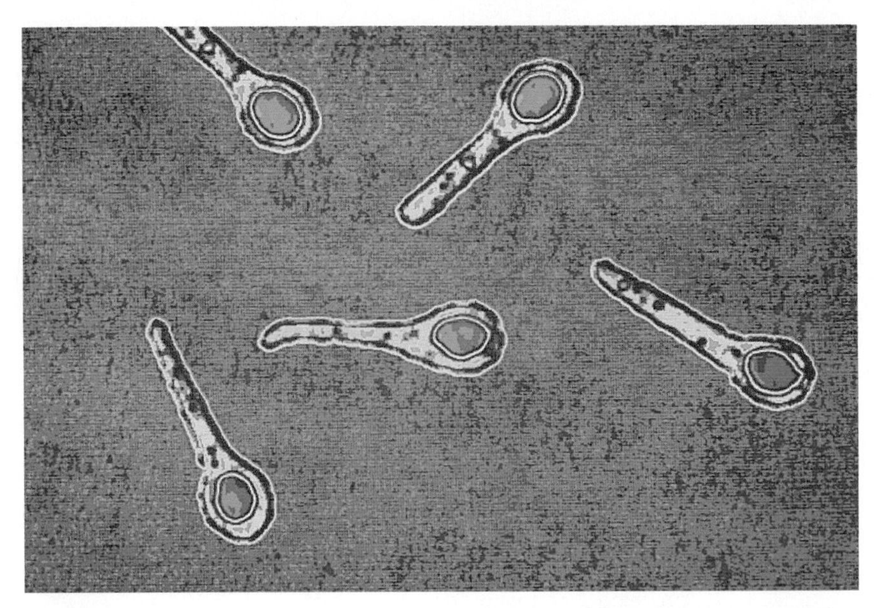

Magnification: 15 000×

Vacuum Packing
A vacuum is a space from which all gas molecules have been removed. Vacuum-packed foods have most of the air removed from around the food. How would this prevent food from spoiling?

Pasteurization

Pasteurization, a process of heating food to a temperature that kills harmful bacteria, is used in the food industry. You are probably most familiar with pasteurized milk, but some fruit juices are also pasteurized. The process is named for Louis Pasteur, who first formulated the process for the wine industry during the nineteenth century in France.

Section Assessment

1. Why are saprophytes helpful and necessary?
2. Why are nitrogen-fixing bacteria important?
3. What makes penicillin an effective antibiotic?
4. **Think Critically:** Why is botulism associated with canned foods and not fresh foods?
5. **Skill Builder**
   Measuring in SI Air may have more than 3500 bacteria per cubic meter. How many bacteria might be in your classroom? If you need help, refer to Measuring in SI in the **Skill Handbook** on page 964.

Using Computers

Spreadsheet Create a spreadsheet that includes: Disease Name, Disease Organism, Method of Transmission, and Symptoms. Enter information for the following diseases: whooping cough, tuberculosis, tetanus, diphtheria, and scarlet fever. Sort your data using Method of Transmission. If you need help, refer to page 974.

Bioremediation

Each year, tons of pollutants are released into ecosystems because of human activities. Many of these pollutants are both poisonous and long lasting. Soil, surface, and groundwater contamination results from the buildup of these harmful compounds. Traditional methods of cleaning up damaged ecosystems, such as the use of landfills and toxic-waste dumps, can be costly and ineffective as long-term solutions.

An Unusual Solution

One approach to cleaning up polluted ecosystems is bioremediation—the use of living organisms, such as bacteria, fungi, and plants, to change pollutants into harmless compounds. Some microorganisms naturally have the ability to break down harmful compounds. Scientists find and isolate these organisms, often stimulating them to clean up polluted areas. Other times, it is necessary to genetically engineer a microorganism to break down specific pollutants. Archaebacteria and eubacteria are the main organisms used in bioremediation efforts. These microorganisms break down polluting substances—even oil and gasoline—and change them into less damaging compounds, such as carbon dioxide and water. At left, technicians spray a fertilizer mix on an oil-soaked shore to promote the growth of oil-eating bacteria. Although bioremediation is not a complete cure, it is a new way to help repair damaged ecosystems.

Uses and Advantages of Bioremediation

About five to ten percent of all industrial, agricultural, and municipal wastes are being treated by bioremediation. To clean water, for example, bacteria are placed in lagoons or large containers. Then, wastewater is pumped through these sites, and the bacteria break down the pollutants in the water into harmless compounds. In another technique, pollutants are mixed into soil and broken down by microorganisms found there. An advantage of bioremediation is that it can eliminate hazardous waste where it occurs, rather than at a distant treatment site. Bioremediation has proven to be safe and effective, and it costs 60 to 90 percent less than many traditional methods.

interNET CONNECTION

Use the Glencoe Science Web Site at **www.glencoe.com/sec/science/ca** to research local waste treatment companies. Do more companies use traditional methods or bioremediation? Try to find out why a company uses a particular method.

Activity 21•2

Are there bacteria in foods?

Materials

- 6 test tubes
- 6 stoppers
- test-tube rack
- felt-tip marker
- 3 droppers
- 3 craft sticks
- Milk, buttermilk, cottage cheese, yogurt, sour cream, water
- bromothymol blue solution (150 mL)

You've learned that bacteria are too small to be seen without a microscope, but is there some way that you can tell if they are present in foods? Because bacteria produce carbon dioxide like other living things, a chemical test that indicates the presence of carbon dioxide can be used to tell if bacteria are growing in foods you eat.

What You'll Investigate

Is there bacteria in the food you eat?

Goals

- **Observe** color changes in test tubes containing food.
- **Determine** which foods contain the most bacteria.

Procedure

1. Use the marker to label the test tubes 1 through 6 and place them in the test tube rack.
2. Add 25 mL of bromothymol blue-indicator solution to each test tube.
3. Using a different dropper each time, add four drops of water to tube 1, four drops of milk to tube 2, and four drops of buttermilk to tube 3. Be careful not to let the drops go down the sides of the tubes.

4. Using a different craft stick each time, add an amount of yogurt about the size of a green pea to tube 4, the same amount of cottage cheese to tube 5, and the same amount of sour cream to tube 6.
5. Loosely place a stopper in each tube and record the color of the contents of each tube in a data table.
6. Leave the tubes undisturbed until the end of the class period. Record the color of the contents of the tubes in the data table.
7. The next time you arrive in class, record the color of the contents of the tubes again.

Conclude and Apply

1. Why was water added to tube 1?
2. What color does bromothymol turn if carbon dioxide is present?
3. Using strength of the color change as a guide, judge which tubes contain the most bacteria.

Data Table for Test of Bacteria in Food

Tube	Contents	Color at Start	Color at End of Class	Color One Day Later	Test + or −	Bacteria Present?
1	Water					
2	Milk					
3	Buttermilk					
4	Yogurt					
5	Cottage Cheese					
6	Sour Cream					

Chapter 21 Reviewing Main Ideas

For a **preview** of this chapter, study this Reviewing Main Ideas before you read the chapter. After you have studied this chapter, you can use the Reviewing Main Ideas to **review** the chapter.

The Glencoe MindJogger, Audiocassettes, and CD-ROM provide additional opportunities for review.

Section 21-1 TWO KINGDOMS OF BACTERIA

Bacteria are prokaryotic cells that usually reproduce by **fission.** All bacteria contain DNA, ribosomes, and cytoplasm but lack membrane-bound organelles. Bacteria are placed into one of two kingdoms—eubacteria and archaebacteria. The eubacteria are considered to be true bacteria and contain a great variety of organisms. Archaebacteria are bacteria that exist in extreme conditions, such as deep-sea vents and hot springs. Most bacteria break down cells of other organisms to obtain food, but cyanobacteria make their own food. **Anaerobes** are bacteria that are able to live without oxygen, whereas **aerobes** need oxygen to survive. ***How do prokaryotic cells differ from eukaryotic cells?***

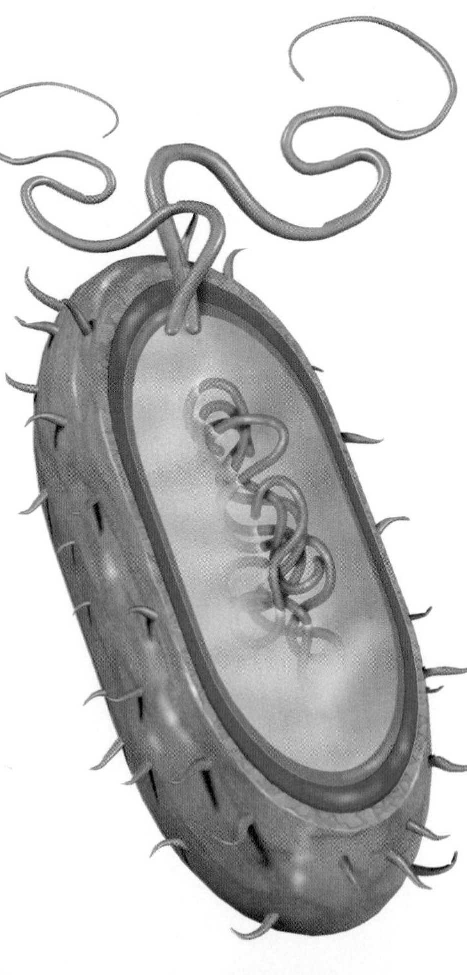

Reading Check ☑
Review **Figure 21-8.** Then, describe the nitrogen-fixing process in your own words, using numbered steps. You will probably have more than four steps.

Section 21-2 BACTERIA IN YOUR LIFE

Bacteria may be helpful or harmful. They may aid in recycling nutrients, fixing nitrogen, or helping in food production. They can even be used to break down harmful pollutants. Other bacteria are harmful because they can cause disease in the organisms they infect. Pasteurization is one process that can prevent harmful bacteria in food. ***What are some diseases caused by harmful bacteria?***

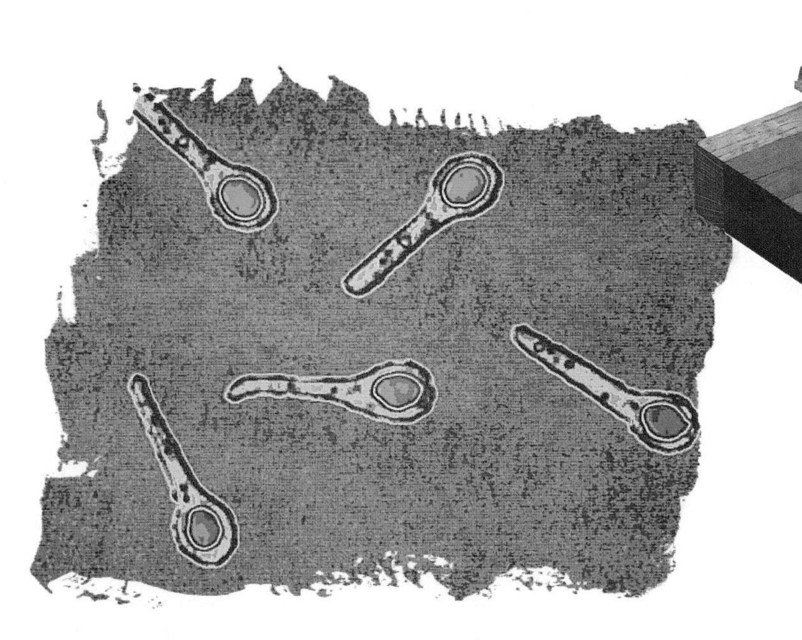

Career CONNECTION

Alice Arellano, Wastewater Operator

Alice Arellano is a wastewater control-room operator responsible for cleaning wastewater in Austin, Texas. Wastewater from peoples' homes in Austin is discharged into the Colorado River, but it first has to be treated. Treatment is a complex process that involves screening, filtering, and chemical treatment. Part of treatment involves using microorganisms, like bacteria, to break down harmful bacteria that live in the wastewater. ***How can understanding the way bacteria live help design water-treatment processes?***

Chapter 21 Assessment

Using Vocabulary

a. aerobe
b. anaerobe
c. antibiotic
d. endospore
e. fission
f. flagella
g. nitrogen-fixing bacteria
h. pathogen
i. saprophyte
j. toxin
k. vaccine

Each phrase below describes a science term from the list. Write the term that matches the phrase describing it.

1. organism that decomposes dead organisms
2. structure by which some organisms move
3. heat-resistant structure in bacteria
4. substance that can prevent, not cure, a disease
5. any organism that produces disease

Checking Concepts

Choose the word or phrase that best answers the question.

6. What is a way of cleaning up an ecosystem using bacteria to break down harmful compounds?
   A) landfills
   B) toxic waste dumps
   C) waste storage
   D) bioremediation
7. What do bacterial cells contain?
   A) nuclei
   B) DNA
   C) mitochondria
   D) no chromosomes
8. What do bacteria that make their own food have?
   A) chlorophyll
   B) lysosomes
   C) Golgi bodies
   D) mitochondria
9. Which of the following describes most bacteria?
   A) anaerobic
   B) pathogens
   C) many-celled
   D) beneficial
10. What is the name for rod-shaped bacteria?
    A) bacilli
    B) cocci
    C) spirilla
    D) colonies
11. What structure(s) allow(s) bacteria to stick to surfaces?
    A) capsule
    B) flagella
    C) chromosome
    D) cell wall
12. What causes blooms in ponds?
    A) archaebacteria
    B) cyanobacteria
    C) cocci
    D) viruses
13. How are nutrients and carbon dioxide returned to the environment?
    A) producers
    B) flagella
    C) saprophytes
    D) pathogens
14. Which of the following is caused by a pathogenic bacterium?
    A) an antibiotic
    B) nitrogen fixation
    C) cheese
    D) strep throat
15. Which organisms do not need oxygen to survive?
    A) anaerobes
    B) aerobes
    C) humans
    D) fish

Thinking Critically

16. What would happen if nitrogen-fixing bacteria could no longer live on the roots of plants?
17. Why are bacteria capable of surviving in all environments of the world?
18. Farmers often rotate crops such as beans, peas, and peanuts with other crops such as corn, wheat, and cotton. Why might they make such changes?
19. One organism that causes bacterial pneumonia is called pneumococcus. What is its shape?
20. What precautions can be taken to prevent food poisoning?

Developing Skills

If you need help, refer to the Skill Handbook.

21. **Concept Mapping:** Use the events chain to sequence the events following a pond bloom.

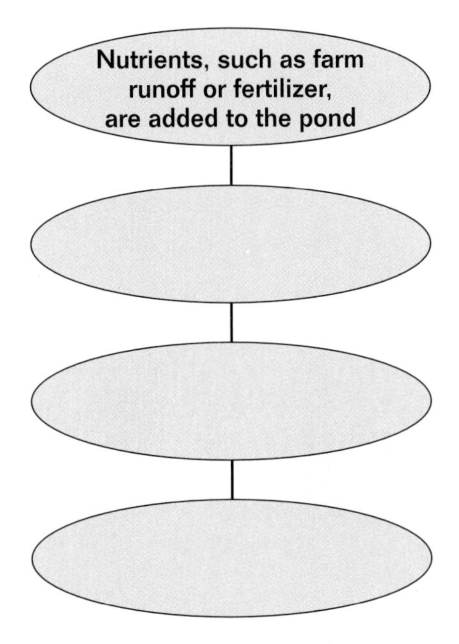

22. **Making and Using Graphs:** Graph the data from the table below. Using the graph, determine where the doubling rate would be at 20°C.

Bacterial Reproduction Rates

Temperature (°C)	Doubling Rate per Hour
20.5	2.0
30.5	3.0
36.0	2.5
39.2	1.2

23. **Interpreting Data:** What is the effect of temperature in question 22?

24. **Design an Experiment:** How could you decide if a kind of bacteria can grow anaerobically?

Test-Taking Tip

Investigate Ask what kinds of questions to expect on the test. Ask for practice tests so that you can become familiar with the test-taking materials.

Test Practice

Use these questions to test your Science Proficiency.

1. One group of bacteria are known as extremophiles, which literally means "lovers of the extreme." Which group of organisms would **BEST** fit this name?
   - **A)** eubacteria
   - **B)** archaebacteria
   - **C)** cyanobacteria
   - **D)** aerobes

2. Bioremediation has been shown to have several advantages over traditional methods of ecosystem cleanup. Which of the following is **NOT** an advantage of bioremediation?
   - **A)** It is less time consuming.
   - **B)** It is less costly.
   - **C)** It is more effective.
   - **D)** It can be done at the site of the pollution.

3. Many bacteria are considered beneficial organisms. Which of the following is **NOT** a reason they are considered beneficial?
   - **A)** They change nitrogen in the air to a form useful for plants.
   - **B)** They cause anthrax in cattle.
   - **C)** They are used in food production.
   - **D)** They are the source of some medicines.

CHAPTER

22 Protists and Fungi

Chapter Preview

Section 22-1
Kingdom Protista

Section 22-2
Kingdom Fungi

Skills Preview

Skill Builders

- Compare and Contrast
- Use Variables, Constants, and Controls

Activities

- Observe
- Compare

MiniLabs

- Predict
- Estimate

Reading Check

As you read this chapter, list three things you already knew about protists and fungi, and ten things you are learning about them.

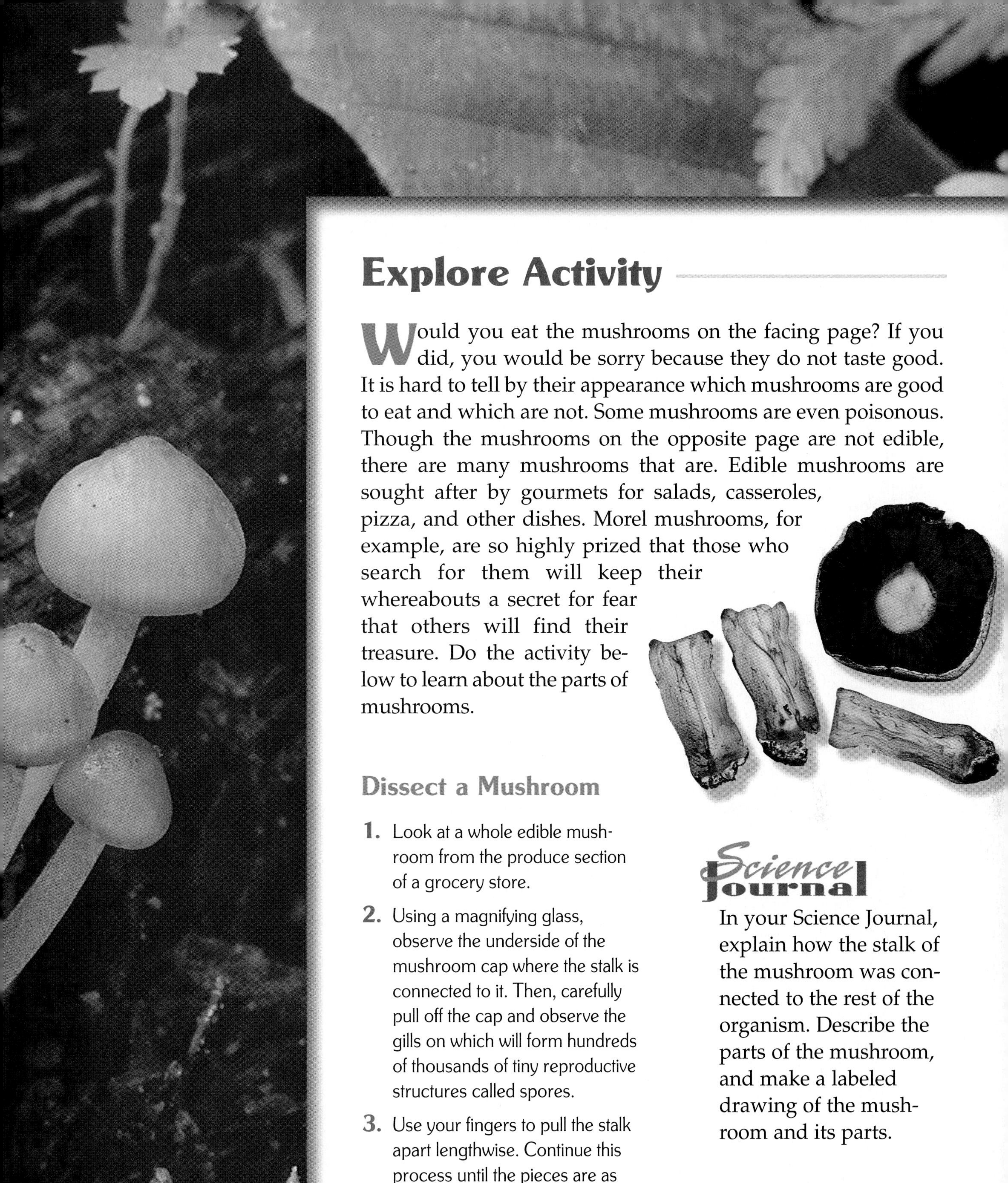

Explore Activity

Would you eat the mushrooms on the facing page? If you did, you would be sorry because they do not taste good. It is hard to tell by their appearance which mushrooms are good to eat and which are not. Some mushrooms are even poisonous. Though the mushrooms on the opposite page are not edible, there are many mushrooms that are. Edible mushrooms are sought after by gourmets for salads, casseroles, pizza, and other dishes. Morel mushrooms, for example, are so highly prized that those who search for them will keep their whereabouts a secret for fear that others will find their treasure. Do the activity below to learn about the parts of mushrooms.

Dissect a Mushroom

1. Look at a whole edible mushroom from the produce section of a grocery store.
2. Using a magnifying glass, observe the underside of the mushroom cap where the stalk is connected to it. Then, carefully pull off the cap and observe the gills on which will form hundreds of thousands of tiny reproductive structures called spores.
3. Use your fingers to pull the stalk apart lengthwise. Continue this process until the pieces are as small as you can get them.

Science Journal

In your Science Journal, explain how the stalk of the mushroom was connected to the rest of the organism. Describe the parts of the mushroom, and make a labeled drawing of the mushroom and its parts.

22•1 Kingdom Protista

What You'll Learn

- The characteristics shared by all protists
- How to describe the three groups of protists
- How to compare and contrast the protist groups

Vocabulary

protist
algae
protozoans
pseudopods
cilia

Why It's Important

- Kingdom Protista shows the importance of variety in the environment.

What is a protist?

Look at the organisms in **Figure 22-1.** Do you see any similarities among them? As different as they appear, all of these organisms belong to the protist kingdom. A **protist** is a single- or many-celled organism that lives in moist or wet surroundings. All protists have a nucleus and are therefore eukaryotic. Despite these similarities, the organisms in Kingdom Protista (proh TIHS tuh) vary greatly. Some protists contain chlorophyll and make their own food, and others don't. Protists are plantlike, animal-like, and funguslike.

Evolution of Protists

Not much evidence of the evolution of protists can be found because many lack hard parts and, as a result, few fossils of these organisms have been found. However, by studying the genes of modern protists, scientists are able to trace their ancestors. Scientists hypothesize that the common ancestor of all protists was a one-celled organism with a nucleus, mitochondria, and other cellular structures. The cellular structures of this organism may have been different from those found in modern protists. Evidence suggests that protists that can't make their own food evolved differently from protists that do make their own food. Some scientists suggest that a cyanobacterium, a bacterium that contains chlorophyll, was taken up by a one-celled organism with mitochondria. As this organism changed over time, the cyanobacterium became the organism's chloroplast, the organelle where photosynthesis occurs. Plantlike protists probably developed from this kind of organism.

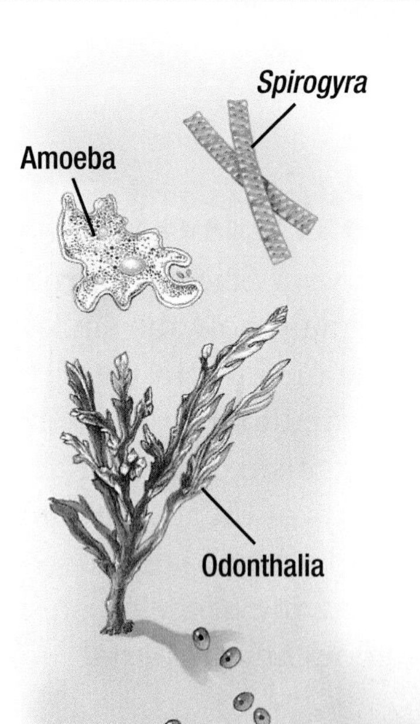

EXAMPLES OF Protists

Figure 22-1 Kingdom Protista is made up of a variety of organisms. **Using what you see in the art, write a description of a protist.**

Plantlike Protists

Plantlike protists are known as **algae** (AL jee). Some species of algae are one celled and others are many celled. All algae can make their own food because they contain the pigment chlorophyll in their chloroplasts. Even though all algae have chlorophyll, not all of them look green. Many have other pigments that cover up their chlorophyll. Species of algae are grouped into six main phyla according to their structure, pigments, and the way in which they store food.

Figure 22-2 How are Euglenas similar to both plants and animals?

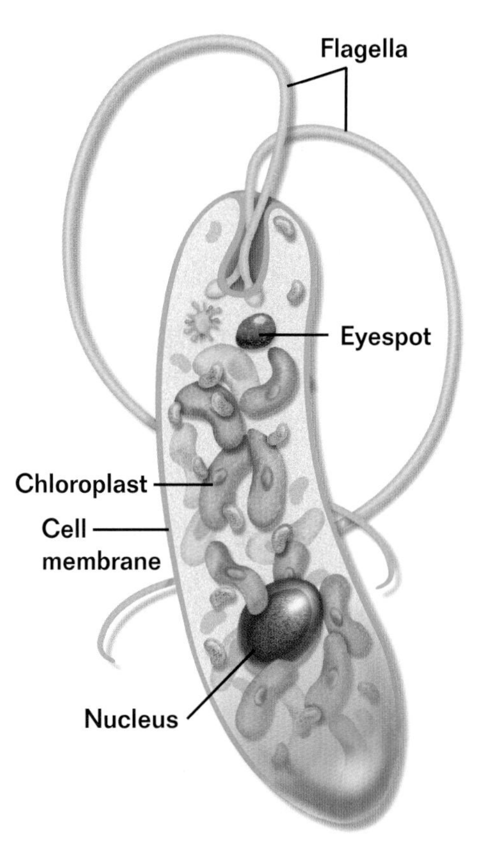

Euglenoids

Algae that belong to the phylum Euglenophyta (yoo GLEE nuh fi tuh) have characteristics of both plants and animals. A typical euglenoid, the Euglena, is shown in **Figure 22-2.** Like plants, these one-celled algae have chloroplasts and produce carbohydrates as food. When light is not present, euglenas feed on bacteria and protists. Although euglenas have no cell walls, they do have a strong, flexible layer inside the cell membrane that helps them move and change shape. Many move by using whiplike tails called flagella. Another animal-like characteristic of euglenas is that they have an adaptation called an eyespot that responds to light.

Diatoms

Diatoms, shown in **Figure 22-3,** belong to the phylum Bacillariophyta (buh sih law ree oh FI tuh) and are found in both freshwater and salt water. Diatoms are photosynthetic, which means they can make their own food. These one-celled algae store food in the form of oil. They have a golden-brown pigment that masks the green chlorophyll. For this reason, they are sometimes referred to as gold-brown algae.

Diatoms reproduce in extremely large numbers. When the organisms die, their small cell walls sink to the floor of the

Figure 22-3 The cell wall of diatoms contain silica, the main element in glass. The body of a diatom is like a small box with a lid. Diatoms are covered with markings and pits that form patterns.

Figure 22-4 Dinoflagellates usually live in the sea. Notice the groove that houses one of the two flagella that mark all members of this group.

Magnification: 3000×

body of water and collect in deep layers. Ancient deposits of diatoms are mined with power shovels and used in insulation, filters, and road paint. The cell walls of diatoms produce the sparkle that makes some road lines visible at night and the crunch you feel when you use toothpaste to brush your teeth.

Dinoflagellates

Phylum Dinoflagellata contains species of one-celled algae called dinoflagellates that have red pigments. Because of their color, they are known as fire algae. The name *dinoflagellate* means "spinning flagellates." One of the flagella moves the cell, and the other circles the cell, causing it to spin with a motion similar to a top. Dinoflagellates, shown in **Figure 22-4,** store food in the form of starches and oils.

VISUALIZING Green Algae

Figure 22-5 There are many different shapes among the species of green algae.

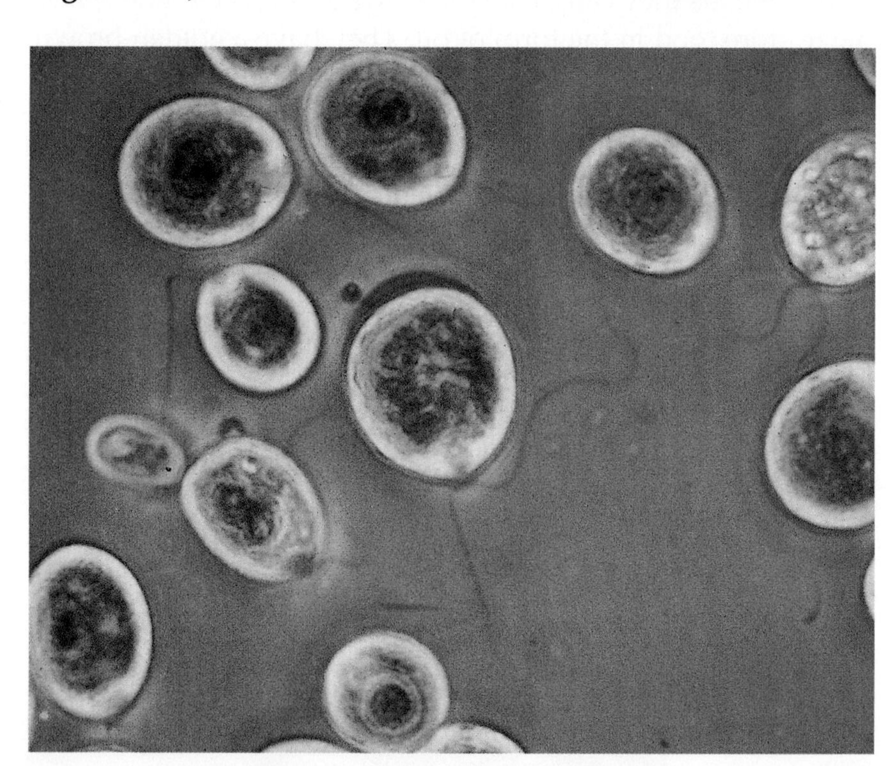

A *Chlamydomonas* is an example of a one-celled green alga. It is found in freshwater ponds and in moist soil.

Magnification: 700×

Almost all dinoflagellates live in salt water. They are important food sources for many saltwater organisms. Some dinoflagellates, however, do live in freshwater and are suspected to have caused health problems for humans and other organisms on the East Coast.

Green Algae

Seven thousand species of green algae form the phylum Chlorophyta (klaw RAHF uh duh), giving it the most variety of any group of protists. The presence of chlorophyll in green algae tells you that they undergo photosynthesis and produce food. They are important because nearly half of the oxygen we consume is a result of the photosynthesis of green algae.

Although most green algae live in water, others can live in many other environments, including tree trunks and other organisms. Green algae can be one-celled or many-celled. **Figure 22-5** shows different forms of green algae.

EXAMPLES OF Green Algae

- **River moss**
- ***Chlamydomonas***
- ***Volvox***
- ***Spirogyra***
- ***Ulva***

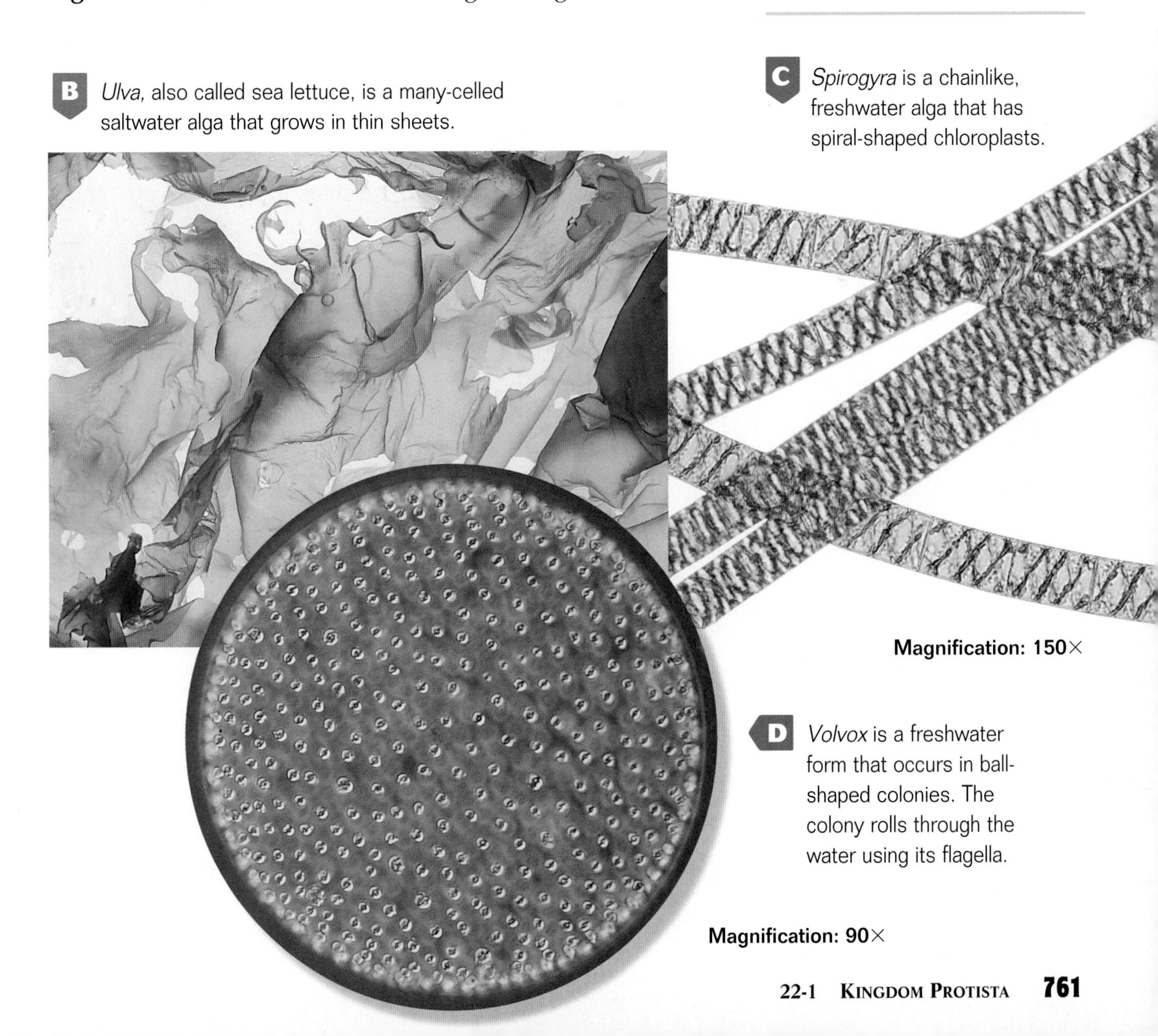

B *Ulva*, also called sea lettuce, is a many-celled saltwater alga that grows in thin sheets.

C *Spirogyra* is a chainlike, freshwater alga that has spiral-shaped chloroplasts.

Magnification: 150×

D *Volvox* is a freshwater form that occurs in ball-shaped colonies. The colony rolls through the water using its flagella.

Magnification: 90×

Figure 22-6 Carrageenan, a substance extracted from the red alga Irish moss, gives some puddings their smooth, creamy texture.

Red Algae

Red algae belong to the phylum Rhodophyta (roh DAHF uh duh). *Rhodo-* means "red" and describes the color of members of this phylum. Pudding and toothpaste are made with red algae. Carrageenan is found in red algae, such as the Irish moss shown in **Figure 22-6.** It gives toothpaste and pudding their smooth, creamy textures. Most red algae are many-celled. Some species of red algae can live up to 175 m deep in the ocean. Their red pigment allows them to absorb the limited amount of light that penetrates to those depths and enables them to produce the starch on which they live.

Brown Algae

Brown algae make up the phylum Phaeophyta (fee AHF uh duh). Members of this phylum are many-celled and vary greatly in size. They are mostly found growing in cool, saltwater environments. Kelp, shown in **Figure 22-7,** is an important food source for many fish and invertebrates. They form a dense mat of stalks and leaflike blades where small fish and other animals live. Giant kelp are the largest organisms in the protist kingdom.

People in many parts of the world eat brown algae. The thick texture of foods such as ice cream and marshmallows is produced by algin, which is found in these algae. Brown algae also are used to make fertilizer. **Table 22-1** summarizes the different phyla of plantlike protists.

Figure 22-7 Giant kelp may be as much as 100 m long and can form forests like this one located off the coast of California. **What are some practical uses for brown algae?**

Table 22-1

The Plantlike Protists			
Phylum	**Example**	**Pigments**	**Other Characteristics**
Euglenophyta Euglenoids		Chlorophyll	One-celled alga that moves with flagella; has eyespot to detect light.
Bacillariophyta Diatoms		Golden Brown	One-celled alga with body made of two halves. Cell walls contain silica.
Dinoflagellata Dinoflagellates		Red	One-celled alga with two flagella. Flagella cause cell to spin. Some species cause red tide.
Chlorophyta Green Algae		Chlorophyll	One- and many-celled species. Most live in water; some live out of water, in or on other organisms.
Rhodophyta Red Algae		Red	Many-celled alga; carbohydrate in red algae is used to give some foods a creamy texture.
Phaeophyta Brown Algae		Brown	Many-celled alga; most live in salt water; important food source in aquatic environments.

Animal-Like Protists

One-celled, animal-like protists are known as **protozoans.** These complex organisms live in water, soil, and in both living and dead organisms. Many types of protozoans are parasites. A parasite is an organism that lives in or on another organism. Protozoans contain special vacuoles for digesting food and getting rid of excess water. Protozoans are separated into groups—rhizopods, flagellates, ciliates, and sporozoans—by how they move. **Figure 22-8** is an example of one type of protozoan.

TRAITS OF Animal-like Protists

- One-celled
- Many are parasites
- Grouped by how they move

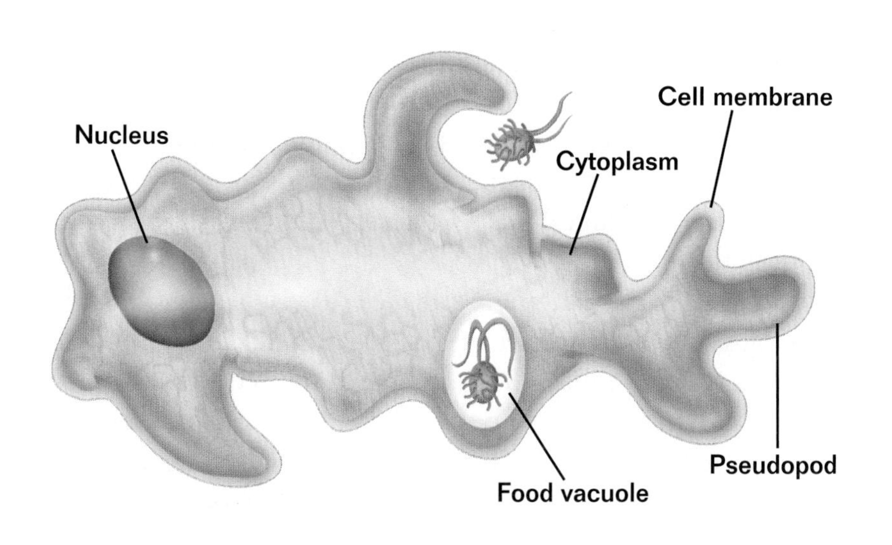

Figure 22-8 An amoeba constantly changes shape as it extends its cytoplasm to capture food and move from place to place. Many areas of the world have a species of amoeba in the water that causes the condition dysentery. Dysentery leads to a severe form of diarrhea. **Why is an amoeba classified as a protozoan?**

Figure 22-9 Many saltwater rhizopods have skeletons made out of calcium carbonate, the material that makes up chalk.

A The White Cliffs of Dover in England are made almost entirely of the shells of billions of rhizopods.

B Rhizopod shells come in a variety of shapes.

Magnification: 100×

Figure 22-10 *Trypanosoma*, responsible for African sleeping sickness, is spread by the tsetse fly in Africa. This flagellate is the gray organism in the photo below. The red disks are blood cells. The disease causes fever, swollen glands, and extreme sleepiness.

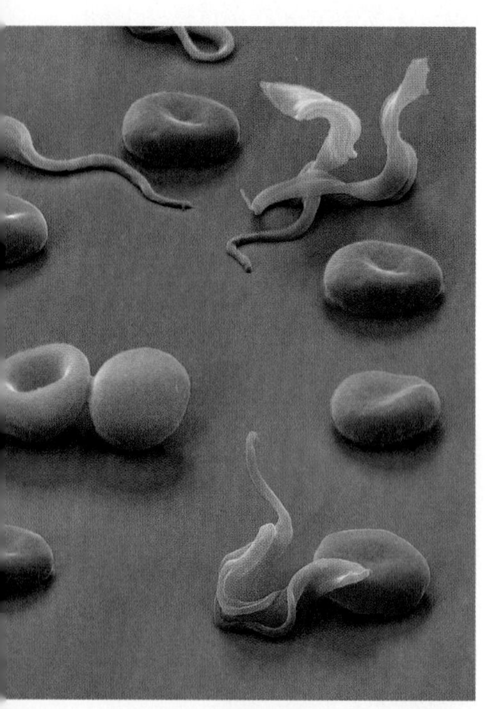

Magnification: 4000×

Rhizopods

The first protozoans were probably similar to members of the phylum Rhizopoda. The amoeba shown in **Figure 22-8** is a typical member of this phylum. Rhizopods move about and feed using temporary extensions of their cytoplasm called **pseudopods** (SEWD uh pahdz). The word *pseudopod* means "false foot." An amoeba extends the cytoplasm of a pseudopod on either side of a food particle such as a bacterium. Then, the pseudopod closes and the particle is trapped. A vacuole forms around the food and it is digested. Members of the phylum Rhizopoda, as shown in **Figure 22-9,** are found in freshwater and saltwater environments, and certain types are found in animals as parasites.

Flagellates

Protozoans that move using flagella are called flagellates and belong to the phylum Zoomastigina (zoe uh mas tuh JINE uh). All of the flagellates have long flagella that whip through a watery environment, moving the organism along. Many species of flagellates live in freshwater, though some are parasites.

Trypanosoma, shown in **Figure 22-10,** is a flagellate that causes African sleeping sickness in humans and other animals. Another flagellate lives in the digestive system of termites. The flagellates are beneficial to the termites because they produce enzymes that digest the wood the termites eat. Without the flagellates, the termites would not be able to digest the wood.

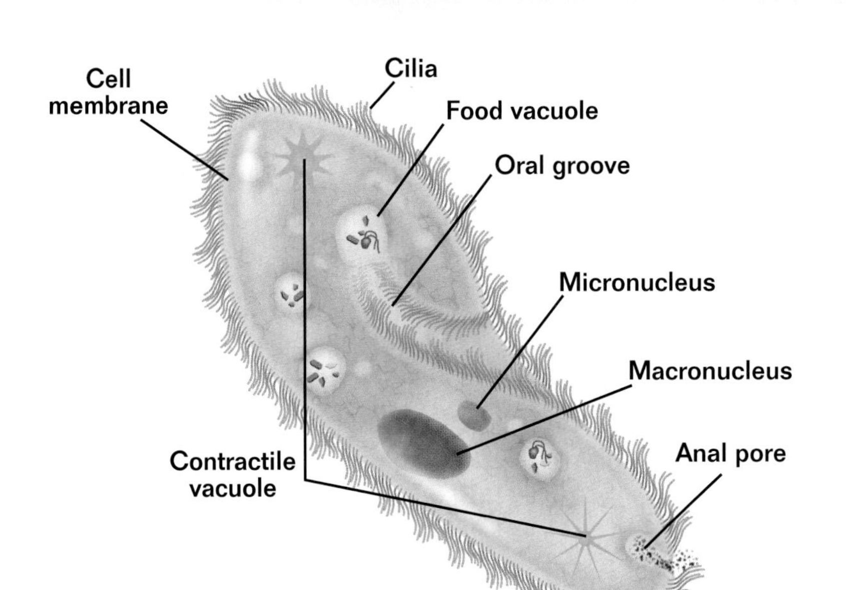

Examples of Ciliates

Figure 22-11 *Paramecium* is a typical ciliate found in many freshwater environments. These rapidly swimming protists consume bacteria. **Can you find the contractile vacuoles in the photo below? What is their function?**

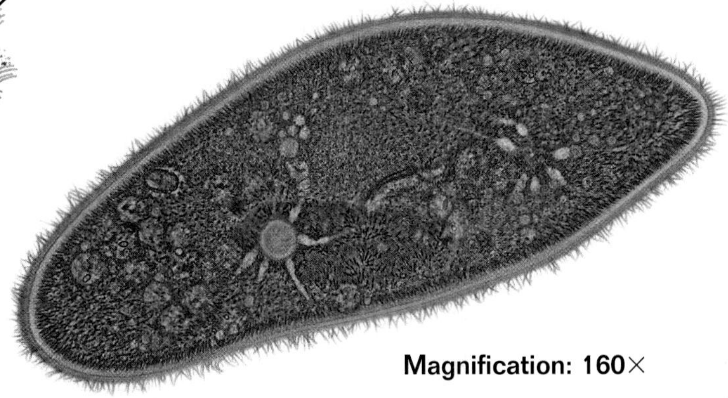

Magnification: 160×

Ciliates

The most complex protozoans belong to the phylum Ciliophora. Members of this phylum move by using cilia. **Cilia** (SIHL ee uh) are short, threadlike structures that extend from the cell membrane. Ciliates may be covered with cilia or have cilia grouped in specific areas of the cell. Cilia beat in an organized way that allows the organism to move swiftly in any direction.

A typical ciliate is *Paramecium,* shown in **Figure 22-11.** In *Paramecium,* you can see another characteristic of the ciliates: each has two nuclei—a macronucleus and a micronucleus. The macronucleus controls the everyday functions of the cell. The micronucleus is used in reproduction. Paramecia usually feed on bacteria swept into the oral groove by the cilia. Once the food is inside the cell, a food vacuole forms and the food is digested. Wastes are removed through the anal pore. As the name implies, a contractile vacuole contracts and excess water is ejected from the cell.

Using Math

A paramecium may be about 0.1 cm long. Giant kelp, a kind of brown algae, may be as much as 100 m long—about the same length as a football field. Using these measurements, how many times larger is a giant kelp than a paramecium?

Sporozoans

The phylum Sporozoa contains only parasitic organisms. Sporozoans have no way of moving on their own. All are parasites that live in and feed on the blood of humans and other animals, as shown in **Figure 22-12.**

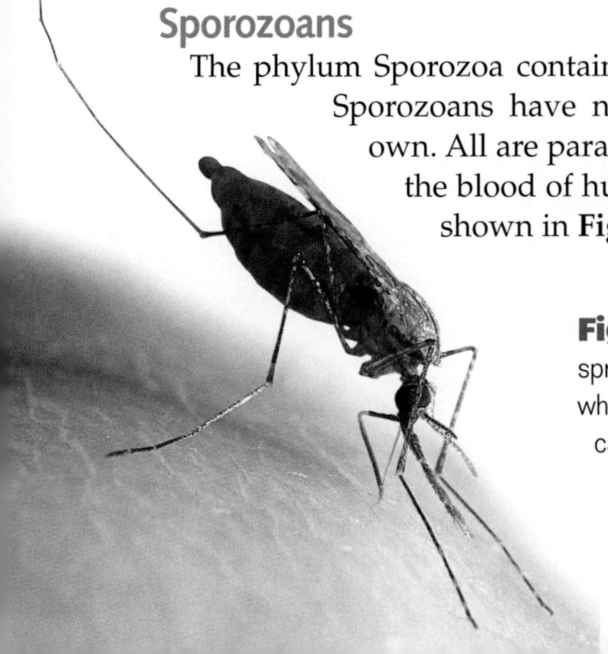

Figure 22-12 Only female *Anopheles* mosquitoes spread the sporozoan that causes malaria. Malaria is spread when an infected mosquito bites a human. This disease still causes about 1 million deaths each year worldwide.

Observing Slime Molds  

Procedure

1. Obtain live specimens of the slime mold *Physarum polycephaalum* from your teacher.
2. Observe the mold for four days.

Analysis

1. Make daily drawings and observations of the mold as it grows. Use a magnifying glass.
2. Predict the conditions under which the slime mold will change from the amoeboid form to the spore-producing form.

Funguslike Protists

Funguslike protists include several small phyla that have features of both protists and fungi. Slime molds and water molds are funguslike protists. They get energy by breaking down organic materials. Examples of slime molds are illustrated in **Figure 22-13.**

Slime Molds

Slime molds are much more attractive than their name sounds. Many are brightly colored. They form a delicate, weblike structure on the surface of their food supply. Slime molds have some protozoan characteristics. During part of their life cycle, the cells of slime molds move by means of pseudopods and behave like amoebas. Slime molds reproduce with spores the way fungi do. You will learn about reproduction in fungi in the next section.

Although most slime molds live on decaying logs or dead leaves in moist, cool, shady woods, one common slime mold is sometimes found crawling across lawns and mulch. It creeps along feeding on bacteria and decayed plants and animals. When conditions become less favorable, reproductive structures form on stalks and spores are produced.

Figure 22-13 Slime molds come in many different forms and colors ranging from brilliant yellow or orange to rich blue, violet, pink, and jet black. **How are slime molds similar to both protists and fungi?**

Blue slime mold

Pink slime mold

Pretzel slime mold

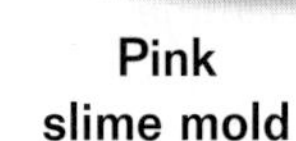

Water Molds and Downy Mildews

Water molds, downy mildews, and white rusts make up another phylum of funguslike protists. Most members of this large and diverse group live in water or moist places. Most water molds appear as fuzzy, white growths on decaying matter. They are called funguslike protists because they grow as a mass of threads over a plant or animal, digest it, and then absorb the organism's nutrients. Water molds have cell walls as do fungi, but their relatively simple cells are more like protozoans. Unlike fungi, they produce reproductive cells with flagella at some point in their reproductive cycles. Some water molds are parasites of plants while others feed on dead organisms. **Figure 22-14B** shows a parasitic water mold that grows on decaying fish. If you have an aquarium, you may see water molds attack a fish and cause its death.

Another important member of this phylum is a downy or powdery mildew that causes a disease on the leaves of many plants when days have been warm and nights become cooler and moist. In fact, the most well-known member of this phylum is the downy mildew, pictured in **Figure 22-14A,** that caused the Irish potato famine in the 1840s. Potatoes were

*inter*NET CONNECTION

Visit the Glencoe Science Web Site at **www.glencoe.com/sec/science/ca** for more information about funguslike protists.

Problem Solving

Puzzled About Slime

At one time, slime molds were classified as fungi. This is because at times, when conditions are unfavorable, they dry up and look like tiny mushrooms. Now, they are classified as protists because they move like protists and have characteristics similar to protists.

Slime molds, such as the scrambled egg slime mold, can be found covering moist wood as in the photograph shown below. They may be white or bright red, yellow, or purple. If you looked at a piece of slime mold on a microscope slide, you would see that the cell nuclei move back and forth as the cytoplasm streams along. This is the method slime mold uses to creep over the wood.

Think Critically: What characteristics do slime molds share with protists? In what ways are slime molds similar to amoebas and fungi? In what ways are they different?

Scrambled egg slime mold

EXAMPLES OF Water Molds

Figure 22-14 The potato plant (A) and the fish (B) show the effects of funguslike protists.

Ireland's main crop and the primary food source for its people. When the potato crop became infected with downy mildew, potatoes rotted in the fields, leaving many people with no food. Nearly 1 million people died in the resulting famine. Many others left Ireland and emigrated to the United States. This downy mildew continues to be a problem for potato growers, even in the United States.

A The Irish potato famine in the 1840s was the result of a downy mildew.

B A parasitic water mold growing on a fish will eventually kill it. Once the fish dies, the water mold will speed the decay of the fish. In this photo, the water mold appears as string coming off the fish.

Section Assessment

1. What are the main characteristics of all protists?
2. Compare and contrast the three groups of protists.
3. How are plantlike protists classified into different phyla?
4. **Think Critically:** Why aren't there many fossils of the different groups of protists?
5. **Skill Builder**
   Making and Using Tables Do the **Chapter 22 Skill Activity** on page 983 and compare and contrast the protist groups.

Using Computers

Spreadsheet Use a spreadsheet to make a table that compares the characteristics of the four phyla of protozoans. Include phylum, example species, method of transportation, and other characteristics. If you need help, refer to page 974.

Activity 22•1

Comparing Algae and Protozoans

Algae and protozoan cells have characteristics that are similar enough to place them within the same kingdom. However, the variety of forms within Kingdom Protista is great. In this activity, you can observe many of the differences that make organisms in Kingdom Protista so diverse.

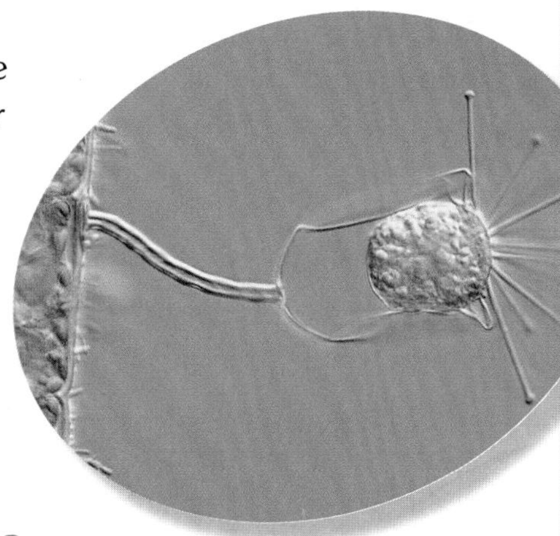

Materials

- Cultures of *Paramecium, Amoeba, Euglena,* and *Spirogyra*
  - * *prepared slides of above organisms*
- Prepared slide of slime mold
- Coverslips (5)
- Microscope
  - * *stereomicroscope*
- Dropper
- Microscope slides (5)

* *Alternate Materials*

What You'll Investigate

What are the differences between algae and protozoans?

Goals

- **Draw and label** the organisms you examine.
- **Observe** the differences between algae and protozoans.

Safety Precautions

Make sure to wash your hands after handling algae and protozoans.

Procedure

1. **Design** a data table in your Science Journal for your drawings and observations.
2. **Make** a wet mount of the *Paramecium* culture. If you need help doing this, refer to Appendix D.
3. **Observe** the wet mount first under low and then under high power. Draw and label the organism.
4. Repeat steps 2 and 3 with the other cultures. Return all preparations to your teacher and wash your hands.
5. **Observe** the slide of slime mold under low and high power. Record your observations.

Conclude and Apply

1. For each organism that could move, **label** the structure that enabled the movement.
2. Which protists make their own food? **Explain** how you know that they make their own food.
3. **Identify** those protists with animal characteristics.

Protist Observations

	Paramecium	Amoeba	Euglena	Spirogyra
Drawing				

22•2 Kingdom Fungi

What You'll Learn

- How to identify the characteristics shared by all fungi
- How to classify fungi into groups based on their methods of reproduction
- The difference between the imperfect fungi and all other fungi

Vocabulary
hyphae
spore
budding
lichen

Why It's Important

- Fungi are important sources of food and medicines, and they recycle Earth's wastes.

What are fungi?

Do you think you can find members of Kingdom Fungi in a quick trip around your house or apartment? You can find fungi in your kitchen if you have mushroom soup or fresh mushrooms. Yeasts are a type of fungi used to make bread and cheese. You also may find mold, a type of fungus, growing on an old loaf of bread, or mildew, another fungus, growing on your shower curtain.

As important as fungi seem in the production of different foods, they are most important in their role as organisms that decompose or break down organic materials. Food scraps, clothing, dead plants, and animals are all made of organic material. Fungi work to decompose, or break down, all these materials and return them to the soil. The materials returned to the soil are then reused by plants. Fungi, along with bacteria, are nature's recyclers. They keep Earth from becoming buried under mountains of waste materials.

Characteristics of Fungi

Fungi were once classified as plants because, like plants, they grow anchored in soil and have cell walls. But, unlike plants, fungi do not make their own food or have the specialized tissues and organs of plants, such as leaves and roots. Most species of fungi are many-celled. The body of a fungus is usually a mass of many-celled, threadlike tubes called **hyphae** (HI fee), as illustrated in **Figure 22-15.**

Fungi don't contain chlorophyll and therefore cannot make their own food. Most fungi feed on dead or decaying tissues. Organisms that obtain food in this way are called *saprophytes.* A fungus gives off enzymes that break down food outside of

Hyphae

Figure 22-15 Most hyphae grow underground, though they also may form reproductive structures such as the mushrooms pictured here.

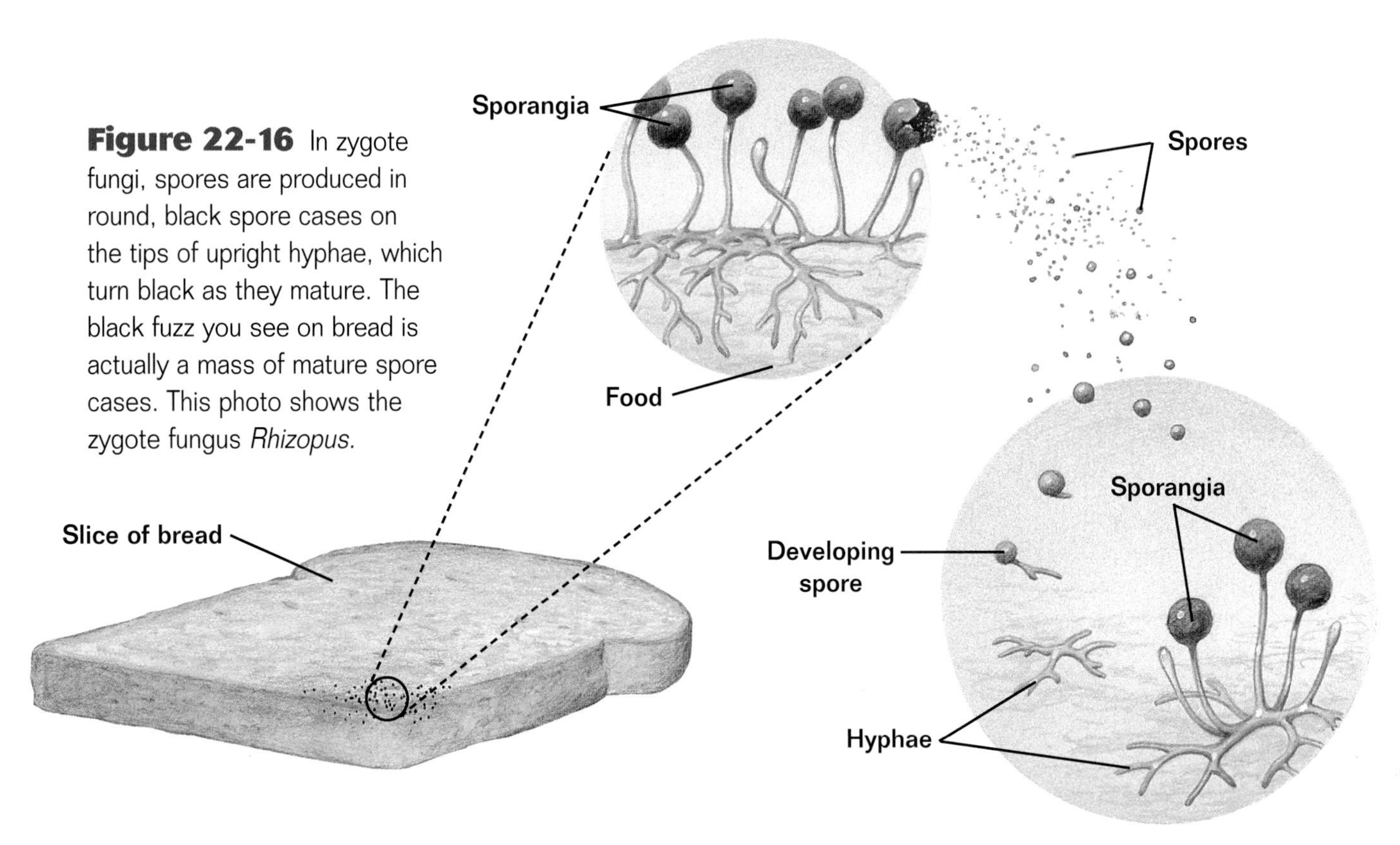

Figure 22-16 In zygote fungi, spores are produced in round, black spore cases on the tips of upright hyphae, which turn black as they mature. The black fuzz you see on bread is actually a mass of mature spore cases. This photo shows the zygote fungus *Rhizopus*.

itself. Then, the fungus cells absorb the digested food. Fungi that cause athlete's foot and ringworm are parasites. They obtain their food directly from living things.

Fungi grow best in warm, humid areas, such as tropical forests or the spaces between your toes.

A **spore** is a reproductive cell that forms new organisms without fertilization. The structures in which fungi produce spores are used to classify fungi into one of four phyla.

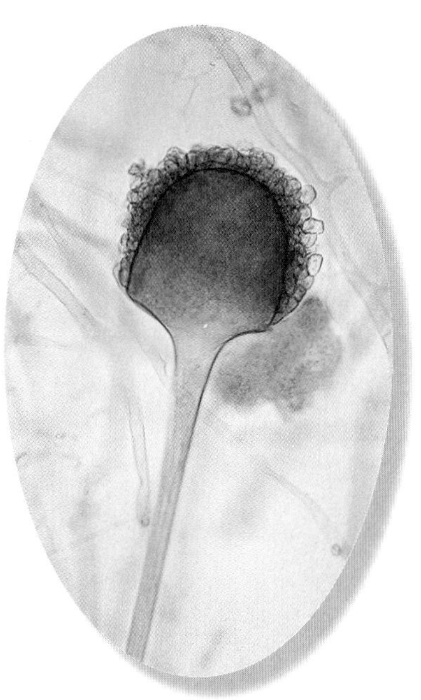

Magnification: 100×

Immature Rhizopus spore

Zygote Fungi

The fuzzy black mold that you sometimes find growing on an old loaf of bread or perhaps a piece of fruit is a type of zygote fungus. Fungi that belong to this division, the phylum Zygomycota, produce spores in round spore cases called sporangia (spuh RAN jee uh) on the tips of upright hyphae, as illustrated in **Figure 22-16.** When each sporangium splits open, hundreds of spores are released into the air. Each spore will grow into more mold if it lands where there is enough moisture, a warm temperature, and a food supply.

Sac Fungi

Yeasts, molds, morels, and truffles are all examples of sac fungi. The spores of these fungi are produced in a little saclike structure called an ascus. The phylum Ascomycota (ahs coh my COH tuh) is named for these sacs. The ascospores are released when the tip of an ascus breaks open.

Interpreting Spore Prints

Procedure

1. Obtain several mushrooms from the grocery store and let them age until the undersides look brown.
2. Remove the stems and arrange the mushroom caps with the gills down on a piece of unlined white paper.
3. Let the mushroom caps sit undisturbed overnight and remove them from the paper the next day.

Analysis

1. Draw and label a sketch of the results in your Science Journal.
2. Describe the marks on the page and what made them.
3. How could you estimate the number of new mushrooms that could be produced from one mushroom cap?

Many sac fungi are well known by farmers because they destroy plant crops. Diseases caused by sac fungi are Dutch elm disease, apple scab, and ergot disease of rye.

Yeast is an economically important sac fungus. Yeasts don't always reproduce by forming spores. They also reproduce asexually by budding, as illustrated in **Figure 22-17. Budding** is a form of asexual reproduction in which a new organism grows off the side of the parent. Yeasts are used in the baking industry. As yeasts grow, they use sugar for energy and produce alcohol and carbon dioxide as waste products. The carbon dioxide causes bread to rise.

Imperfect Fungi

The so-called imperfect fungi, phylum Deuteromycota, are species of fungi in which a sexual stage has never been observed. When a sexual stage of one of these fungi is observed, the species is immediately classified as one of the other three phyla. Instead, imperfect fungi reproduce asexually, most through the use of spores. *Penicillium* is one example from this group. Penicillin, an antibiotic, is an important product of this fungus. Other examples of imperfect fungi are species that cause ringworm and athlete's foot. Because changes in classification now allow asexual fungi to be included in other phyla, *Penicillium* is sometimes considered a sac fungus.

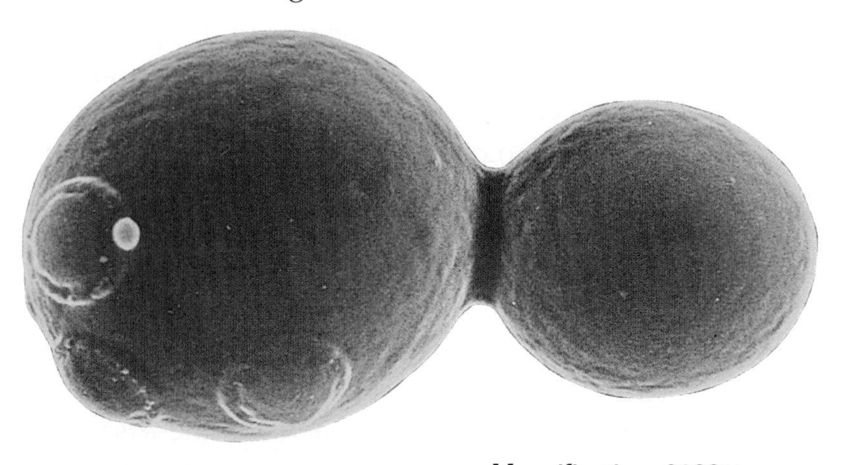

Figure 22-17 Yeasts can reproduce by forming buds off the side of the parents. The bud pinches off and forms an identical cell. **What are yeasts used for?**

Magnification: 6100×

Figure 22-18 A mushroom is the spore-producing structure of a club fungus. The gills are thin sheets of tissue found under the mushroom cap. Spores are contained in many club-shaped structures that line the gills. **What are these club-shaped structures called?**

Club Fungi

The mushrooms shown in **Figure 22-18** are members of the phylum Basidiomycota. These fungi are commonly known as club fungi. The spores of these fungi are produced in a club-shaped structure called a basidium. The spores you observed on the gills of the mushroom in the MiniLab on the previous page were produced in the basidia.

Many of the club fungi are economically important. Rusts and smuts cause billions of dollars worth of damage to food crops each year. Cultivated mushrooms are an important food crop, but you should never eat a wild mushroom because many are poisonous.

Lichens

The colorful organisms in **Figure 22-19** are lichens. A **lichen** (LI kun) is an organism that is made of a fungus and either a green alga or a cyanobacterium. When two organisms live together, they often have a relationship in which both organisms benefit. The cells of the alga live tangled up in the threadlike strands of the fungus. The alga gets a moist, protected place to live, and the fungus gets food made by the green alga or cyanobacterium. Lichens are an important food source for many animals, including caribou and musk oxen.

CHEMISTRY INTEGRATION

pH

The measurement of how much acid or base a substance contains is its pH. Acids are measured on a pH scale that ranges from 1 to 14. Substances that have a pH lower than 7 are considered acidic. Acids become stronger as the pH decreases. The acids produced by lichens are weak, but given enough time, they can erode sedimentary rock. Look up the pH for some common acids, such as stomach acid, lemon juice, and battery acid. In your Science Journal, compare these to the pH of lichen.

Rocks crumble as they weather. Lichens are important in the weathering process because they are able to grow on bare rock. Lichens release acids as part of their metabolism. The acids break down the rock. As bits of rock accumulate and lichens die and decay, soil is formed. This soil supports the growth of other species. Organisms, such as the lichens seen in **Figure 22-19,** that grow on bare rock are called pioneer species because they are the first organisms to appear in a barren area.

Earth scientists also use lichens to monitor pollution levels because many species of lichens quickly die when they are exposed to pollution. When the lichen species return to grow on tree trunks and buildings, it is an indication that the pollution has been cleaned up.

EXAMPLES OF Lichens

Figure 22-19 Lichens can grow upright, appear leafy, or look like a crust on bare rock. All three forms may grow near each other. **Can you think of one way that lichens might be classified?**

Crusty lichen

British soldier lichen

Leafy lichen

Section Assessment

1. How do fungi obtain food?
2. What common characteristics are shared by fungi?
3. What are some important functions of lichens?
4. **Think Critically:** If an imperfect fungus were found to produce basidia under some circumstances, how would the fungus be reclassified?
5. **Skill Builder**
   Comparing and Contrasting
   Organize information about fungi in a table. Use this information to compare and contrast the characteristics of the four divisions of fungi. Include information on lichens as a fifth division in your table. If you need help, refer to Comparing and Contrasting in the **Skill Handbook** on page 956.

Using Math

Of the 100 000 species of fungi, approximately 30 000 are sac fungi. From this information, estimate the percent of sac fungi as a part of the total fungi kingdom.

Monitoring Red Tides

What is a red tide?

Imagine a humpback whale dying and washing up on a beach. Then multiply this death by 14. Add to this grisly scene tons of dead fish littering beaches from Florida to Massachusetts. Such events actually happened in 1987. The cause was a single species of dinoflagellate, a type of microscopic algae (see inset). At times, certain kinds of dinoflagellates reproduce rapidly to form extremely dense populations, or "blooms," that turn the ocean surface red—a condition known as a red tide (see photo at left). Pigments in the dinoflagellates are responsible for the red color. It is not unusual for a red tide to stretch hundreds of kilometers along a coastline. Red tides often occur in warm, shallow parts of the ocean, or where runoff from the land adds nutrients to seawater.

Red tides can be deadly because some dinoflagellates produce poisonous substances called toxins. When a red tide occurs, the algae are so numerous that the amount of toxin in the water is concentrated enough to kill fish and marine mammals such as whales. Toxins also accumulate in the tissues of filter-feeding shellfish such as clams and mussels, making them poisonous. People who eat shellfish contaminated by a red tide can become ill and may die.

How are red tides monitored?

In the past, scientists monitored red tides by sampling seawater and shellfish for the presence of dinoflagellates. Wherever large numbers of dinoflagellates were detected, researchers would alert the public not to eat seafood from those areas. This method of monitoring red tides was not always effective, however, because only small stretches of ocean could be tested at any one time, and red tides often developed before scientists became aware of them.

More recently, satellites equipped with infrared cameras have been used to monitor red tides from space. Satellite images reveal sea-surface temperatures over huge areas of ocean and give scientists clues as to where red tides are most likely to occur. Predicting red tides before they develop can help save lives.

interNET CONNECTION

Visit the Glencoe Science Web Site at **www.glencoe.com/sec/science/ca** for more information about red tides. Determine whether there is an area or time of year in which red tides occur with noticeable frequency.

Activity 22•2

Materials

- Cultures of fungi (bread mold, mushrooms, yeasts, lichens, or *Penicillium*)
- Cellophane tape
- Microscope
- Microscope slides
- Coverslips
- Magnifying lens

Comparing Types of Fungi

Fungi differ mainly in their reproductive structures. The diversity of these structures allows scientists to classify fungi as zygote fungi, club fungi, sac fungi, or imperfect fungi. In this activity, you will compare the reproductive structures in cultures of fungi.

What You'll Investigate

How do reproductive structures of fungi compare?

Goals

- **Observe** the appearance of fungi colonies.
- **Compare** the reproductive structures of fungi cultures.
- **Draw, label, and identify** different types of fungi.

Safety Precautions

Make sure to wash your hands after handling fungi.

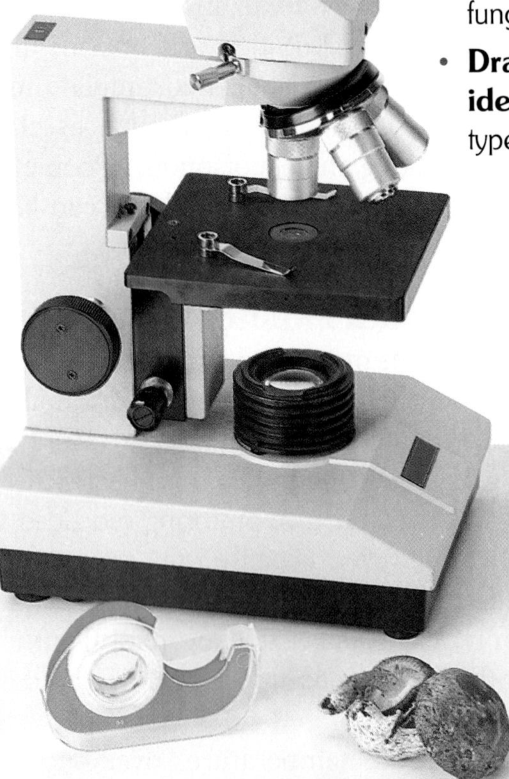

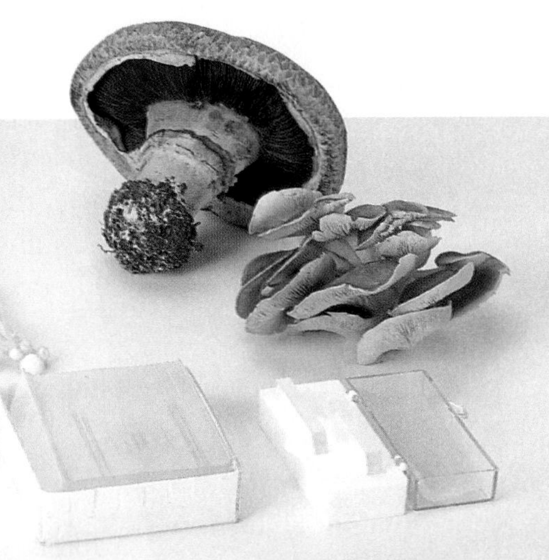

Procedure

1. **Design** a data table like the one below in your Science Journal with columns labeled *Fungus, Colony Appearance, Reproductive Structures,* and *Fungi Division.*
2. **Compare and contrast** the cultures of fungi in drawings that you label.
3. Your teacher will demonstrate how to collect the reproductive structures of fungi with cellophane tape by gently touching the tape to your samples.
4. Place the tape, adhesive side up, on a microscope slide and cover it with a coverslip. If you need help making a wet mount, see **Appendix D.**
5. Draw and label the reproductive structures.
6. Repeat this procedure for each culture of fungus.
7. Fill in the data table you designed. One column has been done for you below.

Conclude and Apply

1. Write a description of the reproductive structures you observed. Include relative numbers, shape of cells, and size.
2. From your descriptions, explain why fungi are classified based on their reproductive structures.
3. List the four divisions of fungi, and give an example of each division.

Fungi Observations

Fungus	Colony Appearance	Reproductive Structures	Fungi Division
mushrooms	rounded stalks with clublike caps	basidia	club fungi

Chapter 22 Reviewing Main Ideas

For a **preview** of this chapter, study this Reviewing Main Ideas before you read the chapter. After you have studied this chapter, you can use the Reviewing Main Ideas to **review** the chapter.

The Glencoe MindJogger, Audiocassettes, and CD-ROM provide additional opportunities for review.

Section

22-1 KINGDOM PROTISTA

Protists are one- or many-celled eukaryotic organisms. They are thought to have evolved from a one-celled organism with a nucleus, mitochondria, and other cellular structures. The protist kingdom has members that are plantlike, animal-like, and funguslike. Plantlike protists are classified by their structure, their pigments, and the way in which they store food. Animal-like protists are separated into groups by how they move. Funguslike protists have characteristics of both protists and fungi. ***What common names are given to each group of protists?***

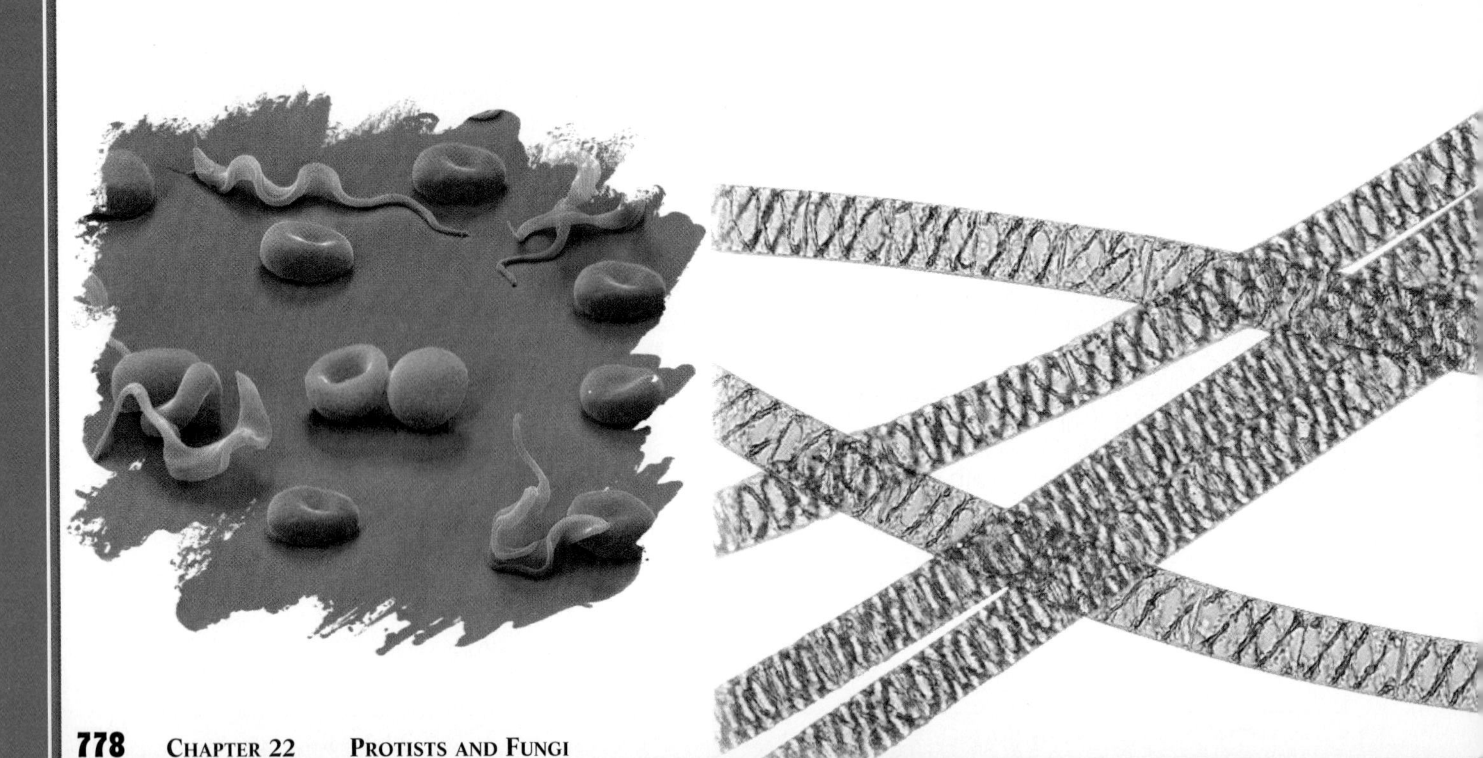

Reading Check

Review "Other Characteristics" in **Table 22-1.** How could you break the information under this heading into at least two columns?

Section

22-2 KINGDOM FUNGI

Fungi are organisms that reproduce using **spores.** They are saprophytes, or parasites, which means they feed off other things because they cannot make their own food. One of the most important roles of fungi is to decompose organic material and return the nutrients to the soil. There are four groups of fungi: zygote fungus, sac fungus, club fungus, and imperfect fungus. Fungi are placed into one of these groups according to the structures in which they produce spores. ***Why are imperfect fungi given that name?***

Dr. Regina Benjamin, Family Practice Physician

Dr. Benjamin runs a family practice in Bayou La Batre, Alabama. She's the only doctor in town, and about 80 percent of her patients live below the poverty level. Dr. Benjamin sees a lot of skin infections caused by fungi because the environment is humid, which promotes the growth of fungus. Fungal infections can be difficult to treat. ***Why is classifying protists and fungi important for health care professionals?***

Chapter 22 Assessment

Using Vocabulary

a. algae
b. budding
c. cilia
d. hyphae
e. lichen
f. protist
g. protozoans
h. pseudopods
i. spore

Each phrase below describes a science term from the list. Write the term that matches the phrase describing it.

1. reproductive cell of a fungus
2. eukaryotic organism that is animal-like, plantlike, or funguslike
3. threadlike structures used for movement
4. plantlike protists
5. organism made up of a fungus and an alga or a cyanobacterium

Checking Concepts

Choose the word or phrase that best answers the question.

6. Which of the following is an example of one-celled algae?
   A) paramecia
   B) lichen
   C) amoeba
   D) diatom
7. What color are members of phylum Bacillariophyta?
   A) green
   B) red
   C) golden-brown
   D) brown
8. Which of the following organisms cause red tides when found in large numbers?
   A) *Euglena*
   B) diatoms
   C) *Ulva*
   D) dinoflagellates
9. What phylum do brown algae belong to?
   A) Rhodophyta
   B) Dinoflagellata
   C) Phaeophyta
   D) Euglenophyta
10. Which of the following moves using cilia?
    A) *Amoeba*
    B) *Paramecium*
    C) *Trypanosoma*
    D) *Euglena*
11. Where would you most likely find funguslike protists?
    A) on decaying logs
    B) in bright light
    C) on dry surfaces
    D) on metal surfaces
12. Decomposition is an important role of which organisms?
    A) protozoans
    B) algae
    C) plants
    D) fungi
13. Which of the following organisms are monitors of pollution levels?
    A) club fungus
    B) lichen
    C) slime mold
    D) imperfect fungus
14. What produce the spores in mushrooms?
    A) sporangia
    B) basidia
    C) asci
    D) hyphae
15. Which of the following is an example of an imperfect fungus?
    A) mushroom
    B) yeast
    C) *Penicillium*
    D) lichen

Thinking Critically

16. What kind of environment is needed to prevent fungal growth?
17. Look at **Figure 22-5C** again. Why is *Spirogyra* a good name for this green alga?
18. Compare and contrast one-celled, colonial, chain, and many-celled algae.
19. Why do scientists find it difficult to trace the origin of fungi? Explain your answer.
20. Explain the adaptations of fungi that enable them to get food.

Developing Skills

If you need help, refer to the Skill Handbook.

21. **Observing and Inferring:** Match the prefix of each alga, *Chloro-, Phaeo-,* and *Rhodo-,* with the correct color: brown, green, and red.
22. **Concept Mapping:** Complete the following concept map on a separate sheet of paper.

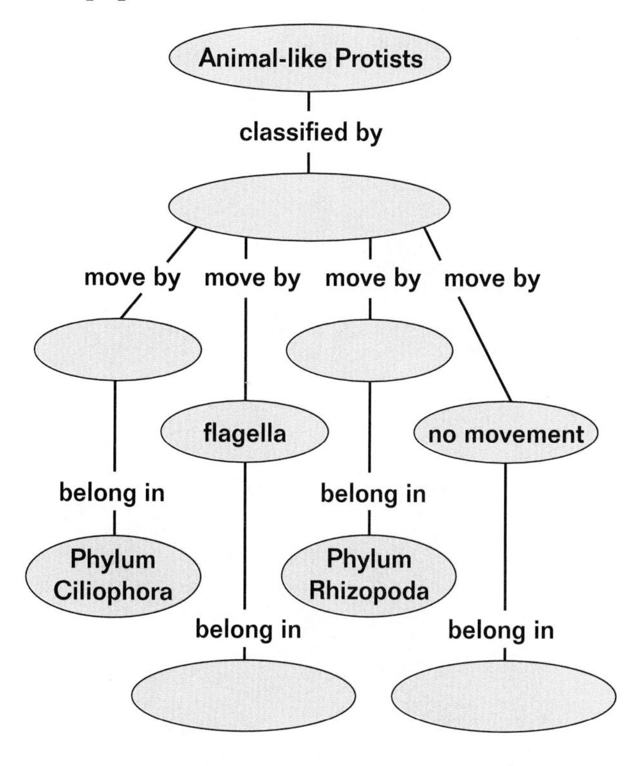

23. **Comparing and Contrasting:** Make a chart comparing and contrasting sac fungi, zygote fungi, club fungi, and imperfect fungi.
24. **Classifying:** Classify the following organisms based on their method of movement: *Euglena,* water molds, *Amoeba,* dinoflagellates, *Paramecium,* slime molds, *Trypanosoma,* and *Volvox.*
25. **Design an Experiment:** You find a new and unusual fungus growing in your refrigerator. Design an experiment to determine what phylum it belongs to.

Test-Taking Tip

Where's the Fire? Slow down! Double-check your math, and go back over reading passages. Remember that doing most of the questions and getting them right is always better than doing all the questions and getting lots of them wrong.

Test Practice

Use these questions to test your Science Proficiency.

1. Algae and plants have some characteristics in common. Which of the following **BEST** represents differences between algae and plants?
   A) Algae have cell walls, but plants do not.
   B) Plants have chlorophyll, but algae do not.
   C) Algae have cell membranes and nuclei, but plants do not.
   D) Plants have roots, stems, and leaves, but algae do not.
2. At one time, some protists were classified as animals because they moved and engulfed food. Which of the following protists are most like animals?
   A) protozoans
   B) algae
   C) slime molds and water molds
   D) zygote fungi
3. Fungi are classified according to how they produce sexual spores. Which of the following groups of fungi are **NOT** known to ever produce sexual spores?
   A) zygote fungi
   B) imperfect fungi
   C) club fungi
   D) sac fungi

CHAPTER

23 Plants

Chapter Preview

Section 23-1
Characteristics of Plants

Section 23-2
Seedless Plants

Section 23-3
Seed Plants

Skills Preview

Skill Builders
- Hypothesize
- Map Concepts

Activities
- Predict
- Compare and Contrast

MiniLabs
- Measure in SI
- Observe and Infer

Reading Check

As you read, list terms that describe parts of both plants and people, such as *vascular tissue, cuticle,* and *epidermis.* Define the terms as they relate to plants and to people.

Explore Activity

Plants are all around—in parks and gardens, by streams and on rocks, in houses, and even on dinner plates. Do you eat salads? Salads are made up of edible plants. What plants would you choose for a salad? Do you know what plant parts you would be eating? In the following activity, find out which plant parts are edible. Then, in the chapter, learn about plant life.

Infer Which Plant Parts Are Edible

1. Make a list of five foods that you might eat during a typical day.
2. Decide whether the foods contain any plant parts.
3. Infer what plant parts were used to make your five foods.

Science Journal

Plants provide many nutrients. List the nutrients from a package of dried fruit in your Science Journal. As a class, compare the nutrients in the dried fruits each student selected.

23•1 Characteristics of Plants

What You'll Learn

- The characteristics of plants
- What plant adaptations make it possible for plants to survive on land
- Similarities and differences between vascular and nonvascular plants

Vocabulary
cellulose
cuticle
vascular plant
nonvascular plant

Why It's Important

- Plants produce food and oxygen for most organisms on Earth. Without plants, there would be no life.

What is a plant?

Do you enjoy walking along nature trails in parks like the one shown in **Figure 23-1?** Maybe you've taken off your shoes and walked barefoot on soft, cool grass. Perhaps you've climbed a tree to see what your world looks like from high in its branches. In every instance, members of the plant kingdom surrounded you.

Now look at **Figure 23-2.** These organisms, mosses and liverworts, have characteristics that identify them as plants, too. What do they have in common with grasses, trees, and ferns? What makes a plant a plant?

Characteristics of Plants

All plants are made of eukaryotic cells that have cell walls. Cell walls provide structure and protection for plant cells. Many plant cells contain the green pigment chlorophyll. Plants range in size from microscopic water ferns to giant sequoia trees that are sometimes more than 100 m in height. They have roots or rootlike structures that hold them in the ground or onto something. Plants have successfully adapted to nearly every environment on Earth. Some grow in frigid, ice-bound polar regions and others grow in hot, dry deserts. Many plants must live in or near water.

About 285 000 plant species have been discovered and identified. Scientists think many more are still to be found, mainly in tropical rain forests. If you were to make a list of all

Figure 23-1 All plants are many celled and nearly all contain chlorophyll. Grasses, trees, and ferns all are members of Kingdom Plantae.

Figure 23-2 Plants include liverworts (A) and mosses (B).

the plants you could name, you probably would include vegetables, fruits, and field crops like wheat, rice, or corn. These plants are important food sources to humans and other consumers. Without plants, most life on Earth as we know it would not be possible.

Origin and Evolution of Plants

Where did the first plants come from? Like all life, early plants probably came from the sea, evolving from plantlike protists. What evidence is there that this is true? Both plants and green algae, a type of protist, have the same types of chlorophyll and carotenoids (KER uh tuh noydz) in their cells. Carotenoids are red, yellow, or orange pigments found in some plants and in all cyanobacteria.

Fossil Record

One way to understand the evolution of plants is to look at the fossil record. Unfortunately, plants usually decay before they form fossils. The oldest fossil plants are from the Silurian period and are about 420 million years old. Fossils of early plants are similar to the plantlike protists. Fossils of *Rhynia major*, illustrated in **Figure 23-3,** represent the earliest land plants. Scientists hypothesize that these kinds of plants evolved into some plants that exist today.

Cone-bearing plants, such as pines, probably evolved from a group of plants that grew about 350 million years ago. Fossils of these plants have been dated to the Paleozoic era, 300 million years ago. Flowering plants did not exist until the Cretaceous period, about 120 million years ago. The exact origin of flowering plants is not known.

Using Computers

Fossil evidence shows that the first land plants lived about 420 million years ago. If Earth is 4.6 billion years old, what percent of Earth's age was Earth without land plants?

Figure 23-3 Fossils of *Rhynia major*, an extinct, small land plant, show that it had underground stems but no true roots or leaves.

CHEMISTRY INTEGRATION

Cellulose

Plant cell walls are made mostly of cellulose, an organic compound. Cellulose is made of long chains of glucose molecules, $C_6H_{12}O_6$. More than half the carbon in plants is in cellulose. Raw cotton is more than 90 percent cellulose. Infer which physical property of cellulose makes it ideal for helping plants survive on land.

Adaptations to Land

Imagine life for a one-celled green alga, a protist, floating in a shallow pool. The water in the pool surrounds and supports it. The alga can make its own food through the process of photosynthesis. Materials enter and leave the cell through the cell membrane and cell wall. The alga has everything it needs to survive.

Now, imagine a summer drought. The pool begins to dry up. Soon, the alga is on damp mud and is no longer supported by the pool's water, as shown in **Figure 23-4.** It won't starve because it still can make its own food. As long as the soil stays damp, the alga can move materials in and out through the cell membrane and cell wall. But, what will happen if the drought continues, and the soil becomes drier and drier? The alga will continue to lose water because water diffuses through the cell membrane and cell wall from where there is more water to where there is less water. Without water in its environment, the alga will dry up and die.

Protection and Support

What adaptations would make it possible for plants to survive on land? Losing water is a major problem for plants. What would help a plant conserve water? Plant cells have cell membranes, but they also have rigid cell walls outside the membrane. Cell walls contain **cellulose** (SEL yuh lohs), an organic compound made up of long chains of glucose molecules. Some woody plants, such as oaks and pines, are as much as 50 percent cellulose. Cell walls provide structure and support and help reduce water loss.

Figure 23-4 Algae must have water to survive.

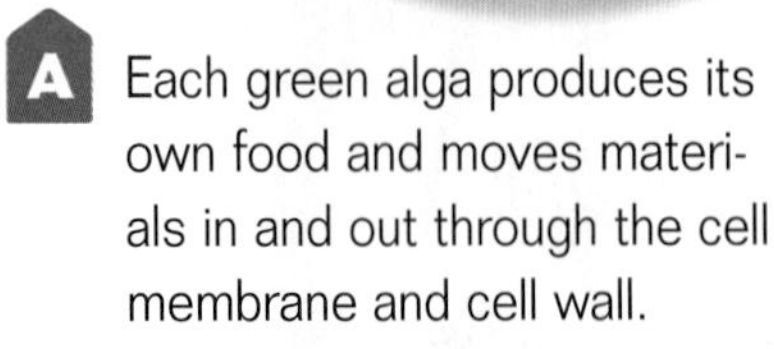

A Each green alga produces its own food and moves materials in and out through the cell membrane and cell wall. **By what process do algae make food?**

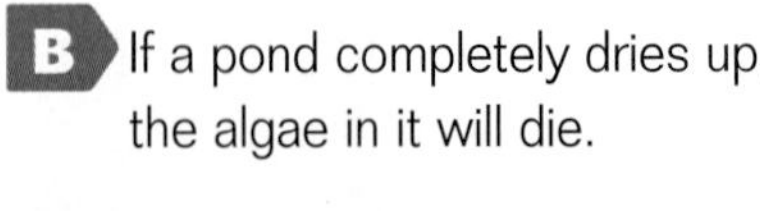

B If a pond completely dries up, the algae in it will die.

Figure 23-5 A waxy cuticle is an adaptation that enables plants to survive on land.

A Rain beads up on the leaves of some plants because of the cuticle. This reduces the amount of moisture on plant surfaces.

B A waxy cuticle prevents moisture loss from this prickly pear cactus. **Why is this important for a cactus?**

C Waxy cuticles are often found on flowers such as this orchid.

Covering the stems, leaves, and flowers of some land plants is a cuticle. The **cuticle** (KYEWT ih kul) is a waxy, protective layer secreted by the cell walls. It slows down the evaporation of water from a plant. After it rains, go outside and see how raindrops bead up on some plant surfaces, as illustrated in **Figure 23-5A.** Removing water from plant surfaces is important because too much moisture on a plant may affect cell functions. Too much surface moisture also may lead to fungal diseases. The cuticle is an adaptation that enabled plants to live on land.

Life on land meant that plant cells could not depend on water to support them or to move substances from one cell to the next. Support came with the evolution of stems and substances that strengthen the cell walls. Eventually, plants developed tissues that distribute materials.

Reproduction

The move to land by plants not only meant changes to reduce water loss and increase support, but it also meant a change in plant reproduction. Plants evolved from organisms that reproduced in water. They completely depended on water for reproduction and survival. Some plants still require water to reproduce, but others do not. The development of cones and flowers that produce seeds allowed these plants to survive on land.

Life on Land

Life on land has some advantages for plants. There is more sunlight and carbon dioxide for plants on land than in water. Plants use sunlight and carbon dioxide for the food-making process, photosynthesis. During photosynthesis, plants give off oxygen. As more and more plants adapted to life on land, the amount of oxygen in Earth's atmosphere increased. This paved the way for the evolution of organisms that depend on oxygen. In some cases, it meant that some organisms evolved together. For example, some flowering plants provided animals with food, and the animals pollinated the plant's flowers.

interNET CONNECTION

Visit the Glencoe Science Web Site at **www.glencoe.com/sec/science/ca** for more information about plants that are sources of medicines. In your Science Journal, list five medicines that come from plants.

Classification of Plants

Today, the plant kingdom is classified into major groups called divisions, as illustrated in **Figure 23-6.** A division is the same as a phylum in other kingdoms, as listed in Appendix E of this book. A less formal way to group plants is as vascular or nonvascular plants. **Vascular plants** have tissues that make up the organ system that carries water, nutrients, and other substances throughout the plant. **Nonvascular plants** have no vascular tissue and use other ways to move water and substances.

Problem Solving

Cause and Effect in Nature

People in all cultures have used and still use plants as medicine. Some Native American cultures used willow bark to cure headaches. Heart problems were treated with foxglove in England and sea onions in Egypt. In Peru, the bark of the cinchona tree was used to treat malaria. Scientists have found that many native cures are medically sound. Willow bark contains salicylates, the main ingredient in aspirin. Foxglove, as seen in the photo to the right, is still the main source of digitalis, a drug prescribed for heart problems. Cinchona bark contains quinine, an antimalarial drug.

Think Critically: Predict how the destruction of the rain forests might affect research for new drugs from plants.

VISUALIZING The Plant Kingdom

Figure 23-6 The diversity of Kingdom Plantae is represented by a branching tree, composed of different divisions. All of these plant groups are related but have differences that separate them. **What differences can you detect among the plant divisions in this illustration?**

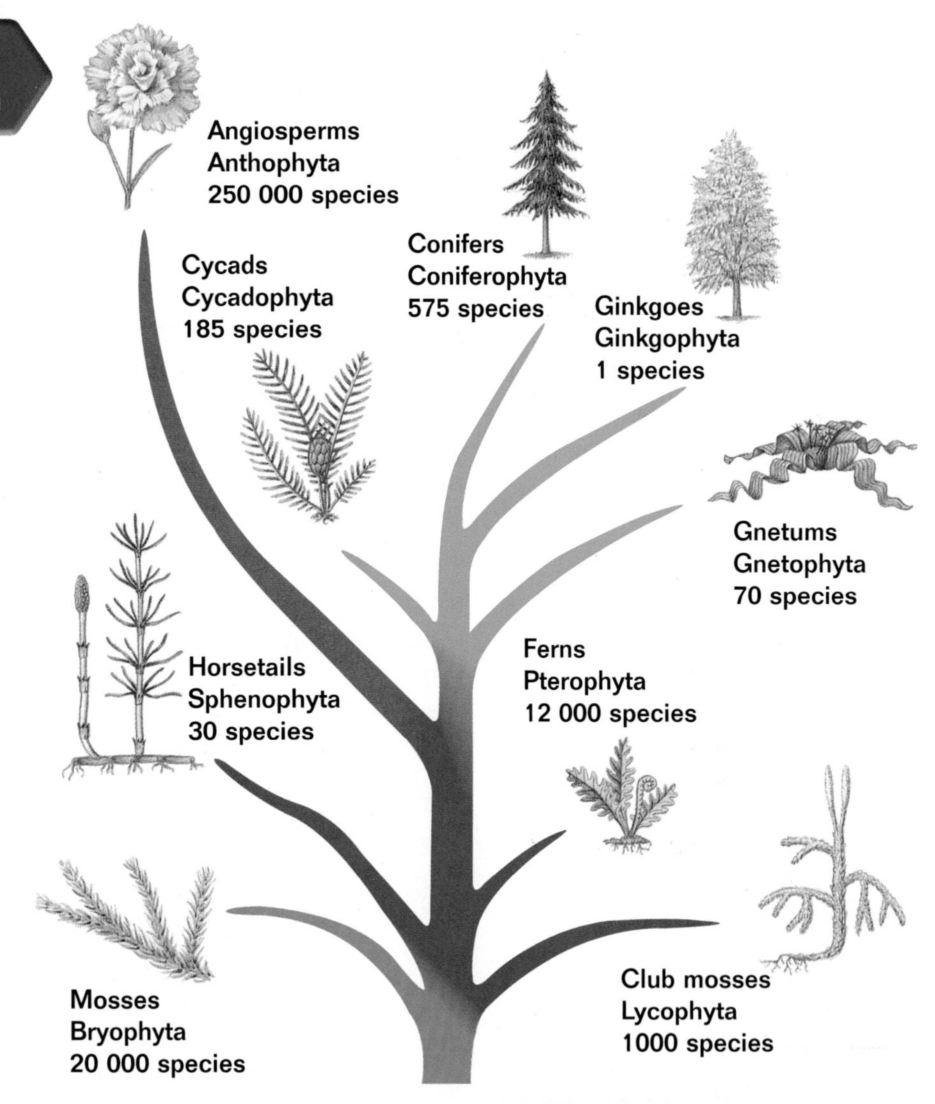

Section Assessment

1. List the characteristics of plants.
2. Compare vascular and nonvascular plants.
3. Name three adaptations that allow plants to survive on land.
4. **Think Critically:** If you left a board lying on the grass for a few days, what would happen to the grass underneath the board? Why?
5. **Skill Builder**
   Forming a Hypothesis From what you have learned about adaptations necessary for life on land, make a hypothesis as to what types of adaptations land plants might have if they had to survive submerged in water. If you need help, refer to Forming a Hypothesis in the **Skill Handbook** on page 958.

The oldest surviving plant species is *Ginkgo biloba.* Research the history of this species, then write about it in your Science Journal.

23•2 Seedless Plants

What You'll Learn

- Characteristics of seedless nonvascular plants and seedless vascular plants
- The importance of some nonvascular and vascular plants

Vocabulary
rhizoid
pioneer species

Why It's Important

- Seedless plants are often the first to grow in damaged or disturbed environments.

Seedless Nonvascular Plants

If you were asked to name the parts of a plant, you probably would list roots, stems, leaves, and perhaps flowers. You also may know that many plants grow from seeds. But, did you know that some plants do not have all of these parts? **Figure 23-7** shows some common types of nonvascular plants.

Liverworts and Mosses (Bryophytes)

The bryophytes (BRI uh fites)—liverworts and mosses—are small, nonvascular plants that are usually just a few cells thick and only 2 cm to 5 cm in height. They have stalks that look like stems and leafy green growths. The threadlike roots of bryophytes are called **rhizoids.** Water is absorbed and distributed directly through their cell walls. Bryophytes grow in damp environments such as the forest floor, the edges of ponds and streams, and near the ocean. Bryophytes usually reproduce by spores because they do not have flowers to produce seeds.

Liverworts get their name because to some people, one type looks like a liver. It is a rootless plant that has a flattened, leaflike body. Liverworts usually have one-celled rhizoids. In the ninth century, liverworts were thought to be useful in treating diseases of the liver. The ending, *-wort,* means "herb," so the word *liverwort* means "herb for the liver." Of approximately 20 000 species of nonvascular plants, most are classified as mosses. Have you ever seen mosses growing on tree trunks, rocks, or the ground in damp or humid areas? Mosses have green, leaflike

A

B

Figure 23-7 The seedless nonvascular plants include the mosses (A) and the liverworts (B).

Figure 23-8 Mosses are often among the first organisms to live in a new environment, such as this lava field. **Where do the mosses come from?**

growths in a spiral around a stalk. Their threadlike rhizoids are only a few cells in length.

EARTH SCIENCE INTEGRATION

Soil Formation

Soil is a mixture of weathered rock and decaying organic matter (plant and animal). Infer what roles pioneer species such as lichens, mosses, and liverworts play in building soil.

The Importance of Bryophytes

Mosses and liverworts are important in the ecology of many areas. Although mosses require moist conditions to grow and reproduce, many of them can withstand long, dry periods. Often, they are among the first plants to grow in new environments, such as lava fields as shown in **Figure 23-8,** or disturbed environments, such as forests destroyed by fire.

When a volcano erupts, lava covers the land and destroys the plants living there. After the lava cools, spores of mosses and liverworts are carried by the wind to the new rocks. The spores will grow into plants if enough water is available and other growing conditions are right. Organisms that are the first to grow in new or disturbed areas like these are called **pioneer species.** As pioneer plants grow and die, decaying plant material builds up. This, along with the breakdown of rocks, begins the formation of soil. Pioneer plants change environmental conditions so that other plants can grow.

Measuring Water Absorption by a Moss

Procedure

1. Place a few teaspoons of *Sphagnum* moss on a piece of cheesecloth. Twist the cheesecloth to form a ball and tie it securely.
2. Weigh the ball.
3. Put 200 mL of water in a container and add the ball.
4. Predict how much water the ball will absorb.
5. Wait 15 minutes. Remove the ball and drain the excess water back into the container.

Analysis

1. Weigh the ball and measure the amount of water left in the container.
2. In your Science Journal, calculate how much water the *Sphagnum* moss absorbed.

Seedless Vascular Plants

The plants in **Figure 23-9** are like mosses because they are seedless plants that reproduce by spores. They are different from mosses because they have vascular tissue. The vascular tissue in the seedless vascular plants is made up of long, tubelike cells. These cells carry water, minerals, and nutrients to cells throughout the plant. Why is having cells like these an advantage to a plant? Remember that bryophytes are only a few cells thick. Each cell absorbs water directly from its environment. As a result, these plants cannot grow large. Vascular plants, on the other hand, can grow bigger and thicker because the vascular tissue distributes water and nutrients.

Reading Check What makes up the vascular tissue in seedless vascular plants?

Types of Seedless Vascular Plants

Seedless vascular plants include the ground pines, spike mosses, horsetails, and ferns. Today, there are about 1000 species of ground pines, spike mosses, and horsetails. Ferns are more abundant, with at least 12 000 species known. Many species of seedless vascular plants are known only from fossils. They flourished during the warm, moist Paleozoic era. Fossil records show that some horsetails grew 15 m tall, unlike modern species that only grow 1 m to 2 m tall.

Figure 23-9 The seedless vascular plants include ground pines, spike mosses, horsetails, and ferns. **Why can these plants grow taller than mosses and liverworts?**

Figure 23-10 Club mosses such as ground pines (A) and spike mosses (B) produce spores at the end of stems in tiny, conelike structures. Photographers once used the dry, flammable spores of club mosses as flash powder. It burned rapidly and produced the light to take photographs.

Ground Pines and Spike Mosses

The photographs in **Figure 23-10** show ground pines and spike mosses. Both groups of plants are often called club mosses. They are seedless vascular plants with needlelike leaves. Spores are produced at the end of the stems in structures that look like tiny pine cones. Ground pines are found from arctic regions to the tropics, but never in large numbers. In some areas, they are endangered because they have been overcollected to make wreaths and other decorations.

Spike mosses resemble ground pines. One species of spike moss, the resurrection plant, is adapted to desert conditions. When water is scarce, the plant curls up and seems dead. When water becomes available, the resurrection plant unfurls its green leaves and begins making food again. The plant can repeat this process whenever necessary.

Figure 23-11 The spores of horsetails are found in conelike structures on the tips of some stems.

Horsetails

Horsetails have a stem structure unique among the vascular plants. Their stems are jointed and have a hollow center surrounded by a ring of vascular tissue. At each joint, leaves grow around the stem. In **Figure 23-11,** you can see these joints easily. If you pull on a horsetail stem, it will pop apart in sections. Like the club mosses, spores from horsetails are produced in a conelike structure at the tips of some stems.

Figure 23-12 Most ferns produce spores in special structures on the leaves, but the spores of the cinnamon fern are on a separate stalk.

The stems of the horsetails contain silica, a gritty substance found in sand. For centuries, horsetails have been used for polishing objects, sharpening tools, and scouring cooking utensils. Another common name for horsetails is scouring rush.

Ferns

Ferns belong to the largest group of seedless vascular plants. Ferns, like those in **Figure 23-12,** have stems, leaves, and roots. They also have characteristics of both nonvascular and vascular plants. Like the bryophytes, ferns produce spores, and they have vascular tissue like vascular plants. Today, thousands of species of ferns grow on Earth, but once there were many more. From clues left in rock layers, scientists know that during the Carboniferous period of the Paleozoic era, much of Earth was tropical. Steamy swamps covered large areas, as illustrated in **Figure 23-13.** The tallest plants were species of ferns. The ancient ferns grew as tall as 25 m—much taller than any fern species alive today. The tallest, modern tree ferns are about 3 m to 5 m in height.

*inter***NET**
CONNECTION

Visit the Glencoe Science Web Site at **www.glencoe.com/sec/science/ca** for more information about which ferns are native to your state. In your Science Journal, list three of these ferns and describe their environments.

Formation of Fuel

When ferns and other plants of the Carboniferous period died, many of them became submerged in water and mud before they could decompose. This plant material built up, became compacted and compressed, and eventually turned into coal. This process took millions of years.

Today, a similar process is taking place in bogs. A bog is a poorly drained area of land that contains decaying plants. The decay process is slow because waterlogged soils do not

contain oxygen. The plants in bogs are mostly seedless plants like mosses and ferns. Peat, the remains of peat mosses, is mined from bogs in some countries for a low-cost fuel. Scientists hypothesize that over time, if additional layers of soil bury, compact, and compress the peat, it will become coal.

Figure 23-13 Many more species of club mosses, horsetails, and ferns grew in carboniferous swamp forests than are alive today.

Section Assessment

1. Compare and contrast the mosses and ferns.
2. What do fossil records tell us about seedless plants?
3. Under what conditions would you expect to find pioneer plants?
4. **Think Critically:** List ways seedless plants affect your life each day. (HINT: Where do electricity and heat for homes come from?)
5. **Skill Builder**
   Concept Mapping Make a concept map showing how seedless nonvascular and seedless vascular plants are related. Include these terms in the concept map: *plant kingdom, bryophytes, seedless nonvascular plants, seedless vascular plants, ferns, ground pines, horsetails, liverworts, mosses,* and *spike mosses.* If you need help, refer to Concept Mapping in the **Skill Handbook** on page 950.

Using Computers

There are approximately 8000 species of liverworts and 9000 species of mosses. Estimate what fraction of bryophytes are mosses.

Comparing Seedless Plants

Materials

One living example of each of these plants:
- Moss
- Liverwort
- Club moss
- Horsetail
- Fern

  * *detailed photographs of the above plant types*
  * *Alternate Material*

Liverworts, mosses, ferns, horsetails, and club mosses have at least one common characteristic—they reproduce by spores. But, do they have other things in common? In this activity, discover their similarities and differences.

What You'll Investigate

How are seedless plants alike and how are they different?

Goals

- **Observe** types of seedless plants.
- **Compare and contrast** seedless plants.

Procedure

1. Copy the Plant Observations table into your Science Journal.
2. Examine each plant and fill in the table using the following guidelines:
   Color—green or not green
   Growth—mostly flat and low or mostly upright
   Root Type—small and fiberlike or rootlike
   Leaf Form—needlelike, scalelike, or leaflike

Conclude and Apply

1. **Observe and infer** what characteristics seedless plants have in common.
2. **Hypothesize** about the differences in growth.
3. **Compare and contrast** the seedless plants.

Plant Observations

Plant	Color	Growth	Root Type	Leaf Form
Moss				
Liverwort				
Club moss				
Horsetail				
Fern				

Preservation in Peat Bogs

A bog is a wetland, characterized by wet, spongy, poorly drained ground. It typically contains a thin layer of living plants overlying a thick layer of partially decomposed plant material called peat. One of the major types of peat is moss peat. It is formed mostly from *Sphagnum* moss. Peat bogs are acidic, low in minerals, and lack oxygen. These conditions provide a unique environment. When some types of organisms become trapped and buried in a peat bog, they do not decay. In Europe and North America, the well-preserved bodies of humans and other animals have been found in peat bogs.

STEP BY STEP

1. Mosses and other wetland plants grow on the surface of a bog.
2. Over time, a layer of partially decayed plant matter accumulates. Eventually, this becomes a thick layer of peat.
3. A substance in the cell walls of *Sphagnum* moss reacts with, and ties up, certain nutrients. These nutrients are essential for the survival of decay-causing bacteria. Without these nutrients, the bacteria cannot live in a bog.
4. When an animal is buried in a bog, its soft tissues, such as skin and internal organs, are not destroyed by decay. But, the animal's bones are dissolved away because of the acidic environment.
5. The skin of animals buried in a peat bog undergoes a sort of tanning process. Human skin becomes leatherlike and coffee colored, as seen in the photograph below.

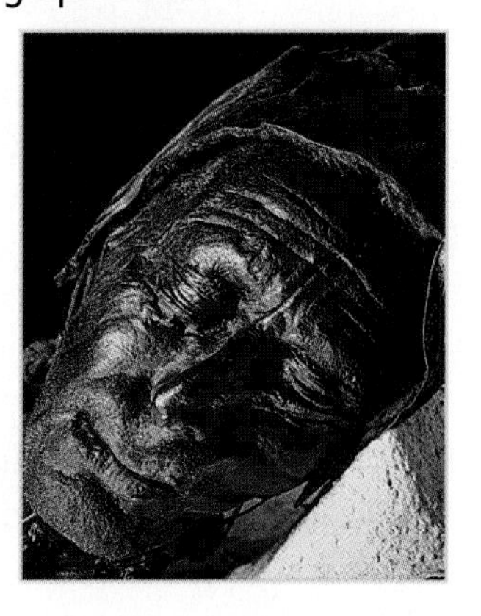

Think Critically

1. What kinds of information might scientists gain by studying bog-preserved ancient humans?
2. Another type of peat is fuel peat. What property of peat do you think makes it usable as a fuel?

Career CONNECTION

Archaeologists have found hundreds of preserved animals in peat bogs. An archaeologist studies ancient peoples, their remains, and their culture. Pretend you are an archaeologist. Imagine what it must be like for archaeologists to discover human remains.

23•3 Seed Plants

What You'll Learn

- The characteristics of seed plants
- The structures and functions of roots, stems, and leaves
- The main characteristics of gymnosperms and angiosperms and their importance
- Similarities and differences of monocots and dicots

Vocabulary

xylem
phloem
cambium
stomata
guard cell
gymnosperm
angiosperm
monocot
dicot

Why It's Important

- Understanding seed plants will help you appreciate how much you depend on them.

What is a seed plant?

Have you ever eaten vegetables like the ones shown in **Figure 23-14?** All of these foods come from seed plants. What fruits and vegetables have you eaten today? If you had an apple, a peanut butter and jelly sandwich, or a glass of orange juice for lunch, you ate foods that came from seed plants.

Nearly all the plants you are familiar with are seed plants. Seed plants have roots, stems, leaves, and vascular tissue and produce seeds. A seed usually contains an embryo and stored food. The stored food is the source of energy for growth of the embryo into a plant. More than 250 000 species of seed plants are known in the world today. Seed plants are generally classified into two major groups: the gymnosperms and the angiosperms.

Figure 23-14 The products of plants, like these being sold at a market in Ecuador, provide food for humans. **How are plants an important part of the world's food supply?**

Figure 23-15 The vascular tissue of some seed plants includes xylem, phloem, and cambium. **Which of these tissues transports food throughout the plant?**

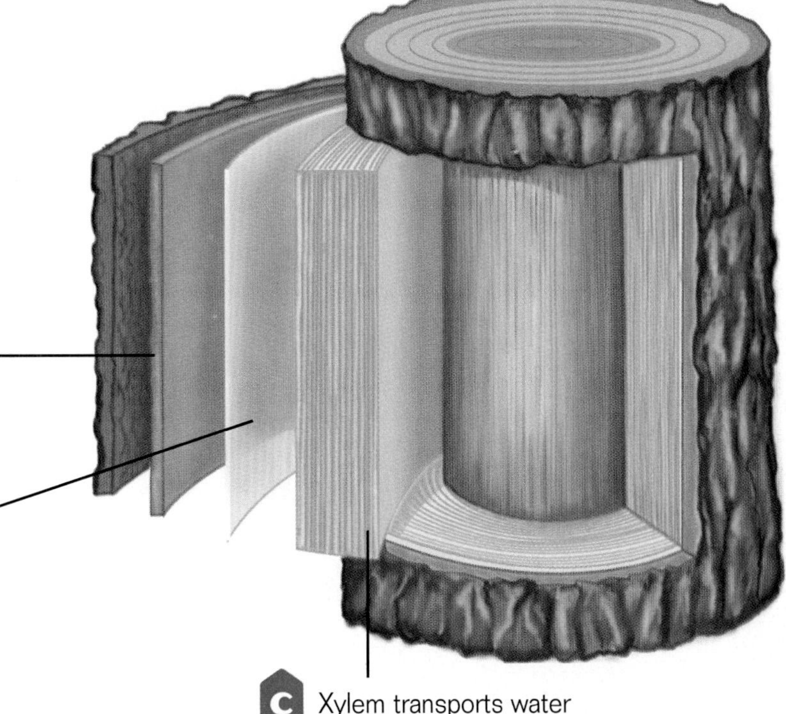

A Phloem transports dissolved sugar throughout the plant.

B Cambium produces xylem and phloem as the plant grows.

C Xylem transports water and dissolved substances throughout the plant.

Vascular Tissue

Three tissues usually make up the vascular system in a seed plant. **Xylem** (ZI lum) tissue transports water and dissolved substances from the roots throughout the plant. **Phloem** (FLOH em) tissue moves food up from where it is made to other parts of the plant where it is used or stored. In some plants, a cambium is between xylem and phloem, as shown in **Figure 23-15**. **Cambium** (KAM bee um) is a tissue that produces new xylem and phloem cells. These three tissues completely circle some stems and roots. Groups of vascular tissue called vascular bundles are found in other plants.

Stems

Did you know that the trunk of a tree is really its stem? Stems are usually above ground and support the branches, leaves, and flowers. Some stems, such as potatoes and onions, are underground. The stem allows movement of materials between leaves and roots. Some stems store food. Sugarcane has an aboveground stem that stores large quantities of food. Stems of cacti are adapted to carry on photosynthesis and make food for the rest of the plant.

MiniLab

Observing Water Moving in a Plant

Procedure

1. Into a clear container, about 10 cm tall and 4 cm in diameter, pour water to a depth of 1.5 cm. Add 15 drops of red food coloring to the water.
2. Put the root end of a whole green onion in the colored water in the container. Do not cut the onion in any way.
3. Let the onion stand overnight.
4. The next day, examine the outside of the onion. Peel off the layers of leaves and examine them.

Analysis

1. In your Science Journal, compare the appearance of the onion before and after it was in the colored water.
2. Describe the location of red color inside the onion.
3. Infer how the red color inside the onion might be related to vascular tissue.

Figure 23-16 The root system of a dandelion is longer than the plant is tall. When you pull up a dandelion, you often pull off the top portion of the plant. The root quickly produces new leaves, and another dandelion grows.

Plant stems are either herbaceous (hur BAY shus) or woody. Herbaceous stems usually are soft and green, like the stems of peppers, corn, and tulips. Oak, birch, and other trees and shrubs have hard, rigid, woody stems.

Roots

Imagine a large tree growing alone on top of a hill. What is the largest part? Maybe you said the trunk or the branches. Did you consider the roots? The root systems of most plants are as large or larger than the aboveground stems and leaves, like the dandelion in **Figure 23-16.**

Roots are important to plants. Water and other substances enter a plant through its roots. Roots have vascular tissue to move water and dissolved substances from the ground up through the stems to the leaves. Roots also anchor plants. If they didn't, plants could be blown away by wind or washed away by water. Each root system must support the plant parts that are above the ground—the stem, branches, and leaves of a tree, for example. Sometimes, part or all of roots are above ground, too.

Roots may store food. When you eat carrots or beets, you eat roots that contain stored food. Root tissues also may perform special functions such as absorbing oxygen that is used in the process of respiration.

Using Computers

The roots of some cacti are shallow but grow horizontally as much as 15 m in all directions from the stem. How much soil surface area do these roots cover?

Leaves

Have you ever rested in the shade of a tree's leaves on a hot, summer day? Leaves are the organs of the plant that usually trap light and make food through the process of photosynthesis. Leaves come in many shapes, sizes, and colors.

Leaf Structure

Look at the structure of a typical leaf shown in **Figure 23-17.** The epidermis is a thin layer of cells that covers and protects both the upper and lower surfaces of a leaf. A waxy cuticle that protects and reduces water loss covers the epidermis of many leaves. A feature of most leaves is stomata. **Stomata** are small pores in the leaf surfaces that allow carbon dioxide, water, and oxygen to enter and leave a leaf. The stomata are surrounded by **guard cells** that open and close the pores. The cuticle, stomata, and guard cells all are adaptations that help plants survive on land.

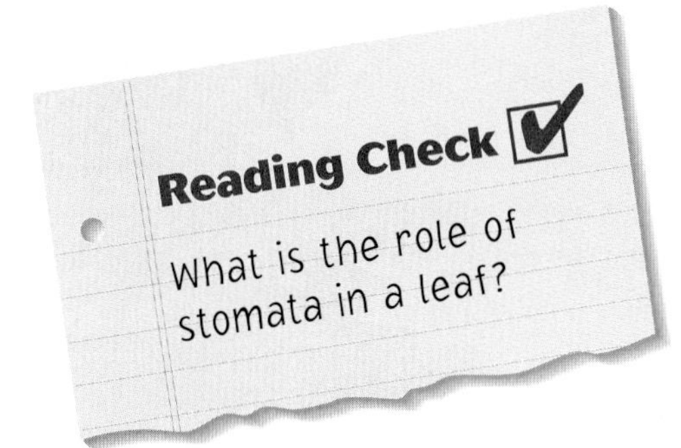

Leaf Cells

A typical leaf is made of different layers of cells. Covering the upper and lower surfaces of a leaf is the epidermis. Just below the upper epidermis is the palisade layer. It consists of closely packed, long, narrow cells that usually contain many chloroplasts. Most of the food produced by plants is made in the palisade cells. Between the palisade layer and the lower epidermis is the spongy layer. It is a layer of loosely arranged cells separated by air spaces. In a leaf, xylem and phloem are in the spongy layer.

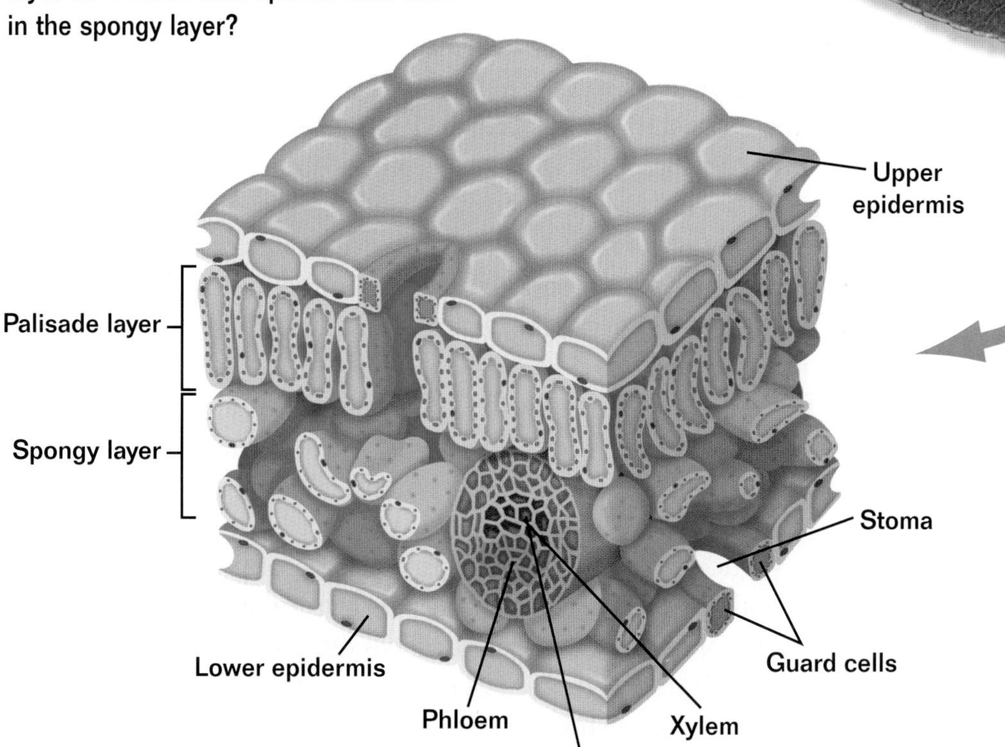

Figure 23-17 The structure of a typical leaf is adapted for photosynthesis. **Why do cells in the palisade layer have more chloroplasts than cells in the spongy layer?**

VISUALIZING Gymnosperms

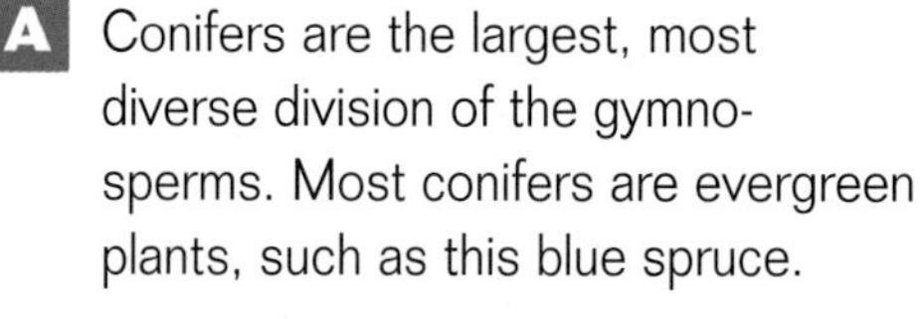

A Conifers are the largest, most diverse division of the gymnosperms. Most conifers are evergreen plants, such as this blue spruce.

B About 100 species of cycads exist today. Only one genus grows naturally in the United States. This sago palm comes from Java, an island in Indonesia.

Figure 23-18 The gymnosperms include conifers (A), cycads (B), ginkgoes (C), and gnetophytes (D).

Gymnosperms

The oldest trees alive today are gymnosperms (JIHM nuh spurmz). A bristlecone pine tree in the White Mountains of eastern California is estimated to be 4900 years old. **Gymnosperms** are vascular plants that produce seeds on the surface of the female reproductive structure. The word *gymnosperm* comes from the Greek language and means "naked seed." Seeds of gymnosperms are not protected by a fruit. Gymnosperms do not produce flowers. Leaves of most gymnosperms are needlelike or scalelike. Gymnosperms are often called evergreens because most keep their leaves for more than one year.

Four divisions of plants—conifers, cycads, ginkgoes, and gnetophytes—are classified as gymnosperms. **Figure 23-18** shows examples of the four divisions. You are probably most familiar with the division Coniferophyta, the conifers. Pines, firs, spruces, redwoods, and junipers belong to this division. It contains the greatest number of gymnosperm species. All conifers produce two types of cones, the male and female reproductive structures. These are usually on the same plant. Seeds develop on the female cone.

EXAMPLES OF Gymnosperms

- Pine
- Hemlock
- Spruce
- Sago Palm
- Ginkgo
- Joint Fir

D The 70 species of gnetophytes are classified into three genera. More than half of the species, such as this joint fir, are in one genus. Another genus has just one species, and the rest of the species are in the third genus.

C Today, the ginkgoes are represented by only one living species. Ginkgoes lose their leaves in the fall. **How is this different from most gymnosperms?**

Angiosperms

When people are asked to name a plant, most people name an angiosperm (AN jee uh spurm). Angiosperms are familiar plants no matter where you live. They grow in parks, fields, forests, jungles, deserts, freshwater, salt water, cracks of sidewalks, or dangling from wires or other plants. One species of orchid even grows underground. Angiosperms make up the plant division Anthophyta. More than eighty-five percent of plant species known today belong to this division.

An **angiosperm** is a vascular plant that flowers and has a fruit that contains seeds. The fruit develops from a part or parts of one or more flowers. The flowers of angiosperms vary in size, shape, and color. Duckweed, an aquatic plant, has a flower that is only 0.1 mm long. A plant in Indonesia has a flower that is nearly 1 m in diameter and can weigh 9 kg. Nearly every color can be found in some flower, although some people would not include black. Multi-colored flowers are common. Some plants have flowers that are not easily recognized as flowers, such as those found on oak and birch trees.

EXAMPLES OF Angiosperms

- Grasses and grains
- Cacti
- Palms
- Garden flowers
- Vegetables
- Fruits
- Nuts (except pine nuts)
- Leafy trees (except ginkgoes)

VISUALIZING
Monocots and Dicots

Figure 23-19 By observing a monocot and a dicot, their plant characteristics can be determined.

A Monocots, such as these lilies, have flower parts in multiples of three. If you had cereal for breakfast, you ate part of a monocot. Corn, rice, oats, and wheat are monocots.

B In monocots, vascular tissues are arranged as bundles scattered throughout the stem. Monocot leaves are usually more narrow than long. The vascular bundles show up as parallel veins in leaves.

Monocots and Dicots

The two classes of angiosperms are the monocots and the dicots. The terms *monocot* and *dicot* are shortened forms of the words *monocotyledon* and *dicotyledon.* The prefix *mono* means "one," and *di* means "two." A cotyledon is a seed leaf inside a seed. Therefore, **monocots** have one seed leaf inside their seeds and **dicots** have two. **Figure 23-19** compares the characteristics of monocots and dicots.

Importance of Seed Plants

Imagine that your class is having a picnic in the park. You cover the wooden picnic table with a red-checked, cotton tablecloth and pass out paper cups and plates. Your lunch includes hot dogs, potato chips, and apple cider. Perhaps you collect leaves or flowers for a science project. Later, you clean up and put leftovers in paper bags.

Now, let's imagine this scene if there were no seed plants on Earth. There would be no wooden picnic table and no

D In dicot stems, vascular bundles occur in rings. These bundles of rings are the annual rings in woody stems. The vascular bundles are the network of veins in dicot leaves.

C Dicots, such as the hibiscus, have flower parts in multiples of four or five. Oaks, maples, and many other trees are dicots. Most vegetables and fruits are dicots, as are many garden flowers.

pulp to make paper products such as cups, plates, and bags. The hot dog came from the meat of animals that eat only plants. Bread for buns, apples for cider, and potatoes for chips all come from plants. The tablecloth is made from cotton, a plant. Without seed plants, there would be no picnic.

Uses of Gymnosperms and Angiosperms

Conifers are the most economically important gymnosperms. Most of the wood used for construction, as in **Figure 23-20,** and for paper production, comes from conifers such as pines and spruces. Resin, a waxy substance secreted by conifers, is used to make chemicals found in soap, paint, varnish, and some medicines.

Figure 23-20 The wood from conifers, such as pines, is commonly used in construction. Resin is used to make household products.

Figure 23-21 Cotton is a flowering plant that yields long fibers that can be woven into a wide variety of fabrics. **What chemical compound makes up these fibers?**

The most common plants on Earth are the angiosperms. They are important to all life because they form the basis for the diets of most animals. Grains such as barley and wheat and legumes such as peas and lentils were among the first plants ever grown by humans. Angiosperms also are the source of many of the fibers used in clothing. Cotton fibers, as seen in **Figure 23-21,** grow from the outer surface of cottonseeds. The fibers of the flax plant are processed and woven into linen fabrics. The production of medicines, rubber, oils, perfumes, pesticides, and some industrial chemicals uses substances found in angiosperms.

Section Assessment

1. What are the characteristics of a seed plant?
2. Compare and contrast the characteristics of gymnosperms and angiosperms.
3. You are looking at a flower with five petals, five sepals, one pistil, and ten stamens. Is it from a monocot or dicot plant?
4. **Think Critically:** The cuticle and epidermis of leaves are transparent. If they were not transparent, what might be the result?
5. **Skill Builder**
   Classifying Conifers have needlelike or scalelike leaves. Do the **Chapter 23 Skill Activity** on page 984 to learn how to use this characteristic to classify conifers.

Using Computers

Word Processing Use a word-processing program to outline the structures and functions that are associated with roots, stems, and leaves. If you need help, refer to page 968.

Using Scientific Methods

Activity 23•2

Comparing Monocots and Dicots

You have read that monocots and dicots are similar because they are both groups of flowering plants. However, you also have learned that these two groups are different. Try this activity to compare and contrast monocots and dicots.

Materials

- Monocot and dicot flowers
- Monocot and dicot seeds
- Scalpel
- Forceps
- Iodine solution

What You'll Investigate

How do the characteristics of monocots and dicots compare?

Goals

- **Observe** similarities and differences between monocots and dicots.
- **Classify** plants as monocots or dicots based on flower characteristics.
- **Infer** what type of food is stored in seeds.

Procedure

1. Copy the Plant Data table in your Science Journal.
2. **Observe** the leaves on the stem of each flower. In your Science Journal, describe the monocot and the dicot leaves.
3. **Examine** the monocot and the dicot flower. For each flower, remove and count the sepals and petals. Enter these numbers on the table.
4. Inside each flower, you should see a pistil(s) and several stamens. **Count** each type and enter these numbers as "Other Observations."
5. **Examine** the two seeds. **Cut** the seeds length-wise, **observe** each half, and **identify** the embryo and cotyledon(s).
6. Place a drop of iodine on different parts of the seed. A blue-black color indicates the presence of starch. **CAUTION:** *Iodine is poisonous. It will stain and can burn your skin.*

Conclude and Apply

1. **Compare** the numbers of sepals and petals of monocot and dicot flowers.
2. What characteristics are the same for monocot and dicot flowers?
3. Distinguish between a monocot and a dicot seed.
4. What type of food is stored in monocot and in

Plant Data

	Number of Sepals	Number of Petals	Number of Cotyledons	Other Observations
Monocot				
Dicot				

Chapter 23 Reviewing Main Ideas

For a **preview** of this chapter, study this Reviewing Main Ideas before you read the chapter. After you have studied this chapter, you can use the Reviewing Main Ideas to **review** the chapter.

The Glencoe MindJogger, Audiocassettes, and CD-ROM provide additional opportunities for review.

Section

23-1 CHARACTERISTICS OF PLANTS

Plants are made up of eukaryotic cells. They usually have some form of leaves, stems, and roots. Plants vary greatly in size and shape. Most plants are adapted to live on land. As plants evolved from aquatic to land forms, changes in structure and function occurred. The changes included how they reproduced, supported themselves, and moved substances from one part of the plant to another. The plant kingdom is classified into groups called divisions. ***What are some plant adaptations for living on land?***

Section

23-2 SEEDLESS PLANTS

Seedless plants include **nonvascular** and **vascular** types. Bryophytes—mosses and liverworts—are seedless **nonvascular plants.** They have no true leaves, stems, roots, or vascular tissues and live in moist environments. For bryophytes, reproduction usually is by spores. Bryophytes may be considered **pioneer species** because they are some of the first plants to grow in new or disturbed environments. They change the environment so that other plant species may grow there. Club mosses, horsetails, and ferns are seedless **vascular plants.** They have vascular tissues, a pipeline that moves substances throughout the plant. Like bryophytes, these plants may reproduce by spores. When ancient forms of these plants died, they underwent a process that, over time, resulted in the formation of coal. ***How are bryophytes and ferns alike?***

Reading Check

Choose a topic in this chapter that interests you. Look it up in a reference book, an encyclopedia or on a CD. Think of a way to share what you learn.

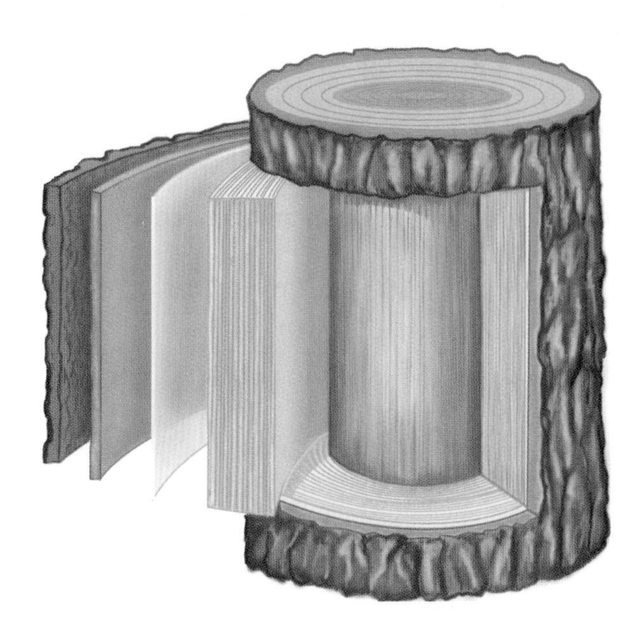

Section
23-3 SEED PLANTS

Seed plants are what most people think of when they hear the word *plants.* These plants have adapted to survive in nearly every environment on Earth. Seed plants produce seeds and have vascular tissue, stems, roots, and leaves. Vascular tissues transport food, water, and dissolved substances in the roots, stems, and leaves. The two major groups of seed plants are gymnosperms and angiosperms. **Gymnosperms** generally have needlelike leaves and some type of cone. **Angiosperms** are plants that flower and are classified as **monocots** or **dicots.** Seed plants provide food, shelter, clothing, and many other products. ***What structures are common to all seed plants?***

Chapter 23 Assessment

Using Vocabulary

a. angiosperm
b. cambium
c. cellulose
d. cuticle
e. dicot
f. guard cell
g. gymnosperm
h. monocot
i. nonvascular plant
j. phloem
k. pioneer species
l. rhizoid
m. stomata
n. vascular plant
o. xylem

Explain the differences between the terms in each of the following sets.

1. xylem, phloem, cambium
2. angiosperm, dicot, monocot
3. guard cell, stomata
4. cuticle, cellulose
5. vascular plant, gymnosperm

Checking Concepts

Choose the word or phrase that best answers the question.

6. Which of the following is a seedless, vascular plant?
   A) moss C) horsetail
   B) liverwort D) pine
7. What are the small openings in the surface of a leaf surrounded by guard cells?
   A) stomata C) rhizoids
   B) cuticles D) angiosperms
8. What is the plant structure that anchors the plant?
   A) stem C) roots
   B) leaves D) guard cell
9. What kind of plants have structures that move water and other substances?
   A) vascular C) nonvascular
   B) protist D) moneran
10. What division has plants that are only a few cells thick?
    A) Anthophyta C) Pterophyta
    B) Cycadophyta D) Bryophyta
11. Where is new xylem and phloem produced?
    A) guard cells C) stomata
    B) cambium D) cuticle
12. Which of the following is **NOT** part of an angiosperm?
    A) flowers C) cones
    B) seeds D) fruit
13. In what part of a leaf does most photosynthesis happen?
    A) epidermis C) stomata
    B) cuticle D) palisade layer
14. Which of these is an advantage to life on land for plants?
    A) more direct sunlight
    B) less carbon dioxide
    C) greater space to grow
    D) less competition for food
15. What do ferns **NOT** have?
    A) fronds C) spores
    B) rhizoids D) vascular tissue

Thinking Critically

16. What might happen if a land plant's waxy cuticle were destroyed?
17. Well-preserved human remains have been found in peat bogs. Explain why this occurs.
18. Plants called succulents store large amounts of water in their leaves, stems, and roots. In what environments would you expect to find succulents growing naturally?
19. Explain why mosses are usually found on moist areas.
20. How do pioneer species change environments so that other plants may grow there?

Developing Skills

If you need help, refer to the Skill Handbook.

21. **Concept Mapping:** Complete this map for the seedless plants of the plant kingdom.

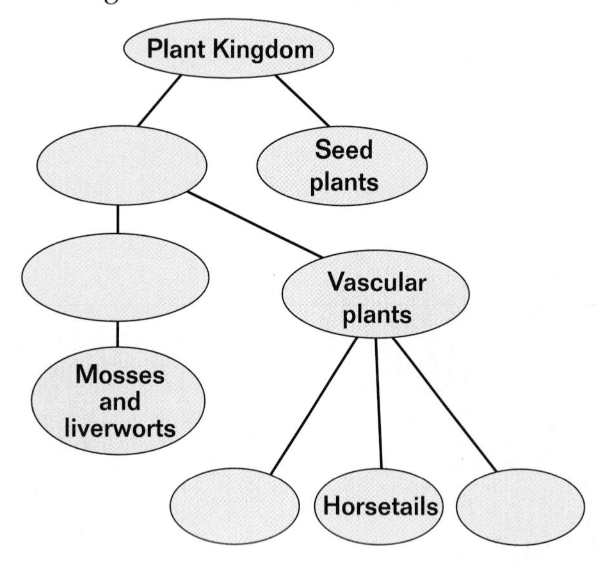

22. **Interpreting Data:** What do the data in this table tell you about where gas exchange occurs in each plant leaf?

Stomata (per mm^2)

	Upper Surface	Lower Surface
Pine	50	71
Bean	40	281
Fir	0	228
Tomato	12	13

23. **Making and Using Graphs:** Make two circle graphs using the table in question 22.
24. **Interpreting Scientific Illustrations:** Using **Figure 23-19,** compare and contrast the *number of seed leaves, bundle arrangement in the stem, veins in leaves,* and *number of flower parts* for monocots and dicots.

Test-Taking Tip

You Are Smarter Than You Think
Nothing on the science tests that you will take this year is so difficult that you can't understand it. You can learn to master any of it. Be confident and just keep practicing your test-taking skills.

Test Practice

Use these questions to test your Science Proficiency.

1. What does the cuticle found on the surface of many plant cells help to do?
   A) increase the carbon dioxide released
   B) change the method of reproduction
   C) reduce water loss for the plant
   D) keep the surface area as small as possible
2. What is one explanation for why bryophytes grow just a few centimeters tall?
   A) They lack reproductive structures.
   B) Their rhizoids are not real roots.
   C) Many creatures trample them on the forest floor.
   D) They do not have vascular tissues.
3. What is one feature that gymnosperms and flowering plants have in common?
   A) reproduce naturally from seeds
   B) have leaves that stay on the plant for more than one year
   C) produce the same types of fruit
   D) are nonvascular plants

CHAPTER

24 Invertebrate Animals

Chapter Preview

Skills Preview

Skill Builders
- Map Concepts

Activities
- Design an Experiment

MiniLabs
- Model

Reading Check

As you read, create an outline of the chapter that includes the headings and subheadings. List important points under each one.

Explore Activity

What is an animal? Is the insect in the photo an animal? What characteristics does the praying mantis have that makes it an animal? More than 1.8 million different kinds of animals have been identified by scientists. How are these animals organized? In the following activity, your class will learn about organizing animals by building a bulletin board display.

Organize Animal Groups

1. Your class is going to make a bulletin board display of different groups of animals. It will look similar to the concept map in **Figure 24-2.**
2. Label large envelopes with the names of different groups.
3. Pick one animal group to study. Make information cards of animals that belong in your group. These cards should have pictures on one side and information on the other.
4. Place your finished cards inside the appropriate envelope on the bulletin board.

In your Science Journal, write down the group of animals you want to study. Collect information on animals that belong to your group. List similarities and differences between your animals and animals of different groups.

24•1 What is an animal?

What You'll Learn

- The characteristics of animals
- The difference between vertebrates and invertebrates
- How the symmetry of animals differs

Vocabulary
vertebrate
invertebrate
symmetry

Why It's Important

- All animals share common characteristics.

Animal Characteristics

Think about the animals shown in **Figure 24-1.** These animals would be described differently. They have a wide variety of body parts, as well as ways to move, get food, and protect themselves. So, what do all animals have in common? What makes an animal an animal?

1. Animals cannot make their own food. Some animals eat plants to supply their energy needs. Some animals eat other animals, and some eat both plants and animals.
2. Animals digest their food. Large food substances are broken down into smaller substances that their cells can use.
3. Most animals can move from place to place. They move to find food, shelter, and mates and to escape from predators.
4. Animals are many-celled organisms that are made of many different kinds of cells. These cells digest food, get rid of wastes, and reproduce.
5. Most animal cells have a nucleus and organelles surrounded by a membrane. This type of cell is called a eukaryotic cell.

Figure 24-1 Animals come in a variety of shapes and sizes.

A The thorny devil lizard lives in the Australian desert. It feeds on ants and survives with little water to drink.

B The largest lion's mane jellyfish was found dead on shore. It had a bell over 2 m across with tentacles that dangled over 36 m long.

C The East African crowned crane is the only crane that will roost in trees. The adults perform spectacular dances when excited.

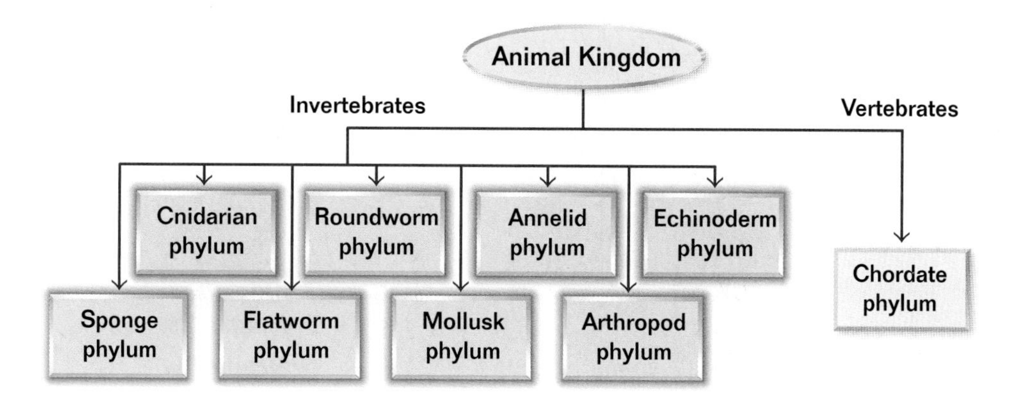

Figure 24-2 This diagram shows the relationships among different groups in the animal kingdom. Different forms of this diagram will appear at the beginning of each section in this and the following chapter. The groups that are highlighted with an orange outline are the groups that will be discussed in that particular section. For example, this section will deal with the invertebrates, which includes the sponge, cnidarian, flatworm, roundworm, mollusk, annelid, arthropod, and echinoderm phylums.

Animal Classification

Deciding whether an organism is an animal is only the first step in classifying it. Scientists place all animals into smaller, related groups. They begin by separating animals into two distinct groups—vertebrates and invertebrates. **Vertebrates** (VURT uh brayts) are animals that have a backbone. **Invertebrates** (ihn VURT uh brayts) are animals that do not have a backbone. There are far more invertebrates than vertebrates. About 97 percent of all animals are invertebrates.

Scientists classify or group the invertebrates into several different phyla (FI lah), as shown in **Figure 24-2.** The animals within each phylum share similar characteristics. These characteristics indicate that the animals within the group descended from a common ancestor. The characteristics also show a change from less complex to more complex animals as you move from phylum to phylum.

Symmetry

As you study the different groups of invertebrates, one feature becomes apparent—symmetry. **Symmetry** (SIH muh tree) refers to the arrangement of the individual parts of an object. Scientists also use body symmetry to classify animals.

Most animals have either radial or bilateral symmetry. Animals with body parts arranged in a circle around a central point have radial symmetry. These animals can locate food and gather other information from all directions. Animals with radial symmetry, such as jellyfish and sea urchins, live in water.

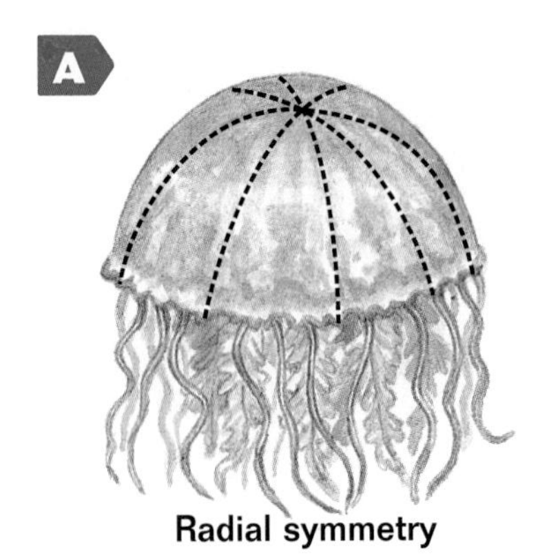

B

Bilateral symmetry

Figure 24-3 Jellyfish (A) have radial symmetry, butterflies (B) have bilateral symmetry, and sponges (C) are asymmetrical. **What type of symmetry do humans exhibit?**

On the other hand, animals with bilateral symmetry have parts that are mirror images of each other. A line can be drawn down the center of their bodies to divide them into two matching parts. Grasshoppers and lobsters are bilaterally symmetrical.

Some animals have no definite shape. They are called asymmetrical. Their bodies cannot be divided into matching halves. Many sponges are asymmetrical (AY suh meh trih kul). As you learn more about invertebrates, see how their body symmetry is related to how they gather food. **Figure 24-3** shows the three ways an animal's body parts can be arranged.

Section Assessment

1. What are the characteristics of animals?
2. How are invertebrates different from vertebrates?
3. What are the types of symmetry? Name an animal that has bilateral symmetry.
4. **Think Critically** Radial symmetry is found among species that live in water. Why might radial symmetry be an adaptation uncommon among animals that live on land?
5. **Skill Builder**
   Concept Mapping Using the information in this section, make a concept map showing the steps a scientist might use to classify a new animal. If you need help, refer to Concept Mapping in the **Skill Handbook** on page 950.

Using Computers

Word Processing
Create a table that you will use as you complete this chapter. Label the following columns: *animal*, *group*, and *body symmetry*. Create ten rows to enter animal names. If you need help, refer to page 968.

Sponges, Cnidarians, Flatworms, and Roundworms

24•2

What You'll Learn

- The structures that make up sponges and cnidarians
- How sponges and cnidarians get food and reproduce
- The body plans of flatworms and roundworms

Vocabulary
cnidarian
polyp
medusa
free-living
parasite

Why It's Important

- Sponges, cnidarians, flatworms, and roundworms exhibit simple cell and tissue organization.

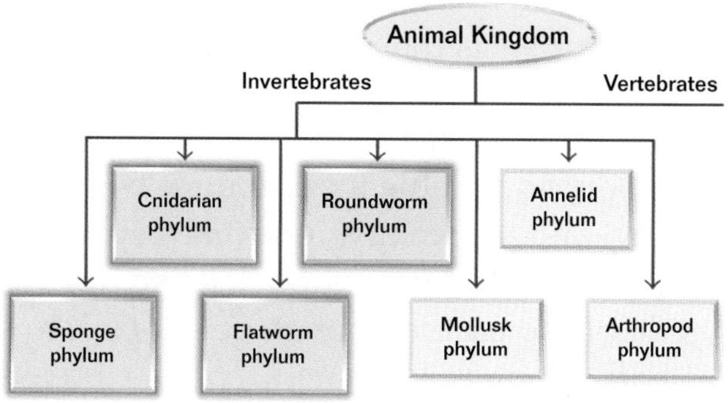

Sponges

Sponges are the simplest of animals. They bridge the gap between single-celled organisms and more complex animals. Their body structure is made of two layers of cells. Adult sponges live attached to one place. Organisms that remain attached to one place during their lifetimes are called sessile (SES ul). Because they do not move about in search of food, scientists used to classify sponges, shown in **Figure 24-4,** as plants. Once scientists found out that sponges can't make their own food, they reclassified them as animals.

Animal Kingdom
Invertebrates
Vertebrates
Cnidarian phylum
Roundworm phylum
Annelid phylum
Sponge phylum
Flatworm phylum
Mollusk phylum
Arthropod phylum

Figure 24-4 Orange finger sponges form long "fingers" from 2 cm to 20 cm in length. They are also called dead man's finger sponges.

Filter Feeders

Sponges live in water. They are called filter feeders because they filter food out of the water that flows through their bodies. Microscopic organisms and oxygen are carried with the water through pores into the central cavity of the sponge. The phylum that sponges belong to, Porifera, gets its name from these pores. The inner surface of the central cavity is lined with specialized cells called collar cells. Thin, whiplike structures, called flagella, extend from the collar cells and keep the water moving through the sponge. Other specialized cells digest the food, carry nutrients to all parts of the sponge, and remove wastes.

CHEMISTRY INTEGRATION

Sponge Spicules

Spicules of "glass" sponges are composed of silica. Other sponges have spicules of calcium carbonate. Where do these organisms get the silica and calcium carbonate that these spicules are made of?

Body Support and Defense

At first glance, you might think that sponges have few defenses against predators. Actually, not many animals eat sponges. The soft bodies of many sponges are supported by sharp, glasslike structures called spicules. Many other sponges have a material called spongin. Spongin can be compared to foam rubber because it makes sponges both soft and elastic. Some sponges have both spicules and spongin, which protects their soft bodies.

Observing Sponge Spicules

Procedure

1. Add a few drops of bleach to a microscope slide. **CAUTION:** *Do not inhale the bleach. Do not spill it on your hands, clothing, or the microscope.*
2. Put a small piece of the sponge into the bleach on the slide. Add a coverslip. Observe the cells of the sponge.

Analysis

1. Are spicules made of the same materials as the rest of the sponge? Explain.
2. What is the function of spicules?

Sponge Reproduction

Sponges are able to reproduce both sexually and asexually. Asexual reproduction occurs when a bud located on the side of the parent sponge develops into a small sponge. The small sponge breaks off, floats away, and attaches itself to a new surface. New sponges also grow when a sponge is cut or broken into pieces. The broken pieces regenerate or grow into a complete new sponge.

Most sponges that reproduce sexually produce both eggs and sperm. The sponge releases sperm into the water. Currents carry the sperm to eggs of another sponge, where fertilization occurs. The fertilized eggs grow into larvae that look different from the adult sponge. The larvae are able to swim to a different area before attaching themselves to a rock or other surface.

Cnidarians

Have you ever cast a fishing line into the water to catch your dinner? In a somewhat similar way, animals in the phylum Cnidaria have tentacles that are used to capture prey. Jellyfish, sea anemones, hydra, and corals belong to this phylum.

Cnidarians (NIH dar ee uns) are a phylum of hollow-bodied animals that have stinging cells. They have radial symmetry that allows them to locate food that floats by from any direction. Their bodies have two cell layers that are organized into tissues. The inner layer forms a digestive cavity where food is broken down. Their tentacles surround the mouth. Stinging cells shoot out to stun or grasp prey. The word *cnidaria* is Latin for "stinging cells." Oxygen moves into the cells from the surrounding water, and carbon dioxide waste moves out of the cells. Nerve cells work together as a nerve net throughout the whole body.

EXAMPLES OF Cnidarians

- Jellyfish
- Sea anemones
- Hydra
- Corals
- Portuguese man-of-war

Two Body Plans

Study the two cnidarians in **Figure 24-5.** They represent the two different body plans found in this animal's phylum. The vase-shaped body of the hydra is called a **polyp** (PAHL up). Although hydras are usually sessile, they can twist to capture prey. They also can somersault to a new location. Jellyfish have a free-swimming, bell-shaped body that is called a **medusa.** Jellyfish are not strong swimmers. Instead, they drift along with the ocean currents. Some cnidarians go through both the polyp and medusa stages during their life cycles.

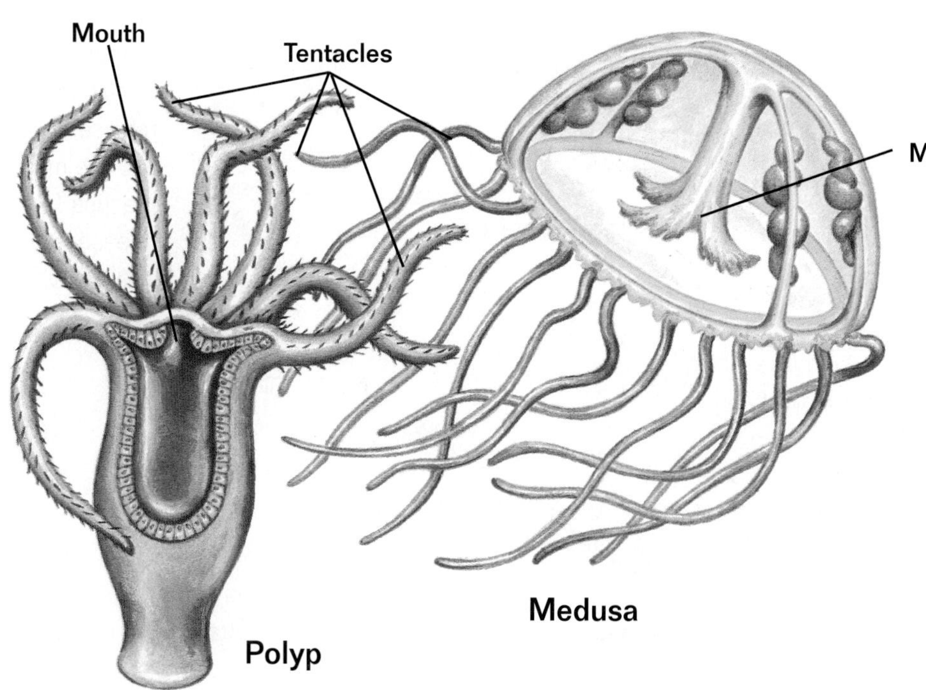

Figure 24-5 The polyp and medusa forms are the two body plans of cnidarians.

Figure 24-6 Polyps, like these hydra, reproduce by budding.

Cnidarian Reproduction

Cnidarians produce both asexually and sexually. Polyp forms of cnidarians, such as hydras, reproduce asexually by budding, as illustrated in **Figure 24-6.** The bud eventually falls off of the parent organism and develops into a new polyp. Some polyps also can reproduce sexually by releasing eggs or sperm into the water. The eggs are fertilized by sperm and develop into a new polyp. Medusa forms of cnidarians, such as jellyfish, have both an asexual and a sexual stage, which are illustrated in **Figure 24-7.** These stages alternate between generations. Medusa reproduce sexually to produce polyps, which in turn, reproduce asexually to form new medusa.

VISUALIZING Cnidarian Reproduction

Figure 24-7 Medusa forms of cnidarians have both a sexual and an asexual stage.

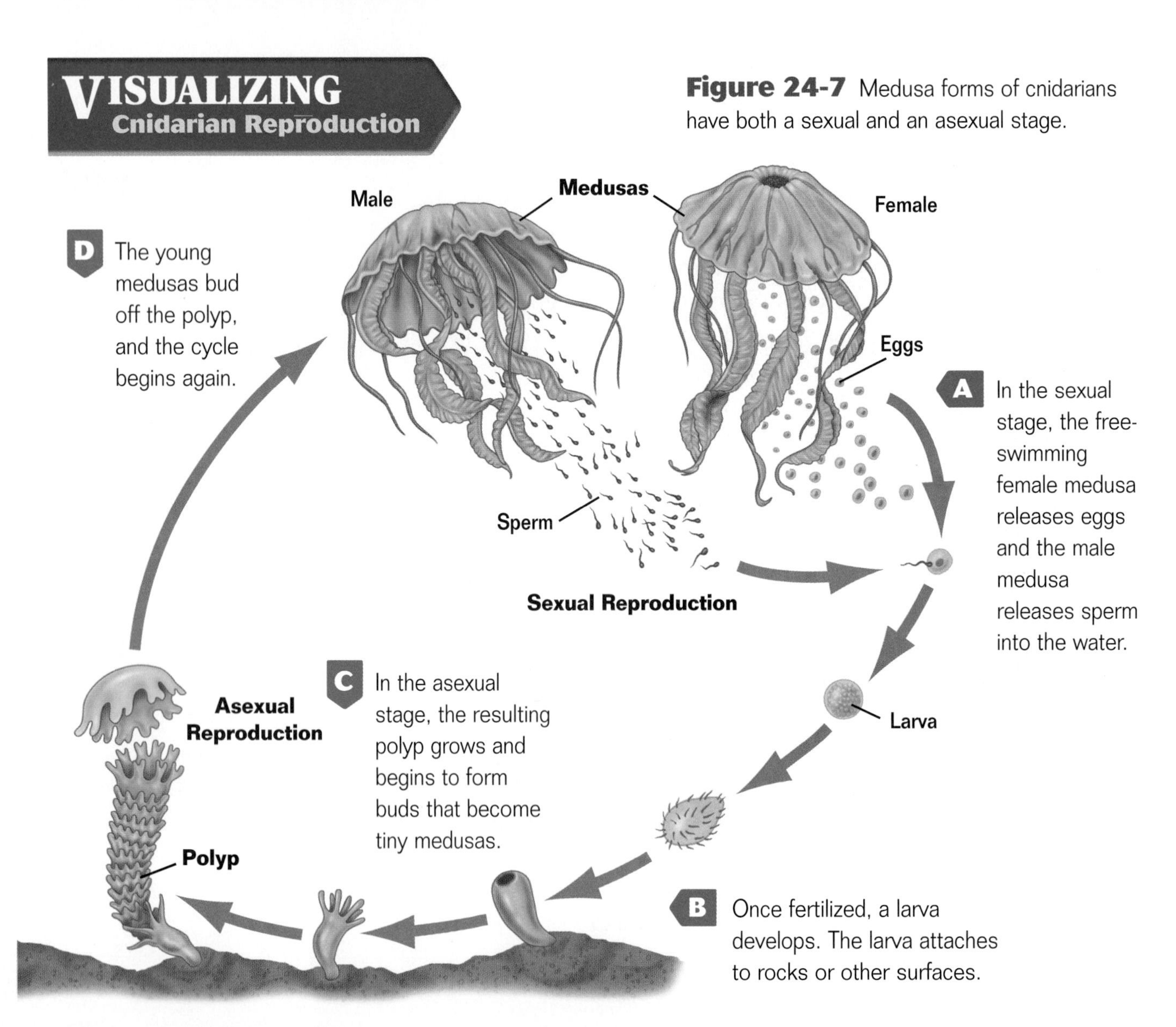

Flatworms

Unlike sponges and cnidarians that wait for food to pass their way, flatworms actively search for their food. Worms are invertebrates with soft bodies and bilateral symmetry. Flatworms are members of the phylum Platyhelminthes (plat ih hel MIHN theez). They have long, flattened bodies. They also have three distinct layers of tissue organized into organs and organ systems.

Some flatworms are free-living, such as the planarian in **Figure 24-8B. Free-living** organisms don't depend on one particular organism for food or a place to live. But, most flatworms are parasites that live in or on their hosts. A **parasite** depends on its host for food and a place to live.

Eyespot
Head
Cilia
Mouth/Anus
Digestive tract
Excretory system

Tapeworms

One parasitic flatworm that lives in humans is called the tapeworm. It lacks a digestive system. To survive, it lives in the intestines of its hosts. The tapeworm absorbs nutrients directly into its body from digested material in the host's intestines. Find the hooks and suckers on the tapeworm's head in **Figure 24-8A.** The hooks and suckers attach the tapeworm to the host's intestines.

B Planarians have eyespots that have been known to respond to light. They also have the power to regenerate. A planarian can be cut in two, and each piece will grow into a new worm.

Figure 24-8 Flatworms have members that are free-living and other members that are parasites.

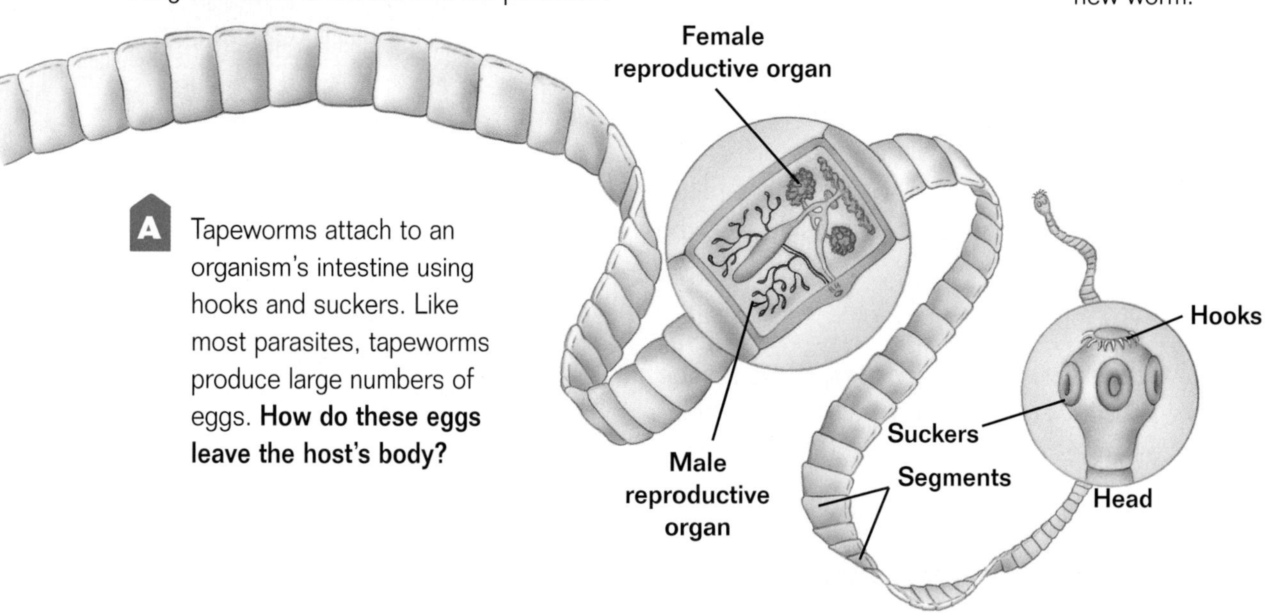

A Tapeworms attach to an organism's intestine using hooks and suckers. Like most parasites, tapeworms produce large numbers of eggs. **How do these eggs leave the host's body?**

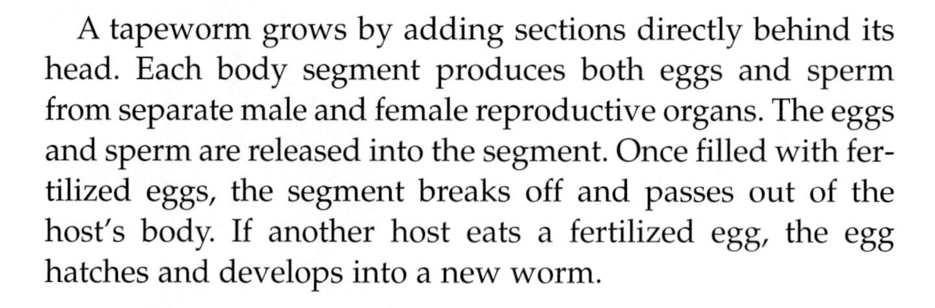

A tapeworm grows by adding sections directly behind its head. Each body segment produces both eggs and sperm from separate male and female reproductive organs. The eggs and sperm are released into the segment. Once filled with fertilized eggs, the segment breaks off and passes out of the host's body. If another host eats a fertilized egg, the egg hatches and develops into a new worm.

Figure 24-9 Mosquitoes are the carriers of dog heartworm. Mosquitoes bite infected dogs and, in turn, infect still other dogs by biting them. The worm larva travels through the circulatory system and lodges in the heart where it interrupts normal blood flow.

Roundworms

Dog owners regularly give their pets a medicine that prevents heartworm disease. Heartworms can kill a dog. They are just one kind of the many thousands of roundworms that make up the phylum Nematoda (nem uh TOH duh). Roundworms are the most widespread animal on Earth. Billions can live in a single acre of soil.

A roundworm's body is described as a tube within a tube, with fluid in between. The cavity separates the digestive tract from the body wall. Roundworms are also more complex than flatworms because their digestive tract is complete with two openings. Food enters through the mouth and wastes exit through an anus.

Roundworms are a diverse group. Some are decomposers. Some are predators. Some are parasites of animals and some are parasites of plants. **Figure 24-9** shows a parasitic heartworm that can infect dogs. What type of body symmetry does a roundworm have?

Section Assessment

1. How do sponges and cnidarians get food?
2. What are three common characteristics of worms?
3. Compare the body plans of flatworms and roundworms.
4. **Think Critically:** Sponges are sessile organisms. They remain attached to one place during their lifetimes. Explain why a sponge is still considered to be an animal.
5. **Skill Builder**
   Comparing and Contrasting Do the **Chapter 24 Skill Activity** on page 985 to compare and contrast types of symmetry found in different animals.

Using Math

A sponge is 1 cm in diameter and 10 cm tall. It can move 22.5 L of water through its body in a day. Calculate the volume of water it pumps through its body in one minute.

Mollusks and Segmented Worms

Mollusks

Imagine yourself walking along the beach at low tide. On the rocks by a small tide pool, you see small conelike shells. The blue-black shelled mussels are exposed along the shore, and one arm of a shy octopus can be seen inside the opening of its den. How could all of these different animals belong to the same phylum? What do they have in common?

Common Characteristics

The snail, slug, mussel, and octopus belong to the phylum Mollusca. **Mollusks** are soft-bodied invertebrates that usually have a shell. Characteristics shared by mollusks include a mantle and a large, muscular foot. The **mantle** is a thin layer of tissue covering the mollusk's soft body. It secretes the protective shell of those mollusks that have a shell. The foot is used for moving the animal or for attaching it to an object.

Between the soft body and the mantel is a space called the mantle cavity. Water-dwelling mollusks have gills in the mantle cavity. **Gills** are organs that exchange oxygen and carbon dioxide with the water. Land-dwelling mollusks have lungs to exchange gases with air. Mollusks have a complete digestive system with two openings. Many also have a scratchy, tonguelike organ called the radula. The **radula** (RAJ uh luh) acts like a file with rows of teeth to break up food into smaller pieces.

What You'll Learn

- The characteristics of mollusks
- The similarities and differences between an open and a closed circulatory system
- The characteristics of segmented worms
- The structures and digestive process of an earthworm

Vocabulary

mollusk
mantle
gills
radula
open circulatory system
closed circulatory system

Why It's Important

- Mollusks and segmented worms have specialized structures that allow them to live in their environments.

Fire Bristleworm

Figure 24-10

Octopus

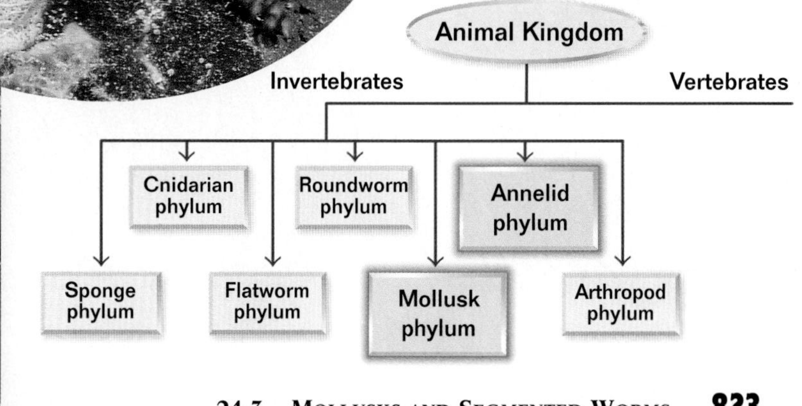

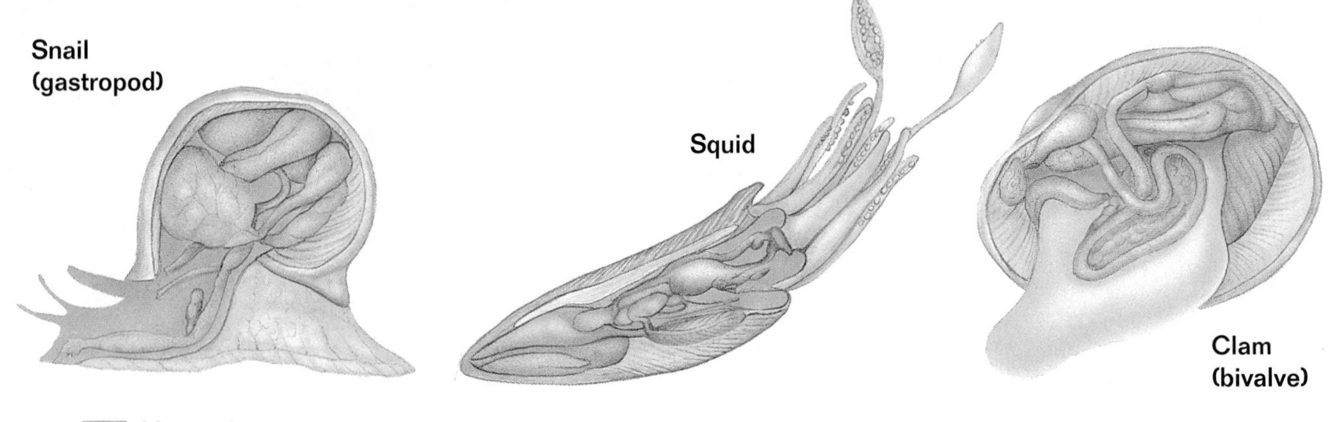

Figure 24-11 All mollusks have the same basic body plan: with a mantle, a shell, a foot, and an area called visceral mass where the body organs are located.

Some mollusks have an open circulatory system. Animals with an **open circulatory system** do not have their blood contained in vessels. Instead, the blood surrounds the organs. These organs are grouped together in a fluid-filled body cavity. **Figure 24-11** shows the basic structure of all mollusks.

Types of Mollusks

To classify mollusks, scientists first find out whether the mollusk has a shell. Then, they look at the kind of shell. They also look at the kind of foot. In this section, you will learn about three kinds of mollusks. **Figure 24-12** shows examples of two groups of mollusks—the gastropods and bivalves.

Gastropods and Bivalves

Gastropods are the largest class of mollusks. Most gastropods, such as the snails and conches, have a single shell. Slugs are also gastropods, but they don't have a shell. All move about on the large, muscular foot. A secretion of mucus allows them to glide across objects. Gastropods live in water or on land.

Bivalves are another class of mollusks. How many shells do you think bivalves have? Think of other words that start

EXAMPLES OF
Bivalves Gastropods

Figure 24-12 Although these animals look different from one another, they are all mollusks.

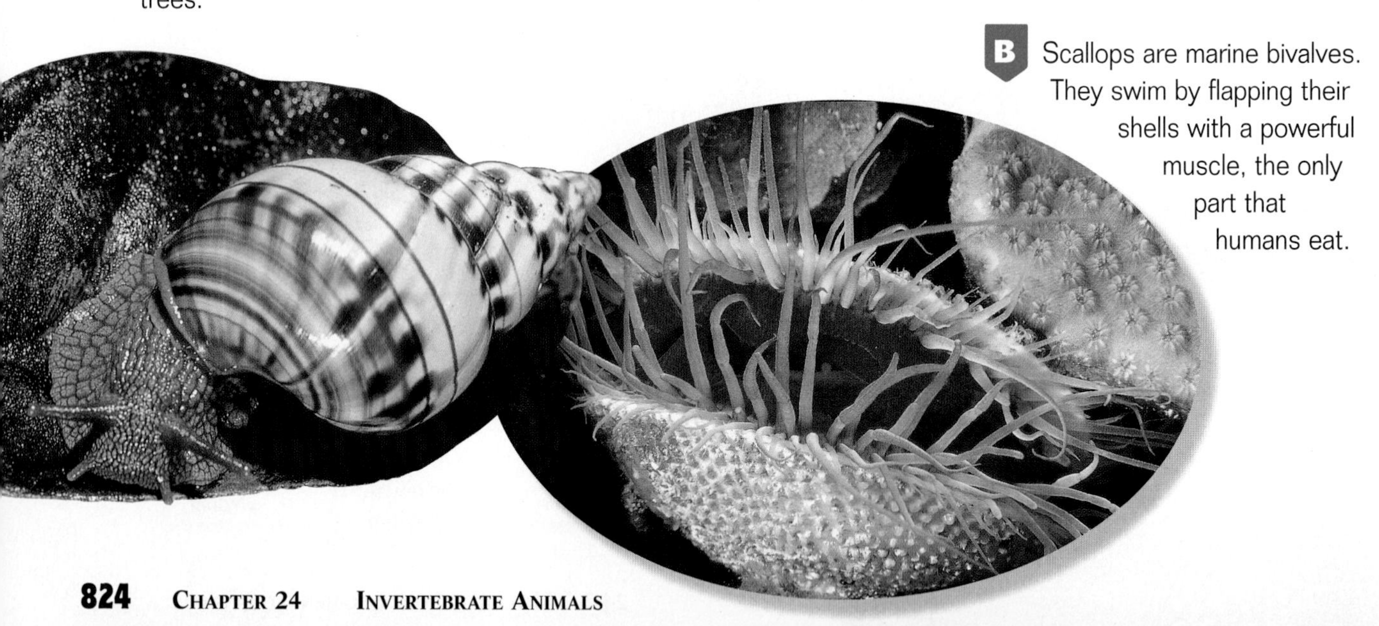

A Tree snails are cone-shaped gastropods ranging in size from 1 cm to 6 cm long. They feed on tiny lichens, fungi, and algae that grow on the bark, leaves, and fruit of trees.

B Scallops are marine bivalves. They swim by flapping their shells with a powerful muscle, the only part that humans eat.

Figure 24-13 Although the chambered nautilus's shell resembles a snail's shell, the nautilus is a cephalopod. Like the octopus and the squid, it swims using jet propulsion, as shown in **Figure 24-14.**

with *bi-*. A clam is a bivalve, or an organism with two shell halves joined by a hinge. Powerful, large muscles open and close the shells. Bivalves are water animals that are also filter feeders. Food is removed from water that is brought into and filtered through the gills.

Cephalopods

Cephalopods (SEF ah loh pawdz) are the most complex type of mollusk. Squid, octopuses, and the chambered nautilus, pictured in **Figure 24-13,** are all cephalopods. Most cephalopods have no shell but they do have a well-developed head. The "foot" is divided into tentacles with strong suckers. These animals also have a **closed circulatory system** in which blood is carried through blood vessels.

Both the squid and octopus are adapted for quick movement in the ocean. The squid's mantle is a muscular envelope that surrounds its internal organs. Water enters the space between the mantle and the other body organs. When the mantle closes around the collar of the squid, the water is squeezed rapidly through a siphon, which is a funnel-like structure. The rapid expulsion of water from the siphon causes the squid to move in the opposite direction of the stream of water. **Figure 24-14** shows how this propulsion system works.

EXAMPLES OF Cephalopods

- Octopus
- Squid
- Chambered nautilus

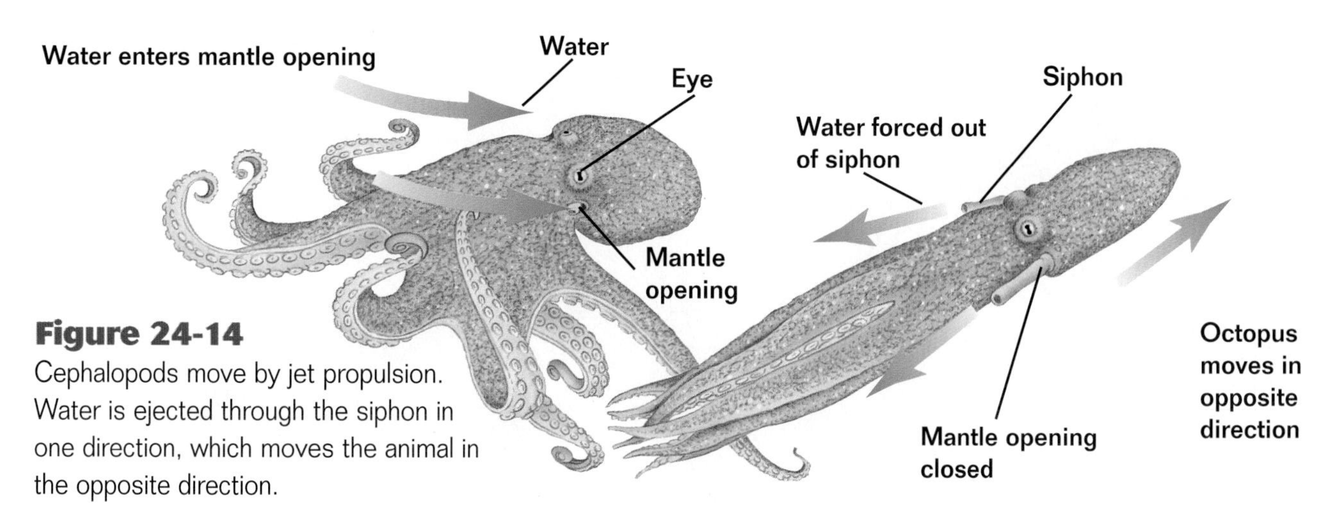

Figure 24-14
Cephalopods move by jet propulsion. Water is ejected through the siphon in one direction, which moves the animal in the opposite direction.

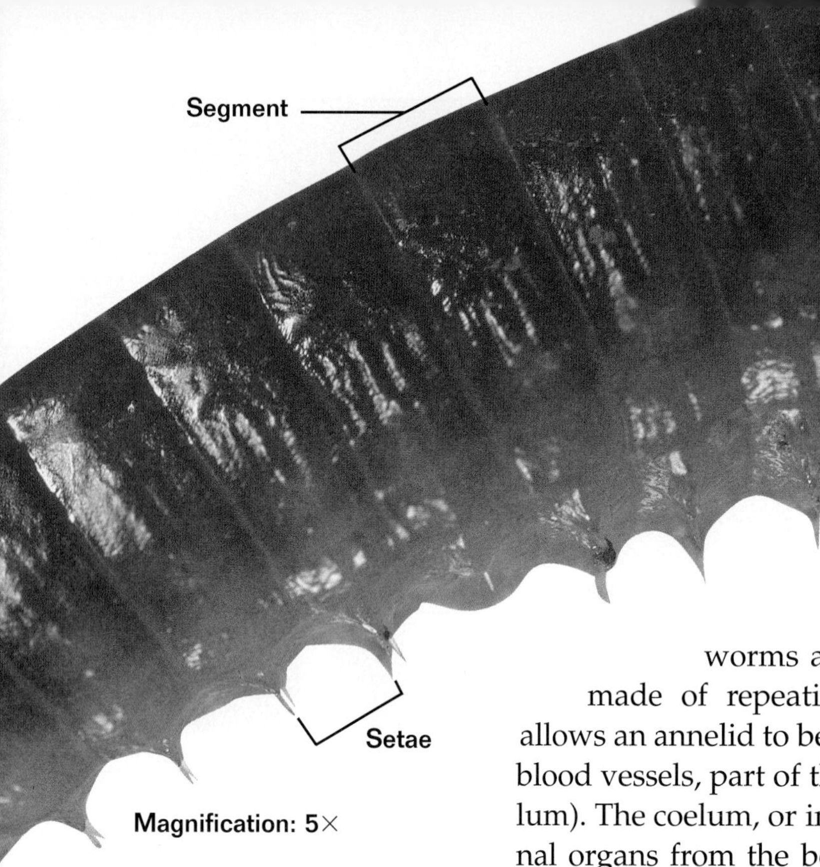

Figure 24-15 Earthworms move using bristlelike hairs called setae. **How would the setae help the earthworms move?**

Segmented Worms

What kind of animal do you think of when you hear the word *worm?* Most likely, you think of an earthworm. Earthworms belong to a group of segmented worms in the phylum Annelida (an NEL ud uh). Leeches and marine worms are also annelids. An annelid's body is made of repeating segments or rings. Segmentation allows an annelid to be flexible. Each segment has nerve cells, blood vessels, part of the digestive tract, and the coelum (SEE lum). The coelum, or internal body cavity, separates the internal organs from the body wall. Annelids also have a closed circulatory system and a complete digestive system with two body openings.

EXAMPLES OF Segmented Worms

- Earthworms
- Leeches
- Marine worms

Earthworms

Earthworms have more than 100 body segments. Setae (SEE tee), or bristlelike structures pictured in **Figure 24-15,** are found on the outside of these segments. Earthworms use the setae and two sets of muscles to move through or hold onto

Figure 24-16 Segmented worms have circulatory, respiratory, excretory, digestive, muscular, and reproductive systems.

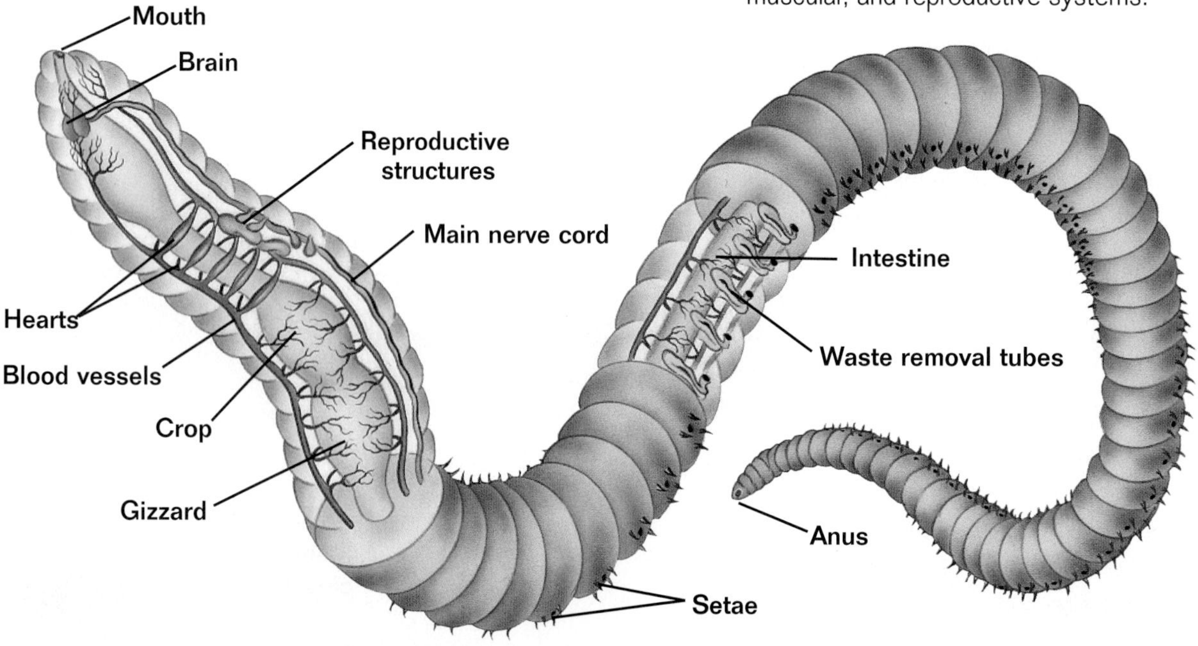

soil. Moving through soil is important for earthworms because they eat it. Earthworms get the energy they need to live from the bits of leaves and other living matter found in the soil. You can trace the path through an earthworm's digestive system in **Figure 24-16.** First, the soil moves to the crop, where it is stored. Behind the crop is a muscular structure called the gizzard. Here, the soil is ground. As the food passes to the intestine, it is broken down and absorbed by the blood. Undigested soil and wastes leave the worm through the anus.

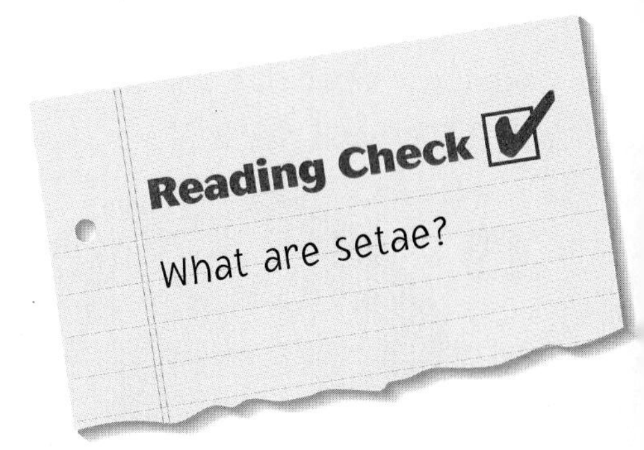

What body structures are not present in the earthworm shown in **Figure 24-16?** Notice that you don't find gills or lungs. An earthworm lives in a thin film of water. It exchanges carbon dioxide and oxygen by diffusion through its skin.

Leeches

Leeches are parasites that have a lifestyle that is different from earthworms'. These worms have flat bodies from 5 mm to 46 cm long and have sucking disks on both ends of their bodies. Leeches attach themselves to and remove blood from the body of a host. Some leeches can store as much as ten times their own weight in blood. The blood can be stored for months and released a little at a time into the digestive system. Leeches are found in freshwater, marine waters, and on land in mild and tropical regions.

Problem Solving

Leeches to the Rescue

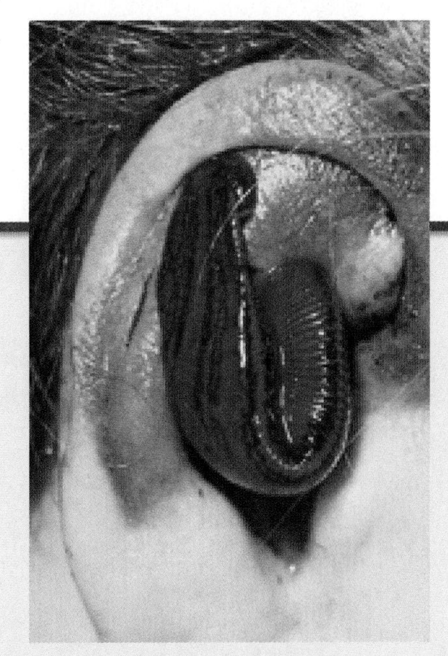

Since ancient times, doctors have used leeches to treat a variety of diseases. Early doctors thought leeches removed the bad blood that resulted in disease. Unfortunately, so many leeches were used sometimes that patients died from blood loss. With the rise of modern medical treatments, the use of leeches was abandoned. People thought it was useless.

Now, the leech is back! Surgeons are able to reattach severed ears or fingers, but it is difficult to keep blood flowing to the reattached body part. If blood clots appear, they stop blood circulation and the cells in the ear or finger die. Medicinal leeches are the key to success. Surgeons place a leech on the reattached ear or finger. It inflicts a painless bite from a sucking disk at each end of its body. As the leech feeds on the blood, chemicals in the saliva break up clots that have already formed and prevent new clots from forming. Eventually, normal circulation is established. The leech is removed and the reattached part survives.

Think Critically: Blood clots are major factors in strokes and some heart and blood vessel diseases. How might research about leeches play an important role in developing treatments for these conditions?

Figure 24-17 Polychaetes come in a variety of forms and colors. The Christmas tree (A) and feather duster (B) use their appendages to filter out food from their watery environments. **How are these organisms similar to cnidarians and sponges?**

Marine Worms

Look at the animals in **Figure 24-17.** You may wonder how these feathery animals can possibly be related to the earthworm and leech. These animals belong to a third group of annelids called polychaetes (PAHL ee kitz). The word *polychaete* means "many spines." There are more species of polychaetes than of any other kind of annelid. More than 6000 known species of polychaetes have been discovered.

The setae of these annelids occur in bundles along their segments. Marine worms are polychaetes that float, burrow, build structures, or walk on the ocean floor. While earthworms find nutrients in the soil and leeches are parasites, polychaetes are predators. Some use powerful jaws or tentacles to catch prey. Some of these strange-looking annelids can even produce their own light.

While annelids may not look complex, they are much more complex than sponges and cnidarians. In the next section, you will learn how they compare to the most complex invertebrates.

Section Assessment

1. Name the three classes of mollusks and identify a member from each class.
2. What are the characteristics of segmented worms?
3. Describe how an earthworm feeds and digests its food.
4. **Think Critically:** How does an annelid's segmentation help it move?
5. **Skill Builder**
   Comparing and Contrasting Compare and contrast an open circulatory system with a closed circulatory system. If you need help, refer to Comparing and Contrasting in the **Skill Handbook** on page 956.

Choose a mollusk and write about it in your Science Journal. Describe its appearance, how it gets food, where it lives, and other interesting facts.

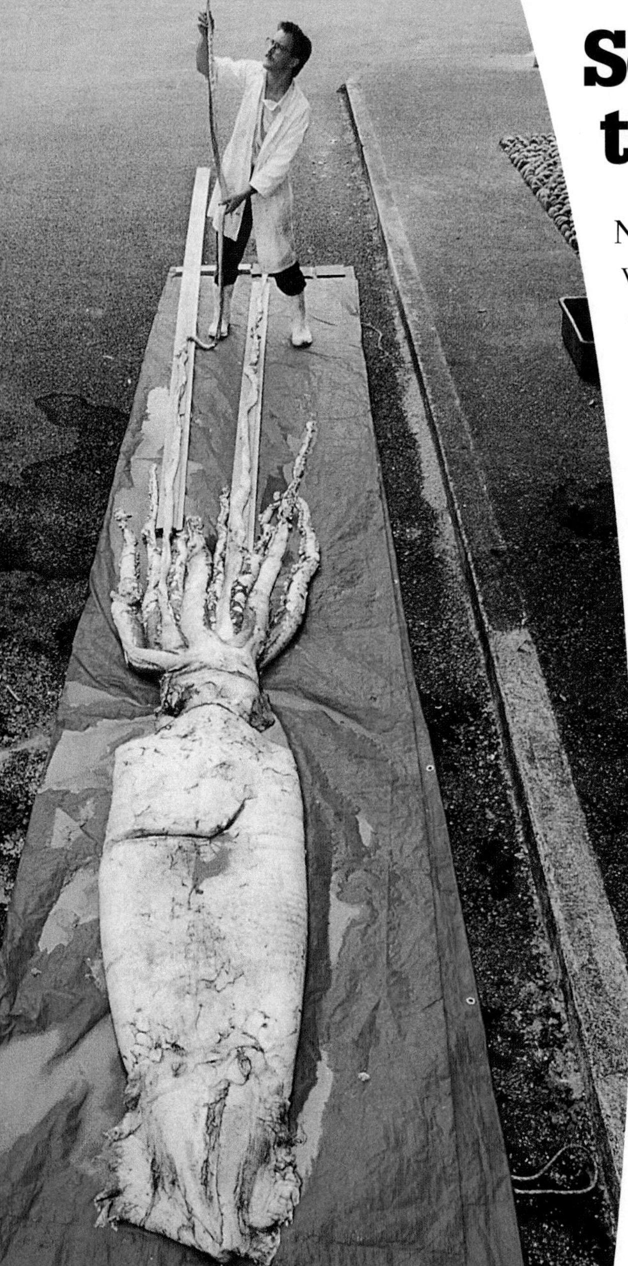

Searching for the Giant Squid

No one has ever seen a giant squid in its natural habitat, which is 300 m to 1500 m below the ocean's surface. Nor has any live, healthy giant squid been kept in an aquarium or research facility to be studied by scientists. The only live specimens of giant squid available for study have been those that washed up on beaches or were brought up in deep-sea commercial fishing nets. These squids have been sick and unsuitable for study.

Rare Find

In the late 1500s, accounts were written about several large sea creatures stranded on Norwegian shores. It was not until 1854 that scientists concluded that these creatures were giant squid. In the late 1800s, a dead giant squid caught by commercial fishers in Newfoundland became the first specimen available for study. The one-metric-ton giant squid at left was netted at a depth of 425 m in the waters off New Zealand. The creature was nearly dead when pulled on board the research vessel. The three-year-old squid measured 8 m from top to tip of tentacle and might have reached a much greater length at maturity.

The Search Goes On

The Smithsonian's Clyde Roper, one of the world's leading experts on the giant squid, has spent more than 30 years studying these remarkable animals. In 1997, Roper and his crew used the *Odyssey*, a robotic underwater vehicle, and a camera to explore the cold, black depths of Kaikoura Canyon, a deep-sea ecosystem located off New Zealand's South Island. Dr. Roper and his colleagues collected valuable information on the temperature, salt content, and depth of the ocean. On a ship at the surface, they viewed many hours of videotapes of this deep-water ecosystem—but alas, no giant squids. One day, perhaps crewed submersibles in the area will be the first to catch a glimpse of the giant squid at home.

Science JOURNAL

How big is a giant squid? Find out the length of the wall in your classroom, a school bus, and an airplane. Record the lengths in your Science Journal. Compare the lengths of these objects to an 18 m giant squid. Which is longest?

Design Your Own Experiment

Activity 24•1

Garbage-eating Worms

Possible Materials

- Worms (red wigglers)
- Plastic containers with drainage holes (4 L) (2)
- Soil (7 L)
- Chopped food scraps including fruit and vegetable peels, pulverized eggshells, tea bags, and coffee grounds
- Shredded newspaper
- Spray bottle

You know that soil conditions can influence the growth of plants. You are trying to decide what factors might improve the soil in your backyard garden. A friend suggests that earthworms improve the quality of the soil. Does the presence of earthworms have any value in improving soil conditions?

Recognize the Problem

How does the presence of earthworms change the condition of the soil?

Form a Hypothesis

Based on your reading and observations, state a hypothesis about how earthworms might improve the conditions of soil.

Goals

- **Design an experiment** that compares the condition of soil in two environments, one with earthworms and one without.
- **Observe** the change in soil conditions for two weeks.

Safety Precautions

Be careful when working with live animals. Always keep your hands wet when handling earthworms. Dry hands will remove the mucus from the earthworms.

Test Your Hypothesis

Plan

1. As a group, agree upon the hypothesis and **decide** how you will test it. **Identify** what results will confirm the hypothesis.
2. **List** the steps you will need to take to test your hypothesis. Be specific. **Describe** exactly what you will do in each step. **List** your materials.
3. Prepare a data table in your Science Journal to **record** your observations.
4. **Read** over the entire experiment to make sure all steps are in logical order.
5. **Identify** all constants, variables, and controls of the experiment.

Do

1. Make sure your teacher approves your plan and your data table before you proceed.
2. Carry out the experiment as planned.
3. While doing the experiment, **record** your observations and complete the data table in your Science Journal.

Analyze Your Data

1. **Compare** the changes in the two sets of soil samples.
2. **Compare** your results with those of other groups.
3. What was your control in this experiment?
4. What were your variables?

Draw Conclusions

1. Did the results support your hypothesis? **Explain.**
2. **Describe** what effect you think rain would have on the soil and worms.

24•4

Arthropods and Echinoderms

What You'll Learn

- Features used to classify arthropods
- How the structure of the exoskeleton relates to its function
- Features of echinoderms

Vocabulary
arthropod
appendage
exoskeleton
metamorphosis

Why It's Important

- Arthropods and echinoderms show great diversity and are found in many different environments.

Arthropods

By far, the largest group of animals belongs in the phylum Arthropoda. More than 900 000 species of arthropods have been discovered. The term **arthropod** comes from *arthros,* meaning "jointed," and *poda,* meaning "foot." Arthropods are animals that have jointed appendages. They are similar to annelids because they have segmented bodies. Yet, in most cases, they have fewer, more specialized segments. Instead of setae, they have different kinds of appendages. **Appendages** are the structures such as claws, legs, and even antennae that grow from the body.

Every arthropod has an **exoskeleton** that protects and supports its body. The exoskeleton also protects the arthropod from drying out. This lightweight body covering is made of a carbohydrate and a protein. As the animal grows, the exoskeleton is shed in a process called molting. The weight of the outer covering increases as the size of the animal increases. Weight and hardness of the exoskeleton produce a problem for the animal. They make it more difficult to move. The jointed appendages solve part of this problem.

Figure 24-18 shows an example of the five different types of arthropods: insects, spiders, centipedes, millipedes, and crustaceans. Find the body segments on these animals. Which arthropods appear most like the annelids?

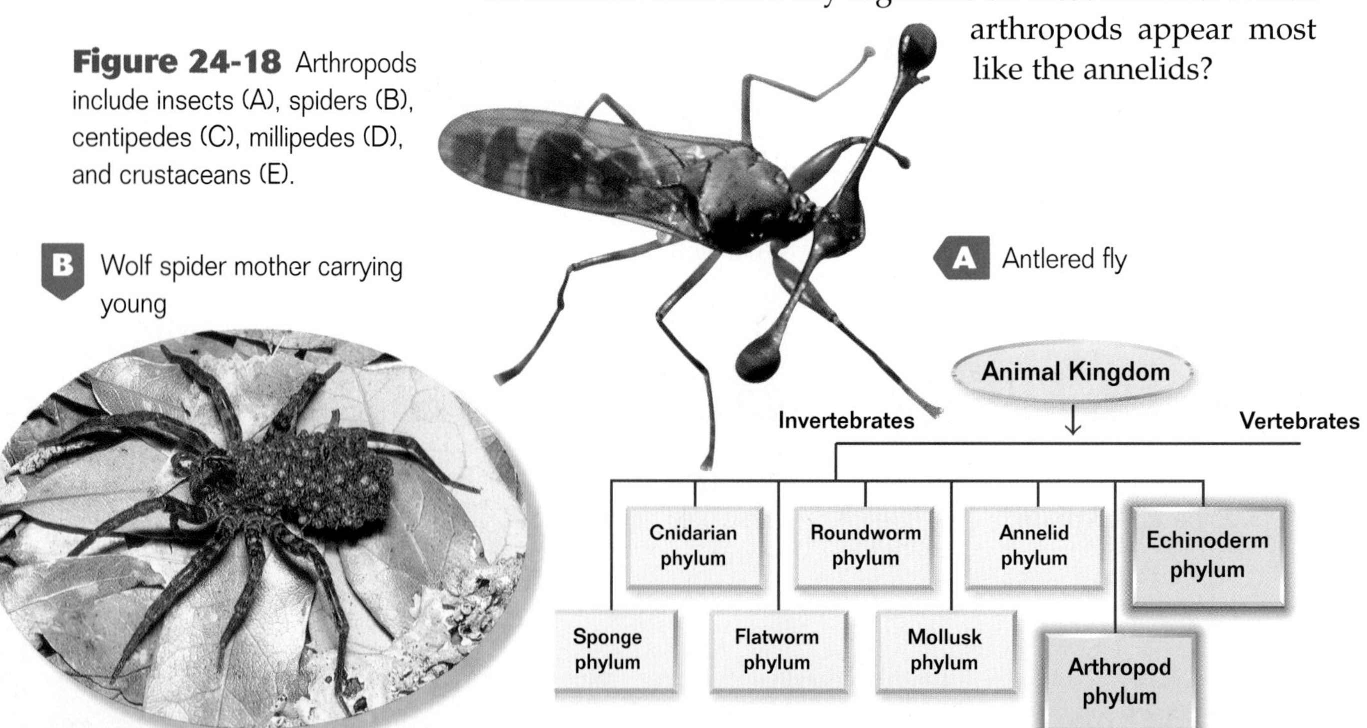

Figure 24-18 Arthropods include insects (A), spiders (B), centipedes (C), millipedes (D), and crustaceans (E).

Insects

When asked to name an insect, your answer might be some kind of flying insect, such as bee, fly, beetle, or butterfly. In fact, insects are the only invertebrates that can fly. Insects make up the largest group of invertebrates. There are more than 700 000 classified species of insects, and scientists describe more each year.

Insects have three distinct body regions, as shown in **Figure 24-18A:** the head, thorax, and abdomen. The head has well-developed sensory organs, including the eyes and antennae. The thorax has three pairs of jointed legs and, in many species, one or two pairs of wings. The wings and legs of insects are highly specialized.

The abdomen is divided into segments and has neither wings nor legs attached to it. Reproductive organs are located in this region. Insects produce many more young than can survive. For example, a single female fly can produce thousands of eggs.

Insects have an open circulatory system. Oxygen is not transported by blood in the system, but food and waste materials are. Oxygen is brought directly to tissues inside of the insect through small holes called spiracles (SPIHR ih kulz) located along the thorax and abdomen.

*inter*NET CONNECTION

Visit the Glencoe Science Web Site at **www.glencoe.com/sec/science/ca** for more information about butterflies.

E Sally lightfoot crab

C Centipede

D Forest floor millipede

VISUALIZING Metamorphosis

Figure 24-19

A Harlequin bugs undergo incomplete metamorphosis.

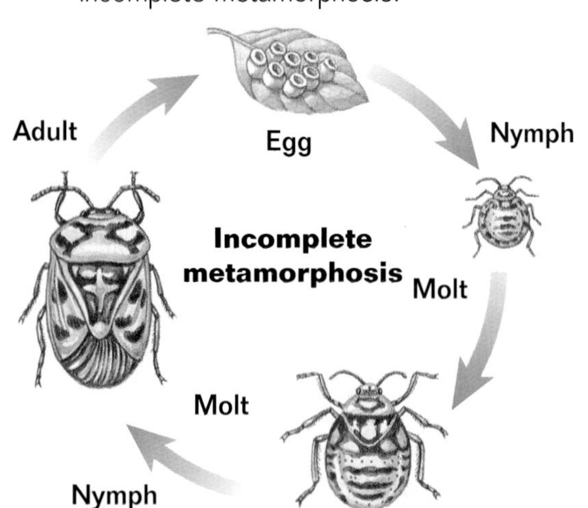

B Butterflies and moths, such as this silk moth, undergo complete metamorphosis.

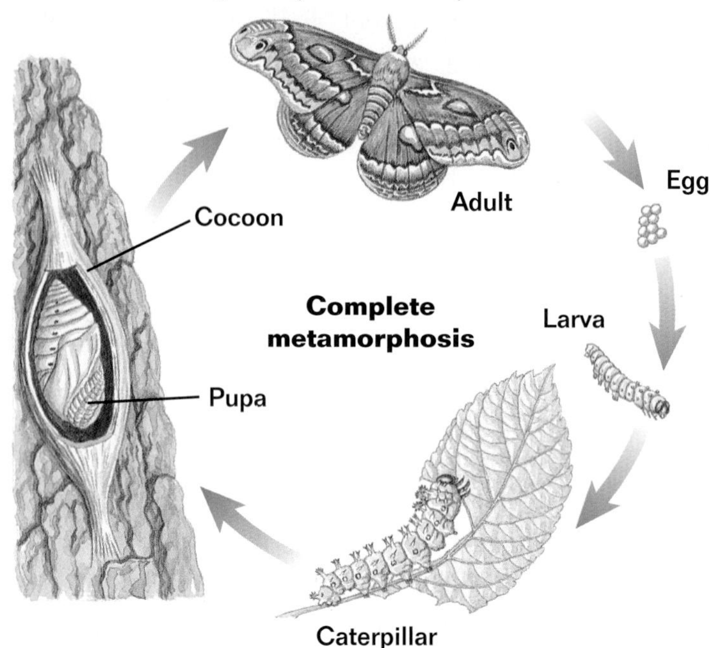

Metamorphosis

Identifying the young of some insects can be difficult. They don't look anything like the adult forms. This happens because many insects completely change their body form as they mature. This change in body form is called **metamorphosis** (met uh MOR fuh sus). There are two kinds of metamorphosis. Butterflies, ants, bees, and moths undergo complete metamorphosis. Complete metamorphosis has four stages: egg, larva, pupa (PYEW puh), and adult. You can trace the stages of this process in **Figure 24-19.** Notice how different the larva and pupa stages are from the adults.

Other insects go through incomplete metamorphosis, which is made up of only three stages: egg, nymph, and adult. Grasshopper nymphs look like a tiny version of the parents except they don't have wings. A nymph molts several times before reaching the adult stage. They replace their old exoskeletons as they grow larger. Grasshoppers get their wings and become adults after their final molt.

Figure 24-20 A spider's web is made from a liquid silk that the arachnid produces in its abdomen. Each kind of spider weaves its own unique style of web.

EXAMPLES OF Arachnids

- Spiders
- Mites
- Ticks
- Scorpions
- Lice

Arachnids

Spiders, ticks, mites, and scorpions are often confused with insects. They actually belong to a separate group of arthropods known as arachnids. Arachnids have two body regions. The first, called the cephalothorax (sef uh luh THOR aks), is made of the fused head and thorax regions. The abdomen is the second region. All arachnids have four pairs of legs attached to the cephalothorax.

Figure 24-21 Millipedes (A) may have more than 100 segments in their long abdomens. Centipedes (B) may have from 15 segments to 181 segments—always an odd number.

Spiders are predators, but they can't chew and eat prey the way insects do. Instead, a spider uses a pair of fanglike appendages in its mouth to inject venom into the prey and paralyze it. The spider releases enzymes that turn its victim into a liquid. The spider then drinks its food. In **Figure 24-20,** a spider is weaving a web that will trap prey.

Centipedes and Millipedes

Centipedes and millipedes are long, thin, segmented arthropods that look like worms. Instead of setae, these arthropods have pairs of jointed legs. Centipedes have one pair of joined legs attached to each body segment. Millipedes have two pairs. Centipedes are predators that use poisonous venom to capture their prey. Millipedes eat plants. Besides the number of legs, how else is the centipede different from the millipede in **Figure 24-21?**

EXAMPLES OF Crustaceans

- Crabs
- Crayfish
- Lobsters
- Shrimp
- Barnacles

Crustaceans

The exoskeleton gets larger and heavier each time an arthropod molts. The weight of the exoskeleton can limit the size of the animal. Now, think about where you can lift the most weight—on land or in water? Water is more buoyant than air, and it provides a greater upward force on an object. Because of this buoyant property, a large, heavy exoskeleton is less limiting for arthropods that live in water. These arthropods belong to a class known as crustaceans.

Most crustaceans live in water. Examples include crabs, crayfish, lobsters, shrimp, barnacles, and water fleas. They have five pairs of jointed legs. The first pair is usually larger and thicker and is used as claws to hold food, as illustrated in **Figure 24-22.** The other four pairs are walking legs. The five pairs of appendages on the abdomen are swimmerets. These are used to help move the animals through water and for reproduction. The swimmerets also force water over the feathery gills. If a crustacean loses an appendage, it can regenerate the lost part.

Figure 24-22 This rock crab, found in the Atlantic Ocean, is using its claws to hold the scallop it eats.

VISUALIZING Echinoderms

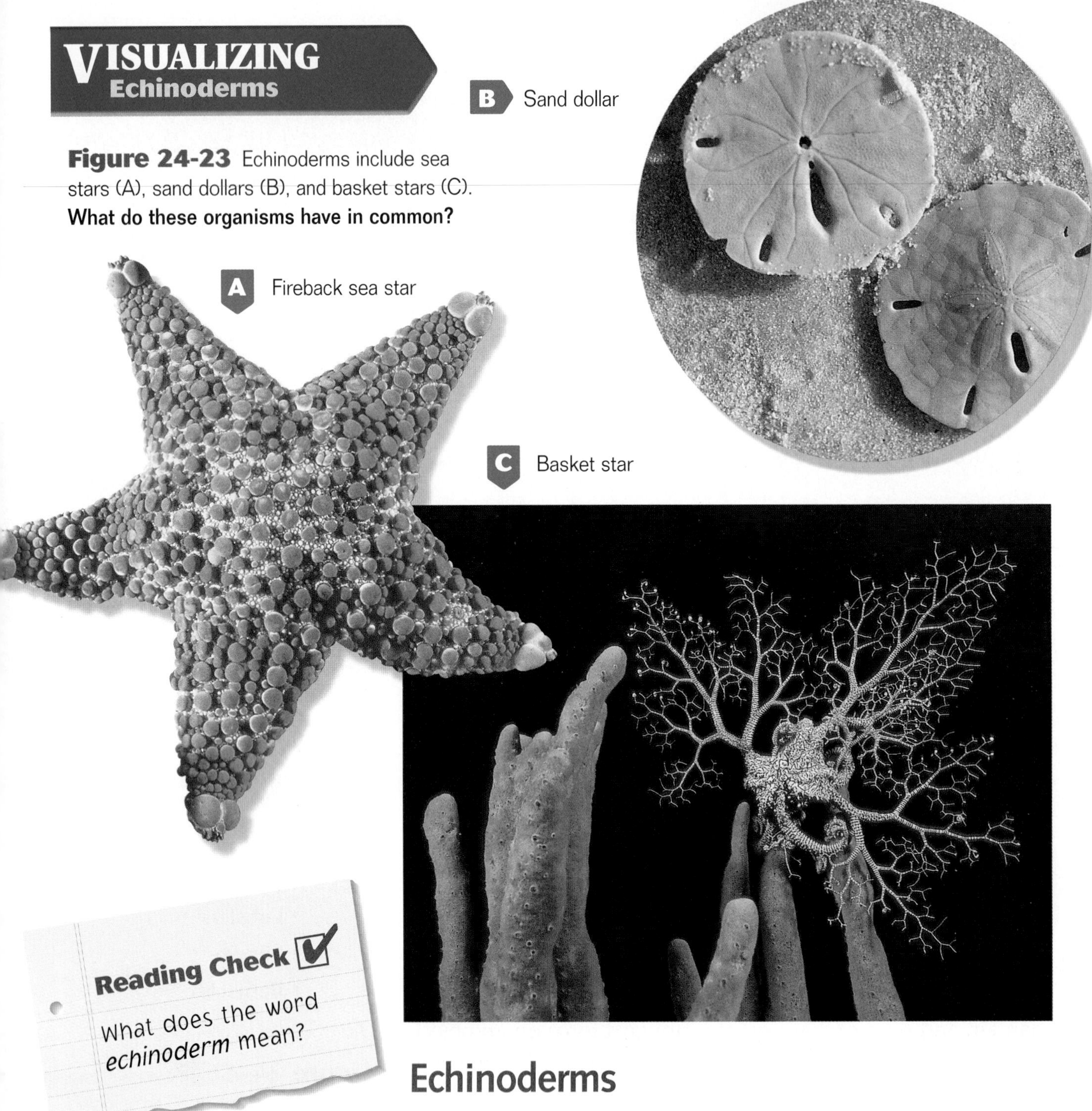

Figure 24-23 Echinoderms include sea stars (A), sand dollars (B), and basket stars (C). **What do these organisms have in common?**

Reading Check What does the word *echinoderm* mean?

EXAMPLES OF Echinoderms

- Sea stars
- Sea urchins
- Sand dollars
- Basket star
- Sea cucumber

Echinoderms

Unless you live near the ocean, you may not have seen an echinoderm (ih KI nuh durm), but most people know what a sea star is. Echinoderms have radial symmetry and are represented by sea stars, brittle stars, sea urchins, sand dollars, and sea cucumbers. They also don't have heads, brains, or advanced nervous systems.

The name *echinoderm* means "spiny skin." You can see from those shown in **Figure 24-23** that echinoderms have spines of various lengths that cover the outside of their bodies. Most echinoderms, such as sea stars, are supported and protected by an internal skeleton made up of calcium carbonate plates. These plates are covered by thin, spiny skin.

Water-Vascular System

Sea stars have a unique characteristic shared by all echinoderms—a water-vascular system. The water-vascular system is a network of water-filled canals. Thousands of tube feet are connected to this system. As water moves into and out of the water-vascular system, the tube feet act as suction cups and help the sea star move and eat. **Figure 24-24** shows these tube feet and how they are used to pry open a dead rock crab.

Sea stars also have a unique way of eating. Think about how you eat. You bring food to your mouth and swallow. The food then travels down to your stomach. The sea star actually pushes its stomach out of its mouth and into the opened shell of the oyster. It then digests the oyster's body while it is still inside the shell.

Like some other invertebrates, sea stars can regenerate damaged parts. Early settlers of the Chesapeake Bay area found the bay teeming with oysters. Eventually, more people moved into the area and deposited their wastes into the bay. Because some sea stars do well in polluted water, their population grew. People who harvested oysters found that the oyster population was decreasing. They decided to kill the sea stars by cutting them into pieces and

Modeling Sea Stars

Procedure

1. Hold your arm straight out, palm up.
2. Place a heavy book on your hand.
3. Have another person time how long you can hold your arm up with the book on it.

Analysis

1. Describe how your arm feels after a few minutes.
2. If the book models the sea star and your arm models the oyster, infer how a sea star successfully overcomes the oyster to obtain food.

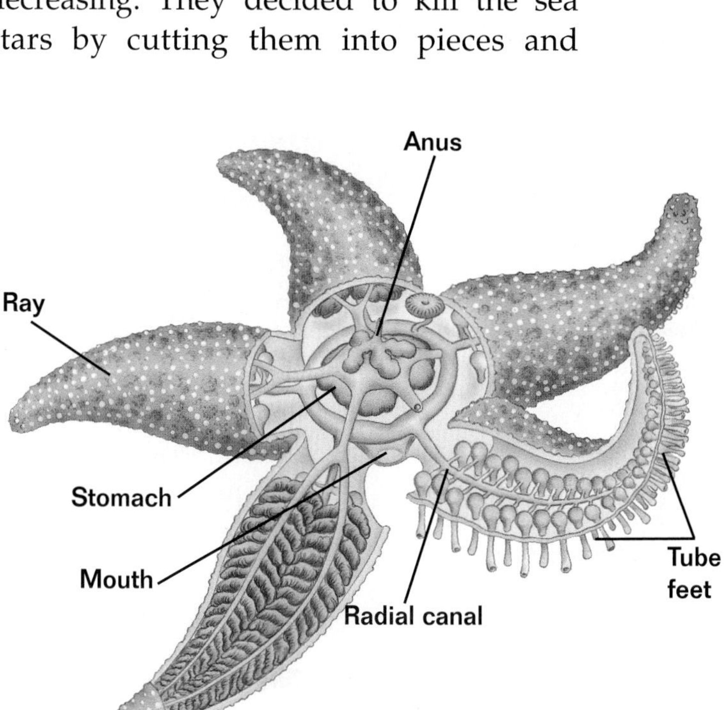

Figure 24-24 Sea bat sea stars use their tube feet to feed on a dead rock crab.

Using Math

Speckled sea cucumbers can grow up to 25 cm in length. The black sea cucumber can grow up to 30 cm. The sea worm sea cucumber can reach 1 m in length. Calculate the average length of these three types of sea cucumbers.

throwing them back into the bay. Within a short time, the sea star population was five times larger than before due to regeneration. The entire oyster bed was destroyed!

Sea Cucumbers

The sea cucumber in **Figure 24-25** looks nothing like the other members of the echinoderm class. They have soft bodies with a leathery covering. They have few calcium carbonate plates. Sea cucumbers have tentacles around their mouths that are used to capture food. Although they have five rows of tube feet on the sides of their bodies, they appear to be more bilaterally symmetrical than the other echinoderms. When threatened, sea cucumbers may expel their internal organs. These organs regenerate in a few weeks.

Scientists continue to study echinoderms to learn more about the process of regeneration. These animals are also important in keeping saltwater environments free of pollution. They feed on dead organisms and help recycle materials within the environment.

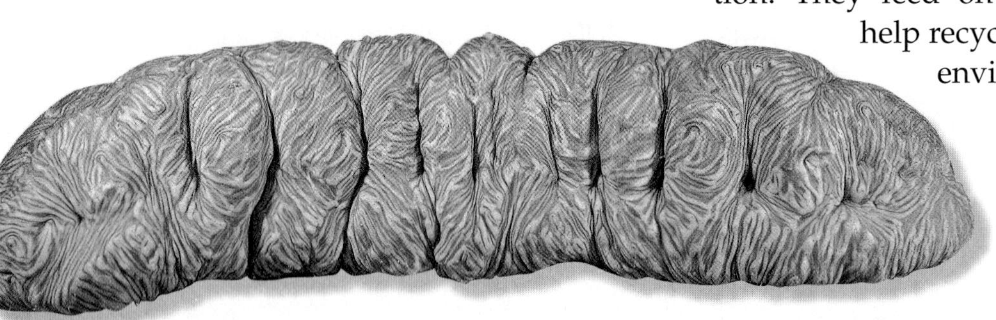

Figure 24-25 A sea cucumber moves along the ocean water using tube feet.

Section Assessment

1. What are three characteristics of all arthropods?
2. What are the advantages and disadvantages of an exoskeleton?
3. What characteristics set echinoderms apart from other invertebrates?
4. **Think Critically:** What might happen to the sea star population after the oyster beds are destroyed? Explain your answer.
5. **Skill Builder**
   Observing and Inferring Observe the echinoderms pictured in **Figure 24-23.** Infer why they are slow moving. If you need help, refer to Observing and Inferring in the **Skill Handbook** on page 956.

Using Math

A flea measuring 4 mm in length can jump 25 cm from a resting position. If a flea were as tall as you are, how far could it jump?

Observing Complete Metamorphosis

Many insects go through the four stages of complete metamorphosis during their life cycles. Chemicals that are secreted by the body of the animal control the changes. How different do the body forms look between the stages of metamorphosis?

Materials

- Large-mouth jar or old fish bowl
- Bran or oatmeal
- Dried bread or cookie crumbs mixed with flour
- Slice of apple or carrot
- Paper towel
- Cheesecloth
- Mealworms
- Rubber band

What You'll Investigate

What do the stages of metamorphosis look like for a mealworm?

Goals

- **Observe** the stages of metamorphosis of mealworms to adult darkling beetles.
- **Compare** the physical appearance of mealworms as they go through two stages of metamorphosis.

Procedure

1. **Set up** a habitat for the mealworms by placing a 1-cm layer of bran or oatmeal on the bottom of the jar. Add a 1-cm layer of dried bread or cookie crumbs mixed with flour. Then, add another layer of bran or oatmeal.
2. **Add** a slice of apple or carrot as a source of moisture. Replace the apple or carrot daily.
3. **Place** 20 to 30 mealworms in the jar. Add a piece of crumpled paper towel.
4. **Cover** the jar with a piece of cheesecloth. Use the rubber band to secure the cloth to the jar.
5. **Observe** the mealworms daily for two to three weeks. **Record** daily observations in your Science Journal.

Conclude and Apply

1. In your Science Journal, **draw** and **describe** the mealworms' metamorphosis to adults.
2. **Identify** the stages of metamorphosis that mealworms go through to become adult darkling beetles.
3. Which of these stages did you not see during this investigation?
4. What are some of the advantages of an insect's young being different from the adult form?
5. Based on the food you placed in the habitat, **infer** where you might find mealworms or the adult darkling beetles in your house.
6. Why do you think pet stores would stock and sell mealworms?

Chapter 24 Reviewing Main Ideas

For a **preview** of this chapter, study this Reviewing Main Ideas before you read the chapter. After you have studied this chapter, you can use the Reviewing Main Ideas to **review** the chapter.

The Glencoe MindJogger, Audiocassettes, and CD-ROM provide additional opportunities for review.

Section 24-1 WHAT IS AN ANIMAL?

Animals are many-celled organisms that must find and digest their own food. **Invertebrates** are animals without backbones. **Vertebrates** have backbones. Animals that have body parts arranged the same way on both sides of their bodies have bilateral **symmetry.** Animals with body parts arranged in a circle around a central point have radial symmetry. Asymetrical animals have no definite shape. *What are five characteristics of animals?*

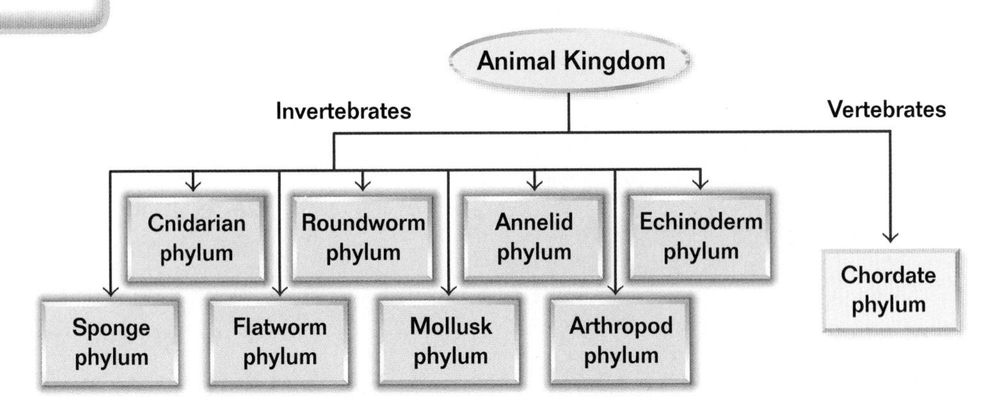

Section 24-2 SPONGES, CNIDARIANS, FLATWORMS, AND ROUNDWORMS

Sponges and cnidarians are only two layers thick. Sponge cells do not form tissues, organs, or organ systems. Sponges are sessile and obtain food and oxygen by filtering water through pores. **Cnidarian** bodies have tissues and are radially symmetrical. Most have tentacles with stinging cells that get food. Regeneration allows an organism to replace lost or damaged parts or to reproduce sexually. Flatworms and roundworms have bilateral symmetry. They have both parasitic and **free-living** members. *Why are sponges considered the least complex of all animals?*

Reading Check ✓

Choose a group of unlike objects, such as the items in your book bag or your locker. Classify these objects into groups and subgroups.

Section

24-3 MOLLUSKS AND SEGMENTED WORMS

Mollusks with one shell are gastropods. Bivalve mollusks have two shells. Cephalopods have a foot divided into tentacles and no outside shell. Except for cephalopods, mollusks have an **open circulatory system** in which the blood surrounds the organs directly. Cephalopods have a **closed circulatory system** with the blood contained in vessels. Annelids have a body cavity that separates the internal organs from the body wall. Setae help annelids move.

How are cephalopods adapted for swimming?

Section

24-4 ARTHROPODS AND ECHINODERMS

Arthropods are classified by the number of body segments and **appendages.** Their **exoskeletons** cover, protect, and support their bodies. Arthropods develop either by complete or incomplete **metamorphosis.** Echinoderms are spiny-skinned invertebrates most closely related to vertebrates. They move by means of a water-vascular system. ***What are some common characteristics for all arthropods?***

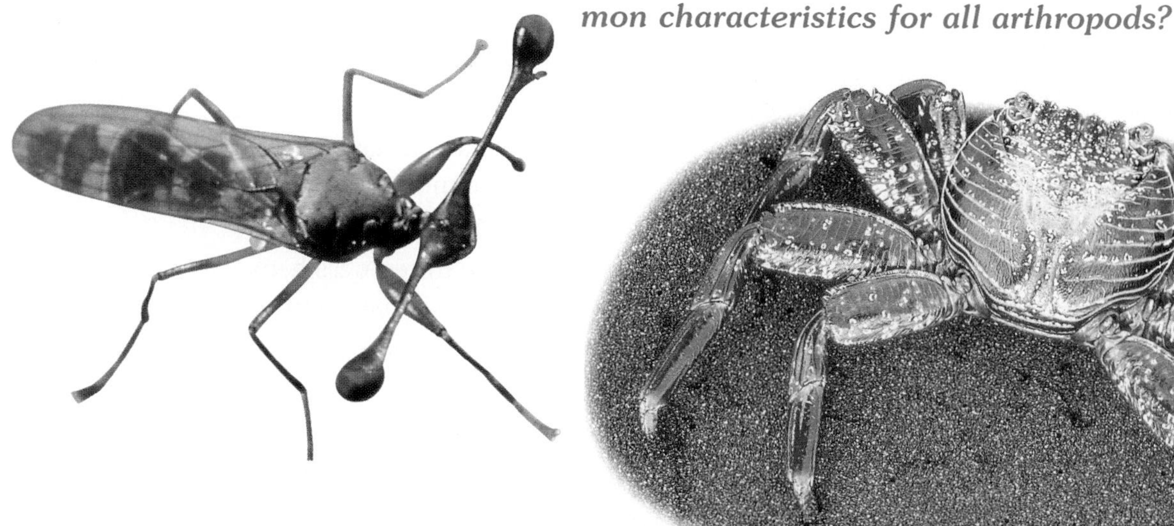

Chapter 24 Assessment

Using Vocabulary

a. appendage
b. arthropod
c. closed circulatory system
d. cnidarian
e. exoskeleton
f. free-living
g. gills
h. invertebrate
i. mantle
j. medusa
k. metamorphosis
l. mollusk
m. open circulatory system
n. parasite
o. polyp
p. radula
q. symmetry
r. vertebrate

Explain the differences between the terms in each of the following sets.

1. medusa, polyp
2. closed circulatory system, open circulatory system
3. vertebrate, invertebrate
4. arthropod, mollusk
5. exoskeleton, mantle

Checking Concepts

Choose the word or phrase that best answers the question.

6. Which of the following refers to animals that can be divided in half along a single line?
   A) asymmetrical
   B) bilaterally symmetrical
   C) radially symmetrical
   D) anterior
7. Which of the following do **NOT** belong to the same group?
   A) fish C) jellyfish
   B) hydras D) sea anemones
8. Which of the following phylums do sponges belong to?
   A) Cnidaria C) Porifera
   B) Nematoda D) Platyhelminthes
9. The body plans of cnidarians are polyp and which of the following?
   A) larva C) ventral
   B) medusa D) bud
10. Which of the following is an example of a parasite?
    A) sponge C) tapeworm
    B) planarian D) jellyfish
11. Which of the following covers the organs of mollusks?
    A) radula C) gill
    B) mantle D) foot
12. Which organism has a closed circulatory system?
    A) octopus C) oyster
    B) snail D) sponge
13. Which organism has two body regions?
    A) insect C) arachnid
    B) mollusk D) annelid
14. Which phylum has many organisms with radial symmetry?
    A) annelids C) echinoderms
    B) mollusks D) arthropods
15. Which of the following are sharp and cause predators to avoid eating sponges?
    A) thorax C) collar cells
    B) spicules D) tentacles

Thinking Critically

16. What aspect of sponge reproduction would be evidence that they are more like animals than plants?
17. What is the advantage for simple organisms to have more than one means of reproduction?
18. What are the differences between the tentacles of cnidarians and cephalopods?
19. What is the difference between budding and regeneration?
20. Centipedes and millipedes have segments. Why are they **NOT** classified as worms?

Developing Skills

If you need help, refer to the Skill Handbook.

21. **Comparing and Contrasting:** Compare and contrast the feeding habits of sponges and cnidarians.
22. **Using Variables, Constants, and Controls:** Design an experiment to test the sense of touch in planarians.
23. **Observing and Inferring:** Why are gastropods sometimes called univalves? Use examples in your answer.
24. **Classifying:** Classify the following animals into arthropod classes: *spider, grasshopper, ladybug, beetle, crab, scorpion, lobster, butterfly, tick,* and *shrimp.*
25. **Concept Mapping:** Complete the concept map of classification in the cnidarian phylum.

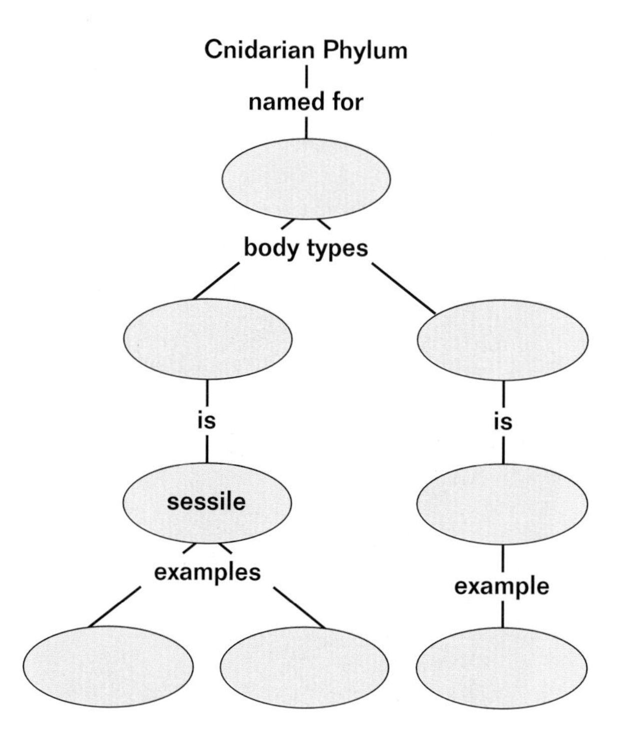

Test-Taking Tip

Words Are Easy to Learn Make a huge stack of vocabulary flash cards and study them. Use your new words in daily conversation. The great thing about learning new words is the ability to express yourself more specifically.

Test Practice

Use these questions to test your Science Proficiency.

1. Symmetry refers to the arrangement of the individual parts of an object. Which of the following organisms have radial symmetry?
   A) cnidarians
   B) sponges
   C) tapeworms
   D) mollusks
2. Echinoderms have a unique way of eating. Which of the following structures are used by echinoderms to move about and open a mollusk's shell?
   A) spicules
   B) arms
   C) spines
   D) tube feet
3. A water-vascular system is a network of water-filled canals. Which of the following phylums of invertebrates possess a water-vascular system?
   A) echinoderms
   B) arthropods
   C) mollusks
   D) cnidarians

CHAPTER

25 Vertebrate Animals

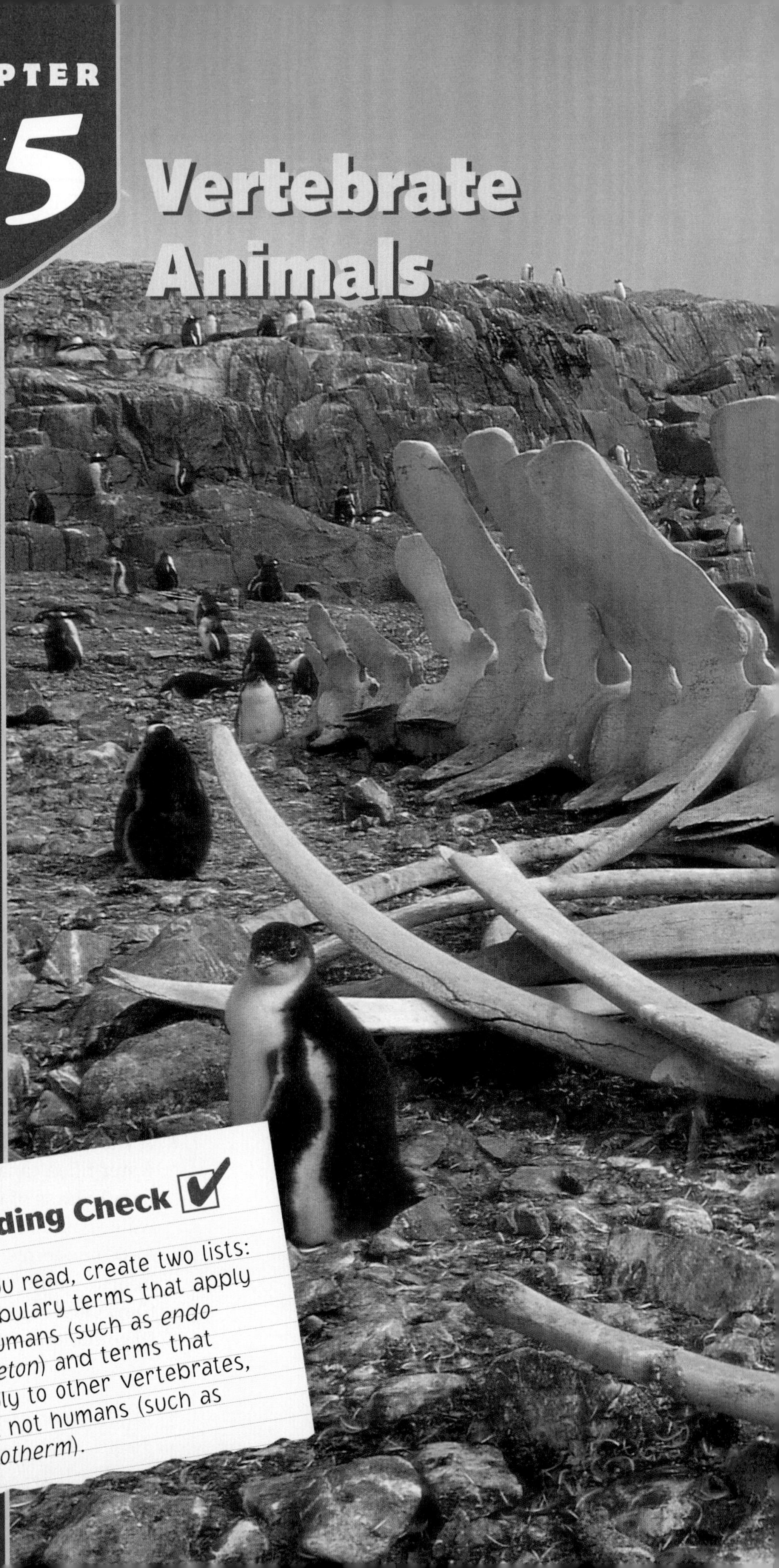

Chapter Preview

Section 25-1
Fish

Section 25-2
Amphibians and Reptiles

Section 25-3
Birds

Section 25-4
Mammals

Skills Preview

Skill Builders
- Map Concepts
- Classify

Activities
- Design an Experiment
- Observe and Infer

MiniLabs
- Make a Model
- Compare and Contrast

Reading Check ✔

As you read, create two lists: vocabulary terms that apply to humans (such as *endoskeleton*) and terms that apply to other vertebrates, but not humans (such as *ectotherm*).

Explore Activity

You have something in common with the whale remains on the opposite page. This common feature protects some of the organs inside your body. It supports and gives your body shape. It also works with your muscles to help move your body. This common feature is your skeleton. Most internal skeletons are made of bone. Bones are many shapes and sizes. They must be strong enough to carry your weight yet light enough for you to move. To learn more about the structure of bones, complete the following Explore Activity.

Model Bones

1. Think about the different shapes of your bones. What shape is your shoulder blade? Your hip bone? Your neck? Your ribs?
2. Use five index cards to make bone models. Fold and bend the cards into different shapes. Use tape to hold the shapes if necessary.
3. Stack books on top of each card to find out which shape supports the most weight.

In your Science Journal, draw a picture of each bone model. Infer which shape would make the strongest bone. Write a paragraph comparing the strengths of each bone model.

25•1 Fish

What You'll Learn

- The major characteristics of chordates
- The difference between ectotherms and endotherms
- The characteristics of the three classes of fish

Vocabulary

chordate
endoskeleton
ectotherm
endotherm
fish
fin
cartilage

Why It's Important

- Fish have many adaptations for living in water.

What is a vertebrate?

Suppose you took a survey in which you asked your classmates to list their pets. Probably dogs, cats, birds, snakes, and fish appear on the list. A large percentage of the animals listed, along with yourself, would belong to a group called vertebrates. Vertebrates are animals with backbones. They are the most complex of three animal groups that belong to the Chordate phylum, as illustrated in **Figure 25-1.** All **chordates** have a notochord, which is a rod of stiffened tissue. Chordates also have a hollow nerve cord in their backs and gill slits. In most vertebrates, a backbone made of vertebra replaces the notochord as the animal develops.

Whereas most invertebrates have exoskeletons, vertebrates have an internal system of bones called an **endoskeleton.** *Endo-* means "within." The vertebrae, skull, and other bones of the endoskeleton support and protect the animal's internal organs. The skeleton also provides a place where muscles are attached.

Vertebrates have two different ways of dealing with internal body temperature. Most vertebrates are ectotherms. **Ectotherms** are vertebrates whose body temperature changes with the temperature of their surroundings. **Endotherms** are animals with a constant body temperature. The body temperature of an endotherm usually remains the same no matter what the temperature of its surrounding environment.

Figure 25-1 This concept map showing the different groups of animals will appear at the beginning of each section. The groups that are highlighted with a red outline are the groups to be discussed. This diagram shows that the Chordate phylum is made up of three groups: the tunicates, the lancelets, and the vertebrates.

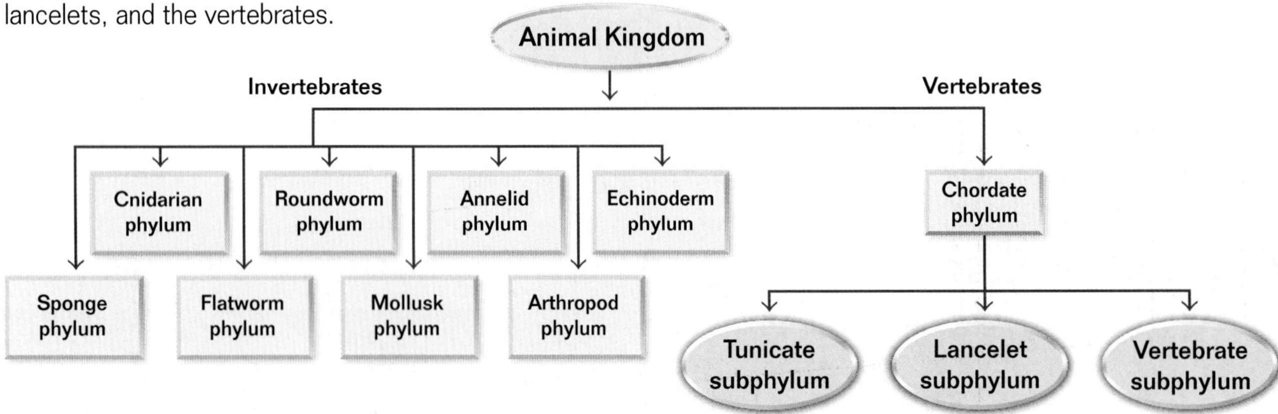

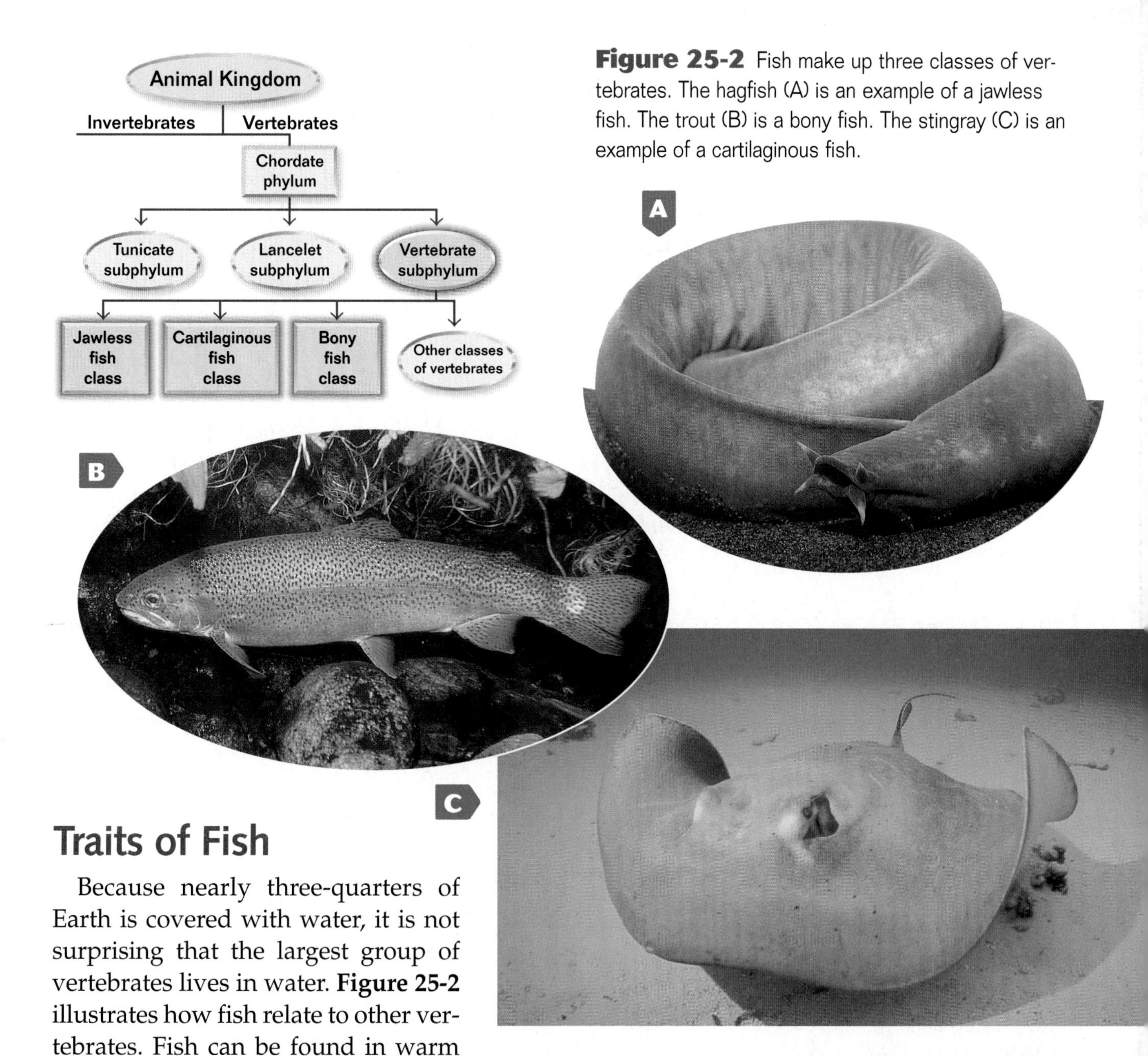

Figure 25-2 Fish make up three classes of vertebrates. The hagfish (A) is an example of a jawless fish. The trout (B) is a bony fish. The stingray (C) is an example of a cartilaginous fish.

Traits of Fish

Because nearly three-quarters of Earth is covered with water, it is not surprising that the largest group of vertebrates lives in water. **Figure 25-2** illustrates how fish relate to other vertebrates. Fish can be found in warm desert pools and the subfreezing Arctic ocean. They swim in shallow streams and far down in the ocean depths.

Fish are ectotherms that live in water and use gills to get oxygen. Gills are fleshy filaments that are filled with tiny blood vessels. The heart of the fish pumps blood to the gills. As blood passes through the gills, it picks up oxygen from water that is passing over the gills. Carbon dioxide is released from the blood into the water.

Most fish have fins. **Fins** are fanlike structures used for steering, balancing, and moving. Usually, they are paired. Those on the top and bottom stabilize the fish. Those on the side steer and move the fish. Scales are another common characteristic of fish although not all fish have scales. Scales are hard, thin, overlapping plates that cover the skin. These protective plates are made of a bony material.

Using Math

Make a circle graph of the number of fish species currently classified. There are 70 species of jawless fish, 820 species of cartilaginous fish, and 23 500 species of bony fish. What percent of this graph is accounted for by cartilaginous fish?

Types of Fish

Scientists group fish into three distinct classes. They are bony fish, jawless fish, and cartilaginous fish. Bony fish have skeletons made of bone, while cartilaginous fish and jawless fish both have endoskeletons made of cartilage. **Cartilage** (KART uh lihj) is a tough, flexible tissue that is similar to bone but is not as hard. Your ears and the tip of your nose are made of cartilage.

EXAMPLES OF Bony Fish

- Trout
- Cod
- Salmon
- Catfish
- Tuna
- Sea horse

Bony Fish

About 95 percent of all fish belong to the class known as bony fish. The body structure of a typical bony fish, a tuna, is shown in **Figure 25-3.** These fish have skeletons made of bone. Their scales are covered with slimy mucus that allows the water to easily flow over the fishes' bodies as they swim in water. The majority of bony fish use external fertilization to reproduce. Females release large numbers of eggs into the water. Males release sperm as they swim over the eggs.

An important adaptation in most bony fish is the swim bladder. This air sac helps control the depth at which the fish swim. Transfer of gases between the swim bladder and the blood, mostly oxygen in deep-water fish and nitrogen in shallow-water fish, changes the inflation of the swim bladder. As the swim bladder fills with gases, the fish becomes more buoyant and rises in the water. When the bladder deflates, the fish becomes less buoyant and sinks lower in the water.

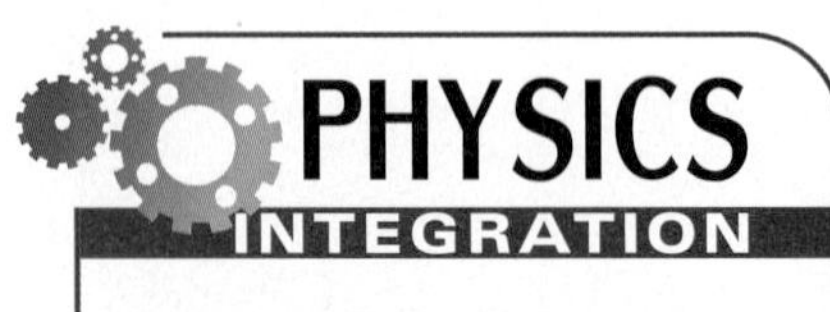

Regulating Buoyancy
Unlike fish that regulate the gas content of their fish bladders, submarines pump water into and out of special chambers to regulate the vertical forces that cause the submarine to sink or rise.

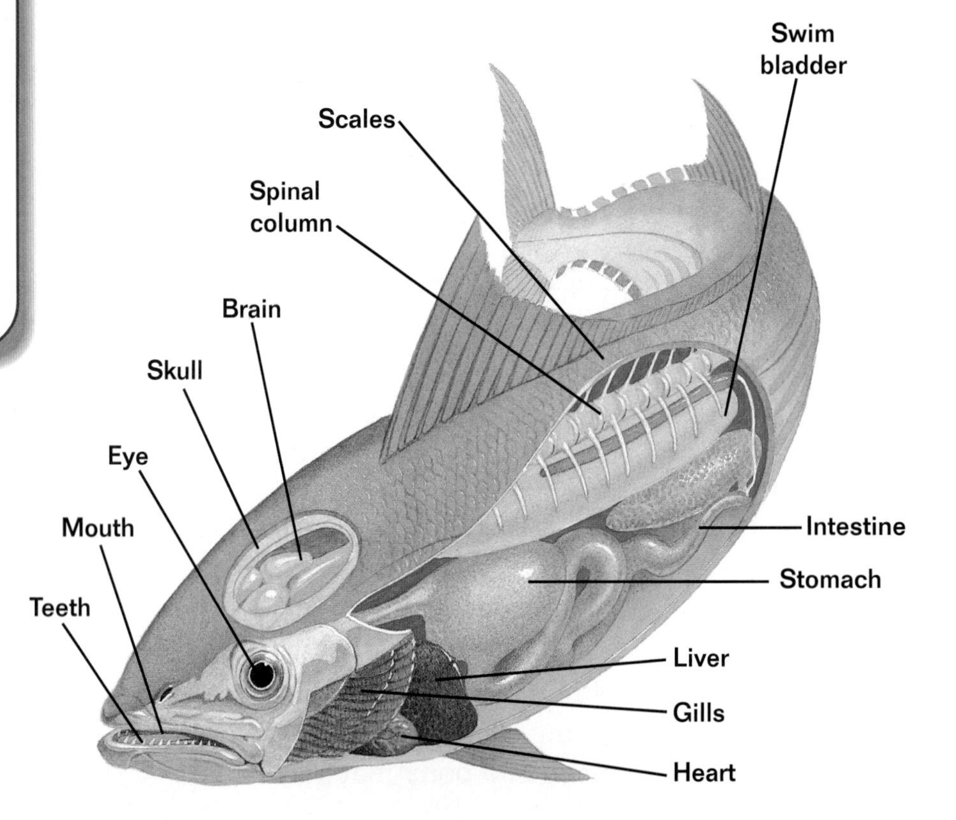

Figure 25-3 Although there are many different kinds of bony fish, they all share basic structures. **What are two unique fish structures?**

Figure 25-4 This sea lamprey (A) with its sucker disk mouth belongs to the class of jawless fish. Sharks (B) belong to the cartilaginous class and are efficient at finding and killing food.

Jawless and Cartilaginous Fish

Few fish belong to the class known as jawless fish. Jawless fish have long, scaleless, tubelike bodies and an endoskeleton made of cartilage. They have round mouths but no jaws, as seen in **Figure 25-4A.** Their mouths act like suckers with sharp toothlike parts. Once a lamprey attaches itself to another larger fish, it uses the toothlike parts to scrape through the host's skin. It then feeds on the blood of the larger fish.

Sharks, skates, and rays are cartilaginous fish. Cartilaginous fish have skeletons made of cartilage just like the jawless fish. However, cartilaginous fish, such as the shark in **Figure 25-4B,** have movable jaws and scales. Their scales feel rough like sandpaper. Most cartilaginous fish are predators.

Section Assessment

1. What are three characteristics of chordates?
2. Name the three classes of fish. What materials make up their skeletons?
3. Compare and contrast ectotherms and endotherms.
4. **Think Critically:** Female fish lay thousands of eggs. Why aren't lakes overcrowded with fish?
5. **Skill Builder**
   Observing and Inferring Fish without swim bladders, such as sharks, must move constantly, or they sink. They need more energy to maintain this constant movement. What can you infer about the amount of food sharks must eat when compared to another fish of similar size that have swim bladders? If you need help, refer to Observing and Inferring in the **Skill Handbook** on page 956.

Using Math

There are 353 known species of sharks. Of that number, only about 30 species have been known to attack humans. What percentage of shark species is known to attack humans?

25•2 Amphibians and Reptiles

What You'll Learn

- How amphibians have adapted to live in water and on land
- What happens during frog metamorphosis
- The adaptations that allow reptiles to live on land

Vocabulary
amphibian, estivation, hibernation, reptile

Why It's Important

- Amphibians are adapted to living in both water and on land while reptiles live only on land.

Amphibians

Have you ever heard of a person leading a double life? Amphibians are animals that lead double lives. In fact, the term *amphibian* comes from the Greek word *amphibios,* which means "double life." **Amphibians** are vertebrates that spend part of their lives in water and part on land. They are also ectotherms, which means that their internal body temperatures changes with their environment. Frogs, toads, and salamanders such as the barred tiger salamander pictured in **Figure 25-5** are the most common kinds of amphibians.

Amphibian Adaptations

Living on land is different from living in water. Air temperature changes more quickly and more often than water temperature. Also, air doesn't support body weight as well as water. Certain adaptations help amphibians survive both in water and on land.

Amphibians have behavioral adaptations that allow them to cope with swings in the air temperature of their particular environment. During cold winter months, they are inactive. They bury themselves in mud or leaves until the temperature warms up. In winter, this period of inactivity and lower metabolic needs

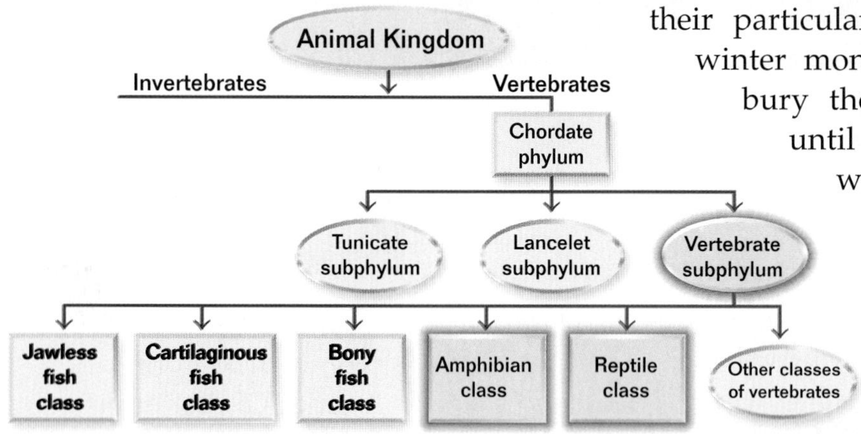

Figure 25-5 This barred tiger salamander has legs that extend straight out from the body.

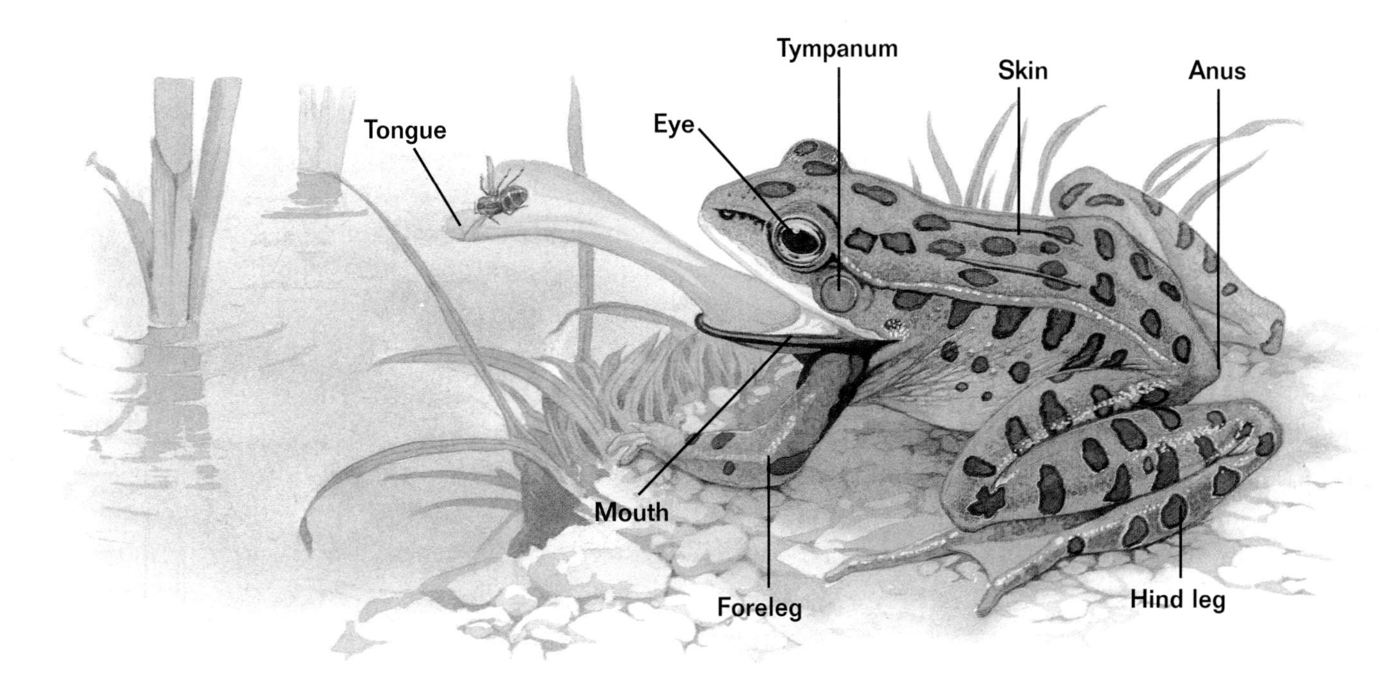

Figure 25-6 A frog's body is adapted for life in the water and on land. **What adaptations can you see in this illustration?**

is called **hibernation.** Metabolic needs refer to the chemical activities in an organism that enable it to live, grow, and reproduce. Amphibians that live in hot, drier environments are inactive and hide in the ground where it is likely to be cooler and more humid. This kind of inactivity during hot, dry summer months is called **estivation.**

Amphibians have a strong endoskeleton made of bones. The skeleton helps to support the bodies of amphibians while on land. Adult frogs and toads have short, broad bodies, with four legs and no neck or tail. The strong hind legs are used for swimming and jumping.

Another adaptation increases amphibians' chances of survival on land. Instead of using gills to obtain oxygen from water, lungs become the primary method of obtaining oxygen from air. To increase the oxygen supply, amphibians exchange oxygen and carbon dioxide through their moist, scaleless skin or the lining of their mouths.

Moving to land provides an increased food supply for adult amphibians. Land habitats offer a variety of insects as food for these organisms. **Figure 25-6** shows some adaptations used to catch prey. The tympanic membranes, or eardrums, vibrate in response to sound and are used for hearing. Large eyes provide excellent vision. The long sticky tongue extends quickly to capture the insect and bring it into the waiting mouth.

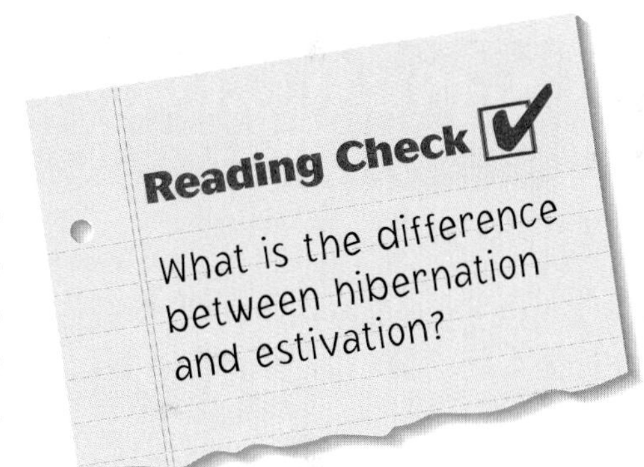

interNET CONNECTION

Visit the Glencoe Science Web Site at **www.glencoe.com/sec/science/ca** for more information about amphibians.

Amphibian Metamorphosis

Although young animals such as kittens and calves are almost miniature duplicates of their parents, young amphibians look nothing like their parents. Metamorphosis is a series of body changes that occur during the life cycle of an amphibian. Most amphibians go through a two-stage metamorphosis as illustrated in **Figure 25-7.** The larval stage lives in water, and the adult lives on land.

Most amphibians mate in water. Here, the eggs hatch, and the young larval forms live. The larvae have no legs and breathe through gills. You can see that as the larval form of frogs, called tadpoles, go through metamorphosis, they change form. The young tadpoles develop body structures needed for life on land, including legs and lungs. The rate at which metamorphosis occurs depends on the species, the water temperature, and the amount of available food. The less available food is and the cooler the water temperatures are, the longer it takes for metamorphosis to occur.

VISUALIZING Frog Metamorphosis

Figure 25-7 Frogs undergo a two-stage metamorphosis from the larval stage that lives in water to the adult stage that lives on land.

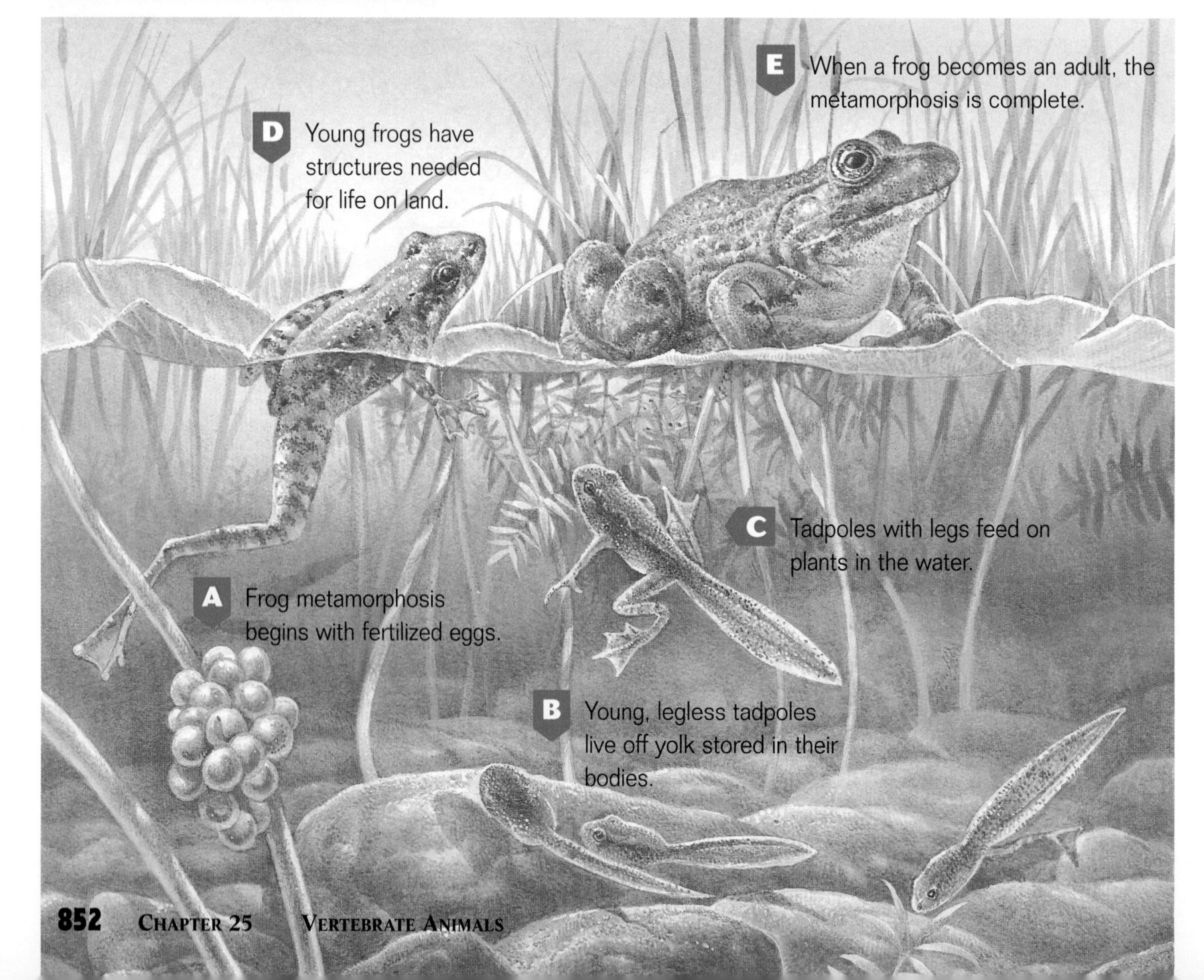

Figure 25-8 The green tree viper snake (A), the collared lizard (B), the spotted turtle (C), and the American alligator (D) are all reptiles.

Reptiles

The snake, lizard, turtle, and crocodile in **Figure 25-8** are all reptiles. A **reptile** is an ectothermic vertebrate with dry, scaly skin. Reptiles are vertebrates that do not depend on water for reproduction. Several adaptations allow reptiles to live on land.

Types of Reptiles

Reptiles vary greatly in size, shape, and color. Turtles are covered with a hard shell. They withdraw into the shell for protection. They eat insects, worms, fish, and plants. Alligators and crocodiles are feared predators that live in and near water. These large reptiles live in tropical climates.

Lizards and snakes are the largest group of reptiles. Lizards have movable eyelids, external ears, and legs with clawed toes. Snakes don't have eyelids, ears, or legs. Instead of hearing sounds, they feel vibrations in the ground. Snakes are also sensitive to chemicals in the air. They use their tongue to "smell" these chemicals.

Reptile Adaptations

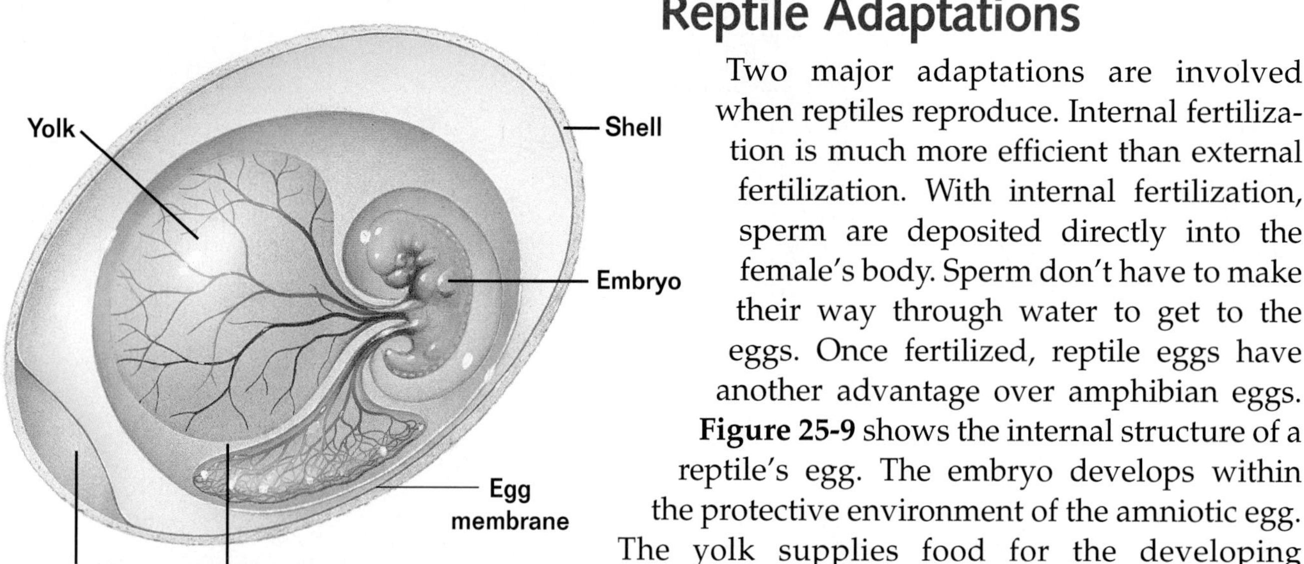

Figure 25-9 The amniotic egg is one of the adaptations reptiles have for living on land. Young reptiles hatch from their eggs fully developed.

Two major adaptations are involved when reptiles reproduce. Internal fertilization is much more efficient than external fertilization. With internal fertilization, sperm are deposited directly into the female's body. Sperm don't have to make their way through water to get to the eggs. Once fertilized, reptile eggs have another advantage over amphibian eggs. **Figure 25-9** shows the internal structure of a reptile's egg. The embryo develops within the protective environment of the amniotic egg. The yolk supplies food for the developing embryo. A leathery shell provides more protection than the jelly-covered frog's egg. When hatched, the young reptiles are fully developed. With some snakes, the young even develop and mature within the female's body. Then, the young snakes are born alive.

Another adaptation for life on land includes a thick, dry, waterproof skin. This skin is covered with scales and prevents dehydration and injury. All reptiles breathe with lungs. Even sea snakes and sea turtles must come to the surface to breathe.

Section Assessment

1. List the adaptations amphibians have for living in water and on land.
2. Sequence the steps of frog metamorphosis.
3. List the adaptations reptiles have for living on land.
4. **Think Critically:** Some harmless snakes have the same red, yellow, and black colors as the poisonous coral snake. How is this coloring an advantage for a nonpoisonous snake?
5. **Skill Builder**
   Comparing and Contrasting Compare and contrast the types of eggs amphibians and reptiles have. If you need help, refer to Comparing and Contrasting in the **Skill Handbook** on page 956.

In your Science Journal, explain why it is important for amphibians to live in moist or wet environments.

Activity 25•1

Frog Metamorphosis

Frogs and other amphibians use external fertilization to reproduce. Female frogs lay hundreds of jellylike eggs in water. Male frogs then fertilize these eggs. Once larvae hatch, the process of metamorphosis begins. Over a period of time, young tadpoles develop into adult frogs.

Materials

- Aquarium or jar (4 L)
- Frog egg mass
- Lake or pond water
- Stereoscopic microscope
- Watch glass
- Small fishnet
- Aquatic plants
- Washed gravel
- Lettuce (previously boiled)
- Large rock

What You'll Investigate

What changes occur as a tadpole goes through metamorphosis?

Goals

- **Observe** how body structures change as a tadpole develops into an adult frog.
- **Determine** how long metamorphosis takes to be completed.

Procedure

1. **Copy** the data table in your Science Journal.
2. As a class, use the aquarium, pond water, gravel, rock, and plants to prepare a water habitat for the frog eggs.
3. **Place** the egg mass in the water of the aquarium. Use the fishnet to separate a few eggs from the mass. **Place** these eggs in the watch glass. The eggs should have the dark side up. **CAUTION:** *Handle the eggs with care.*
4. **Observe** the eggs. **Record** your observations in the data table.
5. **Observe** the eggs twice a week. **Record** any changes that occur.
6. Continue observing the tadpoles twice a week after they hatch. **Identify** the mouth, eyes, gill cover, gills, nostrils, fin on the back, hind legs, and front legs. **Observe** how tadpoles eat boiled lettuce that has been cooled.

Conclude and Apply

1. How long does it take for the eggs to hatch and the tadpoles to develop legs?
2. Which pair of legs appears first?
3. **Explain** why the jellylike coating around the eggs is important.
4. **Compare** the eyes of young tadpoles with the eyes of older tadpoles.
5. **Calculate** how long it takes for a tadpole to change into a frog.

Frog Metamorphosis

Date	Observations

25•3 Birds

What You'll Learn

- The characteristics of birds
- How birds have adapted in order to fly

Vocabulary
bird
contour feather
down feather

Why It's Important

- Many birds demonstrate structural and behavioral adaptations for flight.

Characteristics of Birds

Have you ever heard the term *pecking order?* Originally, it meant the ranking order of all the birds within a flock. High-ranking birds peck at lower-ranking birds to keep them away from food. This action is an example of a behavioral characteristic. Now, let's look at some physical characteristics of birds.

Despite the wide variety of birds, they all share some common characteristics. **Birds** are vertebrates with two legs, two wings, and bills, or beaks. They lay hard-shelled eggs, have feathers, and are endotherms. Recall that endothermic vertebrates keep a constant body temperature no matter what the temperature of the environment. Birds are the only animals that have feathers. The hard-shelled eggs protect the developing birds. Birds often sit on these eggs to keep them warm until they hatch. You learned that endotherms maintain a constant body temperature. A bird's body temperature is about 40°C. Your body temperature is about 37°C. Bird watchers can tell where a bird lives and what it eats by looking at the type of wing, beak, and feet it has. **Figure 25-10** illustrates some of the more than 8600 species of birds.

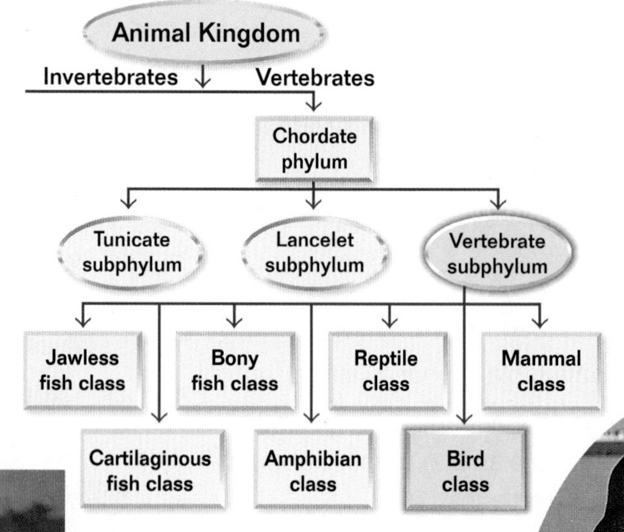

Figure 25-10 Birds are classified into orders based on the characteristic beaks, feet, feathers, and other physical features.

A Flightless land birds, such as ostriches, have their wings reduced in size and strong feet with fused toes for running.

B King penguins use their wings as paddles to propel themselves through water.

C The more than 200 species of ducks, such as this Mandarin duck, have webbed feet and short tails, as do geese and swans.

D Eagles and other birds of prey have sharp, hooked beaks for tearing flesh and large talons for grasping prey.

E Chickens, grouse, quail, turkeys, and this ringneck pheasant are ground-dwelling birds capable of short bursts of flight.

F Long-legged herons, storks, and these flamingos feed on fish and other aquatic organisms. Many of these species form nesting colonies in trees.

G Hummingbirds have specialized beaks for feeding on the nectar of flowers.

H Hairy woodpeckers have long, thin beaks adapted for digging insects out of wood and four toes—two toes in front and two toes in back. Such feet enable them to climb trees effectively.

I Mockingbirds and other perching birds, including crows and jays, have three toes facing forward and one backward. Their feet are adapted for perching on twigs.

J With two toes facing forward and two facing backward, roadrunners are adapted for running.

Using Math

Count the number of different birds you observe outside during a certain time each day for three days. Graph your data.

Adaptations for Flight

Most body adaptations for birds are designed to enable them to fly. Their bodies are streamlined. Their skeletons are light, yet strong. If you could look inside the bone of a bird, you would see that it is hollow. Flying requires that they have a rigid body. Fused vertebrae provide the needed rigidity, strength, and stability. Birds need a good supply of oxygen to fly. Efficient hearts and lungs aid in respiration. The lungs are connected to air sacs that can be found throughout the body. Air sacs make a bird lighter for flight and help bring more oxygen to the blood. Large, powerful flight muscles in the wings are attached to the breastbone or sternum. Birds beat their wings to attain both thrust and lift. Slow motion pictures show that birds beat their wings both up and down as well as forward and back.

A bird's wing provides lift without constant beating. Like the airplane wing in **Figure 25-11,** a bird's wing is curved on top. It is flat or slightly curved on the bottom. A wing with this shape is important. As air moves across the wings, it has a greater distance to move across the top of the wing than along the bottom. The longer path taken by the air moving over the upper surface reduces the air pressure there. As a result, greater pressure is felt on the lower surface of the wing. The difference in air pressure results in lift.

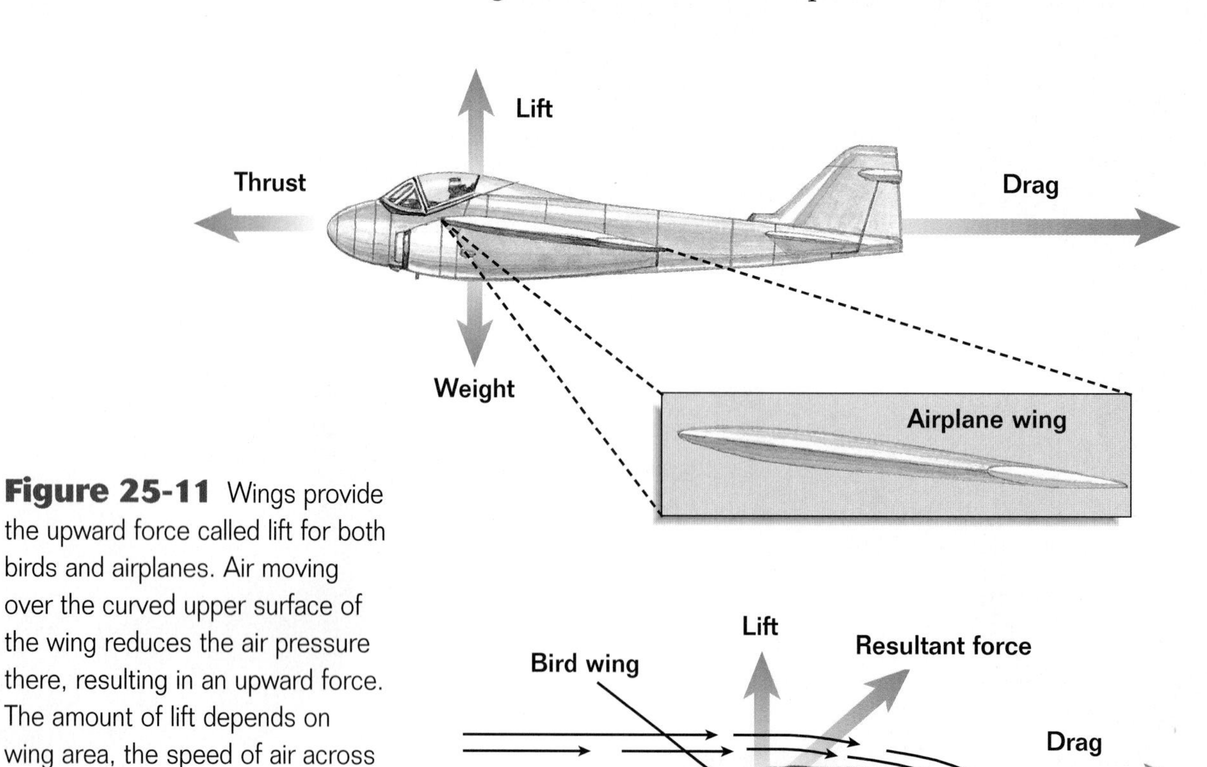

Figure 25-11 Wings provide the upward force called lift for both birds and airplanes. Air moving over the curved upper surface of the wing reduces the air pressure there, resulting in an upward force. The amount of lift depends on wing area, the speed of air across the wing, and the shape and angle of the wing.

Figure 25-12 Adult birds such as this great gray owl have an insulating layer of down feathers under their contour feathers. The owlets, like other young birds, are completely covered with down.

The Function of Feathers

Every body part of a bird is designed with flight in mind. Each feather is designed for flight. A bird's body is covered with two types of feathers, contour feathers and down feathers. Strong, lightweight **contour feathers** give birds their coloring and streamlined shape. Surface contour feathers overlap each other. This means that the bird can move more easily through the air or water. Feather colors and pattern are important because they identify a bird's species and sex. They also serve as protection that helps blend some birds into their surroundings. Contour feathers are also used to fly. It is these long feathers on the wings and tail that help the bird to steer and keep from spinning out of control.

Have you ever noticed that the hair on your arm stands up on a cold day? This response is your body's way to trap and keep warm air next to your skin. Birds have a similar response. This response helps birds maintain a constant body temperature. The birds in **Figure 25-12** have down feathers that trap and keep warm air next to their bodies. Soft, fluffy **down feathers** provide an insulating layer next to the skin of adult birds and cover the bodies of young birds.

MiniLab

Observing Bird Feathers

Procedure

1. Use a hand lens to examine a contour feather.
2. Hold the shaft end while carefully bending the opposite end. Observe what happens when you release the bent end.
3. Examine a down feather with a hand lens.
4. Hold each feather separately. Blow on them. Note any differences in the way each reacts to the stream of air.

Analysis

1. What happens when you release the bent end of the contour feather?
2. Which of the two feathers would you find on a bird's wing?
3. Which type of feather would you find in a pillow? Why?

Figure 25-13 Each barb in a contour feather has many smaller barbules that act like the teeth of a zipper. As a bird smoothes out the feather, the teeth of the barbules catch and zip together.

Care of Feathers

Feathers may be strong but they need to be kept in good condition. Only then can they keep birds warm, dry, and able to fly. Birds preen their feathers to take care of them. When they preen, they run their beaks through the feathers, much like people run their hands through their hair. Preening reorganizes the feathers and repairs the breaks, or gaps, in them. A close look at the contour feather in **Figure 25-13** shows the parallel strands, called barbs, that branch off the main shaft.

In addition to repairing and reorganizing feathers, preening makes feathers water-repellent. The bird rubs its beak against an oil gland found at the base of the tail. It then rubs off the oil from its beak and onto its feathers. Making sure that the feathers stay water-repellent is important. Watersoaked birds can't fly or maintain their body temperature.

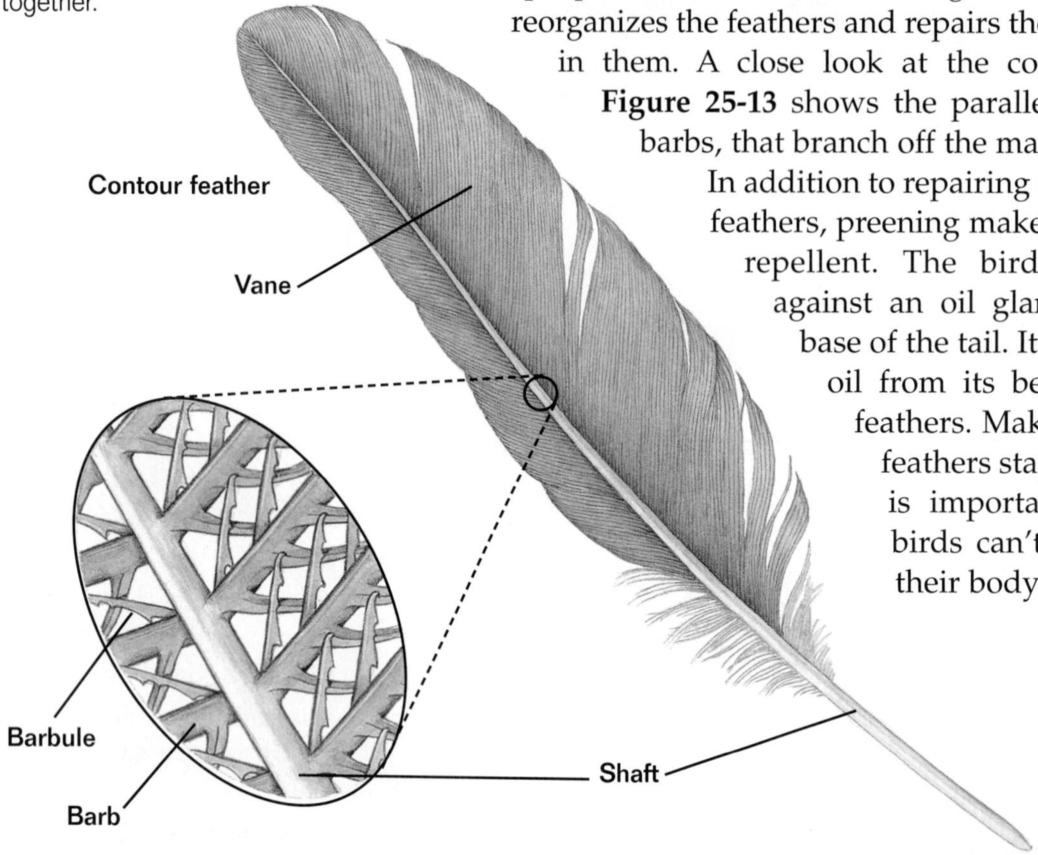

Section Assessment

1. List four characteristics shared by all birds.
2. Explain how a bird's skeleton is adapted for flight.
3. **Think Critically:** Explain why birds can reproduce in the arctic but reptiles cannot.
4. **Skill Builder**
   Concept Mapping Make a network tree concept map that details the characteristics of birds. Use the following terms in your map: *birds, adaptations for flight, air sacs, beaks, eggs, feathers, hollow bones,* and *wing.* If you need help, refer to Concept Mapping in the **Skill Handbook** on page 950.

Using Computers

Spreadsheet Every 10 s a crow beats its wings 20 times, a robin 23 times, a chickadee 270 times, and a hummingbird 700 times. Using a spreadsheet, find out how many times the wings of each bird beat during a five-minute flight? If you need help, see page 974.

Flight Through the Ages

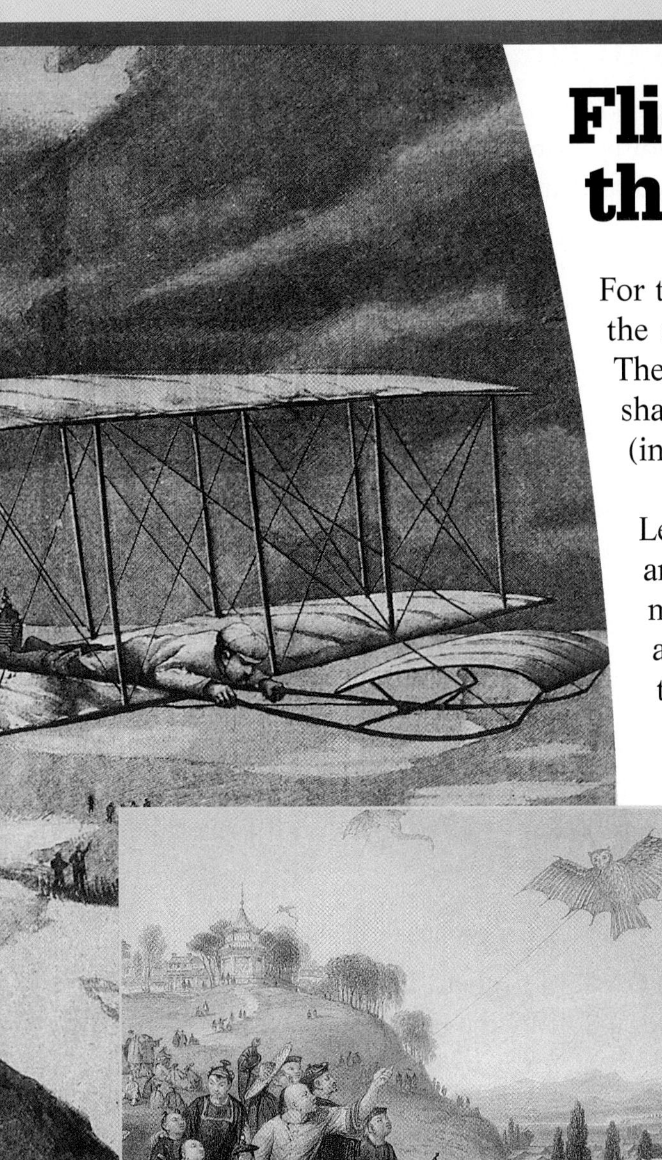

For thousands of years, people watched birds soar through the sky and yearned to experience the freedom of flight. The Maori people of what is now New Zealand made kites shaped like birds. The ancient Chinese loved kites, too (inset), and made them in all shapes and sizes.

In the early sixteenth century, artist and inventor Leonardo da Vinci made notes and diagrams about birds and flying machines. He reasoned that a bird's wings must work according to certain laws of physics and math and that therefore people should be able to build a device that could imitate the action of a bird in flight.

Da Vinci's drawings of flying machines inspired the invention of the ornithopter, or flapping-wing machine. People continued to experiment with these odd-looking devices—made out of willow, silk, and feathers—but never managed to get more than a few feet off the ground.

In the early 1800s, English scientist Sir George Cayley carried out his own studies of birds and bird flight. He concluded that it was impossible for people to fly using artificial flapping wings. Eventually, Cayley designed the first successful fixed-wing glider that could carry a person—a milestone that inspired Wilbur and Orville Wright.

Only after the Wright brothers solved a number of problems with gliding aircraft and built several gliders themselves did they focus on building an engine-powered aircraft. The Wright brothers identified the successful features of other aircraft and then added their own ideas about lift, the action of air currents, and the shape of wings. On December 17, 1903, Orville and Wilbur Wright made the world's first powered, sustained, and controlled flights in an airplane, the longest of which was 260 m. That momentous day set the stage for the evolution of many different kinds of engine-powered craft, from biplanes to supersonic jets and space shuttles.

Science JOURNAL

Think of how a bird flies. In your Science Journal, record the similarities and differences between airplane flight and the flight of birds.

25•4 Mammals

What You'll Learn

- The characteristics of mammals
- How mammals adapt to different environments
- The difference among monotremes, marsupials, and placental mammals

Vocabulary

mammal
monotreme
marsupial
placental mammal
herbivore
carnivore
omnivore

Why It's Important

- Mammals—which include humans—all share many structural characteristics.

Characteristics of Mammals

How many different kinds of mammals can you name? Cats, dogs, bats, dolphins, horses, and people are all mammals. They live on land and in water, in cold and in hot climates. They burrow through the ground or fly through the air. Mammals have many characteristics that they share with other vertebrates. For example, they all have an internal skeleton with a backbone. But what characteristics make mammals unique?

Mammals are endotherms that have hair and produce milk to nourish their young. Being endothermic is not unique. Birds also are endotherms. However, mammals are unique because their skin is covered with hair or fur. Hair is mostly made of a protein called keratin. Some mammals, such as bears, are covered with thick fur. Others, like humans, have patches of hair. Still others, like the whale pictured in **Figure 25-14,** are almost hairless. Hair insulates the mammal's body from both cold and heat. It also protects the animal from wind and rain. Wool, spines, quills, and certain horns are made of keratin. What function do you think quills and spines serve?

Mammary Glands

Mammals put a great deal of time and energy into the care of their young. This begins at birth. Female mammals have mammary glands that form in the skin. During pregnancy, they increase in size. After birth, milk is produced and released in these glands. For the first weeks or months, the milk provides all of the nutrition that the young mammal needs.

Figure 25-14 Unlike other mammals, whales, such as this humpback whale, are practically hairless with the exception of a few sensory whiskers on their snouts.

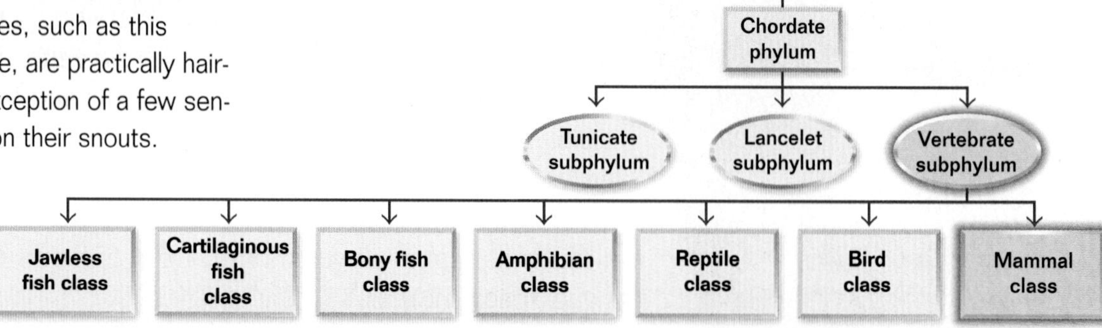

Body Systems

Think of all the different activities that mammals do. They run, swim, climb, hop, fly, and so on. They live active lives. Their body systems must be able to support all of these activities. Well-developed lungs made of millions of microscopic sacs called alveoli allow the exchanges of carbon dioxide and oxygen.

Mammals also have a more complex nervous system than other animals. The brain, spinal cord, and nerves allow these animals to utilize their senses and to gather information from their surrounding environment. They quickly sense and react to changes in their environment. Mammals are able to learn and remember more than other animals. The large brain plays an important part in this ability. In fact, the brain of a mammal is usually larger than the brain of other animals of the same size. Another factor in a mammal's ability to learn is the time spent by its parents to care for and teach it as it matures.

All mammals reproduce sexually and have internal fertilization. Most mammals give birth to live young after a period of development inside an organ called a uterus. While some mammals are nearly helpless when born, others must be able to stand and move quickly after birth. Why do you think a young deer must be able to run soon after it is born?

Observing Hair

Procedure

1. Brush or comb your hair to remove a few loose hairs.
2. Take two hairs from your brush that look like they still have the root attached.
3. Make a wet mount slide of the two hairs, being sure to include the root.
4. Focus on the hairs with the low-power objective. Draw what you see.
5. Switch to the high-power objective and focus on the hairs. Draw what you see.

Analysis

1. Describe the characteristics of hair and root.
2. Infer how hair keeps an organism warm.

Mammal Classification

Once an egg is fertilized, the developing mammal is called an embryo. Mammals can be divided into three groups based on how their embryos develop.

Monotremes

Look at the animal in **Figure 25-15.** The duck-billed platypus looks like someone took parts from several different animals and put them together as a practical joke.

Figure 25-15 A duck-billed platypus is a mammal, yet it lays eggs. **Why is it classified as a mammal?**

But, in fact, the duck-billed platypus belongs to the smallest group of mammals called monotremes. **Monotremes** lay eggs with tough leathery shells. The female incubates the eggs for about ten days. Mammary glands that produce the milk of monotremes lack nipples. When the young hatch, they nurse by licking up the milk that seeps through the skin surrounding the glands. The duck-billed platypus and two species of spiny anteaters are the only surviving members of this group.

Figure 25-16 Marsupials carry their developing young in a pouch on the outside of their bodies. Opossums are the only marsupials found in North America.

Marsupials

Can you think of an animal that carries its young in a pouch? Mammals that do this are called marsupials. **Marsupials** are pouched mammals that give birth to immature offspring. Their embryos develop for only a few weeks within the uterus. When the young are born, they are naked, blind, and not fully formed. Using their sense of smell, the young crawl into the pouch and attach themselves to a nipple. Here they complete their development. Most marsupials live in Australia, Tasmania, and New Guinea. Kangaroos, koalas, Tasmanian devils, and wallabies are marsupials. The opossum in **Figure 25-16** is a marsupial that lives in North America.

Problem Solving

Predicting Bat Behavior

Bats are acrobats of the night. They can fly around obstacles and can find insects to eat in complete darkness. Have you ever wondered how they do this? Some bats emit, or send out, extremely high-pitched sounds through the mouth and nose when hunting for food. These sounds are usually too high pitched for humans to hear. Bats also make noises that people hear, from whining sounds to loud twitters and squeaks. Bats can catch fast-flying insects or darting fish and at the same time avoid branches, wires, and other obstacles in a process called echolocation. The sound waves they send out travel in front of them, and this helps them locate objects.

The diagram illustrates what happens when a sound wave emitted by a bat comes in contact with an object.

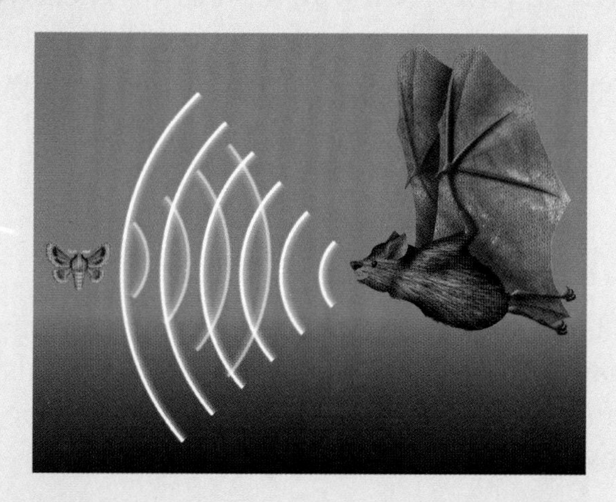

Think Critically: How does a bat locate an object in the dark? Explain what might happen to bats if they were allowed to search for food in a soundproof room, where walls absorb most of the sound. Infer what would happen if a bat's mouth and nose are covered.

Placental Mammals

By far, the largest number of mammals belongs to the third group known as placental mammals. The most important characteristic of **placental mammals** is that their embryos develop in the uterus of the female. This time of development, from fertilization to birth, is the gestation period. Gestation periods vary greatly among placental mammals. Imagine waiting almost two years for the young elephant in **Figure 25-17** to be born! Placental mammals are named for the placenta, a saclike organ developed by the growing embryo that is attached to the uterus. The placenta absorbs oxygen and food from the mother's blood. An umbilical cord, **Figure 25-18,** attaches the embryo to the placenta. Several blood vessels in the umbilical cord act as a transportation system. Food and oxygen are transported from the placenta to the embryo. Waste products are taken away.

Figure 25-17 Gestation periods vary among mammals. While an elephant carries its young for 624 days, a golden hamster's gestation period is about 16 days.

*inter***NET**
CONNECTION

Visit the Glencoe Science Web Site at **www.glencoe.com/sec/science/ca** for more information about small mammals.

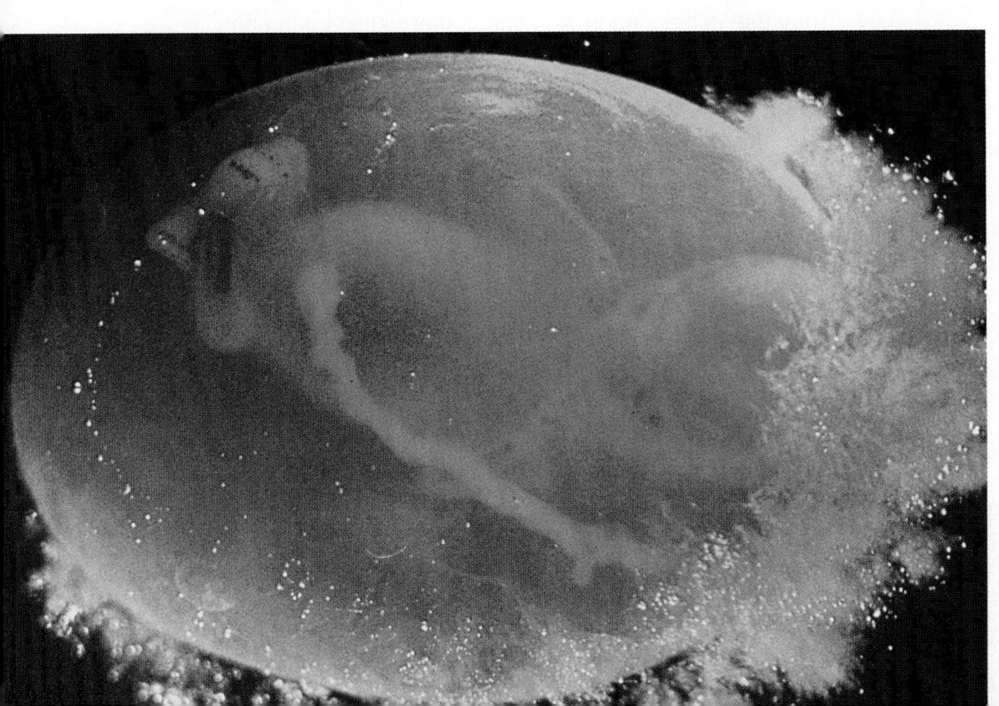

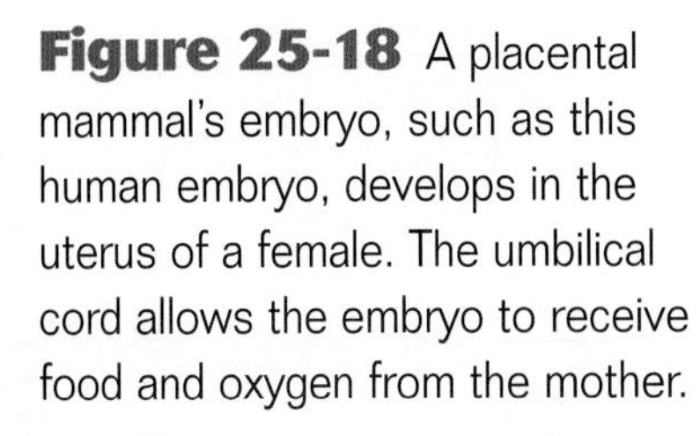

Figure 25-18 A placental mammal's embryo, such as this human embryo, develops in the uterus of a female. The umbilical cord allows the embryo to receive food and oxygen from the mother.

You have learned the basic characteristics that distinguish mammals—vertebrae, hair or fur, mammary glands that produce milk, type of teeth, and the ability of young to learn. In addition, each kind of animal has certain adaptations that enable it to live successfully within its environment. Some of the 4000 species of mammals are shown in **Figure 25-19.**

Figure 25-19 In addition to monotremes (A) and marsupials (B), many of the major orders of placental mammals are shown here.

A **Monotremata** (mahn uh tru MAH tah): Monotremes, such as this duck-billed platypus, are the only egg-laying mammals.

B **Marsupiala** (mar sew pee AH luh): Pouched mammals include kangaroos, shown here, and opossums.

C **Insectivora** (ihn sek tih VOR ah): Burrowing woodland moles have poor eyesight but an excellent sense of touch to catch insects.

D **Edentata** (ee duhn TAH tuh): Armadillos, shown here, anteaters, and tree sloths are toothless or have few teeth with which to eat insects.

E **Chiroptera** (cher OP ter uh): Bats are the only true flying mammals. Their front limbs are designed for flight. They use echolocation, a process that uses sound and echoes, to navigate while flying.

F **Carnivora** (kar NIH vor uh): The household cat and dog are meat-eaters that have canine teeth used to capture prey. This red fox is also a carnivore.

G **Cetacea** (sih TAY shuh): Marine mammals, including dolphins, spend their entire lives in the ocean.

H **Proboscidea** (proh boh SIH dee uh): Elephants are the largest land mammals. They have an elongated nose that forms a trunk.

I **Perissodactyla** (per ih soh DAHK tih luh): Herbivorous hoofed mammals with an odd number of toes. Horses, zebras, tapirs (shown here), and rhinoceroses belong to this group.

J **Artiodactyla** (ar tee oh DAHK tih luh): Herbivorous, hoofed mammals have an even number of toes. They also have large, flat molars and complex stomachs. Cows, camels, deer, giraffes, and the moose (shown here) belong to this group.

K **Rodentia** (roh DEN cha): The largest order, these gnawing mammals have two pairs of chisel-shaped teeth that never stop growing. These teeth wear down through use. This golden mouse, along with squirrels, beavers, porcupines, and gophers are in this group.

L **Lagomorpha** (lah gah MOR fuh): Lagomorphs include herbivorous rabbits, hares, and pikas. This Eastern cottontail rabbit has long hind legs that are adapted for jumping and running. It also has two pairs of upper incisors.

M **Primates** (PRI maytz): Humans, apes, monkeys, and this orangutan are representative of this group. They have long arms with grasping hands and feet, and opposable thumbs. They are omnivores and the most intelligent of mammals.

Figure 25-20 Mammals have teeth specialized for the food they eat. **How would you classify a horse (A), a hyena (B), and a human (C)? Herbivore? Carnivore? Omnivore?**

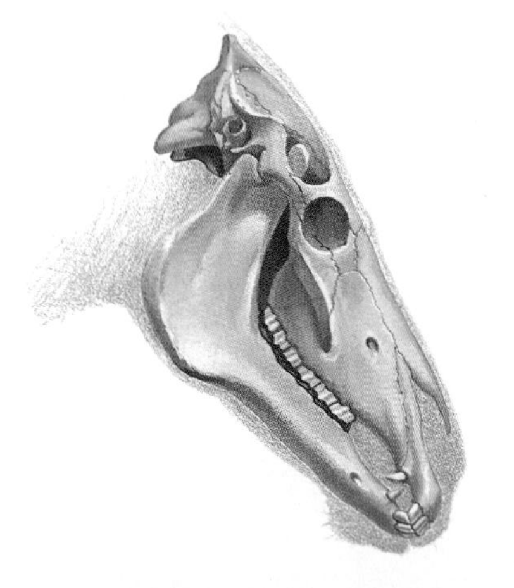

Different Teeth

Mammals have teeth that are specialized for the type of food they eat. There are four types of teeth: incisors, canines, premolars, and molars. Incisors are the sharp, chisel-shaped front teeth used to bite and cut off food. Grazing mammals, which eat plants, are called **herbivores.** They have sharp incisors to grab and cut grass. Horses, buffalo, and rabbits are some mammals that eat plants. Some mammals, such as lions and tigers, are predators and eat flesh. Flesh-eating mammals are called **carnivores.** They use long and pointed canine teeth to stab, grip, and tear flesh. They also have sharp-edged premolars that cut and shred food. Large premolars and molars shred, crush, and grind food. Horses have large, flat molars that grind both grains and grasses.

Some mammals eat both plants and animals. These mammals are called **omnivores.** Humans are capable of being omnivores. They have all four types of teeth. You usually can tell whether a mammal eats plants, other animals, or both from the kind of teeth it has. Look at **Figure 25-20.**

Mammals Today

Mammals are important in maintaining a balance in the environment. Large carnivores, such as lions, help control populations of grazing animals. Bats help pollinate flowers, and some pick up plant seeds in their fur and distribute them. But mammals are in trouble today. As millions of acres of wildlife habitat are developed for housing and recreational areas, many mammals are left without food, shelter, and space to survive. The Bengal tiger pictured in **Figure 25-21** lives in India and is considered an endangered species.

Figure 25-21 Illegal poaching and decreasing habitat help account for the extreme decline in the Bengal tiger population in nature. In the early 1900s, there were around 100 000 tigers, but that has declined by roughly 95 percent this century.

Section Assessment

1. Describe five characteristics of all mammals and explain how these characteristics allow mammals to survive in different environments.
2. Compare and contrast herbivores with omnivores.
3. **Think Critically:** Compare reproduction in placental mammals with that of monotremes and marsupials.
4. **Skill Builder**
   Observing and Inferring Mammals have many adaptations to their environments. Do the **Chapter 25 Skill Activity** on page 986 to observe tracks to infer how mammals' feet are adapted.

Using Math

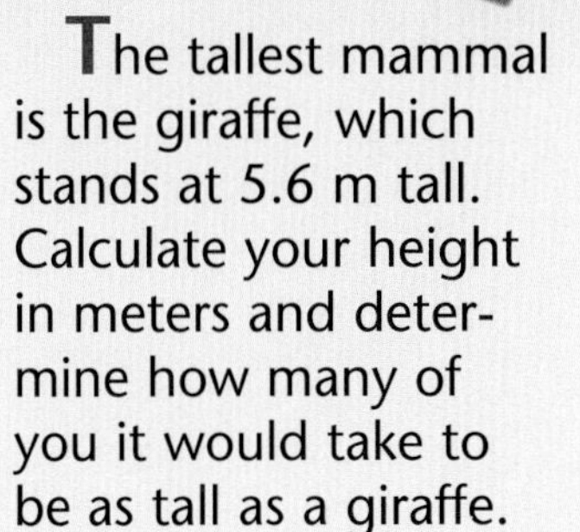

The tallest mammal is the giraffe, which stands at 5.6 m tall. Calculate your height in meters and determine how many of you it would take to be as tall as a giraffe.

Activity 25•2

Bird Counts

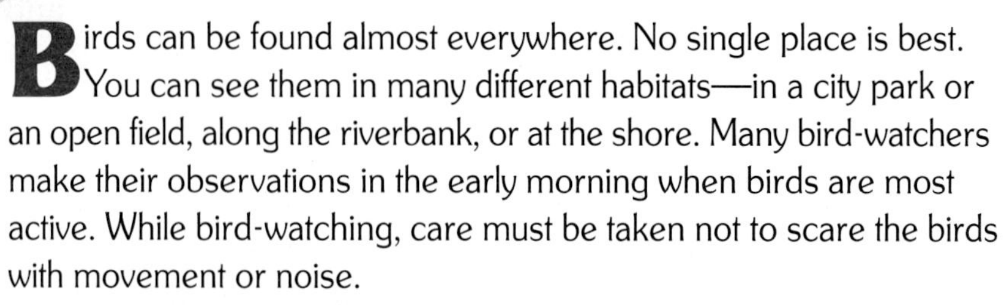

Birds can be found almost everywhere. No single place is best. You can see them in many different habitats—in a city park or an open field, along the riverbank, or at the shore. Many bird-watchers make their observations in the early morning when birds are most active. While bird-watching, care must be taken not to scare the birds with movement or noise.

It's simple to get started bird-watching. You can attract birds to your yard at home or at school by filling a bird feeder with seeds that birds like most. Then, sit back and observe the birds while they enjoy your hospitality.

Recognize the Problem

What type of bird is present in your neighborhood in the largest number?

Form a Hypothesis

Think about the types of birds that you observe around your neighborhood. What types of food do they eat? Do all birds come to a bird feeder? Make a hypothesis about the type of bird that you think you will see most often at your bird feeder.

Goals

- **Observe** the types of birds in your neighborhood.
- **Research** how to attract birds to a bird feeder.
- **Build** a bird feeder.
- **Identify** the types of birds observed.
- **Graph** your results in order to communicate them with other students.

Data Source

Go to the Glencoe Science Web Site at **www.glencoe.com/sec/science/ca** for more information about how to build a bird feeder, hints on bird watching, and data from other students.

Test Your Hypothesis

Plan

1. **Research** general information about how to attract and identify birds. Determine where you will make your observations.
2. **Search** reference materials to find out how to build a bird feeder. Do all birds eat the same types of seeds?
3. What variables can you control in this activity? How long will you make your observations? Does the season or the weather conditions affect your observations?
4. What will you do to **identify** the birds that you do not recognize?

Do

1. Make sure your teacher approves your plan before you start.
2. **Record** your data in your Science Journal each time you **observe** your bird feeder.

Analyze Your Data

1. **Describe** the location where you made your observations and the time of year.
2. **Calculate** the total number of each type of bird by adding the numbers you recorded each day.
3. **Graph** your data. Will your results be best displayed in a line, circle, or bar graph?
4. **Post** your data on the Glencoe Science Web Site.

Draw Conclusions

1. What type of bird was present in your neighborhood in the largest number?
2. Did all of your classmates' data agree with yours? Why or why not?
3. **Compare and contrast** your observations with the observations posted by other students on the Glencoe Science Web Site. **Map** the data you collect from the Web site to **recognize** patterns in bird populations.
4. Many birds include an enormous number of insects in their diet. **Infer** the need for humans to maintain a healthy environment for birds.

Chapter 25 Reviewing Main Ideas

For a **preview** of this chapter, study this Reviewing Main Ideas before you read the chapter. After you have studied this chapter, you can use the Reviewing Main Ideas to **review** the chapter.

The Glencoe MindJogger, Audiocassettes, and CD-ROM provide additional opportunities for review.

Section

25-1 VERTEBRATES AND FISH

All animals in the Chordate Phylum have a notochord, dorsal hollow nerve cord, and gill slits. The body temperature of an **ectotherm** changes with its environment. **Endothermic** animals maintain body temperature. **Fish** are ectotherms that have scales and **fins.** Classes of fish include jawless fish, cartilaginous fish, and bony fish. ***Why can't jawless fish be predators?***

White sha

Section

25-2 AMPHIBIANS AND REPTILES

Amphibians are vertebrates that spend part of their lives in water and part on land. Most frogs, toads, and salamanders are amphibians that go through metamorphosis from a water-living larva to a land-living adult. **Reptiles** are ectothermic land animals that have dry, scaly skin. Turtles, crocodiles, alligators, snakes, and lizards are reptiles. Reptiles lay eggs with a leathery skin. ***Why does the reptile's egg provide better protection for the embryo than a frog's egg?***

Collared lizard

Barred tiger salamander

Reading Check ☑

Explain the major differences among the five groups of vertebrates described in this chapter in a way that a child could understand. (You might create a chart).

Hummingbird

Section

25-3 BIRDS

Birds are endotherms that are covered with feathers and lay eggs. Their front legs are modified into wings. Adaptations birds have for flight include wings, feathers, and a light, strong skeleton. Birds lay eggs enclosed in hard shells. Most birds keep their eggs warm until they hatch. ***How do down feathers keep a bird warm?***

Mandarin duck

Flamingo

Bat

25-4 MAMMALS

Mammals are endotherms with hair. Female mammals have mammary glands that produce milk. There are three groups of mammals. **Monotremes** are mammals that lay eggs. **Marsupials** are mammals that have pouches for the development of their embryos. **Placental mammals** have offspring that develop within the female's uterus. ***What are some adaptations of mammals that allow them to be endothermic?***

Red fox

Chapter 25 Assessment

Using Vocabulary

a. amphibian
b. bird
c. carnivore
d. cartilage
e. chordate
f. contour feather
g. down feather
h. ectotherm
i. endoskeleton
j. endotherm
k. estivation
l. fin
m. fish
n. herbivore
o. hibernation
p. mammal
q. marsupial
r. monotreme
s. omnivore
t. placental mammal
u. reptile

Define the following Vocabulary terms and give two examples of each.

1. fish
2. amphibian
3. reptile
4. bird
5. mammal

Checking Concepts

Choose the word or phrase that best answers the question.

6. Which of the following animals have fins, scales, and gills?
   A) amphibians
   B) crocodiles
   C) reptiles
   D) fish
7. Which of the following stuctures is used for steering and balancing?
   A) cartilage
   B) endoskeleton
   C) bone
   D) fin
8. Which of the following is **NOT** an example of a bony fish?
   A) trout
   B) bass
   C) shark
   D) goldfish
9. Which of the following has a swim bladder?
   A) shark
   B) lamprey
   C) trout
   D) skate
10. Which of the following is **NOT** an adaptation that helps a bird fly?
    A) hollow bones
    B) fused vertebrae
    C) hard-shelled eggs
    D) feathers
11. Which of the following does **NOT** have scales?
    A) birds
    B) snakes
    C) frogs
    D) fish
12. Which of the following are vertebrates with lungs and moist skin?
    A) amphibians
    B) fish
    C) reptiles
    D) lizards
13. Which of the following are mammals that lay eggs?
    A) carnivores
    B) marsupials
    C) monotremes
    D) placental mammals
14. Which of the following have mammary glands but no nipples?
    A) marsupials
    B) placental mammals
    C) monotremes
    D) omnivores
15. Which of the following animals eat only plant materials?
    A) carnivores
    B) herbivores
    C) omnivores
    D) endotherms

Thinking Critically

16. Why do you think there are fewer species of amphibians on Earth than any other type of vertebrate?
17. What important adaptation allows a reptile to live on land while an amphibian must return to water to live out part of its life cycle?
18. Give two reasons why whales have little hair.
19. You observe a mammal catching and eating a rabbit. What kind of teeth does this animal probably have? Tell how it uses its teeth.

20. Explain how the development of the amniotic egg led to the early success of reptiles.

Developing Skills

If you need help, refer to the Skill Handbook.

21. **Comparing and Contrasting:** Compare and contrast the eggs of fish, reptiles, birds, and mammals. How well does each egg type protect the developing embryo?
22. **Concept Mapping:** Complete the concept map describing groups of mammals.

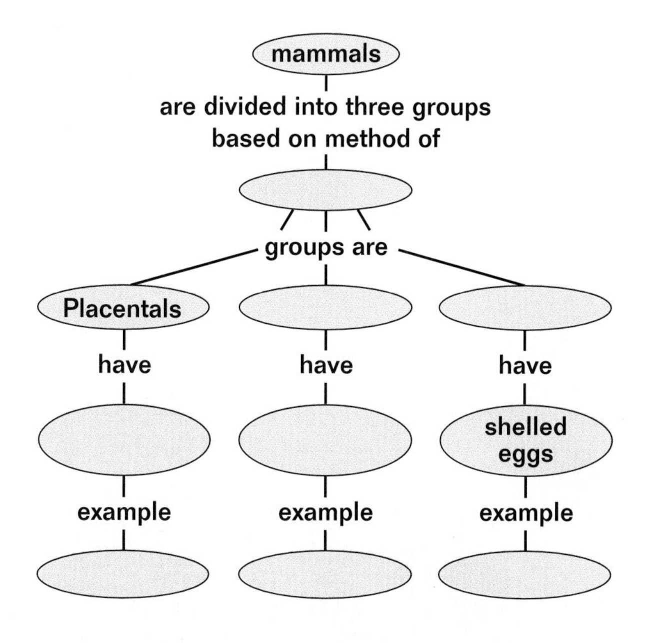

23. **Designing an Experiment:** Design an experiment to find out the effect of water temperature on frog egg development.
24. **Observing and Inferring:** How could you use the feet of a bird to identify it?
25. **Comparing and Contrasting:** Compare and contrast the teeth of herbivores, carnivores, and omnivores. How is each tooth type adapted to the animal's diet?

Test-Taking Tip

Let Bygones Be Bygones Once you have read a question, consider the answers and choose one. Then, put that question behind you. Don't try to keep the question in the back of your mind, thinking that maybe a better answer will come to you as the test continues.

Test Practice

Use these questions to test your Science Proficiency.

1. Vertebrates make up a large percentage of animals. Which of the following statements is true of all vertebrates?
   A) Vertebrates are animals without backbones.
   B) All vertebrates have a notochord.
   C) Only fish have gill slits.
   D) Dorsal hollow nerve cords always develop into a spinal cord with a brain at the front end.
2. Placental mammals, along with monotremes and marsupials, are the orders that make up mammals. Which of the following animals is an example of a placental mammal?
   A) elephant
   B) koala
   C) duck-billed platypus
   D) turtle
3. Which of the following terms describes inactivity during the summer?
   A) estivation
   B) hibernation
   C) metamorphosis
   D) preening

UNIT 7

You & the Environment

NATIONAL GEOGRAPHIC

What's Happening Here?

The ocean is Earth's last frontier. Only recently have explorers searched its remotest depths to reveal some of its special secrets. In places, the water is so deep that if Mount Everest were to rise from the ocean floor, its peak would still be 2000 meters from the surface. With so much water, can't the ocean wash away whatever is dumped into it? Not any longer. Each year in the United States, thousands of oil spills are reported. When the tanker *Megaborg* exploded in the Gulf of Mexico in 1990 (left), it dumped 4.6 million gallons and threatened wetlands bordering Galveston Bay. Some environmental problems are not accidental—people discarding trash in the wrong place, for instance. The rings of a six pack holder will cut short the life of this young Western Gull (below). As the human population grows, the wear and tear on our planet is showing. How serious are the consequences, and how can we help? These are some of the questions addressed in this unit.

interNET CONNECTION

Explore the Glencoe Science Web Site at **www.glencoe.com/sec/science/ca** to find out more about topics found in this unit.

CHAPTER

26 Our Impact on Land

Chapter Preview

Skills Preview

Skill Builders

- Use a Graph
- Communicate

Activities

- Design an Experiment
- Make a Model

MiniLabs

- Classify
- Make a Model

Reading Check

As you read this chapter, choose two illustrations and explain the purpose of each. Describe other types of illustrations that could replace the two that you choose.

Explore Activity

Have you ever considered the impact that each of us has on the land? Each person on Earth competes for space and resources. Each one generates trash; consumes products made in factories; uses natural resources such as water, soil, and energy; and creates pollution. Do you think our impact on land is significant?

Draw a Population Growth Model

1. Use a piece of paper and a pencil to draw a square that is 10 cm on each side. This represents 1 km^2 of Earth's land surface.
2. In 1965, the average number of people for every square kilometer of land was 21. Draw 21 small circles inside your square to represent this.
3. In 1990, the average was 35. Add 14 circles to illustrate this increase.
4. In 2025, there will be an estimated 52 people per km^2. Add circles to represent the average number of people per square kilometer of land in 2025.
5. Prepare a bar graph that shows population density for each year discussed above.

Science Journal

In your Science Journal, explain whether or not human population is increasing more rapidly as time goes on. How do you think population growth affects the environment?

26•1 Population Impact on the Environment

What You'll Learn

- How to interpret data from a graph that shows human population growth
- Reasons for Earth's rapid increase in human population
- Several ways each person in an industrialized nation affects the environment

Vocabulary
carrying capacity
population
population explosion

Why It's Important

- Humans directly impact the environment. The more humans there are, the greater the impact.

The Human Population Explosion

At one time, people thought of Earth as a world with unlimited resources. They thought the planet could provide them with whatever materials they needed. Earth seemed to have an endless supply of metals, fossil fuels, and rich soils. Today, we know this isn't true. Earth has a carrying capacity. The **carrying capacity** is the maximum number of individuals of a particular species that the planet will support. Thus, Earth's resources are limited. Unless we treat those resources with care, they will disappear.

Many years ago, few people lived on Earth. Fewer resources were used and less waste was produced than today. But, in the last 200 years, the number of people on Earth has increased at an extremely rapid rate. The increase in the world population has changed the way we must view our world and how we care for it for future generations, like the babies in **Figure 26-1.**

Figure 26-1 The human population is growing at an increasingly rapid rate. **Why does Earth have a carrying capacity?**

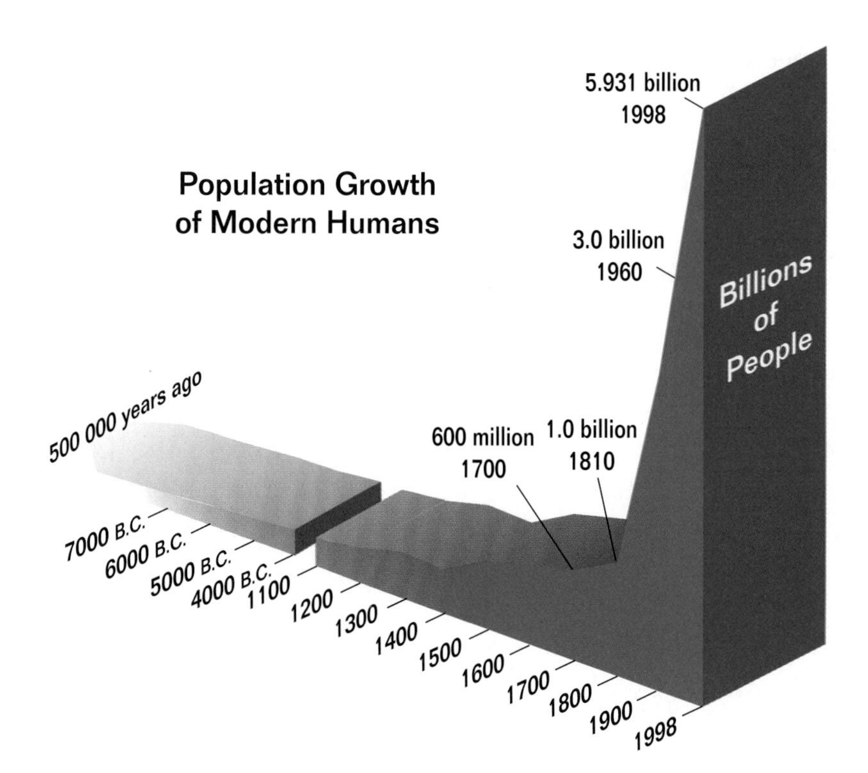

Figure 26-2 The human species, *Homo sapiens*, may have appeared about 500 000 years ago. Our population numbers remained relatively steady until about 200 years ago. **Why have we experienced such a sharp increase in growth rate since about 1800?**

Human Population

A **population** is the total number of individuals of a particular species in a particular area. The area can be small or large. For example, we can talk about the human population of one particular community, such as Los Angeles, or about the human population of the entire planet.

Have you ever wondered how many people live on Earth? The global population in 1998 was 5.9 billion. Each day, the number of humans increases by approximately 215 000. Earth is now experiencing a **population explosion.** The word *explosion* is used because the rate at which the population is growing has increased rapidly in recent history.

Our Increasing Population

Look at **Figure 26-2.** You can see that it took hundreds of thousands of years for Earth's population to reach 1 billion people. After that, the population increased much faster. Population has increased so rapidly in recent years because the death rate has been slowed by modern medicine, and we have better sanitation and better nutrition. This means that more people are living longer. Also, the number of births has increased because more people survive to the age at which they can have children.

The population explosion has seriously affected the environment. Scientists predict even greater changes as more people use Earth's limited resources. The population is predicted to be about 11 billion by 2100—nearly twice what it is now.

Carrying Capacity

One of the things that affects carrying capacity is food. When a region does not have enough food, animals either migrate or starve. Infer what other factors determine the carrying capacity of a particular region for a species.

Using Math

The population density of a region is the average number of people per unit of area. Find the population density of Pennsylvania, which has a population of about 12 million people and an area of about 117 000 km^2.

We need to be aware of the effect such a large human population will have on our environment. We need to ask ourselves whether we have enough natural resources to support such a large population.

How People Affect the Environment

By the time you're 75 years old, you will have produced enough garbage to equal the mass of six African elephants (43 000 kg). You will have consumed enough water to fill 100 000 bathtubs (26 million L). If you live in the United States, you will have used five times as much energy as an average person living elsewhere in the world.

Our Daily Activities

In your daily activities, you use electricity, some of which is generated by the burning of fuels. The environment changes when fuels are mined and again, later, when they are burned. The water that you use must be made as clean as possible before being returned to the environment. You eat food, which takes land to grow. Much of the food you eat is grown using chemical substances, such as pesticides and herbicides, to kill insects and weeds. These chemicals can get into water supplies and threaten the health of living things if they become too concentrated. How else do you and other people affect the environment?

Many of the products you buy are packaged in plastic and paper. Plastic is made from oil. The process of refining oil produces pollutants. Producing paper requires cutting down trees, using gasoline to transport them to a paper mill, and producing pollutants in the process of transforming the trees into paper. **Figure 26-3** shows some items that may require these activities to produce them.

We change the land when we remove resources from it, and we further impact the environment when we shape those resources into usable products. Then, once we've produced and consumed products, we must dispose of them. Look at **Figure 26-4.** Unnecessary packaging is only one of the problems associated with waste disposal.

Figure 26-3 Every day, you use many of Earth's resources. **What resources were consumed to produce the items shown in this photograph?**

The Future

As the population continues to grow, more demands will be made on the environment. Traffic-choked highways, overflowing garbage dumps, shrinking forests, and vanishing wildlife are common. What can we do? People are the problem, but we also are the solution. As you learn more about how we affect the environment, you'll discover what you can do to help make the future world one that everyone can live in and enjoy. An important step that we can take is to think carefully about our use of natural resources. If everyone learns to conserve resources, we can make a positive impact on the environment.

Figure 26-4 This toy car is overpackaged. Because of consumer demands, many products now come in environmentally friendly packages.

Section Assessment

1. Using **Figure 26-2,** estimate how many years it took for the *Homo sapiens* population to reach 1 billion. How long did it take to triple to 3 billion?
2. Why is human population increasing so rapidly?
3. **Think Critically:** In nonindustrial nations, individuals have less negative impact on the environment than citizens in industrialized nations. In your Science Journal, explain why you think this is so.
4. **Skill Builder**
   Making and Using Graphs Use **Figure 26-2** to answer the questions below. If you need help, refer to Making and Using Graphs in the **Skill Handbook** on page 953.
   a. Early humanlike ancestors existed more than 4 million years ago. Why does the graph indicate that it should extend back only 500 000 years?
   b. How would the slope of the graph change if, in the near future, the growth rate were cut in half?

Using Math

Make a line graph of the data shown below. Plot years on the *x*-axis and population on the *y*-axis. Use your completed graph to infer the population of humans in the year 2040.

Human Population in Billions

1998	2010	2025
5.931	6.849	7.923

Activity 26•1

Using Scientific Methods

Materials

- Many small objects, such as dried beans, popcorn, or paper clips
- Beaker (250 mL)
- Clock or watch

A Crowded Encounter

Think about the effects of our rapidly increasing human population. One of these is overcrowding. Every second, five people are born, and two people die. The result is a net increase of three people every second, or 180 people every minute.

What You'll Investigate

Goals

- **Make a model** of human population growth over a ten-minute time period.
- **Observe** the effects of a population increase on a limited space.
- Record, graph, and interpret population data.

Safety Precautions

Never eat or taste anything from a lab, even if you are confident that you know what it is.

Procedure

1. Use the empty beaker to represent the space left on Earth that is unoccupied by humans at the moment you begin.
2. Let each of your small objects represent five people.
3. **Design** a table with two columns. One column will show the time (1 to 10 minutes), and the other column will show the population at the designated time.
4. **Begin timing** your first minute. At the end of one minute, place the appropriate number of small items in your beaker. **Record** the data in your table. Continue for each minute of time.
5. After completing your table, **make a graph** that shows the time in minutes on the horizontal axis and the population on the vertical axis.

Conclude and Apply

1. At the end of ten minutes, what is the net increase in human population?
2. **Compare and contrast** the graph you just made with the graph shown in **Figure 26-2.** How do you account for the differences?
3. Today, approximately 5.9 billion people inhabit Earth. That number will double in about 40 years. Assuming the rate remains unchanged, **predict** what the population will be 80 years from now.
4. Suggest ways in which the net increase in human population affects Earth's limited resources.

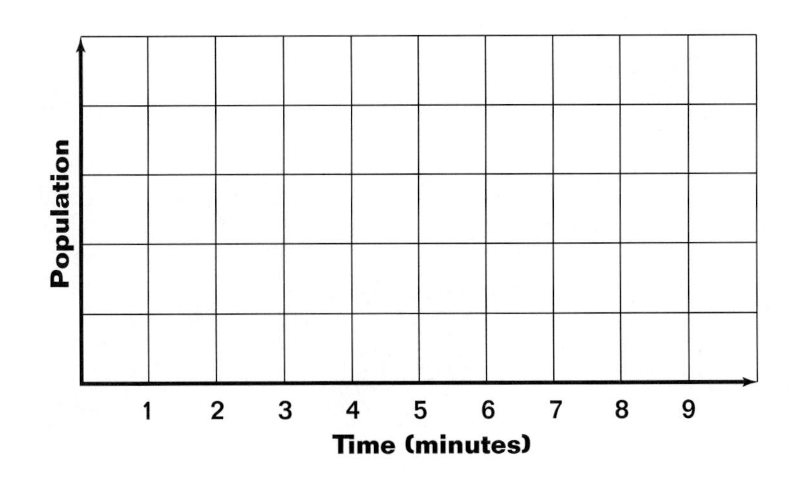

26•2 Using Land

What You'll Learn

- Ways that we use land
- Environmental problems created because of land use
- Things you can do to help protect the environment

Vocabulary
landfill
hazardous waste
conservation
composting

Why It's Important

- Land is a resource that we need to use responsibly.

Land Usage

You may not think of land as a natural resource. Yet, it is as important to people as oil, clean air, and clean water. Through agriculture, logging, garbage disposal, and urban development, we use land—and sometimes abuse it.

Farming

Earth's total land area is 149 million km^2. We use about 16 million km^2 as farmland. Even so, about 20 percent of the people living in the world are hungry. Millions starve and die each year. To fight this problem, some farmers work to increase the productivity of croplands by using higher-yield seeds and chemical fertilizers. Herbicides and pesticides also are used to reduce weeds, insects, and other pests that can damage crops.

Other farmers rely on organic farming techniques to lessen the environmental impact of chemicals on the land and to increase yield. **Figure 26-5** shows an organic farm in China that has been farmed for many centuries.

Figure 26-5 Organic farming techniques can rebuild topsoil rather than deplete it. Organic farmers use natural fertilizers, crop rotation, and biological pest controls to help their crops thrive.

Figure 26-6 Farmers reduce erosion with contour plowing, as shown on this farm in Washington State. Erosion is reduced because the path of plowing follows the shape of the land. **How can contour plowing control the direction that water flows in a farm field?**

Whenever vegetation is removed from an area, such as on construction sites, mining sites, or tilled farmland, the soil can erode easily. With plants gone, nothing prevents the soil from being carried away by running water and wind. Several centimeters of topsoil may be lost in one year. In some places, it can take more than 1000 years for new topsoil to develop and replace eroded topsoil. Some farmers practice no-till farming, which reduces erosion because land is not loosened by plowing. **Figure 26-6** shows another way farmers work to reduce erosion.

Figure 26-7 Corn, as shown on this farm in Lancaster, Pennsylvania, is used for human food, for livestock feed, and for industrial products such as ceramics, textiles, ethanol, and paint. About half the corn grain raised in the United States is fed to livestock.

Grazing Livestock

Land also is used for grazing livestock. Animals such as cattle eat vegetation and then often are used as food for humans. In the United States, the majority of land used for grazing is unsuitable for crops. However, about 20 percent of the total cropland in our country is used to grow feed for livestock, such as the corn shown in **Figure 26-7.**

A square kilometer of vegetable crops can feed many more people than a square kilometer used to raise livestock. Some people argue that a more efficient use of the land would be to grow crops directly for human consumption, rather than for livestock. For many, however, meat and dairy products are an important part of their diet. They also argue that livestock have ecological benefits that justify livestock production.

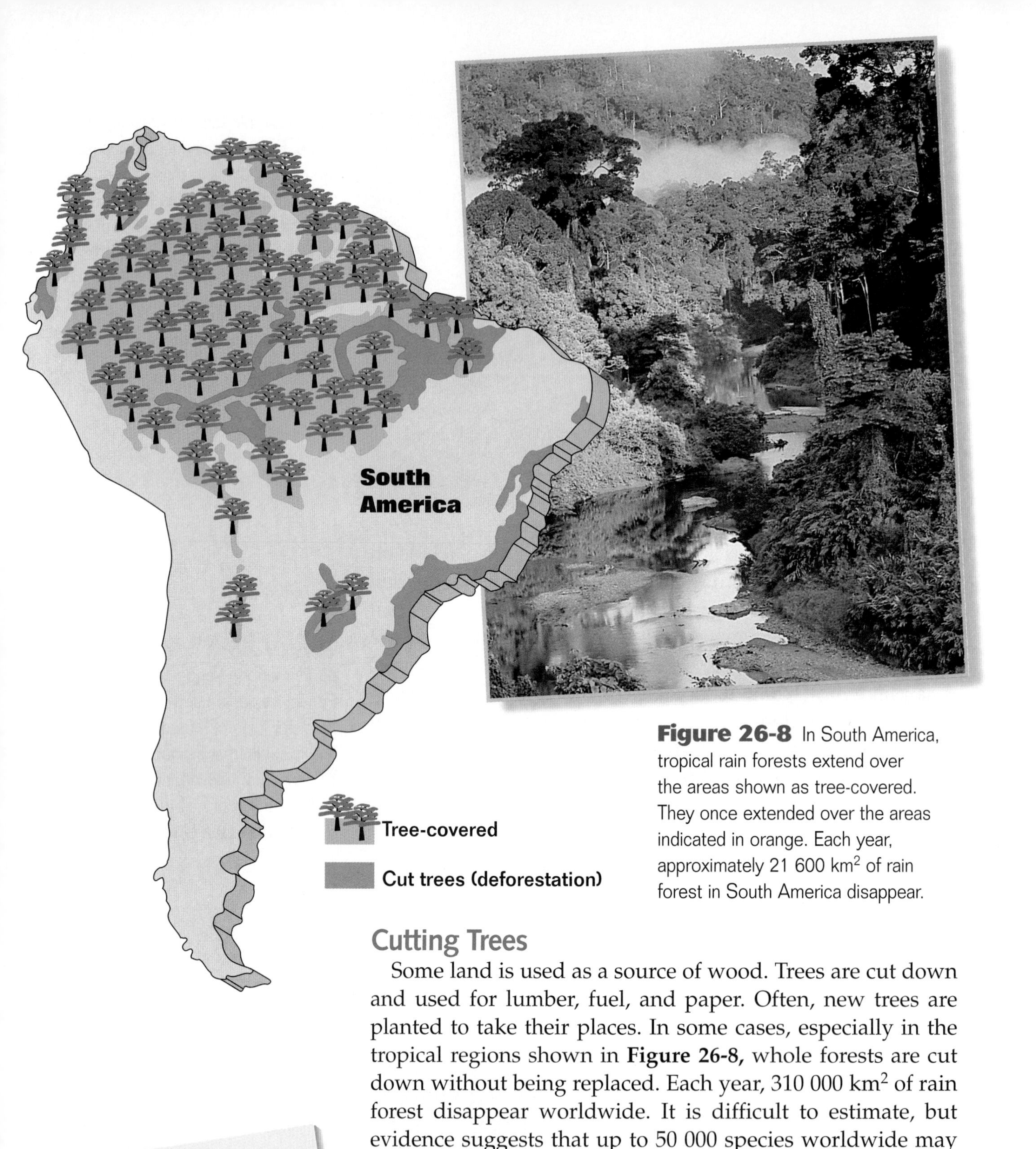

Figure 26-8 In South America, tropical rain forests extend over the areas shown as tree-covered. They once extended over the areas indicated in orange. Each year, approximately 21 600 km^2 of rain forest in South America disappear.

Cutting Trees

Some land is used as a source of wood. Trees are cut down and used for lumber, fuel, and paper. Often, new trees are planted to take their places. In some cases, especially in the tropical regions shown in **Figure 26-8,** whole forests are cut down without being replaced. Each year, 310 000 km^2 of rain forest disappear worldwide. It is difficult to estimate, but evidence suggests that up to 50 000 species worldwide may become extinct each year due to loss of habitat.

Organisms living outside of the tropics also suffer because of the lost vegetation. Plants remove carbon dioxide from the air when they photosynthesize. The process of photosynthesis also produces oxygen that organisms need to breathe. Therefore, reduced vegetation may result in higher levels of carbon dioxide in the atmosphere. Carbon dioxide is a gas that may contribute to a rise in temperatures on Earth.

Reading Check

How do plants remove carbon dioxide from the air?

Landfills

Land also is used when we dispose of the products we consume. About 60 percent of our garbage goes into landfills. A **landfill** is an area where waste is deposited. In a *sanitary landfill,* such as the one illustrated in **Figure 26-9,** each day's deposit is covered with dirt. The dirt prevents the deposit from blowing away and reduces the odor produced by the decaying waste. Sanitary landfills also are designed to prevent liquid wastes from draining into the soil and groundwater below. A sanitary landfill is lined with plastic, concrete, or clay-rich soils that trap the liquid waste.

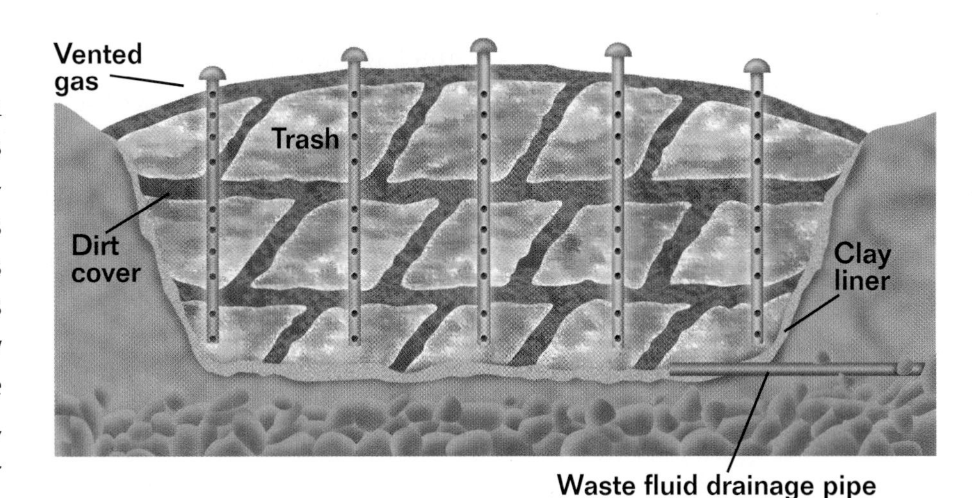

Figure 26-9 The vast majority of our garbage is deposited in landfills. **What are some problems associated with landfill disposal?**

Sanitary landfills greatly reduce the chance that pollutants will leak into the surrounding soil and groundwater. However, some may still find their way into the environment.

Another problem is that we're filling up our landfills and running out of acceptable areas to build new ones. Many materials placed into landfills decompose slowly.

Hazardous Wastes

Some of the wastes we put into landfills are dangerous to organisms. Poisonous, cancer-causing, or radioactive wastes are called **hazardous wastes.** Hazardous wastes are put into landfills by everyone—industries and individuals alike. We contribute to this problem when we throw away insect sprays, batteries, drain cleaners, bleaches, medicines, and paints.

It may seem that when we throw something in the garbage can, even if it's hazardous, it's gone and we don't need to be concerned with it anymore. Unfortunately, our garbage does not disappear. It can remain in a landfill for hundreds of years. In the case of radioactive waste, it

Try at Home

MiniLab

Classifying Your Trash for One Day

Procedure

1. Prepare a table for yourself with the following column headings: *Paper, Plastic, Glass, Metal, Food Waste.*
2. During the day, record everything you throw out in the appropriate column.
3. At the end of the day, determine the number of trash items in each column.

Analysis

1. Rank each column by number from the least trash items (number 5) to the most trash items (number 1).
2. Compare your rankings with those of others in your household.
3. Compare your daily activities with others to account for differences in the tables.
4. What activities can you change to decrease the amount of trash you produce?

may remain harmful for thousands of years, creating problems for many future generations. Fortunately, industries and individuals are becoming more aware of the problems associated with landfills and are disposing of their wastes in a more responsible manner. You can help by disposing of hazardous wastes you generate at home at special hazardous waste-collection sites. Contact your local government to find out about dates, times, and locations of collections in your area. You can learn more about disposing wastes in the **Field Guide to Waste Management** at the end of this chapter.

Phytoremediation

Earlier, you learned that hazardous substances sometimes contaminate soil. These contaminants may come from nearby industries, residential areas, or landfills. Water contaminated from such a source can filter into the ground and leave behind the toxic substances within soil. Did you know that plants are sometimes used to help fix this problem? Methods of phytoremediation (*phyto* means "plant"; *remediation* means "to fix, or remedy a problem") are being studied to help decontaminate soil.

Extracting Metals

Certain varieties of plants can help remove metals from soil. When soil becomes too concentrated with metallic elements, human health may be at risk. Plant roots can absorb certain metals such as copper, nickel, and zinc. **Figure 26-10** shows how metals are absorbed from the soil and taken into plant tissue. Plants that become concentrated with metals from soil must eventually be harvested and either composted to obtain and recycle the metals or incinerated. If incineration is used to dispose of the plants, the ash residue must be handled carefully and disposed of at a hazardous waste site.

Figure 26-10 Metals such as copper can be removed from soil and incorporated into the tissues of plants. **How does this process illustrate the law of conservation of matter?**

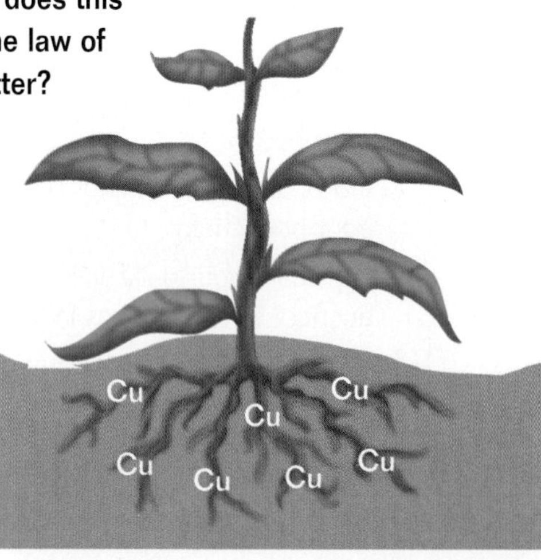

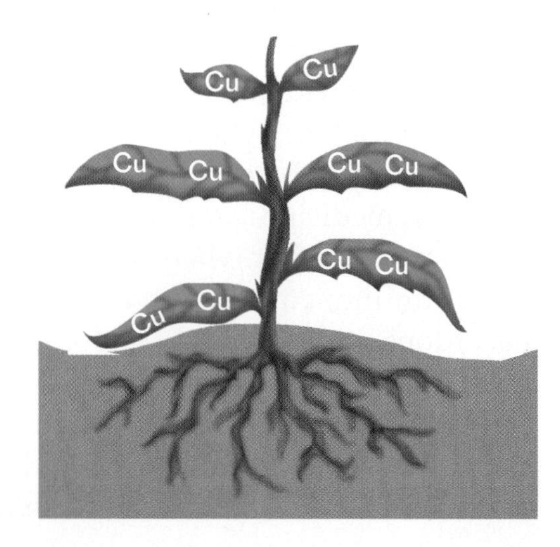

Breaking Down Organic Contaminants

Organic contaminants are hazardous wastes that contain carbon, hydrogen, and other elements such as oxygen, nitrogen, or chlorine. Some common examples of hazardous wastes are gasoline, oil, and solvents. Enzymes are chemical substances that can speed chemical reactions. Some enzymes that can break down organic pollutants are found in plant tissue. Similar to metals extraction, this type of cleanup occurs at the root of the plant. The enzyme is released by the root and causes the organic pollutant in the soil to break down into harmless substances, some of which are useful to the plant and promote its growth.

Human-Built Structures

Concrete and asphalt are quickly replacing grass and woodlands in our communities. The impact on the environment, particularly in urban and suburban areas, is easy to observe. Asphalt and concrete absorb solar radiation. The atmosphere is then heated by conduction and convection, which causes the air temperature to rise. You may have observed this if you've ever traveled from a rural area to the city and noticed a rise in temperature.

The Effects of Trash Disposal

In the early days of the United States, the population was sparse and few people considered the impact of their actions on the environment. They threw their trash into rivers, buried it, or burned it. Today, we must consider the consequences of our methods of trash disposal. The graph at right shows how we deposit our waste.

Think Critically: More than half of the states in our country are running out of landfill space. New landfills will have to be made, but most people have a NIMBY attitude. NIMBY means "Not In My BackYard." People don't want to live near a landfill. What percent of our trash presently goes into landfills? If we reduce the amount of trash in landfills, what alternatives do we have for disposal? How could these alternatives influence the environment? List the pros and cons for each alternative you think of in your Science Journal.

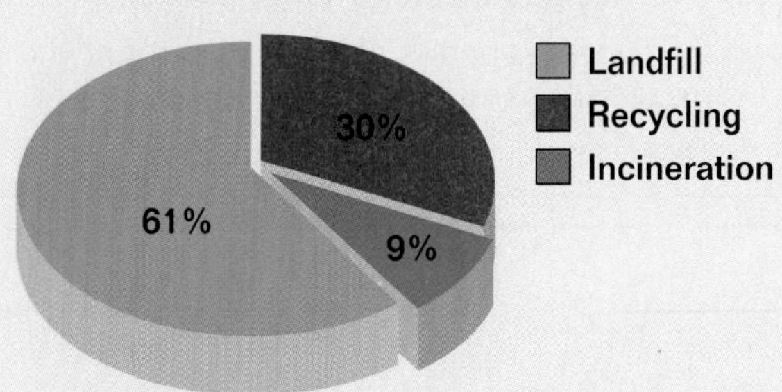

Figure 26-11 Some cities are working to preserve green space within city limits, such as this area in Portland, Oregon. **How does more green space in the city improve the environment?**

Paving over the land prevents water from easily soaking into the soil. Instead, it runs off into sewers or streams. During heavy rainstorms in paved areas, sewer pipes can overflow or become clogged with debris. This causes increased runoff of rainwater directly into streams, and increases the risk of flooding in urban and suburban areas.

A stream's discharge increases when more water enters its channel. Stream discharge is the volume of water flowing past a point per unit of time. For example, the Mississippi River discharges an average of about 19 000 m^3 of water into the Gulf of Mexico every second. This is a large volume of moving water, but the Mississippi is a major river. Many thousands more cubic meters flow per second when the Mississippi is flooding. If discharge increases too rapidly, as happens in urban areas from time to time, a stream can flow over its banks and flood a populated area. This happened to the Mississippi and Missouri Rivers and their tributaries during the summer of 1993.

Increased runoff also influences groundwater. Some of the water that does not soak into the soil evaporates. This reduces the amount of water in groundwater aquifers. Many communities rely on groundwater for drinking water. But covering more and more land with roads, sidewalks, and parking lots prevents the water from reaching aquifers.

Some cities are actively preserving more space that cannot be paved over. This type of activity, shown in **Figure 26-11,** beautifies the urban environment, increases the area into which water can soak, and provides more space for recreation.

MiniLab

Modeling Runoff

Procedure

1. Divide into groups of four or five.
2. Obtain two buckets of water for each group from your teacher.
3. With your teacher present, carefully take your buckets outside.
4. Find a paved area and a grassy area on your school grounds.
5. Pour one bucket of water on the paved area and observe how the water flows on the pavement.
6. Repeat step 5 for the grassy area.

Analysis

1. Describe how the water flowed over each area.
2. Infer what properties of the pavement and the grassy area control how the water flows over each.

Natural Preserves

Not all land on Earth is being utilized to produce usable materials or for storing waste. Look at **Figure 26-12.** Some land remains mostly uninhabited by people. National forest lands, grasslands, and parks in the United States are protected from many of the problems that you've read about in this section. In many countries throughout the world, land is set aside as natural preserves. As the world population continues to rise, the strain on our environment is likely to increase. Preserving some land in its natural state should continue to benefit future generations.

Conserving Resources

In the United States and other industrialized countries, people have a throwaway lifestyle. When we are done with something, we throw it away. This means more products must be produced to replace what we've thrown away, more land is used, and landfills overflow. You can help by conserving resources. **Conservation** is the careful use of resources to reduce damage to the environment.

Reduce, Reuse, Recycle

The United States makes up only five percent of the world's human population, yet it consumes 25 percent of the world's natural resources. Each of us can reduce our consumption of materials in simple ways, such as using both sides of notebook paper or carrying lunch to school in a nondisposable container. Ways to conserve resources include reducing our use of materials and reusing and recycling materials. Reusing an item means finding another use for it instead of throwing it away. You can reuse old clothes by giving them to someone else or by cutting them into rags. The rags can be used in place of paper towels for cleaning jobs around your home.

Figure 26-12 Many countries set aside land as natural preserves. **How do these natural preserves benefit humans and other living things?**

Using Math

Assume 17 fewer trees are cut down when 1000 kg of paper are recycled. Calculate the number of trees conserved per year if 150 000 kg of paper are recycled each month.

Reusing plastic and paper bags is another way to reduce waste. Some grocery stores even pay a few cents when you return and reuse paper grocery bags.

Outdoors, there are things you can do, too. If you cut grass or rake leaves, you can compost these items instead of putting them into the trash. **Composting** means piling yard wastes where they can gradually decompose. The decomposed matter can be used as fertilizer in gardens or flower beds. Some cities no longer pick up yard waste to take to landfills. In these places, composting is common. If everyone in the United States composted, it would reduce the trash put into landfills by 20 percent.

The Population Outlook

The human population explosion already has had devastating effects on the environment and the organisms that inhabit Earth. It's unlikely that the population will begin to decline in the near future. To compensate, we must use our resources wisely. Conserving resources by reducing, reusing, and recycling is an important way that you can make a difference.

Section Assessment

1. In your Science Journal, list six ways that people use land.
2. Discuss environmental problems that are sometimes created by agriculture, mining, and trash disposal.
3. How can phytoremediation positively impact the environment?
4. **Think Critically:** Choose one of the following items, and list three ways it can be reused: an empty milk carton, vegetable scraps, used notebook paper, or an old automobile tire. Be sure your uses are environmentally friendly.
5. **Skill Builder**
Communicating Do the **Chapter 26 Skill Activity** on page 987 to find out ways in which an environmental problem can be communicated.

Using Computers

Word Processing
Suppose that a new landfill is needed in your community. Where do you think it should be located? Now, suppose that you want to convince people that you've selected the best place for the landfill. Use your word-processing skills to write a letter to the editor of the local newspaper, listing reasons in favor of your choice. If you need help, refer to page 968.

Recycling

26-3

Recyclable Objects

Did you know that any object is **recyclable** if it can be processed and then used again? Look at **Figure 26-13.** Glass and aluminum are two of the many things that can be recycled.

Paper makes up about 40 percent of the mass of our trash. If it is recycled, landfill space and trees are conserved. Also, the production of recycled paper takes 58 percent less water and generates 74 percent fewer air pollutants than the production of brand-new paper made from trees.

How much energy do you think is saved when you recycle one aluminum can? Answer: enough energy to keep a TV running for about three hours. Twenty aluminum cans can be recycled with the energy that is needed to produce a single brand-new can from aluminum ore.

What You'll Learn

- The advantages of recycling
- The advantages and disadvantages of required recycling

Vocabulary
recyclable

Why It's Important

- Recycling helps conserve resources and reduces solid waste.

VISUALIZING Recycling

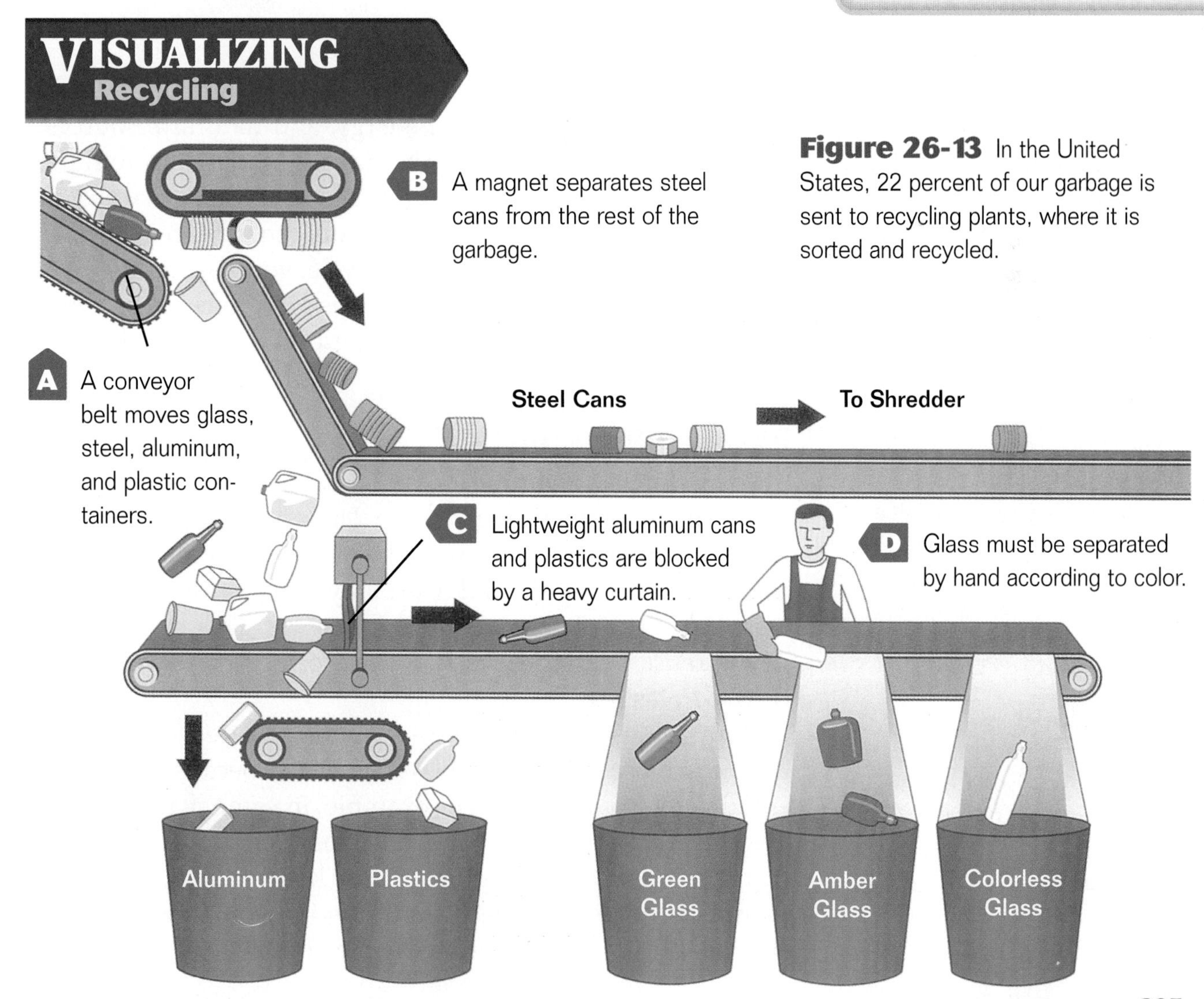

Figure 26-13 In the United States, 22 percent of our garbage is sent to recycling plants, where it is sorted and recycled.

Figure 26-14 Recycling saves landfill space, energy, and natural resources. Many community volunteers adopt sections of a highway. They pick up trash and recycle the salvageable part.

Everyone agrees that recycling is good for the environment. It saves landfill space, energy, and natural resources. Recycling also helps reduce the damage caused by mining, cutting trees, and manufacturing. Did you know that if you recycle, you will reduce the trash you generate in your lifetime by 60 percent? If you don't recycle, you'll generate trash equal to at least 600 times your mass. No one argues that recycling is not a good thing. The question is should recycling be required?

Required Recycling

Many things are thrown away because some people aren't in the habit of recycling. In the United States, much less garbage is recycled than in countries with mandatory recycling, such as Japan and Germany. Mandatory recycling means that people are required to recycle. This creates new jobs in reuse industries, such as the production of items from recycled plastics.

Many states already have some form of recycling laws. People in these states comply with the laws because they benefit directly in some way. For example, in some places people who recycle pay lower trash-collection fees. In other places, garbage is not collected if it contains items that should have been recycled. **Figure 26-14** shows typical containers used to help people organize their recyclable objects.

In some states, a refundable deposit is made on all beverage containers. This means paying extra money at the store for a drink. You get your money back if you return the container to the store for recycling. Some people suggest that if we had a national container law, we could save enough energy to light up a large city for four years. ☑

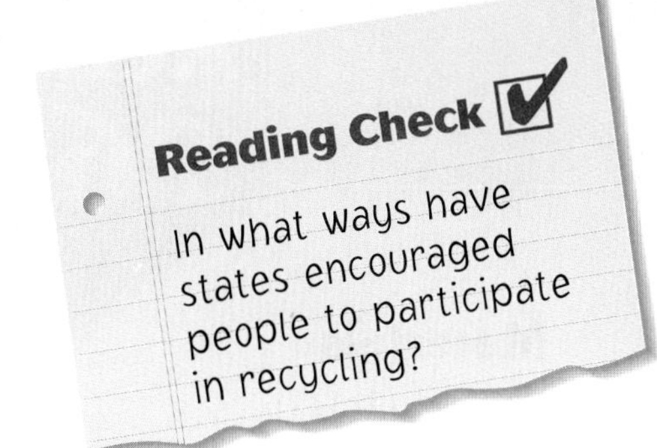

Voluntary Recycling

Today, many people already recycle voluntarily because their cities provide curbside collection or convenient drop-off facilities. In this case, people have the freedom to decide whether or not to recycle, without government intervention.

Some people argue that the cost of recycling outweighs the benefits. Recycling requires money to pay for workers, trucks, and buildings. Also, some workers, such as miners and manufacturers who make brand-new containers, might lose their jobs.

Another problem is what to do with all of the recyclable items. Recycling businesses must make a profit, or they can't exist. The only way to make a profit in recycling is to sell the recycled material, so there must be a market for the material. Whether voluntary or mandatory, recycling conserves resources. In addition to saving landfill space, recycling also protects our environment by minimizing our need to extract raw materials from Earth.

interNET CONNECTION

Visit the Glencoe Science Web Site at **www.glencoe.com/sec/science/ca** to learn more about conservation. Make a list of conservation tips for individuals.

Section Assessment

1. List at least four advantages of recycling.
2. What are the advantages and disadvantages of mandatory recycling?
3. **Think Critically:** Spend a day at home keeping track of what you throw away and what you recycle. Record these items in your Science Journal. Did you throw away anything that could have been recycled?
4. **Skill Builder**
   Making and Using Tables As you will see in the **Field Guide to Waste Management** at the end of this chapter, plastics must be carefully sorted before they can be reprocessed into new usable items. Do the Activity in the field guide to find out how to organize your recyclable plastic items. If you need help, refer to Making and Using Tables in the **Skill Handbook** on page 952.

In your Science Journal, write a letter to your local chamber of commerce suggesting ways to encourage businesses to recycle.

Activity 26•2

Using Scientific Methods

A Model Landfill

Materials

- Bottles (2L) (2)
- Soil
- Thermometer
- Plastic wrap
- Graph paper
- Rubber band
- Trash (including fruit and vegetable scraps, a plastic item, a metal item, a foam cup, and notebook paper or newsprint)

When garbage is put into landfills, it is covered under other trash and soil and isn't exposed to sunlight and other things that help decomposition. When examined by a researcher, one landfill was found to contain grass clippings that were still green and bread that had not molded.

What You'll Investigate

At what rates do different materials decompose in a landfill?

Goals

- **Make a model** of a sanitary landfill.
- **Compare and contrast** the decomposition of different materials in a landfill.

Safety Precautions

CAUTION: *Be especially careful not to expose your skin or eyes to garbage items.*

Procedure

1. **Cut** off the tops of two 2-L bottles.
2. **Add** soil to each bottle until it is half filled.
3. On graph paper, **trace** the outline of all the garbage items that you will place into each bottle. **Label** each outline and keep the tracings.
4. **Place** the items, one at a time, in each bottle. Completely **cover** each item with soil.
5. **Add** water to your landfill until the soil is slightly moist. **Place** a thermometer in each bottle and seal the bottle with the plastic wrap and a rubber band. **Store** one bottle in a cold place and put the other on a shelf.
6. **Check** the temperature of your landfill on the shelf each day for two weeks. **Record** the temperatures in a data table that you design.
7. After two weeks, **remove** all of the items from the soil in both bottles. Trace the outlines of each on a new sheet of graph paper. **Compare** the sizes of the items with their original sizes.
8. **Wash** your hands thoroughly after cleaning up your lab space. Be sure to dispose of each item properly as instructed by your teacher.

Conclude and Apply

1. Most decomposition in a landfill is due to the activity of microorganisms. The organisms can live only under certain temperature and moisture conditions.
   Explain how the decomposition rates would have differed if the soil had been completely dry.
2. **Compare** your results with the results from the bottle that was stored at a cold temperature. **Explain** the differences you observe.
3. Why do some items decompose more rapidly than others?
4. What problems are created in landfills by plastics?

Using Plants to Reduce Pollution

Pollution-Absorbing Plants

Plants are helping clean up hazardous chemicals in soil and water. By taking in pollutants through their roots, some plants can make hazardous substances less harmful to humans and other organisms. These helpful plants include poplar trees, mustard (left), and fescue grass (below).

Fescue to the Rescue

High concentrations of the metal selenium (suh LEE nee uhm) are harmful to the environment. In central California, soil became contaminated when irrigation water containing selenium flowed through fields. Farmers in the area planted fescue grass and Indian mustard to absorb selenium from the contaminated irrigation water. Researchers have found that mustard and fescue are able to convert selenium metal into a gas that is eventually given off by the plants. Scientists suggest that the gas is many times less harmful to the environment than concentrated levels of selenium in soils.

Advantages of Using Plants

Using plants to control or eliminate certain types of pollution is becoming increasingly popular. Cost is one reason. It is often less expensive to use plants than other methods of reducing pollutants. Plants clean up contaminated soil or water on the site, so there is no expense of digging up soil or removing water. Plants also can make an area more attractive. Finally, few, if any, people object to using plants to reverse the negative effects of pollution.

interNET CONNECTION

To find information about the Environmental Protection Agency's Citizen's Guide to Phytoremediation, visit the Glencoe Science Web Site at **www.glencoe.com/sec/science/ca.**

FIELD GUIDE to Waste Management

FIELD *ACTIVITY*

The type of plastic contained in a recyclable item is indicated by a coded number placed on the item. Arrange collection centers at your school for plastic to be recycled. Name your collection activity and advertise it with posters. Operate the collection of recyclable plastics for one week. Use the Plastics Code System Table in this field guide to organize the plastic products by code number so they can be recycled. Arrange to have your plastics taken to a recycling center. Make a bar graph that shows how many pieces of each type of plastic you collected. In your Science Journal, list examples of products that can be made from the collected plastics.

Managing waste properly can reduce the use of resources and prevent pollution. People can do three things to cut down on waste production and reduce harm to the environment. They can follow the three Rs of waste management: reduce, reuse, and recycle. For example, a 450-g family-size box of cereal uses a lot less cardboard than 18 single-serving boxes that each contain 25 g of cereal. Finding another function for used items such as wrapping gifts with old magazines or newspapers greatly reduces waste. And, you can use many products every day that are recyclable. You can also help complete the cycle by purchasing items that are made from recycled materials.

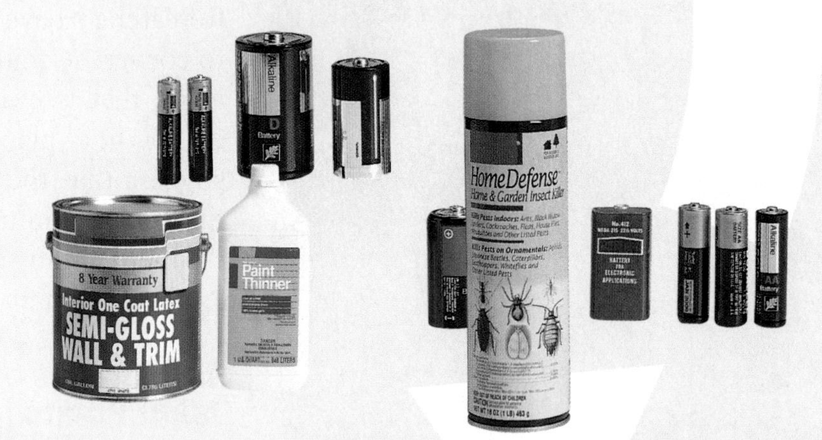

Household Hazardous Wastes

- Household Hazardous Wastes (HHWs) are products containing chemicals that can cause injury or are harmful if used, stored, or disposed of improperly. Some of these products include household and car batteries, bleach and household cleaners, paint, paint thinner, old motor oil, old gasoline, herbicides and pesticides.
- These chemicals pose a threat to people (especially children, firefighters, and refuse workers) and to our environment.
- HHWs have caution words, skull and crossbones, or special handling directions.
- Some communities provide information to help people dispose of HHWs properly.
- Follow these steps to reduce HHWs:
  1. Whenever possible, buy nontoxic alternatives to hazardous products.
  2. If you buy a hazardous product, buy only what you need to do the job.
  3. Before you put leftover products on the shelf, try to find someone who can use them.

Plastics

- Plastics are among the most difficult products to recycle. Most plastics are composed of complex molecules that tend not to break down easily.
- Many different types of plastics exist, and they often cannot be recycled together.
- **Table 26-1** below lists the codes used to identify specific types of plastics used in products. This helps people sort common plastic items for proper recycling.
- Plastic beverage containers are recycled into insulation, carpet yarn, strapping, and packing material.

Table 26-1

The Plastics Code System

Code	Material	% of Containers	Reclaimed For
1 PET	Polyethylene terephthalate	7	Carpet, food packaging, fiberfill, fibers, and auto parts
2 HDPE	High-density polyethylene	31	Drainage pipes, drums, traffic cones, plastic lumber, and combs
3 V	Vinyl chloride	5	Pipes, hoses, mud flaps, and tile
4 LDPE	Low-density polyethylene	33	Mixed with HDPE to produce cases, recycling bins, and garbage bags
5 PP	Polypropylene	9	Household and janitorial products
6 PS	Polystyrene	11	Insulation and food trays
7 Other	All others and mixed	4	Storage containers, lumber, and animal-pen floors

Glass

- Glass is often separated by color into green, brown, or colorless types before recycling.
- Most glass bottles are recyclable, but some glassware is not because it is too thin. For example, broken or burned-out lightbulbs cannot be recycled.
- New products made from recycled glass include beverage containers.

Metals

- A variety of metals are recyclable, such as aluminum beverage cans and steel used in a variety of canned goods.
- Aluminum is processed to make lawn chairs, siding, cookware, or new beverage cans.
- Even precious metals such as silver, gold, and platinum used in laboratories or in jewelry, for example, are recyclable.

Paper

- Plain white paper, newspaper, magazines, and telephone books are common paper goods that can be recycled. New products made from these items include newsprint, cardboard, egg cartons, and building materials.
- Not all glossy and colored papers are recyclable at all recycling centers.

- As for any recycled material, you should check with your neighborhood recycling center for specific instructions about properly sorting your paper goods.

Yard Waste

- Grass clippings, leaves, sticks, and other yard wastes can be placed in bags and taken to your local recycling center. Some communities provide for the collection of yard wastes from your home after you gather them together.
- Another approach is to practice your own mulching. Rake your leaves and then place them on a garden plot to compost over the winter. This will enrich the soil in your garden when you're ready to plant in the spring.
- Some communities shred sticks and leaves to make mulch. Whatever the approach, recycling yard waste reduces the amount of material we send to landfills.

Chapter 26 Reviewing Main Ideas

For a **preview** of this chapter, study this Reviewing Main Ideas before you read the chapter. After you have studied this chapter, you can use the Reviewing Main Ideas to **review** the chapter.

The Glencoe MindJogger, Audiocassettes, and CD-ROM provide additional opportunities for review.

Section 26-1 POPULATION IMPACT ON THE ENVIRONMENT

The rapid increase in human **population** in recent years is due to an increase in the birthrate, advances in medicine, better sanitation, and better nutrition. ***How does an increase in the number of humans affect Earth's carrying capacity for other organisms?***

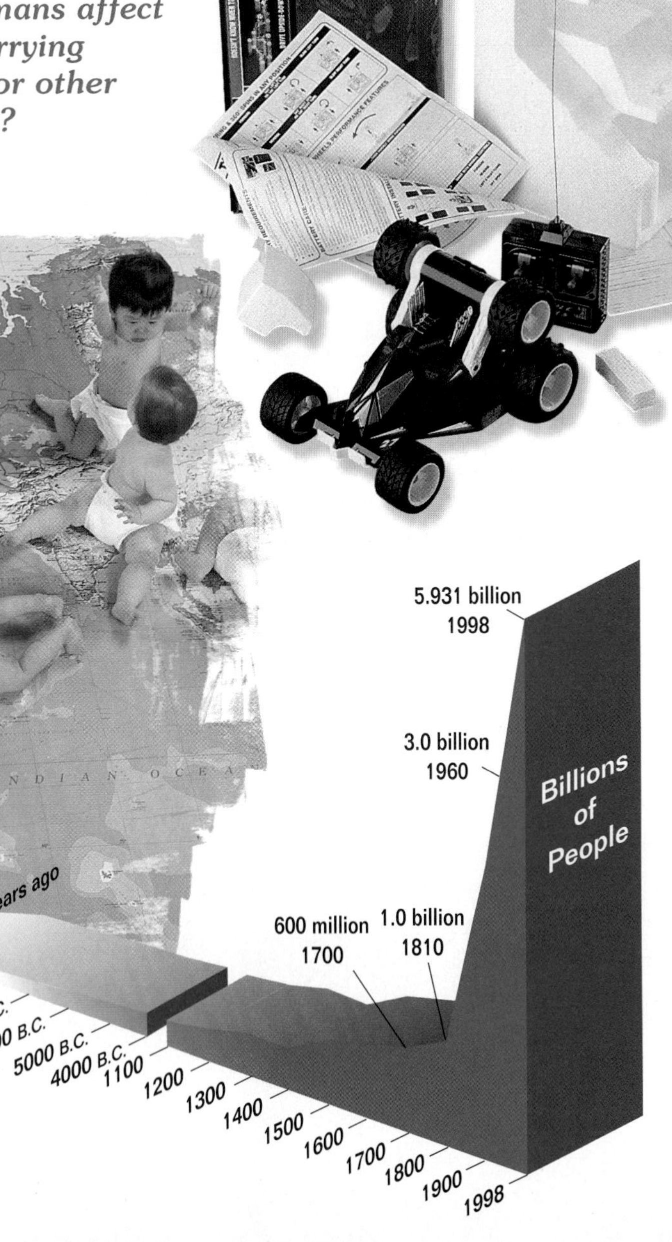

Reading Check

List at least two facts and two opinions related to population growth or related to recycling.

Section

26-2 USING LAND

Land is used for farming, grazing livestock, lumber, and mining coal and mineral ores. We also build structures and **landfills** on land. Land becomes polluted by **hazardous wastes** thrown away by industries and individuals. Fertilizers and pesticides pollute groundwater and soil. ***What happens to soil quality and atmospheric carbon dioxide when trees are cut down?***

Section

26-3 RECYCLING

Recycling, reducing, and reusing materials are important ways we can conserve natural resources. Recycling saves energy and much-needed space in landfills. Some parts of the world have mandatory recycling, while other parts have voluntary programs. ***Why do some people oppose having mandatory recycling programs?***

Chapter 26 Assessment

Using Vocabulary

a. carrying capacity
b. composting
c. conservation
d. hazardous waste
e. landfill
f. population
g. population explosion
h. recyclable

Which vocabulary word describes the phrase or process given below?

1. total number of individuals of a particular species in an area
2. careful use of resources
3. area lined with plastic, concrete, or clay where garbage is dumped
4. items that can be processed and used again
5. maximum number of individuals of a particular type that the planet will support

Checking Concepts

Choose the word or phrase that best answers the question.

6. Where is most of the trash in the United States disposed of?
A) recycling centers
B) landfills
C) hazardous waste sites
D) old mine shafts

7. Between 1960 and 1998, world population increased by how many billions of people?
A) 5.9
B) 3.2
C) 1.0
D) 2.9

8. What percent of Earth's resources does the United States use?
A) 5
B) 10
C) 25
D) 50

9. About what percent of U.S. cropland is used to grow feed for livestock?
A) 100
B) 1
C) 50
D) 20

10. What do we call an object that can be processed in some way so that it can be used again?
A) trash
B) recyclable
C) disposable
D) hazardous

11. What is about 40 percent of the mass of our trash made up of?
A) glass
B) aluminum
C) yard waste
D) paper

12. In which type of facility do humans cover trash with soil?
A) recycling center
B) surface mine
C) sanitary landfill
D) coal mine

13. By what order of magnitude are people starving each year?
A) the hundreds
B) the thousands
C) the millions
D) the billions

14. Organisms living outside the tropics suffer when rain forests are cut down. This is because fewer trees are available to produce which?
A) carbon dioxide
B) methane
C) water
D) oxygen

15. Which of the following is an example of a hazardous waste?
A) piece of glass
B) plastic jug
C) steel can
D) can of paint

Thinking Critically

16. How would reducing the packaging of consumer products impact our disposal of solid wastes?

17. Renewable resources are those resources that can be replenished by nature in the foreseeable future. Nonrenewable resources cannot be replenished. Which kind of resource is oxygen? Explain.

18. Although land is farmable in many developing countries, hunger is a major problem in many of these places. Give some reasons why this might be so.
19. Forests in Germany are dying due to acid rain. What effects might this loss of trees have on the environment?
20. Describe how you could encourage your neighbors to recycle their aluminum cans.

Developing Skills

If you need help, refer to the Skill Handbook.

21. **Making and Using Graphs**: In a population of snails, each snail produces two offspring each month. Each offspring also produces two offspring. Using the graph below, determine how many new snails would be produced during the fifth month if the initial population were only two snails.
22. **Interpreting Scientific Illustrations:** Why does the curve of the line graph below change its slope over time? Suppose half of the snails died after six months. Draw a new graph to illustrate the effect.

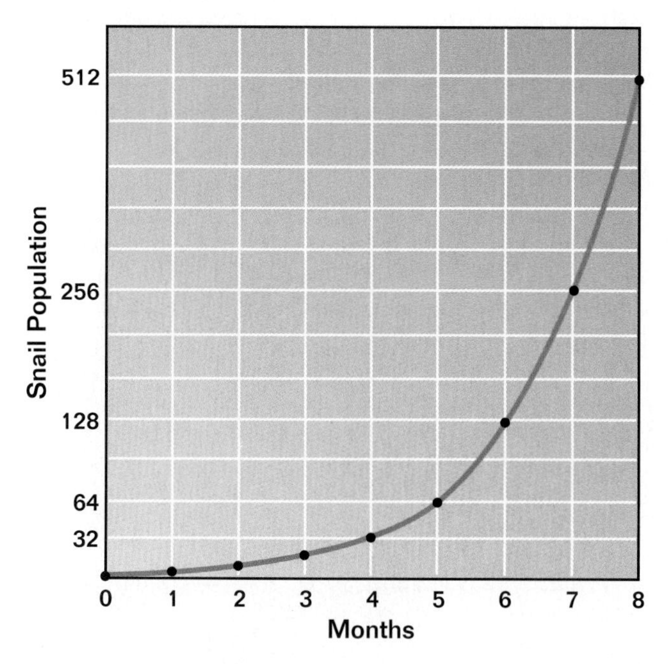

Test-Taking Tip

Don't Be Afraid to Ask for Help Ask for advice on things you don't understand. If you're practicing for a test and find yourself stuck, unable to understand why you got a question wrong, or unable to do it in the first place, ask for help.

Test Practice

Use these questions to test your Science Proficiency.

1. In some areas of the world, when rain forests are destroyed for lumber, a few fast-growing species of trees are planted in their place. Why is this a problem?
   A) The trees won't grow as quickly as the original rain forest trees.
   B) The tree farm won't produce oxygen.
   C) The roots of the new trees won't hold the soil.
   D) The biodiversity is decreased.
2. In 1946, there were 2.4 billion people on Earth. In 1998, there were 5.9 billion people. By how much did world population increase in 52 years?
   A) 226 percent
   B) 41 percent
   C) 146 percent
   D) 69 percent
3. Which of the following must be true for a recycling center to be profitable?
   A) The center must recycle glass.
   B) Mandatory recycling is enforced.
   C) Glossy and colored paper are recycled.
   D) There is a market for the recycled items.

CHAPTER

27 Our Impact on Air and Water

Chapter Preview

Skills Preview

Skill Builders

- Map Concepts
- Interpret Scientific Illustrations

Activities

- Collect and Analyze Data
- Make and Use a Data Table

MiniLabs

- Experiment
- Observe and Infer

Reading Check

As you read this chapter, create a timeline of the federal laws that have been enacted to help control our impact on air and water.

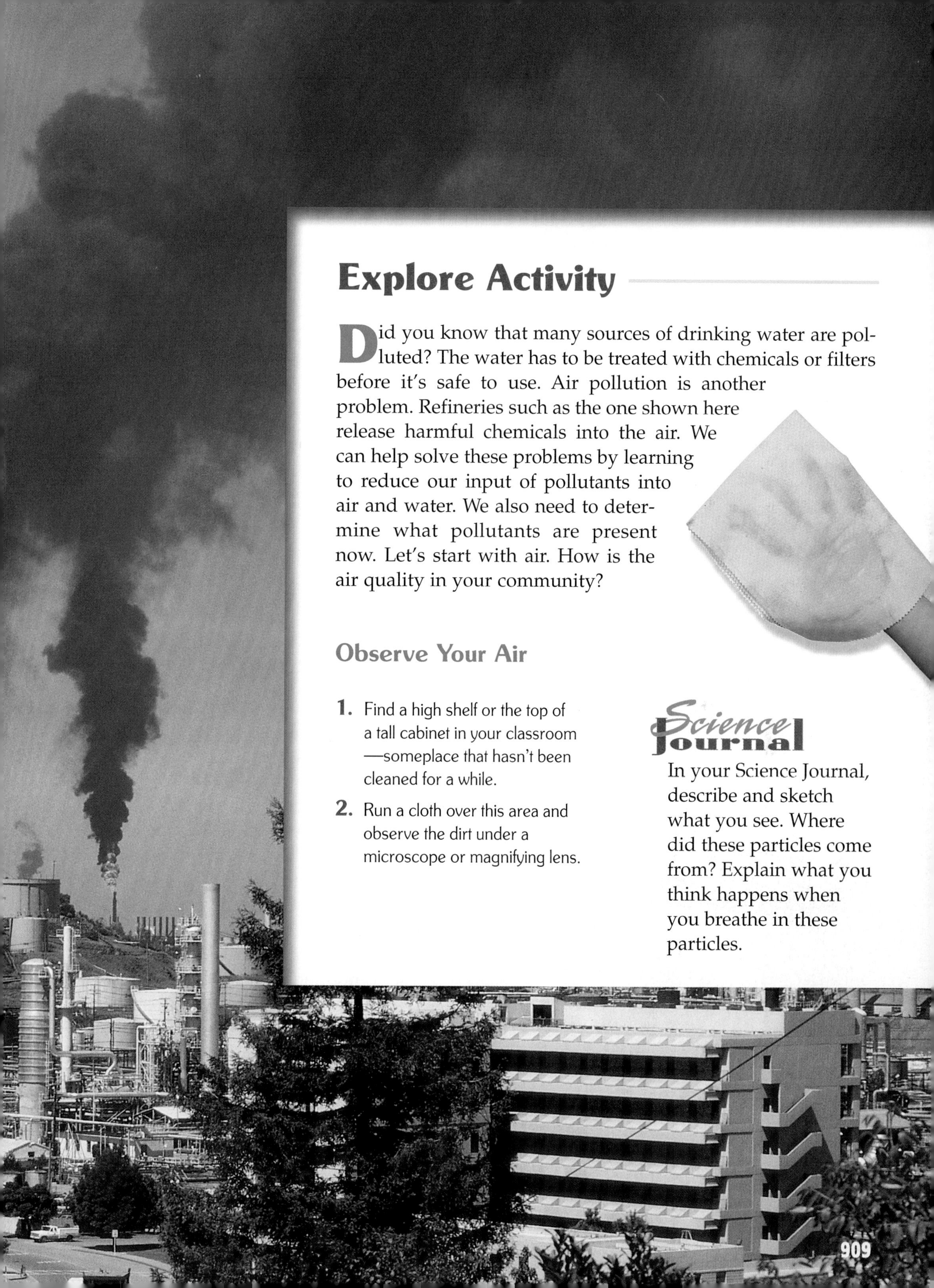

Explore Activity

Did you know that many sources of drinking water are polluted? The water has to be treated with chemicals or filters before it's safe to use. Air pollution is another problem. Refineries such as the one shown here release harmful chemicals into the air. We can help solve these problems by learning to reduce our input of pollutants into air and water. We also need to determine what pollutants are present now. Let's start with air. How is the air quality in your community?

Observe Your Air

1. Find a high shelf or the top of a tall cabinet in your classroom —someplace that hasn't been cleaned for a while.
2. Run a cloth over this area and observe the dirt under a microscope or magnifying lens.

Science Journal

In your Science Journal, describe and sketch what you see. Where did these particles come from? Explain what you think happens when you breathe in these particles.

27•1 Air Pollution

What You'll Learn

- The different sources of air pollutants
- How air pollution affects people and the environment
- How air pollution can be reduced

Vocabulary
photochemical smog
sulfurous smog
acid rain
pH scale
acid
base
Clean Air Act
scrubber

Why It's Important

- Air pollution can affect your health and the health of others.

What causes air pollution?

Have you ever noticed that the air looks hazy on some days? Do you know what causes this haziness? Some industries generate dust and chemicals. Other human activities add pollutants to the air, too. Look at **Figure 27-1.** Cars, buses, trucks, trains, and planes all burn fossil fuels for energy. Their exhaust—the waste products from burning the fossil fuels—adds polluting chemicals to the air. Other sources include smoke from burning trash and dust from plowed fields, construction sites, and mines.

Natural sources also add pollutants to the air. Volcanic eruptions, forest fires, and grass fires all emit dust and chemicals into the air. Volcanic eruptions even cause temporary changes in climate by blocking out sunlight when ash erupts.

Smog

Figure 27-2 shows the major sources of air pollution. Around cities, polluted air is called *smog,* a word made by combining the words *smoke* and *fog.* Two types of smog are common—photochemical smog and sulfurous smog.

Photochemical Smog

In areas such as Los Angeles, Denver, and New York City, a hazy, brown blanket of smog is created when sunlight reacts with pollutants in the air. This brown smog is called **photochemical smog** because it forms with the aid of light. The pollutants get into the air when fossil fuels are burned. Coal, natural gas, and gasoline are burned by factories, airplanes, and cars. Burning fossil fuels causes nitrogen and oxygen to combine chemically to form nitrogen compounds. These compounds react in the presence of sunlight and produce other substances. One of the substances produced is ozone. Ozone in the stratosphere protects us

Figure 27-1 Cars, like these in New York City, are one of the main sources of air pollution in the United States. **Describe other sources of air pollution where you live.**

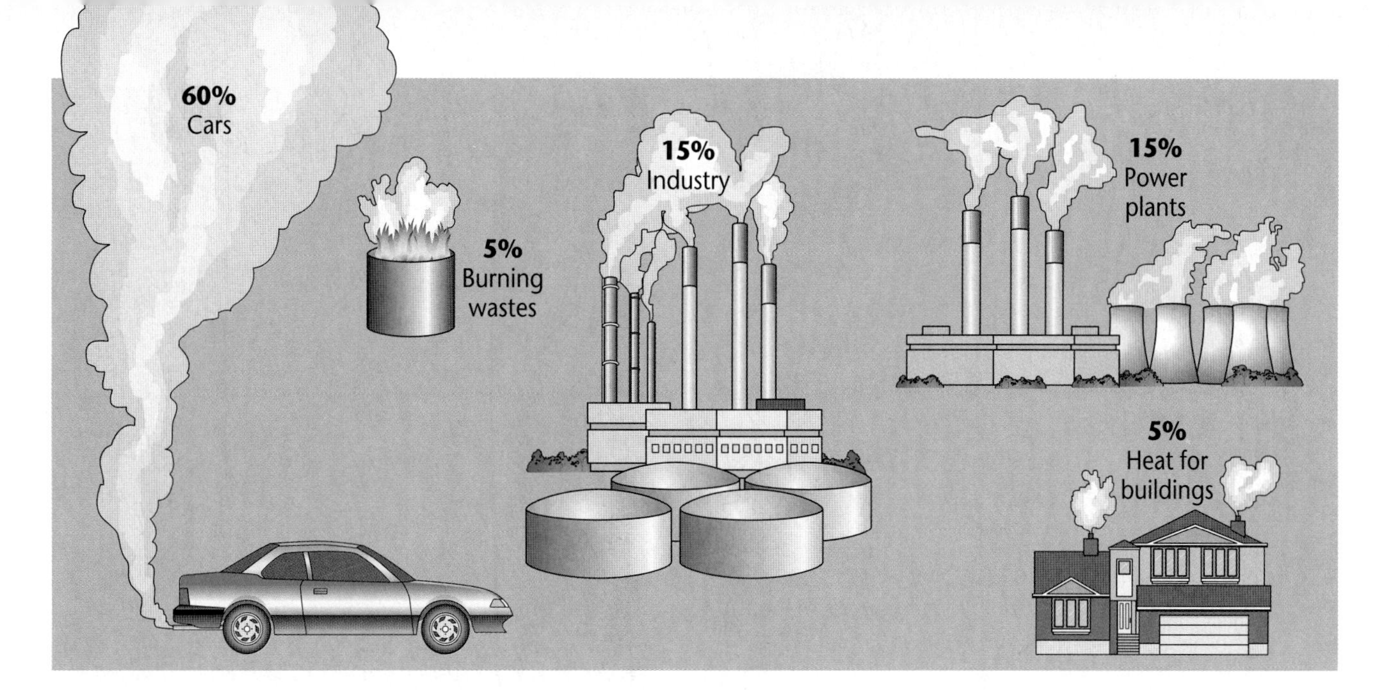

Figure 27-2 There are five major sources of human-created smog. **Which three sources combined produce 90 percent of human-created smog?**

from the sun's ultraviolet radiation. But ozone that forms in smog near Earth's surface causes health problems.

Sulfurous Smog

A second type of smog is called **sulfurous smog.** It's created when coal is burned in electrical power plants and home furnaces. The burning releases sulfur compounds, dust, and smoke particles into the air. Sulfurous smog forms when these substances collect in an area where there's little or no wind. A blanket of gray smog may hang over a city for several days and be hazardous to breathe.

Nature and Smog

Nature plays an important role in creating smog. Sunlight helps form photochemical smog. Sulfurous smog forms when weather systems are calm and the air is not being moved around. Normally, warmer air is near Earth's surface. But, sometimes warm air overlies cool air, trapping cool air mixed with pollutants near the ground. Eventually, the weather changes and cleaner air is blown in, dispersing the pollutants in the air.

Landforms also enhance smog development. For example, air with smog can be blocked by surrounding mountains. This prevents smog from being dispersed by winds. Dense, dirty air tends to collect in valleys in this way.

Smog isn't the only air pollution problem we have. Chlorofluorocarbons (CFCs) from air conditioners and refrigerators are thought to be destroying the ozone layer in the stratosphere. Some scientists suggest that carbon dioxide released from burning coal, oil, natural gas, and forests could contribute to increasing temperatures on Earth.

Visit the Glencoe Science Web Site at **www.glencoe.com/sec/science/ca** for more information about smog.

Identifying Acid Rain

Procedure

1. The next time it rains or snows, use a glass or plastic container to collect a sample of the precipitation.
2. Use pH paper to determine the acidity level of your sample. If you have collected snow, melt it before measuring its pH.
3. Record the indicated pH of your sample and compare it with the results of other classmates who have followed the same procedure.

Analysis

1. What is the average pH of the samples obtained from this precipitation?
2. Compare and contrast the pH of your samples with those of the substances shown on the pH scale in **Figure 27-4.**

Figure 27-3 These trees are dying because acids in the soil have lowered the trees' resistance to diseases, insects, and bad weather. Acid rain also increases the acidity of streams, rivers, and lakes, killing fish. Acid rain even damages the surfaces of buildings and cars.

Acid Rain

Another major pollution problem is acid rain. Acid rain is created when sulfur dioxide from coal-burning power plants combines with moisture in the air to form sulfuric acid. It also is created when nitrogen oxides from car exhausts combine with moisture in the air to form nitric acid. The acidic moisture falls to Earth as rain or snow. We call this **acid rain.** Acid rain can poison organisms, as shown by the dying trees in **Figure 27-3.**

To understand what is meant by an acid, we use the **pH scale,** shown in **Figure 27-4.** Substances with a pH lower than seven are **acids.** The lower the number, the greater the acidity. Substances with a pH above seven are **bases.** Acid rain is sometimes as acidic as lemon juice.

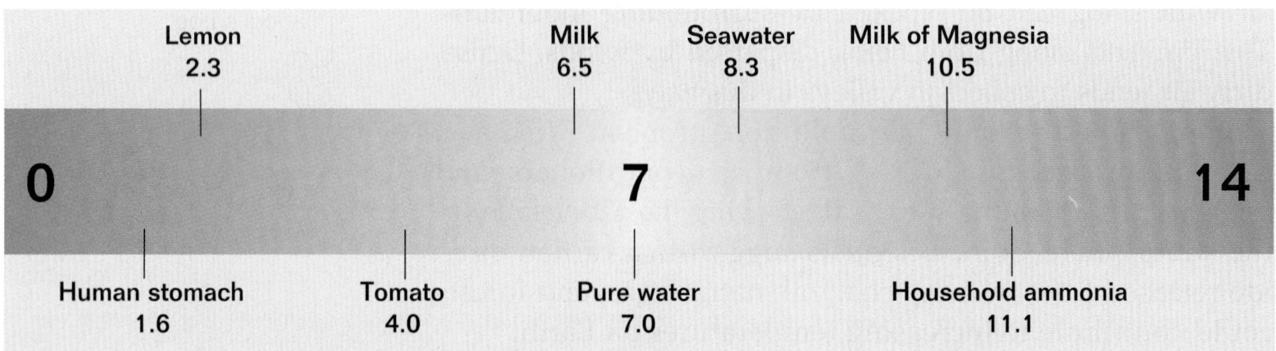

Figure 27-4 The natural pH of rainwater is about 5.6. Acid rain is precipitation with a pH below 5.6.

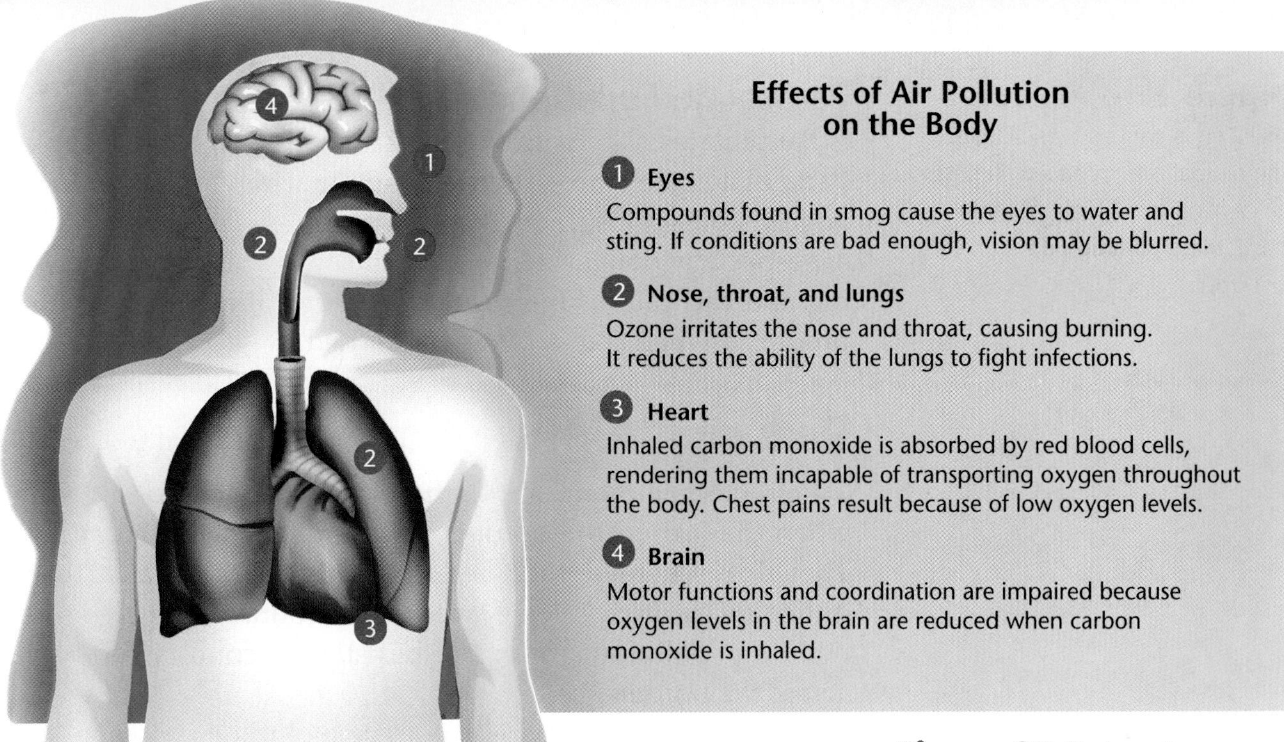

Figure 27-5 Air pollution is a health hazard. Compounds in the air can affect your body.

How Air Pollution Affects Your Health

Suppose you're an athlete in a large city and you're training for a big, upcoming competition. You have to get up at 4:30 A.M. to exercise. Later in the day, the smog levels will be so high that it won't be safe for you to do strenuous exercise. In southern California, in Denver, and in other areas, athletes adjust their training schedules to avoid exposure to ozone and other smog. Schools schedule football games for Saturday afternoons when smog levels are low. Parents are warned to keep their children indoors when smog exceeds certain levels. **Figure 27-5** shows how breathing dirty air, especially taking deep breaths of it, can cause health problems.

Health Disorders

How hazardous is dirty air? Approximately 250 000 people in the United States suffer from pollution-related breathing disorders. About 60 000 deaths each year in the United States are blamed on air pollution. Ozone damages lung tissue, making people more susceptible to diseases such as pneumonia and asthma. Less severe symptoms of breathing ozone include burning eyes, dry throat, and headache. ✓

Carbon monoxide also contributes to air pollution. A colorless, odorless gas, carbon monoxide makes people ill, even in small concentrations.

What do you suppose happens when you inhale the humid air from acid rain? Acid is deposited deep inside your lungs. This causes irritation, reduces your ability to fight respiratory infections, interferes with oxygen absorption, and puts stress on your heart.

Using Math

The pH scale is a logarithmic scale. This means that there is a tenfold difference for each pH unit. For example, pH 4 is ten times more acidic than pH 5 and 100 times more acidic than pH 6. Calculate how much more acidic pH 1 is than pH 4.

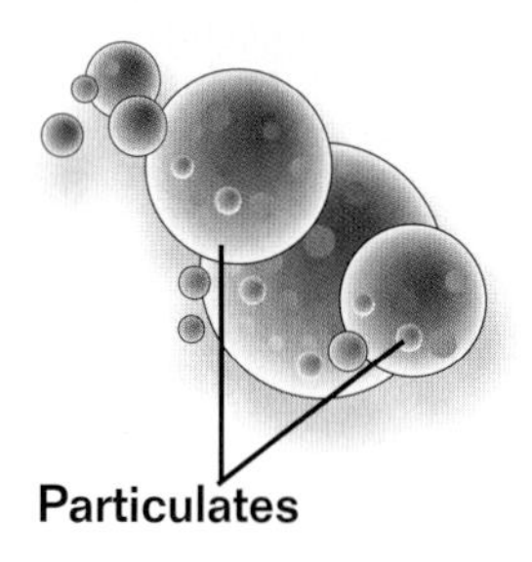

Figure 27-6 Particulate pollution is caused by solids in the air that are produced, in part, by burning fossil fuels. **Why is particulate pollution difficult to control?**

Particulate Pollution

Particulates shown in **Figure 27-6,** can also harm people. Particulates are fine airborne solids that range in size from large visible grains to microscopic particles. The fine particles are especially dangerous because they disrupt normal breathing and can cause lung disease. Some of these particles are produced when coal and oil are burned.

Reducing Air Pollution

Pollutants moving through the atmosphere don't stop when they reach the borders between states and countries. They float wherever the wind carries them. This makes them difficult to control. Even if one state or country reduces its air pollution, pollutants from another state or country can blow across the border.

When states and nations cooperate, pollution problems can be reduced. Diplomats from around the world have met on several occasions since 1990 to try to eliminate some kinds of air pollution. Of particular concern are chlorofluorocarbons and carbon dioxide.

Air Pollution in the United States

The Congress of the United States has passed several laws to protect the air. The 1990 **Clean Air Act** attacked the problems of smog, chlorofluorocarbons, particulates, and acid rain by regulating car manufacturers, coal technologies, and other industries. In **Table 27-1,** you can read about some of these regulations.

Table 27-1

Clean Air Regulations

Urban Air Pollution	Acid Rain	Airborne Toxins	Ozone-Depleting Chemicals
By 1996, all new cars had to have their nitrogen oxide emissions reduced by 60 percent and hydrocarbons reduced by 35 percent from 1990 levels.	In 1990, nitrogen oxide emissions had to be reduced by several million tons immediately. Sulfur dioxide emissions must be reduced by 14 million tons from 1990 levels by the year 2000.	Beginning in 1995, industries had to limit the emission of 200 compounds that cause cancer and birth defects.	In 1990, industries were required to immediately phase out ozone-depleting chemicals.

The good news is that since the passage of the Clean Air Act, the quality of the air in some regions of the United States has improved. The bad news is that one of four U.S. citizens still breathes unhealthy air.

It is the role of the federal Environmental Protection Agency to monitor progress toward the goals of the Clean Air Act. However, consumers must pay increased prices and taxes and change their habits in order to really help protect the environment. The Clean Air Act can work only if we all cooperate. You can conserve energy and reduce trash in several ways. When you do these things, you also are reducing air pollution. We all must do our share to clean up the air.

Reducing Emissions

The main source of the nitric acid in acid rain is car exhaust. Better emission-control devices on cars will help reduce acid rain. So will car pooling and public transportation because they reduce the number of trips and, therefore, the amount of fuel used.

Coal-burning power plants can help reduce air pollutants, too. Some coal has a lot of sulfur in it. When the coal is burned, the sulfur combines with moisture in the air to form sulfuric acid. Power plants can wash coal to remove some sulfur before the coal is burned. Burning cleaner coal produces less sulfur in the smoke. Power plants also can run the smoke through a scrubber. A **scrubber** lets the gases in the smoke dissolve in water, as they would in nature, until the smoke's pH increases to a safe level. **Figure 27-7** illustrates how an electrostatic separator removes particulates.

Using Math

Suppose a car travels 18 000 miles per year. How many gallons of gas must it burn in one year if it gets 20 miles per gallon? 30 miles per gallon? If a car emits 20 pounds of carbon dioxide for each gallon of gas burned, how much more carbon dioxide is emitted by a 20-mile-per-gallon car than a 30-mile-per-gallon car in one year? Convert your answer from pounds to kilograms.

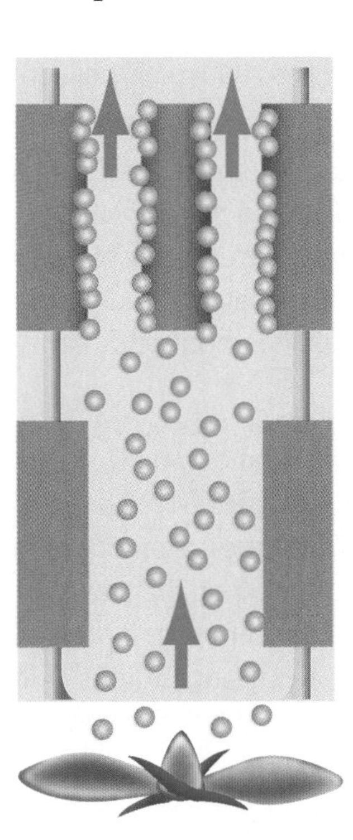

Figure 27-7
Smokestack scrubbers and electrostatic separators remove the pollutants from industrial smoke.

Figure 27-8 This geyser in Yellowstone Geyser Basin, Wyoming, indicates that a magma chamber, a potential source of geothermal power, exists in this area.

Alternative Sources of Power

Another thing humans could do to reduce air pollution is to switch to other power sources such as solar, wind, nuclear, and geothermal power. **Figure 27-8** shows a geyser that indicates a possible source of geothermal power. However, these alternative sources have disadvantages, too. And, even if everyone agreed to make changes, it would take years for some areas to change. This is because many people, especially in the midwestern states, depend on coal-burning power plants for home heating and electricity. Changing the kind of power used would be costly.

The 1990 Clean Air Act requires great reductions in auto exhaust and sulfur dioxide emissions. This will cost billions of dollars. Thousands of people have lost jobs in mining, factories, and in coal-burning power plants. However, new jobs are created as humans discover alternative sources of power.

interNET CONNECTION

Visit the Glencoe Science Web Site at **www.glencoe.com/sec/science/ca** for more information about solar cars and solar cookers. How does a solar car work? How do solar cookers concentrate solar energy?

Section Assessment

1. In what ways does air pollution affect the health of people?
2. How can changes in human activities reduce air pollution?
3. **Think Critically:** The Clean Air Act of 1970 required that coal-burning power plants use tall smokestacks so that air pollutants would be ejected high into the sky, where high-altitude winds would disperse them. Power plants in the midwestern states complied with that law, and people in eastern Canada began complaining about acid rain. Explain the connection.
4. **Skill Builder**
   Making and Using Graphs Make a bar graph of **Figure 27-2** that shows sources of smog on the *x*-axis and percent contribution of smog on the *y*-axis. How much more smog is created by cars than industries? If you need help, refer to Making and Using Graphs in the **Skill Handbook** on page 953.

In your Science Journal, create a crossword puzzle using at least 12 important terms found in this section.

How it Works

Bee Probes

Honeybee colonies have been used for centuries to provide honey and pollinate flowers, fruit trees, and other crops. But now, scientists have found a new use for the busy insect. Honeybee colonies are used globally to indicate the presence of hazardous materials in the environment. Millions of established colonies provide constant monitoring. Because honeybees can live under many different environmental conditions, small colonies can be introduced almost anywhere hazardous substances are suspected.

Scientists at the University of Montana have designed electronic beehives (left) that provide useful information about the environment. Electronic hives record the behavior of every bee, including how often it flies, the pollen it gathers, and how the bees control the environment in the hives. Pollutants brought into the hives by the bees are detected using electronic instruments attached to the hives.

1. Bees leave the hives and pick up water, nectar, pollen, and airborne water particles.
2. When bees return to the hives, they fan their wings to control the air temperature in the hives.
3. Pollutants in the environment that were picked up by the bees are released into the air of the hives as the bees fan their wings.
4. Pollutants released by the bees are measured using chemical probes attached to the hives.
5. The chemical data are analyzed to determine what pollutants were brought into the hives from the local environment.

Career CONNECTION

Behavioral biologists usually have a bachelor's degree in biology or zoology. They enjoy observing animals for long periods of time. Write a letter to a local zoo or animal park. Ask biologists who work there to send you information about their careers and their education.

Think Critically

1. Why are bees useful animals for detecting pollution?
2. What are common causes of pollution in your area?
3. Research how a miner's canary was used to warn about hazardous substances. How is this similar to how honeybee colonies are being used?
4. Think about other environmentally sensitive organisms. In your Science Journal, write how you think other organisms could be used to protect the environment.

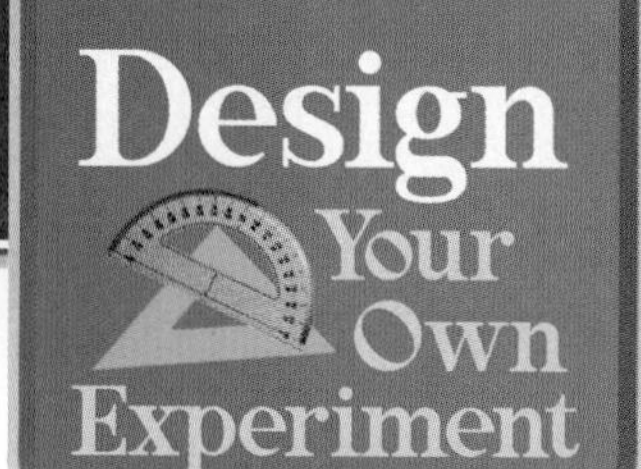

Activity 27 • 1

What's in the air?

Possible Materials

- Small box of plain gelatin
- Hot plate
- Pan or pot
- Water
- Marker
- Refrigerator
- Plastic lids (4)
- Microscope
  *Hand lens

**Alternate materials*

Have you ever gotten a particle of dust in your eye? Before it got there, it was one of the many pieces of particulate matter in the air. Whenever you dust off items in your household, you are cleaning up dust particles that settled out of the air. How often do you have to dust to keep your furniture clean? Just imagine how many pieces of particulate matter the air must hold.

Recognize the Problem

What kinds of particulate matter are in your environment? Are some areas of your environment more polluted with particulates than others?

Form a Hypothesis

Based on your knowledge of your neighborhood, hypothesize what kinds of particulate matter you will find in your environment. Will all areas in your community contain the same types and amounts of particulate matter?

Goals

- **Design an experiment** to collect and analyze particulate matter in the air in your community.
- **Use** gelatin to collect particulate matter present in the air.
- **Observe** and describe the particulate matter you collect.

Safety Precautions

 Wear a thermal mitt, safety goggles, and an apron while working with a hot plate and while pouring the gelatin from the pan or pot into the lids. Don't eat anything in the lab.

Test Your Hypothesis

Plan

1. As a group, agree upon and **write** out your hypothesis.
2. As a group, **list** the steps you need to take to test your hypothesis. Be specific, describing exactly what you will do at each step.
3. **List** your materials.
4. **Design** a data table in your Science Journal so that it is ready to use as your group collects data.
5. **Mix** the gelatin according to the directions on the box. Carefully pour a thin layer of gelatin into each lid. Use this to collect air particulate matter.
6. **Decide** where you will place each plastic lid in order to collect particulate matter in the air.
7. **Read** over your entire experiment to make sure that all steps are in a logical order.
8. **Identify** any constants, variables, and controls of the experiment.

Do

1. Make sure your teacher approves your plan before you proceed.
2. Carry out the experiment as planned.
3. While the experiment is going on, write down any observations that you make and complete the data table in your Science Journal.

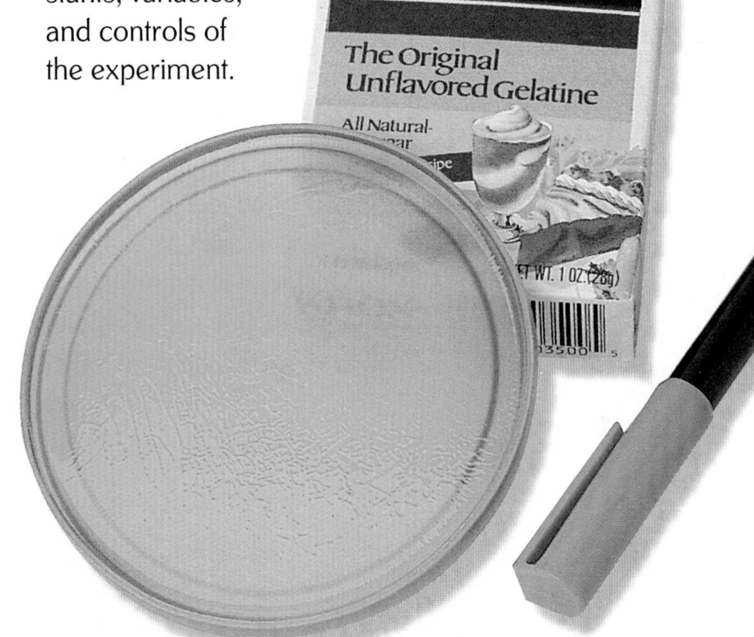

Analyze Your Data

1. **Describe** the types of materials you collected in each lid.
2. **Graph** your results using a bar graph. Place the number of particulates on the *y*-axis and the test-site location on the *x*-axis.

Draw Conclusions

1. Which test-site location yielded the most particulates? **Infer** why this is so.
2. Which of the particulates can you relate directly to the activities of humans?

27·2 Water Pollution

What You'll Learn

- Types of water pollutants and their sources
- Ways that international agreements and U.S. laws are designed to reduce water pollution
- Ways that you can help reduce water pollution

Vocabulary
Safe Drinking Water Act
Clean Water Act

Why It's Important

- Many human activities cause water pollution. There are ways you can help reduce the problem.

Causes and Effects of Water Pollution

Suppose you were hiking along a stream or lake and became thirsty. Do you think it would be safe to drink the water? In most cases, it wouldn't. Many streams and lakes in the United States are polluted, such as the one shown in **Figure 27-9.** Even streams that look clear and sparkling may not be safe for drinking.

Pollutants from humans or other organisms can get into the oceans, streams, groundwater, and lakes. Sometimes pollutants travel from one source of water to another, such as when a contaminated stream flows into a lake. There is strong reason to believe that some of these pollutants cause birth defects and health problems such as cancer, dysentery, and liver damage in humans and other animals.

Pollution Sources

How do you think pollutants get into the water? Bacteria and viruses get into the water because some cities illegally dump untreated sewage directly into the water supply. Underground septic tanks can leak, too. Radioactive materials can get into the water from leaks at nuclear power plants and radioactive waste disposal sites.

Pesticides, herbicides, and fertilizers from farms and lawns are picked up by rainwater and carried into streams. Some people dump motor oil into sewers after

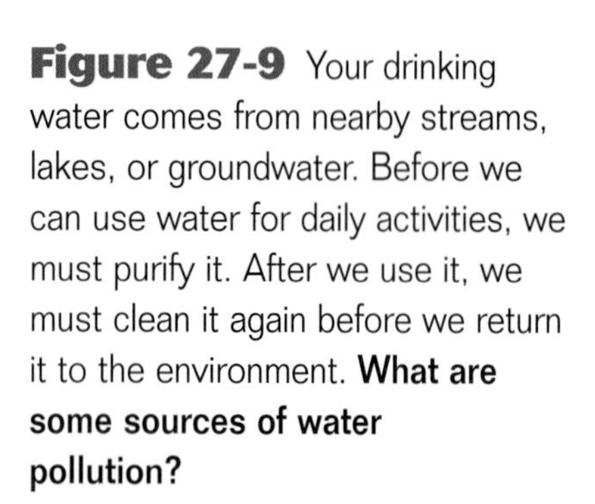

Figure 27-9 Your drinking water comes from nearby streams, lakes, or groundwater. Before we can use water for daily activities, we must purify it. After we use it, we must clean it again before we return it to the environment. **What are some sources of water pollution?**

Figure 27-10 The water hyacinth plant removes many pollutants from water. Water hyacinths can be used at wastewater-treatment facilities (shown at left) to clean water before it flows back into streams and aquifers.

they've changed the oil in their cars. Water running through mines also carries pollutants to streams and underground aquifers. Some factories illegally dump industrial chemicals directly into water. Waste from landfills and hazardous waste facilities leaks into the surrounding soil and groundwater.

Most water pollution is caused by legal, everyday activities. If left untreated, water would remain polluted after we flush our toilets, wash our hands, brush our teeth, and water our lawns. Nitrogen and phosphorus from household detergents, soaps, and other cleaning agents must be removed before water is returned to a source, such as a stream or reservoir. Water also is polluted when oil and gasoline run off of pavement, down storm sewers, and into streams. These pollutants must be removed at water-treatment facilities like those in **Figures 27-10** and **27-11.**

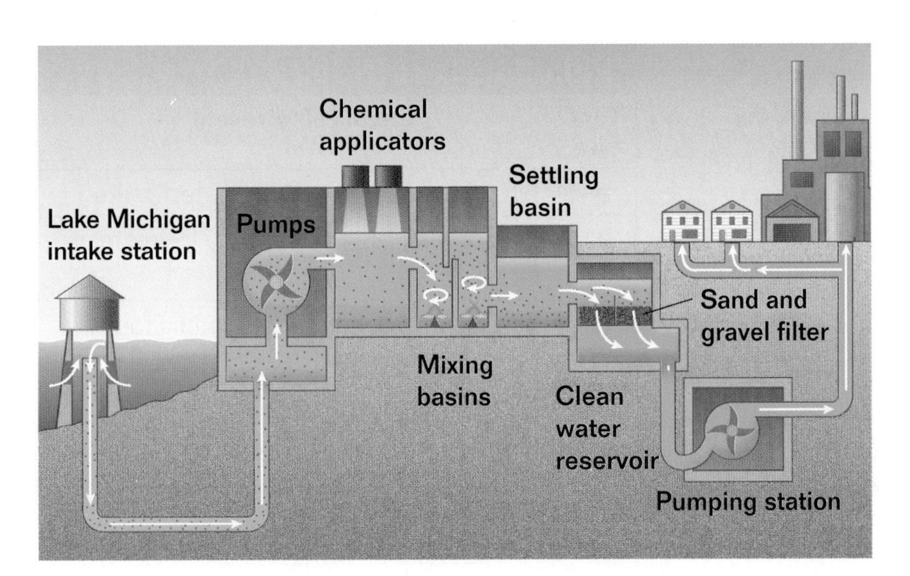

Figure 27-11 This water-purification plant in Chicago provides drinking water for millions of people. Water taken from Lake Michigan is pumped into a tank where alum, chlorine, lime, and other compounds are added to kill microorganisms. The water is thoroughly mixed, and the large particles of matter settle out. Some smaller particles are filtered by sand and gravel. Clean water is then pumped to consumers.

Reducing Water Pollution

Several countries have worked together to reduce water pollution. Let's look at one example. Lake Erie is on the border between the United States and Canada. In the 1960s, Lake Erie was so polluted by phosphorus from sewage, soaps, and fertilizers that it was turning into a green, soupy mess. Large areas of the lake bottom no longer had oxygen and, therefore, no life.

International Cooperation

In the 1970s, the United States and Canada made two water quality agreements. The two countries spent $15 billion to stop the sewage problem. Today, the green slime is gone and the fish are back. However, more than 300 human-made chemicals can still be found in Lake Erie, and some of them are hazardous. The United States and Canada are studying ways to get them out of the lake.

Problem Solving

Interpreting Pollution Sources

Water pollution comes in a variety of forms: heavy metals like lead and manganese from mines, bacteria from septic tanks, herbicides and pesticides from agriculture, thermal pollution from factories, acids from power plants and automobiles, sediments from construction sites, and so on.

In analyzing a possible source of water pollution in a river, chemists look for two types: point source and nonpoint source. Point sources occur where factories and cities pipe their untreated wastes directly into lakes and rivers. Nonpoint sources are runoff from farms, cities, mines, and construction sites. Analyze the map below and the chart of pollution test results to answer the Think Critically questions below.

Think Critically: What is the likely source of the nitrates and bacteria found at sites c and d that weren't present at sites a and b? Is there enough information to tell if this is a case of point-source or nonpoint-source pollution? Explain.

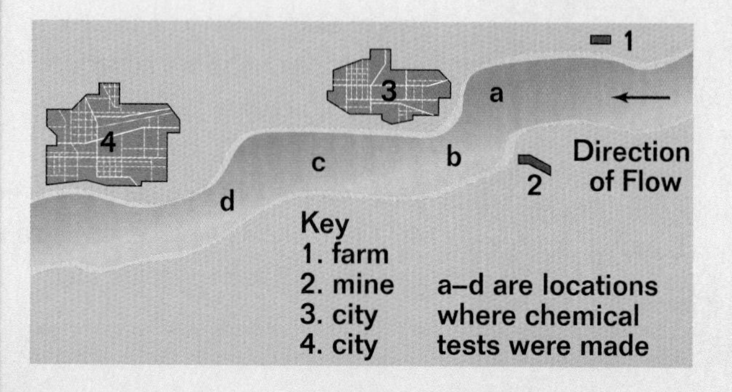

Pollution Test Results

Test Site	Chemicals Present in Water
a	nitrates commonly found in fertilizers
b	lead and nitrates commonly found in fertilizers
c	nitrates and bacteria commonly found in sewage, lead, nitrates commonly found in fertilizers
d	nitrates and bacteria commonly found in sewage, lead, nitrates commonly found in fertilizers

The U.S. Congress also has reduced water pollution by passing several laws, including the 1996 Safe Drinking Water Act amendments and the 1987 Clean Water Act.

The 1996 **Safe Drinking Water Act** amendments aim to strengthen health standards for drinking water and to protect rivers, lakes, and streams that are sources of drinking water. These amendments also provide the public with a right to know about contaminants that could be in their tap water.

Figure 27-12 Sewage, industrial wastes, and solid wastes pollute many rivers and lakes. However, these sources of pollution can be controlled and the water made safe for recreational purposes. **How does the 1987 Clean Water Act encourage communities to clean up their water?**

Clean Water Act

The 1987 **Clean Water Act** gives money to states for building sewage and wastewater-treatment facilities. The money is also for controlling runoff from streets, mines, and farms. Runoff caused up to half of the water pollution in the United States before 1987. This act also requires states to develop quality standards for all their streams.

The U.S. Environmental Protection Agency (EPA) makes sure that cities comply with both the Safe Drinking Water Act and the Clean Water Act. Most cities and states are working hard to clean up their water. Look at **Figure 27-12.** Many streams that once were heavily polluted by sewage and industrial wastes are now safe for recreation.

However, much remains to be done. For example, the EPA recently discovered that 30 percent of the nation's rivers, 42 percent of its lakes, and 32 percent of its estuaries are still polluted from farm runoff and municipal sewage overflows from cities. An estimated 40 percent of the country's freshwater supply is still not usable because of pollution. Since 1972, the U.S. government has spent more than 260 billion dollars on sewage system improvements. However, more than 1000 cities still have substandard water-treatment facilities.

Amphibian Decline

All over the world, the amphibian population is declining. Scientists do not know for sure what is causing the decline, but some suspect it is caused by pollution. What are amphibians? What types of pollution might affect amphibians?

Bioremediation

Bioremediation (*bio* = "life"; *remediation* = "the act of remedying, or fixing a problem") uses organisms to consume or make a hazardous substance harmless. Examples of resources cleaned by bioremediation include soil, sediment, groundwater, and surface water. Some hazardous substances that are removed by bioremediation include oil, gasoline, and other organic pollutants.

Microorganisms

Did you know that bacteria are organisms that are helpful in cleaning up the environment? Although these organisms are so small you would need a microscope to see them, they often are able to consume or make some toxic wastes harmless. Bacteria already may be present in a contaminated site or may be brought in from the outside. For these microorganisms to be successful, they must be kept healthy enough to consume waste in a reasonable amount of time.

One way that water is treated to remove pollutants like oil and gasoline is to inject it with oxygen. The oxygen creates a healthy environment for some types of bacteria. Nutrients such as nitrogen and phosphorus also are necessary for the bacteria. These nutrients may be in the contaminated site already or pumped in if the site does not contain enough of them. Contaminated groundwater is first pumped to the surface using extraction wells, then pretreated with concentrated bacteria to remove some of the waste. The groundwater is then injected back underground and oxygenated. The oxygen

Figure 27-13 Bioremediation can help clean water right at the location of a contaminated site.

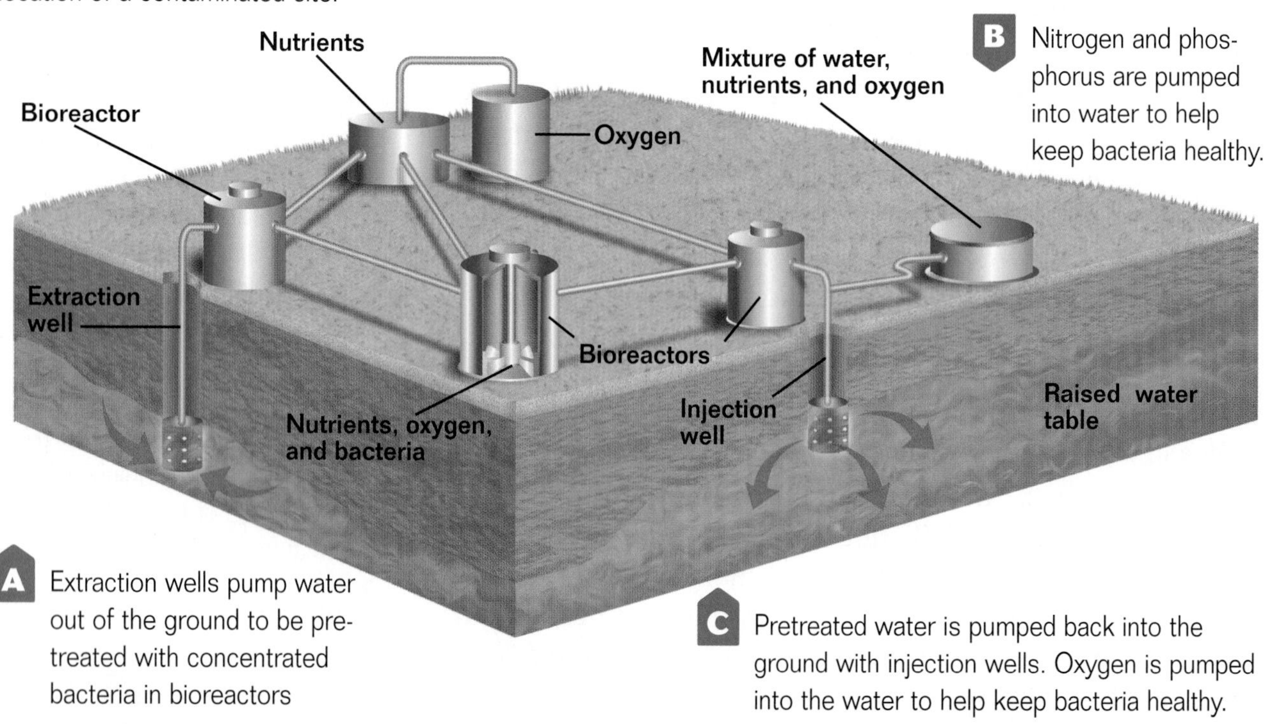

B Nitrogen and phosphorus are pumped into water to help keep bacteria healthy.

A Extraction wells pump water out of the ground to be pretreated with concentrated bacteria in bioreactors

C Pretreated water is pumped back into the ground with injection wells. Oxygen is pumped into the water to help keep bacteria healthy.

stimulates bacteria to consume or break down the remaining waste. **Figure 27-13** shows the basic components of *in situ* bioremediation, which means that the decontamination can take place right at the field site.

Observing Water Hardness

Procedure

1. When minerals such as calcium carbonate, magnesium carbonate, or sulfates are dissolved in water, the water is said to be *hard.* This is a type of natural pollution that occurs in some areas.
2. Use small containers such as baby food jars to collect samples of water from the tap, a nearby pond or well, and a local stream.
3. Add one drop of liquid soap to each jar.
4. Cap each container tightly and shake it rapidly.
5. Observe how many soapsuds are produced in each container.

Analysis

1. Which of your water samples had the hardest water? (Hint: The container with the most suds contains the softest water.)
2. Infer what problems might be caused by having a hard water supply in your home or community.

How can you help?

As you have discovered in this chapter, humans often are the cause of our environmental problems. But, we also are the solution. What can you do to help?

Dispose of Wastes Safely

When you dispose of household chemicals such as paint and motor oil, don't pour them down the drain or onto the ground. Also, don't put them out to be picked up with your other trash.

Hazardous wastes poured directly onto the ground move through the soil and eventually reach the groundwater below. When you pour them down the drain, they flow through the sewer, through the wastewater-treatment plant, and into wherever the wastewater is drained, usually a stream. This is how rivers become polluted. If you put hazardous wastes out with the trash, they end up in landfills, where they may leak out.

What should you do with these wastes? First, read the label on the container for instructions on disposal. Don't throw the container into the trash if the label specifies a different method of disposal. Recycle if you can. Many cities have recycling facilities for metal, glass, and plastic containers. Store chemical wastes so that they can't leak. If you live in a city, call the sewage office, water office, or garbage disposal service and ask them how to safely dispose of these wastes in your area.

We all must do our part to help conserve water and reduce water pollution. Consider some changes you can make in your life that will make a difference.

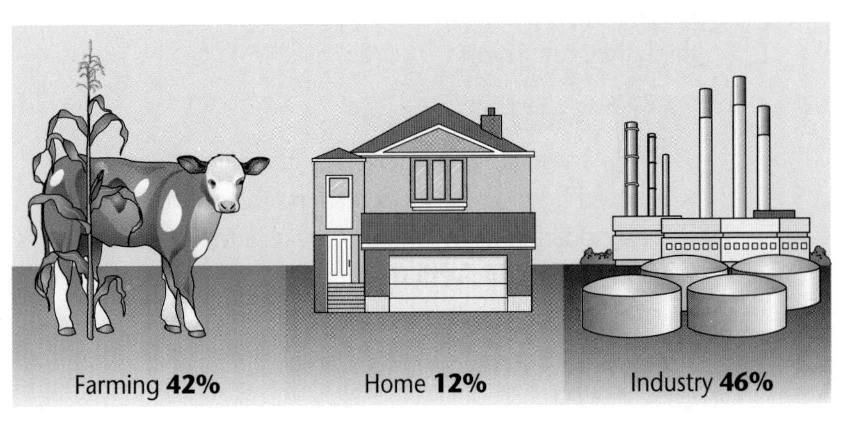

Figure 27-14 The industries that produce the products you use each day consume nearly half of the fresh water used in the United States.

Figure 27-15 Simple things you can do to use less water include taking a shower instead of a bath and turning off the water while brushing your teeth.

Conserve Energy and Water

Another way you can reduce water pollution is to conserve energy. Decreasing the use of fuels reduces the amount of acid rain that will fall into forests and streams. Decreasing your power usage will help reduce the input of hazardous materials into the environment.

Another way you can help is to conserve water. Look at **Figure 27-14.** How much water do you use every day? You use water every time you flush a toilet, take a bath, clean your clothes, wash dishes, wash a car, or use a hose or lawn sprinkler. Typical U.S. citizens, like the one shown in **Figure 27-15,** use from 380 L to 950 L of water every day.

All of this water must be purified before it reaches your home. It takes a lot of energy to treat water and pump it to your home. Remember, when you use energy, you add to the pollution problem.

Section Assessment

1. What are three things you can do to help reduce water pollution?
2. What is the difference between point-source and nonpoint-source pollution?
3. What hazardous substances can be removed from water using bioremediation?
4. **Think Critically:** Southern Florida is home to millions of people, dairy farms, and sugarcane fields. It is also the location of Everglades National Park—a shallow river system with highly polluted waters. What kinds of pollutants do you think are in the Everglades? How do you think they got there?
5. **Skill Builder**
Interpreting Data Have you ever wondered how scientists determine the sources of water pollution in a lake or a river? Do the **Chapter 27 Skill Activity** on page 988 to see an example of how this is done.

Using Computers

Word Processing Design a pamphlet to inform people how they can reduce the amount of water they use. Be creative and include graphics in your pamphlet. Use word-processing utilities to check your spelling and grammar. If you need help, refer to page 968.

Water Use

Materials

- Home water meter

How much water goes down the drain at your house? Did you know that up to 75 percent of the water used in homes is used in the bathroom? Flushing the toilet accounts for 50 percent of that water. The rest is for bathing, showering, washing hands, and brushing teeth. By learning to read a water meter, you can find out how much water your family uses.

What You'll Investigate

How much water does your family use?

Goals

- **Calculate** your family's water usage.
- **Infer** how your family can conserve water.

Background

There are several different types of water meters. Meter A has six dials. As water moves through the meter, the pointers on the dials rotate. To read a meter like A, find the dial in A with the lowest denomination, which in this case is 10. Record the last number that the pointer on that dial has passed. Continue this process for each dial in the meter. Meter A therefore shows 28 853 gallons. Meter B is read like a digital watch. It indicates 1959.9 cubic feet. Meter C is similar to meter B but indicates water use in cubic meters. If you have a meter that is different from these, contact your area's water department for help on reading your meter.

A

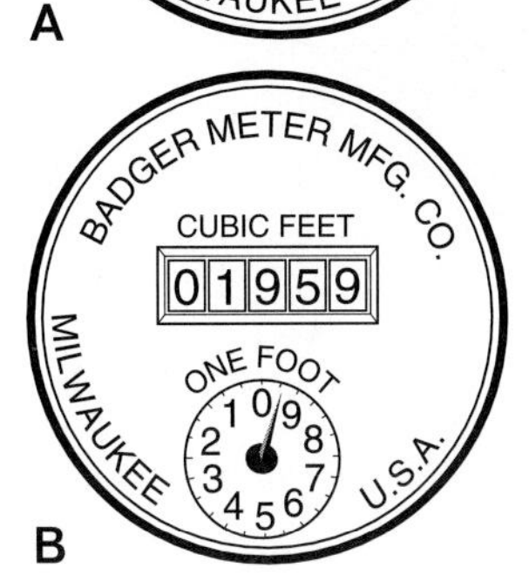

B

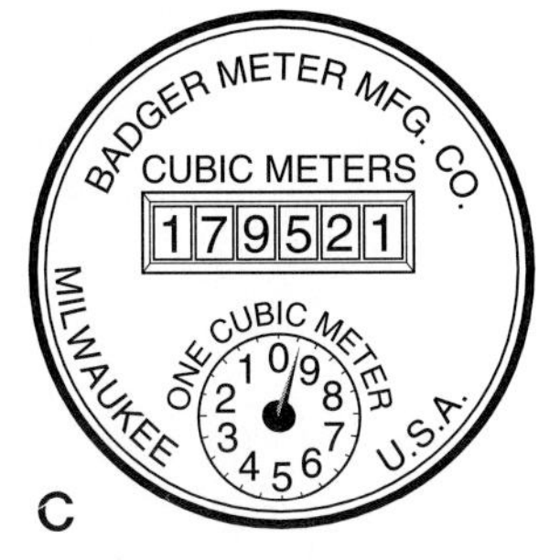

C

Procedure

1. **Design** a data table and **record** your home water meter reading at the same time of the day for eight days.
2. **Subtract** the previous day's reading to determine the amount of water used each day.
3. **Record** how much water is used in your home each day. Also, record the activities in your home that use water each day.
4. **Plot your data** on a graph like the one shown below. Label the vertical axis with the units used by your meter.

Conclude and Apply

1. **Calculate** the average amount of water each person in your family used during the week by dividing the total amount of water used by the number of persons.
2. **Infer** how the time of year might affect the rate at which your family uses water.
3. What are some things your family could do to conserve water?

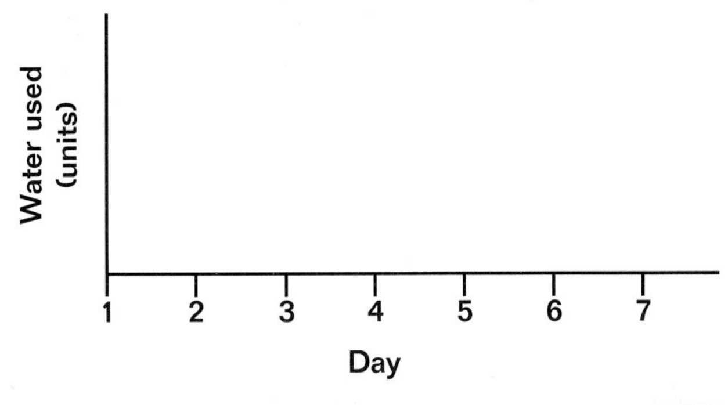

Chapter 27 Reviewing Main Ideas

For a **preview** of this chapter, study this Reviewing Main Ideas before you read the chapter. After you have studied this chapter, you can use the Reviewing Main Ideas to **review** the chapter.

The Glencoe MindJogger, Audiocassettes, and CD-ROM provide additional opportunities for review.

Section
27-1 CAUSES OF AIR POLLUTION

Many human activities impact our air and water. **Smog, acid rain,** and water pollution are consequences of our activities. When fossil fuels are burned, polluting chemicals are added to the air. Construction dust and smoke from burning fuels pollute the air. Nature also contributes to air pollution. Air pollutants don't have boundaries. They float between states and countries. National and international cooperation is necessary to reduce the problem. The purpose of the **Clean Air Act** is to reduce problem chemicals in the air. ***Which national agency has the job ofmonitoring progress toward the goals of the Clean Air Act?***

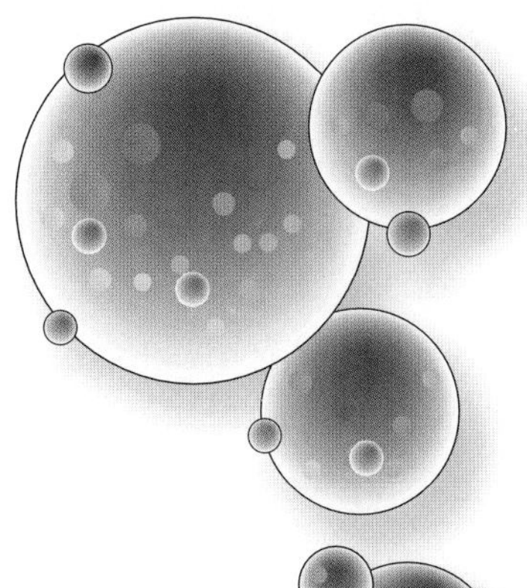

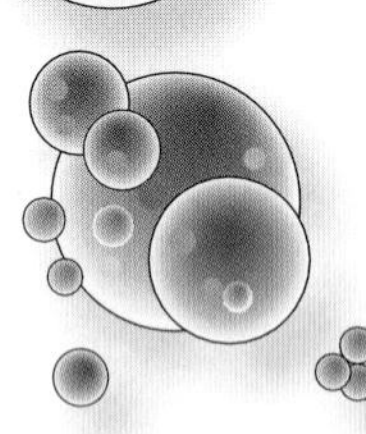

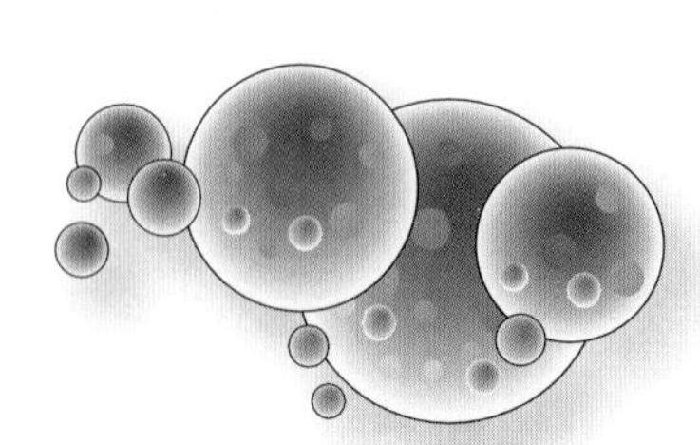

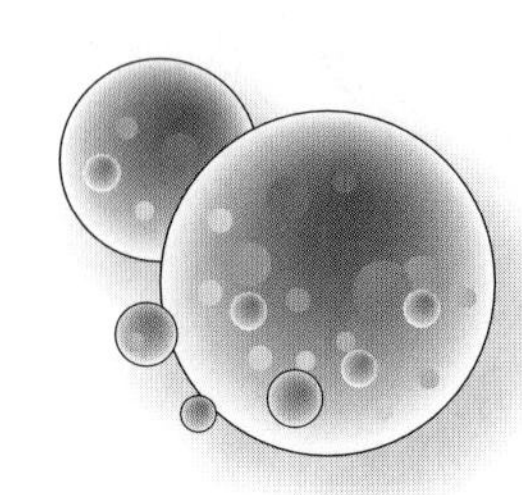

Reading Check

Explain how the topics of air and water pollution might be approached differently in a health textbook than in a science book.

Section

27-2 WATER POLLUTION

Water pollution has many sources. A few of these sources include underground septic tanks that leak; runoff of pesticides, herbicides, and fertilizers from lawns and farms; and even water flushed down toilets. National and international cooperation is necessary if water pollution is to be reduced. In the United States, the **Safe Drinking Water Act** and the **Clean Water Act** set up standards for sewage and wastewater-treatment facilities and for runoff from roadways and farms. Most waterways are cleaner now than before these acts were voted on by Congress. But, many of the nation's streams, rivers, and lakes are still polluted. ***How can oil dripping from a car eventually pollute a stream?***

Career CONNECTION

Craig Cox, Hydrogeologist

As a hydrogeologist, Craig Cox works with companies to help prevent groundwater contamination. Unused chemicals can soak into the ground, just like water can, contaminating the water table. Craig examines how industries dispose of dangerous materials to ensure they don't drain into the water table, contaminating drinking water. ***What would a hydrogeologist look for to determine the danger of groundwater being contaminated by a chemical spill?***

Chapter 27 Assessment

Using Vocabulary

a. acid
b. acid rain
c. base
d. Clean Air Act
e. Clean Water Act
f. pH scale
g. photochemical smog
h. Safe Drinking Water Act
i. scrubber
j. sulfurous smog

Using the list above, replace the underlined words with the correct Vocabulary words.

1. Smog that forms with the aid of light contains ozone near Earth's surface.
2. Acidic rain, snow, sleet, or hail is created when sulfur dioxide combines with moisture in the air.
3. A law passed to protect air in the United States regulates car manufacturers.
4. A device that lowers sulfur emissions from coal-burning power plants increases the pH of smoke.
5. A substance with a low pH number can be toxic to organisms.

Checking Concepts

Choose the word or phrase that best answers the question.

6. What causes more smog pollution than any other source?
   A) power plants
   B) burning wastes
   C) industries
   D) cars
7. What forms when chemicals react with sunlight?
   A) pH
   B) photochemical smog
   C) sulfurous smog
   D) acid rain
8. What are substances with a low pH known as?
   A) neutral
   B) acidic
   C) dense
   D) basic
9. What combines with moisture in the air to form acid rain?
   A) ozone
   B) sulfur dioxide
   C) lead
   D) oxygen
10. The industries that produce the products you use each day consume how much of the freshwater used in the United States?
    A) one-tenth
    B) one-half
    C) one-third
    D) two-thirds
11. Which law was enacted to reduce the level of car emissions?
    A) Clean Water Act
    B) Clean Air Act
    C) Safe Drinking Water Act
    D) Hazardous Waste Act
12. What is the pH of acid rain?
    A) less than 5.6
    B) between 5.6 and 7.0
    C) greater than 7.0
    D) greater than 9.5
13. What kind of pollution are airborne solids that range in size from large grains to microscopic?
    A) pH
    B) ozone
    C) particulate
    D) photo
14. What causes most water pollution?
    A) illegal dumping
    B) industrial chemicals
    C) everyday water use in the home
    D) wastewater-treatment facilities
15. Which act gives money to local governments to treat wastewater?
    A) Clean Water Act
    B) Clean Air Act
    C) Safe Drinking Water Act
    D) Hazardous Waste Act

Thinking Critically

16. How might cities with smog problems lessen the dangers to people who live and work in the cities?
17. How are industries both helpful and harmful to humans?

18. How do plants help reduce water pollution?
19. Thermal pollution occurs when heated water is dumped into a nearby body of water. What effects does this type of pollution have on organisms living in the water?
20. What steps might a community in a desert area take to cope with water-supply problems?

Developing Skills

If you need help, refer to the Skill Handbook.

21. **Hypothesizing:** Earth's surface is nearly 75 percent water. Yet, much of this water is not available for many uses. Explain.
22. **Recognizing Cause and Effect:** What effect will an increase in the human population have on the need for freshwater?
23. **Concept Mapping:** Complete a concept map of the water cycle. Indicate how humans interrupt the cycle. Use the following phrases: *evaporation occurs, purified, drinking water, atmospheric water, wastewater, precipitation falls,* and *groundwater or surface water.*

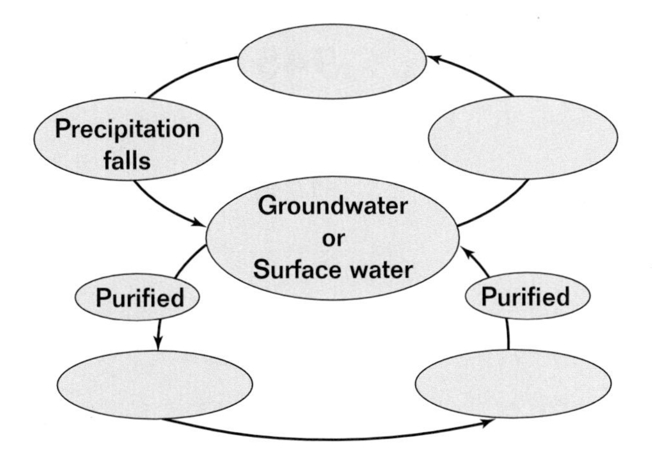

Test-Taking Tip

Use as Much Time as You Can You will not get extra points for finishing early. Work slowly and carefully on any test and make sure you don't make careless errors because you are hurrying to finish.

Test Practice

Use these questions to test your Science Proficiency.

1. Both acid rain and photochemical smog can be reduced by limiting emissions of a certain chemical from the exhaust of cars. Which chemical is it?
   A) sulfur
   B) ozone
   C) carbon
   D) nitrogen oxide
2. Determine approximately how much more acidic lemon juice is than milk. Use **Figure 27-4** and the information in Using Math in Section 27-1 to help you answer this question.
   A) 100
   B) 10 000
   C) 1000
   D) 100 000
3. All of the following events happen when you inhale acid rain. Which event is the **LAST** in the series of events?
   A) Stress is put on your heart.
   B) Acid is deposited deep inside your lungs.
   C) Your lungs become irritated.
   D) Oxygen absorption by the lungs is difficult.

Appendices

Appendix A

Safety in the Science Classroom

1. Always obtain your teacher's permission to begin an investigation.
2. Study the procedure. If you have questions, ask your teacher. Be sure you understand any safety symbols shown on the page.
3. Use the safety equipment provided for you. Goggles and a safety apron should be worn during an investigation.
4. Always slant test tubes away from yourself and others when heating them.
5. Never eat or drink in the lab, and never use lab glassware as food or drink containers. Never inhale chemicals. Do not taste any substances or draw any material into a tube with your mouth.
6. If you spill any chemical, wash it off immediately with water. Report the spill immediately to your teacher.
7. Know the location and proper use of the fire extinguisher, safety shower, fire blanket, first aid kit, and fire alarm.
8. Keep all materials away from open flames. Tie back long hair and loose clothing.
9. If a fire should break out in the classroom, or if your clothing should catch fire, smother it with the fire blanket or a coat, or get under a safety shower. NEVER RUN.
10. Report any accident or injury, no matter how small, to your teacher.

Follow these procedures as you clean up your work area.

1. Turn off the water and gas. Disconnect electrical devices.
2. Return all materials to their proper places.
3. Dispose of chemicals and other materials as directed by your teacher. Place broken glass and solid substances in the proper containers. Never discard materials in the sink.
4. Clean your work area.
5. Wash your hands thoroughly after working in the laboratory.

Table A-1

First Aid	
Injury	**Safe Response**
Burns	Apply cold water. Call your teacher immediately.
Cuts and bruises	Stop any bleeding by applying direct pressure. Cover cuts with a clean dressing. Apply cold compresses to bruises. Call your teacher immediately.
Fainting	Leave the person lying down. Loosen any tight clothing and keep crowds away. Call your teacher immediately.
Foreign matter in eye	Flush with plenty of water. Use eyewash bottle or fountain.
Poisoning	Note the suspected poisoning agent and call your teacher immediately.
Any spills on skin	Flush with large amounts of water or use safety shower. Call your teacher immediately.

Appendix B

SI/Metric to English Conversions

	When you want to convert:	To:	Multiply by:
Length	inches	centimeters	2.54
	centimeters	inches	0.39
	feet	meters	0.30
	meters	feet	3.28
	yards	meters	0.91
	meters	yards	1.09
	miles	kilometers	1.61
	kilometers	miles	0.62
Mass and Weight*	ounces	grams	28.35
	grams	ounces	0.04
	pounds	kilograms	0.45
	kilograms	pounds	2.2
	tons (short)	tonnes (metric tons)	0.91
	tonnes (metric tons)	tons (short)	1.10
	pounds	newtons	4.45
	newtons	pounds	0.23
Volume	cubic inches	cubic centimeters	16.39
	cubic centimeters	cubic inches	0.06
	cubic feet	cubic meters	0.03
	cubic meters	cubic feet	35.30
	liters	quarts	1.06
	liters	gallons	0.26
	gallons	liters	3.78
Area	square inches	square centimeters	6.45
	square centimeters	square inches	0.16
	square feet	square meters	0.09
	square meters	square feet	10.76
	square miles	square kilometers	2.59
	square kilometers	square miles	0.39
	hectares	acres	2.47
	acres	hectares	0.40
Temperature	Fahrenheit	5/9 (°F − 32) =	Celsius
	Celsius	9/5 (°C) + 32 =	Fahrenheit

*Weight as measured in standard Earth gravity

Appendix C

SI Units of Measurement

Table C-1

SI Base Units					
Measurement	**Unit**	**Symbol**	**Measurement**	**Unit**	**Symbol**
length	meter	m	temperature	kelvin	K
mass	kilogram	kg	amount of substance	mole	mol
time	second	s			

Table C-2

Units Derived from SI Base Units		
Measurement	**Unit**	**Symbol**
energy	joule	J
force	newton	N
frequency	hertz	Hz
potential difference	volt	V
power	watt	W
pressure	pascal	Pa

Table C-3

Common SI Prefixes					
Prefix	**Symbol**	**Multiplier**	**Prefix**	**Symbol**	**Multiplier**
	Greater than 1			Less than 1	
mega-	M	1 000 000	*deci-*	d	0.1
kilo-	k	1 000	*centi-*	c	0.01
hecto-	h	100	*milli-*	m	0.001
deca-	da	10	*micro-*	μ	0.000 001

Appendix D

Care and Use of a Microscope

Eyepiece Contains a magnifying lens you look through

Arm Supports the body tube

Low-power objective Contains the lens with low-power magnification

Stage clips Hold the microscope slide in place

Coarse adjustment Focuses the image under low power

Fine adjustment Sharpens the image under high and low magnification

Body tube Connects the eyepiece to the revolving nosepiece

Revolving nosepiece Holds and turns the objectives into viewing position

High-power objective Contains the lens with the highest magnification

Stage Supports the microscope slide

Light source Allows light to reflect upward through the diaphragm, the specimen, and the lenses

Base Provides support for the microscope

Care of a Microscope

1. Always carry the microscope holding the arm with one hand and supporting the base with the other hand.
2. Don't touch the lenses with your fingers.
3. Never lower the coarse adjustment knob when looking through the eyepiece lens.
4. Always focus first with the low-power objective.
5. Don't use the coarse adjustment knob when the high-power objective is in place.
6. Store the microscope covered.

Using a Microscope

1. Place the microscope on a flat surface that is clear of objects. The arm should be toward you.
2. Look through the eyepiece. Adjust the diaphragm so that light comes through the opening in the stage.
3. Place a slide on the stage so that the specimen is in the field of view. Hold it firmly in place by using the stage clips.
4. Always focus first with the coarse adjustment and the low-power objective lens. Once the object is in focus on low power, turn the nosepiece until the high-power objective is in place. Use ONLY the fine adjustment to focus with the high-power objective lens.

Making a Wet-Mount Slide

1. Carefully place the item you want to look at in the center of a clean, glass slide. Make sure the sample is thin enough for light to pass through.
2. Use a dropper to place one or two drops of water on the sample.
3. Hold a clean coverslip by the edges and place it at one edge of the drop of water. Slowly lower the coverslip onto the drop of water until it lies flat.
4. If you have too much water or a lot of air bubbles, touch the edge of a paper towel to the edge of the coverslip to draw off extra water and force out air.

Appendix E

Diversity of Life: Classification of Living Organisms

Scientists use a six-kingdom system of classification of organisms. In this system, there are two kingdoms of organisms, Kingdoms Archaebacteria and Eubacteria, which contain organisms that do not have a nucleus and lack membrane-bound structures in the cytoplasm of their cells. The members of the other four kingdoms have cells which contain a nucleus and structures in the cytoplasm that are surrounded by membranes. These kingdoms are Kingdom Protista, Kingdom Fungi, the Kingdom Plantae, and the Kingdom Animalia.

Kingdom Archaebacteria

One-celled prokaryotes; absorb food from surroundings or make their own food by chemosynthesis; found in extremely harsh environments including salt ponds, hot springs, swamps, and deep-sea hydrothermal vents.

Kingdom Eubacteria

Cyanobacteria one-celled prokaryotes; make their own food; contain chlorophyll; some species form colonies; most are blue-green

Bacteria one-celled prokaryotes; most absorb food from their surroundings; some are photosynthetic; many are parasites; round, spiral, or rod-shaped

Kingdom Protista

Phylum Euglenophyta one-celled; can photosynthesize or take in food; most have one flagellum; euglenoids

Phylum Bacillariophyta one-celled; make their own food through photosynthesis; have unique double shells made of silica; diatoms

Phylum Dinoflagellata one-celled; make their own food through photosynthesis; contain red pigments; have two flagella; dinoflagellates

Phylum Chlorophyta one-celled, many-celled, or colonies; contain chlorophyll; make their own food; live on land, in fresh water, or salt water; green algae

Phylum Rhodophyta most are many-celled; photosynthetic; contain red pigments; most live in deep saltwater environments; red algae

Phylum Phaeophyta most are many-celled; photosynthetic; contain brown pigments; most live in saltwater environments; brown algae

Phylum Foraminifera many-celled; take in food; primarily marine; shells constructed of calcium carbonate, or made from grains of sand; forams

Phylum Myxomycota
Slime Mold
Magnification: 5×

Phylum Chlorophyta
Desmids Magnification: 50×

Appendix E

Phylum Rhizopoda one-celled; take in food; move by means of pseudopods; free-living or parasitic; amoebas

Phylum Zoomastigina one-celled; take in food; have one or more flagella; free-living or parasitic; zoomastigotes

Phylum Ciliophora one-celled; take in food; have large numbers of cilia; ciliates

Phylum Sporozoa one-celled; take in food; no means of movement; parasites in animals; sporozoans

Phylum Myxomycota and Acrasiomycota: one- or many-celled; absorb food; change form during life cycle; cellular and plasmodial slime molds

Phylum Oomycota many-celled; live in fresh or salt water; are either parasites or decomposers; water molds, rusts and downy mildews

Kingdom Fungi

Phylum Zygomycota many-celled; absorb food; spores are produced in sporangia; zygote fungi; bread mold

Phylum Ascomycota one- and many-celled; absorb food; spores produced in asci; sac fungi; yeast

Phylum Basidiomycota many-celled; absorb food; spores produced in basidia; club fungi; mushrooms

Phylum Deuteromycota: members with unknown reproductive structures; imperfect fungi; penicillin

Lichens organisms formed by symbiotic relationship between an ascomycote or a basidiomycote and green alga or cyanobacterium

Kingdom Plantae

Non-seed Plants

Division Bryophyta nonvascular plants; reproduce by spores produced in capsules; many-celled; green; grow in moist land environments; mosses and liverworts

Division Lycophyta many-celled vascular plants; spores produced in conelike structures; live on land; are photosynthetic; club mosses

Division Sphenophyta vascular plants; ribbed and jointed stems; scalelike leaves; spores produced in conelike structures; horsetails

Division Pterophyta vascular plants; leaves called fronds; spores produced in clusters of sporangia called sori; live on land or in water; ferns

Division Bryophyta
Liverwort

Lichens
British soldier lichen × 3

Appendix E

Seed Plants

Division Ginkgophyta: deciduous gymnosperms; only one living species; fan-shaped leaves with branching veins; reproduces with seeds; ginkgos

Division Cycadophyta: palmlike gymnosperms; large featherlike leaves; produce seeds in cones; cycads

Division Coniferophyta: deciduous or evergreen gymnosperms; trees or shrubs; needlelike or scalelike leaves; seeds produced in cones; conifers

Division Gnetophyta: shrubs or woody vines; seeds produced in cones; division contains only three genera; gnetum

Division Anthophyta: dominant group of plants; ovules protected in an ovary; sperm carried to ovules by pollen tube; produce flowers and seeds in fruits; flowering plants

Kingdom Animalia

Phylum Porifera: aquatic organisms that lack true tissues and organs; they are asymmetrical and sessile; sponges

Phylum Cnidaria: radially symmetrical organisms; have a digestive cavity with one opening; most have tentacles armed with stinging cells; live in aquatic environments singly or in colonies; includes jellyfish, corals, hydra, and sea anemones

Phylum Platyhelminthes: bilaterally symmetrical worms; have flattened bodies; digestive system has one opening; parasitic and free-living species; flatworms

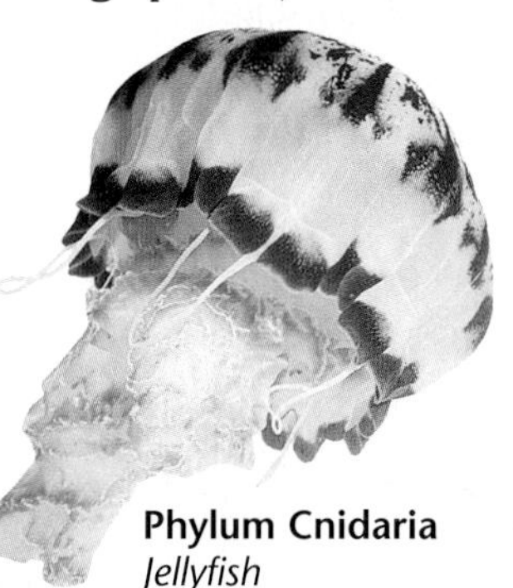

Phylum Cnidaria
Jellyfish

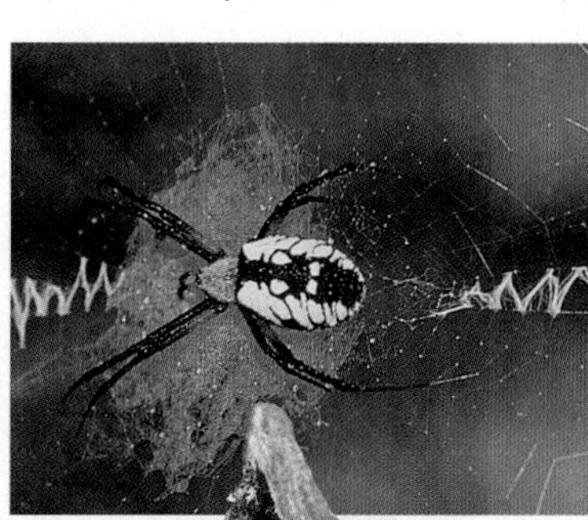

Phylum Arthopoda
Orb Weaver Spider

Phylum Arthropoda
Hermit Crab

Division Coniferophyta
Pine cone

Division Anthophyta
Strawberry Blossoms

Division Anthophyta
Strawberries

Phylum Mollusca
Florida Fighting Conch

Phylum Annelida
Sabellid Worms Feather Duster

Appendix E

Phylum Nematoda: round, bilaterally symmetrical body; digestive system with two openings; many parasitic forms but mostly free-living roundworms

Phylum Mollusca: soft-bodied animals, many with a hard shell; a mantle covers the soft body; aquatic and terrestrial species; includes clams, snails, squid, and octopuses

Phylum Annelida: bilaterally symmetrical worms; have round, segmented bodies; terrestrial and aquatic species; includes earthworms, leeches, and marine polychaetes

Phylum Arthropoda: largest phylum of organisms; have segmented bodies; pairs of jointed appendages; have hard exoskeletons; terrestrial and aquatic species; includes insects, crustaceans, spiders, and horseshoe crabs

Phylum Echinodermata: marine organisms; have spiny or leathery skin; water-vascular system with tube feet; radial symmetry; includes sea stars, sand dollars, and sea urchins

Phylum Chordata: organisms with internal skeletons; specialized body systems; paired appendages; all at some time have a notochord, dorsal nerve cord, gill slits, and a tail; include fish, amphibians, reptiles, birds, and mammals

Phylum Arthropoda
Giant Swallowtail Butterfly

Phylum Echinodermata
Blood Sea Star and Red Sea Urchin

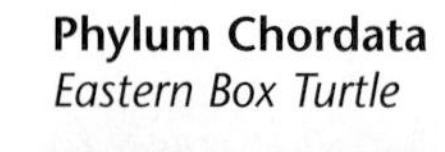

Phylum Chordata
Eastern Box Turtle

Phylum Chordata
Lemon Butterfly fish

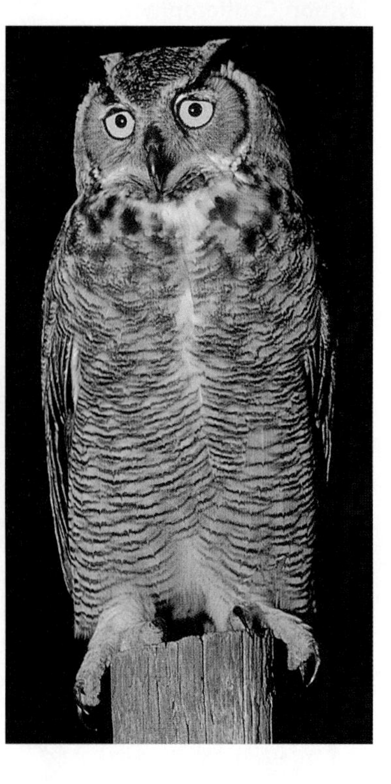

Phylum Chordata
Great Horned Owl

Appendix F

Minerals

Mineral (formula)	Color	Streak	Hardness	Breakage pattern	Uses and other properties
graphite (C)	black to gray	black to gray	1–1.5	basal cleavage (scales)	pencil lead, lubricants for locks, rods to control some small nuclear reactions, battery poles
galena (PbS)	gray	gray to black	2.5	cubic cleavage perfect	source of lead, used in pipes, shields for X rays, fishing equipment sinkers
hematite (Fe_2O_3)	black or reddish brown	reddish brown	5.5–6.5	irregular fracture	source of iron; converted to "pig" iron, made into steel
magnetite (Fe_3O_4)	black	black	6	conchoidal fracture	source of iron, naturally magnetic, called lodestone
pyrite (FeS_2)	light, brassy, yellow	greenish black	6–6.5	uneven fracture	source of iron, "fool's gold"
talc ($Mg_3Si_4O_{10}(OH)_2$)	white greenish	white	1	cleavage in one direction	used for talcum powder, sculptures, paper, and tabletops
gypsum ($CaSO_4 \cdot 2H_2O$)	colorless, gray, white brown	white	2	basal cleavage	used in plaster of paris and dry wall for building construction
sphalerite (ZnS)	brown, reddish brown, greenish	light to dark brown	3.5–4	cleavage in six directions	main ore of zinc; used in paints, dyes and medicine
muscovite ($KAl_3Si_3O_{10}(OH)_2$)	white, light gray, yellow, rose, green	colorless	2–2.5	basal cleavage	occurs in large flexible plates; used as an insulator in electrical equipment, lubricant
biotite ($K(Mg, Fe)_3(AlSi_3O_{10})(OH)_2$)	black to dark brown	colorless	2.5–3	basal cleavage	occurs in large flexible plates
halite (NaCl)	colorless, red, white, blue	colorless	2.5	cubic cleavage	salt; soluble in water; a preservative

Appendix F

Minerals

Mineral (formula)	Color	Streak	Hardness	Breakage pattern	Uses and other properties
calcite ($CaCO_3$)	colorless, white, pale blue	colorless, white	3	cleavage in three directions	fizzes when HCl is added; used in cements and other building materials
dolomite ($CaMg(CO_3)_2$)	colorless, white, pink green, gray black	white	3.5–4	cleavage in three directions	concrete and cement; used as an ornamental building stone
fluorite (CaF_2)	colorless, white, blue green, red yellow, purple	colorless	4	cleavage in four directions	used in the manufacture of optical equipment; glows under ultraviolet light
hornblende ($(CaNa)_{2\text{-}3}(Mg,Al,Fe)_5(Al,Si)_2Si_6O_{22}(OH)_2$)	green to black	gray to white	5–6	cleavage in two directions	will transmit light on thin edges; 6-sided cross section
feldspar ($KAlSi_3O_8$) ($NaAlSi_3O_8$) ($CaAl_2Si_2O_8$)	colorless, white to gray, green	colorless	6	two cleavage planes meet at ~90° angle	used in the manufacture of ceramics
augite ($(Ca, Na)(Mg, Fe, Al)(Al, Si)_2O_6$)	black	colorless	6	cleavage in two directions	square or 8-sided cross section
olivine ($(Mg, Fe)_2SiO_4$)	olive, green	none	6.5–7	conchoidal fracture	gemstones, refractory sand
quartz (SiO_2)	colorless, various colors	none	7	conchoidal fracture	used in glass manufacture, electronic equipment, radios, computers, watches, gemstones

Appendix G

Rocks

Rock Type	Rock Name	Characteristics
Igneous (intrusive)	Granite	Large mineral grains of quartz, feldspar, hornblende, and mica. Usually light in color.
	Diorite	Large mineral grains of feldspar, hornblende, mica. Less quartz than granite. Intermediate in color.
	Gabbro	Large mineral grains of feldspar, hornblende, augite, olivine, and mica. No quartz. Dark in color.
Igneous (extrusive)	Rhyolite	Small mineral grains of quartz, feldspar, hornblende, and mica or no visible grains. Light in color.
	Andesite	Small mineral grains of feldspar, hornblende, mica or no visible grains. Less quartz than rhyolite. Intermediate in color.
	Basalt	Small mineral grains of feldspar, hornblende, augite, olivine, mica or no visible grains. No quartz. Dark in color.
	Obsidian	Glassy texture. No visible grains. Volcanic glass. Fracture looks like broken glass.
	Pumice	Frothy texture. Floats. Usually light in color.
Sedimentary (detrital)	Conglomerate	Coarse-grained. Gravel or pebble-sized grains.
	Sandstone	Sand-sized grains 1/16 to 2 mm in size.
	Siltstone	Grains are smaller than sand but larger than clay.
	Shale	Smallest grains. Usually dark in color.
Sedimentary (chemical or biochemical)	Limestone	Major mineral is calcite. Usually forms in oceans, lakes, rivers, and caves. Often contains fossils.
	Coal	Occurs in swampy. low-lying areas. Compacted layers of organic material, mainly plant remains.
Sedimentary (chemical)	Rock Salt	Commonly forms by the evaporation of seawater.
Metamorphic (foliated)	Gneiss	Well-developed banding because of alternating layers of different minerals, usually of different colors. Common parent rock is granite.
	Schist	Well-defined parallel arrangement of flat, sheet-like minerals, mainly micas. Common parent rocks are shale, phyllite.
	Phyllite	Shiny or silky appearance. May look wrinkled. Common parent rocks are shale, slate.
	Slate	Harder, denser, and shinier than shale. Common parent rock is shale.
Metamorphic (non-foliated)	Marble	Interlocking calcite or dolomite crystals. Common parent rock is limestone.
	Soapstone	Composed mainly of the mineral talc. Soft with a greasy feel.
	Quartzite	Hard and well cemented with interlocking quartz crystals. Common parent rock is sandstone.

Appendix H

Topographic Map Symbols

Primary highway, hard surface
Secondary highway, hard surface
Light-duty road, hard or Improved surface
Unimproved road
Railroad: single track and multiple track
Railroads in juxtaposition

Buildings
Schools, church, and cemetery — cem
Buildings (barn, warehouse, etc)
Wells other than water (labeled as to type) — oil, gas, water
Tanks: oil, water, etc. (labeled only if water)
Located or landmark object; windmill
Open pit, mine, or quarry; prospect

Marsh (swamp)
Wooded marsh
Woods or brushwood
Vineyard
Land subject to controlled inundation
Submerged marsh
Mangrove
Orchard
Scrub
Urban area

Spot elevation — ×7369
Water elevation — 670

Index contour
Supplementary contour
Intermediate contour
Depression contours

Boundaries: National
State
County, parish, municipal
Civil township, precinct, town, barrio
Incorporated city, village, town, hamlet
Reservation, National or State
Small park, cemetery, airport, etc.
Land grant
Township or range line, United States land survey
Township or range line, approximate location

Perennial streams
Elevated aqueduct
Water well and spring
Small rapids
Large rapids
Intermittent lake
Intermittent streams
Aqueduct tunnel
Glacier
Small falls
Large falls
Dry lake bed

Appendix I

Weather Map Symbols

Sample Plotted Report at Each Station

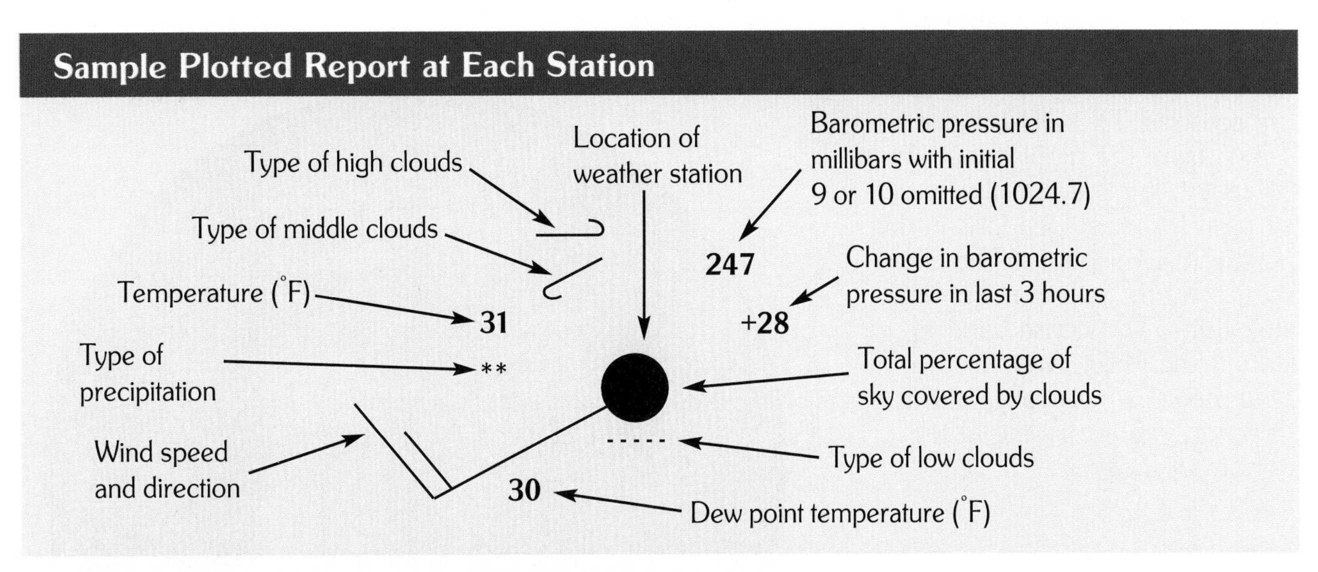

Sample Plotted Report at Each Station

Precipitation	Wind Speed and direction	Sky coverage	Some types of high clouds
≡ Fog	0 knots; calm	No cover	Scattered cirrus
★ Snow	1-2 knots	1/10 or less	Dense cirrus in patches
● Rain	3-7 knots	2/10 to 3/10	Veil of cirrus covering entire sky
Thunder-storm	8-12 knots	4/10	Cirrus not covering entire sky
, Drizzle	23-17 knots	1/2	
▽ Showers	17-22 knots	6/10	
	23-27 knots	7/10	
	48-52 knots	Overcast with openings	
	1 knot = 1.852 km/h	Complete overcast	

Some types of middle clouds	Some types of low clouds	Fronts and pressure systems	
Thin altostratus layer	Cumulus of fair weather	(H) or High (L) or Low	Center of high-or low-pressure system
Thick altostratus layer	Stratocumulus		Cold front
Thin altostratus in patches	Fractocumulus of bad weather		Warm Front
Thin altostratus in bands	Stratus of fair weather		Occluded front
			Stationary front

Appendix J

Star Charts

Shown here are star charts for viewing stars in the northern hemisphere during the four different seasons. These charts are drawn from the night sky at about 35° north latitude, but they can be used for most locations in the northern hemisphere. The lines on the charts outline major constellations. The dense band of stars is the Milky Way. To use, hold the chart vertically, with the direction you are facing at the bottom of the map.

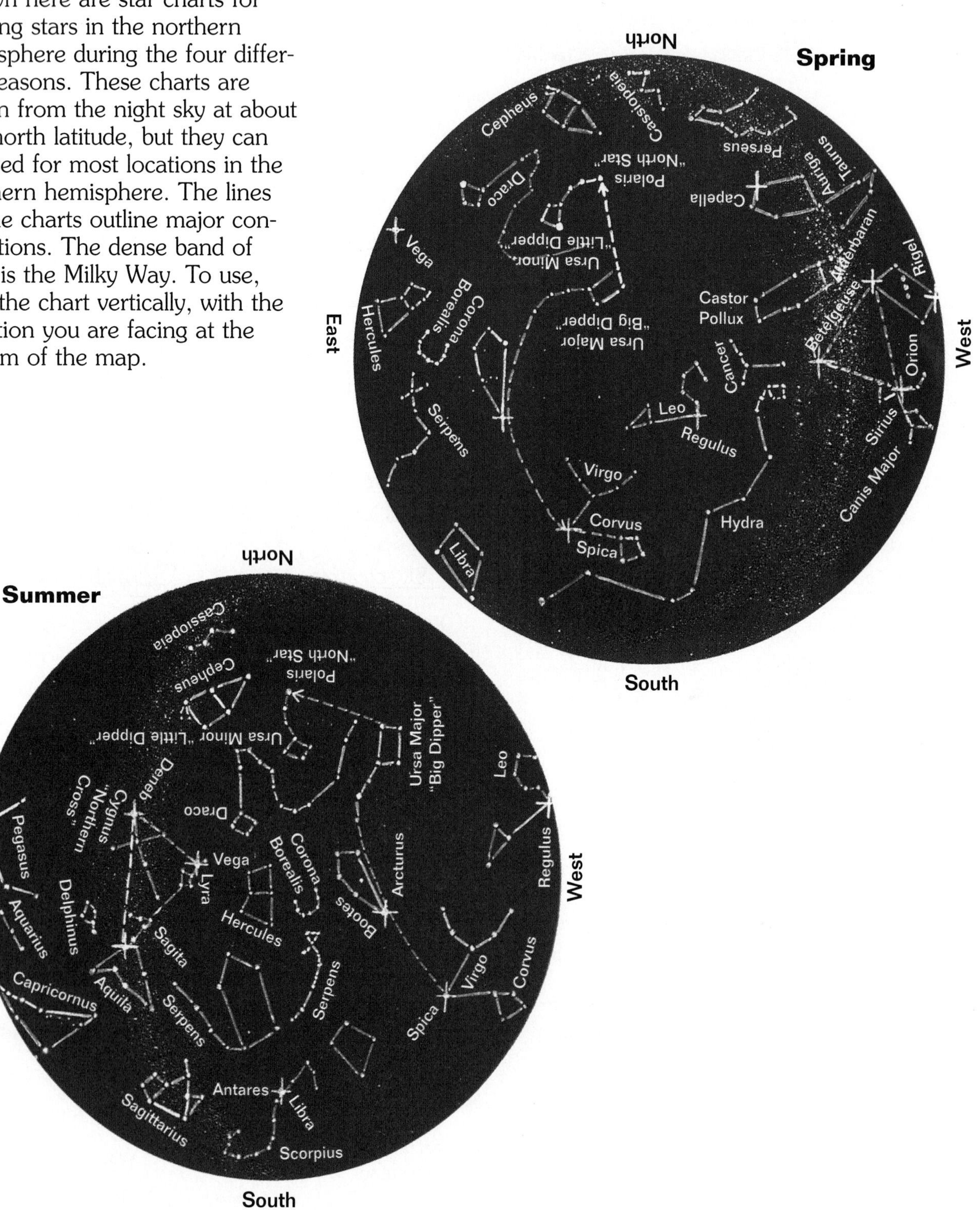

Appendix J

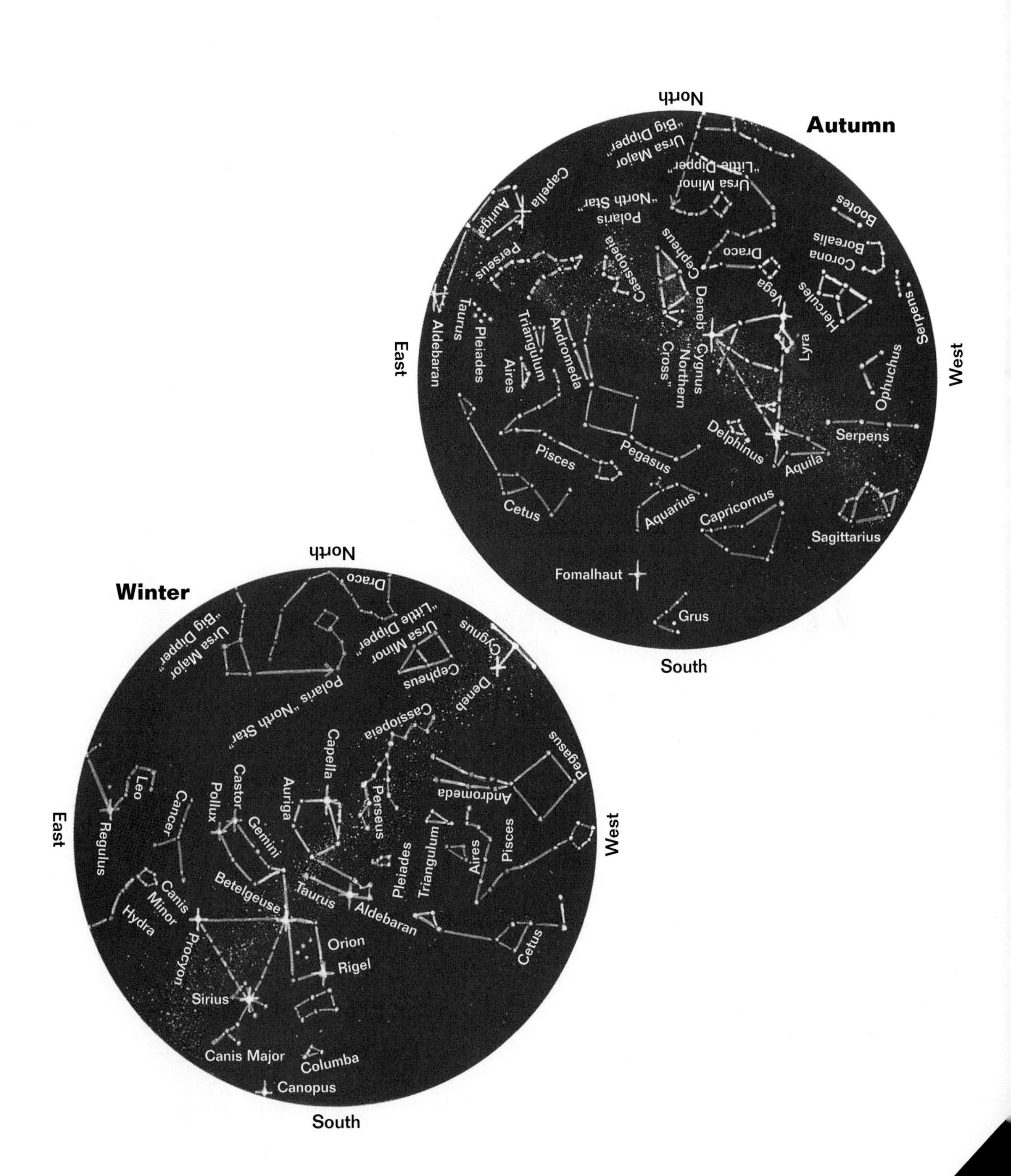

Autumn
North
East
West
South
Ursa Major "Big Dipper"
Ursa Minor "Little Dipper"
Polaris "North Star"
Capella
Auriga
Perseus
Cassiopeia
Cepheus
Draco
Bootes
Corona Borealis
Hercules
Serpens
Vega
Lyra
Deneb
Cygnus "Northern Cross"
Taurus
Aldebaran
Pleiades
Triangulum
Aires
Andromeda
Ophuchus
Pisces
Pegasus
Delphinus
Aquila
Cetus
Aquarius
Capricornus
Sagittarius
Fomalhaut
Grus
Winter
North
East
West
South
Draco
Ursa Major "Big Dipper"
Ursa Minor "Little Dipper"
Cygnus
Cepheus
Deneb
Polaris "North Star"
Cassiopeia
Pegasus
Andromeda
Capella
Castor
Pollux
Auriga
Perseus
Leo
Cancer
Gemini
Regulus
Triangulum
Aires
Pisces
Pleiades
Betelgeuse
Taurus
Aldebaran
Canis Minor
Hydra
Procyon
Orion
Rigel
Cetus
Sirius
Canis Major
Columba
Canopus

Skill Handbook

Table of Contents

Science Skill Handbook

Organizing Information

Thinking Critically

Practicing Scientific Processes

Representing and Applying Data

Technology Skill Handbook

Software

Hardware

Organizing Information

Communicating

The communication of ideas is an important part of our everyday lives. Whether reading a book, writing a letter, or watching a television program, people everywhere are expressing opinions and sharing information with one another. Writing in your Science Journal allows you to express your opinions and demonstrate your knowledge of the information presented on a subject. When writing, keep in mind the purpose of the assignment and the audience with which you are communicating.

Examples Science Journal assignments vary greatly. They may ask you to take a viewpoint other than your own; perhaps you will be a scientist, a TV reporter, or a committee member of a local environmental group. Maybe you will be expressing your opinions to a member of Congress, a doctor, or to the editor of your local newspaper, as shown in **Figure 1.** Sometimes, Science Journal writing may allow you to summarize information in the form of an outline, a letter, or in a paragraph.

Figure 1 A Science Journal entry

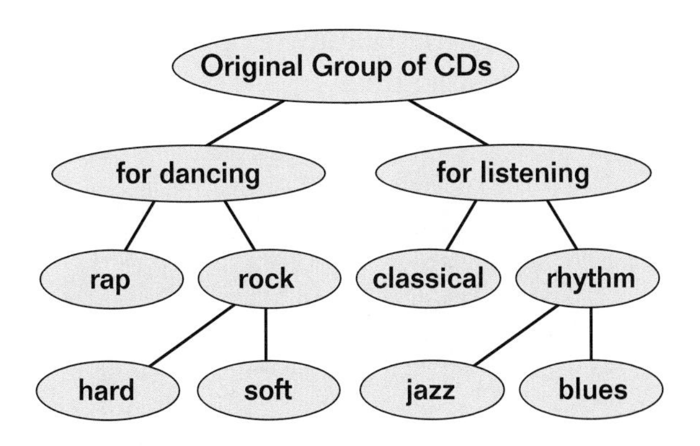

Figure 2 Classifying CDs

Classifying

You may not realize it, but you make things orderly in the world around you. If you hang your shirts together in the closet or if your favorite CDs are stacked together, you have used the skill of classifying.

Classifying is the process of sorting objects or events into groups based on common features. When classifying, first observe the objects or events to be classified. Then, select one feature that is shared by some members in the group, but not by all. Place those members that share that feature into a subgroup. You can classify members into smaller and smaller subgroups based on characteristics.

Remember, when you classify, you are grouping objects or events for a purpose. Keep your purpose in mind as you select the features to form groups and subgroups.

Example How would you classify a collection of CDs? As shown in **Figure 2,** you might classify those you like to dance to in one subgroup and CDs you like to listen to in the next subgroup. The CDs you like to dance to could be subdivided into a rap subgroup and a rock subgroup. Note that for each feature selected, each CD fits into only one subgroup. You would keep selecting features until all the CDs are classified. **Figure 2** shows one possible classification.

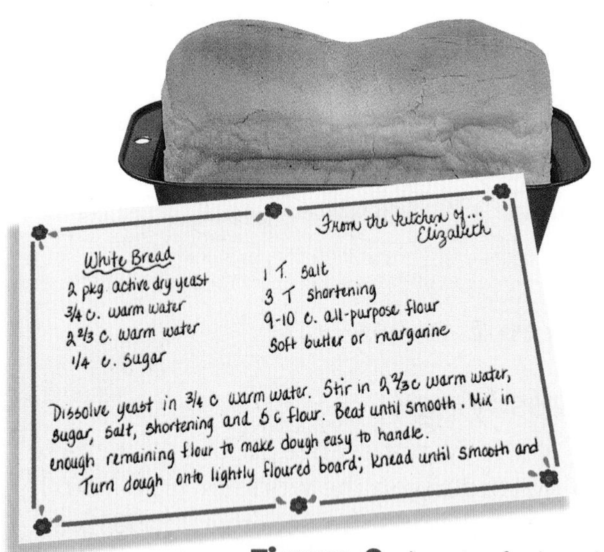

Figure 3 A recipe for bread contains sequenced instructions

Sequencing

A sequence is an arrangement of things or events in a particular order. When you are asked to sequence objects or events within a group, figure out what comes first, then think about what should come second. Continue to choose objects or events until all of the objects you started out with are in order. Then, go back over the sequence to make sure each thing or event in your sequence logically leads to the next.

Example A sequence with which you are most familiar is the use of alphabetical order. Another example of sequence would be the steps in a recipe, as shown in **Figure 3.** Think about baking bread. Steps in the recipe have to be followed in order for the bread to turn out right.

Concept Mapping

If you were taking an automobile trip, you would probably take along a road map. The road map shows your location, your destination, and other places along the way. By looking at the map and finding where you are, you can begin to understand where you are in relation to other locations on the map.

A concept map is similar to a road map. But, a concept map shows relationships among ideas (or concepts) rather than places. A concept map is a diagram that visually shows how concepts are related. Because the concept map shows relationships among ideas, it can make the meanings of ideas and terms clear, and help you understand better what you are studying.

There is usually not one correct way to create a concept map. As you construct one type of map, you may discover other ways to construct the map that show the

Figure 4 Network tree describing U.S. currency

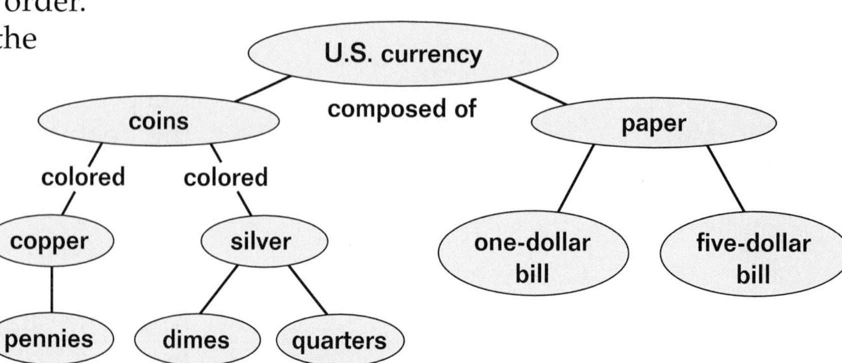

relationships between concepts in a better way. If you do discover what you think is a better way to create a concept map, go ahead and use the new one. Overall, concept maps are useful for breaking a big concept down into smaller parts, making learning easier.

Examples

Network Tree Look at the concept map about U.S. currency in **Figure 4.** This is called a network tree. Notice how some words are in ovals while others are written across connecting lines. The words inside the ovals are science concepts. The lines in the map show related concepts. The words written on the lines describe the relationships between concepts.

When you are asked to construct a network tree, write down the topic and list the major concepts related to that topic on a piece of paper. Then look at your list and begin to put them in order from general to specific. Branch the related concepts from the major concept and describe the relationships on the lines. Continue to write the more specific concepts. Write the relationships between the concepts on the lines until all concepts are mapped. Examine the concept map for relationships that cross branches, and add them to the concept map.

Events Chain An events chain is another type of concept map. An events chain map, such as the one describing a typical morning routine in **Figure 5,** is used to describe ideas in order. In science, an events chain can be used to describe a sequence of events, the steps in a procedure, or the stages of a process.

When making an events chain, first find the one event that starts the chain. This event is called the initiating event. Then, find the next event in the chain and continue until you reach an outcome. Suppose you are asked to describe what happens when your alarm rings. An events chain map describing the steps might look like **Figure 5.** Notice that connecting words are not necessary in an events chain.

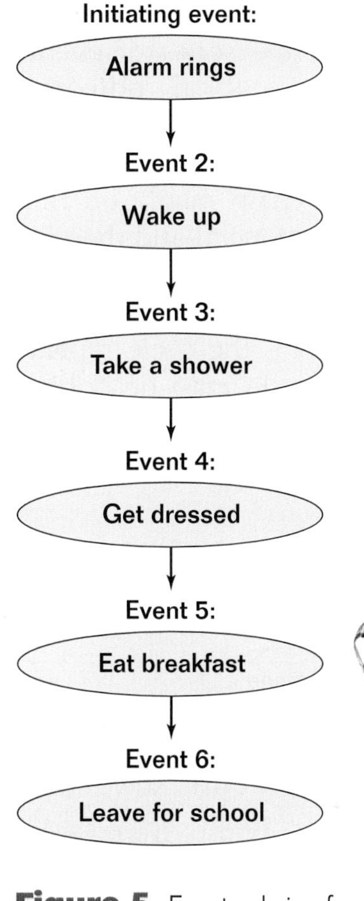

Figure 5 Events chain of a typical morning routine

Cycle Map A cycle concept map is a special type of events chain map. In a cycle concept map, the series of events does not produce a final outcome. Instead, the last event in the chain relates back to the initiating event.

As in the events chain map, you first decide on an initiating event and then list each event in order. Because there is no outcome and the last event relates back to the initiating event, the cycle repeats itself. Look at the cycle map describing the relationship between day and night in **Figure 6.**

Figure 6 Cycle map of day and night.

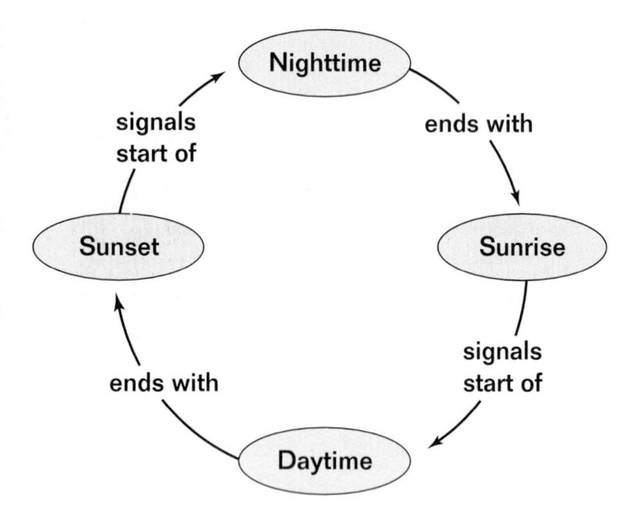

Spider Map A fourth type of concept map is the spider map. This is a map that you can use for brainstorming. Once you have a central idea, you may find you have a jumble of ideas that relate to it, but are not necessarily clearly related to each other. As illustrated by the homework spider map in **Figure 7,** by writing these ideas outside the main concept, you may begin to separate and group unrelated terms so that they become more useful.

Figure 7 Spider map about homework.

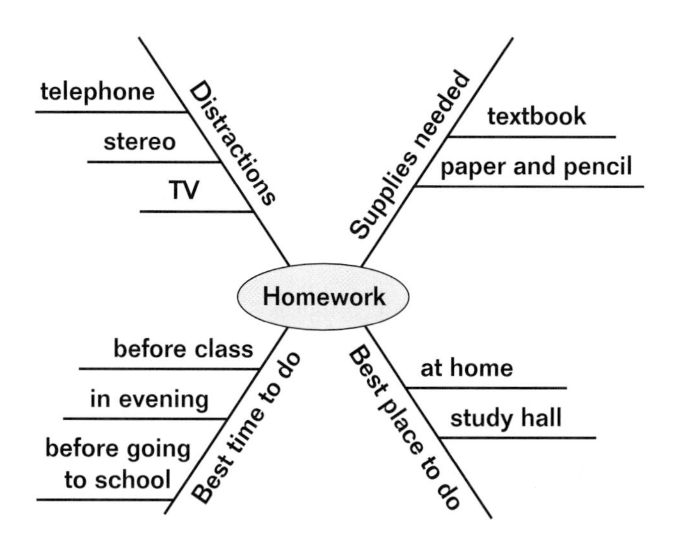

Making and Using Tables

Browse through your textbook and you will notice tables in the text and in the activities. In a table, data or information is arranged in a way that makes it easier for you to understand. Activity tables help organize the data you collect during an activity so that results can be interpreted.

Examples Most tables have a title. At a glance, the title tells you what the table is about. A table is divided into columns and rows. The first column lists items to be compared. In **Figure 8,** the collection of recyclable materials is being compared in a table. The row across the top lists the specific characteristics being compared. Within the grid of the table, the collected data are recorded.

What is the title of the table in **Figure 8?** The title is "Recycled Materials." What is being compared? The different materials being recycled and on which days they are recycled.

Making Tables To make a table, list the items to be compared down in columns and the characteristics to be compared across in rows. The table in

Figure 8 Table of recycled materials

Recycled Materials			
Day of Week	Paper (kg)	Aluminum (kg)	Plastic (kg)
Mon.	4.0	2.0	0.5
Wed.	3.5	1.5	0.5
Fri.	3.0	1.0	1.5

Figure 8 compares the mass of recycled materials collected by a class. On Monday, students turned in 4.0 kg of paper, 2.0 kg of aluminum, and 0.5 kg of plastic. On Wednesday, they turned in 3.5 kg of paper, 1.5 kg of aluminum, and 0.5 kg of plastic. On Friday, the totals were 3.0 kg of paper, 1.0 kg of aluminum, and 1.5 kg of plastic.

Using Tables How much plastic, in kilograms, is being recycled on Wednesday? Locate the column labeled "Plastic (kg)" and the row "Wed." The data in the box where the column and row intersect is the answer. Did you answer "0.5"? How much aluminum, in kilograms, is being recycled on Friday? If you answered "1.0," you understand how to use the parts of the table.

Making and Using Graphs

After scientists organize data in tables, they may display the data in a graph. A graph is a diagram that shows the relationship of one variable to another. A graph makes interpretation and analysis of data easier. There are three basic types of graphs used in science—the line graph, the bar graph, and the circle graph.

Examples

Line Graphs A line graph is used to show the relationship between two variables. The variables being compared go on two axes of the graph. The independent variable always goes on the horizontal axis, called the *x*-axis. The dependent variable always goes on the vertical axis, called the *y*-axis.

Suppose your class started to record the amount of materials they collected in one week for their school to recycle. The collected information is shown in **Figure 9.**

You could make a graph of the materials collected over the three days of the school week. The three weekdays are the independent variables and are placed on the *x*-axis of your graph. The amount of materials collected is the dependent variable and would go on the *y*-axis.

After drawing your axes, label each with a scale. The *x*-axis lists the three weekdays. To make a scale of the amount of materials collected on the *y*-axis, look at the data values. Because the lowest amount collected was 1.0 and the highest was 5.0, you will have to start numbering at least at 1.0 and go through 5.0. You decide to start numbering at 0 and number by ones through 6.0, as shown in **Figure 10.**

Next, plot the data points for collected paper. The first pair of data you want to plot is Monday and 5.0 kg of paper.

Figure 9 Amount of recyclable materials collected during one week

Materials Collected During Week		
Day of Week	Paper (kg)	Aluminum (kg)
Mon.	5.0	4.0
Wed.	4.0	1.0
Fri.	2.5	2.0

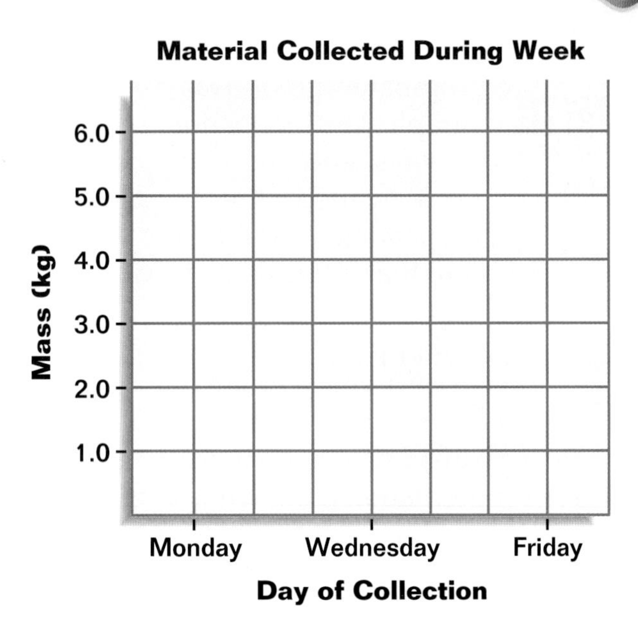

Figure 10 Graph outline for material collected during week

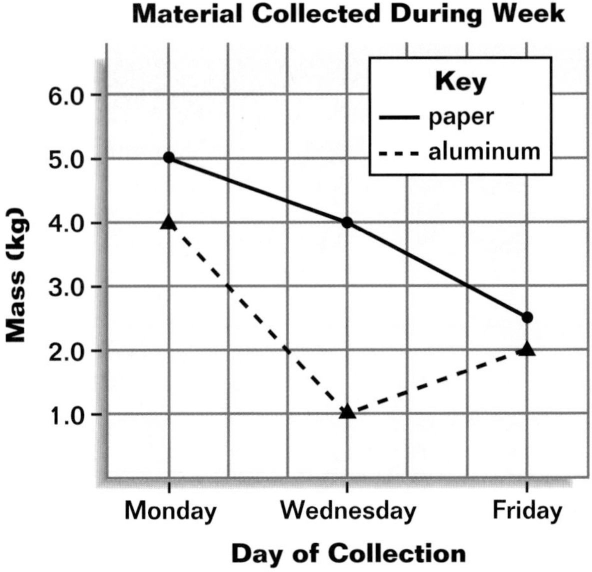

Figure 11 Line graph of materials collected during week

Locate "Monday" on the x-axis and locate "5.0" on the y-axis. Where an imaginary vertical line from the x-axis and an imaginary horizontal line from the y-axis would meet, place the first data point. Place the other data points the same way. After all the points are plotted, connect them with the best smooth curve. Repeat this procedure for the data points for aluminum. Use continuous and dashed lines to distinguish the two line graphs. The resulting graph should look like **Figure 11.**

Bar Graphs Bar graphs are similar to line graphs. They compare data that do not continuously change. In a bar graph, vertical bars show the relationships among data.

To make a bar graph, set up the x-axis and y-axis as you did for the line graph. The data is plotted by drawing vertical bars from the x-axis up to a point where the y-axis would meet the bar if it were extended.

Look at the bar graph in **Figure 12** comparing the mass of aluminum collected over three weekdays. The x-axis is the days on which the aluminum was collected. The y-axis is the mass of aluminum collected, in kilograms.

Circle Graphs A circle graph uses a circle divided into sections to display data. Each section represents part of the whole. All the sections together equal 100 percent.

Suppose you wanted to make a circle graph to show the number of seeds that germinated in a package. You would count the total number of seeds. You find that there are 143 seeds in the package. This represents 100 percent, the whole circle.

You plant the seeds, and 129 seeds germinate. The seeds that germinated will make up one section of the circle graph, and the seeds that did not germinate will make up the remaining section.

To find out how much of the circle each section should take, divide the number of seeds in each section by the total number of seeds. Then, multiply your answer by 360, the number of degrees in a circle, and round to the nearest whole number. The

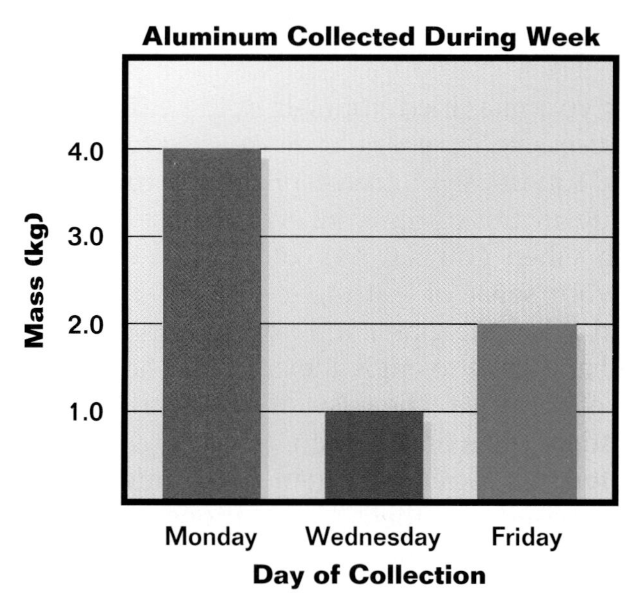

Figure 12 Bar graph of aluminum collected during week

section of the circle graph in degrees that represents the seeds germinated is figured below.

$$\frac{129}{143} \times 360 = 324.75 \text{ or } 325 \text{ degrees (or } 325°)$$

Plot this group on the circle graph using a compass and a protractor. Use the compass to draw a circle. It will be easier to measure the part of the circle representing the non-germinating seeds, so subtract 325° from 360° to get 35°. Draw a straight line from the center to the edge of the circle. Place your protractor on this line and use it to mark a point at 325°. Use this point to draw a straight line from the center of the circle to the edge. This is the section for the group of seeds that did not germinate. The other section represents the group of 129 seeds that did germinate. Label the sections of your graph and title the graph as shown in **Figure 13.**

Figure 13 Circle graph of germinated seeds

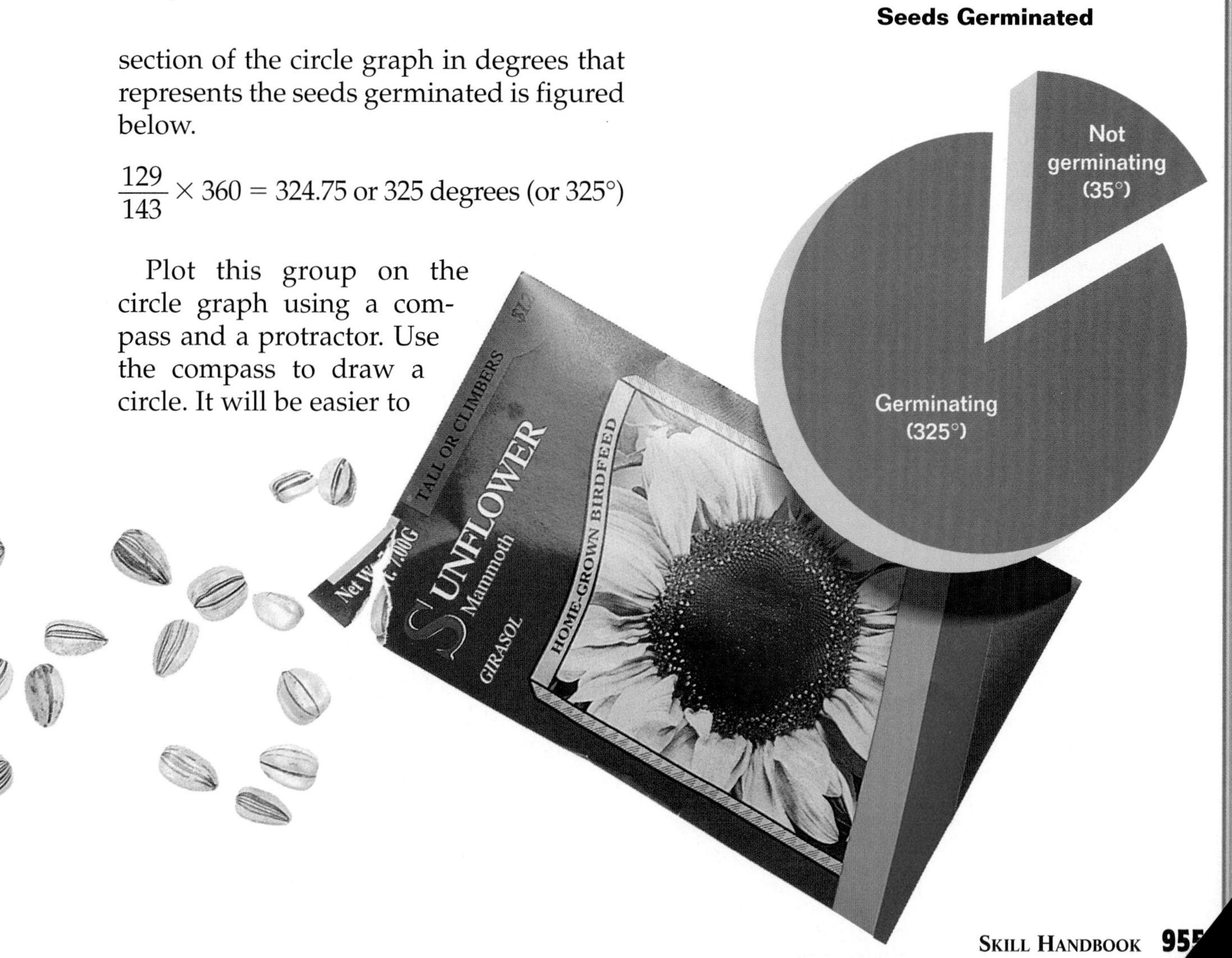

Thinking Critically

Observing and Inferring

Observing Scientists try to make careful and accurate observations. When possible, they use instruments such as microscopes, thermometers, and balances to make observations. Measurements with a balance or thermometer provide numerical data that can be checked and repeated.

When you make observations in science, you'll find it helpful to examine the entire object or situation first. Then, look carefully for details. Write down everything you observe.

Example Imagine that you have just finished a volleyball game. At home, you open the refrigerator and see a jug of orange juice on the back of the top shelf. The jug, shown in **Figure 14,** feels cold as you grasp it. Then, you drink the juice, smell the oranges, and enjoy the tart taste in your mouth.

Figure 14 Why is this jug of orange juice cold?

As you imagined yourself in the story, you used your senses to make observations. You used your sense of sight to find the jug in the refrigerator, your sense of touch when you felt the coldness of the jug, your sense of hearing to listen as the liquid filled the glass, and your senses of smell and taste to enjoy the odor and tartness of the juice. The basis of all scientific investigation is observation.

Inferring Scientists often make inferences based on their observations. An inference is an attempt to explain or interpret observations or to say what caused what you observed.

When making an inference, be certain to use accurate data and observations. Analyze all of the data that you've collected. Then, based on everything you know, explain or interpret what you've observed.

Example When you drank a glass of orange juice after the volleyball game, you observed that the orange juice was cold as well as refreshing. You might infer that the juice was cold because it had been made much earlier in the day and had been kept in the refrigerator, or you might infer that it had just been made, using both cold water and ice. The only way to be sure which inference is correct is to investigate further.

Comparing and Contrasting

Observations can be analyzed by noting the similarities and differences between two or more objects or events that you observe. When you look at objects or events to see how they are similar, you are comparing them. Contrasting is looking for differences in similar objects or events.

Figure 15 Table comparing the nutritional value of *Cereal A* and *Cereal B*

Nutritional Value		
	Cereal A	Cereal B
Serving size	103 g	105 g
Calories	220	160
Total Fat	10 g	10 g
Protein	2.5 g	2.6 g
Total Carbohydrate	30 g	15 g

Example Suppose you were asked to compare and contrast the nutritional value of two kinds of cereal, *Cereal A* and *Cereal B.* You would start by looking at what is known about these cereals. Arrange this information in a table, like the one in **Figure 15.**

Similarities you might point out are that both cereals have similar serving sizes, amounts of total fat, and protein. Differences include *Cereal A* having a higher calorie value and containing more total carbohydrates than *Cereal B.*

Recognizing Cause and Effect

Have you ever watched something happen and then made suggestions about why it happened? If so, you have observed an effect and inferred a cause. The event is an effect, and the reason for the event is the cause.

Example Suppose that every time your teacher fed the fish in a classroom aquarium, she or he tapped the food container on the edge of the aquarium. Then, one day your teacher just happened to tap the edge of the aquarium with a pencil while making a point. You observed the fish swim to the surface of the aquarium to feed, as shown in **Figure 16.** What is the effect, and what would you infer to be the cause? The effect is the fish swimming to the surface of the aquarium. You might infer the cause to be the teacher tapping on the edge of the aquarium. In determining cause and effect, you have made a logical inference based on your observations.

Perhaps the fish swam to the surface because they reacted to the teacher's waving hand or for some other reason. When scientists are unsure of the cause of a certain event, they design controlled experiments to determine what causes the event. Although you have made a logical conclusion about the behavior of the fish, you would have to perform an experiment to be certain that it was the tapping that caused the effect you observed.

Figure 16 What cause-and-effect situations are occurring in this aquarium?

Practicing Scientific Processes

You might say that the work of a scientist is to solve problems. But when you decide how to dress on a particular day, you are doing problem solving, too. You may observe what the weather looks like through a window. You may go outside and see whether what you are wearing is heavy or light enough.

Scientists use an orderly approach to learn new information and to solve problems. The methods scientists may use include observing to form a hypothesis, designing an experiment to test a hypothesis, separating and controlling variables, and interpreting data.

Forming Operational Definitions

Operational definitions define an object by showing how it functions, works, or behaves. Such definitions are written in terms of how an object works or how it can be used; that is, what is its job or purpose?

Example Some operational definitions explain how an object can be used.

- A ruler is a tool that measures the size of an object.
- An automobile can move things from one place to another.

Or such a definition may explain how an object works.

- A ruler contains a series of marks that can be used as a standard when measuring.
- An automobile is a vehicle that can move from place to place.

Forming a Hypothesis

Observations You observe all the time. Scientists try to observe as much as possible about the things and events they study so they know that what they say about their observations is reliable.

Some observations describe something using only words. These observations are called qualitative observations. Other observations describe how much of something there is. These are quantitative observations and use numbers, as well as words, in the description. Tools or equipment are used to measure the characteristic being described.

Example If you were making qualitative observations of the dog in **Figure 17,** you might use words such as *furry, yellow,* and *short-haired.* Quantitative observations of this dog might include a mass of 14 kg, a height of 46 cm, ear length of 10 cm, and an age of 150 days.

Hypotheses Hypotheses are tested to help explain observations that have been made. They are often stated as *if* and *then* statements.

Figure 17 What observations can be made about this dog?

Examples Suppose you want to make a perfect score on a spelling test. Begin by thinking of several ways to accomplish this. Base these possibilities on past observations. If you put each of these possibilities into sentence form, using the words *if* and *then*, you can form a hypothesis. All of the following are hypotheses you might consider to explain how you could score 100 percent on your test:

If the test is easy, then I will get a perfect score.

If I am intelligent, then I will get a perfect score.

If I study hard, then I will get a perfect score.

Perhaps a scientist has observed that plants that receive fertilizer grow taller than plants that do not. A scientist may form a hypothesis that says: If plants are fertilized, then their growth will increase.

Designing an Experiment to Test a Hypothesis

In order to test a hypothesis, it's best to write out a procedure. A procedure is the plan that you follow in your experiment. A procedure tells you what materials to use and how to use them. After following the procedure, data are generated. From this generated data, you can then draw a conclusion and make a statement about your results.

If the conclusion you draw from the data supports your hypothesis, then you can say that your hypothesis is reliable. *Reliable* means that you can trust your conclusion. If it did not support your hypothesis, then you would have to make new observations and state a new hypothesis—just make sure that it is one that you can test.

Example Super premium gasoline costs more than regular gasoline. Does super premium gasoline increase the efficiency or fuel mileage of your family car? Let's figure out how to conduct an experiment to test the hypothesis, "*if* premium gas is more efficient, *then* it should increase the fuel mileage of our family car." Then a procedure similar to **Figure 18** must be written to generate data presented in **Figure 19** on the next page.

These data show that premium gasoline is less efficient than regular gasoline. It took more gasoline to travel one mile (0.064) using premium gasoline than it does to travel one mile using regular gasoline (0.059). This conclusion does not support the original hypothesis made.

PROCEDURE

1. Use regular gasoline for two weeks.
2. Record the number of miles between fill-ups and the amount of gasoline used.
3. Switch to premium gasoline for two weeks.
4. Record the number of miles between fill-ups and the amount of gasoline used.

Figure 18 Possible procedural steps

Figure 19 Data generated from procedure steps

Gasoline Data			
	Miles traveled	**Gallons used**	**Gallons per mile**
Regular gasoline	762	45.34	0.059
Premium gasoline	661	42.30	0.064

Separating and Controlling Variables

In any experiment, it is important to keep everything the same except for the item you are testing. The one factor that you change is called the *independent variable.* The factor that changes as a result of the independent variable is called the *dependent variable.* Always make sure that there is only one independent variable. If you allow more than one, you will not know what causes the changes you observe in the independent variable. Many experiments have *controls*—a treatment or an experiment that you can compare with the results of your test groups.

Example In the experiment with the gasoline, you made everything the same except the type of gasoline being used. The driver, the type of automobile, and the weather conditions should remain the same throughout. The gasoline should also be purchased from the same service station. By doing so, you made sure that at the end of the experiment, any differences were the result of the type of fuel being used—regular or premium. The type of gasoline was the *independent factor* and the gas mileage achieved was the *dependent factor.* The use of regular gasoline was the *control.*

Interpreting Data

The word *interpret* means "to explain the meaning of something." Look at the problem originally being explored in the gasoline experiment and find out what the data show. Identify the control group and the test group so you can see whether or not the variable has had an effect. Then, you need to check differences between the control and test groups.

Figure 20 Which gasoline type is most efficient?

These differences may be qualitative or quantitative. A qualitative difference would be a difference that you could observe and describe, while a quantitative difference would be a difference you can measure using numbers. If there are differences, the variable being tested may have had an effect. If there is no difference between the control and the test groups, the variable being tested apparently has had no effect.

Example Perhaps you are looking at a table from an experiment designed to test the hypothesis: If premium gas is more efficient, then it should increase the fuel mileage of our family car. Look back at **Figure 19** showing the results of this experiment. In this example, the use of regular gasoline in the family car was the control, while the car being fueled by premium gasoline was the test group.

Data showed a quantitative difference in efficiency for gasoline consumption. It took 0.059 gallons of regular gasoline to travel one mile, while it took 0.064 gallons of the premium gasoline to travel the same distance. The regular gasoline was more efficient; it increased the fuel mileage of the family car.

What are data? In the experiment described on these pages, measurements were taken so that at the end of the experiment, you had something concrete to interpret. You had numbers to work with. Not every experiment that you do will give you data in the form of numbers. Sometimes, data will be in the form of a description. At the end of a chemistry experiment, you might have noted that one solution turned yellow when treated with a particular chemical, and another remained colorless, as water, when treated with the same chemical. Data, therefore, are stated in different forms for different types of scientific experiments.

Figure 21

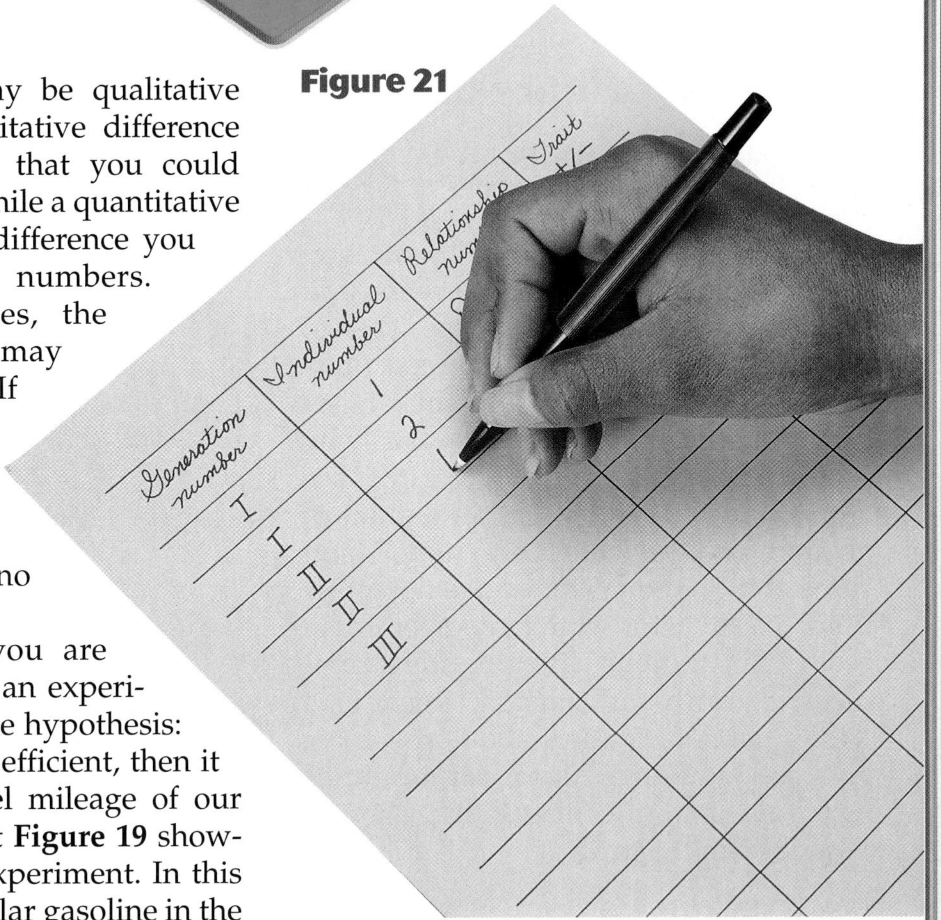

Are all experiments alike? Keep in mind as you perform experiments in science that not every experiment makes use of all of the parts that have been described on these pages. For some, it may be difficult to design an experiment that will always have a control. Other experiments are complex enough that it may be hard to have only one dependent variable. Real scientists encounter many variations in the methods that they use when they perform experiments. The skills in this handbook are here for you to use and practice. In real situations, their uses will vary.

Representing and Applying Data

Interpreting Scientific Illustrations

As you read a science textbook, you will see many drawings, diagrams, and photographs. Illustrations help you to understand what you read. Some illustrations are included to help you understand an idea that you can't see easily by yourself. For instance, we can't see atoms, but we can look at a diagram of an atom and that helps us to understand some things about atoms. Seeing something often helps you remember more easily. Illustrations also provide examples that clarify difficult concepts or give additional information about the topic you are studying. Maps, for example, help you to locate places that may be described in the text.

Figure 23 The orientation of a dog is shown here.

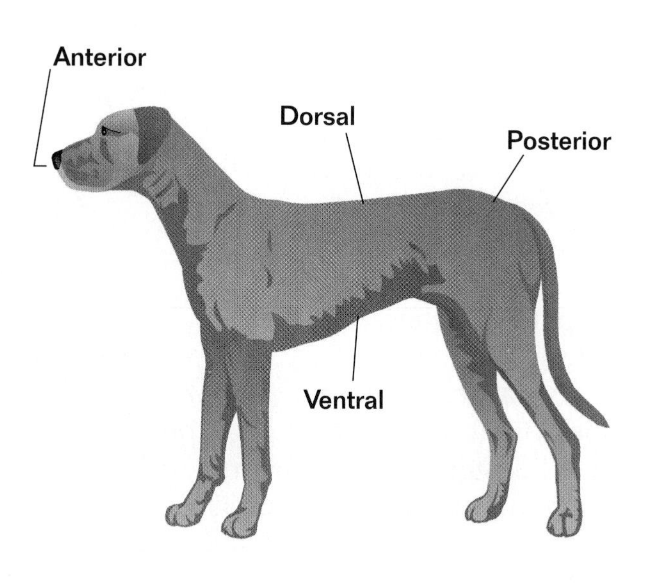

Examples

Captions and Labels Most illustrations have captions. A caption is a comment that identifies or explains the illustration. Diagrams, such as **Figure 22,** often have labels that identify parts of the organism or the order of steps in a process.

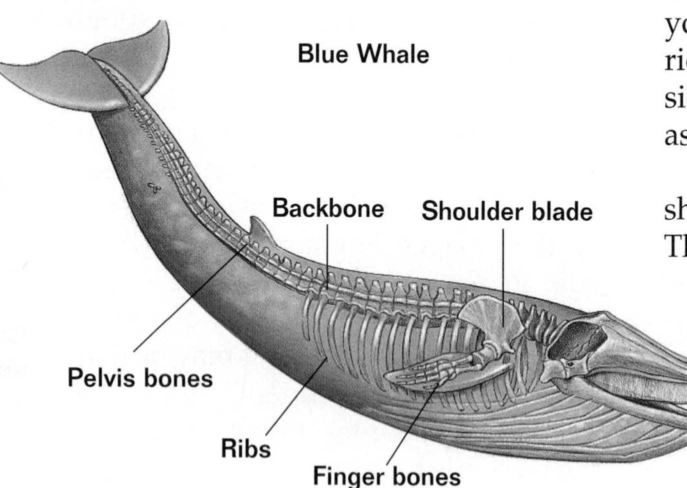

Figure 22 A labeled diagram of a blue whale

Learning with Illustrations An illustration of an organism shows that organism from a particular view or orientation. In order to understand the illustration, you may need to identify the front (anterior) end, tail (posterior) end, the underside (ventral), and the back (dorsal) side, as shown in **Figure 23.**

You might also check for symmetry. A shark in **Figure 24** has bilateral symmetry. This means that drawing an imaginary line through the center of the animal from the anterior to posterior end forms two mirror images.

Radial symmetry is the arrangement of similar parts around a central point. An object or organism, such as a hydra, can be divided anywhere through the center into similar parts.

Some organisms and objects cannot be divided into two similar parts. If an

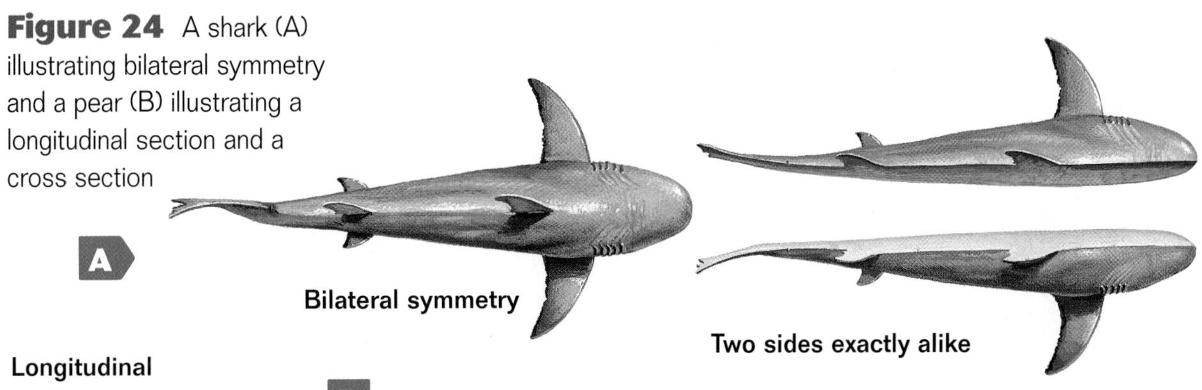

Figure 24 A shark (A) illustrating bilateral symmetry and a pear (B) illustrating a longitudinal section and a cross section

organism or object cannot be divided, it is asymmetrical. Regardless of how you try to divide a natural sponge, you cannot divide it into two parts that look alike.

Some illustrations enable you to see the inside of an organism or object. These illustrations are called sections. **Figure 24** also illustrates some common sections.

Look at all illustrations carefully. Read captions and labels so that you understand exactly what the illustration is showing you.

Making Models

Have you ever worked on a model car, plane, or rocket? These models look, and sometimes work, much like the real thing, but they are often on a different scale than the real thing. In science, models are used to help simplify large or small processes or structures that otherwise would be difficult to see and understand. Your understanding of a structure or process is enhanced when you work with materials to make a model that shows the basic features of the structure or process.

Example In order to make a model, you first have to get a basic idea about the structure or process involved. You decide to make a model to show the differences in size of arteries, veins, and capillaries. First, read about these structures. All three are hollow tubes. Arteries are round and thick. Veins are flat and have thinner walls than arteries. Capillaries are small.

Now, decide what you can use for your model. Common materials are often most useful and cheapest to work with when making models. As illustrated in **Figure 25** on the next page, different kinds and sizes of pasta might work for these models. Different sizes of rubber tubing might do just as well. Cut and glue the different noodles or tubing onto thick paper so the openings can be seen. Then label each. Now you have a simple, easy-to-understand model showing the differences in size of arteries, veins, and capillaries.

What other scientific ideas might a model help you to understand? A model of a molecule can be made from balls of modeling clay (using different colors for the different elements present) and toothpicks (to show different chemical bonds).

Figure 25 Different types of pasta may be used to model blood vessels

A working model of a volcano can be made from clay, a small amount of baking soda, vinegar, and a bottle cap. Other models can be devised on a computer. Some models are mathematical and are represented by equations.

Measuring in SI

The metric system is a system of measurement developed by a group of scientists in 1795. It helps scientists avoid problems by providing standard measurements that all scientists around the world can understand. A modern form of the metric system, called the International System, or SI, was adopted for worldwide use in 1960.

The metric system is convenient because unit sizes vary by multiples of 10. When changing from smaller units to larger units, divide by 10. When changing from larger units to smaller, multiply by 10. For example, to convert millimeters to centimeters, divide the millimeters by 10. To convert 30 millimeters to centimeters, divide 30 by 10 (30 millimeters equal 3 centimeters).

Prefixes are used to name units. Look at **Figure 26** for some common metric prefixes and their meanings. Do you see how the prefix *kilo-* attached to the unit *gram* is *kilogram,* or 1000 grams? The prefix *deci-* attached to the unit *meter* is *decimeter,* or one-tenth (0.1) of a meter.

Examples

Length You have probably measured lengths or distances many times. The meter is the SI unit used to measure length. A baseball bat is about one meter long. When measuring smaller lengths, the meter is divided into smaller units called centimeters and millimeters. A centimeter is one-hundredth (0.01) of a meter, which is about the size of the width of the fingernail on your ring finger. A millimeter is one-thousandth of a meter (0.001), about the thickness of a dime.

Most metric rulers have lines indicating centimeters and millimeters, as shown in

Figure 26 Common metric prefixes

Metric Prefixes			
Prefix	Symbol	Meaning	
kilo-	k	1000	thousand
hecto-	h	100	hundred
deca-	da	10	ten
deci-	d	0.1	tenth
centi-	c	0.01	hundredth
milli-	m	0.001	thousandth

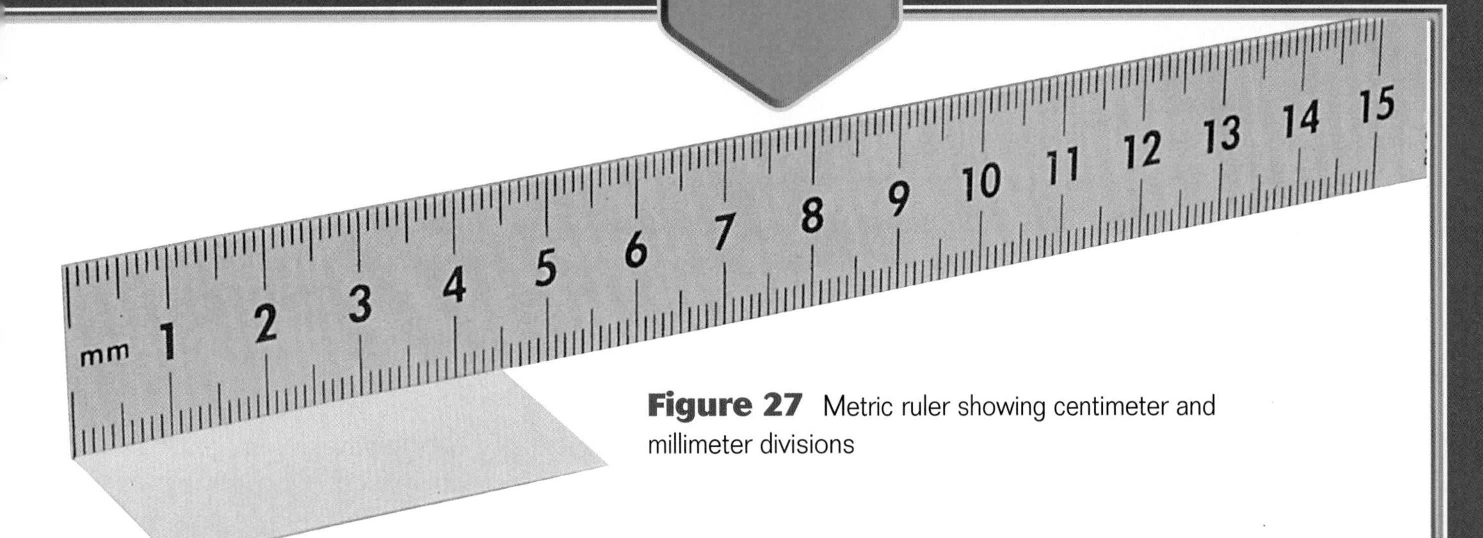

Figure 27 Metric ruler showing centimeter and millimeter divisions

Figure 27. The centimeter lines are the longer, numbered lines; the shorter lines are millimeter lines. When using a metric ruler, line up the 0-centimeter mark with the end of the object being measured, and read the number of the unit where the object ends, in this instance 4.5 cm.

Surface Area Units of length are also used to measure surface area. The standard unit of area is the square meter (m^2). A square that's one meter long on each side has a surface area of one square meter. Similarly, a square centimeter, (cm^2), shown in **Figure 28,** is one centimeter long on each side. The surface area of an object is determined by multiplying the length times the width.

Volume The volume of a rectangular solid is also calculated using units of length. The cubic meter (m^3) is the standard SI unit of volume. A cubic meter is a cube one meter on each side. You can determine the volume of rectangular solids by multiplying length times width times height.

Liquid Volume During science activities, you will measure liquids using beakers and graduated cylinders marked in milliliters, as illustrated in **Figure 29.** A graduated cylinder is a cylindrical container marked with lines from bottom to top.

Liquid volume is measured using a unit called a liter. A liter has the volume of 1000 cubic centimeters. Because the prefix *milli-* means thousandth (0.001), a milliliter equals one cubic centimeter. One milliliter of liquid would completely fill a cube measuring one centimeter on each side.

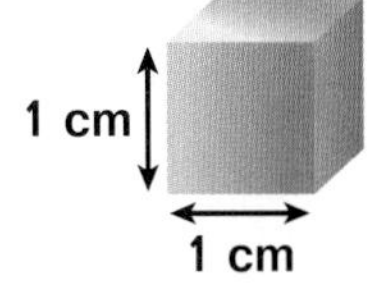

Figure 28 A square centimeter

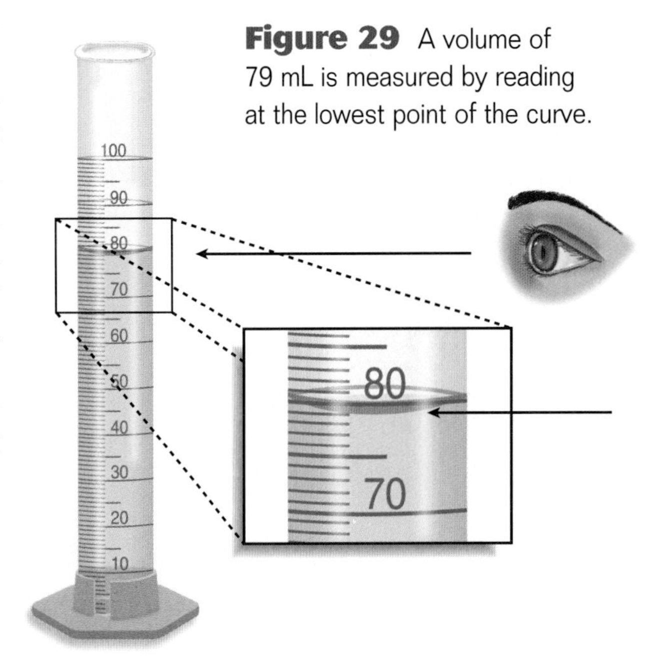

Figure 29 A volume of 79 mL is measured by reading at the lowest point of the curve.

Mass Scientists use balances to find the mass of objects in grams. You might use a beam balance similar to **Figure 30.** Notice that on one side of the balance is a pan and on the other side is a set of beams. Each beam has an object of a known mass called a *rider* that slides on the beam.

Before you find the mass of an object, set the balance to zero by sliding all the riders back to the zero point. Check the pointer on the right to make sure it swings an equal distance above and below the zero point on the scale. If the swing is unequal, find and turn the adjusting screw until you have an equal swing.

Place an object on the pan. Slide the rider with the largest mass along its beam until the pointer drops below zero. Then move it back one notch. Repeat the process on each beam until the pointer swings an equal distance above and below the zero point. Add the masses on each beam to find the mass of the object.

You should never place a hot object or pour chemicals directly onto the pan. Instead, find the mass of a clean beaker or a glass jar. Place the dry or liquid chemicals in the container. Then find the combined mass of the container and the chemicals. Calculate the mass of the chemicals by subtracting the mass of the empty container from the combined mass.

Predicting

When you apply a hypothesis, or general explanation, to a specific situation, you predict something about that situation. First, you must identify which hypothesis fits the situation you are considering.

Examples People use prediction to make everyday decisions. Based on previous observations and experiences, you may form a hypothesis that if it is wintertime, then temperatures will be lower. From past experience in your area, temperatures are lowest in February. You may then use this hypothesis to predict specific temperatures and weather for the month of February in advance. Someone could use these predictions to plan to set aside more money for heating bills during that month.

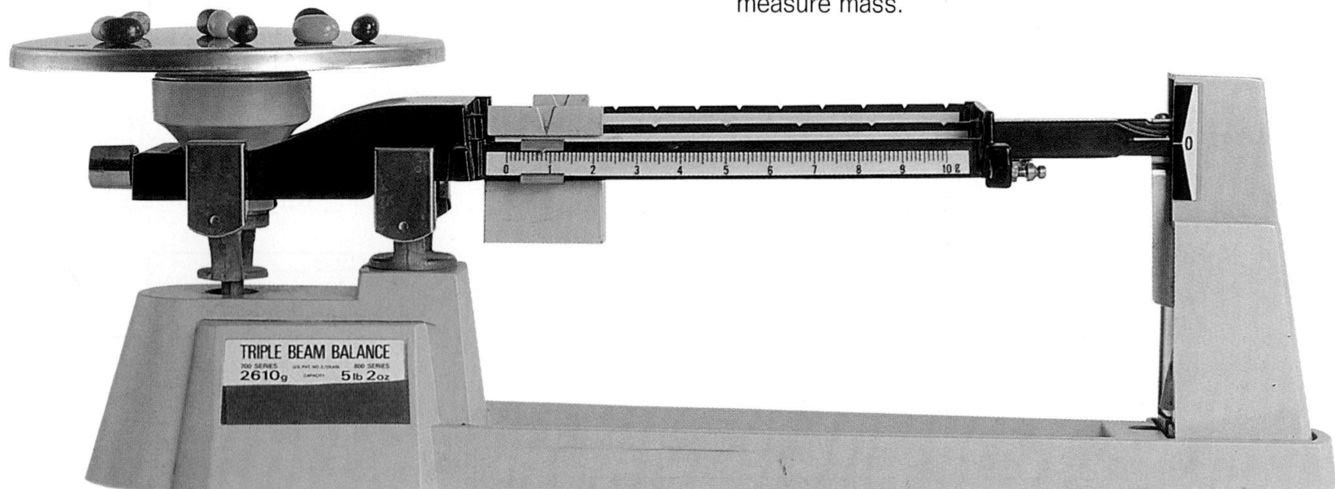

Figure 30 A beam balance is used to measure mass.

Using Numbers

When working with large populations of organisms, scientists usually cannot observe or study every organism in the population. Instead, they use a sample or a portion of the population. To sample is to take a small representative portion of organisms of a population for research. By making careful observations or manipulating variables within a portion of a group, information is discovered and conclusions are drawn that might then be applied to the whole population.

Scientific work also involves estimating. To estimate is to make a judgment about the size of something or the number of something without actually measuring or counting every member of a population.

Examples Suppose you are trying to determine the effect of a specific nutrient on the growth of black-eyed Susans. It would be impossible to test the entire population of black-eyed Susans, so you would select part of the population for your experiment. Through careful experimentation and observation on a sample of the population, you could generalize the effect of the chemical on the entire population.

Here is a more familiar example. Have you ever tried to guess how many beans were in a sealed jar? If you did, you were estimating. What if you knew the jar of beans held one liter (1000 mL)? If you knew that 30 beans would fit in a 100-milliliter jar, how many beans would you estimate to be in the one-liter jar? If you said about 300 beans, your estimate would be close to the actual number of beans. Can you estimate how many jelly beans are on the cookie sheet in **Figure 31?**

Scientists use a similar process to estimate populations of organisms from bacteria to buffalo. Scientists count the actual number of organisms in a small sample and then estimate the number of organisms in a larger area. For example, if a scientist wanted to count the number of bacterial colonies in a petri dish, a microscope could be used to count the number of organisms in a one-square-centimeter sample. To determine the total population of the culture, the number of organisms in the square-centimeter sample is multiplied by the total number of square centimeters in the culture.

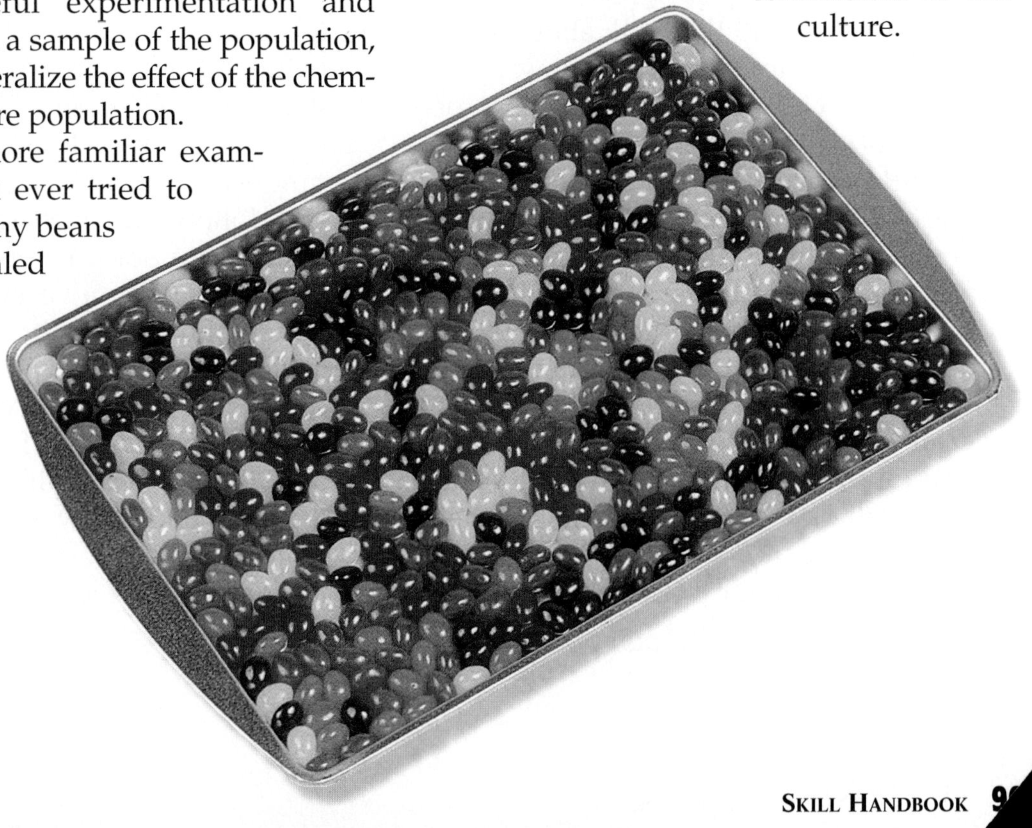

Figure 31
Sampling a group of jelly beans allows for an estimation of the total number of jelly beans in the group.

Using a Word Processor

Suppose your teacher has assigned you to write a report. After you've done your research and decided how you want to write the information, you need to put all that information on paper. The easiest way to do this is with a word processor.

A word processor is a computer program in which you can write your information, change it as many times as you need to, and then print it out so that it looks neat and clean. You can also use a word processor to create tables and columns, add bullets or cartoon art, include page numbers, and even check your spelling.

Example Last week in Science class, your teacher assigned a report on the history of the atom. It has to be double spaced and include at least one table. You've collected all the facts, and you're ready to write your report. Sitting down at your computer, you decide you want to begin by explaining early scientific ideas about the atom and then talk about what scientists think about the atom now.

After you've written the two parts of your report, you decide to put a heading or subtitle above each part and add a title to the paper. To make each of these look different from the rest of your report, you can use a word processor to make the words bigger and bolder. The word processor also can double space your entire report, so that you don't have to add an extra space between each line.

You decide to include a table that lists each scientist that contributed to the theory of the atom along with his or her contribution. Using your word processor, you can create a table with as many rows and columns as you need. And, if you forget to include a scientist in the middle, you can go back and insert a row in the middle of your table without redoing the entire table.

When you've finished with your report, you can tell the word processor to check your spelling. If it finds misspelled words, it often will suggest a word you can use to replace the misspelled word. But, remember that the word processor may not know how to spell all the words in your report. Scan your report and double check your spelling with a dictionary if you're not sure if a word is spelled correctly.

After you've made sure that your report looks just the way you want it on the screen, the word processor will print your report on a printer. With a word processor, your report can look like it was written by a real scientist.

Helpful Hints

- If you aren't sure how to do something using your word processor, look under the help menu. You can look up how to do something, and the word processor will tell you how to do it. Just follow the instructions that the word processor puts on your screen.
- Just because you've spelled checked your report doesn't mean that the spelling is perfect. The spell check can't catch misspelled words that look like other words. So, if you've accidentally typed *mind* instead of *mine,* the spell checker won't know the difference. Always reread your report to make sure you didn't miss any mistakes.

Using a Database

Imagine you're in the middle of research project. You are busily gathering facts and information. But, soon you realize that its becoming harder and harder to organize and keep track of all the information. The tool to solve "information overload" is a database. A database is exactly what it sounds like—a base on which to organize data. Similar to how a file cabinet organizes records, a database also organizes records. However, a database is more powerful than a simple file cabinet because at the click of a mouse, the entire contents can be reshuffled and reorganized. At computer-quick speeds, databases can sort information by any characteristic and filter data into multiple categories. Once you use a database, you will be amazed at how quickly all those facts and bits of information become manageable.

Example For the past few weeks, you have been gathering information on living and extinct primates. A database would be ideal to organize your information. An entry for gorillas might contain fields (categories) for fossil locations, brain size, average height, earliest fossil, and so on. Later on, if you wanted to know which primates have been found in Asia, you could quickly filter all entries using Asia in the field that listed locations. The database will scan all the entries and select the entries containing Asia. If you wanted to rank all the primates by arm length, you would sort all the entries by arm length. By using different combinations of sorting and filtering, you can discover relationships between the data that otherwise might remain hidden.

Helpful Hints

- Before setting up your own database, it's easier to learn the features of your database software by practicing with an established database.
- Entering the data into a database can be time consuming. Learn shortcuts such as tabbing between entry fields and automatic formatting of data that your software may provide.
- Get in the habit of periodically saving your database as you are entering data. That way, if something happens and your computer locks up or the power goes out, you won't lose all of your work. Most databases have specific words you can use to narrow your search.
- AND: If you place an AND between two words in your search, the database will look for any entries that have both the words. For example, "blood AND cell" would give you information about both blood and cells.
- OR: If you place an OR between two words, the database will show entries that have at least one of the words. For example, "bird OR fish" would show you information on either birds or fish.
- NOT: If you place a NOT between two words, the database will look for entries that have the first word but do not have the second word. For example, "reproduction NOT plant" would show you information about reproduction but not about plant reproduction.

Using Graphics Software

Having trouble finding that exact piece of art you're looking for? Do you have a picture in your mind of what you want but can't seem to find the right graphic to represent your ideas? To solve these problems, you can use graphics software. Graphics software allows you to change and create images and diagrams in almost unlimited ways. Typical uses for graphics software include arranging clip-art, changing scanned images, and constructing pictures from scratch. Most graphics-software applications work in similar ways. They use the same basic tools and functions. Once you master one graphics application, you can use any other graphics application relatively easily.

Example For your report on bird adaptations, you want to make a poster displaying a variety of beak and foot types. You have acquired many photos of birds, scanned from magazines and downloaded off the Internet. Using graphics software, you separate the beaks and feet from the birds and enlarge them. Then, you use arrows and text to diagram the particular features that you want to highlight. You also highlight the key features in color, keeping the rest of the graphic in black and white. With graphics software, the possibilities are endless. For the final layout, you place the picture of the bird next to enlarged graphics of the feet and beak. Graphics software allows you to integrate text into your diagrams, which makes your bird poster look clean and professional.

Helpful Hints

- As with any method of drawing, the more you practice using the graphic software, the better your results.
- Start by using the software to manipulate existing drawings. Once you master this, making your own illustrations will be easier.
- Clip art is available on CD-ROMs, and on the Internet. With these resources, finding a piece of clip art to suit your purposes is simple.
- As you work on a drawing, save it often.
- Often you can learn a lot from studying other people's art. Look at other computer illustrations and try to figure out how the artist created it.

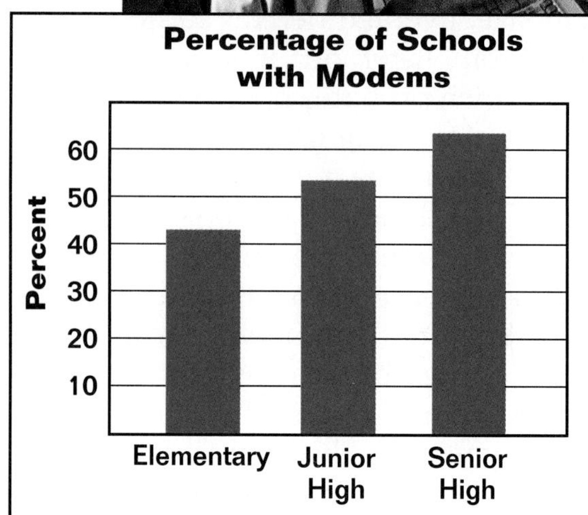

Using a Computerized Card Catalog

When you have a report or paper to research, you go to the library. To find the information, skill is needed in using a computerized card catalog. You use the computerized card catalog by typing in a subject, the title of a book, or an author's name. The computer will list on the screen all the holdings the library has on the subject, title, or author requested.

A library's holdings include books, magazines, databases, videos, and audio materials. When you have chosen something from this list, the computer will show whether an item is available and where in the library to find it.

Example You have a report due on dinosaurs, and you need to find three books on the subject. In the library, follow the instructions on the computer screen to select the "Subject" heading. You could start by typing in the word *dinosaurs.* This will give you a list of books on that subject. Now you need to narrow your search to the kind of dinosaur you are interested in, for example, *Tyrannosaurus rex.* You can type in *Tyrannosaurus rex* or just look through the list to find titles that you think would have information you need. Once you have selected a short list of books, click on each selection to find out if the library has the books. Then, check on where they are located in the library.

Helpful Hints

- Remember that you can use the computer to search by subject, author, or title. If you know a book's author, but not the title, you can search for all the books the library has by that author.
- When searching by subject, it's often most helpful to narrow your search by using specific search terms. If you don't find enough, you can then broaden your search.
- Pay attention to the type of materials found in your search. If you need a book, you can eliminate any videos or other resources that come up in your search.
- Knowing how your library is arranged can save a lot of time. The librarian will show you where certain types of material are kept and how to find something.

Developing Multimedia Presentations

It's your turn—you have to present your science report to the entire class. How do you do it? You can use many different sources of information to get the class excited about your presentation. Posters, videos, photographs, sound, computers, and the Internet can help show our ideas. First, decide the most important points you want your presentation to make. Then, sketch out what materials and types of media would be best to illustrate those points. Maybe you could start with an outline on an overhead projector, then show a video, followed by something from the Internet or a slide show accompanied by music or recorded voices. Make sure you don't make the presentation too complicated, or you will confuse yourself and the class. Practice your presentation a few times for your parents or brothers and sisters before you present it to the class.

Example Your assignment is to give a presentation on bird-watching. You could have a poster that shows what features you use to identify birds, with a sketch of your favorite bird. A tape of the calls of your favorite bird or a video of birds in your area would work well with the poster. If possible, include an Internet site with illustrations of birds that the class can look at.

Helpful Hints

- Carefully consider what media will best communicate the point you are trying to make.
- Keep your topic and your presentation simple.
- Make sure you learn how to use any equipment you will be using in your presentation.
- Practice the presentation several times.
- If possible, set up all of the equipment ahead of time. Make sure everything is working correctly.

Using E-Mail

It's science fair time and you want to ask a scientist a question about your project, but he or she lives far away. You could write a letter or make a phone call. But you can also use the computer to communicate. You can do this using electronic mail (E-mail). You will need a computer that is connected to an E-mail network. The computer is usually hooked up to the network by a device called a *modem.* A modem works through the telephone lines. Finally, you need an address for the person you want to talk with. The E-mail address works just like a street address to send mail to that person.

Example There are just a few steps needed to send a message to a friend on an E-mail network. First, select Message from the E-mail software menu. Then, enter the E-mail address of your friend. Next, type your message. Make sure you check it for spelling and other errors. Finally, click the Send button to mail your message and off it goes! You will get a reply back in your electronic mailbox. To read your reply, just click on the message and the reply will appear on the screen.

Helpful Hints

- Make sure that you have entered the correct address of the person you're sending the message to.
- Reread your message to make sure it says what you want to say, and check for spelling and grammar.
- If you receive an E-mail message, respond to it as soon as possible.
- If you receive frequent email messages, keep them organized by either deleting them, or saving them in folders according to the subject or sender.

Using an Electronic Spreadsheet

Your science fair experiment has produced lots of numbers. How do you keep track of all the data, and how can you easily work out all the calculations needed? You can use a computer program called a *spreadsheet* to keep track of data that involve numbers. A spreadsheet is an electronic worksheet. Type in your data in rows and columns, just as in a data table on a sheet of paper. A spreadsheet uses some simple math to do calculations on the data. For example, you could add, subtract, divide, or multiply any of the values in the spreadsheet by another number. Or you can set up a series of math steps you want to apply to the data. If you want to add 12 to all the numbers and then multiply all the numbers by 10, the computer does all the calculations for you in the spreadsheet. Below is an example of a spreadsheet that is a schedule.

Test Run Data

	A	B	C	D
1	Test Runs	Time	Distance	Speed
2	Car 1	5 mins.	5 miles	60 mph
3	Car 2	10 mins.	4 miles	24 mph
4	Car 3	6 mins.	3 miles	30 mph
5				
6				
7				
8				
9				
10				
11				
12				
13				
14				

Example Let's say that to complete your project, you need to calculate the speed of the model cars in your experiment. Enter the distance traveled by each car in the rows of the spreadsheet. Then enter the time you recorded for each car to travel the measured distance in the column across from each car. To make the formula, just type in the equation you want the computer to calculate; in this case, *speed* = *distance* ÷ *time*. You must make sure the computer knows what data are in the rows and what data are in the columns so the calculation will be correct. Once all the distance and time data and the formula have been entered into the spreadsheet program, the computer will calculate the speed for all the trials you ran. You can even make graphs of the results.

Helpful Hints

- Before you set up the spreadsheet, sketch out how you want to organize the data. Include any formulas you will need to use.
- Make sure you have entered the correct data into the correct rows and columns.
- As you experiment with your particular spreadsheet program you will learn more of its features.
- You can also display your results in a graph. Pick the style of graph that best represents the data you are working with.

Using a CD-ROM

What's your favorite music? You probably listen to your favorite music on compact discs (CDs). But, there is another use for compact discs, called CD-ROM. CD-ROM means Compact Disc-Read Only Memory. CD-ROMs hold information. Whole encyclopedias and dictionaries can be stored on CD-ROM discs. This kind of CD-ROM and others are used to research information for reports and papers. The information is accessed by putting the disc in your computer's CD-ROM drive and following the computer's installation instructions. The CD-ROM will have words, pictures, photographs, and maybe even sound and video on a range of topics.

Example Load the CD-ROM into the computer. Find the topic you are interested in by clicking on the Search button. If there is no Search button, try the Help button. Most CD-ROMs are easy to use, but refer to the Help instructions if you have problems. Use the arrow keys to move down through the list of titles on your topic. When you double-click on a title, the article will appear on the screen. You can print the article by clicking on the Print button. Each CD-ROM is different. Click the Help menu to see how to find what you want.

Helpful Hints

- Always open and close the CD-ROM drive on your computer by pushing the button next to the drive. Pushing on the tray to close it will stress the opening mechanism over time.
- Place the disc in the tray so the side with no printing is facing down.
- Read through the installation instructions that come with the CD-ROM.
- Remember to remove the CD-ROM before you shut your computer down.

Using Probeware

Data collecting in an experiment sometimes requires that you take the same measurement over and over again. With probeware, you can hook a probe directly to a computer and have the computer collect the data about temperature, pressure, motion, or pH. Probeware is a combination sensor and software that makes the process of collecting data easier. With probes hooked to computers, you can make many measurements quickly, and you can collect data over a long period of time without needing to be present. Not only will the software record the data, most software will graph the data.

Example Suppose you want to monitor the health of an enclosed ecosystem. You might use an oxygen and a carbon dioxide sensor to monitor the gas concentrations or humidity or temperature. If the gas concentrations remain stable, you could predict that the ecosystem is healthy. After all the data is collected, you can use the software to graph the data and analyze it. With probeware, experimenting is made efficient and precise.

Helpful Hints

- Find out how to properly use each probe before using it.
- Make sure all cables are solidly connected. A loose cable can interrupt the data collection and give you inaccurate results.
- Because probeware makes data collection so easy, do as many trials as possible to strengthen your data.

Using a Graphing Calculator

Science can be thought of as a means to predict the future and explain the past. In other language, if x happens, can we predict y? Can we explain the reason y happened? Simply, is there a relationship between x and y? In nature, a relationship between two events or two quantities, x and y, often occurs. However, the relationship is often complicated and can only be readily seen by making a graph. To analyze a graph, there is no quicker tool than a graphing calculator. The graphing calculator shows the mathematical relationship between two quantities.

Example If you have collected data on the position and time for a migrating whale, you can use the calculator to graph the data. Using the linear regression function on the calculator, you can determine the average migration speed of the whale. The more you use the graphing calculator to solve problems, the more you will discover its power and efficiency.

Graphing calculators have some keys that other calculators do not have. The keys on the bottom half of the calculator are those found on all scientific calculators. The keys located just below the screen are the graphing keys. You will also notice the up, down, left, and right arrow keys. These allow you to move the cursor around on the screen, to "trace" graphs that have been plotted, and to choose items from the menus. The other keys located on the top of the calculator access the special features such as statistical computations and programming features.

A few of the keystrokes that can save you time when using the graphing calculator are listed below.

- The commands above the calculator keys are accessed with the 2nd or ALPHA key. The 2nd key and its commands are yellow and the ALPHA and its commands are green.
- 2nd [ENTRY] copies the previous calculation so you can edit and use it again.
- Pressing ON while the calculator is graphing stops the calculator from completing the graph.
- 2nd [QUIT] will return you to the home (or text) screen.
- 2nd [A-LOCK] locks the ALPHA key, which is like pressing "shift lock" or "caps lock" on a typewriter or computer. The result is that all letters will be typed and you do not have to repeatedly press the ALPHA key. (This is handy for programming.) Stop typing letters by pressing ALPHA again.
- 2nd [OFF] turns the calculator off.

Helpful Hints

- Mastering the graphing calculator takes practice. Don't expect to learn it all in an afternoon.
- Programming a graphing calculator takes a plan. Write out all of the steps before entering them.
- It's easiest to learn how to program the calculator by first using programs that have already been written. As you enter them, figure out what each step is telling the calculator to do.

Skill Activities

Table of Contents

Skill Activity

Use After Section 17-3

Using Numbers

Background

The length of time it takes for a satellite to complete one orbit is called the orbital period. The greater the altitude of a satellite, the longer its orbital period. Satellites that stay above the same spot on Earth's surface are called geostationary satellites. Communication systems for telephone and television use geostationary satellites.

What is the altitude of a geostationary orbit? Try the following procedure to determine the altitude of a geostationary orbit.

Orbital Data

Altitude of orbit (km)	Orbital velocity (km/hr)	Orbital circumference (km)	Orbital period (hr)
10 000	26 470	46 400	
20 000	17 770	103 000	
30 000	11 920	229 000	
40 000	10 560	292 000	
50 000	9575	354 000	

Procedure

1. The Orbital Data table lists the altitude, speed, and circumference of six different orbits. The orbital period can be calculated by dividing the circumference by the speed. Calculate the orbital periods for each altitude and record the data.
2. Make a line graph that compares the altitude and orbital period.

Orbital Periods of Earth Satellites

Orbital Period (h): 0, 10, 20, 30, 40

Orbital Altitude (km): 10 000, 30 000, 50 000

Practicing the SKILL

1. What is the relationship between the altitude and the orbital speed?
2. What is the approximate altitude of a satellite in a geostationary orbit?

For more skill practice, do the Chapter 17 Interactive Exploration on the **Science Voyages Level Blue CD-ROM.**

Interpreting Scientific Illustrations

Background

During a total solar eclipse, the moon's shadow falls on Earth. The darkest part of the shadow, the umbra, traces a narrow, curved path across Earth's surface. By plotting the moon's orbit and phases, scientists are able to predict the umbra's path for future total solar eclipses. The world map below shows the times and locations of all total solar eclipses until the year 2020.

When and where will future total solar eclipses occur?

Procedure

1. Study the map of future eclipses.
2. Answer the questions in the Practicing the Skill box.

Practicing the SKILL

1. When will the next total solar eclipse occur in the United States? How old will you be at this time?
2. Which eclipse path will be located mostly over the ocean?
3. How many total solar eclipses will occur between the years 1999 and 2020?

For more skill practice, do the Chapter 18 Interactive Exploration on the **Science Voyages Level Blue CD-ROM.**

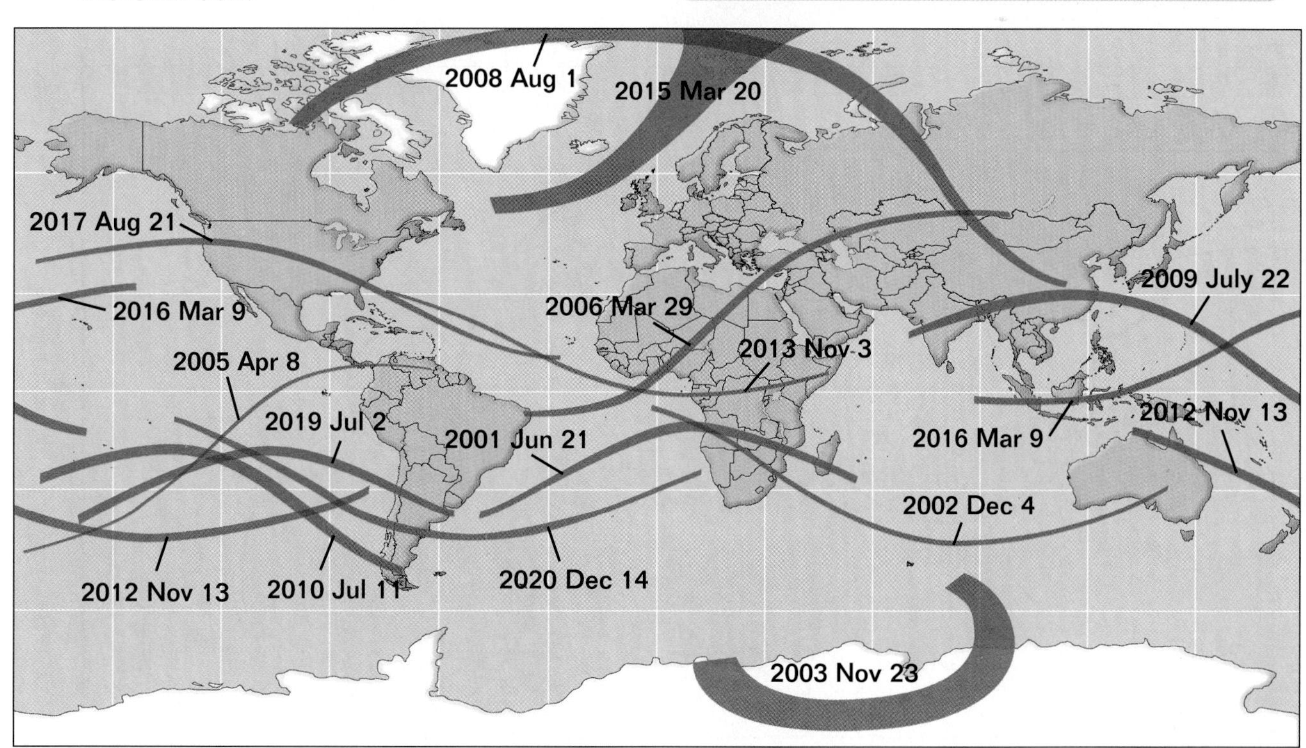

Chapter 19

Skill Activity

Use After Section 19-4

Inferring

Background

The surfaces of Earth's moon, Mercury, and other planetary bodies often are covered with craters. Scientists usually are unable to determine the exact age of the craters because they do not have actual rock samples. However, photographs taken by satellites help scientists determine the rough ages of the craters. For example, if two craters overlap, the crater that appears to be underneath is the older of the two.

Procedure

1. The diagram below shows an area containing several craters. Each crater is labeled by a letter in its center. Study the relationships between the craters and determine their relative ages.

Practicing the SKILL

1. Which crater occurred first, crater A or crater C?
2. Can the rough age of crater J be determined? Why or why not?
3. What is the estimated diameter of crater D?
4. List craters A through I in order of increasing age (youngest crater first).

For more skill practice, do the Chapter 19 Interactive Exploration on the **Science Voyages Level Blue CD-ROM.**

GLENCOE TECHNOLOGY

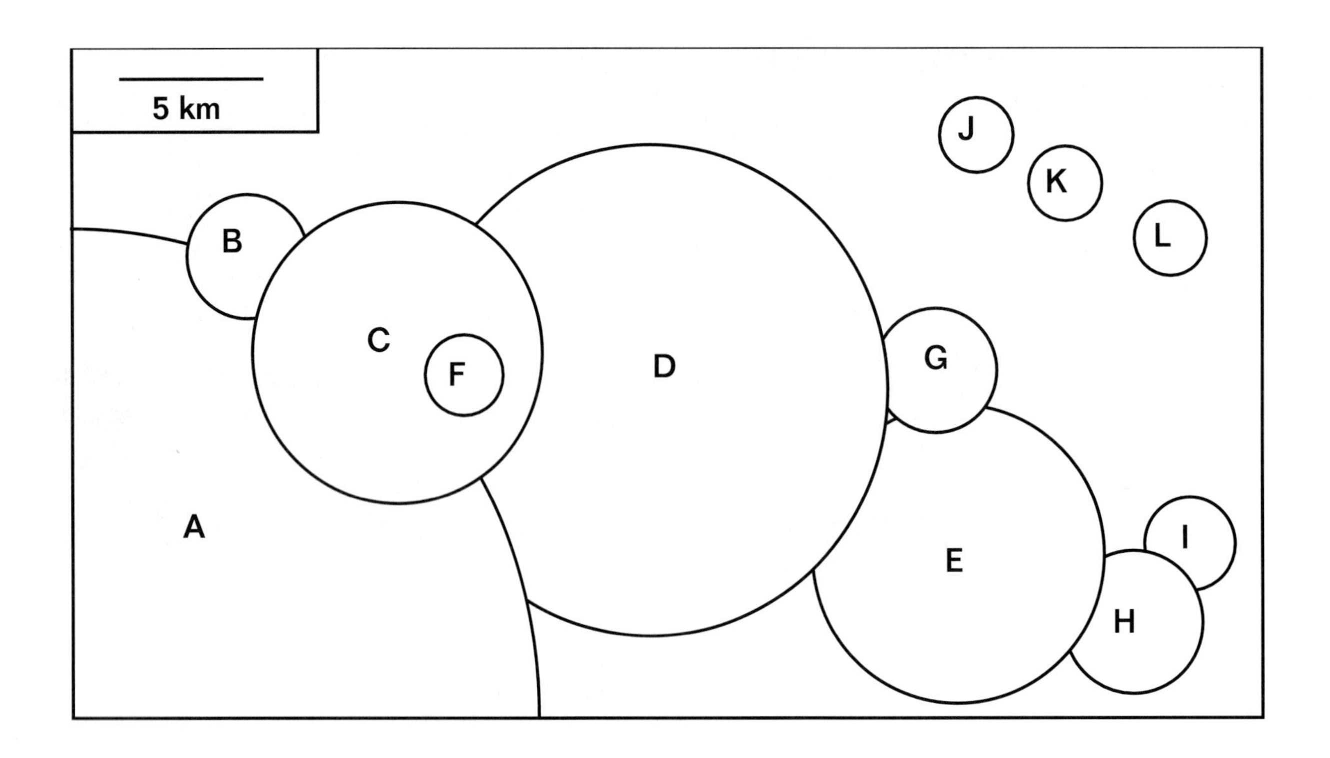

Predicting

Background

Astronomical distances are measured in light-years. A light-year is the distance that light can travel in one year. Proxima Centauri is a star that is 4.2 light-years away from Earth. When astronomers observe Proxima Centauri, they are seeing what occurred 4.2 years ago. In other words, when you look at the stars, you are looking back in time. The light astronomers observe for Proxima Centauri left the star 4.2 years ago.

What was happening on Earth when a star's light began its journey?

Star Distances

Star	Distance from Earth in light-years	Star	Distance from Earth in light-years
Sirius	8.8	Deneb	1800
Arcturus	36	Barnard's Star	5.9
Rigel	920	Wolf 359	7.6
Betelgeuse	310	Procyon	11
Antares	330	Altair	17
Vega	26	Regulus	85

Procedure

1. The Star Distances table lists the distances to several different stars. Study these distances to determine how long the light has been traveling toward Earth.
2. Using your history references, find a significant event that occurred when light from a particular star began its journey to Earth.
3. Make a data table that lists the significant historical events that occurred when light from the stars began the journey to Earth. Include the historical event, date, and the star in your table. Use at least six of the stars listed.

Practicing the SKILL

1. On July 20, 1969, astronauts landed on the moon. If a television signal showing this landing had been broadcast out to space, which stars would it have reached by the year 2000? by 2005? (Television signals travel at the speed of light, which is 300 000 km/s in a vacuum.)
2. Describe a historic event that took place when light from Rigel began traveling toward Earth.
3. How many times farther is Arcturus from Earth than Barnard's Star is?

For more skill practice, do the Chapter 20 Interactive Exploration on the **Science Voyages Level Blue CD-ROM.**

GLENCOE TECHNOLOGY

Interpreting Data

Background

Bacteriologists are people who study microorganisms, grow bacteria in dishes, and perform experiments on them. Although individual bacteria are too small to see with the naked eye, colonies that contain large numbers of bacteria are visible. The color and shape of the colony can help to identify the type of bacteria.

Scientists often use tables to organize data from experiments. Having data laid out in a logical way makes it easier to interpret. To interpret means to explain why something is the way it is. Interpreting data is determining why you got the results you did. Reading the following procedure and studying the data table will help you learn to interpret data.

Procedure

1. Imagine you are a bacteriologist trying to determine which household item is most effective in preventing the growth of bacteria. You design an experiment in which you have three sterile petri dishes that contain nutrient agar. You rub your finger over the entire surface of the agar in dishes 1 and 2 to introduce bacteria.
2. Next, you cut four small squares of filter paper, soaking them each in one of the following substances: hydrogen peroxide, mouthwash, alcohol, and disinfectant. They are labeled and placed in dish 1, without touching or overlapping. All three petri dishes are covered and placed in a warm, dark place for two days.
3. At the end of two days, you take out each dish to observe any growth. The Bacterial Growth table is a record of your observations.

Bacterial Growth

Dish	Square	Observations
1	hydrogen peroxide	a few colonies are observed
	mouthwash	many colonies are observed
	alcohol	very little growth under square or in surrounding area
	disinfectant	no growth under square or in surrounding area
2	none	hundreds of colonies are present
3	none	no colonies are observed

Practicing the SKILL

1. According to the data above, which substance was most effective in preventing bacterial growth? Which was least effective?
2. In dish 2, bacteria were added but no substance was placed in the dish. What was the purpose of this?
3. Dish 3 contained neither bacteria nor a substance. What purpose did this dish serve?

For more skill practice, do the Chapter 21 Interactive Exploration on the **Science Voyages Level Blue CD-ROM.**

Making and Using Tables

Background

Tables are used to record information so that it can be understood easily. Tables help you find information quickly by summarizing information given in the text. A table is similar to a system of classification. Information is grouped in vertical columns so that similarities and differences can be recognized easily. A table has three main parts: a title, vertical columns, and column headings. Sometimes, horizontal lines are used to group the information further.

Procedure

1. Study **Table 22-1** in the Protists and Fungi chapter. Examine the title. Look down the four columns to see if the information is related to the title and to each of the column headings.
2. Examine the information in **Table 22-1.** Notice how all four columns contain information on plantlike protists.
3. Using **Table 22-1,** answer the questions under Practicing the Skill.
4. Make a table of your own, similar to **Table 22-1,** in which you compare the different types of fungi discussed in Section 22-2.

Practicing the SKILL

1. What is the purpose of **Table 22-1?**
2. Which plantlike protist is used to give food a creamy texture?
3. What two plantlike protists have flagella?
4. Which plantlike protist has an eye-spot?
5. What groups of protists contain one-celled organisms, and which contain many-celled organisms?
6. Which plantlike protist can cause red tide?
7. Which has cell walls that contain silica?
8. Which protist is an important food source?
9. Why are tables used?

For more skill practice, do the Chapter 22 Interactive Exploration on the **Science Voyages Level Blue CD-ROM.**

Chapter 23

Skill Activity

Use after Section 23-3

Classifying

Background

Keys are used to identify things that are already classified.

In this Skill Activity, you will learn about some trees and how they have been classified. For this activity you need to know that needlelike leaves are shaped like needles and scalelike leaves are like the scales on a fish or a lizard.

How can you use a key to classify plants?

Procedure

1. Look at illustrations or actual examples of gymnosperm leaves.
2. Make a data table and record the number of each leaf down one side.
3. Use the key below to identify the leaves. There may be differences among the leaves. Choose the statement that describes most of the leaves on the branch. By following the key, the numbered steps will lead you to the name of the plant.

Key to Classifying Leaves

1. All leaves are needlelike.
   a. yes, go to 2
   b. no, go to 8
2. Needles are in clusters.
   a. yes, go to 3
   b. no, go to 4
3. Clusters contain 2, 3, or 5 needles.
   a. yes, pine
   b. no, cedar
4. Needles grow on all sides of the stem.
   a. yes, go to 5
   b. no, go to 7
5. Needles grow from a woody peg.
   a. yes, spruce
   b. no, go to 6
6. Needles appear to grow from the branch.
   a. yes, Douglas fir
   b. no, hemlock
7. Most of the needles grow upward.
   a. yes, fir
   b. no, redwood
8. All needles are scalelike but not prickly.
   a. yes, arborvitae
   b. no, juniper

Practicing the SKILL

1. What trait was used to separate the gymnosperm leaves into two groups?
2. What are two traits of a hemlock?
3. What gymnosperms have scalelike leaves?
4. Describe a spruce leaf.
5. How are pine and cedar leaves alike?

For more skill practice, do the Chapter 23 Interactive Exploration on the **Science Voyages Level Blue CD-ROM.**

Skill Activity

Use After Section 24-2

Comparing and Contrasting

Background

Determining the type of symmetry an animal has will help you describe the animal, as well as to determine what other animals it might be related to. In this Skill Activity, you will make some decisions about the type of symmetry of several animals.

Procedure

1. Review the discussion of symmetry in Section 24-1 of your textbook. Observe the animals pictured on this page.
2. Decide if the animal has radial symmetry, bilateral symmetry, or no symmetry.
3. Make a copy of the table below and record your answers in this table. If you need additional help, read about the animal's structure in reference books.
4. Explain how you decided what type of symmetry the animal has. Write your explanation in the table column labeled "Reason."

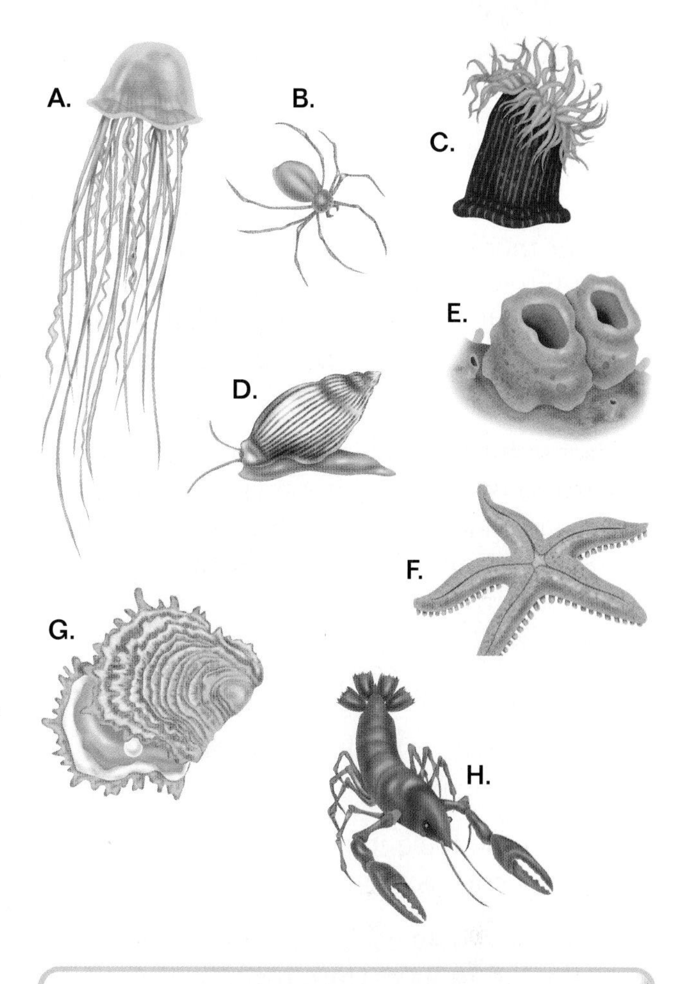

Animal Symmetry

Animal	Symmetry	Reason
jellyfish		
crayfish		
sponge		
spider		
sea star		
oyster		
snail		
sea anemone		

Practicing the SKILL

1. Which animals have radial symmetry? Bilateral symmetry? No symmetry?
2. What kind of symmetry do you think most animals have?
3. If an animal has a front and hind end, what kind of symmetry does it have?

For more skill practice, do the Chapter 24 Interactive Exploration on the **Science Voyages Level Blue CD-ROM.**

Chapter 25

Skill Activity

Use After Section 25-4

Observing and Inferring

Background

Have you ever seen an animal track in the snow or mud? If you have, you probably tried to identify what animal left it there. You probably inferred what type of animal left it there based on observations you made about the area you were in.

Scientists also draw conclusions based on observations of the environment. In this activity, you will identify animal tracks and determine which animal made the tracks.

Procedure

1. Look at the figure below.
2. Decide which track belongs to which type of animal.
3. Copy the table in your Science Journal and record your answers.
4. Describe how each animal's foot is adapted to its environment.

Identifying Animal Tracks

Animal	Track	Adaptation
Bear		
Beaver		
Cheetah		
Deer		
Horse		
Moose		
Raccoon		

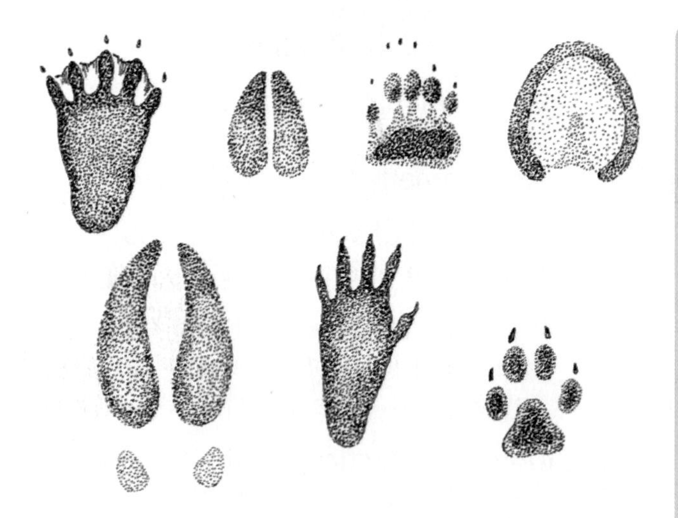

Practicing the SKILL

1. Could you expect to find a raccoon track in the same area you found a cheetah track? Explain.
2. What are the differences between track **b** and **e**? How does that help you identify the track?

For more skill practice, do the Chapter 25 Interactive Exploration on the **Science Voyages Level Blue CD-ROM.**

Chapter 26 **Skill Activity** Use After Section 26-2

Communicating

Background

Not all of the information that we read is presented honestly or accurately. In order to make informed decisions, you must be able to evaluate critically the information you read to make sure that the information is not only accurate but also that it is not biased or slanted to one particular view. Use the following guidelines to determine if the scientific information you read is reliable.

Procedure

1. Check the background of the author. Most articles written in journals or magazines give a brief biographical sketch of the author. Is the author a professional in the field about which he or she is writing, or is the author trained in another, unrelated field? Has the author earned awards in that field or awards from any of the major scientific societies?
2. Check the source of the article. Has the article been written for a scientific journal or has the article appeared in a popular magazine or local newspaper?
3. Evaluate the emotional level of the information. Scientific information is generally written in a straightforward style. When you read an article, consider the question: Does the headline or title make you angry, sad, or happy?
4. Read the article for how the content is presented. Check to see that concepts are clearly explained and supported by research. Be wary if many conclusions are drawn from only one, limited experiment. Also watch for overuse of such comments as "I think," or "In my opinion."
5. Determine whether the information has been taken out of context. Is the scientist writing the article or has someone reinterpreted the scientist's comments? Is it possible that only parts of the quoted comments are reported?

Practicing the SKILL

1. Read the following headlines. Which one do you think would contain more reliable information?
   - **Strange Fish Kill Has Public Upset**
   - **Scientists Investigate the Death of Fish in Plum River**
2. Which of the following three periodicals would be the best source of information for the situations below?
   - *An environmental periodical*
   - *A consumer periodical*
   - *An encyclopedia*

   a. Which detergent will clean your clothes the best?

   b. What new compounds are being used in making detergents?

   c. What effect do phosphate detergents have on the environment?

For more skill practice, do the Chapter 26 Interactive Exploration on the **Science Voyages Level Blue CD-ROM.**

GLENCOE TECHNOLOGY

Chapter 27 **Skill Activity** Use After Section 27-2

Interpreting Scientific Illustrations and Data

Background

Over the last ten years, people have begun to build houses around Maple Lake. Forty percent of the shoreline now has been developed. Recently, the residents have begun to complain about excessive algae growth and poor fishing. A scientific study indicates high levels of phosphates and nitrates in the lake. In an effort to locate the source of these chemicals, scientists collected and analyzed water samples. The sample locations are shown and the analyses are listed in the table below.

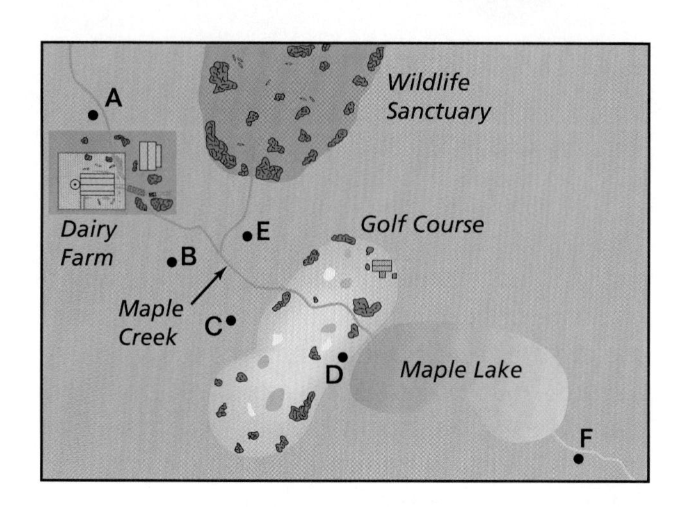

Procedure

1. Study the map of the Maple Lake area.
2. Study the table that lists location by letter and the amount of nitrates and phosphates at each location.
3. Use the map and the table to answer the questions in Practicing the Skill.

Location of Chemicals in Maple Lake

Location	Nitrates	Phosphates
A	2 ppm*	1 ppm
B	16 ppm	2 ppm
C	8 ppm	1 ppm
D	25 ppm	12 ppm
E	<1 ppm	<1 ppm
F	30 ppm	15 ppm

*The abbreviation "ppm" means parts per million. For example, 2 ppm here means 2 parts nitrates per million parts water in Maple Lake.

Practicing the SKILL

1. What might be the source of pollution at B?
2. Why do you think the level of chemicals dropped from B to C?
3. How do you explain the data at D?
4. The level of chemicals at F are higher than D. Where do you think the extra nitrates and phosphates are coming from?
5. A scientist has proposed to create a large water hyacinth pond on the creek between the golf course and Maple Lake. Do you think this will help with the algae problem in the lake? Why or why not?

For more skill practice, do the Chapter 27 Interactive Exploration on the **Science Voyages Level Blue CD-ROM**

GLENCOE TECHNOLOGY

English Glossary

This glossary defines each key term that appears in bold type in the text. It also shows the chapter and page number where you can find the word used.

Pronunciation Key

a...**ba**ck (bak)	oh...g**o** (goh)	sh...**sh**elf (shelf)
ay...d**ay** (day)	aw...s**o**ft (sawft)	ch...na**t**ure (nay chur)
ah...f**a**ther (fahth ur)	or...**or**bit (or but)	g...**g**ift (gihft)
ow...fl**ow**er (flow ur)	oy...c**oi**n (coyn)	j...**g**em (jem)
ar...c**ar** (car)	oo...f**oo**t (foot)	ing...s**ing** (sing)
e...l**e**ss (les)	ew...f**oo**d (fewd)	zh...vi**s**ion (vihzh un)
ee...l**ea**f (leef)	yoo...p**u**re (pyoor)	k...ca**k**e (kayk)
ih...tr**i**p (trihp)	yew...f**ew** (fyew)	s...**s**eed, **c**ent (seed, sent)
i (i + con + e)...**i**dea (i dee uh), l**i**fe (life)	uh...comm**a** (cahm uh)	z...**z**one, rai**s**e (zohn, rayz)
	u (+ con)...flow**er** (flo ur)	

A

absolute magnitude: measure of the amount of light a star actually emits. (ch. 20, p. 702)

acid rain: rain, snow, sleet, or hail with a pH below 5.6 that is created when sulfur dioxide or nitrogen oxides combine with moisture in the air; can kill plants, trees, and fish, and damage the surfaces of cars and buildings. (ch. 27, p. 912)

acids: substances that contain hydrogen and produce positively charged hydronium ions when they dissolve in water, forming acidic solutions (ch. 27, p. 912)

aerobes: organisms that require oxygen to survive—for example, humans and most bacteria. (ch. 21, p. 742)

algae (AL gee): one- or many-celled plantlike protists, all of which contain chlorophyll and can make their own food; organized into six main phyla based on their structure, their pigments, and the way they store food. (ch. 23, p. 759)

amphibian: ectothermic vertebrate that spends part of its life in water and part on land. (ch. 25, p. 850)

anaerobes: organisms that are able to live without oxygen—for example, methanogens and thermophiles. (ch. 21, p. 742)

angiosperms (AN jee uh spurmz): vascular plants that flower, have their seeds contained in a fruit, and are the most common form of plant life on Earth. (ch. 23, p. 803)

antibiotic: substance, such as penicillin, produced by one organism that inhibits or kills another organism. (ch. 21, p. 746)

apparent magnitude: measure of the amount of light that is received on Earth from a star. (ch. 20, p. 702)

appendages: jointed structures, such as legs, claws, and antennae, that grow from a body. (ch. 24, p. 832)

arthropod: animals that have jointed appendages, such as an insect or a crustacean, that is classified by the number of body segments and appendages, and that has a protective exoskeleton. (ch. 24, p. 832)

asteroid: piece of rock usually found in the asteroid belt between the orbits of Mars and Jupiter. (ch. 19, p. 691)

astronomical unit: average distance from Earth to the sun (150 million km), which is used to measure distances to objects in the solar system. (ch. 19, p. 676)

axis: imaginary line around which Earth spins. (ch. 18, p. 641)

B

bases: substances that produce negatively charged hydroxide ions when they dissolve in water, forming basic solutions (ch. 27, p. 912)

big bang theory: states that approximately 15 billion years ago, the universe began expanding out of an enormous explosion. (ch. 20, p. 723)

binary system: system in which two stars orbit each other. (ch. 27, p. 708)

bird: endothermic vertebrate with feathers, two legs, two wings, and bills, or beaks, and that lays hard-shelled eggs. (ch. 25, p. 856)

black hole: remnant of a star that is so dense that nothing can escape its gravity. (ch. 20, p. 714)

budding: form of asexual reproduction in which a new organism grows off the side of the parent. (ch. 22, p. 772)

C

cambium (KAM bee um): vascular plant tissue that produces new xylem and phloem cells. (ch. 23, p. 799)

carnivore: flesh-eating animals. (ch. 25, p. 868)

carrying capacity: maximum number of individuals of a particular species that the planet will support. (ch. 26, p. 880)

cartilage: tough, flexible tissue that is similar to bone but is not as hard. (ch. 25, p. 848)

cellulose (SEL yuh lohs): organic compound made of long chains of glucose molecules; forms the rigid cell walls of plants. (ch. 23, p. 786)

chordate: animal with a notochord, a dorsal hollow nerve cord, and gill slits. (ch. 25, p. 846)

chromosphere: layer of the sun's atmosphere above the photosphere and below the corona. (ch. 20, p. 705)

cilia (SIHL ee uh): short, threadlike structures that extend from the cell membrane of ciliates and are used for movement. (ch. 22, p. 765)

Clean Air Act: protects air quality by regulating car manufacturers, coal technologies, and other industries. (ch. 27, p. 914)

Clean Water Act: provides money to states for building sewage and wastewater-treatment facilities and for controlling runoff; also requires states to develop quality standards for their streams. (ch. 27, p. 923)

closed circulatory system: type of blood-circulation system in which blood is carried through blood vessels. (ch. 24, p. 825)

cnidarians (NIH dar ee uns): phylum of hollow-bodied, water-dwelling animals with stinging cells, radial symmetry, a body two layers thick, and both sexual and asexual reproduction. (ch. 24, p. 819)

comet: mass of dust and rock particles mixed in with frozen water, ammonia, and methane; consists of a nucleus, a coma, and a tail. (ch. 19, p. 688)

composting: piling yard wastes where they can gradually decompose. (ch. 26, p. 894)

conservation: careful use of resources to reduce damage to the environment by means such as reducing our use of materials, reusing items, and recycling materials. (ch. 26, p. 893)

constellation: group of stars that forms a pattern that looks like a familiar object, animal, or character. (ch. 20, p. 700)

contour feathers: strong, lightweight feathers that give birds their coloring and streamlined shape and that are used to fly and to steer. (ch. 25, p. 859)

corona: largest layer of the sun's atmosphere that extends millions of miles into space. (ch. 20, p. 705)

cuticle (KYEWT ih kul): waxy, protective layer covering the stems, leaves, and flowers of some land plants; is secreted by the plant's cell walls and slows the evaporation of water. (ch. 23, p. 787)

D

dicot: class of angiosperm that has two seed leaves inside its seeds, vascular bundles that occur in rings, and flower parts in multiples of four or five. (ch. 23, p. 804)

down feathers: soft, fluffy feathers that provide an insulating layer next to the skin of adult birds and that cover the bodies of young birds. (ch. 25, p. 859)

E

Earth: third planet from the sun; surface temperatures allow water to exist as a solid, liquid, and gas and atmosphere protects life from the sun's radiation. (ch. 19, p. 676)

ectotherm: vertebrate whose body temperature changes with the temperature of its surroundings. (ch. 25, p. 846)

electromagnetic spectrum: arrangement of electromagnetic radiation according to wavelength. (ch. 17, p. 613)

ellipse (ee LIHPS): elongated, closed curve that describes Earth's orbit. (ch. 18, p. 643)

endoskeleton: internal system of bones that protects and supports an animal's internal organs and also provides a place for muscle attachment. (ch. 25, p. 846)

endospores: heat-resistant, thick-walled structures many bacteria can produce around themselves when conditions are unfavorable. (ch. 21, p. 747)

endotherm: vertebrate that maintains a constant body temperature. (ch. 25, p. 846)

equinox (EE kwuh nahks): twice-yearly time when the sun is directly above Earth's equator and the number of nighttime hours equals the number of daylight hours worldwide. (ch. 18, p. 645)

estivation: behavioral adaptation for survival during hot, dry summer months, during which an animal becomes inactive; in amphibians, involves hiding in cooler, more humid ground. (ch. 25, p. 851)

exoskeleton: lightweight body covering that protects and supports an arthropod's body, prevents it from drying out, and is shed by molting. (ch. 24, p. 832)

F

fins: fanlike structures of most fish that are used for balancing, steering, and moving, and usually are paired. (ch. 25, p. 847)

first quarter: moon phase in which one-quarter of the moon's surface that faces Earth is lit up; occurs about a week after a new moon. (ch. 18, p. 651)

fish: ectotherm that lives in water and uses gills to get oxygen; usually has fins and scales. (ch. 25, p. 847)

fission: simplest form of asexual reproduction in which two cells are produced with genetic material identical to that of the parent cell; the method by which bacteria reproduce. (ch. 21, p. 742)

flagella: whiplike tails that help many types of bacteria move around in moist environments. (ch. 21, p. 739)

free-living: organism, such as a planarian, that doesn't depend on one particular organism for food or a place to live. (ch. 24, p. 821)

full moon: moon phase in which all of the moon's surface that faces Earth is lit up. (ch. 18, p. 651)

G

galaxy: large group of stars, gas, and dust held together by gravity. (ch. 20, p. 717)

giant: stage in a star's life cycle where hydrogen in the core is used up, the core contracts, and temperatures inside the star increase, causing the outer layers of the star to expand. (ch. 20, p. 713)

gills: organs that exchange oxygen and carbon dioxide with water. (ch. 24, p. 823)

Great Red Spot: high-pressure storm generated by huge thunderstorms in Jupiter's atmosphere. (ch. 19, p. 680)

guard cells: in a plant leaf, the cells that surround the stomata and that open and close them. (ch. 23, p. 801)

gymnosperms (JIHM nuh spurmz): vascular plants that produce seeds on the surface of the female reproductive structures, do not have flowers, and generally have needlelike or scalelike leaves. (ch. 23, p. 802)

hazardous wastes: poisonous, cancer-causing, or radioactive wastes that are dangerous to living things. (ch. 26, p. 889)

herbivore: grazing animal that eats only plants. (ch. 25, p. 868)

hibernation: behavioral adaptation for survival during cold, winter months, where an animal becomes inactive and its metabolic needs are lowered; in amphibians, involves burying themselves in mud or leaves until temperatures become warmer. (ch. 25, p. 851)

hyphae (HI fee): mass of many-celled, threadlike tubes that usually make up the body of a fungus. (ch. 22, p. 770)

inner planets: four solid, rocky planets that are closest to the sun—Mercury, Venus, Earth, and Mars. (ch. 19, p. 671)

invertebrates (ihn VURT uh brayts): animals lacking a backbone; about 97 percent of animals are invertebrates. (ch. 24, p. 815)

Jupiter: largest planet and fifth planet from the sun; composed mostly of hydrogen and helium; has continuous storms of high-pressure gas. (ch. 19, p. 680)

L

landfill: area where waste is deposited; the majority of U.S. garbage goes into landfills. (ch. 26, p. 889)

lichen (LI kun): organism that is made up of a fungus and a green alga or a cyanobacterium; an important food source for many animals; used by scientists to monitor pollution levels. (ch. 22, p. 773)

light-year: distance that light travels in one year (9.5 trillion km), which is used to measure distances in space. (ch. 20, p. 703)

lunar eclipse: eclipse that occurs when Earth's shadow falls on the moon. (ch. 18, p. 654)

M

main sequence: in an H-R diagram, the diagonal band of stars that runs from hot, bright stars in the upper-left corner of the diagram to cool, faint stars in the lower-right corner. (ch. 20, p. 710)

mammal: endothermic vertebrate that has hair and produces milk to feed its young. (ch. 25, p. 862)

mantle: thin tissue layer covering a mollusk's soft body; secretes the protective shell of those mollusks having a shell. (ch. 24, p.823)

maria: dark-colored, relatively flat areas of the moon that were formed when ancient lava filled basins on the moon's surface. (ch. 18, p. 655)

Mars: fourth planet from the sun; appears red due to the iron oxide content in its weathered rocks. (ch. 19, p. 676)

marsupial: mammal that gives birth to immature offspring and that has a pouch in which its young complete their development. (ch. 25, p. 864)

mascon: concentration of mass on the moon located beneath an impact basin. (ch. 18, p. 659)

medusa: free-swimming, bell-shaped body plan of a cnidarian, such as a jellyfish, that allows it to drift with the ocean currents. (ch. 24, p. 819)

Mercury: planet closest to the sun; has many craters, low gravitational pull, and is the second-smallest planet in our solar system. (ch. 19, p. 674)

metamorphosis (met uh MOR fuh sus): process in which insects change their body form as they mature; can be complete (egg, larva, pupa, and adult) or incomplete (egg, nymph, and adult). (ch. 24, p. 834)

meteor: meteoroid that burns up in Earth's atmosphere. (ch. 19, p. 690)

meteorite: meteoroid that does not completely burn up in Earth's atmosphere and strikes Earth. (ch. 19, p. 690)

mollusk: soft-bodied invertebrate that has a mantle, a large muscular foot, a complete digestive system with two openings, and usually has a protective shell. (ch. 24, p. 823)

monocot: class of angiosperm that has one seed leaf inside its seeds, vascular tissues arranged as bundles scattered throughout the stem, and flower parts in multiples of three. (ch. 23, p. 804)

monotreme: mammal that lays eggs with tough, leathery shells; the duckbilled platypus and two species of spiny anteaters. (ch. 25, p. 864)

moon phase: changing appearance of the moon as seen from Earth, which depends on the relative positions of the moon, Earth, and sun. (ch. 18, p. 651)

N

nebula: large cloud of gas and dust that can fragment into smaller pieces, each of which will collapse and form stars. (ch. 20, p. 712)

Neptune: large, gaseous planet similar to Uranus; is usually the eighth planet from the sun. (ch. 19, p. 684)

neutron star: collapsed core of a supernova that shrinks to about 10 km to 15 km in diameter and has only neutrons in the dense core. (ch. 20, p. 714)

new moon: moon phase that occurs when the lighted half of the moon faces the sun and the dark side faces Earth. (ch. 18, p. 651)

nitrogen-fixing bacteria: bacteria that live in the root nodules of certain kinds of plants and change nitrogen from the air into forms useful for animals and plants. (ch. 21, p. 746)

nonvascular plant: plant lacking vascular tissue and that absorbs water and other dissolved substances directly through its cell walls. (ch. 23, p. 788)

O

observatory: specially designed building, often with a dome-shaped roof that opens up to admit light; used to house optical telescopes. (ch. 17, p. 614)

omnivore: animals that eat both plants and animals. (ch. 25, p. 868)

Oort Cloud: cloud of comets that completely surrounds the solar system and that is located beyond the orbit of Pluto. (ch. 19, p. 689)

open circulatory system: type of blood-circulation system in which the blood is not contained in vessels but instead surrounds the organs. (ch. 24, p. 824)

orbit: curved path of a satellite as it revolves around an object in space. (ch. 17, p. 620)

outer planets: five planets that are farthest from the sun—Jupiter, Saturn, Uranus, Neptune, and Pluto. (ch. 19, p. 671)

P

parallax: apparent shift in position of an object when it is viewed from two different positions. (ch. 20, p. 703)

parasite: organism, such as a tapeworm, that depends on its host for food and a place to live. (ch. 24, p. 821)

pathogen: any organism that produces disease. (ch. 21, p. 746)

pH scale: scale used to describe how acidic or basic a substance is; ranges from 0 to 14, with 0 being the most acidic and 14 being the most basic. (ch. 27, p. 912)

phloem (FLOH em): vascular plant tissue made up of tubular cells that transport food from where it is made to other parts of the plant where it is used or stored. (ch. 23, p. 799)

photochemical smog: hazy, brown smog that is created when sunlight reacts with pollutants in the air; contains ozone near Earth's surface. (ch. 27, p. 910)

photosphere: lowest layer of the sun's atmosphere and the layer that gives off light. (ch. 20, p. 705)

pioneer species: first plants to grow in new or disturbed environments and that change environmental conditions so that other plant species can grow there. (ch. 23, p. 791)

placental mammal: mammal whose embryo develops in the uterus of the female. (ch. 25, p. 865)

Pluto: smallest planet and considered the ninth planet from the sun; has a thin, changing atmosphere and icy-rock surface. (ch. 19, p. 684)

polyp (PAHL up): vase-shaped body plan of a cnidarian, such as a hydra, that allows it to twist to capture prey and to somersault to a new location. (ch. 24, p. 819)

population: total number of individuals of a particular species in a specific area. (ch. 26, p. 881)

population explosion: rapidly increasing number of humans on Earth due to factors such as modern medicine, better sanitation, better nutrition, and more people surviving to the age when they can have children. (ch. 26, p. 881)

Project Apollo: final stage in the U.S. effort to reach the moon—on July 20, 1969, Neil Armstrong was the first human to set foot on the lunar surface. (ch. 17, p. 625)

Project Gemini: second stage in the U.S. program to reach the moon, in which a team of astronauts met and connected with another spacecraft while in orbit. (ch. 17, p. 624)

Project Mercury: first step in the U.S. effort to reach the moon, in which a piloted spacecraft successfully orbited around Earth and returned safely. (ch. 17, p. 624)

protist: single- or many-celled eukaryotic organism that lives in a moist or wet environment; can be plantlike, animal-like, or funguslike. (ch. 22, p. 758)

protozoans: complex, one-celled, animal-like protists that contain special vacuoles for digesting food and eliminating excess water; classified by their method of movement. (ch. 22, p. 763)

pseudopods (SEWD uh pahdz): temporary, footlike extensions of cytoplasm used by rhizopods for movement and for trapping food. (ch. 22, p. 764)

R

radio telescope: type of telescope that uses a large, curved dish to collect and record radio waves traveling through space and that can be used during the day or at night and during bad weather. (ch. 17, p. 615)

radula (RAJ uh luh): scratchy, tongue-like organ in many mollusks that acts like a file with rows of teeth to break up food into smaller pieces. (ch. 24, p. 823)

recyclable: any item that can be processed and used again in order to conserve natural resources and reduce solid waste. (ch. 26, p. 895)

reflecting telescope: optical telescope that uses a mirror (or mirrors) to focus light and produce an image at the focal point. (ch. 17, p. 614)

refracting telescope: optical telescope that uses a double convex lens to focus light and form an image at the focal point. (ch. 17, p. 614)

reptile: ectothermic vertebrate that has thick, dry, scaly skin, and does not depend on water for reproduction. (ch. 25, p. 853)

revolution: yearly orbit of Earth around the sun. (ch. 18, p. 643)

rhizoids: threadlike roots that are only a few cells in length and that anchor liverworts and mosses in place. (ch. 23, p. 790)

rotation: spinning of Earth on its axis, which causes day and night to occur. (ch. 18, p. 641)

S

Safe Drinking Water Act: strengthens health standards for drinking water; protects rivers, lakes, and streams; gives the public a right to know about contaminants that might be in their tap water. (ch. 27, p.923)

saprophyte: any organism that uses dead material as a food and energy source; sprophytes decompose dead organisms and recycles nutrients so that they are available for use by other organisms; saprophytic bacteria keep dead material from building up over all of Earth. (ch. 21, p. 745)

satellite: any object that revolves around another object; can be natural (Earth's moon) or artificial (*Sputnik I*). (ch. 17, p. 620)

Saturn: sixth planet from the sun; has a complex ring system made of hundreds of ringlets. (ch. 19, p. 681)

scrubber: device used in coal-burning power plants that allows the gases in the smoke to dissolve in water until the pH of the smoke increases to a safe level. (ch. 27, p. 915)

solar eclipse (ih KLIPS): eclipse that occurs when the moon moves directly between the sun and Earth and casts a shadow on part of Earth. (ch. 18, p. 652)

solar system: system of nine planets, including Earth and many smaller objects, that orbit the sun. (ch. 19, p. 669)

solstice: point at which the sun reaches its greatest distance north or south of the equator. (ch. 18, p. 645)

space probe: instrument that travels out into the solar system to gather information and sends the data back to Earth. (ch. 17, p. 621)

space shuttle: reusable spacecraft that carries astronauts, satellites, and other materials to and from space. (ch. 17, p. 628)

space station: large artificial satellite that provides support systems, living quarters, and equipment so that humans can live and work in space and conduct research not possible on Earth. (ch. 17, p. 629)

sphere (SFIHR): round, three-dimensional object whose surface at all points is the same distance from its center. (ch. 18, p. 640)

spore: reproductive cell that forms new organisms without fertilization. (ch. 22, p. 771)

stomata: small pores in the leaf surfaces surrounded by guard cells; allow carbon dioxide, oxygen, and water to enter and leave a leaf. (ch. 23, p. 801)

sulfurous smog: smog formed when burning fuel releases sulfur compounds in the air; may collect in an area where there's little or no wind. (ch. 27, p. 911)

sunspot: dark, relatively cool area on the surface of the sun. (ch. 20, p. 706)

supergiant: late stage in the life cycle of a massive star where the core reaches very high temperatures, heavy elements form by fusion, and the star expands. (ch. 20, p. 714)

symmetry: arrangement of the individual parts of an object; animals with bilateral symmetry have mirror image body parts; animals with radial symmetry have body parts arranged in a circle around a central point; asymmetrical animals have no definite shape. (ch. 24, p. 815)

third quarter: moon phase in which only half of the lighted side of the moon is visible. (ch. 18, p. 652)

toxin: poison produced by a bacterial pathogen. (ch. 28, p. 747)

Uranus: large, gaseous planet and seventh planet from the sun; has a magnetic pole tilted 60 degrees and rotates on an axis nearly parallel to the plane of its orbit. (ch. 19, p. 683)

V

vaccine: substance that is made from killed bacteria or damaged bacterial particles and can prevent, but not cure, many bacterial diseases. (ch. 21, p. 746)

vascular plant: plant with vascular tissue, a "pipeline" that moves water, food, and dissolved substances to cells throughout the plant. (ch. 23, p. 788)

Venus: second planet from the sun; has a dense atmosphere of carbon dioxide and sulfuric acid. (ch. 19, p. 675)

vertebrates (VURT uh brayts): animals with a backbone; only about 3 percent of animals are vertebrates. (ch. 24, p. 815)

waning: occurs after a full moon, when the amount of the moon's lighted side that can be seen becomes smaller. (ch. 18, p. 652)

waxing: occurs shortly after a new moon, when more and more of the moon's lighted side becomes visible. (ch. 20, p. 651)

white dwarf: late stage in a star's life cycle where its core uses up its supply of helium, it contracts, and its outer layers escape into space, leaving behind the hot dense core. (ch. 20, p. 714)

xylem (ZI lum): vascular plant tissue made up of tubular vessels that transport water and dissolved substances up from the roots throughout the plant. (ch. 23, p. 799)

Glossary/Glosario

Este glossario define cada término clave que aparece en **negrillas** en el texto. También muestra el número de página donde se usa dicho término.

A

absolute magnitude / magnitud absoluta: Medida de la cantidad de luz que una estrella emite verdaderamente. (Cap. 20, pág. 702)

acid / ácido: Sustancia con un pH menor de 7 en la escala de pH. (Cap. 27 pág. 912)

acid rain / lluvia ácida: Lluvia, nieve, cellisca o granizo con un pH menor que 5.6 que se forma cuando el dióxido sulfuroso o los óxidos de hidrógeno se combinan con la humedad del aire; puede matar plantas, árboles y peces, y además causar daños a las superficies de los carros y edificios. (Cap. 27, pág. 912)

aerobes / aerobios: Organismos que requieren oxigeno para sobrevivir, por ejemplo, los seres humanos y la mayoria de las bacterias. (Cap. 21, pág. 742)

algae / algas: Protistas unicelulares o multicelulares que parecen plantas, contienen clorofila y pueden fabricar su propio alimento; organizadas en seis filos principales con base en sus estructuras, sus pigmentos y la manera en que fabrican alimento. (Cap. 22, pág. 759)

amphibian / anfibio: Vertebrado de sangre fría que pasa parte de su vida en agua y parte sobre tierra. (Cap. 25, pág. 850)

anaerobes / anaerobios: Organismos con variaciones que les permiten vivir sin oxígeno, por ejemplo los metanógenos y los termófilos. (Cap. 21, pág. 742)

angiosperms / angiospermas: Plantas vasculares que florecen y producen frutos que contienen semillas. Son la forma más común de vida vegetal sobre la Tierra. (Cap. 23, pág. 803)

antibiotic / antibiótico: Sustancia producida por un organismo que inhibe o destruye otro organismo. La penicilina es un antibiótico muy conocido, el cual impide que las bacterias produzcan nuevas paredes celulares. (Cap. 21, pág. 746)

apparent magnitude / magnitud aparente: Medida de la cantidad de luz de una estrella que llega hasta la Tierra. (Cap. 20, pág. 702)

appendages / apéndices: Estructuras, tales como garras, patas o incluso antenas que crecen del cuerpo. (Cap. 24, pág. 832)

arthropod / artrópodo: Animal de patas articuladas, tal como un insecto o un crustáceo, que se clasifica de acuerdo con el número de segmentos corporales y apéndices y el cual tiene un exoesqueleto protector. El término artrópodo proviene de la palabra arthros que significa "unido" y de la palabra poda que significa "pata". (Cap. 24, pág. 832)

asteroid / asteroide: Fragmento rocoso semejante al material que formó los planetas. (Cap. 19, pág. 691)

astronomical unit / unidad astronómica: Medida que se usa para medir distancias hacia los objetos en el sistema solar; corresponde a 150 millones de kilómetros, lo cual es la distancia promedio entre la Tierra y el sol. (Cap. 19, pág. 676)

axis / eje: Línea imaginaria alrededor de la cual gira la Tierra. (Cap. 18, pág. 641)

B

bases / bases: Sustancias que producen iones hidroxilos negativos cuando se disuelven en agua, formando soluciones básicas ; sustancias con un pH mayor que siete. (Cap. 27, pág. 912)

big bang theory / teoría de la gran explosión: Teoría que enuncia que hace unos 15 billones de años, el universo comenzó con una enorme explosión. (Cap. 20, pág. 723)

binary system / sistema binario: Sistema en el cual dos estrellas giran una alrededor de la otra. (Cap. 20, pág. 708)

bird / ave: Vertebrado de sangre caliente con plumas, dos patas, dos alas y un pico, que pone huevos con cáscara dura. (Cap. 25, pág. 856)

black hole / agujero negro: Núcleo restante de una estrella de neutrones, el cual es tan denso y masivo que nada puede escapar de su campo de gravedad, ni siquiera la luz. (Cap. 20, pág. 714)

budding / gemación: Es una forma de reproducción asexual en que un nuevo organismo crece de un lado del organismo progenitor. (Cap. 22, pág. 772)

C

cambium / cambium: Tejido que produce nuevas células de xilema y de floema. (Cap. 23, pág. 799)

carnivore / carnívoro: Animal que se alimenta de la carne de otros animales. (Cap. 25, pág. 868)

carrying capacity / capacidad de carga: El mayor número de individuos, de una especie en particular, que el planeta puede soportar y mantener. (Cap. 26, pág. 880)

cartilage / cartílago: Tejido flexible fuerte que se parece al hueso, pero que no es tan duro como el hueso. (Cap. 25, pág. 848)

cellulose / celulosa: Compuesto orgánico hecho de cadenas largas de moléculas de glucosa, del cual están formadas las paredes celulares de las plantas. (Cap. 23, pág. 786)

chordate / cordado: Animal con notocordio, cordón nervioso dorsal hueco en sus espaldas y hendiduras branquiales. (Cap. 25, pág. 846)

chromosphere / cromosfera: Capa que se encuentra encima de la fotosfera y que se extiende por encima de esta unos 2000 km. (Cap. 20, pág. 705)

cilia / cilios: Estructuras cortas que parecen hilos y se extienden desde la membrana celular de los ciliados. (Cap. 22, pág. 765)

Clean Air Act / Ley para el Control de la Contaminación del Aire: Protege la calidad del aire al regular la industria automotriz, las tecnologías del carbón y otras industrias. (Cap. 27, pág. 914)

Clean Water Act / Ley para el Control de la Contaminación del Agua: Otorga fondos a los estados para la construcción de instalaciones de tratamiento de aguas negras y residuales y para el control de las aguas de desagüe. También requiere que los estados desarrollen estándares de calidad para sus corrientes de agua. (Cap. 27, pág. 923)

closed circulatory system / sistema circulatorio cerrado: Sistema circulatorio en que la sangre se transporta por el cuerpo a través de vasos sanguíneos. (Cap. 24, pág. 825)

cnidarians / cnidarios: Filo de animales acuáticos de cuerpo hueco que poseen células urticantes que usan para aturdir o atrapar presas de alimento; también poseen simetría radial. (Cap. 24, pág. 819)

comet / cometa: Objeto compuesto de polvo y partículas rocosas mezclados con agua congelada, metano y amoníaco. (Cap. 19, pág. 688)

composting / abono orgánico: Desechos vegetales que se apilan para que se descompongan paulatinamente. (Cap. 26, pág. 894)

conservation / conservación: Uso cuidadoso de los recursos, lo cual disminuye el daño al ambiente. (Cap. 26, pág. 893)

constellation / constelación: Grupo de estrellas en el firmamento. Las constelaciones recibieron nombres de animales, figuras mitológicas u objetos cotidianos. (Cap. 20, pág. 700)

contour feathers / plumas de contorno: Plumas fuertes y livianas que les dan a las aves sus bellos coloridos y sus perfiles aerodinámicos y las cuales usan para volar y para navegar. (Cap. 25, pág. 859)

corona / corona: La capa más grande de la atmósfera solar, la cual se extiende millones de kilómetros en el espacio. (Cap. 20, pág. 705)

cuticle / cutícula: Capa cerosa protectora que cubre los tallos, hojas y flores de algunas plantas terrestres; es secretada por las paredes celulares de la planta y disminuye la evaporación de agua. (Cap. 23, pág. 787)

dicot / dicotiledónea: Tipo de angiosperma que contiene dos cotiledones dentro de sus semillas. (Cap. 23, pág. 804)

Earth / la Tierra: El tercer planeta a partir del sol; tiene temperaturas superficiales que permiten que el agua exista como sólido, líquido y gas y una atmósfera que protege la vida de la radiación solar. (Cap. 19, pág. 676)

ectotherm / de sangre fría: Animal vertebrado cuya temperatura corporal cambia con la del ambiente. (Cap. 25, pág. 846)

electromagnetic spectrum / espectro electromagnético: Arreglo de radiación electromagnética, de acuerdo con sus longitudes de onda. (Cap. 17, pág. 613)

ellipse / elipse: Curva cerrada y alargada. La órbita de la Tierra forma un elipse. (Cap. 18, pág. 643)

endoskeleton / endoesqueleto: Sistema óseo interno de los vertebrados que apoya y protege los órganos internos del animal y al cual se adhieren los músculos. (Cap. 25, pág. 846)

endospores / endoesporas: Estructuras con paredes gruesas que rodean a muchas bacterias que producen toxinas, cuando las condiciones son desfavorables. (Cap. 21, pág. 747)

endotherm / de sangre caliente: Animal que mantiene una temperatura corporal constante. (Cap. 25, pág. 846)

equinox / equinoccio: Época del año cuando el sol está directamente encima del ecuador terrestre y las horas de luz solar son iguales a las horas de oscuridad. (Cap. 18, pág. 645)

estivation / estivación: Período de inactividad durante los meses calurosos y secos del verano. (Cap. 25, pág. 851)

exoskeleton / exoesqueleto: Cubierta corporal externa que protege y apoya el cuerpo de los artrópodos y que también impide que se seque el animal. (Cap. 24, pág. 832)

F

fins / aletas: Estructuras en forma de abanico que usan los peces para cambiar de dirección, equilibrarse y moverse. (Cap. 25, pág. 847)

first quarter / cuarto creciente: Fase de la luna cuando, desde la Tierra, se puede observar la mitad de su faz iluminada o un cuarto de la superficie lunar. (Cap. 18, pág. 651)

fish / pez: Animal de sangre fría que usa sus branquias para obtener oxígeno. (Cap. 25, pág. 847)

fission / fisión: La forma más simple de reproducción asexual, en la que se producen dos células con material genético idéntico al de la célula progenitora; es el método de reproducción más común de las bacterias. (Cap. 21, pág. 742)

flagella / flagelos: Estructuras en forma de látigo que poseen algunas bacterias para poder moverse en condiciones húmedas. (Cap. 21, pág. 739)

free-living / de vida libre: Organismo que no depende de otro organismo en particular para su alimentación o morada. (Cap. 24, pág. 821)

full moon / luna llena o plenilunio: Fase lunar durante la cual toda la superficie lunar que da a la Tierra está totalmente iluminada. (Cap. 18, pág. 651)

galaxy / galaxia: Grupo inmenso de estrellas, gas y polvo que se mantiene unido gracias a la gravedad. Nuestra galaxia, la Vía Láctea contiene unos 200 billones de estrellas. (Cap. 20, pág. 717)

giant / gigante: Etapa en el ciclo de vida de una estrella en que se agota el hidrógeno del núcleo, el núcleo estelar se contrae y las temperaturas dentro de la estrella aumentan, haciendo que las capas externas de la estrella se expandan. (Cap. 20, pág. 713)

gills / branquias: Órganos de los moluscos que intercambian oxígeno y dióxido de carbono con el agua. (Cap. 24, pág. 823)

Great Red Spot / la Gran Mancha Roja: Espectacular tormenta de gas turbulento y de alta presión que se puede observar continuamente en Júpiter. (Cap. 19, pág. 680)

guard cells / células guardianas: Células alrededor del estoma que lo abren y lo cierran. Junto con la cutícula y los estomas, son adaptaciones que ayudan a las plantas a sobrevivir sobre tierra. (Cap. 23, pág. 801)

gymnosperms / gimnospermas: Plantas vasculares que producen semillas en la superficie de las estructuras reproductoras femeninas. (Cap. 23, pág. 802)

hazardous wastes / desechos peligrosos: Desechos venenosos, cancerígenos o radiactivos que causan daño a los seres vivos. (Cap. 26, pág. 889)

herbivore / herbívoro: Animal de pastoreo que come plantas. (Cap. 25, pág. 868)

hibernation / hibernación: Período de inactividad y bajas necesidades metabólicas durante el invierno. (Cap. 25, pág. 851)

hyphae / hifas: Masas filamentosas multicelulares que, por lo general, componen el cuerpo de los hongos. (Cap. 22, pág. 770)

inner planets / planetas interiores: Planetas sólidos rocosos situados más cerca del sol: Mercurio, Venus, la Tierra y Marte. (Cap. 19, pág. 671)

invertebrates / invertebrados: Animal sin columna vertebral. (Cap. 24, pág. 815)

Jupiter / Júpiter: El planeta más grande del sistema solar y está ubicado en quinto lugar a partir del sol. (Cap. 19, pág. 680)

L

landfill / vertedero controlado: Área en donde se depositan los residuos. (Cap. 26, pág. 889)

lichen / liquen: Organismo compuesto de un hongo y un alga verde o una cianobacteria. (Cap. 22, pág. 773)

light-year / año luz: Distancia que viaja la luz en un año. Es también la unidad que se usa para medir distancias en el espacio. (Cap. 20, pág. 703)

lunar eclipse / eclipse lunar: Ocurre cuando la sombra de la Tierra cae sobre la luna. (Cap. 18, pág. 654)

main sequence / secuencia principal: En el diagrama H-R, la banda diagonal de estrellas que corre desde las estrellas calientes y brillantes, en la parte superior izquierda del diagrama, hasta las estrellas frías y tenues, en la parte inferior derecha. (Cap. 20, pág. 710)

mammal / mamífero: Vertebrado de sangre caliente que tiene pelo y produce leche para amamantar a las crías. (Cap. 25, pág. 862)

mantle / manto: Capa fina de tejido que cubre el cuerpo blando de los moluscos y secreta la concha protectora de los moluscos que poseen concha. (Cap. 24, pág. 823)

maria / maria: Regiones oscuras y relativamente planas de la superficie lunar. (Cap. 18, pág. 655)

Mars / Marte: Denominado el planeta rojo, Marte es el cuarto planeta a partir del sol. (Cap. 19, pág. 676)

marsupial / marsupio: Mamífero con bolsa que tiene crías inmaduras, las cuales completan su desarrollo en dicha bolsa. (Cap. 25, pág. 864)

mascon / concentración de masa: Concentración de masa ubicada debajo de las cuencas de impacto en la Luna. (Cap. 18, pág. 659)

medusa / medusa: Animal de vida libre, con cuerpo en forma de campana. (Cap. 24, pág. 819)

Mercury / Mercurio: El planeta más cercano al sol y es también el segundo planeta más pequeño. (Cap. 19, pág. 674)

metamorphosis / metamorfosis: Cambios por los que pasan muchos insectos y otros animales. Existen dos tipos de metamorfosis: completa e incompleta. (Cap. 24, pág. 834)

meteor / meteoro: Meteoroide que se quema en la atmósfera terrestre. (Cap. 19, pág. 690)

meteorite / meteorito: Meteoroide lo suficientemente grande como para caer sobre la superficie terrestre. (Cap. 19, pág. 690)

mollusk / molusco: Invertebrado de cuerpo blando, generalmente, con concha; posee un manto y una pata muscular grande. (Cap. 24, pág. 823)

monocot / monocotiledónea: Tipo de angiosperma que contiene un cotiledón dentro de sus semillas. (Cap. 23, pág. 804)

monotreme / monotrema: Mamífero que pone huevos con cáscara fuerte y correosa. (Cap. 25, pág. 864)

moon phase / fase lunar: Apariencia cambiante de la luna vista desde la Tierra. La fase que vemos depende de las posiciones relativas de la luna, la Tierra y el sol. (Cap. 18, pág. 651)

N

nebula / nebulosa: Nube extensa de gas y polvo que corresponde a la etapa inicial de formación de una estrella. (Cap. 20, pág. 712)

Neptune / Neptuno: Planeta grande y gaseoso descubierto en 1846; por lo general es el octavo planeta a partir del sol. (Cap. 19, pág. 684)

neutron star / estrella de neutrones: La etapa de una supernova cuando el núcleo denso y colapsado de la estrella se encoge hasta unos 10 a 15 km en diámetro y solo pueden existir neutrones en él. (Cap. 20, pág. 714)

new moon / luna nueva: Ocurre cuando la cara iluminada de la luna mira hacia el Sol y la cara oscura mira hacia la Tierra. La luna se encuentra en el firmamento, pero no podemos verla desde la Tierra. (Cap. 18, pág. 651)

nitrogen-fixing bacteria / bacterias nitrificantes: Bacterias que convierten el nitrógeno del aire en una forma útil para ciertas clases de plantas y animales. (Cap. 21, pág. 746)

nonvascular plant / planta no vascular: Planta que carece de tejido vascular y que usa otros medios para mover agua y sustancias a través de la planta. (Cap. 23, pág. 788)

observatory / observatorio: Edificio que alberga la mayoría de los telescopios ópticos usados por astrónomos profesionales. (Cap. 17, pág. 614)

omnivore / omnívoro: Animal que come plantas y también come otros animales. (Cap. 25, pág. 868)

Oort Cloud / Nube de Oort: Nube que, según el astrónomo holandés Jan Oort, está ubicada más allá de la órbita de Plutón y la cual rodea completamente el sistema solar. (Cap. 19, pág. 689)

open circulatory system / sistema circulatorio abierto: Sistema circulatorio que no posee vasos sanguíneos y en el cual la sangre rodea los órganos. (Cap. 24, pág. 824)

orbit / órbita: Trayectoria curva que sigue un objeto a medida que gira alrededor de otro objeto en el espacio. Por ejemplo, los planetas giran, en órbitas, alrededor del Sol. (Cap. 17, pág. 620)

outer planets / planetas exteriores: Planetas más alejados del sol: Júpiter, Neptuno, Saturno, Urano y Plutón. (Cap. 19, pág. 671)

P

parallax / paralaje: Cambio aparente en la posición de un objeto cuando uno lo observa desde dos posiciones diferentes. (Cap. 20, pág. 703)

parasite / parásito: Organismo que depende de su huésped para obtener alimento y morada. (Cap. 24, pág. 821)

pathogen / patógeno: Cualquier organismo causante de enfermedades. (Cap. 21, pág. 746)

pH scale / escala de pH: Escala que describe la acidez o basicidad de una sustancia; varía de 0 a 14, siendo 0 el rango más ácido y 14 el más básico. (Cap. 27, pág. 912)

phloem / floema: Tejido vegetal compuesto de células tubulares. Transporta alimentos desde el lugar en donde se fabrican hasta otras partes de la planta, en donde es usado o almacenado. (Cap. 23, pág. 799)

photochemical smog / smog fotoquímico: Smog color café que se forma cuando la luz solar reacciona con los contaminantes del aire. (Cap. 27, pág. 910)

photosphere / fotosfera: Capa más baja de la atmósfera del sol y desde la cual se emite la luz solar. A menudo llamada superficie solar. (Cap. 20, pág. 705)

pioneer species / especie pionera: Organismos que son los primeros en crecer en áreas nuevas o que han sido alteradas. (Cap. 23, pág. 791)

placental mammal / mamífero placentario: Animal cuyos embriones se desarrollan dentro del útero de la hembra. (Cap. 25, pág. 865)

Pluto / Plutón: El planeta más pequeño del sistema solar y del cual tenemos menos información. Se le considera el noveno planeta a partir del sol. (Cap. 19, pág. 684)

polyp / pólipo: Animal que tiene forma de jarrón y que generalmente es sésil. (Cap. 24, pág. 819)

population / población: Número total de individuos de cierta especie en un área particular. (Cap. 26, pág. 881)

population explosion / explosión demográfica: Rápido crecimiento de la población humana. (Cap. 26, pág. 881)

Project Apollo / Proyecto Apolo: Etapa final del programa americano de viajar a la luna. (Cap. 17, pág. 625)

Project Gemini / Proyecto Gemini: Segunda etapa en la meta de viajar a la luna. (Cap. 17, pág. 624)

Project Mercury / Proyecto Mercurio: Proyecto que inició el programa americano de viajar a la luna. (Cap. 17, pág. 624)

protist / protista: Organismo unicelular o multicelular que vive en ambientes húmedos o lluviosos. (Cap. 22, pág. 758)

protozoans / protozoarios: Protistas unicelulares que parecen animales; son complejos y viven en agua, tierra y tanto en organismos vivos como muertos. (Cap. 22, pág. 763)

pseudopods / seudopodios: Extensiones temporales del citoplasma, o patas falsas, de los Rhizopoda, que usan para moverse y alimentarse. (Cap. 22, pág. 764)

R

radio telescope / radiotelescopio: Tipo de telescopio que se usa para estudiar ondas radiales que viajan a través del espacio. (Cap. 17, pág. 617)

radula / rádula: Órgano de los moluscos que parece una lengua y que actúa como una lima con hileras de dientes para romper los alimentos en pedazos más pequeños. (Cap. 24, pág. 823)

recyclable / reciclable: Cualquier artículo que se puede procesar y volver a usar, para así conservar los recursos naturales y disminuir los desechos sólidos. (Cap. 26, pág. 895)

reflecting telescope / telescopio reflector: Telescopio que usa un espejo como objetivo para enfocar la luz del objeto bajo observación. (Cap. 17, pág. 614)

refracting telescope / telescopio refractor: Telescopio en que la luz del objeto pasa a través de una lente convexa doble, en donde la luz se dobla formando una imagen sobre el punto focal; luego el ocular magnifica la imagen. (Cap. 17, pág. 614)

reptile / reptil: Vertebrado de sangre fría con piel seca y escamosa y el cual no depende del agua para su reproducción. (Cap. 25, pág. 853)

revolution / revolución: Órbita anual de la Tierra alrededor del sol. (Cap. 18, pág. 643)

rhizoids / rizoides: Raíces filamentosas con solo unas cuantas células de grosor que anclan las hepáticas y los musgos en su lugar. (Cap. 23, pág. 790)

rotation / rotación: Movimiento de la Tierra alrededor de su eje, el cual causa el día y la noche. (Cap. 18, pág. 641)

S

Safe Drinking Water Act / Ley sobre la Seguridad del Agua Potable: Fortalece los estándares de salud para el agua potable, protege los ríos, lagos y corrientes de agua y otorga a los ciudadanos el derecho de saber acerca de los contaminantes que pueda contener el agua potable. (Cap. 27, pág. 923)

saprophyte / saprofito: Cualquier organismo que usa materia muerta como su fuente alimenticia y energética; las bacterias saprofitas evitan la acumulación de materias muertas, por todo el mundo. (Cap. 21, pág. 745)

satellite / satélite: Cualquier objeto que gira alrededor de otro objeto. (Cap. 17, pág. 620)

Saturn / Saturno: Conocido como el planeta anular, es el sexto planeta a partir del sol. (Cap. 19, pág. 681)

scrubber / depurador: Dispositivo que hace que los gases en el humo se disuelvan en agua, así como sucedería en la naturaleza, hasta aumentar el pH del humo a un nivel seguro. (Cap. 27, pág. 915)

solar eclipse / eclipse solar: Ocurre cuando la luna se mueve directamente entre el sol y la Tierra y proyecta una sombra sobre parte de la Tierra. (Cap. 18, pág. 652)

solar system / sistema solar: Sistema compuesto de nueve planetas, incluyendo la Tierra, y muchos objetos más pequeños que giran alrededor del sol. (Cap. 19, pág. 669)

solstice / solsticio: Punto en que el sol alcanza su mayor distancia al norte o al sur del ecuador. (Cap. 18, pág. 645)

space probe / sonda espacial: Instrumento que viaja por el sistema solar; reúne información y la envía a la Tierra. (Cap. 17, pág. 621)

space shuttle / transbordador espacial: Nave espacial reutilizable que transporta a astronautas, satélites y otros materiales hacia el espacio y desde el mismo. (Cap. 17, pág. 628)

space station / estación espacial: Estación en el espacio que posee viviendas, áreas de trabajo y de ejercicio, y todo el equipo y sistemas auxiliares que necesitan los seres humanos para vivir y trabajar en el espacio. (Cap. 17, pág. 629)

sphere / esfera: Objeto redondo tridimensional cuya superficie en cualquiera de sus puntos está a la misma distancia de su centro. (Cap. 18, pág. 640)

spore / espora: Célula reproductora que forma nuevos organismos sin ayuda de la fecundación. (Cap. 22, pág. 771)

stomata / estomas: Pequeños poros en la superficie de las hojas de las plantas, que permiten que el dióxido de carbono, el agua y el oxígeno entren y salgan de la hoja. (Cap. 23, pág. 801)

sulfurous smog / smog sulfuroso: Tipo de smog que se forma cuando la quema de combustibles libera compuestos de azufre en el aire; este smog sulfuroso se puede acumular en un área donde no sopla el viento o sopla muy poco. (Cap. 27, pág. 911)

sunspot / mancha solar: Área de la superficie solar que parece oscura porque es más fría que las áreas que la rodean. (Cap. 20, pág. 706)

supergiant / supergigante: Etapa en la formación de una estrella en la cual se forman elementos cada vez más pesados por medio de la fusión, haciendo que a la larga, se forme hierro en su núcleo. (Cap. 20, pág. 714)

symmetry / simetría: Se refiere al arreglo de las partes individuales de un objeto; los animales con simetría bilateral tienen partes corporales que son imágenes especulares una de la otra; los animales con simetría radiada poseen partes corporales arregladas en forma de círculo alrededor de un punto central y los animales asimétricos no tienen una forma corporal definitiva. (Cap. 24, pág. 815)

T

third quarter / cuarto menguante: Cuando se ve solo la mitad de la faz iluminada de la luna. (Cap. 18, pág. 652)

toxin / toxina: Veneno que producen los patógenos bacteriales. (Cap. 21, pág. 747)

Uranus / Urano: El séptimo planeta a partir del sol, descubierto en 1781. Es un planeta grande y gaseoso, con 17 satélites y un sistema de anillos oscuros y delgados. (Cap. 19, pág. 683)

vaccine / vacuna: Sustancia que se produce a partir de partículas dañadas de las paredes celulares de bacterias o de bacterias muertas; puede prevenir, pero no curar muchas enfermedades causadas por bacterias. (Cap. 21, pág. 746)

vascular plant / planta vascular: Planta con tejidos que forman un sistema que transporta agua, nutrientes y otras sustancias a lo largo de la planta. (Cap. 23, pág. 788)

Venus / Venus: A veces llamado el gemelo de la Tierra, Venus es el segundo planeta a partir del sol; tiene una atmósfera densa de dióxido de carbono y ácido sulfúrico. (Cap. 19, pág. 675)

vertebrates / vertebrados: Animal con columna vertebral; solo un 3 por ciento de todos los animales son vertebrados. (Cap. 24, pág. 815)

waning / octante menguante: Cuando la cantidad de la faz iluminada de la luna, que se puede ver desde la Tierra, comienza a disminuir. (Cap. 18, pág. 652)

waxing / octante creciente: Cuando se hace cada vez más visible la cara iluminada de la luna. (Cap. 18, pág. 651)

white dwarf / enana blanca: Etapa tardía en el ciclo de vida de una estrella, en que su núcleo agota su abastecimiento de helio, se contrae y sus capas externas se escapan hacia el espacio, dejando un núcleo denso y caliente. (Cap. 20, pág. 714)

xylem / xilema: Tejido compuesto de vasos tubulares que transportan agua y sustancias disueltas desde las raíces, a través de toda la planta. (Cap. 23, pág. 799)

Index

The index for *Science Voyages* will help you locate major topics in the book quickly and easily. Each entry in the index is followed by the numbers of the pages on which the entry is discussed. A page number given in **boldface type** indicates the page on which that entry is defined. A page number given in *italic type* indicates a page on which the entry is used in an illustration or photograph. The abbreviation *act.* indicates a page on which the entry is used in an activity.

A

B

D

E

F

K

L

M

S

T

V

W

Art Credits

TABLE OF CONTENTS
viii (b)Rolin Graphics; **xi**(l) Barbara Hoopes-Ambler; **xii** Morgan-Cain & Associates.

Chapter 17 - **612-3** Rolin Graphics; **614** George Bucktell; **620 622-3** John Edwards.

Chapter 18 - **641** John Edwards; **642** Rolin Graphics; **643** Bruce Sanders; **644 645** John Edwards; **650** John Edwards/Morgan-Cain & Associates; **651** Morgan-Cain & Associates; **652** John Edwards/Morgan-Cain & Associates; **653 654 656-7** Rolin Graphics; **662** John Edwards; **665** Glencoe/McGraw-Hill.

Chapter 19 - **668-9** Morgan-Cain & Associates; **670 671** Dave Fischer/John Edwards; **673** Dartmouth Publishing; **682** Morgan-Cain & Associates; **683 689** John Edwards; **690-1** (t)Morgan-Cain & Associates; **691** John Edwards; **694** John Edwards; **694** Dave Fischer/John Edwards; **695** Morgan-Cain & Associates; **697** Glencoe/McGraw-Hill.

Chapter 20 - **700** (l)Morgan-Cain & Associates, (r)Precision Graphics; **701 703** John Edwards; **705 710** Morgan-Cain & Associates; **711 712 713** John Edwards; **718** Morgan-Cain & Associates; **719** John Edwards; **720-1** Morgan-Cain & Associates; **721** (b)Jim Shough; **722** John Edwards; **726 727 728 729** Morgan-Cain & Associates; **730** John Edwards; **733** Glencoe/McGraw-Hill.

Chapter 21 - **739 740** Morgan-Cain & Associates; **746-7** Morgan-Cain & Associates/Pond & Giles; **752** Morgan-Cain & Associates; **755** Glencoe/McGraw-Hill.

Chapter 22 - **758** Felipe Passalacqua/Morgan-Cain & Associates; **759** Morgan-Cain & Associates; **763** (t)Felipe Passalacqua, (b)Morgan-Cain & Associates; **765** Morgan-Cain & Associates; **770 771 779** Dave Fischer; **781** Glencoe/McGraw-Hill.

Chapter 23 - **785** Morgan-Cain & Associates; **789** Pond & Giles/Morgan-Cain & Associates; **799** Pond & Giles; **801** Morgan-Cain & Associates; **804 805 809** Pond & Giles; **811** Glencoe/McGraw-Hill.

Chapter 24 - **815** Glencoe/McGraw-Hill; **816** Cende Hill; **817** Glencoe/McGraw-Hill; **819** Cende Hill; **820** Morgan-Cain & Associates; **821** Sarah Woodward; **823** Glencoe/McGraw-Hill; **824** Laurie O'Keefe; **825 826** Sarah Woodward; **832** Glencoe/McGraw-Hill; **834** David Ashby; **837** Sarah Woodward; **840 843** Glencoe/McGraw-Hill.

Chapter 25 - **846 847** Glencoe/McGraw-Hill; **848** Michael Woods; **850** Glencoe/McGraw-Hill; **851** Michael Woods; **852** Robert Hynes; **854** Dave Fischer; **856** Glencoe/McGraw-Hill; **858** David Ashby; **860** Pond & Giles; **862** Glencoe/McGraw-Hill; **864** Morgan-Cain & Associates; **868** Barbara Hoopes-Ambler; **875** Glencoe/McGraw-Hill.

Chapter 26 - **881** Dartmouth Publishing; **885** Glencoe/McGraw-Hill; **888** Tom Kennedy; **889 890** Morgan-Cain & Associates; **891** Glencoe/McGraw-Hill; **895** Tom Kennedy; **904** Dartmouth Publishing; **907** Morgan-Cain & Associates.

Chapter 27 - **911** Thomas Gagliano; **913** John Edwards; **914** Thomas Gagliano, (br)Morgan-Cain & Associates; **915** Morgan-Cain & Associates; **921** John Edwards; **922** Glencoe/McGraw-Hill; **924** Morgan-Cain & Associates; **925** Thomas Gagliano; **927** (l) Dartmouth Publishing; **928** Thomas Gagliano; **931** Glencoe/McGraw-Hill.

Photo Credits

TABLE OF CONTENTS
v Jack Zehrt/FPG International; **viii** (l)Matt Meadows, (r)NASA/Science Source/Photo Researchers; **ix** TSADO/JPL/NASA/Tom Stack & Associates; **x** (t)Jan Hinsch/Science Photo Library/Photo Researchers, (b) Visuals Unlimited; **xi** (r)Jack Wilburn/Animals Animals; **xiii** (r)Nigel Cattlin/Holt Studios International/Photo Researchers, (l)The New Zealand Herald; **xiv** Matt Meadows; **xv** Matt Meadows; **xvi** Kazuaki Iwasaki/The Stock Market; **xvii** (tr)Richard L. Carton/Photo Researchers; **xviii** Matt Meadows.

UNIT 5

Opener - **608-9** NASA; **609** NASA/Corbis Media.

Chapter 17 - **610-1** Jack Zehrt/FPG International; **611** Matt Meadows; **612** (l)Mark Reinstein/FPG International, (r)Mark E. Gibson; **613** (l)Daedalus Enterprises/Peter Arnold, Inc., (c)Rob Atkins/The Image Bank, (r)David M. Dennis/Tom Stack & Associates; **614** Matt Meadows; **615** NASA; **616** (t)Eric Sander/Liaison International, (b)Science Photo Library/Photo Researchers; **618** Matt Meadows; **621** (l)NASA/Science Source/Photo Researchers, (lc)NASA, (rc)NASA/Science Source/Photo Researchers, (r)Martin Marietta Corporation/Science Photo Library/Photo Researchers; **624** NASA; **625** NASA/Mark Marten/Photo Researchers; **626** NASA; **627** International Dark Sky Association; **628-9** Mark M. Lawrence/The Stock Market; **630-1** NASA/Science Photo Library/Photo Researchers; **632** NASA; **633** NASA/Newell Colour Imaging; **634** (t)Rafael Macia/Photo Researchers, (bl)NASA, (br)NASA/Mark Marten/Photo Researchers; **635** (t)NASA, (b)Mark M. Lawrence/The Stock Market.

Chapter 18 - **638-9** NASA/TSADO/Tom Stack & Associates; **639** Matt Meadows; **640** Jerry Schad/Photo Researchers; **643** Skip Comer; **644** (t)Rafael Macia/Photo Researchers, (b)Richard Price/FPG International; **646** NASA/GSFC/Tom Stack & Associates; **647** Tom Croke/Liaison International; **648 649** Matt Meadows; **651** Dr. Fred Espenak/Science Photo Library/Photo Researchers; **653** Bruce Herman/Tony Stone Images; **655** Kazuaki Iwasaki/The Stock Market; **658** NASA; **659** Zuber et al/Johns Hopkins University/NASA/Photo Researchers; **660** BMDO/NRL/LLNL/Science Photo Library/Photo Researchers; **662** (t)Rafael Macia/Photo Researchers, (b)Kazuaki Iwasaki/The Stock Market; **663** (t)NASA, (b)courtesy Gibor Basri.

Chapter 19 - **666-7** Telegraph Colour Library/FPG International; **667** Matt Meadows; **672** Scala/Art Resource, NY; **674** (l)US Geological Survey/Science Photo Library/Photo Researchers, (r)JPL/TSADO/Tom Stack & Associates; **675** JPL/TSADO/Tom Stack & Associates; **676** NASA; **677** (l)USGS/NASA/TASDO/Tom Stack & Associates, (r)NASA/TSADO/Tom Stack & Associates; **678** (l)Science Photo Library/Photo Researchers, (r)TSADO/JPL/NASA/Tom Stack & Associates; **679** USGS/TSADO/Tom Stack & Associates; **680** (t)NASA/Mark Marten/Photo Researchers, (b)NASA/Tom Stack & Associates; **681** (right-1)USGS/TSADO/Tom Stack & Associates, (right-2)TSADO/NASA/Tom Stack & Associates, (right-3)TSADO/NASA/Tom Stack & Associates, (right-4)JPL, (b)Space Telescope Science Institute/NASA/Science Photo Library/Photo Researchers; **683** NASA/JPL/Tom Stack & Associates; **684** (t)NASA, (b)NASA/Photo Researchers; **685** NASA/ESA/Tom Stack & Associates; **687** Tom McHugh/Photo Researchers; **690** David Parker/Science Photo Library/Photo Researchers; **691** Planet Earth Pictures/FPG International; **692** JPL/TSADO/Tom Stack & Associates; **693** NASA; **694** (t)JPL/TSADO/Tom Stack & Associates, (b)NASA; **695** NASA/Mark Marten/Photo Researchers.

Chapter 20 - **698-9** Space Telescope Science Institute/NASA/Science Photo Library/Photo Researchers; **699** Matt Meadows; **701** Bill & Sally Fletcher/Tom Stack & Associates; **702** Tim Courlas; **704** David Parker/Science Photo Library/Photo Researchers; **706** (l)NOAO/TSADO/Tom Stack & Associates, (r)ESA/TSADO/Tom Stack & Associates; **707** (l)Chris Butler/SPL/Photo Researchers, (r)NASA; **708** Bill & Sally Fletcher/Tom Stack & Associates; **709** Tim Courlas; **714** Celestial Image Co./Science Photo Library/Photo Researchers; **715** Bill & Sally Fletcher/Tom Stack & Associates; **716** (l)National Geographic Photographer Sam Abell, (r)David Robert Austen; **717** ©Jerry Lodriguss/Photo Researchers; **718** Telegraph Colour Library; **719** Celestial Image Co./Science Photo Library/Photo Researchers; **723** NASA/Science Source/Photo Researchers; **724** Matt Meadows; **726-9** David S. Addison/Visuals Unlimited; **730** NASA; **731** (t)Celestial Image Co./Science Photo Library/Photo Researchers, (b)©Jerry Lodriguss/Photo Researchers.

UNIT 6

Opener - **734-5** ©Chris Newbert; **735** ©David Young/Tom Stack & Associates.

Chapter 21 - **736-7** Manfred Kage/Peter Arnold, Inc.; **737** Michael Abbey/Photo Researchers; **738** R. Calentine/Visuals Unlimited; **741** Matt Meadows; **742** (t)Tom E. Adams/Peter Arnold, Inc., (b)Visuals Unlimited; **743** D. Foster/Visuals Unlimited; **744** (tl)Michael Abbey/Photo Researchers, (tr)Michael Abbey/Photo Researchers, (bl)Winston Patnode/Photo Researchers, (br)Michael Abbey/Photo Researchers; **745** (t)David R. Frazier/Photo Researchers, (b)Bob Mullenix; **748** Alfred Pasieka/Science Photo Library/Photo Researchers; **749** Bryan Hodgson; **750 751** KS Studio; **752** (t)R. Calentine/Visuals Unlimited, (b)Visuals Unlimited; **753** (l)Alfred Pasieka/Science Photo Library/Photo Researchers, (r)Bob Mullenix; (b)Daniel Schaefer.

Chapter 22 - **756-7** Amanita Pictures; **757** Mark Burnett; **759** Jan Hinsch/Science Photo Library/Photo Researchers; **760** (t)Dr. David M. Phillips/Photo Researchers, (b)Biophoto Associates/Photo Researchers; **761** (tl)Runk/Schoenberger from Grant Heilman, (tr)Runk/Schoenberger from Grant Heilman, (b)Michael Abbey/Photo Researchers; **762** (t)Walter H. Hodge/Peter Arnold, Inc., (b)Gregory Ochoki/Photo Researchers; **764** (tl)Ronald Gorbutt/Britstock, (tr)Alfred Pasieka/Science Photo Library/Photo Researchers,(b)Oliver Meckes/Photo Researchers; **765** (t)M.I.Walker/Photo Researchers, (b)Sinclair Stammers/Science Photo Library/Photo Researchers; **766** (l)Scott Camazine/Photo Researchers, (c)Amanita Pictures, (r)Matt Meadows; **767** David M. Dennis/Tom Stack & Associates; **768** (l)Nigel Cattlin/Holt Studios International/Photo Reasearchers, Inc., (r)Noble Proctor/Photo Researchers; **769** Paul Johnson/BPS/Tony Stone Images; **770** Amanita Pictures; **771** Ed Reschke/Peter Arnold, Inc.; **772** J. Forsdyke,Gene Cox/Science Photo Library/Photo Researchers; **773** David M. Dennis/Tom Stack & Associates; **774** (l)Stephen J. Krasemann/DRK Photo, (c)Runk/Schoenberger from Grant Heilman, (r)L.West/Photo Researchers; **775** Emory Kristof, (inset)Manfred Kage/Peter Arnold, Inc.; **776** Matt Meadows; **777** Matt Meadows; **778** (t)Jan Hinsch/Science Photo Library/Photo Researchers, (l)Oliver Meckes/Photo Researchers, (r)Runk/Schoenberger from Grant Heilman; **779** The Birmingham News.

Chapter 23 - **782-3** Aaron Haupt; **783** file photo; **784** Michael P. Gadomski/Photo Researchers; **785** (t)Jan Hirsch/Science Photo Library/Photo Researchers, (b)Doug Sokell/Visuals Unlimited, (l)Pat O'Hara/DRK Photo, (r)John Shaw/Tom Stack & Associates; **787** (l)Runk/Schoenberger from Grant Heilman, (c)Harold

Photo Credits

Hofman/Photo Researchers, (r)Kevin Schafer/Peter Arnold, Inc.; **788** David Cavagnaro/DRK Photo; **790** (l)John Kaprielian/Photo Researchers, (r)Barry L. Runk from Grant Heilman; **791** Kevin Schafer/Peter Arnold, Inc.; **792** (tr)Jane Grushow from Grant Heilman, (c)Stephen J. Krasemann/Photo Researchers, (l)Rod Planck/Photo Researchers, (br)David S. Addison/Visuals Unlimited; **793** (t)Runk/Schoenberger from Grant Heilman, (c)Sydney Karp/Photos/NATS, (b)Richard L. Carton/Photo Researchers; **794** Walter H. Hodge/Peter Arnold, Inc.; **795** Ludek Pesek/Science Photo Library/Photo Researchers; **796** Aaron Haupt; **797** (l)John D. Cunningham/Visuals Unlimited, (r)Ira Block, Courtesy Silkeborg Museum, Denmark; **798** Jeff Greenberg/Visuals Unlimited; **800** Runk Schoenberger from Grant Heilman; **802** (l)Richard Shiel/Earth Scenes, (r)Kenneth W. Fink/Photo Researchers; **803** (l)Joyce Photographics/Photo Researchers, (r)M.A. Chappell/Earth Scenes; **804** (l)Photo/NATS, (r)George E. Jones III/Photo Researchers; **805** (t)Mark E. Gibson, (bl)Aaron Haupt, (br)Frank Siteman/Stock Boston; **806** (l)Aaron Haupt, (r)Angelina Lax/Photo Researchers; **807** Matt Meadows; **808** (t)Michael P. Gadomski/Photo Researchers, (b)Walter H. Hodge/Peter Arnold, Inc.; **809** (t)Richard Shiel/Earth Scenes, (b)Aaron Haupt.

Chapter 24 - **812-3** Roger K. Burnard; **813** KS Studio; **814** (l)Mitsuaki Iwago/Minden Pictures, (c)Lynn Stone, (r)Fred Bavendam/Minden Pictures; **817** Fred Bravendam/Minden Pictures; **820** Carolina Biological Supply/Phototake; **821** Breck P. Kent/Animals, Animals; **822** James E. Hayden/Phototake; **823** (l)Zig Leszczynski/Animals, Animals, (r)Andrew J. Martinez/Photo Researchers; **824** (l)William J. Weber, (r)Sharon M. Kurgis; **825** Flip Nicklin/Minden Pictures; **826** Runk/Schoenberger from Grant Heilman; **827** NMSB/Custom Medical Stock Photo; **828** (l)Geri Murphy, (r)Geri Murphy; **829** The New Zealand Herald; **830 831** KS Studio; **832** (l)David M. Dennis, (r)Mark Moffett/Minden Pictures; **833** (t)Frans Lanting/Minden Pictures, (c)Jack Wilburn/Animals, Animals, (b)Sinclair Stammers/Animals, Animals; **834** Lynn Stone; **835** (t)G.I. Bernard/Animals, Animals, (c)E. R. Degginger/Animals, Animals, (b)Fred Bravendam/Minden Pictures; **836** (tr)Ruth Dixon, (l)Fred Bavendam/Minden Pictures, (br)Fred Bavendam/Minden Pictures; **837** Fred Bavendam/Minden Pictures; **838** Dave Fleetham/Tom Stack & Associates; **839** KS Studio; **841** (tl)William J. Weber, (tr)Geri Murphy, (bl)Mark Moffett/Minden Pictures, (br)Frans Lanting/Minden Pictures.

Chapter 25 - **844-5** Roland Seitre/Peter Arnold, Inc.; **845** Dan Rest; **847** (t)Brian Parker/Tom Stack & Associates, (c)David R. Frazier, (b)Jesse Cancelmo; **849** (t)Breck P. Kent/Animals, Animals, (b)Kelvin Aitken/Peter Arnold, Inc.; **850** David M. Dennis; **853** (t)Mark Moffett/Minden Pictures, (lc)Michael Collier, (rc)Alvin R. Staffan, (b)Lynn Stone; **855** Hans Pfletschinger/Peter Arnold, Inc.; **856** (l)Roger K. Burnard, (r)Lynn Stone; **857** (left-1)Don C. Nieman, (left-2)Alan Carey, (left-3)Roy Morsch/The Stock Market, (left-4)Alvin E. Staffan, (right-1)David R. Frazier, (right-2)William J. Weber, (right-3)Alan Nelson, (right-4)William J. Weber; **859** Michael Quinton/Minden Pictures; **861** (l)Mary Evans Picture Library/Photo Researchers, (r)Culver Pictures; **862** Johnny Johnson; **863** Tom McHugh/Photo Researchers; **864** Roger K. Burnard; **865** (t)Sharon Remmen, (b)CNRI/Phototake; **866** (left-1)Tom McHugh/Photo Researchers, (left-2)William J. Weber, (left-3)Stephen Dalton/Animals, Animals, (left-4)Sharon M. Kurgis, (right-1)Sharon Remmen, (right-2)Alvin Staffan, (right-3)V. Berns; **867** (left-1)Tom Pantages, (left-2)Lynn Stone, (left-3)Alvin E. Staffan, (right-1)Alan Carey, (right-2)William J. Weber, (right-3)Frans Lanting/Minden Pictures; **868** (tr)Lynn M. Stone, (l)David R. Frazier, (br)Michael A. Keller/The Stock Market; **869** Gerard Lacz/Peter Arnold, Inc.; **870** Maslowski Photo; **872** (t)Kelvin Aitken/Peter Arnold, Inc., (c)Michael Collier, (b)David M. Dennis; **873** (t)Alan Nelson, (l)William J. Weber, (right-1)Don C. Nieman, (right-2)Stephen Dalton/Animals, Animals, (right-3)V. Berns.

UNIT 7

Opener - **876-7** Sam C. Pierson/Photo Researchers; **877** Keith H. Murakami/Tom Stack & Associates.

Chapter 26 - **878-9** Ray Pfortner/Peter Arnold, Inc.; **879** Mark Burnett; **880** Jon Feingersh/The Stock Market; **882** Matt Meadows; **883** Richard Hutchings; **884** Matt Meadows; **886** (l)Roy Morsch/The Stock Market, (r)Michael Ableman; **887** (t)Jim Wark/Peter Arnold, Inc., (b)Larry Lefever from Grant Heilman; **888** Frans Lanting/Minden Pictures; **891** Mark Burnett; **892** Rick Iwasaki/Tony Stone Images; **893** Jack Dykinga; **896** (l,r)Kenji Kerins, (c)file photo; **898** Matt Meadows; **899** (l)ARS-Banuelos, (r)Nigel Cattlin/Holt Studios International/Photo Researchers; **900** KS Studio; **900-3** file photo; **901** file photos; **902** (tl)Telegraph Colour Library/FPG International, (tr)Hank Morgan/Science Source/Photo Researchers, (bl)file photo, (br)Jose Fuste Raga/The Stock Market; **903** (tl)Mark Burnett, (tr, bl, br)file photos; **904** (l)Jon Feingersh/The Stock Market, (r)Richard Hutchings; **905** (t)Rick Isasaki/Tony Stone Images, (b)Kenji Kerins.

Chapter 27 - **908-9** Mark E. Gibson; **909** Tim Courlas; **910** Rafael Macia/Photo Researchers; **912** Oliver Strewe/Tony Stone Images; **915** Lionel Delevingue/PhotoTake; **916** Mark E. Gibson; **917** University of Montana/Photo by Todd Goodrich; **918** Matt Meadows; **919** file photo; **920** (l)Kenji Kerins, (r)Tom Stack/Tom Stack & Associates; **921** (t)courtesy of the city of San Diego, (b)John Eastcott/Yva Momatiuk/DRK Photo; **923** (l)Tom Ives/The Stock Market, (r)Ian Adams; **926** Doug Martin; **928** Rafael Macia/Photo Researchers; **929** (tl)Kenji Kerins, (tr)Tom Stack/Tom Stack & Associates, (b)Doug Martin.

PERIODIC TABLE OF THE ELEMENTS

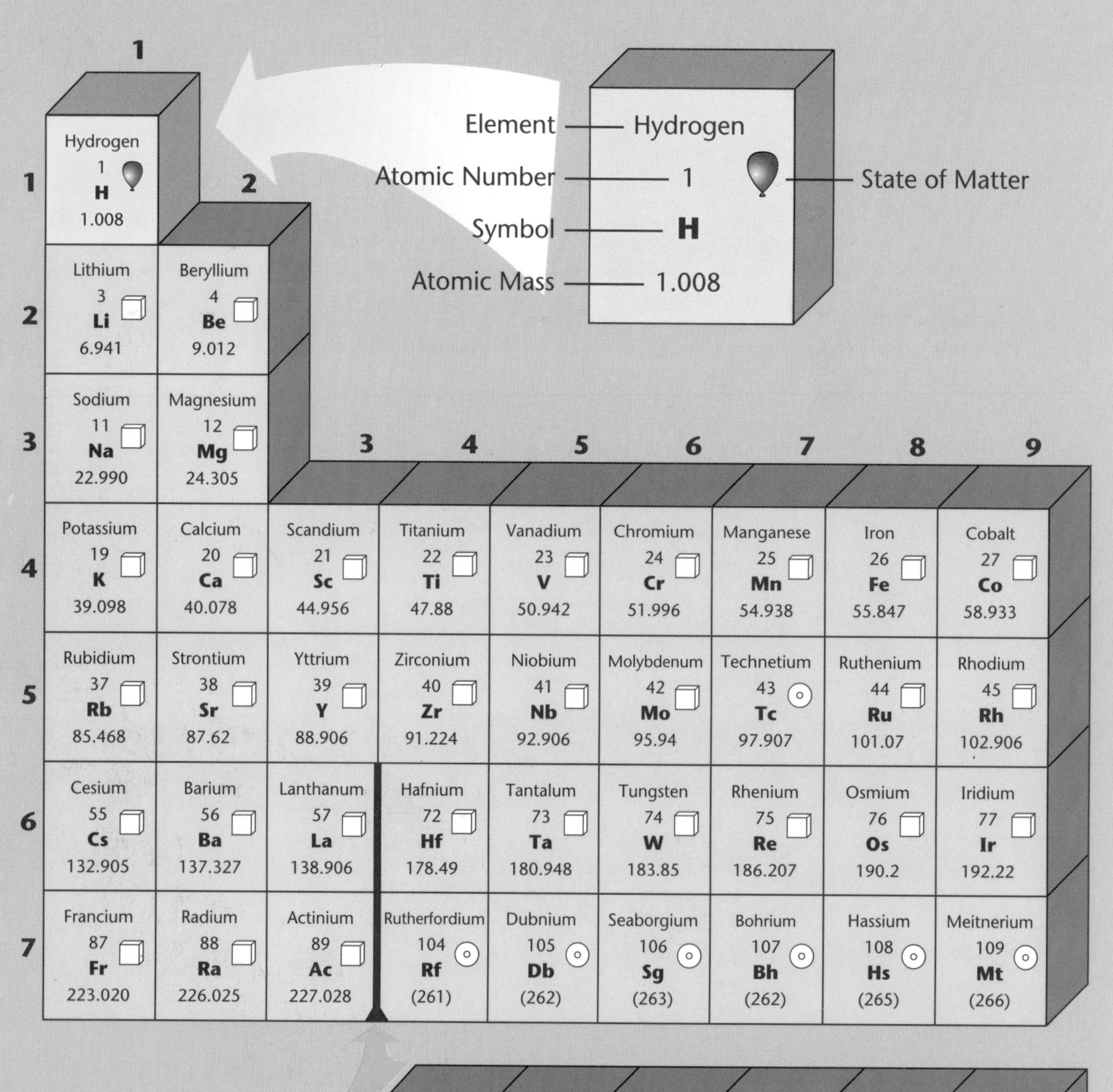

	1	2	3	4	5	6	7	8	9
1	Hydrogen 1 **H** 1.008								
2	Lithium 3 **Li** 6.941	Beryllium 4 **Be** 9.012							
3	Sodium 11 **Na** 22.990	Magnesium 12 **Mg** 24.305							
4	Potassium 19 **K** 39.098	Calcium 20 **Ca** 40.078	Scandium 21 **Sc** 44.956	Titanium 22 **Ti** 47.88	Vanadium 23 **V** 50.942	Chromium 24 **Cr** 51.996	Manganese 25 **Mn** 54.938	Iron 26 **Fe** 55.847	Cobalt 27 **Co** 58.933
5	Rubidium 37 **Rb** 85.468	Strontium 38 **Sr** 87.62	Yttrium 39 **Y** 88.906	Zirconium 40 **Zr** 91.224	Niobium 41 **Nb** 92.906	Molybdenum 42 **Mo** 95.94	Technetium 43 **Tc** 97.907	Ruthenium 44 **Ru** 101.07	Rhodium 45 **Rh** 102.906
6	Cesium 55 **Cs** 132.905	Barium 56 **Ba** 137.327	Lanthanum 57 **La** 138.906	Hafnium 72 **Hf** 178.49	Tantalum 73 **Ta** 180.948	Tungsten 74 **W** 183.85	Rhenium 75 **Re** 186.207	Osmium 76 **Os** 190.2	Iridium 77 **Ir** 192.22
7	Francium 87 **Fr** 223.020	Radium 88 **Ra** 226.025	Actinium 89 **Ac** 227.028	Rutherfordium 104 **Rf** (261)	Dubnium 105 **Db** (262)	Seaborgium 106 **Sg** (263)	Bohrium 107 **Bh** (262)	Hassium 108 **Hs** (265)	Meitnerium 109 **Mt** (266)

Lanthanide Series	Cerium 58 **Ce** 140.115	Praseodymium 59 **Pr** 140.908	Neodymium 60 **Nd** 144.24	Promethium 61 **Pm** 144.913	Samarium 62 **Sm** 150.36	Europium 63 **Eu** 151.965
Actinide Series	Thorium 90 **Th** 232.038	Protactinium 91 **Pa** 231.036	Uranium 92 **U** 238.029	Neptunium 93 **Np** 237.048	Plutonium 94 **Pu** 244.064	Americium 95 **Am** 243.061